$30

CONSUMER BEHAVIOR

second edition

CONSUMER

PRENTICE-HALL, INC., Englewood Cliffs, New Jersey 07632

Leon G. Schiffman
Baruch College
City University of New York

Leslie Lazar Kanuk
Baruch College
City University of New York

BEHAVIOR

Library of Congress Cataloging in Publication Data

SCHIFFMAN, LEON G.
    Consumer behavior.

    Includes bibliographical references and index.
    1. Consumers. 2. Motivation research (Marketing)
I. Kanuk, Leslie Lazar. II. Title.
HF5415.3.S29 1983   658.8'342   82–22966
ISBN 0–13–168880–4

Editorial/production supervision by Esther S. Koehn
Interior design by Suzanne Behnke
Cover design by Suzanne Behnke
Assistant Art Director: Linda Conway
Manufacturing buyer: Ed O'Dougherty

CONSUMER BEHAVIOR, *Second Edition*
by Leon G. Schiffman and Leslie Lazar Kanuk

Printed in the United States of America

10 9 8 7

ISBN 0-13-168880-4

Prentice-Hall International, Inc., *London*
Prentice-Hall of Australia Pty. Limited, *Sydney*
Editora Prentice-Hall do Brasil, Ltda., *Rio de Janeiro*
Prentice-Hall Canada Inc., *Toronto*
Prentice-Hall of India Private Limited, *New Delhi*
Prentice-Hall of Japan, Inc., *Tokyo*
Prentice-Hall of Southeast Asia Pte. Ltd., *Singapore*
Whitehall Books Limited, *Wellington, New Zealand*

To Janet and David Schiffman
and
Jack, Randi, and Alan Kanuk

CONTENTS

Preface xvii

Contents

viii

Personality and Consumer Behavior   84

Consumer Psychographics   111

Consumer Attitude Formation and Change   219

Communication and Consumer Behavior   247

PART THREE
CONSUMERS IN THEIR SOCIAL AND CULTURAL SETTINGS

11   Group Dynamics and Consumer Reference Groups   285

12   The Family   315

13 Social Class and Consumer Behavior   347

14 The Influence of Culture on Consumer Behavior   386

15 Subcultural and Cross-Cultural Aspects of Consumer Behavior   425

PART FOUR
THE CONSUMERS' DECISION-MAKING PROCESS

16 Personal Influence and the Opinion Leadership Process   465

17 Diffusion of Innovations   500

18 Consumer Decision Making   533

19 Comprehensive Models of Consumer Decision Making   552

PART FIVE
BROADENING THE CONCEPT OF CONSUMER BEHAVIOR

20 Consumer Behavior Applications for Public Policy and Nonprofit Organizations   571

PREFACE

From the day we finished writing the first edition of *Consumer Behavior,* our friends in the academic and publishing communities told us that future editions would be a "snap." At that time we took comfort in their prognosis. Now that we have completed the second edition, we would like to suggest that the statement "Revisions are easy" be placed alongside such classic academic exaggerations as: "The term paper must have gotten lost in the mail," "My typewriter broke down as I was starting the report," and "You will receive an advance copy of the paper three weeks before the conference."

Part of the difficulty in preparing a revision was the fact that the field of consumer behavior has become so dynamic and its researchers so prolific since we completed the original manuscript. Indeed, given the number and diversity of consumer behavior research articles that continue to appear at an ever-increasing pace, it was difficult to decide when to "cut off" the review of new articles, which new streams of research to include, and where to include them since they often fit into more than one topical area.

Because we truly do believe in the marketing concept, an overriding consideration throughout the preparation of this edition has been to meet the needs of *our* consumers—students, practitioners, and professors of consumer behavior—by providing a text that is highly readable and that clearly explains the relevant concepts and theories upon which the discipline of consumer behavior is based. We have also endeavored to illustrate with pragmatic examples how these concepts are used by marketing practitioners to develop and implement effective marketing strategies.

We have tried to make this second edition comprehensive without becoming encyclopedic. To make the book as useful as possible to both graduate and undergraduate students, we sought to maintain a firm balance between basic behavioral concepts, supporting research findings, and marketing illustrations and applications.

We continue to be convinced that the major contribution of consumer behavior studies to the practice of marketing is the provision of structure and direction for effective market segmentation. To this end, we have included a greatly expanded discussion of market segmentation in this second edition (see Chapter 2). We have also increased the number of market segmentation examples given throughout the book.

This second edition of *Consumer Behavior* is divided into five parts, consisting of twenty chapters (an addition of five chapters over the original edition). Part I introduces the reader to the study of consumer behavior. It discusses what consumer behavior is, how and why it developed, and how consumer behavior research findings are used by marketing practitioners. This is followed by an in-depth discussion of how consumer behavior principles provide the conceptual framework and strategic direction for the segmentation of markets.

Part II discusses the consumer as an individual. It begins with an exploration of consumer needs and motivations, and is followed by a discussion of personality and by an expanded examination of consumer psychographics. A comprehensive discussion of the impact of consumer perception on marketing strategies is followed by an entirely new chapter on consumer learning which stresses the influence of consumer information processing on consumer behavior. Two new chapters on consumer attitudes reflect the latest state-of-the-art knowledge and theory in this area. Part II concludes with a discussion of communication, and relates consumers as individuals to the world and the people around them. Thus, this chapter serves as a natural bridge between Parts II and III.

Part III is concerned with the social and cultural dimensions of consumer behavior. It begins with a discussion of group dynamics and consumer reference groups, followed by an examination of the influence of the family and the influence of social class on consumer behavior. It examines consumers in their cultural milieu and investigates the impact of societal and subcultural values, beliefs and customs on consumer behavior. Part III concludes with an exploration of consumer behavior in other countries and indicates the need for careful cross-cultural analyses in this era of increasing multinational marketing.

Part IV provides a greatly expanded treatment of various aspects of consumer decision making. It begins with a discussion of personal influence and opinion leadership, followed by an examination of the diffusion of innovations. Next it describes how consumers make product decisions and offers the reader a simple model of consumer decision making which ties together the psychological, social, and cultural concepts examined throughout the book. Part IV concludes with an overview of various models of consumer behavior that have received attention in consumer behavior literature over the years. In this section, as in our discussion of consumer learning, we have been particularly mindful of the importance of consumer information processing.

Part V, which is new to this edition, explores the implications of consumer behavior research for public policy issues and concludes with a discussion of the application of consumer behavior principles to nonprofit marketing.

Of the many people who have been enormously helpful in the preparation of this new edition of *Consumer Behavior*, we are especially grateful to our own consumers—the graduate and undergraduate students of consumer behavior, and their professors, who have provided us with invaluable experiential feedback from the first edition.

We would particularly like to thank our close friend and colleague, Professor Conrad Berenson, Chairman of the Department of Marketing at Baruch College, for his encouragement, his advice, and his unfailing support. Other colleagues at Baruch who deserve special recognition for their invaluable suggestions include Professors Benny Barak, Bernard Belasco, Jean Boddewyn, Maureen Coughlin, David Rachman, Gary Soldow and Joe Wisenblit. Professors William Dillon of the University of Massachusetts, Harold Kassarjian of the University of California at Los Angeles, Michael Mills of the University of Southern California, and Robert Settle of San Diego State University have provided us with critical and highly constructive comments for which we are very grateful.

Among the many other individuals who have provided us with valuable advice and assistance in the preparation of this manuscript, we would like to acknowledge Royce Anderson, Margaret Crowson, Nancy Flavin, Stanley Garfunkel, Elaine Romano, Barry Katz, Ben Morris, Carol Neustadt, Jeanne Pereira, C. Jerome Greenberg, Angela Schwimmer, Elaine Sherman, Avichai Shuv-Ami, Mat Stover, Lucille Streeter, and Susan Raul Weiner.

We would like to extend special thanks to Miss Ray Hessen, marketing vice-president of Professional Products, Revlon Corporation, for her insightful comments. And we would also like to acknowledge Marvin Roscoe and John Veltri of the American Telephone and Telegraph Company and Michael Jones and Elizabeth Slaughter of the New York Telephone Company for their consistent support and cooperation. To the many others whom we have not specifically named, we think of you, we thank you, and we love you nonetheless.

Leon G. Schiffman
Leslie Lazar Kanuk

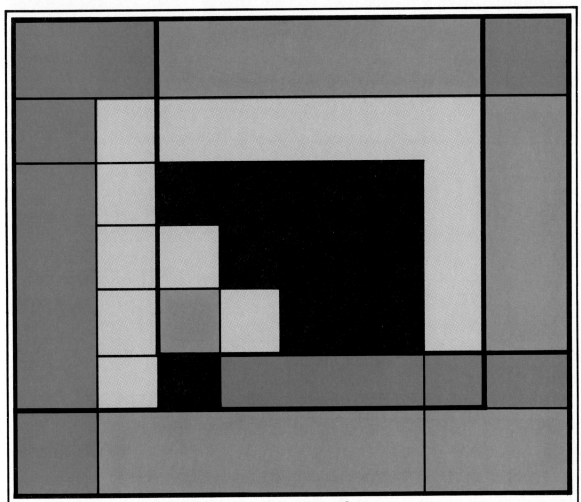

part one

INTRODUCTION

Part I is designed to introduce the reader to the study of consumer behavior. Chapter 1 sets the stage for the remainder of the book by focusing on (1) what consumer behavior is, (2) why we study consumer behavior, (3) how firms apply consumer behavior findings, and (4) how and why consumer behavior has developed as a theoretical and applied discipline. Chapter 2 discusses the theory and practice of market segmentation and demonstrates how consumer behavior provides both the conceptual framework and the strategic direction for the practical segmentation of markets.

ONE

Consumer Behavior:
Introduction

introduction

COSMETICS for men? A flourishing business today, but ten, or even five years ago no self-respecting cosmetics manufacturer would have attempted anything so foolhardy as marketing a line of cosmetics or skin-care products for men.

What has happened to make such products acceptable today? Have men become more vain? Have they become less masculine? Have sex roles become so blurred as to obscure the market for gender-specific products?

More to the point: What cues were there in the environment to signal marketers that the time was ripe to develop male-targeted skin-care products? What elements in a man's personality or lifestyle make cosmetics suddenly acceptable? What needs do they fulfill? How do they affect his self-image? How does he "learn" to use cosmetics? What influence do his family, his friends, or his social class have on his willingness to try or to buy cosmetics?

These are the types of questions that consumer behaviorists address as they try to understand what it is that influences consumers in their consumption-related decisions.

This book is designed to give the reader a strong understanding of the basic principles of consumer behavior, an insight into the scientific investigations on which our knowledge of consumer behavior is based, and an awareness of how these consumer behavior findings can be practically applied to the professional practice of marketing. For one of the few common denominators among all of us—no matter what our education, our politics, or our commitments—is that, above all, we are consumers. That is, we use or consume—on a regular basis—food, clothing, shelter, transportation, education, brooms, dishes, vacations, necessities, luxuries, services, even ideas. As consumers, we play a vital role in the health of the economy—local, national, and international. The decisions we make concerning our consumption behavior affect the demand for basic raw materials, for transportation, for production, for banking; they affect the employment of workers and the deployment of resources, the success of some industries and the failure of others. Thus, consumer behavior is an integral

Behavior is a mirror in which everyone displays his own image.

GOETHE,
Elective Affinities, 1809

4

FIGURE 1-1   Advertisement for Skin-Care Products for Men

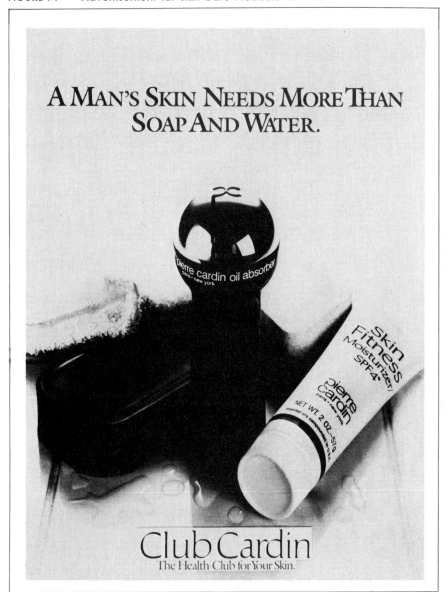

Courtesy of Pierre Cardin

factor in the ebbs and flows of *all* business in a consumer-oriented society such as
our own.

　　This chapter introduces the reader to the notion of consumer behavior as
an interdisciplinary science designed to investigate the decision-making activities
of individuals in their consumption roles. It describes the reasons for the
development of consumer behavior as an academic discipline and an applied
science. The role and scope of the research process in the study of consumer

behavior is considered. The chapter discusses the evolution of marketing in this country from a production orientation to a selling orientation to a consumer orientation, and briefly examines the importance of situational factors and level of consumer involvement on the consumer decision-making process.

WHAT IS CONSUMER BEHAVIOR?

The term *consumer behavior* can be defined as *the behavior that consumers display in searching for, purchasing, using, evaluating, and disposing of products, services and ideas which they expect will satisfy their needs.* The study of consumer behavior is the study of how individuals make decisions to spend their available resources (money, time, effort) on consumption-related items. It includes the study of *what* they buy, *why* they buy it, *how* they buy it, *when* they buy it, *where* they buy it, and *how often* they buy it. Thus the study of an individual's consumption behavior in the area of toothpaste products might include a study of his level of involvement (how important the purchase of toothpaste is to him), which brand of toothpaste he buys (e.g., Close-Up), why he buys it (because he believes that it will whiten his teeth better than competing brands), how he buys it (for cash and coupon), when he buys it (when he does the food shopping), where he buys it (in a supermarket), and how often he buys it (approximately every three weeks).

A study of another individual's consumption behavior regarding a more durable item, such as a rug, might include a study of what kind of rug she buys (e.g., a handloomed six-by-nine-foot rug), why she buys it (to give physical and visual warmth to her living room and to impress her friends), how she buys it (on credit), when she buys it (on home-furnishings sale days), where she buys it (in a well-known department store), how often she buys or replaces it (when it is worn or when she refurnishes her living room), and where she discards it (in a hospital thrift shop).

Although this text will focus on how and why consumers make decisions to buy goods and services, consumer behavior research today goes far beyond these facets of consumer behavior. Research also considers the uses that consumers make of the goods they buy and their evaluations of these goods after use. What happens after the consumer makes a purchase can have many repercussions. For example, a woman may feel remorse or dissatisfaction with her choice of a particular automobile—perhaps because she had to forgo an equally attractive purchase in order to pay for it, or because it has continuing service problems. She may communicate her dissatisfaction to a friend and may in turn influence his next purchase of an automobile. She may vow never to buy the same brand of auto again. Each of these possible consequences has significant ramifications for the marketer.

In addition to studying consumers' use and post-purchase evaluations of the products they buy, consumer researchers are also interested in how individuals dispose of their once-new purchases.[1] For example, after consumers have used a product, do they store it, throw it or give it away, sell it, rent it, or lend it out? The answer to this question is important to marketers because they must match their production to the frequency with which consumers buy replacements. But it is also important to society as a whole because scarce resources (both economic and natural resources) are forcing all of us to reevaluate our use of products and services, and because solid-waste disposal is a troubling environmental problem. Research into current disposal practices can enable marketers to develop and effectively promote environmentally sound and economically efficient products.

Types of Consumers

The term *consumer* is often used to describe two different kinds of consuming entities: (1) the personal consumer and (2) the organizational consumer. The *personal consumer* is the individual who buys goods and services for his or her own use (e.g., shaving cream or lipstick), for the use of the household (a cake mix), for just one member of the household (a shirt), or as a gift for a friend (a book). In all of these contexts, the goods are bought for final use by individuals, who are referred to as "end users" or "ultimate consumers."

The second category of consumer, the *organizational consumer*, encompasses private businesses, government agencies (local, state, and national), and institutions (schools, churches, prisons), all of which must buy products, equipment, and services in order to run their organizations—whether for profit or nonprofit. Manufacturing companies must buy the raw materials and other components to manufacture and sell their own products; service companies must buy the equipment necessary to render the services they sell; government agencies must buy the variety of products they need to operate their departments; and institutions must buy the materials they need to maintain themselves and their populations.

Despite the importance of both categories of consumers—individuals and organizations—this book will focus on the individual consumer, who purchases for his or her own personal use or for household use. End-use consumption is perhaps the most pervasive of all types of consumer behavior, since it involves every individual, of every age and every background, in the role of either buyer or user, or both.

Buyers versus Users

Inherent in the notion that individuals buy products for themselves and their families is the distinction that exists between buyers and users. The person who makes the actual purchase is not always the user, or the only user, of the product in question. Nor is the purchaser necessarily the person who makes the product decision. A mother may buy toys for her children (who are the users); she may buy food for dinner (and be one of the users); she may buy a handbag (and be the only user). She may buy a record that one of her teenagers requested, or a magazine that her husband requested, or she and her husband together may buy a car that they both selected. The various influences on family product-related decisions are discussed in detail in Chapter 12; suffice it here to stress the fact that buyers are not always the users, or the only users, of the products they buy, nor are they necessarily the persons who make the product selection decisions.

Prospects

Marketers must decide at whom to direct their promotional efforts; in so doing, they must identify the best *prospect* for the product they want to sell. Some marketers believe that the buyer of the product is the best prospect, others believe it is the user of the product, while still others play it safe by directing their promotional efforts to both buyers and users. For example, some toy manufacturers advertise their products on children's television shows to reach the users, others advertise in *Parents' Magazine* to reach the buyers, while still others run dual campaigns designed to reach both children and their parents. Because such toy marketers are uncertain as to how much influence children exert on their parents, they try to favorably influence parents in an effort to make them more receptive to their children's requests for particular toys.

Situational Factors

Specific consumer choices often depend on the buying situation. In gift buying, for example, individuals may select different qualities or brands (either higher or lower) when buying for a friend than they would for their own personal consumption. They may spend more on individual items of clothing when waited on by a salesperson than they would in self-service situations. The ability to charge a purchase may reduce the influence of price as a consideration, so that consumers may spend more on a specific item (e.g., a dress) charged to their account than they would if they had to actually count out the dollars in payment.

Level of Involvement

How important the product or product category is to the consumer in terms of image, self-concept, salience, and so forth, is reflected in the decision-making process. To some consumers, for example, bath soap is a low-involvement product to which they give almost no conscious thought in terms of brand selection. To other consumers, however, bath soap may be symbolic of personal luxury and pampering and overall beauty skin care, and these people will carefully search for a bath soap that they believe possesses the qualities they seek. Thus the level of involvement affects the entire purchase process, from the degree of search and evaluation of product alternatives to actual product selection.

WHY WE STUDY CONSUMER BEHAVIOR

The study of consumer behavior is concerned not only with *how* consumers behave but with *why* they behave as they do. As consumers, it is important for us to study consumer behavior so that we may gain greater insight into our own consumer-related decisions: what we buy, why we buy, and how we buy. The study of consumer behavior enables us to analyze our own consumption decisions and makes us aware of the subtle influences that persuade us to make the product choices we do.

As students of human behavior, it is important for us to understand the internal and external influences that impel individuals to act in certain consumption-related ways. Consumer behavior is simply a subset of the larger field of human behavior. As scientists, we are interested in understanding every aspect of human behavior. Certainly, as scientists, we should also want to understand the special aspect of human behavior known as consumer behavior.

As future marketers, it is important for us to be sufficiently well versed in the field of consumer behavior so that we can make significant contributions to the development of marketing strategy when we enter our chosen profession. Without doubt, marketers who do understand consumer behavior have a great competitive advantage in the marketplace.

HOW MARKETING FIRMS USE CONSUMER BEHAVIOR

To operate successfully, marketing firms must have a thorough understanding—explicit rather than implicit—of what makes consumers buy. They have to know *why* they buy, what *needs* they are trying to fulfill, and what outside *influences* affect their product choices in order to design marketing strategies that will favorably influence related consumer decisions.

Designing Marketing Strategies

Marketers use an understanding of consumer behavior to anticipate future behavior based on the implementation of specific marketing strategies. For example, awareness of consumers' predispositions, needs, and present attitudes toward certain products enables marketers to design effective marketing mixes, using variables that they control (such as advertising, packaging, pricing, retail outlets.) As depicted in Figure 1-2, *understanding* (and this is true of any human phenomenon) permits *prediction,* which in turn permits the development of strategies designed to achieve favorable results.

FIGURE 1-2   Knowledge of Consumer Behavior Facilitates Development of Successful Marketing Strategies

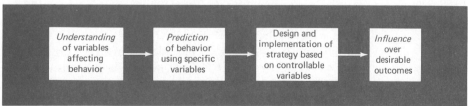

Measuring Marketing Performance

Clearly, a knowledge of consumer behavior serves as a strong basis for the development of marketing strategies. However, not only does consumer behavior *affect* marketing strategy, it also serves to *reflect* marketing strategy. A careful monitoring of consumer behavior in the marketplace enables the marketer to measure the success or failure of a specific marketing strategy. For example, if an advertising campaign that stresses a product's convenience does not produce the anticipated sales volume, the marketer may conclude that convenience is not a major factor in the decision to buy the product and endeavor to find a more effective marketing strategy.

Segmenting Markets

Marketers also use a knowledge of consumer behavior to segment their markets. The American consumer market is made up of some 222 million consumers who consume over $1.6 trillion worth of products and services each year. With such a vast market, made up of individuals who vary significantly in terms of education, age, interests, income, occupation, tastes, attitudes, residence, and so forth, it would be close to impossible for the average marketer to design a marketing mix (product, price, promotion, and distribution strategy) with sufficiently universal appeal to influence the purchase decisions of all.

The strategy that most marketers have developed to handle their vast potential market is to divide it up into smaller subgroups—or segments—each of which is similar (i.e., homogeneous) regarding some characteristic that is relevant to the purchase or the usage of the product or product category. This process is called market segmentation. One of the major contributions of consumer behavior to marketers is the identification of meaningful variables upon which to segment markets.

CONSUMER BEHAVIOR IS INTERDISCIPLINARY

The field of consumer behavior is based upon concepts and theories about people that were originally developed by scientists in disciplines and fields of inquiry other than marketing. This "interdisciplinary" nature of consumer behavior is perhaps its greatest strength: it serves to integrate existing knowledge from other fields into a comprehensive body of information about the consumer. Although the study of consumer behavior is of relatively recent origin, its underpinnings are rooted in strong scientific evidence that has emerged from many years of research by scientists specializing in the study of human behavior.

The major disciplines on which consumer behavior is based (i.e., from which it "borrows") include psychology, sociology, social psychology, cultural anthropology, and economics. In addition, a strong body of research specifically conducted by consumer behaviorists is now being developed.

Psychology

Psychology is the study of the individual. It includes the study of motivation, perception, attitudes, personality, and learning patterns. All of these factors are integral to an understanding of consumer behavior. They enable us to understand the various consumption needs of individuals, their actions and reactions in response to different products and product messages, and the way personality characteristics and previous experiences affect their product choices.

Sociology

Sociology is the study of groups. Group behavior—the actions of individuals in groups—often differs from the actions of individuals operating alone. The influence of group memberships, family structure, and social class on consumer behavior are all relevant to the study of consumer segments in the marketplace.

Social Psychology

Social psychology is an amalgam of sociology and psychology. It is the study of how an individual operates in a group. The study of consumer behavior is not only the study of how groups operate in terms of market behavior; it is also the study of how individuals are influenced in their personal consumption behavior by those whose opinions they respect: their peers, their reference groups, their families, and opinion leaders.

Cultural Anthropology

The study of human beings in society is the study of cultural anthropology. It traces the development of the core beliefs, values, and customs that are passed down to individuals from their parents and grandparents and influence their purchase and consumption behavior. It also includes the study of subcultures (subgroups within the larger society) and lends itself to a comparison of consumers of different nationalities with diverse cultures and customs.

Economics

An important component of the study of economics is the study of consumers: how they spend their funds, how they evaluate alternatives, and how they make decisions to maximize their satisfactions. Many of the early theories concerning consumer behavior were based on economic theory. For example, the "economic man" theory postulates that individuals act rationally to maximize their utilities (i.e., their benefits) in the purchase of goods and services. More recent consumer studies have indicated that individuals often act less than rationally (i.e., emotionally) to fulfill their psychological needs.[2]

To gain a greater understanding of consumers and their lifestyles, consumer researchers engage in extensive behavioral research into consumers and their consumption practices. As in any science, consumer behavior theories must be tested and either supported or rejected before conclusions can be generalized and applied to marketing practice. Some consumer behavior research is conducted on the basis of observations of actual behavior in the marketplace, other research is conducted under controlled conditions in the laboratory, still other research is based on the manipulation of marketing variables within a simulated marketing context.[3] Only through the constant testing, evaluation, rejection, and support of related hypotheses can a conceptual framework be developed that permits us to understand consumer behavior in depth. Consumer behavior research also enables marketers to carve out new market segments based on variables that emerge as important discriminators among consumers for a specific product or product category.

Scope of Consumer Behavior Research

Consumer behavior research takes place at every phase of the consumption process: from *before the purchase* takes place (when the consumer first becomes aware of a need), to the *actual purchase decision* (including product and brand choice, store choice, and method of payment), which may be either routine or based on careful search and evaluation of alternatives, to *after the purchase* takes place (through any periods of uncertainty, satisfaction, dissatisfaction, repurchase, or further search in the marketplace).

DEVELOPMENT OF CONSUMER BEHAVIOR AS A DISCIPLINE

There are a number of reasons why consumer behavior has developed as a separate discipline. Marketing scientists had long noted that consumers did not always act or react as economic theory would suggest. The size of the consumer market in this country was vast and still growing. Billions of dollars were being spent on goods and services by millions of people. The development of consumer behavior studies was in fact an outgrowth of the evolution of marketing philosophy and practice.

Impact of the Marketing Concept

At the end of World II, marketers found that they could sell almost any goods they could produce to consumers who had long done without because the nation's manufacturing facilities had been dedicated to the production of war materials. After consumer production had been resumed for a number of years, the public's appetite for consumer goods became somewhat sated, and consumers began to exercise discrimination in their selection of products.

At this point, many companies went from a production orientation to a selling orientation; that is, they switched their primary focus from production to selling. During this period, companies exerted a tremendous "hard sell" on consumers in order to move the goods that they unilaterally decided to produce.

Finally, in the early 1950s, many marketers began to realize that they could sell more goods, more easily, if they produced only those goods they had predetermined that consumers would buy. Instead of trying to persuade customers to buy what the firm has already produced, marketing-oriented firms try to produce and sell only what they have already determined that customers want. Thus consumers' needs become the firm's primary focus. This consumer-oriented marketing philosophy has come to be known as the "marketing concept."

The widespread adoption of the marketing concept by American business provided the impetus for the study of consumer behavior. To identify unsatisfied needs of consumers, companies had to engage in extensive marketing research. In so doing, they discovered that consumers were highly complex individuals, subject to a variety of psychological and social needs quite apart from their survival needs. They discovered that individuals' needs and their priorities differed dramatically. And they discovered that in order to design new products and marketing strategies that would fulfill the needs of consumers, they had to study consumers and their consumption behavior in depth. Thus the stage was set for the development of a new discipline called consumer behavior.

Fast Pace of New-Product Introduction

The technological explosion that hit this country soon after World War II has resulted in the introduction of new products at an ever-increasing rate. Many of these new products—some experts estimate over 80 percent—fail badly. To increase the likelihood of success, many marketers search for better information about what consumers are willing to buy, and try to discover new consumer needs. To find out what consumers want in the way of new products, how acceptable the new-product idea is, and how best to introduce it so that it will receive wide consumer acceptance, marketers try to learn as much as they can about consumers and what makes them "tick." In this way they hope to reduce new-product failures.

Shorter Product Life Cycles

Because of the fast pace of new-product introductions, products tend to have a shorter life cycle, since they are constantly subjected to modification, improvement, and replacement by new and substitute products. Faced with a much shorter product life cycle, companies constantly seek new-product ideas and concepts that will satisfy consumer needs. They also try to anticipate consumer lifestyles in an effort to develop products that will satisfy future needs. To do so, they must engage in careful research to try to discover consumer wants, needs, wishes, and lifestyles—both present and anticipated. Furthermore, they must engage in research designed to reveal how best to reach consumers in order to influence their purchase behavior. For all of these reasons, successful marketers have ongoing programs designed to study consumers and their consumption behavior.

Growth of Segmentation as a Marketing Strategy

As marketers began to study the behavior of consumers, they soon realized that despite overriding similarities, consumers were not all alike; nor did they wish to use the identical products that everyone else used. Rather, many consumers preferred differentiated products, which they felt closely reflected their own personal needs, wishes, personalities, lifestyles, and so forth. To better cater to the specialized needs of selected groups of consumers, marketers adopted a policy of market segmentation, in which they divided their total potential market into smaller, homogeneous segments for which they could design a specific marketing mix. A market segmentation strategy is based on satisfying the needs and wants of specific groups of consumers; thus it requires a great deal of insight into the consumption habits of selected market segments. The collection and analysis of such information is the province of the field of consumer behavior.

Increased Interest in Consumer Protection

The increased interest in consumerism and the growth of private consumer groups concerned with protecting the rights of the consuming public have created a much greater need to understand consumer behavior in depth. For example, it is important to discover how consumers perceive various marketing and promotional appeals in order to identify potential sources of consumer confusion and deception. A large, half-filled package of noodles may be purchased by consumers who are deceived into thinking that it contains a greater quantity than more tightly packaged competitive brands. Consumer research that reveals such erroneous consumer perceptions provides the basis for recommendations concerning new consumer protection legislation.

Setting of Public Policy

Parallel with the growth of the consumer protection movement, public policy-makers at the local, state, and federal levels became more aware of their responsibility to sponsor legislation designed to protect the interests and the well-being of their consumer constituents. At the federal level, such agencies as the Federal Trade Commission, Federal Communications Commission, and Food and Drug Administration are increasingly undertaking research to discover the impact of products and promotional campaigns on the consuming public. As the surge of interest in consumer protection increases, these agencies are likely to undertake increasing numbers of consumer-oriented studies in order to determine the public's reaction to proposed legislation.

Environmental Concerns

Increasing public concern over dangers to the environment has made both marketers and public policymakers aware of the potentially negative impact of a number of consumer products, such as high-suds detergents, aerosol sprays, disposable bottles, and nonbiodegradable packages. Research into consumer needs and practices has enabled marketers to develop and effectively promote environmentally sound product substitutes for the socially concerned consumer.

Growth of Nonprofit Marketing

Organizations in the public and the nonprofit sectors have begun to realize the importance of adopting marketing practices in order to bring their services to the attention of their relevant publics. For example, organizations such as private and public colleges, welfare agencies, hospitals, and museums have found that to successfully identify their appropriate markets and to adequately satisfy the needs of these markets, they have to undertake in-depth consumer behavior research.

Computer and Statistical Techniques

The development of appropriate tools and techniques has encouraged and facilitated research into consumer behavior. For example, the computer enables scientists to process and store vast amounts of data concerning consumer activities, and the use of sophisticated statistical techniques enables researchers to analyze masses of information concerning consumers.

PLAN OF THE BOOK

In order to build a useful conceptual framework that both enhances understanding and permits practical application of consumer behavior principles, this book is divided into five parts. The following chapter supplements this introduction by describing market segmentation as an effective marketing strategy and illustrates how consumer behavior research can be used to identify homogeneous target markets. Market segmentation is the basic theme that underlies the balance of the book.

Part II explores the consumer as an individual. It discusses how individuals are motivated (Chapter 3); the impact of individual personality characteristics (Chapter 4) and lifestyles (Chapter 5) on consumer behavior; and the process and importance of perception (Chapter 6) and learning (Chapter 7) on consumer attitudes (Chapters 8 and 9). This part concludes with an examination of the communication process and its impact on consumer behavior (Chapter 10).

Part III focuses on consumers as members of society, subject to varying external influences on their buying behavior, such as their group memberships (Chapter 11), families (Chapter 12), social class (Chapter 13), and the broad cultural and specific subcultural groups to which they belong (Chapters 14 and 15).

Part IV examines the consumer decision-making process. It explores the impact of respected "others" whose product opinions influence consumer choices (Chapter 16) and describes the process by which new products are adopted by consumers and "diffused" throughout the target population (Chapter 17). The various steps in the consumer decision-making process are presented in Chapter 18, and various models of this process are examined in Chapter 19.

Part V concludes with a discussion of the broad application of consumer behavior research to public policy and other nonprofit marketing endeavors (Chapter 20).

summary

Consumer behavior can be defined as *the behavior that consumers display in searching for, purchasing, using, evaluating, and disposing of products, services, and ideas which they expect will satisfy their needs.* The study of consumer behavior is concerned not only with *what* consumers buy but with *why* they buy it, *when, where,* and *how* they buy it, and *how often* they buy it. Consumer behavior research takes place at every phase of the consumption process: before the purchase, during the purchase, and after the purchase.

There are two kinds of consumers: *personal* (or *ultimate*) *consumers,* who buy goods and services for their own use or for household use, and *organizational consumers,* who buy products, equipment, and services in order to run their organizations, which may be operated for profit (e.g., commercial enterprises) or nonprofit (e.g., governmental agencies, museums, or hospitals).

Consumer behavior is interdisciplinary; that is, it is based upon concepts and theories about people which have been developed by scientists in such diverse disciplines as psychology, sociology, social psychology, cultural anthropology, and economics.

Marketing firms use their knowledge of consumer behavior to design marketing strategies, to measure marketing performance, and to segment markets. The development of consumer behavior studies was an outgrowth of the evolution of marketing philosophy from a production orientation to a selling orientation to a marketing orientation (the so-called marketing concept). Other factors that have contributed to the development of consumer behavior studies include the fast pace of new-product introduction, shorter product life cycles, the high rate of new-product failures, increased interest in consumer protection by private groups and public policy decisionmakers, concern over the environment, the adoption of marketing practices by nonprofit organizations, the availability of computers and sophisticated statistical techniques, and the growth of segmentation as a marketing strategy.

discussion questions

1. Mrs. Jones, a housewife, is buying a can of Campbell's soup. Mr. Jones, her husband, a buyer for a quality men's store, is ordering a new line of men's leisure suits. Describe the consumer behavior aspects of each purchase in terms of
   a. What, why, how, when, how often
   b. Personal versus organizational buying
   c. Buyer versus user
2. In the 1920s, Henry Ford remarked that his customers could have any color car they wanted as long as it was black. Why won't the president of Ford Motor Company make the same statement today? In your answer, discuss the changes in marketing philosophy that have occurred since the 1920s.
3. You are the product manager of a line of toys for preschool children. Describe how an understanding of consumer behavior can be useful to you in terms of
   a. Market segmentation strategy
   b. New-product introduction
   c. Product life cycle
   d. Consumer protection
4. Name three ways in which an understanding of consumer behavior can help the marketer design effective marketing strategies.
5. Consumer behavior has been said to both *affect* and *reflect* marketing strategy. Discuss.
6. Consumer behavior is based on principles "borrowed" from other disciplines. Name five such disciplines and explain how they contribute to the study of consumer behavior.
7. "Consumers don't need more laws to protect them; they need more knowledge." Discuss.
8. An argument often used against the application of consumer behavior research in the nonprofit sector is that you can't sell "brotherhood" like you do soap. Do you agree? Why or why not?

endnotes

1. See Jacob Jacoby, Carol K. Berning, and Thomas F. Dietvorst, "What about Disposition?" *Journal of Marketing*, 41 (April 1977), 22–28, and Jacob Jacoby, "Consumer Research: A State of the Art Review," *Journal of Marketing*, 42 (April 1978), esp. 94–95.
2. See, for example, Otto Pollack, "Symptomatic Factors in Consumer Behavior," in Wroe Alderson, Stanley Shapiro, and Reavis Cox, eds., *Theory in Marketing*, 2nd ed. (Homewood, Ill.: Richard D. Irwin, 1964), 281–87.
3. For a critical article on current behavioral research techniques and practices, see Jacoby, "Consumer Research," esp. 87–94.

TWO

Market Segmentation

introduction

IN the preceding chapter we saw how the development of the marketing concept gave impetus to the study of consumer behavior. As marketers began to study the behavior of consumers, they soon realized that despite overriding similarities, consumers were not all alike; nor did they wish to use the identical products that everyone else used. Rather, many consumers preferred differentiated products that they felt more closely reflected their own personal needs, personalities, lifestyles, and so forth. To better satisfy the specialized needs of selected groups of consumers, marketers adopted a policy of market segmentation.

Though the concept of segmentation is relatively new, it has spread very fast. As evidence, we need only point to the great variety of automobiles—of every color and style—that can be found on the street, or note the vast array of magazines—for every conceivable interest from tennis to auto repair to astrology—that can be found at the corner newsstand.

Consumer behavior findings have direct application to effective market segmentation. This chapter will examine some of the key elements of segmentation strategy and explore the criteria marketers use to determine when and if a segmentation approach is feasible. The chapter concludes with an evaluation of the strengths and weaknesses of this key marketing strategy.

WHAT IS MARKET SEGMENTATION?

Before the widespread adoption of the marketing concept, the prevailing way of doing business with consumers was through mass marketing; that is, offering the identical product to all consumers. The essence of this strategy was summed up by entrepreneur Henry Ford, who offered the Model T automobile to the public "in any color it wanted, as long as it was black." The public could also have any refrigerator it wanted, as long as it was white, and any boots it wanted, as long as they were high-buttoned.

By nature, men are nearly alike; by practice, they get to be wide apart.

CONFUCIUS
Analects, 5th c. BC

If all potential customers did indeed have the same needs, *mass marketing*—the practice of offering a single product or marketing mix to everyone—would be a logical strategy. A few companies, primarily those that deal in agricultural products or very simple manufactured goods (such as needles), do use a mass-marketing approach. The primary advantage of mass marketing is that it saves money. One advertising campaign is all that is needed; one marketing strategy is all that is developed; and usually, one standardized product is all that is offered.

There are, of course, drawbacks to such a strategy for both producers and consumers. In trying to sell their products to every prospect by using a single advertising campaign, marketers must try to represent their products as being all things to all people and may end up by appealing to no one. Without market differentiation, the bachelor and the family of six would have to make do with the same standard-sized refrigerator.

Segmentation developed as an answer to the problems of both marketers and consumers. A good statement of the essence of segmentation strategy is the slogan General Motors used for years—"A car for every price, purpose, and personality." More formally, *market segmentation* is *the process of dividing a potential market into distinct subsets of consumers and selecting one or more segments as a market target to be reached with a distinct marketing mix.*

The strategy of segmentation allows producers to avoid head-on competition in the marketplace by differentiating their offerings, not just on the basis of price, but through styling, packaging, promotional appeal, or a unique mode of distribution. By offering distinctively styled cars with many options, for example, General Motors no longer has to undercut the price of Ford to have a wide market appeal. Manufacturing many different models does, of course, raise costs because engineering costs are higher and production runs are shorter. But sales are likely to increase, offsetting the higher costs, because many more consumers can find just what they want. Consumers are thereby better off as well.

Users of Segmentation

Because the strategy of market segmentation benefits both sides of the marketplace, it has quickly caught on. Manufacturers of consumer goods are eager practitioners of market segmentation. Today nearly every product category in the consumer market is highly segmented. To take just one example, the $359 million vitamin market is subdivided by age (adults, children), place of distribution (drugstores, grocery stores, health food stores), and formulation (multivitamins, special combinations of vitamins, liquids, and tablets).[1]

But the makers of consumer goods are not the only users of segmentation. The manufacturers of products that are used by business and industry also segment their markets. Xerox produces different copiers to meet the needs of small-, medium-, and large-sized firms. IBM produces different computer models to meet the needs of banks, retailers, and industrial firms.

The concept of market segmentation has also been adopted by retailers. Sears, Roebuck has carved out a specific market segment—the blue-collar shopper looking for economy and practicality—as its target market. The company's attempt a few years back to become a fashion merchandiser failed, precisely because it could not shake the image that had long made it a success. In contrast, stores like Neiman-Marcus and Saks Fifth Avenue deliberately carry high-priced and high-fashion clothing, and actively cultivate an image designed to appeal to the opposite end of the market spectrum—the affluent consumer.

As noted in Chapter 1, the nonprofit sector has recently begun to realize the importance of marketing, and it too has adopted segmentation strategies. Charities such as the March of Dimes frequently concentrate their fund-raising efforts on heavy givers. Theater companies, such as the American Conservatory Theatre of San Francisco, have been able to segment their subscribers on the basis of benefits sought in subscribing and have succeeded in increasing attendance through specialized promotional appeals.[2]

Finally, various media vehicles—magazines, cable TV stations, radio stations—deliberately single out highly specific target segments to whom they appeal through special-interest programming. For example, classical music stations, disco stations, and all-news stations attract very different radio audiences. The major advantage of capturing a specialized or unique audience segment is that the medium can then "sell" that audience to advertisers interested in reaching the same segment.

Uses of Segmentation

Not only are the *users* of segmentation quite diverse, but the strategic *uses* of segmentation are equally wide-ranging. Basically, segmentation strategies are designed to discover the needs and wants of specific groups of consumers so that specialized goods and services can be developed and promoted to satisfy their needs. Many new products have been developed to fill product gaps in the marketplace revealed through segmentation research. For example, the Aurora Toy Company discovered through research that youngsters five to eight years of age liked to play with their older brothers' electric slot cars but were themselves not capable of assembling the models then on the market. By simplifying the design, Aurora "scooped" its competitors, which until then had provided only nonelectric, mechanical models for younger children.[3]

Besides aiding in the development of new products, segmentation studies are also used to guide the redesign or repositioning of old products as sales of a brand begin to taper off. Very often all that is needed is to find a new market segment for the product. Repositioning the product can be accomplished either by changing some features of the product itself or simply by changing its promotion, distribution, or price. For example, Revlon repositioned its Natural Wonder line of cosmetics from the teenage market to the slightly older, cost-conscious woman, a segment that market studies showed to be more promising. New black-and-white, no-nonsense packaging, and distribution through drugstores and supermarkets rather than department stores, were part of the repositioning effort.[4]

Advertising, aided by segmentation research, plays a major role in the positioning of any product. Advertisers can better tailor their messages if they know exactly whom they are targeting and what these consumers are seeking in the way of product benefits. Segmentation studies reveal the characteristics and needs of potential product users. For example, segmentation research in a medium-sized city of three hundred thousand inhabitants revealed a distinct segment of primarily younger men who sought convenience and a range of financial services in their banking institutions, rather than the friendly atmosphere or community services that appealed to older citizens.[5] Depending upon which segment a bank preferred to target, it could develop commercials featuring the bank's express lines or information concerning bank-assisted auto loans, mortgages, or life insurance, or it could feature senior citizens meeting or socializing on the bank's premises.

In addition to shaping advertising messages, segmentation research is used by advertisers to identify the most appropriate media in which to place their advertisements. Almost all media vehicles—from TV and radio stations to newspapers and magazines—use segmentation research to determine the characteristics of their audiences, and they then publicize their findings to attract advertisers seeking similar audiences. Independent groups are also interested in discovering the audience characteristics of various media. For example, a study of female magazine readership in the Syracuse area discovered three distinct segments of readers, which the researchers identified as (1) *feminists* (primarily young, well-educated readers, either working or still in school, who were strongly supportive of women's issues); (2) *traditionalists* (primarily older readers with somewhat less education, who thought of themselves as housewives and supported more traditional female roles); and (3) *moderates* (primarily younger readers who were more likely to hold full-time jobs than the traditionalists and who were divided on feminist issues).[6]

The reading habits of these three segments are summarized in Table 2-1. The table suggests that an advertiser who wants to appeal to a broad cross-section of women (e.g., a marketer of panty hose) can use fashion magazines or local newspapers, since all three female segments read these media. However, if the marketer wished to appeal primarily to working women (as might be the case if the product were briefcases), news, business, and consumer magazines would be more appropriate.

CRITERIA FOR EFFECTIVE MARKET SEGMENTATION

Several criteria must be met if a market segmentation strategy is to be successful: (1) The total market must contain significant subgroups; (2) these subgroups must be identifiable; and (3) they must be reachable through specialized media.

Identification

Segments must be identifiable; that is, a significant proportion of a firm's potential market must have a common need or characteristic that can be identified by the marketer. For example, if a sufficient number of people in the

TABLE 2-1   Magazine Readership Habits for Three Segments of the Female Market

TYPE OF PUBLICATION	SEGMENT(S) TO WHICH IT APPEALS
1. Homemaker magazines (Family Circle, Woman's Day, Better Homes and Gardens, Good Housekeeping, McCall's, House Beautiful)	1. Moderates and traditionalists
2. Movie and romance magazines (True Story Magazine, Modern Romances, True Confessions, Modern Screen)	2. Moderates and traditionalists
3. National and international news (New York Times [Sunday], New York Times [daily], Newsweek)	3. Feminists
4. Business and consumer magazines (Consumer Bulletin, Consumer Reports, Business Week)	4. Moderates and feminists
5. Fashion magazines (Cosmopolitan, Glamour)	5. Moderates, traditionalists, feminists
6. Cultural and intellectual magazines (Saturday Review, New Yorker, Harper's Magazine, U.S. News & World Report, Atlantic, Ms.)	6. None
7. Local news (Syracuse Post-Standard, Syracuse Herald Journal, Business Week)	7. Moderates, traditionalists, feminists

Source: Adapted from Alladi Venkatesh and Clint B. Tankersley, "Magazine Readership by Female Segments," *Journal of Advertising Research*, 19 (August 1979), 36–38.

household detergent market have newborn infants, then mothers of newborn infants can become a feasible market segment for a differentiated detergent product, promoted through a campaign carefully tailored to appeal to their special needs and interests. If a substantial number of families in a community own homes in the $50,000 to $80,000 range, then middle-income homeowners can become a feasible market segment for a local home maintenance service.

Some segmentation characteristics are easily identifiable, such as age, occupation, race, or geographic location. Other characteristics can be determined through questioning, such as education, income, or marital status. Still other characteristics are more difficult to identify, such as attitudes, personality, or lifestyle. A knowledge of consumer behavior is especially useful to marketers who wish to segment their markets on the basis of such elusive or intangible consumer characteristics.

Sufficiency

There must be a sufficient number of people with the same characteristics to make it profitable for a marketer to adopt a policy of market segmentation. For example, few shoe manufacturers have found it worthwhile to market shoes for people who have two different-sized feet, because the number of people who require two different-sized shoes is apparently not large enough to warrant special treatment. On the other hand, some manufacturers do market shoes for men with very large or very wide feet, presumably because there are enough men with outsized feet to make it a profitable market segment.

Accessibility

A third requirement for effective market segmentation is accessibility, which means that marketers must be able to reach the market segment with specially tailored promotional messages. If a segment is found of invalids whose main interests consist of reading the classics, but there is no known advertising medium with which to reach this segment, dividing the market on that basis would be impractical. On the other hand, if the preferred reading material consisted of paperback spy novels, the segment could possibly be reached by placing advertising inserts in the books.

It may not be worthwhile for advertisers to use media with a mass-audience appeal to reach a specific market segment, because they would have to pay for wasted circulation coverage. For example, manufacturers of expensive lawn furniture may be able to reach owners of luxury homes through advertising in *TV Guide,* but they are also paying good advertising dollars to reach many readers who have no use for the product. If no specialized medium is available to communicate with a specific market segment, it might be wise for the marketer to eliminate that segment.

BASES FOR SEGMENTATION

Although the criteria for effective market segmentation are essentially the same, the consumer characteristics that serve as bases for segmentation strategies are quite diverse. Five major classes of such characteristics can be distinguished, as shown in Table 2-2. They include *geographic* characteristics, *demographic* characteristics, *psychological* characteristics, *social-cultural* characteristics, and *user-behavior* characteristics. Recent consumer research suggests two additional bases for segmentation: *level of consumer involvement* in the product category and *situational factors* surrounding the purchase decision.

Geographic Segmentation

In geographic segmentation, the market is divided in terms of different locations. The theory behind such a strategy is that people who live in the same locale have similar needs and wants, and that these needs and wants differ from

TABLE 2-2   Market Segmentation Categories and Selected
Segmentation Variables

VARIABLES	EXAMPLES
geographic characteristics	
Region	North, South, East, West
City size	Major metropolitan areas, small cities, towns
Density of area	Urban, suburban, exurban, rural
Climate	Temperate, hot, humid
demographic characteristics	
Age	Under 11, 12–17, 18–34, 35–49, 50 +
Sex	Male, female
Marital status	Single, married, divorced
Income	Under $10,000, $10,000–14,999, $15,000–$24,999, $25,000–$40,000, over $40,000
Occupation	Professional, blue-collar, white-collar, agricultural
Education	Some high school, high-school graduate, some college, college graduate
psychological characteristics	
Personality	Extroverts, introverts, aggressives, compliants
Lifestyle	Swingers, straights, conservatives, status seekers
Benefits sought	Convenience, prestige, economy
social-cultural characteristics	
Culture	American, Italian, Chinese, Mexican
Subculture	
Religion	Jewish, Catholic, Protestant, other
Race	Black, Caucasian, Oriental, Hispanic
Social class	Lower, middle, upper
Family life cycle	Bachelors, young marrieds, empty nesters
user-behavior characteristics	
Usage rate	Heavy, medium, light users, nonusers
Brand loyalty status	None, medium, strong

those of people in other areas. That assumption is not as valid today as it was in the past when, lacking good transportation, television, and other means of communication, communities tended to grow up in isolation from one another and developed distinctive tastes and customs. Beer, for example, was once brewed almost entirely on a local basis.

Although Americans, as a people, are much more unified today, regional differences still exist. For example, certain food products sell better in one region than in others (e.g., cream cheese and frozen waffles tend to sell better in the Northeast, Japanese food with plenty of soy sauce in the Northwest, and cake mixes and cottage cheese in the Midwest and Mountain States). Other product categories that show regional differences are appliances (home freezers sell best in the Southeast, garbage disposals on the West Coast); automotive products (snow tires in the Northeast, power house trailers in the Northwest, motorcycles and foreign cars on the West Coast); and clothing (down clothing in the Northwest, full slips and very narrow women's shoes in the Southeast).[7]

Some of the regional differences can be accounted for by climate. The Sunbelt regions of the South and the West represent better opportunities for selling swimming pools and suntan lotion than the Snowbelt regions of the North and East, where quilts and snow shovels are likely to be better sellers.

But beyond regional and climatic differences, researchers have found that product usage differs even between cities. Some of these differences are listed in Table 2-3. Such findings are important to marketers, especially in planning their advertising. Many companies that market nationally would prefer to allocate their advertising dollars to those areas where they can get the best results. Some advertising firms now offer their clients just such an option in market-by-market ad plans. Thus a company like Prudential, which sells life insurance nationally, might devote more of its advertising budget to Pittsburgh (the best market for such insurance, according to the table) than to Miami (the worst).[8]

Besides differences between cities, marketers are also conscious of diver-

TABLE 2-3   Product Purchases by City—the Best and the Worst

PRODUCT	THE BEST	THE WORST
Beer & ale (% of drinkers who consume)	Milwaukee (67.9)	Dallas/Fort Worth (44.2)
Bicycles (% adults who ever bought)	Minneapolis/St. Paul (30)	Atlanta (18.5)
Brief cases (% adults who ever bought)	Los Angeles (12.9)	Cincinnati (6.2)
Canned chili (% of homemakers who use)	Dallas/Forth Worth (72.7)	Boston (6)
Deodorants & antiperspirants (% adults who use once a day)	Baltimore (88.1)	Minneapolis/St. Paul (78.3)
Foreign travel (% adults who traveled in past three years)	Seattle/Tacoma (38)	Cincinnati (10.8)
Fur coats (% adults who ever bought)	Detroit (11)	Cincinnati (6.4)
Insecticides (% of homemakers who use at least once a month)	Houston (61.9)	New York (26.4)
Life Insurance (% adults who currently have)	Pittsburgh (80.3)	Miami (53.4)
Lipstick (% of women using at least twice a day)	Seattle/Tacoma (58.2)	Cincinnati (35.6)
Men's neckties (% men who bought one within 12 months)	Cleveland (18)	Pittsburgh (10.2)

TABLE 2-3   Continued

PRODUCT	THE BEST	THE WORST
Motor oil (% adults who buy)	Dallas/Fort Worth (64.8)	New York (40.8)
Panty hose (% women who bought in past month)	Houston (61.1)	Miami (39.7)
Paperback books (% adults who bought in last 30 days)	Seattle/Tacoma (53.2)	Dallas/Fort Worth (31.3)
Popcorn (% adults who buy for home use)	Minneapolis/St. Paul (54.3)	Miami (26.5)
Restaurants (% adults who visited in past month)	Seattle/Tacoma (72.6)	Washington, D.C. (54.9)
Scotch whisky (% of drinkers who consume)	New York (35.9)	Cincinnati (9.6)
Shotguns (% adults who ever bought)	Minneapolis/St. Paul (12)	New York (3.1)
Tennis racquets (% adults who ever bought)	Los Angeles (17.5)	Cincinnati (9.8)

Source: Major Market Index 1977; reprinted from Niles Howard, "More Bang for the Dollar," *Dun's Review*, 112 (October 1978), 107.

gent consumer purchasing patterns in rural, suburban, and urban areas. Throughout the United States, more furs and expensive jewelry are sold in cities than in small towns. Even within a large metropolitan area, different types of household furnishings and leisure products are sold in the central city and in the suburbs. For example, convertible sofas and small appliances are more likely to be bought by the city apartment dweller than the suburban homeowner, who may in turn call for more outdoor furniture or king-sized beds. This, of course, is a function of available living space and of lifestyle, both characteristics that lend themselves to segmentation.

One firm that has capitalized on the differences between small-town and metropolitan areas is Wal-Mart. While its major competitors, K-Mart and J.C. Penney, have battled for market share in areas with populations of at least one hundred thousand, Wal-Mart has concentrated its stores in rural areas of twenty-five thousand or less, especially in the South Central States. Compared with the other chains, Wal-Mart stores are smaller and carry fewer items, mainly budget-priced staple goods such as motor oil and cosmetics. But Wal-Mart stores meet the needs of the lower-income rural consumers they serve, and they are expected to grow as rural areas of the Sunbelt benefit from the influx of new industry.[9]

Market Segmentation

Geographic segmentation, therefore, can be a profitable strategy. It is relatively easy to find geographically based differences for some products; in addition, geographic segments are usually readily accessible through local media, including newspapers, TV, and radio, and through regional editions of magazines. Its main limitation is that while segments for product categories can readily be distinguished, segments for specific brands (other than local brands) cannot. Other consumer characteristics must be used for that purpose.

Demographic Segmentation

Demographic characteristics, such as age, sex, marital status, income, occupation, and education, are most often used as the basis for market segmentation. *Demography* refers to the vital and measurable statistics of a population. Demographic characteristics are generally easy to identify and to measure; furthermore, they can often be associated—either singly or in composite—with the usage of specific products and with specific media.

AGE

Because product needs often vary with age, marketers have found age to be a useful variable in distinguishing segments. Many producers have carved out a place in the market by concentrating on a specific age segment. For example, Fisher-Price produces toys exclusively for preschoolers, and K-tel records are aimed at album buyers 7 to 15 years of age.[10]

Since expanding market segments usually represent the best marketing opportunities, marketers in the 1980s are particularly interested in people aged 35–44, and those over 65. The former segment consists of individuals born in the baby boom immediately following World War II, which constitutes a large percentage of today's population. The over-65 group is also large and growing, primarily because of medical advances that have increased the average life span. When the group now in the 35–44 age bracket were in their teens (in the 1960s), they helped make the fortunes of record, jeans, and soft drink producers. These manufacturers are trying to hold on to that now older segment by modifying their offerings. Levi has begun to promote slacks with fuller proportions for men who have outgrown their teen dimensions. Coca-Cola has diversified into diet sodas and other drinks for more mature tastes (e.g., Coke now owns Minute Maid). In addition, new-product categories are beginning to thrive because they are now of interest to the "aging" baby boom segment. Home furnishings and do-it-yourself products fall into this category.

The "gray market," as those over 65 have been called, is the second fastest-growing segment today.[11] It is the target market for such services as auto maintenance and home repairs. Since members of this segment are often retirees, they are also a ready target for travel promotions. Tours by train and bus have special appeal because many senior citizens are on limited budgets. Magazines such as *Modern Maturity* and *50 Plus* make this segment easily accessible to advertisers.

SEX

Sex has always been a distinguishing segmentation variable. Women have traditionally been the main users of such products as hair coloring and cosmetics; and men, of cigars and shaving preparations.

In recent years, however, sex roles have been breaking down, and gender may no longer be an accurate way to distinguish consumers in some product categories. The hair-care market, which used to be divided strictly along sex lines, with barbershops for men and beauty salons for women, is becoming much more homogeneous with the advent of unisex beauty shops and unisex hair products.

Role changes may have limited *gender* as a segmentation variable in some markets, but they have created new opportunities in others. For example, the market for men's fragrances and skin-care products has grown tremendously in the past ten years, as has the market for life insurance for women.

Much of the change in sex roles has come about because of the upsurge in the number of working women (see Chapter 15). One consequence for marketers is that women are not as readily accessible through traditional media as they once were. Since working women do not have as much time to watch TV or listen to the radio as those who do not work, many advertisers now emphasize magazines in their media schedules, especially those specifically aimed at working women (such as *Savvy, Self,* and *Working Mother.*)[12]

MARITAL STATUS

Marital status is an increasingly important variable for segmenting markets, now that more and more people are choosing to remain single or are divorcing. In the past, the focus of most marketing efforts was the family, but marketers are gradually discovering the benefits of targeting special promotional efforts to singles. Campbell's now has a line of Soups-for-One, and Stouffer's has promoted a line of frozen entrees to people living away from home for the first time. Marketers are also offering "mini-appliances," such as burger makers and two-cup coffee makers, to singles. To reach this growing segment, new magazines (e.g., *Your Place*) have emerged.

INCOME

Income has long been an important variable for distinguishing market segments. Marketers are usually interested in the higher-income brackets—and for good reason. The 30 percent of families at the highest-income levels in this country control 54 percent of total purchasing power. Moreover, while there are perhaps 20 million families in that category now, their number is expected to increase over the next ten years, bringing in many more people in the 25–44 age bracket.[13]

As real income rises, individuals tend to spend less of their total earnings on necessities and more on luxuries. Some marketers of luxury products are already reaping the benefits of increased affluence. Cadillac, for example, now markets four models—two for younger upscale customers and two for older and slightly more affluent customers. Cadillac sales continue to climb despite generally hard economic times.

OCCUPATION AND EDUCATION

Marketers have found that occupational category (white-collar, blue-collar, etc.) and educational level can also be used to distinguish market segments. For example, beer is more likely to be marketed to less-educated, blue-collar workers; Scotch and fine wines, on the other hand, are generally targeted at college-educated, white-collar workers or professionals.

Just as income level is rising, so too is the level of education. By 1985, one out of every three Americans is expected to have at least some college background. The composition of the work force is changing as the amount of education rises. Today over 50 percent of the work force is engaged in white-collar occupations (in schools, offices, banks, etc.), and that percentage is expected to increase. Cultural organizations such as museums, operas, and theaters—which have traditionally catered to upper-income groups—are now broadening their appeals to reach new segments.

COMBINING DEMOGRAPHIC VARIABLES

Although some marketers rely on a single demographic variable to define significant market segments, marketers often combine consumer characteristics to identify likely groups of consumers. The automobile market provides an illustration. Table 2-4 shows the demographic profiles of buyers of various Chevrolet models. Age, income, educational status, and sex are the distinguishing characteristics. The Monza buyer, for example, is about the same age as the Corvette buyer but is more likely to be female, earn less money, and have less education than the Corvette buyer. Both of these segments contrast sharply with the Nova buyer, who tends to be an older, less-educated male with a relatively low income.

Demographic variables are particularly useful when combined to pinpoint a target market. Combined (or composite) variables are also used to identify stages in the family life cycle and social classes (see Chapters 12 and 13). But demographic variables do not always provide sufficient information to fine-tune a marketing effort. Two individuals with the same demographic profile may still

TABLE 2-4   Chevrolet Purchaser Demographics

	CHEVETTE	MONZA	CAMARO	NOVA	MALIBU	MONTE CARLO	REGULAR	CORVETTE
Median age...........	37	30	26	49	47	39	50	32
Income...............	$21,000	18,000	20,000	16,500	20,500	20,000	23,100	29,500
Some college..........	60%	54%	61%	42%	55%	55%	54%	69%
Female	44%	53%	46%	39%	39%	38%	27%	24%

Source: William B. Ruxlow, "Demographics Lay Out a Giant Puzzle," *Advertising Age*, September 17, 1979, S-30.

purchase different brands. To understand why, marketers often have to turn to other consumer characteristics, such as psychological makeup.

Psychological Segmentation

Psychological characteristics refer to the intrinsic qualities of an individual, such as personality and lifestyle. Individual differences of this sort are important bases for segmentation. Unlike demographic research, which sometimes provides marketers with a superficial view of their customers, psychological research delves into consumer motives and beliefs for a more in-depth understanding of why certain product choices are made. (Chapter 4 focuses on personality characteristics, and Chapter 5 explores the elusive quality of psychographics, also known as lifestyle.)

PERSONALITY

The earliest psychological segmentation studies concentrated on the relationship between personality characteristics and product choice. The object was to find one or more personality traits that could reliably predict the selection of one brand over another. Consumers were given standard personality tests that measured such traits as dominance or aggression and were also asked—in an addendum, as it were—to specify their brand preferences in certain product categories. Researchers then looked for correlations between personality traits and brand preferences. A few studies turned up some interesting correlations. For example, it was found that aggressive men were more likely than compliant men to use after-shave lotion and manual razors and to buy Old-Spice aftershave.[14] Most studies of this sort, however, were inconclusive.

The problem seemed to be that correlations were sought with traits that had no intrinsic relationship to the products under study. The traits were selected primarily because they were included in standardized personality tests and could easily be measured. More promising research resulted from letting relevant consumer characteristics come to the surface during product-related discussions.

PSYCHOGRAPHICS

The distinctive lifestyles that individuals adopt are the basis for psychographic segmentation. There are three principal indicators of lifestyle: *activities,* or how consumers spend their time; *interests,* or what preferences consumers have; and *opinions,* or where consumers stand on social issues, products, or a variety of other issues. Researchers conduct psychographic research by asking consumers to express their agreement or disagreement with statements covering their activities, interests, and opinions (called a psychographic inventory). Statistical techniques are then used to group together consumers with similar responses and to contrast them with groups of consumers who hold dissimilar views. (See Chapter 5 for a fuller description of this technique.)

Lifestyle studies can be either generic or product-specific.[15] A product-specific study, as the name implies, is used to determine the psychological profile of users or potential users of a specific product. For example, a study conducted by Revlon found potential users of the perfume *Charlie* to be irreverent and unpretentious, rule breakers, pace setters, relaxed about sex, and highly individual in taste and judgment. When the perfume was introduced, commercials showed a fresh-faced young girl in a pantsuit striding boldly down a city street. The image caught on and sent the perfume to the top of the market.[16]

Unlike product-specific studies, generic studies are conducted with no specific product in mind. Their purpose is to reveal broad-based patterns in the marketplace, and they are used by marketers to uncover new-product opportunities or new ways to promote existing products.

One generic study of the TV market revealed fourteen categories of viewers. Ten of them—three segments consisting predominantly of men, four of women, and three of youth—are described in Table 2-5. The study provides clues for television advertisers as to who is watching what. For example, a surprising number of teenagers watch children's programming, particularly cartoons. The research suggests that teenage products might benefit from advertising in those program slots. The research also provides network programmers with insights on how to attract and retain audiences, given the increasing competition from cable TV. For example, the researchers found that some cultural programs are watched by a segment of disadvantaged people, who look to TV to expand their intellectual horizons. More programming in this area may be indicated.[17]

BENEFITS SOUGHT

Another form of psychological segmentation is based on the kinds of benefits consumers seek in products. The classic case of successful segmentation on the basis of benefits sought is the market for toothpaste. Research has discovered that children look for flavor or product appearance; teens and young marrieds look for brighteners; large families, for decay-prevention qualities; and men, for a good deal on price. Marketers of brands that have been introduced since that study was published have generally gone after one or more of these segments. For example, Aim, introduced in 1974, stresses good taste and tooth-decay prevention in its commercials—an appeal to both young children and families.[18]

Benefit segmentation has been used not only to find a niche for new products but to reposition established brands. Research done by Colgate Palmolive for Irish Spring soap provides a case in point. The research uncovered three segments for deodorant soap: (1) males who wanted a light-fragrance deodorant soap; (2) females who wanted a gentle, mild-fragrance bar; and (3) a mixed segment (but predominantly male) who looked for a strong-fragrance, refreshing deodorant soap. Irish Spring was found to do well with the last segment, but the company saw a bigger sales opportunity in the second segment. As a result, the soap was reformulated and ads began to stress the family appeal of the product.

Benefit segmentation, like the other types of psychological segmentation discussed above, is a useful way of identifying new market segments; however,

TABLE 2-5   Psychographic Segments of Television Viewers

a. males
1. Mechanics and outdoor life (7 percent)
   —average age 29; blue-collar workers; interested in noncompetitive activities such as fishing, camping, and auto repair
   —above-average viewers of science fiction, adventure, crime dramas
2. Money and nature's products (7 percent)
   —average age 53; suburban or rural residents; interested in business investments, fishing, hunting; traditional values
   —above-average viewers of adventure programs, crime dramas, documentaries, professional sports, variety shows, daily news, news commentaries, religious shows
3. Family/community-centered (8 percent)
   —average age 47; married; nonmetropolitan residents; interested in outdoor pursuits, business investments, community activities; expressed need for family ties
   —above-average viewers of sports, daily news, news commentaries, religious shows

b. females
4. Elderly concerns (7 percent)
   —average age 61; retirees and/or widows; biggest problem is loneliness
   —above-average viewers of dramas, game shows, soap operas, religious shows, news commentaries, talk shows, variety shows
5. Arts and cultural activities (7 percent)
   —average age 44; highly educated; professional or white-collar workers; need for intellectual stimulation, understanding others
   —above-average viewers of theatrical and musical performances, documentaries, news commentaries, daily news, sports
6. Home- and community-centered (8 percent)
   —average age 44; married; interested in homemaking and the local community; need for family ties and understanding others
   —above-average viewers of soap operas, religious programming, game shows, talk shows
7. Family-integrated activities (8 percent)
   —average age 34; white suburban residents; have school-age children
   —above-average viewers of children's educational shows, dramas, movies, documentaries, game shows, soap operas, specials

c. youth
8. Competitive sports and science engineering (8 percent)
   —teenage; male; interested in sports, mechanical activities; need for intellectual stimulation, status enhancement, escape from boredom
   —above-average viewers of sports, children's programs, situation comedies, science fiction
9. Athletic and social activities (5 percent)
   —teenage; female; interested in home life responsibilities and in finding outside activities
   —above-average viewers of children's programs, TV movies, science fiction, situation comedies
10. Indoor games and social activities (6 percent)
    —average age 22; female; income $11,000; beginning to set up own home; need for status enhancement, social stimulation; interested in indoor games
    —above-average viewers of musical performances, science fiction, adventure, children's programs, crime dramas, situation comedies

Source: Derived from Ronald E. Frank and Marshall G. Greenberg, "Zooming in on TV Audiences," *Psychology Today*, October 1979, 92–103; and "Interest-Based Segments of TV Audiences," *Journal of Advertising Research*, 19 (October 1979), 43–52.

results have not always lived up to expectations. Problem segmentation (segmentation of the market according to problems uncovered in talking to consumers) may be a promising alternative.[19] Because the whole field is relatively new, disputes about the most effective form of psychological segmentation will no doubt continue for some time.

Social-Cultural Segmentation

Sociological (i.e., group) and *anthropological* (i.e., cultural) variables provide further bases for market segmentation. For example, consumer markets have been successfully subdivided into segments on the basis of cultural and subcultural membership, social-class membership, and stage in the family-life-cycle.

CULTURE

Some marketers have found it useful to segment their markets on the basis of cultural heritage, since members of the same society tend to share the same values, beliefs, and customs. This strategy is particularly successful if marketing takes place in an international context.

Very often a product must be altered or reformulated in some way in order for it to do well in several cultures. For example, Nestlé sells coffee worldwide, but the Italian segment of its coffee market (which prefers a strong, black brew) would not buy the same blend that is sold in the United States. Sometimes climatic conditions necessitate distinctive product offerings. The type of gasoline sold in Iceland and the type of gasoline sold in the Sahara must be radically different. Sometimes it is merely custom that divides cultural segments. Greeting cards, sold with a verse in the United States, are sold without one in Europe.

Culturally distinct segments may be prospects for the very same product, but it may be necessary to promote the product in quite different ways. For example, bicycles might be promoted as an efficient means of transportation in the Far East and as a recreational vehicle in the United States. International marketers who engage in segmentation studies can often better target their products and their promotional efforts.

SUBCULTURE

Within a particular culture there are sometimes distinct groups or subcultures that are united by certain experiences, values, or beliefs. Such groups can also provide fertile segments for selected marketing efforts. For example, various religious, racial, and ethnic subcultures have served as bases for market segmentation.

Some marketers give a great deal of attention to the black subculture. Although the income of blacks tends to be lower than that of whites, blacks account for a disproportionate share of market in some product categories (e.g., 43 percent of the shaver market and 39 percent of the rice market).[20] In such product categories, it pays to target blacks for special marketing efforts. As Figure 2-1 indicates, Kraft has directed a special promotional campaign for condiments to the black market. (More information on the black consumer can be found in Chapter 15.)

FIGURE 2-1   Advertisement Aimed at the Black Subculture

Courtesy of Kraft Foods, Inc.

SOCIAL CLASS

Social class has been particularly amenable to treatment as a market segmentation variable. It is usually measured by an index composed of several demographic variables, such as education, income, and occupation.

The concept of social class implies that there are people higher or lower on the social scale. Studies have shown that consumers in different social classes vary in terms of their values, product preferences, and buying habits. For example, researchers have found that women at the top of the class structure value elegance, prefer tailored clothes, and buy designer originals; middle-class women, on the other hand, tend to value status and buy cheaper, mass-produced designer labels to imitate the upper class.

Marketers have used their knowledge of social-class patterns to appeal to specific classes. For example, the Chase Manhattan Bank, in an effort to secure the patronage of new arrivals to the upper middle class, ran a series of ads featuring young people who were getting ahead in life (e.g., a newly promoted young executive, a young couple at the country club) and urged readers to "get the Chase advantage" in managing their finances. The campaign represented an about-face from previous ads aimed at lower-class patrons, who were told "You have a friend at Chase."[21]

FAMILY LIFE CYCLE

Another frequently used sociological basis for market segmentation is stage-in-the-family-life-cycle. The life-cycle concept is based on the premise that families pass through several phases in their formation, growth, and final dissolution. At each phase the family unit needs different products. Young marrieds, for example, need basic furniture to start a home; an older, more established family may want more elaborate furnishings. Each is a distinct segment for marketers.

The family-life-cycle concept has been used by Lever Brothers to market a variety of toothpastes, each for a different segment. Pepsodent is aimed at families whose children have left home; Close-Up, at young adults and teenagers who want a breath freshener and whitening agent; and Aim, as we have seen, at families with small children in the cavity-prone years.[22]

Bases for segmenting the market are often combined to produce a sharper picture of the target audience. As in the case of toothpaste, where benefits sought and stage-in-the-family-life-cycle both serve to delineate likely segments, social-cultural variables are often combined with one or more of the other bases to achieve more precise market segmentation.

User-Behavior Segmentation

Markets can also be segmented by the *rate of usage* of a particular product category and by the degree of *loyalty* to a particular brand.

Rate of usage refers to the volume of purchases a consumer makes of a particular product, and it generally differentiates between heavy users, light users, and nonusers. Marketers who rely on usage rate to segment their markets also seek demographic or psychological information to distinguish subgroups. For example, one study of male beer drinkers utilized psychographic variables to distinguish heavy drinkers from nondrinkers and light drinkers. Compared with the other two segments, heavy drinkers were found to be more self-indulgent, less accepting of responsibility, more sports minded, and to have a very masculine view of life.[23]

Research indicates that 50 percent of the beer drinkers account for 88 percent of all beer consumed.[24] For this reason, most marketers would prefer to target a campaign to the heavy users, rather than spend considerably more money trying to attract the light users.

Sometimes *brand loyalty* is a useful basis for segmentation. Marketers often try to identify the characteristics of their brand-loyal consumers so that they can direct their promotional efforts to people with similar characteristics in the larger population. Or they may decide to go after consumers who show no brand loyalty, since such people may represent greater market potential than consumers who are loyal to competing brands. Non-brand-loyal consumers also suggest a different type of marketing mix to the marketing practitioner (low price, consumer "deals," point-of-purchase displays, etc.). Identifying brand-loyal consumers and distinguishing them from those that are not brand loyal by means of demographic or psychological or social-cultural characteristics is seldom an easy task. Therefore, brand loyalty is less frequently used than usage rate to differentiate market segments.

CONDUCTING A SEGMENTATION STUDY

The amount of research needed to implement a segmentation strategy depends on the bases used for segmentation. If the basis is demographic, the task may be relatively easy, since secondary sources for such information are often readily available. If bases other than demographic are utilized, then primary research involving surveys, interviews, and questionnaires may be called for. A decision must be made at the completion of such studies as to whether to pursue just one or several of the segments uncovered by the research.

Locating Secondary Data

A great deal of geographic, demographic, and sociocultural information is available from government sources. For example, the U.S. Census of Housing and Population collects data on the age, education, occupation, and income of residents of areas as small as a city block. Additional information on rents, places of work, automobile ownership, and patterns of migration is provided by the government in studies of census tracts within major metropolitan areas.

Private marketing research firms and advertising agencies are also sources of secondary market data. The A.C. Nielsen Company, for instance, will supply a variety of product usage information for a fee. In addition, a number of marketing guides are published by marketing firms. To give just two examples, *Census Update* shows annual changes in key demographic data by census tracts, and *ZIProfile* breaks down such data by ZIP code areas.[25]

Retailers and nonprofit organizations often have directly relevant demographic, sociocultural, and usage information available in their own customer or client records. For example, retailers can use their own credit and charge account data or mail-order records to identify just who their customers are and what products and/or brands they have purchased. Subscription and donor lists serve the same purpose for nonprofit organizations and charities.

Collecting Primary Data

If more detailed information on purchasing patterns and product attitudes is needed—for example, when psychological and usage behavior are used as segmentation bases—then primary data (data collected for the specific purpose of the study) must be gathered. Research to secure such information is usually expensive, but it often yields a more accurate picture of potential segments than studies based on generally available data.

Detailed segmentation studies are often conducted in three phases, as summarized in Table 2-6.[26] In the *exploratory qualitative* phase, researchers carry out depth interviews and focus group discussions to gather ideas about consumers' rate of use, frequency of purchase, and degree of loyalty to specific brands within a given product category. They also look for general attitudes toward products within the category, and for the principal benefits sought by consumers. This research is *qualitative,* rather than quantitative, because it seeks to gather ideas and tentative generalizations about the product qualities

TABLE 2-6   Phases of an In-Depth Segmentation Study

phase 1	Exploratory qualitative	Examines the usage patterns, buying habits, benefits sought, and attitudes about a product class
phase 2	Exploratory quantitative	Measures brand similarities, attitudes, perceptions of brand images, and preferences
phase 3	Quantitative probability	Identifies the prime segments to be pursued in terms of members' behavior, attitudes, demographic characteristics, and media habits

Source: Adapted from Larry Percy, "How Market Segmentation Guides Advertising Strategy," *Journal of Advertising Research,* 16 (October 1976), 11–22.

consumers prefer, without attaching hard numbers or percentages to the ideas obtained.

In the *exploratory quantitative* phase, numbers are sought to support or refute the findings that emerged from the first phase. A representative sample of consumers are interviewed concerning the similarities they see among various brands, their perceptions of different brand images, their attitudes, and their preferences. Researchers then apply appropriate statistical techniques to analyze and synthesize the information gathered. On the basis of this analysis, researchers identify prime segments for a new-product idea or a revised marketing mix.

In the *quantitative probability* phase, individuals are grouped together into likely segments, not only on the basis of various demographic traits but also by media habits, attitudes, perceptions, and personality characteristics.

Concentrated versus Differentiated Marketing

Once an organization has identified its most promising market segments, it must then decide whether to pursue several segments or just one. Marketing to several segments, using a distinct product, promotional appeal, price, and/or method of distribution for each, is called *differentiated marketing*. Marketing to a single segment with a unique marketing mix is called *concentrated marketing*.

Examples of firms that practice differentiated marketing are not difficult to find. Anheuser-Busch appeals to the calorie-conscious segment of the beer market with two different light beers (Natural Light and Michelob Light), to the regular beer market with both a medium-priced and a higher-priced brand (Busch and Budweiser), and to the upscale market with a premium-priced brand (Michelob). The company's strategy is to offer one or more alternatives to every offering of Miller—its closest competitor—in order to gain more exposure in supermarkets.[27]

Differentiated marketing is a wise segmentation decision if a company is financially strong, well established in a product category, and competitive with other firms that are also strong in the category. However, if a company is small or new to a field, concentrated marketing is a better bet. By finding a niche not occupied by stronger competitors, such a company can survive and prosper. For example, in the market for tea, the Celestial Seasonings Company has been able to thrive in a field dominated by such giants as Lipton and Salada by offering caffeine-free herb teas, which appeal to a health-conscious market segment. There is some risk in concentrated marketing, however, because if the market for that product should contract for any reason, the firm has no other product on which to rely. But that risk may be an unavoidable one for a new company.

IS SEGMENTATION WORTHWHILE?

A variety of organizations have found market segmentation to be an effective way to increase sales and profits. Insofar as this strategy also produces market offerings that better meet the needs of individuals, it is a boon to consumers as well.

However, segmentation strategies are not necessarily problem-free. Expensive, time-consuming segmentation studies may turn up nothing more than obvious results.[28] Moreover, in some situations, segmentation has led to fragmentation rather than useful division of the market. In an attempt to cater to every interest, some marketers have allowed their product lines, and the corresponding costs of production, to increase needlessly.

Some researchers now suggest that it may be more profitable to implement a "countersegmentation" strategy for a number of product categories. The goal of such a strategy would be to combine existing segments instead of seeking new ones. Because of inflation, shortages, and a new respect for a simpler way of life, many consumers may be willing to accept a little less than they previously were if that means savings. A countersegmentation strategy could involve dropping some products and simplifying others in a manufacturer's product line.[29]

This idea has some merit, especially in the resource-scarce environment we are likely to inhabit in the future. The essence of market segmentation is to uncover consumer needs. But those needs can fluctuate with changing economic tides, and it is up to marketers to monitor such variations carefully. The study of consumer behavior can aid in the search for new ways to further divide or to combine subgroups in the marketplace.

summary

Before the widespread adoption of the marketing concept, mass marketing—offering the same product or marketing mix to everyone—was the marketing strategy most widely used. Market segmentation followed as a more logical way to meet the specific needs of subsets of consumers.

Segmentation research is designed to identify such subsets within a larger consumer market and to identify the needs and wants of one or more such groups so that specific goods and services can be developed to satisfy their needs. Besides aiding in the development of new products, segmentation studies assist in the redesign and repositioning of existing products, as well as in the creation of advertising appeals and the selection of advertising media.

Since segmentation strategies benefit both marketers and consumers, they have received wide support from both sides of the marketplace. Market segmentation is now widely used by manufacturers, by retailers, and by the nonprofit sector. Important criteria for the successful use of market segmentation strategies are the ability to identify, measure, and reach significant subgroups of the total potential market.

Five major classes of consumer characteristics serve as the most common bases for market segmentation. These include geographic variables (e.g., region, density, climate); demographic variables (e.g., age, sex, education); psychological variables (e.g., personality, lifestyle); social-cultural variables (e.g., race, religion, social class); and user-behavior variables (e.g., usage rate and brand loyalty).

The methodologies used in segmentation research are dependent upon the segmentation bases used. For example, demographic data are often available through secondary sources (that is, from data that have been collected for other purposes), while psychological segmentation usually requires primary research, such as interviews or questionnaires specifically designed for the study in question.

Once an organization has identified promising market segments, it must decide whether to pursue several segments (differentiated marketing) or just one segment (concentrated marketing).

While segmentation has generally been a useful marketing strategy, it has occasionally led to needless fragmentation of markets, resulting in increased production and marketing costs. Various researchers are now suggesting that some marketers consider implementing a countersegmentation strategy, which would combine existing segments and thus achieve savings in production and marketing that could be passed on to consumers.

discussion questions

1. Define *market segmentation*. What are the major advantages and disadvantages of this marketing strategy for marketers and for consumers?
2. You are the manufacturers of semiconductor chips for computers. What criteria will enable you to implement a successful market segmentation strategy?
3. Describe the relative importance of each of the five segmentation bases in marketing the following products: lawnmowers, health spas for citizens over fifty-five years of age, home computers, and video cassettes.
4. Which, if any, government agencies could effectively use a policy of market segmentation? Why?
5. The marketing manager of a large cigarette company wants to differentiate its menthol cigarette. Plan a research program designed to identify relevant segments for this cigarette.
6. Could you segment a market for novels based on situational factors? Explain your answer.
7. What is psychographic segmentation, and on what variables is it based?
8. Can a museum use market segmentation to improve attendance on weekdays? Discuss.

endnotes

1. Nancy F. Millman, "Vitamins Make the Teen Scene as Market Continues to Fragment," *Advertising Age*, December 26, 1977, 2.
2. Gloria Bordeaux Mitchel, "American Conservatory Theatre: A Case Study" (Unpublished paper, 1979).

Market Segmentation

41

3. "Toy Marketing Isn't Kid Stuff," *Media Decisions,* 11 (May 1976), 69.

4. Pat Sloan, "Natural Wonder Turns New Face to Post-Teen Bid," *Advertising Age,* February 26, 1979, 6, 77.

5. C.R. Laurent, "Image Segmentation in Bank Marketing," *Bankers Magazine,* 162 (July 1979), 32–37.

6. Alladi Venkatesh and Clint B. Tankersley, "Magazine Readership by Female Segments," *Journal of Advertising Research,* 19 (August 1979), 31–38.

7. S. Baker, *Advertising Creativity* (New York: McGraw-Hill, 1979), 44–45.

8. Niles Howard, "More Bang for the Ad Dollar," *Dun's Review,* 112 (October 1978), 106–10.

9. "Wal-Mart: A Discounter Sinks Deep Roots in Small Town, U.S.A.," *Business Week,* November 5, 1979, 145–46.

10. "How Fisher-Price Sells All Those Toys," *Business Week,* March 3, 1973, 40–41; and Jacques Nehen, "K-tel Turns Down Volume in Shift to Music Market," *Advertising Age,* May 7, 1979, 34, 36.

11. Betsy Gelb, "Gray Market," *MSU Business Topics,* 26 (Spring 1978), 41–46.

12. "Magazines Targeted at the Working Woman," *Business Week,* February 18, 1980, 150–52.

13. Fabian Linden, "The Classes: Upward," *Across the Board,* 14 (April 1977), 59–62; and "The Great Reshuffle of Spending Power: The Ages of Affluence," *Across the Board,* 15 (December 1978), 61–65.

14. Joel B. Cohen, "An Interpersonal Orientation to the Study of Consumer Behavior," *Journal of Marketing Research,* August 1967, 270–80.

15. For a discussion of this distinction and the relative merits of each type, see William D. Wells, "Psychographics: A Critical Review," *Journal of Marketing Research,* 12 (May 1975), 196–213; and Stuart Van Auken, "General versus Product-Specific Life Style Segmentations," *Journal of Advertising,* 7 (Fall 1978), 31–35.

16. See E.B. Weiss, "Creative Advertising Moves toward the New Society," *Advertising Age,* July 3, 1973, 32–34; and Karen Boiko, "Jontue: Revlon Does It Again," *Product Marketing,* 6 (March 1977), 26–30.

17. Ronald E. Frank and Marshall G. Greenberg, "Zooming in on TV Audiences," *Psychology Today,* October 1979, 92–103; and "Interest-Based Segments of TV Audiences," *Journal of Advertising Research,* 19 (October 1979), 43–52.

18. Russell I. Haley, "Benefit Segmentation: A Decision-Oriented Research Tool," *Journal of Marketing,* 32 (July 1968), 30–35.

19. Richard H. Evans, "Benefit Analysis or Problem Analysis," *Journal of Advertising,* 9 (Winter 1980), 27–31.

20. Barbara Proctor, "Black, It's Beautiful," *Media Decisions,* 12 (April 1977), 73–75.

21. Christopher Gilson and Harold W. Berkman, *Advertising: Concepts and Strategies* (New York: Random House, 1980), 112–13.

22. "Marketing-Oriented Lever Uses Research to Capture Bigger Dentifrice Market Shares," *Marketing News,* January 27, 1978, 9.

23. J.T. Plummer, "Life Style and Advertising: Case Studies," in Fred Allvine, ed., *1971 Proceedings of the American Marketing Association* (Chicago: American Marketing Association, 1971), 294.

24. Dick Warren Twedt, "How Important to Marketing Strategy Is the 'Heavy User'?" *Journal of Marketing,* 28 (January 1964), 71–72.

25. "Census Update & ZIProfile Offer Detailed Demographics," *Marketing News,* November 30, 1979, 5.

26. The suggestion that three phases are involved is derived from Larry Percey, "How Market Segmentation Guides Advertising Strategy," *Journal of Advertising Research,* 16 (October 1976), 11–22.

27. Bob Lederer, "Anheuser-Busch's Two-against-One Strategy," *Beverage World,* 98 (September 1979), 38–41.
28. For these and other criticisms of segmentation studies, see Neil Holbert, "The Segmentation Trap," *Marketing Review,* 34 (May–June 1979), 11–17; and Alfred D. Remson, "Mistakes I Have Made in Segmentation Studies," *Marketing News,* January 27, 1978, 8.
29. Alan J. Resnik, Peter P. B. Turney, and J. Barry Mason, "Marketers Turn to Countersegmentation," *Harvard Business Review,* 57 (September 1979), 100–106.

part two

THE CONSUMER
AS AN INDIVIDUAL

Chapters 3 through 10 are designed to provide the reader with a comprehensive picture of consumer psychology. The objectives of these chapters are (1) to explain the basic psychological concepts that account for individual behavior, and (2) to show how these concepts influence the individual's consumption-related behavior. Chapter 10, "Communication and Consumer Behavior," provides the bridge between the individual and his or her connection with the outside world.

THREE

Consumer Needs
and Motivation

introduction

WE have all grown up "knowing" that people are different. They seek different pleasures, spend their money in different ways. A couple may spend their vacation traveling in Europe; their friends are content with two weeks in a cottage by the sea. A doting father may buy his son a set of encyclopedias; another may buy his son a set of electric trains. A woman may save her household money to carpet her bedrooms; her neighbor may save hers to buy a second car. Different modes of consumer behavior—different ways of spending money—do not surprise us. We have been brought up to believe that the differences in people are what makes life interesting.

However, this apparent diversity in human behavior often causes us to overlook the fact that people are really very much alike. There are underlying similarities—*constants* that tend to operate across many types of people—which serve to explain and to clarify their consumption behavior. Psychologists and consumer behaviorists agree that basically most people experience the same kinds of needs and motives; they simply express these motives in different ways. For this reason, an understanding of human motives is very important to marketers: It enables them to understand, and even anticipate, human behavior in the marketplace.

This chapter will discuss the basic needs that operate in most people to motivate behavior. It explores the influence that such needs have on consumption behavior. Later chapters in this section explain why and how these basic human motives are expressed in so many diverse ways.

WHAT IS MOTIVATION?

Several basic concepts are integral to an understanding of human motivation. Before we discuss these, it is necessary to agree on some basic definitions.

> *Understanding human needs is half the job of meeting them.*
>
> *ADLAI STEVENSON:*
>
> *Speech, Columbus, Ohio (October 3, 1952)*

Motivation

Motivation can be described as *the driving force within individuals that impels them to action.* This driving force is produced by a state of tension, which exists as the result of an unfilled need. Individuals strive—both consciously and subconsciously—to reduce this tension through behavior that they anticipate will fulfill their needs and thus relieve them of the stress they feel. The specific goals they select and the patterns of action they undertake to achieve their goals are the results of individual thinking and learning. Figure 3-1 presents a model of the motivational process. It portrays motivation as a state of need-induced tension, which exerts a "push" on the individual to engage in behavior that he or she expects will gratify needs and thus reduce tension. Whether gratification is actually achieved depends on the course of action pursued. (If a high-school girl pins her hopes of being asked to the senior prom on her switch to a highly advertised "sexy" toothpaste, she may be disappointed. If her brother pins his hopes of making the tennis team on his purchase of a tennis racquet endorsed by Vitas Gerulaitis, he too may be disappointed.)

The specific courses of action undertaken by consumers and the specific goals chosen are selected on the basis of their thinking processes (i.e., cognition) and previous learning. Thus marketers who understand motivational theory attempt to influence the consumer's thinking or cognitive processes.

Needs

Every individual has needs; some are innate, others are acquired. Innate needs are physiological (i.e., biogenic); they include the needs for food, for water, for air, for clothing, for shelter, and for sex. Because all of these factors are needed to sustain biological life, the biogenic needs are considered *primary* needs or motives.

Acquired needs are needs that we learn in response to our culture or environment. These may include needs for esteem, for prestige, for affection,

FIGURE 3-1   A Model of the Motivation Process

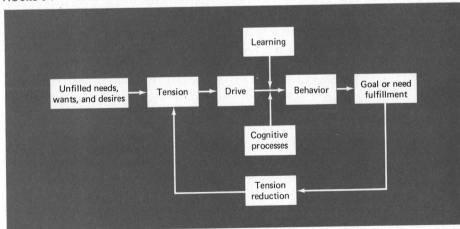

for power, and for learning. Because acquired needs are generally psychological (i.e., psychogenic), they are considered *secondary* needs or motives. They result from the individual's subjective psychological state and from his or her relationships with others. For example, all individuals need shelter from the elements; thus, finding a place to live fulfills an important primary need for a newly transferred executive. However, the kind of house she buys may be the result of secondary needs. She may seek a house where she can entertain large groups of people (and fulfill her social needs); furthermore, she may want to buy a house in an exclusive community in order to impress her friends and family (and fulfill her ego needs). The house that an individual ultimately purchases thus may serve to fulfill both primary and secondary needs.

Goals

Goals are the sought-after results of motivated behavior. As Figure 3-1 indicates, all behavior is goal-oriented. Our discussion of motivation in this chapter is in part concerned with consumers' *generic* goals; that is, the general classes or categories of goals they select to fulfill their needs. Marketers are even more concerned with consumers' *product-specific* goals; that is, the specifically branded or labeled products they select to fulfill their needs. For example, the Thomas J. Lipton Company wants consumers to view iced tea as a good way to quench summer thirst (i.e., as a generic goal). However, it is even more interested in having consumers view *Lipton's* iced tea as the *best* way to quench summer thirst (i.e., as a product-specific goal). As trade association advertising indicates, marketers recognize the importance of promoting both types of goals. The American Dairy Association advertises that "milk is a natural," while Borden's, a member of the Association, advertises its own brand of milk.

Positive and Negative Motivation

Motivation can be either positive or negative in direction. We may feel a driving force *toward* some object or condition, or a driving force *away* from some object or condition. For example, a person may be impelled toward a restaurant to fulfill a hunger need and away from airplane transportation to fulfill a safety need. Some psychologists refer to positive drives as needs, wants, or desires, and negative drives as fears or aversions. However, though negative and positive motivational forces seem to differ dramatically in terms of physical (and sometimes emotional) activity, they are basically similar in that they both serve to initiate and sustain human behavior. For this reason, researchers often refer to both kinds of drives or motives as needs, wants, and desires.[1]

Goals, too, can be either positive or negative. A positive goal is one toward which behavior is directed, and thus it is often referred to as an *approach* object. A negative goal is one from which behavior is directed away, and thus it is sometimes referred to as an *avoidance* object. Since both approach and avoidance goals can be considered objectives of motivated behavior, most researchers refer to both types simply as *goals*. Consider this example. A middle-aged woman may wish to remain as attractive as possible to male acquaintances. Her positive goal is to appear desirable, and therefore she may use a perfume advertised to make her "irresistible." A negative goal may be to prevent her skin from aging, and therefore she may buy and use face creams advertised to prevent wrinkles. In the former case, she uses perfume to help her achieve her positive goal—sexual attractiveness; in the latter case, she uses face creams to help avoid a negative goal—wrinkled skin.

The Selection of Goals

For any given need, there are many different and appropriate goals. The goals selected by individuals depend on their personal experiences, physical capacity, prevailing cultural norms and values, and the goal's accessibility in the physical and social environment.[2] For example, an individual may have a strong hunger need. If he is a young American athlete, he may envision a rare sirloin steak as his goal-object; however, if he is also an orthodox Jew, he may require that the steak be kosher to conform to Jewish dietary laws. If the individual is old or infirm, he may not have the physical capacity to chew or digest a steak; therefore, he may select hamburger instead. If he has never tasted steak—if it is out of his realm of personal experience—he will probably not even think of steak as a goal-object but instead will select a food that has satisfied his hunger before (perhaps fish or chicken).

Finally, the goal-object has to be both physically and socially accessible. If the individual were shipwrecked on an island with no food provisions or living animals, he could not realistically select steak as his goal-object, though he might fantasize about it. If he were in India where cows are considered sacred deities, he could not realistically hope to consume steak because to do so might be considered sacrilegious. Therefore he would have to select a substitute goal more appropriate to the social environment.

The individual's own conception of himself or herself also serves to influence the specific goals selected. The products that a person owns, would like to own, or would not like to own are often perceived in terms of how closely they reflect (are congruent with) the person's self-image. A product that is perceived as fitting an individual's self-image has a greater probability of being selected than one that is not.[3] Thus a man who perceives himself as young and "swinging" may drive a Corvette; a woman who perceives herself as rich and conservative may drive a Mercedes. The types of houses people live in, the cars they drive, the clothes they wear, the very foods they eat—these specific goal-objects are often chosen because symbolically they reflect the individual's own self-image while they satisfy specific needs.[4] (The relationship of self-concept to product choice is explained more fully in Chapter 6.)

Rational versus Emotional Motives

Some consumer researchers distinguish between so-called rational motives and emotional (or nonrational) motives. They use the term *rationality* in the traditional economic sense that assumes that consumers behave rationally when they carefully consider all alternatives and choose those that give them the greatest utility (i.e., satisfaction).[5] In a marketing context, the term *rationality* implies that the consumer selects goals based on totally objective criteria, such as size, weight, price, or miles per gallon. *Emotional* motives imply the selection of goals according to personal or subjective criteria (the desire for individuality, pride, fear, affection, status).

The assumption underlying this distinction is that subjective or emotional criteria do not maximize utility or satisfaction. However, it is reasonable to assume that consumers always attempt to select alternatives that, *in their view,* serve to maximize satisfaction. Obviously, the assessment of satisfaction is a very personal process, based upon the individual's own need structure as well as on past behavioral, social, and learning experiences. What may appear as irrational to an outside observer may be perfectly rational within the context of the consumer's own psychological field. For example, a product purchased to enhance one's self-image (such as a fragrance) is a perfectly rational form of consumer behavior. If behavior did not appear rational to the person who undertakes it at the time that it is undertaken, obviously he or she would not do it. Therefore the distinction between rational and emotional motives does not appear to be warranted.

Indeed, some researchers go so far as to suggest that emphasis on "needs" obscures the rational, or conscious, nature of most consumer motivation.[6] They claim that consumers act consciously to maximize their gains and minimize their losses; that they act not from subconscious drives but from rational preferences, or what they perceive to be in their own best interests.

Marketers who agree with this view are reluctant to spend either time or money to uncover subconscious buyer motives. Instead, they try to identify problems that consumers experience with products then on the market.[7] For example, instead of trying to identify any special needs that consumers may have for dog food, the marketer will try to discover any problems that consumers are experiencing with existing brands of dog food. If the marketer discovers that many dog foods leave an unpleasant odor in the refrigerator, he or she can develop a new product that solves this consumer problem and then run advertisements that announce to dog owners that the new product does not impart unpleasant odors. Thus, rather than address consumers' expressed needs, such marketers attempt to discover and solve consumers' problems and thereby achieve market success.

Interdependency of Needs and Goals

Needs and goals are interdependent. One does not exist without the other.[8] However, people are often not as aware of their needs as they are of their goals. For example, a teenager may not be consciously aware of her social needs but may join many clubs to meet new friends. A local politician may not be consciously aware of a power need but may regularly run for public office. A woman may not recognize her ego needs but may strive to have the most successful real estate office in town.

Individuals are usually somewhat more aware of their physiological needs than they are of their psychological needs. Most people know when they are hungry or thirsty or cold, and they take appropriate steps to satisfy these needs. Sometimes they may subconsciously engage in behavior designed to fulfill their bodily needs, even though they are not consciously aware of such needs. For example, medical researchers have reported the case of a young child who had an overwhelming craving for salt almost from the time of his birth. All the foods he liked were salty; in addition, he ate about a teaspoonful of salt daily. When he was about three and one-half years old, he was placed in a hospital for observation and was restricted to a routine hospital diet. Within seven days he was dead. A postmortem examination revealed a glandular deficiency, which had caused excessive loss of salt from his body through urination. The boy had literally kept himself alive for three and one-half years by eating great quantities of salt to compensate for his salt deficiency. When he no longer had free access to salt, he died.[9]

THE DYNAMIC NATURE OF MOTIVATION

Needs and Goals Are Constantly Changing

Needs and goals are constantly growing and changing in response to an individual's physical condition, environment, interactions with others, and experiences. As individuals attain their goals, they develop new goals. If they do not attain their goals, they continue to strive for old goals or they develop substitute goals. Some of the reasons why human activity never ceases include the following: (1) existing needs are never completely satisfied and thus constantly require activity designed to attain or maintain fulfillment; (2) as needs become satisfied, new, higher-order needs emerge which must be fulfilled; and (3) people who achieve their goals set new and higher goals for themselves.

NEEDS ARE NEVER FULLY SATISFIED

Most human needs are never completely, or finally, satisfied. For example, people experience hunger needs at regular intervals that must be satisfied by eating. Most people regularly seek companionship and approval from others in order to satisfy their social needs. Even more complex psychological needs are rarely satisfied. For example, a person may partially or temporarily satisfy her power need by serving on the town council, but this small taste of power may not sufficiently satisfy her need, so she may run for successively higher public office. In this instance, temporary goal achievement does not fully satisfy the need for power, and the individual keeps striving to more fully satisfy that need.

NEW NEEDS EMERGE AS OLD NEEDS ARE SATISFIED

Some motivational theorists believe that a hierarchy of needs exists and that new, higher-order needs emerge as lower-order needs are fulfilled.[10] For example, a man who has largely satisfied his basic physiological needs may turn his efforts to achieving acceptance among his new neighbors by joining their clubs and supporting their candidates. Having achieved such acceptance, he may then seek recognition by winning tennis trophies or by giving lavish parties.

Marketers must stay attuned to changing needs. Car manufacturers who stress the prestige value of their product fail to recognize that many consumers now look elsewhere to satisfy their need for prestige—for example, by installing hot tubs in their backyards or taking exotic trips abroad. For this reason, manufacturers of prestige cars may do better if they were to stress other satisfactions as reasons for buying a new model.[11]

SUCCESS AND FAILURE INFLUENCE GOALS

A number of researchers have explored the nature of the goals that individuals set for themselves.[12] In general, they have concluded that individuals who successfully achieve their goals usually set new and higher goals for themselves; that is, they raise their *levels of aspiration*. This is probably due to the fact that they become more confident of their ability to reach their goals. Conversely, those who do not reach their goals sometimes lower their levels of aspiration. Thus goal selection is often a function of success and failure experiences. For example, a college senior who is not accepted into medical school may try, instead, to go to dental school; failing that, he or she may train to be a pharmacist.

The nature and persistence of an individual's behavior are often influenced by expectations of success or failure in reaching certain goals. Those expectations, in turn, are often based upon the individual's past experiences in attaining goals. A person who takes good snapshots with an inexpensive camera may be motivated to buy a more expensive camera in the belief that it will enable her to take even better photographs. In this way, she may eventually upgrade her camera by several hundred dollars. On the other hand, a person who cannot take good pictures is just as likely to keep the same camera or may even lose all interest in photography.

These effects of success and failure on goal selection have strategy implications for the marketer. Goals should be reasonably attainable. Advertisements should not promise more than the product will deliver. Even a good product will not be repurchased if it does not live up to the consumer's expectations. Research shows that a disappointed consumer will regard a product that has not lived up to expectations with even less satisfaction than its objective performance warrants.[13] Thus advertisers who create unrealistic expectations for their products are likely to cause dissatisfaction among consumers. It has been suggested that the frustration and disappointment that result from just such consumer dissatisfaction have been the driving force behind consumerism.[14]

SUBSTITUTE GOALS

When, for one reason or another, an individual cannot attain a particular goal or type of goal that he or she anticipates will satisfy certain needs, behavior may be directed to a substitute goal. Although the substitute goal may not be as satisfactory as the primary goal, it may be sufficient to dispel uncomfortable tension. Continued deprivation of a primary goal may result in the substitute goal assuming primary-goal status. A man who has stopped drinking whole milk because he is dieting may actually begin to prefer skimmed milk. A person who cannot afford a Cadillac may convince herself that an Oldsmobile has an image she clearly prefers. Of course, in this latter instance, the substitute goal may be a defensive reaction to frustration.

Frustration

Failure to achieve a goal often results in feelings of frustration. Everyone has at one time or another experienced the frustration that comes from an inability to attain one's goal. The barrier that prevents attainment of a goal may be personal to the individual (i.e., it can be a physical or financial limitation, or a psychological barrier such as conflicting goals), or it can be an obstacle in the physical or social environment. Regardless of the cause, individuals react differently to frustrating situations. Some people are adaptive and manage to cope by finding their way around the obstacle or, if that fails, by selecting a substitute goal. Others are less adaptive and may regard their inability to achieve their goals as a personal failure and may experience feelings of anxiety. An example of adaptive behavior would be the college student who would prefer a sports car but settles for a secondhand jalopy. If he cannot afford the insurance for a used car, he may settle for a bike on which to ride around campus.

People who cannot cope with frustration often mentally redefine the frustrating situation in order to protect their self-images and defend their self-esteem. For example, a newly married woman may yearn for a genuine leather sofa which she cannot afford. The coping individual may have the same sofa copied by a local upholsterer for less money, or have it made up in a synthetic leather fabric, or settle for a different model altogether. The person who cannot cope may react with anger toward her boss for not paying her enough money to afford it, or she may ask her parents to buy it for her. These last two possibilities are examples, respectively, of aggression and regression, defense mechanisms that people sometimes adopt to protect their egos from feelings of failure when they cannot attain their goals. Other defense mechanisms include rationalization, withdrawal, projection, autism, identification, and repression.[15]

RATIONALIZATION

Sometimes individuals redefine the frustrating situation by inventing plausible reasons for not being able to attain their goals. Or they may decide that the goal really wasn't worth pursuing. Rationalizations are not deliberate lies, since the individual is not fully aware of the cognitive distortion that arises as a result of the frustrating situation. Thus a consumer who cannot give up smoking may convince himself that he is smoking less if he smokes fewer (though longer) cigarettes each day.

WITHDRAWAL

Frustration is often resolved by simply withdrawing from the frustrating situation. A person who has difficulty using a sewing machine may simply stop sewing. Furthermore, she may rationalize her withdrawal by deciding that it really is cheaper to buy ready-made clothing; in addition, she may decide she can use her time more constructively in other activities.

PROJECTION

The individual may redefine the frustrating situation by assigning (or "projecting") blame for his or her own failures and inabilities on other objects or persons. Thus the golfer who misses a stroke may blame his caddy or his ball; the driver who has an automobile accident may blame the other driver or the condition of the road.

AUTISM

Autism, or autistic thinking, refers to thinking that is almost completely dominated by needs and emotions, with no effort being made to relate to reality. Such daydreaming, or fantasizing, enables the individual to attain imaginary gratification of unfulfilled needs. Thus a person who is dieting may daydream about gorging with ice cream and candy bars, or an office clerk may dream of marrying a millionairess. (Figure 3-2 illustrates an autism appeal that suggests that ownership of a tuxedo will enable the reader to marry an heiress.)

IDENTIFICATION

Sometimes people resolve their feelings of frustration by subconsciously identifying with other persons or situations that they consider relevant. Marketers have long recognized the importance of this defense mechanism and often use it as the basis for advertising appeals. That is why "slice-of-life" commercials or advertisements are so popular. Such advertisements usually portray a stereotypical situation in which an individual experiences a frustration and then overcomes the problem (i.e., the resulting frustration) by using the advertised product (see Figure 3-3). If the viewer can identify with the frustrating situation, he or she may very likely adopt the proposed solution and buy the product advertised. For example, a boy who has difficulty attracting a girl he likes may decide to use the same mouthwash or shampoo or deodorant that "worked" for the fellow in the commercial. Interestingly enough, use of the product may increase his self-confidence sufficiently to enable him to achieve his goal.

AGGRESSION

Individuals who experience frustration may resort to aggressive behavior in an attempt to protect their self-esteem. This was aptly illustrated during the 1976 Olympics by two British yachtsmen who, disappointed at their poor showing in the sailing competition, burned their boat and swam ashore. Frustrated consumers have boycotted manufacturers in their efforts to improve product quality and boycotted retailers in their efforts to have prices lowered.

FIGURE 3-2   Autism Appeal

HOW TO MARRY AN HEIRESS ON A $129.50 INVESTMENT.

Your own tux.

It'll take you anywhere.

Make you feel relaxed in any surroundings.

Help you look as if you belong.

And once you're on the scene, you're on your own.

After all, it's just as easy to develop a meaningful relationship with a rich girl.

To be certain that no man is deprived of his chance to be in the right place at the right time in the right clothes, After Six is making a very special offer: the $129.50 investment. It includes this trim, classic tuxedo, the graceful bowtie in the latest shape and elegant flyfront shirt with ruffles and matching link cuffs.

If you have accessories, you can buy the tux alone for about $110. Or you can buy the shirt and tie separately.

At the fine stores listed opposite, or write After Six Inc., 1290 Avenue of the Americas, N.Y. 10019.

The After Six $129.50 investment. Even if you're happily married, it's worth it for celebrating your good fortune.

after Six FORMALS

AFTER SIX FORMAL
A DIVISION OF AFTER SIX, INC.
AMERICAN STOCK EXCHANGE SYMBOL TUX

FIGURE 3-3   Identification Appeal

"**You know the feeling. I thought everyone was staring at my hands.**"

"Those horrid weathered age spots made me so self-conscious I hated to play cards. Then the girls told me about this cream Esoterica. What a blessing. It's just made to fade age spots. And it creams your hands beautiful besides. You'll see."

Esoterica. It's made to fade age spots

(and it creams your hands beautiful besides).

Cream and Lotion

REPRESSION

Another way that the individual avoids the tension arising from frustration is by repressing the unsatisfied need. Thus individuals may "forget" a need; that is, they force the need out of their conscious awareness. Sometimes repressed needs manifest themselves indirectly. A couple who cannot have children may surround themselves with plants or pets. The wife may teach school or work in a library; the husband may do volunteer work in a boys' club. The manifestation of repressed needs in a socially acceptable form of behavior is called *sublimation*, another type of defense mechanism.

REGRESSION

Sometimes people react to frustrating situations by adopting childish or immature behavior. A woman attending a bargain sale, for example, may fight over merchandise and resort to tearing a garment that another woman will not relinquish, rather than allow her to have it.

This listing of defense mechanisms is far from exhaustive. People have virtually limitless ways of redefining frustrating situations so that they can protect their self-esteem from the anxieties that result from experiencing failure. Based on their early experiences, individuals tend to develop their own characteristic ways of handling frustration.

Marketers often consider this fact in their selection of advertising appeals. For example, a flour manufacturer may convince consumers that their baking failures were caused by the ingredients they used rather than the ineptness of their efforts.

Multiplicity of Needs

Consumer behavior is often designed to fulfill more than one need. In fact, it is more likely that specific goals are selected because they fulfill several needs. We buy clothing for protection and for modesty; in addition, our clothing fulfills an enormous range of both personal and social needs. Usually, however, there is one overriding (i.e., prepotent) need that initiates behavior. For example, a man may stop smoking because he wants to rid himself of a chronic cough; he may also be concerned about the cigarette-cancer controversy. In addition, his girlfriend may be "turned off" by the smell of cigarette smoke. If the cumulative amount of tension produced by each of these three reasons is sufficiently strong, he will stop smoking; however, just one of the reasons (e.g., his girlfriend's influence) may serve as the triggering mechanism. That one would be called the *prepotent* need.

Needs and Goals Vary Among Individuals

One cannot accurately infer motives from behavior. People with different needs may seek fulfillment through selection of the same goals, while people with the same needs may seek fulfillment through different goals. Consider the following examples. Five people who are active in a consumer organization may each belong for a different reason. The first may be genuinely concerned with protecting consumer interests, the second may be personally concerned with rising prices, the third may seek the social contacts that derive from organizational meetings, the fourth may enjoy the power inherent in directing a large group, and the fifth may enjoy the status provided by membership in a powerful organization.

Similarly, five people may be driven by the same need (e.g., an ego need) to seek fulfillment in different ways. The first may seek advancement and recognition through a professional career, the second may become a director of the League of Women Voters, the third may join a health club in an effort to maintain his youthful physique, the fourth may become a gang leader, and the fifth may seek attention by monopolizing conversations.

Arousal of Motives

Most of the specific needs of an individual are dormant much of the time. The arousal of any particular set of needs at a specific point in time may be caused by internal stimuli found in the individual's physiological condition or cognitive processes, or by external stimuli in the outside environment.

PHYSIOLOGICAL AROUSAL

A person's bodily needs at any one specific moment are rooted in his or her physiological condition at that moment. A drop in blood-sugar level or stomach contractions will trigger awareness of a hunger need. Secretion of sex hormones will awaken the sex need. A drop in body temperature will induce shivering, which makes the individual aware of the need for warmth. Most of these physiological cues are involuntary; however, they arouse related needs which cause uncomfortable tensions until they are satisfied. For example, a shivering man may turn up the heat in his home to relieve his discomfort; he may also make a mental note to buy a new overcoat.

COGNITIVE AROUSAL

Sometimes thinking or daydreaming results in the arousal or stimulation of latent needs. People who are bored or frustrated in their attempts to achieve their goals often engage in daydreaming (autistic thinking), in which they imagine themselves in all sorts of desirable situations. These thoughts tend to arouse dormant needs, which may produce uncomfortable tensions that "push" them into goal-oriented behavior. A young girl who dreams of becoming a writer may identify with her favorite author and enroll in a writing course. Similarly, a young man who wants to play football professionally may identify with a major league player and use the products he recommends commercially.

ENVIRONMENTAL AROUSAL

The set of needs activated at a particular time are often determined by specific cues in the environment. Without these cues, the needs would remain dormant. Thus the six o'clock news, the vision or smell of food, food commercials on television, the children's return from school—all of these may arouse the "need" for food. In such cases, modification of the environment may be necessary in order to reduce the arousal of hunger.

A most potent form of situational cue is the goal-object itself. A couple may experience an overwhelming need for a new dishwasher when they see their neighbor's new dishwasher; a person may suddenly experience a need for a new car when passing a dealer's display window. Sometimes an advertisement or other environmental cue produces a psychological imbalance in the viewer's mind. For example, a man who prides himself on his gardening may see an advertisement for a tractor mower that apparently works more efficiently than his own rotary mower. The ad may make him so unhappy with his old mower that he experiences severe tension until he buys himself a new tractor model.

When people live in a complex and highly varied environment, they experience many opportunities for need arousal. Conversely, when their environment is poor or deprived, fewer needs are activated. This explains why television has had such a mixed effect on the lives of the ghetto poor. It exposes them to various lifestyles and expensive products that they would not otherwise see, and it awakens wants and desires that they have little opportunity or even hope of attaining. Thus, while it enriches their lives, television may also serve to frustrate their lives and sometimes results in the adoption of antisocial defense mechanisms such as aggression.

TYPES AND SYSTEMS OF NEEDS

Diversity of Need Systems

For many years, psychologists and others interested in human behavior have attempted to develop exhaustive lists of human needs or motives. These lists have proved to be as diverse in content as they have been in length. Although there is little disagreement about specific *physiological* needs, there is considerable disagreement about specific *psychogenic* needs. For example, in 1923 a professor of business psychology at the Harvard Business School compiled a list of forty-four human motives for use as copy appeals (see Table 3-1).[16]

In 1938 psychologist Henry Murray prepared a detailed list of twenty-eight psychogenic needs, which have served as the basic constructs for a number of widely used personality tests (for example, the Thematic Apperception Technique and Edwards Personal Preference Schedule).[17] Murray believed that

TABLE 3-1   Motives in Male and Female Adults

Appetite—Hunger	Respect for Deity
Love of Offspring	Sympathy for Others
Health	Protection of Others
Sex Attraction	Domesticity
Parental Affection	Social Distinction
Ambition	Devotion to Others
Pleasure	Hospitality
Bodily Comfort	Warmth
Possession	Imitation
Approval of Others	Courtesy
Gregariousness	Play—Sport
Taste	Managing Others
Personal Appearance	Coolness
Safety	Fear—Caution
Cleanliness	Physical Activity
Rest—Sleep	Manipulation
Home Comfort	Construction
Economy	Style
Curiosity	Humor
Efficiency	Amusement
Competition	Shyness
Cooperation	Teasing

Source: Daniel Starch, Principles of Advertising (Chicago: A.W. Shaw & Co., 1923), 273.

everyone has the same basic set of needs, but that individuals differ in their priority ranking of these needs. Murray's basic needs include many motives that are assumed to play an important role in consumer behavior, such as acquisition, achievement, recognition, and exhibition (see Table 3-2).

Lists of human motives are often too long to be of practical use to marketers. The most useful kind of list is a limited one in which needs are sufficiently generic in title to subsume more detailed human needs. For example, one consumer behaviorist grouped the various lists of psychogenic needs into just three broad categories: affectional needs, ego-bolstering needs, and ego-defensive needs.[18]

Affectional needs are described as the needs to form and maintain warm, harmonious, and emotionally satisfying relations with others.

Ego-bolstering needs are the needs to enhance or promote the personality (to achieve, to gain prestige and recognition, and to satisfy the ego through domination of others).

Ego-defensive needs are the needs to protect the personality (to avoid physical and psychological harm, to avoid ridicule and "loss of face," to prevent loss of prestige, and to avoid or obtain relief from anxiety).[19]

While some psychologists have suggested that people have different need priorities based on their personalities, their experiences, their environments, and so forth, others believe that most human beings assign a similar priority ranking to their basic needs.

TABLE 3-2   Murray's List of Psychogenic Needs

Needs Associated with Inanimate Objects
  Acquisition
  Conservance
  Order
  Retention
  Construction
Needs That Reflect Ambition, Power, Accomplishment, and Prestige
  Superiority
  Achievement
  Recognition
  Exhibition
  Inviolacy (inviolate attitude)
  Infavoidance (to avoid shame, failure, humiliation, ridicule)
  Defendance (defensive attitude)
  Counteraction (counteractive attitude)
Needs Concerned with Human Power
  Dominance
  Deference
  Similance (suggestible attitude)
  Autonomy
  Contrarience (to act differently from others)
Sado-Masochistic Needs
  Aggression
  Abasement
Needs Concerned with Inhibition
  Blamavoidance (to avoid blame)
Needs Concerned with Affection between People
  Affiliation
  Rejection
  Nurturance (to nourish, aid, or protect the helpless)
  Succorance (to seek aid, protection, or sympathy)
  Play
Needs Concerned with Social Intercourse (the Needs to Ask and Tell)
  Cognizance (inquiring attitude)
  Exposition (expositive attitude)

Source: Adapted from Henry A. Murray, "Types of Human Needs," in David C. McClelland, Studies in Motivation (New York: Appleton-Century-Crofts, 1955), 63–66. Reprinted by permission of Irvington Publishers, Inc.

Hierarchy of Needs

The first proponent of the theory of a universal hierarchy of human needs was Dr. Abraham Maslow, a psychologist who formulated a widely accepted theory of human motivation after some twenty years of clinical practice.[20] Maslow's theory postulates five basic levels of human needs, which rank in order of importance from low-level (biogenic) needs to higher-level (psychogenic) needs. It suggests that individuals seek to satisfy lower-level needs before higher-level needs emerge. The lowest level of chronically unsatisfied need that an individual experiences serves to motivate his or her behavior; when that need is fairly well satisfied, a new (and higher) need emerges which the individual is motivated to fulfill. When this need is satisfied, a new (and still higher) need emerges, and so on. Of course, if a lower-level need experiences some renewed deprivation, it may temporarily become dominant again. Figure 3-4 presents Maslow's *hierarchy of needs* in diagrammatic form. For clarity, each level of need is depicted as mutually exclusive; however, according to the theory, there is some overlap between each level, as no need is ever completely satisfied. For this reason, though all levels of need below the dominant level continue to motivate behavior to some extent, the *prime* motivator—the major driving force within the individual—is the lowest level of need that remains largely unsatisfied.

PHYSIOLOGICAL NEEDS

In the hierarchy-of-needs theory, the first and most basic level of needs is physiological. These needs, which are required to sustain biological life, include food, water, air, shelter, clothing, sex—all of the biogenic needs, in fact, that were listed as primary needs earlier. According to Maslow, physiological needs are dominant when they are chronically unsatisfied: "For the man who is extremely and dangerously hungry, no other interest exists but food. He dreams food, he remembers food, he thinks about food, he emotes only about food, he perceives only food and he wants only food."[21] In this country, for most citizens most of the time, the biogenic needs are generally satisfied. Thus the higher-level needs are usually dominant.

SAFETY NEEDS

After the first level of needs is satisfied, safety and security needs become the driving force behind an individual's behavior. These needs are concerned with much more than physical safety. They include order, stability, routine, familiarity, and certainty—the knowledge, for example, that the individual will eat dinner not only that day and the following day but also far into the future. The

FIGURE 3-4   Maslow's Hierarchy of Human Needs

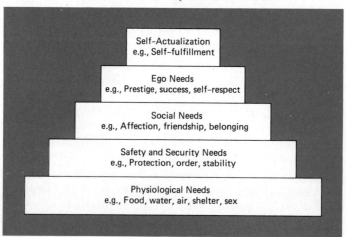

impetus for the growth of labor unions in the United States derives from the safety need, since unions provide members with the security of knowing that their employment does not depend on the day-to-day whims of their employers. The social welfare programs enacted by this country (e.g., social security, unemployment insurance, medicare) have traditionally provided some degree of security to American citizens. Savings accounts, insurance policies, education, and vocational training are all means by which individuals satisfy the need for security. Like the physiological need level, the safety level tends to be fairly well satisfied for many American citizens. However, in times of real or threatened cutbacks in federal spending for social programs, such as those enacted or proposed by the Reagan administration, the security need becomes manifest among the poor and the elderly.

SOCIAL NEEDS

The third level of Maslow's hierarchy includes such needs as love, affection, belonging, and acceptance. People seek warm and satisfying human relationships with other people. (The importance of group acceptance and group influence on consumer behavior is examined more fully in Chapter 11.) Because of the importance of social motives in our society, advertisers of personal-care products often emphasize this appeal in their advertisements (see Figure 3-5).

EGOISTIC NEEDS

When the social needs are more or less satisfied, the fourth level of Maslow's hierarchy becomes operative. This level is concerned with egoistic needs. These needs can take either an inward or an outward orientation, or both. Inwardly directed ego needs reflect an individual's need for self-acceptance, for self-esteem, for achievement, for success, for independence, for personal satisfaction with a job well done. Outwardly directed ego needs include the need for prestige, for reputation, for status, for recognition from others. The desire to "keep up with the Joneses" is a reflection of an outwardly oriented ego need. Figure 3-6 presents an advertisement designed to appeal to the ego need.

NEED FOR SELF-ACTUALIZATION

According to Maslow, most people do not satisfy their ego needs sufficiently to ever move to the fifth level—the need for self-actualization or self-fulfillment. This need refers to an individual's desire to fulfill his or her own potential—to become everything he or she is capable of becoming. "What a man *can* be, he must be."[22] This need is expressed in different ways by different people. A young man may desire to be the best athlete he possibly can (e.g., Eric Heiden, who won more gold medals in speed skating in the 1980 Olympics than any individual in history, worked single-mindedly for years to become the best in his sport). An artist may need to express herself on canvas; a business executive may try to build an empire. Maslow noted that the self-actualization need is not necessarily a creative urge, but that in people with some capacity for creativity, it is likely to take that form. Advertisements for art lessons, for luxury cars, and

FIGURE 3-5   Social Appeal

Courtesy of American Telephone & Telegraph Company, Long Lines Department.

even for diamond watches often try to appeal to the self-actualization need. Figure 3-7 presents an advertisement designed to appeal to this need.

In summary, the hierarchy-of-needs theory postulates that there is a five-level hierarchy of prepotent human needs. Higher-order needs become the driving force behind human behavior as lower-level needs are satisfied. The theory says, in effect, that satisfaction does not motivate behavior, only dissatisfaction does.

An Evaluation of the Need Hierarchy

The need hierarchy has received wide acceptance in many social disciplines because it appears to reflect the assumed or inferred motivations of many people in our society. The five levels of need postulated by the need hierarchy are

FIGURE 3-6   Egoistic Appeal

**Your suit
won't impress anyone
if your shirt doesn't.**

You're not going to make any points with
a fine suit of clothes unless you have a fine
shirt to go with it.

Arrow's Kent is that fine shirt. It's styled to
compliment a gentleman's taste in suits.

It has room to move in, with a seven-
button front. The sleeves and neck come in
exact sizes.

And the patterns and color go with anything you're wearing now and anything you
may want to buy tomorrow.

Kent. Because behind every impressive
suit is an impressive shirt.

►Arrow►

Courtesy of The Arrow Company

FIGURE 3-7   Self-actualization Appeal

generic enough to encompass most lists of individual needs. Some critics, however, maintain that Maslow's concepts are too general. To say that hunger and self-esteem are similar, in that both are needs, is to obscure the urgent, involuntary nature of the former and the largely conscious, voluntary nature of the latter.[23] The major problem with the theory is that it cannot be empirically tested; there is no way to measure precisely how well satisfied one need is before the next higher need becomes operative. The need hierarchy also appears to be very closely bound to our contemporary American culture (i.e., it appears to be culture and time bound).

Despite these criticisms, the hierarchy is a useful tool for understanding consumer motivations and is readily adaptable to marketing strategy, primarily because consumer goods often serve to satisfy each of the need levels. For example, individuals buy houses, food, and clothing to satisfy their physiological needs; they buy insurance and radial tires and vocational training to satisfy their safety and security needs. Almost all personal-care products (cosmetics, toothpaste, shaving cream) are bought to satisfy social needs. Luxury products such as furs or jewels or big cars are usually bought to fulfill ego needs, and college training and art lessons are sold as ways to achieve self-fulfillment.

The hierarchy provides a useful, comprehensive framework for marketers trying to establish appropriate advertising appeals for their products. It is adaptable in two ways: first, it enables marketers to focus their advertising appeals on a need level that is likely to be shared by a large segment of the prospective audience; second, it facilitates product positioning.

SEGMENTATION APPLICATIONS

The need hierarchy is often used as the basis for market segmentation, as specific advertising appeals are directed to individuals on one or more need levels. For example, soft-drink ads directed to teenagers may stress a social appeal by showing a group of young people mutually sharing good times as well as the advertised product.

Figure 3-8 shows how supermarkets can use Maslow's categories to segment their customers and develop appropriate marketing strategies. As the figure notes, the so-called need-driven customers—those primarily motivated by physical and security needs—are quite different from the "belongers," the "achievers," and the "inner-directed" customers in terms of the foods they buy, the advertising appeals to which they respond, and the kinds of store decor in which they feel most comfortable. Thus supermarkets located in the inner city would appeal to their *need-driven* customers by stressing price in their advertisements, by stocking store brands, and by decorating their stores with showy displays. In contrast, supermarkets in affluent suburban areas would stress quality and variety in their ads, carry "natural" or exotic foods, strive for a subtle, artistic store atmosphere, and downplay the need for security personnel. Stores with a mixture of customers would have to strive for a harmonious blend.[24]

POSITIONING APPLICATIONS

Another way to utilize the hierarchy is for "positioning" products; that is, deciding how the product is to be perceived by prospective consumers. The key to positioning is to find a niche that is not occupied by any competing brand. This application of the need hierarchy relies on the notion that no need is ever fully satisfied, that it always continues to be somewhat motivating. For example, most manufacturers of luxury cars use status appeals ("Impress your friends"), or self-actualizing appeals ("You deserve the very best"), or even social appeals ("The whole family can ride in luxurious comfort"). To find a unique position

FIGURE 3-8   Segmentation Applications of Maslow's Need Hierarchy

	Demographics	**Values & Buying Emphasis**
Need-Driven 	**19 Million Adults** • Average family income $5,500. • One-third of the group is black. • Average education: nine years. • One-third under 30; 39% over 50. • 63% female. • Over 70% in one- or two-person households. Forecast: no change in number.	Dominated by worries about survival and security. Farthest removed from the American cultural mainstream of any large consumer group. Forced by low incomes to buy more in accord with what they *need* than what they *want.* Concerned with price. Buy staples, functional items. Occasional splurges.
Belongers 	**58 Million Adults** • Median family income around $13,000. • Blacks definitely underrepresented. • Hold hard-hat and clerical jobs. • 35% keep house and 17% are retired. • Average age over 50. • Almost two-thirds are women. Forecast: very mild growth.	Prime drive is to fit in, not stand out. A conforming, nonexperimental kind of person. Tend to be puritanical, formal, matriarchal, suspicious of the new, dutiful, following, nostalgic and sentimental. Aura of old-fashionedness, reliability, and dependability. Seeks to become part of the group via his or her purchases. The heart of much family buying. Joining in the fads of the times in the third or fourth wave—not innovators.
Achievers 	**37 Million Adults** • 40% have family incomes over $25,000 and 5% over $50,000. • 97% white. • Live in city suburbs. • Average age about 42. • Most male of groups. • 60% have attended college, and 14% have graduate training. • Dominate professional, managerial professions. Forecast: very mild growth.	The driving and driven person, oriented to success. Expends wealth, activity, and energy on good things of life. Wants the best and willing to work hard for it. Work and Puritan ethic central—even leisure must be busy and productive. Competetive, self-confident, and willing to try the new, especially if the newness smacks of technological innovation. Support a large share of high-profity luxury and gift market. Buy top of the line. Open to "new and improved."
Inner-Directed 	**26 Million Adults** • Average age about 32 • Almost half have family incomes over $20,000. • 39% professional or technical. • More likely to live in West than other segments. • Evenly divided between sexes. • 89% white, 9% black, and 2% other nonwhite. • Best educated group. • Many singles. Forecast: rapid growth, especially among two subsegments: • **Experiential** (seek direct experience; active in vigorous outdoor sports like hang-gliding; seek inner revelation and understanding). • **Societally Conscious** (dominant in such movements as consumerism, conservation, health and safety; pro "voluntary simplicity").	Most liberal and permissive group. Strongly favor many nontradtional political and moral views. A principal force for change in the U.S. society. Importantly motivated by social and cultural, rather than personal, concerns. Buy to meet own inner wants and pleasures as distinct from responding primarily to norms of others. Dominant feature is self-expressive diversity. Create frgmented, varied markets. Hence, hard to spot and track.

Supermarket Behavior	Store Environment
Buy loss-leader items. Respond to ads emphasizing price, coupons. Buy store brands. Prefer ethnic foods and starchy, fill-up foods. Spend 10% of budget on foods eaten away from home.	Blaring facades Contrasty merchandise Price dominant Clear warranty Bright music and color Displays changed regularly Obvious store security
Prepare home-cooked, from-scratch meals. Respond to ad themes like "The family that eats together, stays together." Prefer hearty meat-and-potato meals.	Traditional facades Bland merchandise Provide specific information Heavy display (little atmosphere) Traditional fixtures Less obvious store security
Buy gourmet and convenience foods. Respond to ads stressing quality, appearance, convenience. Are concerned with dieting and nutrition. Buy cheeses, wines, fresh meat, and fish. Spend up to one-third of budget on food away from home.	Classical/modern facades High-quality merchandise Information on request Much atmosphere Wood/chrome/glass fixtures Unobtrusive store security
Experientials: Cook from scratch and go for elegant dining. Respond to ads for the modish or stylish. Buy exotic foods and recreational foods (e.g., for camping). Spend up to one-third of budget on away-from-home meals. **Societally Conscious:** Grow and prepare food from scratch. Are conscious of health and nutrition. Respond to ads stressing aesthetics and one-of-a-kind appeals. Eat vegetarian fare.	Natural, homey facades Subtle, muted, artistic atmosphere Personal/informal presentation No evidence of store security

Source: Adopted from Arnold Mitchell, "A Further Splintering in Buying Styles," *Progressive Grocer,* 58 (November 1979), 102–4.

among its luxury competitors, Mercedes Benz adopted the safety appeal in advertisements to well-to-do executives ("When your wife is driving the two children home on a dark and stormy night, you can relax if she's driving the Mercedes").

It is interesting, in light of the cigarette/cancer controversy, to recall that in the late 1940s, most cigarette commercials stressed medical endorsements ("Two out of three doctors interviewed smoke Camels"). Cigarette smoking was advertised as relaxing, soothing, and good for the nervous system; in effect, as a means of fulfilling physiological needs. Then a new competitive campaign broke upon the scene which repositioned a cigarette brand by suggesting social fulfillment. The advertisement showed a young man surrounded by a bevy of beautiful girls with a headline that read, "For a treat instead of a treatment, smoke Old Golds." By repositioning its product to fulfill social needs, Old Gold snared a significant share of the market.

VERSATILITY OF THE NEED HIERARCHY

One way to illustrate the usefulness of the need hierarchy in designing promotional programs is to show how workable appeals for a single product can be developed from each level. Consider, for example, the following potential promotional appeals for a microwave oven. An appeal to *physiological* needs would show how quickly food can be prepared (i.e., satisfy hunger needs) in a microwave oven. A *safety* appeal would demonstrate how safe the microwave oven is in comparison with other cooking appliances (e.g., no burned fingers). *Social* appeals can be invoked by illustrations of party and holiday dinners prepared in a microwave oven. *Status* is easily demonstrated through such standard appeals as "Impress your friends" or "For a truly luxurious kitchen, you need a microwave oven." Finally, appeals to *self-actualization* may point out to career couples how easy it is to prepare last-minute dinners after a long and challenging workday.

A Trio of Needs

Several psychologists have written extensively on the existence of a trio of basic needs: the needs for power, for affiliation, and for achievement.[25] These needs can each be subsumed in Maslow's need hierarchy; however, considered individually, they each have a unique relevance to consumer motivation.

POWER NEEDS

The power need relates to an individual's desire to control his or her environment. It includes the need to control other persons and various objects. This need appears to be closely related to the ego need, in that many individuals experience increased self-enhancement when they exercise power over objects or people. A number of products lend themselves to promises of power or superiority for their users. An automobile advertisement might stress enormous speed capability even though this capability can rarely be exercised because of legal or practical limits. Nevertheless, the implied promise of power will attract individuals with strong power needs.

AFFILIATION NEEDS

Affiliation is a well-known and well-researched social motive which has far-reaching influence on consumer behavior. The affiliation need suggests that individuals' behavior is highly influenced by the desire for friendship, for acceptance, for belonging. People with high affiliation needs tend to have a strong social dependence on others. They often select goods that they feel will meet with the approval of friends. People who go to crafts fairs or to garage sales, teenagers who hang out at malls on Saturdays, car buffs who congregate at automobile shows, often do so more for the satisfaction of being with others than for making a purchase. Such individuals appreciate the assistance and the opinions of friendly salespeople and may purchase clothing or even household goods in order to merit the approval of an encouraging salesperson. People with high affiliation needs often adapt their purchase behavior to the norms and standards of their reference groups (see Chapter 11).

ACHIEVEMENT NEEDS

A number of research studies have focused on the achievement need.[26] Individuals with a strong need for achievement regard personal accomplishment as an end in itself. The achievement need is closely related to the egoistic need, in that satisfaction with a job well done serves to enhance the individual's self-esteem. People with a high need for achievement have certain traits that make them vulnerable to relevant appeals. They are more self-confident, enjoy taking calculated risks, research their environment actively, and are very much interested in feedback. (Their interest in money rewards or profits is primarily due to the feedback that money provides as to how well they are doing.) They like situations in which they can take personal responsibility for finding problem solutions.[27]

High-achievement people are often good prospects for cleverly presented innovative products, for do-it-yourself projects, for older houses, and even for moderately speculative stock issues. They are also likely to be receptive to appeals from advertisers in whom they recognize similar needs (i.e., with whom they can identify). For example, the Datsun slogan "We are driven" might strike a responsive note in individuals with high achievement needs.

Several research studies indicate that individuals with a high need for achievement may constitute a special market segment for certain products. For example, one study found that men with a high need for achievement tend to favor products considered virile and masculine, such as boating equipment, straight razors, and skis. Men with low-need achievement scores preferred to buy products characterized as meticulous or fastidious, such as mouthwash, deodorants, and automatic dishwashers.[28] Another study suggested that many of the people who engage in active outdoor sports have a high need for achievement.[29] People with a high need for achievement are also more likely to patronize stores that not only use appeals of excellence but liberally use positive achievement words.[30]

In summary, then, individuals with specific psychological needs tend to be receptive to advertising appeals directed to those needs. They also tend to be receptive to certain kinds of products. Thus, such needs provide marketers with additional bases on which to divide their markets into smaller, homogeneous market segments.

THE MEASUREMENT OF MOTIVES

How are motives identified? How are they measured? How do researchers know which motives are responsible for certain kinds of behavior? These are difficult questions to answer because motives are hypothetical constructs; that is, they cannot be seen or touched, handled, smelled, or otherwise tangibly observed. For this reason, no one measurement method can be considered a reliable index of motivation. Instead, researchers usually rely on a combination of methods used in tandem to try to establish the presence and/or the strength of various motives. These methods are complementary and include observation and inference, self-reports, and projective techniques.

Observation and Inference

Motivations are often inferred from the actions and statements of individuals.[31] If a person undertakes extensive search behavior for a specific kind of product and continues such activity until he or she makes a purchase selection, then inferences are often made as to the need that motivated the search behavior.[32] For example, prior to buying a washing machine, if a couple visits appliance stores to examine and to price washing machines, and if they study appliance advertisements and seek relevant information from *Consumer Reports,* the logical inference is that they have a need for an efficient, practical way to wash clothes. Of course, motive identification through inference can be somewhat circular in reasoning; that is, a motive may be attributed to observed behavior and then be used to explain the behavior from which it was inferred. For example, observers may assume that a man's purchase of a mink coat is motivated by his need for prestige, and then they "explain" his wearing of mink as a reflection of his need for prestige. Mink, however, is actually an extremely warm, durable, and lightweight fur. For someone who can afford it, a mink coat may simply be the most practical way to keep warm in the winter.

Although we may feel that we can plausibly infer a motive from certain kinds of behavior, we cannot validly claim to do so. For example, it may seem reasonable to assume that people who devote time and effort to school board activities do so out of esteem or self-actualization needs; however, in reality they may find such activities a way of fulfilling social needs. Similarly, it may seem reasonable to assume that a person who works long hours in business has a strong achievement motive, but in reality he or she may have an overwhelming need for security which is satisfied through the accumulation of money. Or he or she may simply be setting aside a nest egg in order to fulfill a secret wish to take a world cruise.

In addition to observation, another source of inference about the motives of individuals is the nonstructured, or "depth," interview. In this type of interview, respondents are questioned singly or in small groups for several hours by an interviewer who is trained to establish rapport, and not to guide the discussion excessively. Respondents are encouraged to talk freely about their activities or interests, or about a specific subject or brand under study (in which case the interview is termed a "focus" interview). A verbatim account of the interview is then carefully studied, together with reports of the respondents' moods and any gesture or body language they may have used to convey their attitudes or motives.[33] Such studies are very useful, especially for giving marketers a lead on appeals they might use. For example, interviews done for Pizza Hut revealed that people considered eating pizza a sensual, sharing, uninhibiting experience, which researchers used to create the successful ad slogan "Let yourself go at Pizza Hut."[34] Because informal group interviews are relatively inexpensive and can be completed in much less time than other research techniques, they are gaining in popularity. But obviously, analysis of responses elicited in an interview requires a great deal of skill on the part of researchers, and critics warn that the technique can be overused.[35]

To avoid errors of inference, a motivational analysis that is based on observation or in-depth interviews is often supplemented with other methods, such as subjective or self-reports.

Self-Reports

Some researchers claim that the best way to find out about the needs and goals of individuals is simply to ask them. A number of pencil-and-paper "tests" given to consumers inquire directly about their wants, desires, fears, goals, successes, failures. The information so obtained is then quantified (assigned a numerical score) to yield a measure of the strength of a specific need or motive.

There are two potential problems with self-reports of this nature. First, individuals may not themselves be aware of the actual reasons or motives underlying their behavior and they may unconsciously rationalize their actions; that is, they may assign reasons or motives that are acceptable to their personalities but are not, in fact, accurate. They do this with no awareness that they are rationalizing. A couple may justify their move to the suburbs by saying that they want to have more room and fresh air for the children when their actual motive is to escape the anonymity of big-city apartment life. Or they may send their children to summer camp because "the fresh air and organized activities are good for them," but they may not consciously realize that they do so primarily to free themselves from oppressive child-care responsibilities for two months.

Aside from unconsciously rationalizing their own motives, people may also deliberately falsify self-report inventories to impress the researcher, to please the researcher, or to avoid personal embarrassment. It is difficult for a researcher to distinguish among true reports, rationalized reports, or deliberately falsified reports. For this reason, psychologists and other researchers interested in motivation have developed techniques designed to delve below the consumers' level of conscious awareness, to tap the underlying motives of individuals despite their unconscious rationalizations or conscious concealment. These methods are called projective techniques.

Projective Techniques

Projective techniques are designed to reveal a person's true feelings and motivations. They consist of a variety of disguised tests that contain ambiguous stimuli, such as incomplete sentences, untitled pictures or cartoons, inkblots, word-association tests, and other-person characterizations. (See Figure 3-9 and Table 3-3 for examples of projective tests.) The respondent is asked to complete, describe, or explain the meaning of various stimuli. The theory behind projective tests is that individuals' own needs and motives will influence how they perceive ambiguous stimuli. Thus the stories they tell or the sentences they complete are actually projections of their own feelings, though they attribute their responses to something or someone else. In this way, respondents are expected to reveal their underlying needs, wants, fears, aspirations, and motives, whether or not they are fully aware of them. For example, if a subject looks at a picture of a man wearing a business suit and describes him as a "big-shot," one may infer that the subject is concerned with ego needs.

The basic assumption underlying projective techniques is that respondents are unaware that they are exposing their own feelings. This is sometimes

FIGURE 3-9   Example of Thematic Apperception Test

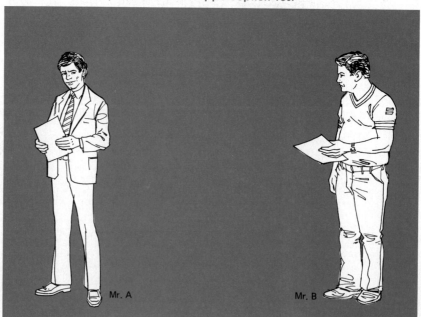

Mr. A   Mr. B

TABLE 3-3   Examples of Projective Techniques Used in Consumer Research

word association
> What is the first word you think of when I say:
>> Hammer?
>> Roof?
>> Faucet?
>> Ladder?

incomplete sentences
> Please complete the following sentences:
>> Do-it-yourselfers are............
>> Investing in the stock market is...........

narrative projection
> A friend of yours has just inherited $10,000. She asks you how to invest it. What would you advise?

cartoons
> Look at this picture of a man holding a wrench beneath a sink. What is the man saying to his friend standing nearby?

thematic apperception test
> Look at this drawing of a two-story house. (Drawing indicates various hazardous conditions: an icy path to the door, a partially obscured bicycle lying on its side in the driveway, a crumbling chimney.) If you were an insurance agent, what would you note in a report?

illustrated by the old joke about a psychologist who shows a subject a series of geometric figures and asks him to describe what he sees. In each case, the subject reports seeing a lewd or lascivious scene. When the psychologist comments that the subject has an obvious sexual fixation, the latter retorts, "It's not *my* fixation; after all; it's *you* who are showing me the dirty pictures."

Obviously, the identification and measurement of human motives is still a very inexact process. Some psychologists point out that most measurement techniques do not meet the crucial test criteria of validity and reliability.[36] *Validity* ensures that the test measures what it purports to measure; *reliability* refers to the consistency with which the test measures what it does measure. By using a combination of assessments based on behavioral data (e.g., observation), subjective data (e.g., self-reports), and projective techniques, many consumer researchers feel confident that they gain valuable insights into consumer motivations. Though some analysts complain that such research does not produce hard numbers that objectively "prove" a point under investigation, others believe that qualitative studies can be just as revealing, and often less expensive, than quantitative studies.[37] However, there is clearly a need for improved methodological procedures for measuring human motives.

MOTIVATIONAL RESEARCH

The term *motivational research*, which should include all types of research into human motives, is generally used to refer to qualitative research designed to uncover the consumer's subconscious or hidden motivations.[38] Operating on the premise that consumers are not always fully aware of the basic reasons for their actions, motivational research attempts to discover underlying feelings, attitudes, and emotions concerning product, service, or brand usage.

Methodology and Analysis

Because emotional feelings are not easily or accurately revealed by consumers upon direct questioning, motivational researchers utilize clinical psychological methods such as the nondirective (depth) interview and projective techniques (word-association tests, sentence completion tests, inkblot and cartoon tests, other-person characterizations). Careful analysis of the data generated by these techniques provides researchers with varying degrees of insight into the underlying reasons why consumers buy or do not buy products or product categories under study.

Motivational research analyses often suggest new ways for marketers to present their products to the public. For example, a study prepared for a hair-coloring manufacturer revealed that women regarded becoming blond as a way of changing their image and personality. Respondents considered blonds to be attractive and sexy women, leading "fun" and "swinging" lives. These and other findings provided the company with substantial material on which to base a new advertising campaign.

Development of Motivational Research

Motivational research became popular in the early 1950s when Dr. Ernest Dichter, formerly a psychoanalyst in Vienna, adapted his psychoanalytic techniques to the study of consumer buying habits. Marketing research up to this time had focused on *what* consumers did (i.e., quantitative, descriptive studies) rather than on *why* they did it. Marketers were quickly fascinated by the glib, entertaining, and usually surprising explanations offered for consumer behavior, especially since many of these explanations were rooted in sex. (Most early motivational researchers were Freudian in their thinking and took the approach that all behavior is sexually motivated [see Chapter 4].) Thus marketers were told that cigarettes and lifesaver candies were bought because of their sexual symbolism, that men regarded convertible cars as surrogate mistresses, that women baked cakes to fulfill their reproductive yearnings.[39] Before long, almost every advertising agency on Madison Avenue had a psychologist on its staff in charge of motivational research studies.

Shortcomings of Motivational Research

By the early 1960s, marketers realized that motivational research had some drawbacks. Because of the intensive nature of qualitative research, samples were necessarily small; thus there was concern about generalizing findings to the total market. Also, marketers soon realized that the analysis of projective tests and depth interviews was highly subjective. The same data given to three different analysts could produce three different reports, each offering its own explanation of the consumer behavior examined. Critics noted that many of the projective tests that were used had originally been developed for clinical purposes, rather than for studies of marketing or consumption behavior. (One of the basic criteria for test development is that tests be developed and validated for the specific purpose and on the specific audience from which information is desired.)

Finally, too many motivational researchers imputed highly exotic reasons to rather prosaic consumer purchases, and marketers began to question their recommendations (e.g., Is it better to sell a man a pair of suspenders as a means of holding up his pants or as a "reaction to castration anxiety"?[40] Is it easier to persuade a woman to buy a garden hose to water her lawn or as a symbol of the "futility of genital competition for the female"?[41]) Motivational researchers often came up with sexual explanations for the most mundane activities. For example, an ad showing a hostess behind a beverage table filled with large bottles of soft drinks was commended by a leading motivational researcher for its "clever use of phallic symbolism."[42]

Motivational Research Today

Despite these criticisms, motivational research is still being used by marketers who are concerned with gaining deeper insights into the whys of consumer behavior than conventional marketing research techniques can yield. As one agency professional pointed out, motivational research is a "chance to experience a 'flesh and blood' customer...to experience the emotional framework in which the product is being used."[43]

Since motivational research often reveals unsuspected consumer motivations concerning product or brand usage, its principal use is in the development of new ideas for promotional campaigns, ideas that can penetrate the consumer's conscious awareness by appealing to his or her unrecognized needs. Thus manufacturers of house paint were able to convince Minnesota consumers to try more vivid colors on the exteriors of their homes after researchers discovered a latent "color hunger" among people living in that gray, wintry climate.[44] Such research also provides marketers with a basic orientation for new-product categories and enables them to explore consumer reactions to ideas and copy at an early stage so that costly errors can be avoided. Furthermore, motivational research provides marketers with the basic cues for more structured, quantitative marketing research studies—studies that can be conducted on larger, more representative samples of consumers.

Motivation research has also been used "profitably" by nonprofit organizations. For example, Dichter found that people unconsciously resist making charitable donations because they feel that once they have given, they will no longer be the objects of attention. Using that insight, the United Way and other fund-raisers now spend almost as much time thanking people for their donations as soliciting new donations, in order to generate goodwill for future campaigns.[45]

Motivational research continues to be a useful tool for many marketers who are concerned with knowing the actual reasons underlying consumer behavior.

However, it is no longer considered the *only* method for uncovering human motivation, but rather one of a variety of research techniques available to the consumer researcher.

summary

Motivation is the driving force within individuals that impels them to action. This driving force is produced by a state of uncomfortable tension, which exists as the result of an unfilled need. All individuals have needs, wants, and desires. The individual's subconscious drive to reduce need-induced tension results in behavior that he or she anticipates will satisfy needs and thus bring about a more comfortable state.

All behavior is goal oriented. Goals are the sought-after results of motivated behavior. The form or direction that behavior takes—the goal that is selected—is a result of thinking processes (cognition) and previous learning. Marketers talk of two types of goals: generic goals and product-specific goals. A *generic* goal is a general category of goal that may fulfill a certain need; a *product-specific* goal is a specifically branded or labeled product that the individual sees as a way to fulfill a need.

Innate needs—those an individual is born with—are primarily physiological (biogenic); they include all the factors required to sustain physical life (e.g., food, water, clothing, shelter, sex). Acquired needs—those an individual develops after birth—are primarily psychological (psychogenic); they include esteem, fear, love, and acceptance. For any given need, there are many different and appropriate goals. The specific goal selected depends on the individual's experiences, physical capacity, prevailing cultural norms and values, and the goal's accessibility in the physical and social environment.

Needs and goals are interdependent, and change in response to the individual's physical condition, environment, interaction with other people, and experiences. As needs become satisfied, new, higher-order needs emerge which must be fulfilled.

Failure to achieve a goal often results in feelings of frustration. Individuals react to frustration in two ways: They may cope by finding a way around the obstacle that prohibits goal attainment or by finding a substitute goal, or they may adopt a defense mechanism that enables them to protect their self-esteem. Defense mechanisms include aggression, regression, rationalization, withdrawal, projection, autism, identification, and repression.

Motives cannot be easily inferred from consumer behavior. People with different needs may seek fulfillment through selection of the same goals; people with the same needs may seek fulfillment through different goals.

While some psychologists have suggested that individuals have different need priorities, others believe that most human beings experience the same basic needs, to which they assign a similar priority ranking. Maslow's hierarchy-of-needs theory proposes five levels of prepotent human needs: physiological needs, safety needs, social needs, egoistic needs, and self-actualization needs. A trio of other needs widely used in consumer appeals are the needs for power, affiliation, and achievement.

There are three commonly used methods for identifying and "measuring" human motives: observation and inference, subjective reports, and projective techniques. None of these methods is completely reliable by itself; therefore, researchers often use a combination of two or three techniques in tandem to assess the presence or strength of consumer motives.

Motivational research is qualitative research designed to delve below the consumer's level of conscious awareness. Despite some shortcomings, motivational research has proved to be of great value to marketers concerned with developing new ideas and new copy appeals.

discussion questions

1. What is motivational research? What are its strengths and its weaknesses? How can it best be utilized in the development of marketing strategy?
2. How can a marketer design a promotional strategy to reduce consumer frustrations? Find an advertisement that illustrates this attempt.
3. Choose five magazine advertisements for different consumer goods. Carefully review Murray's list of human needs. Identify, through advertising appeal, which need(s) each product is presumed to satisfy.
4. Briefly explain how marketers can employ Maslow's need hierarchy in their marketing strategies. Give at least two examples.
5. Explain briefly the needs for power, affiliation, and achievement. Find three advertisements, each aimed at satisfying one of these needs through the purchase of the advertised product.
6. Suppose you are the vice-president of consumer research for a large U.S. liquor distributor. A new project assigned to you requires you to determine *why* people drink alcoholic beverages. Discuss the measurement techniques you would employ.
7. Develop five different advertising appeals—one for each level of Maslow's need hierarchy—that the General Motors marketing staff might employ for its new fall line of automobiles.
8. Consumers have both innate needs and acquired needs. Give examples of each kind of need and show how the same purchase can serve to fulfill either or both kinds of needs.

endnotes

1. David Krech, Richard S. Crutchfield, and Egerton L. Ballachey, *Individual in Society* (New York: McGraw-Hill, 1962), 69.
2. Ibid., 76–77.

3. Harold H. Kassarjian, "Personality and Consumer Behavior: A Review," *Journal of Marketing Research,* 8 (November 1971), 413; and E. Laird Landon, Jr., "Self Concept, Ideal Self Concepts and Consumer Purchase Intentions," *Journal of Consumer Research,* 1 (September 1974), 44–51.

4. Edward L. Grubb and Bruce L. Stern, "Self-Concept and Significant Others," *Journal of Marketing Research,* 8 (August 1971), 382.

5. George Katona, "Rational Behavior and Economic Behavior," *Psychological Review,* 60 (September 1953), 307–18.

6. See, for example, Thomas V. Bonoma, "Who Needs Needs? Marketing Is Power!" (Unpublished paper, University of Pittsburgh, October 1977).

7. "Forget Wants, Needs, Listen to Consumers' Problems: Dillon," *Marketing News,* June 2, 1978, 6.

8. Krech et al., *Individual in Society,* 69.

9. L. Wilkens and C.P. Richter, "A Great Craving for Salt by a Child with Cortico-Adrenal Insufficiency," *Journal of the American Medical Association,* 14 (1940), 866–68.

10. See Abraham H. Maslow, "A Theory of Human Motivation," *Psychological Review,* 50 (1943), 370–96; Abraham H. Maslow, *Motivation and Personality* (New York: Harper & Row, 1954); and Abraham H. Maslow, *Toward a Psychology of Being* (New York: Van Nostrand Reinhold, 1968), 189–215.

11. Ernest Dichter, "Interpretative versus Descriptive Research," in *Research in Marketing* (New York: JAI Press, 1978), I, 73.

12. A number of studies have focused on human levels of aspiration. See, for example, Kurt Lewin, et al., "Level of Aspiration," in J. McV. Hunt, *Personality and Behavior Disorders* (New York: Ronald Press, 1944); and I.L. Child and J. William Whiting, "Determinants of Level of Aspiration: Evidence from Everyday Life," *Journal of Abnormal Social Psychology,* 44 (1949), 303–14.

13. Rolph E. Anderson, "Consumer Dissatisfaction: The Effect of Disconfirmed Expectancy on Perceived Product Performance," *Journal of Marketing Research,* 10 (February 1973), 38–44.

14. Richard H. Buskirk and James T. Rothe, "Consumerism—An Interpretation," *Journal of Marketing,* 34 (October 1970), 61–62, 65. See also George S. Day and David A. Aaker, "A Guide to Consumerism," *Journal of Marketing,* 34 (July 1970), 12–19.

15. Krech et al., *Individual in Society,* 119–23.

16. Daniel Starch, *Principles of Advertising* (Chicago: A.W. Shaw, 1923), 273.

17. Henry A. Murray et al., *Explorations in Personality* (New York: Oxford University Press, 1938), 80–85, 109–15.

18. James A. Bayton, "Motivation, Cognition, Learning—Basic Factors in Consumer Behavior," *Journal of Marketing,* 23 (January 1958), 282–89.

19. Ibid.

20. Maslow, "A Theory of Human Motivation," 380.

21. Ibid.

22. Ibid.

23. Bonoma, "Who Needs Needs?" 9.

24. Arnold Mitchell, "A Further Splintering in Buying Styles," *Progressive Grocer,* 58 (November 1979), 101–04.

25. See, for example, Edward M. Tauber, "Why Do People Shop?" *Journal of Marketing,* 36 (October 1972), 46–59.

26. David C. McClelland, *Studies in Motivation* (New York: Appleton-Century-Crofts, 1955).

27. David C. McClelland, "Business Drive and National Achievement," *Harvard Business Review,* July-August 1962, 99; "Achievement Motivation Can Be Developed,"

Harvard Business Review, November–December 1965, 5–24, 178; and Abraham K. Korman, *The Psychology of Motivation* (Englewood Cliffs, N.J.: Prentice-Hall, 1974), 190.

28. E. Laird Landon, Jr., "A Sex Role Explanation of Purchase Intention Differences of Consumers Who Are High and Low in Need for Achievement," in M. Venkatesan, ed., *Proceedings of the Third Annual Conference* (Association for Consumer Research, 1972), 1–8.

29. David M. Gardner, "An Exploratory Investigation of Achievement Motivation Effects on Consumer Behavior," in Venkatesan, *Proceedings of the Third Annual Conference,* 20–33.

30. Charles D. Schewe, "Selected Social Psychological Models for Analyzing Buyers," *Journal of Marketing,* 37 (July 1973), 31–39; and David C. McClelland and Alvin M. Liberman, "The Effect of Need for Achievement on Recognition of Need-Related Words," *Journal of Personality,* 18 (December 1949), 236–51.

31. The use of observation as a way of measuring or determining motivation has been called an unobtrusive measure by some psychologists, since the subjects do not know they are being measured. See, for example, E.J. Webb, D.T. Campbell, R.D. Schwartz, and L. Sechrest, *Unobtrusive Measures: Nonreactive Research in the Social Sciences* (Chicago: Rand McNally, 1966).

32. Krech et al., *Individual in Society,* 87.

33. Darlene Miskovic, "Behind the Mirror: Here Are Some Rules That Can Help Sharpen the Value of Focus Groups," *Advertising Age,* November 17, 1980, 49.

34. Nancy F. Millman, "Don't Shoot Till You Know the Whys of Their Buys," *Advertising Age,* January 16, 1978, 36.

35. See George J. Szybillo and Robert Berger, "What Advertising Agencies Think of Focus Groups," *Journal of Advertising Research,* 19 (June 1979), 29–33; and Theodore J. Gage, "Theories Differ on Use of Focus Group," *Advertising Age,* February 4, 1980, 19–22

36. Korman, *Psychology of Motivation,* 124–51.

37. Fred D. Reynolds and Deborah K. Johnson, "Validity of Focus Group Findings," *Journal of Advertising Research,* 18 (June 1978), 21–24.

38. Ernest Dichter, *A Strategy of Desire* (Garden City, N.Y.: Doubleday, 1960).

39. For additional reports of motivational research findings, see Dichter, *Strategy of Desire;* Vance Packard, *The Hidden Persuaders* (New York: Pocket Book, Inc., 1957); and Pierre Martineau, *Motivation in Advertising* (New York: McGraw-Hill, 1957).

40. R. Ferber and H.G. Wales, eds., *Motivation and Market Behavior* (Homewood, Ill.: Richard D. Irwin, 1958), 20.

41. Ibid.

42. Leslie Kanuk, "Emotional Persuasion in Print Advertising," (Master's thesis, City College of New York, 1964).

43. "Qualitative Is Most Vulnerable Research: Axelrod," *Advertising Age,* May 13, 1974, 82.

44. Dichter, "Interpretative versus Descriptive Research," 72.

45. Rena Bartos, "Ernest Dichter: Motive Interpreter," *Journal of Advertising Research,* 17 (June 1977), 8.

FOUR

Personality
and Consumer Behavior

introduction

FOR several decades marketers have been interested in identifying specific market segments in terms of how these segments differ in personality characteristics. Their objective has been to isolate the personality traits of market segments they would like to reach so that they can develop marketing strategies that will attract their desired target market. Interest in segmenting consumers on the basis of personality is founded upon the belief that consumers' purchase behavior is in part a reflection of their personality.

This chapter examines what personality is, and how personality interrelates with other consumer behavior concepts. It reviews several major personality theories and describes how they have stimulated marketers' interest in the study of consumer personality.

Particular attention is given to how a knowledge of consumer personality characteristics can be employed by marketers to segment markets.

WHAT IS PERSONALITY?

The examination of personality has been approached by theorists in a variety of ways. Some theorists have emphasized the dual influence of heredity and early childhood experiences on personality development, while others have stressed broader social and environmental influences and the fact that personalities continuously develop over time. Some theorists prefer to view personality as a unified whole, while others focus on specific traits. The wide variation in viewpoints makes it somewhat difficult to arrive at a single definition of personality. However, we propose that *personality* be defined as *those inner psychological characteristics that both determine and reflect how a person responds to his or her environment.*

The emphasis in this definition is on the person's *inner* characteristics— those specific qualities, attributes, traits, factors, and mannerisms that distin-

A man is like a bit of labrador spar, which has no lustre as you turn it in your hand, until you come to a particular angle; then it shows deep and beautiful colors.

EMERSON:

"Experience," *Essays: Second Series (1844)*

guish one individual from other individuals. As we will discover later in this chapter, the deeply ingrained characteristics that we call personality are likely to influence the individual's product and store choices; they also affect the way the consumer responds to a firm's communication efforts. Therefore the identification of specific personality characteristics that are associated with consumer behavior may be highly useful in the development of a firm's market segmentation strategies.

THE NATURE OF PERSONALITY

In approaching the study of personality, three distinct properties are of central importance: (1) personality is the essence of individual differences, (2) personality is consistent and enduring, and (3) personality can change.[1]

Personality Reflects Individual Differences

Because the inner characteristics that constitute an individual's personality are a unique combination of factors, no two individuals are exactly alike. Nevertheless, many individuals tend to be similar in terms of a single personality characteristic. For instance, many people can be described as "high" in sociability (the degree of interest they display in social or group activities), while others can be described as "low" in sociability. Personality is a useful consumer behavior concept because it enables us to categorize people into different groups on the basis of a single trait or a few traits. If each person were different in *all* respects, it would be impossible to segment people into similar consuming groups; thus there would be little reason to develop standardized products and promotional campaigns.

Personality Is Consistent and Enduring

An individual's personality is commonly thought to be both consistent and enduring. Indeed, the mother who comments that her child "has been stubborn from the day he was born" is supporting the contention that personality has both consistency and endurance. Both of these qualities are essential if marketers are to explain or predict consumer behavior in terms of personality.

The stable nature of personality suggests that it is unreasonable for marketers to attempt to change consumers' personalities to conform to certain products. At best, they may learn which personality characteristics influence specific consumer responses, and attempt to appeal to relevant personality traits inherent in their target group of consumers.

Even though an individual's personality may be consistent, consumption behavior may vary considerably because of psychological, social-cultural, and environmental factors that affect behavior. For instance, while an individual's personality may be largely stable, specific needs or motives, attitudes, reaction to group pressures, and even responses to the brands that are now available may cause a change in the person's behavior. Therefore personality is only one of a combination of factors that influence how a consumer behaves.

Personality Can Change

Although personality tends to be consistent and enduring, it may still change under various circumstances. For instance, an individual's personality may be altered because of major life events (the birth of a child, the death of a loved one, a divorce, a major career promotion). An individual's personality changes not only in response to abrupt events in his or her life but also as part of a gradual maturing process.

THEORIES OF PERSONALITY

In this section we will briefly review three major theories of personality: (1) Freudian theory, (2) neo-Freudian theory, and (3) trait theory. These theories have been chosen for discussion from among many theories of personality because each has played a prominent role in the study of the relationship between consumer behavior and personality.[2]

Freudian Theory

Sigmund Freud's psychoanalytic theory of personality is the cornerstone of modern psychology. This theory was built on the premise that unconscious needs or drives, especially biological and sexual drives, are at the heart of human motivation and personality. Freud constructed his theory on the basis of patients' recollections of early childhood experiences, analysis of their dreams, and the specific nature of their mental and physical adjustment problems.

ID, SUPEREGO, AND EGO

Based upon his analyses, Freud proposed that the human personality consists of three interacting systems—the *id*, the *superego*, and the *ego*. The *id* was conceptualized as a "warehouse" of primitive and impulsive drives—basic physiological needs such as thirst, hunger, and sex—for which the individual seeks immediate satisfaction without concern for the specific means of satisfaction.

In contrast, the *superego* is conceptualized as the individual's internal expression of society's moral and ethical codes of conduct. The superego's role is to see that the individual satisfies needs in a socially acceptable fashion. Thus the superego is a kind of "brake" that restrains or inhibits the impulsive forces of the id.[3]

Finally, the *ego* is the individual's conscious control. It functions as an internal monitor that attempts to balance the impulsive demands of the id and the social-cultural constraints of the superego.

STAGES OF PERSONALITY DEVELOPMENT

In addition to specifying a structure for personality, Freud emphasized that an individual's personality is formed as he or she passes through a number of distinct stages of infant and childhood development. Freud labeled these stages of development to conform to the area of the body on which he believed the child's sexual instincts are focused at the time. They include the oral, anal, phallic, latent and genital stages:

1. *Oral stage*—The infant first experiences social contact with the outside world through the mouth (e.g., eating, drinking, and sucking). A crisis develops at the end of this stage as the child is weaned from the mother's breast or from the bottle.

2. *Anal stage*—During this stage, the child's primary source of pleasure is the process of elimination. A second crisis develops at the end of this stage as the parents try to toilet-train the child.

3. *Phallic stage*—The child experiences self-oriented sexual pleasure during this phase with discovery of the sexual organs. A third crisis occurs as the child experiences sexual desire for the parent of the opposite sex. How the child resolves this crisis affects later relationships with persons of the opposite sex and with authority figures.

4. *Latency stage*—Freud believed that the sexual instincts of the child lie dormant from about the age of five till the beginning of adolescence and that no important personality changes occur during this dormant stage.

5. *Genital stage*—At the age of adolescence, the individual develops a sexual interest in persons of the opposite sex, beyond self-oriented love and love for parents. If this crisis is adequately resolved, the individual's personality enters into the genital stage.

According to Freud, an adult's personality is determined by how well an individual deals with the crises that are experienced as the child passes through each of these stages (particularly the first three). For instance, if a child's oral needs are not adequately satisfied at the first stage of development, the person may become fixated at this stage and display an adult personality that includes such "oral" traits as "...dependence, passivity, greediness, and excessive tendencies toward oral activities, as in smoking, chewing, or garrulous speech."[4] If an individual is fixated at the anal stage, the adult personality may display traits of stinginess, obstinacy, excessive need for neatness, and problems in relating to other people.[5]

APPLICATIONS OF FREUDIAN THEORY TO CONSUMER BEHAVIOR

Motivational researchers have applied Freud's psychoanalytic theory to the study of consumer behavior by underscoring the belief that human drives are largely *unconscious,* and that consumers are not consciously aware of their true motives. Thus the emphasis of motivational research studies has been on discovering the underlying motivations for specific consumer behavior. To discover consumers' basic motivations, researchers use a variety of clinical measurement procedures, such as observation and inference, self-reports, projective techniques, focus group sessions, and depth interviews (discussed in Chapter 3). The same basic measurement procedures are used to study motivations and personality, since both areas are usually treated by motivational researchers as unified or complementary psychological concepts.

In applying psychoanalytic personality theory, the motivational researcher tends to focus on the consumer's purchases, treating them as a reflection and an extension of the consumer's own personality. In essence, the motivational researcher tries to determine the product's personality and then works backward to determine the consumer's personality. The following comment captures this viewpoint: "Indications of a person's personality can be gained not only from the type of food he eats, but also from the way in which he eats it. Food habits are among the first ones we acquire. Any mother of several children knows how early in life these habits are developed and how they vary with different children."[6] Table 4-1 briefly describes the general "personalities" that a leading motivational researcher has attributed to several product categories. This view of product personality is illustrated in Figure 4-1 where a magazine ad for Chanel No. 19 characterizes the product as "The Outspoken Chanel" and "Witty. Confident. Devastatingly feminine"—personality traits that the female model is dynamically acting out.

Neo-Freudian Personality Theory

Several of Freud's colleagues disagreed with his contention that personality is primarily instinctual and sexual in nature. Instead, these neo-Freudians believed that *social relationships* are fundamental in the formation and development of personality. For instance, Alfred Adler viewed human beings as seeking to attain various rational goals, which he called *style of life*. He also placed much emphasis

TABLE 4-1   Selective Product Personality Profiles

PRODUCT	DESCRIPTION OF PRODUCT PERSONALITY
prunes	Long identified with their laxative properties, prunes are a symbol of old age; they are like dried-out spinsters, and have none of the soft pleasurableness of plums.
rice	Rice is viewed as a feminine food. It typically suggests a strong, healthy, fertile female. Throwing rice at newly married couples symbolizes the wish that the marriage be blessed with children.
power tools	Power tools are a symbol of manliness. They represent masculine skill and competence, and are often bought more for their symbolic value than for active do-it-yourself applications. Ownership of a good power tool or circular saw provides a man with feelings of omnipotence.
ice cream	Ice cream is often associated with love and affection. It derives particular potency from childhood memories, when it was given to a child for being "good," and withheld as an instrument of punishment. People refer to ice cream as something they "love" to eat.

Adapted from Handbook of Consumer Motivations, by Ernest Dichter. Copyright 1964. McGraw-Hill Book Company. Used with permission of McGraw-Hill Book Company.

Courtesy of Chanel, Inc.

on the individual's effort to overcome feelings of inferiority (i.e., to strive for superiority).

Harry Stack Sullivan, another neo-Freudian, stressed that people continuously attempt to establish significant and rewarding relationships with others. He was particularly concerned with the individual's efforts to reduce tensions such as anxiety.

Like Sullivan, Karen Horney was also interested in anxiety. She focused on the impact of child-parent relationships, especially the individual's desire to conquer feelings of anxiety. Horney proposed that individuals can be classified into three personality groups.[7]

1. *Compliant* individuals are those who move *toward* others (they desire to be loved, wanted, and appreciated).
2. *Aggressive* individuals are those who move *against* others (they desire to excel and win admiration).
3. *Detached individuals* are those who move *away* from others (they desire independence, self-sufficiency, and freedom from obligations).

Neo-Freudian theories of personality have received surprisingly little attention from consumer researchers, despite their emphasis on the importance of the individual's social-cultural environment as a determinant of personality. However, several researchers have applied Horney's classification system to the study of consumer behavior. For example, one consumer researcher developed a test based on Horney's theory and found some tentative relationships between college students' responses and their product and brand usage patterns.[8] Highly compliant students were found to prefer name brand products, such as Bayer aspirin; students classified as aggressive showed a preference for Old Spice deodorant over other brands (seemingly because of its masculine appeal); and highly detached students were heavy tea drinkers (possibly reflecting their desire not to conform). More recent studies employing the same personality test have also found Horney's scheme to be useful in exploring selective aspects of consumer behavior.[9] However, additional work is necessary to refine and assess the appropriate conditions under which this personality measure can be fruitfully used.[10]

Although neo-Freudian theories of personality have not received wide attention, it is likely that marketers have employed some of these theories intuitively. For example, marketers who position their products as providing "unexcelled" craftsmanship or quality seem to be guided by Adler's theory that individuals constantly strive for superiority.

Trait Theory

Trait theory now represents the most popular approach to measuring consumer personality. It constitutes a major departure from the basically qualitative or subjective measures that typify the Freudian and neo-Freudian movements (personal observation, self-reported experiences, dream analysis, and projective techniques).

The orientation of trait theory is primarily *quantitative* or empirical; it focuses on the measurement of personality in terms of specific psychological characteristics of the individual called traits. *Trait* is defined as "...any distinguishing, relatively enduring way in which one individual differs from another."[11] Accordingly, trait theorists are concerned with the construction of personality tests or inventories that pinpoint individual differences in terms of specific traits.

Viewing personality as a set of enduring traits has a natural appeal because it conforms to many commonly held practices. For example, many individuals distinguish between friends as "reserved" or "outgoing." In this way, they are intuitively evaluating and "labeling" them in terms of traits.

To more fully understand what is meant by a personality trait, and why the trait approach is considered quantitative rather than qualitative, we will briefly consider how a personality test is developed.

A personality test usually consists of one or more scales, each of which measures a specific personality trait. A *scale* is a series of questions or items that are designed to measure a single personality trait. The scores achieved by an individual on each of the items in the scale are combined to produce a single index, which reflects the degree to which he or she possesses that trait. Some personality tests consist of a single scale; that is, they are designed to measure only one trait, such as "dogmatism" (how willing a person is to accept a different viewpoint).[12] Other personality tests include more than one scale, with each scale measuring a different trait. An example of a multitrait personality test is the 480-item California Psychological Inventory, which consists of eighteen scales, each measuring a specific trait (e.g., dominance, sociability, self-acceptance, tolerance).[13] Later in this chapter we will examine how single-trait and multitrait personality inventories have been employed in the study of consumer behavior.

In constructing a scale to measure a specific trait, test developers start by observing the behavior of people who they feel typify the personality trait that they wish to measure. They then develop a large number of questions that they believe reflects the actual observed behavior, and they administer these questions to samples of people who might reasonably be expected to score either high or low on the trait under study. For example, if the researchers were developing a scale to measure "outgoingness," they might administer their questions to a sample of salespeople and a sample of laboratory scientists. If they have developed questions that appropriately measure the trait "outgoingness," they should find that salespeople (who might be expected to score "high" on outgoingness) do in fact score "high," and that laboratory scientists (who might be expected to score "low" on outgoingness) do in fact score "low." After repeated testing on different samples with similar results, the researchers can conclude that their series of questions constitute a valid scale for the measurement of outgoingness. They will then try to reduce the number of questions (through factor analyses) without impairing the scale's ability to measure the trait in question.[14]

Because personality scales are easy to combine and administer in the form of a questionnaire, such "paper-and-pencil" personality tests have become the most popular approach for assessing consumer personality.

PROBLEMS AND PROMISES OF PERSONALITY TRAITS AND CONSUMER BEHAVIOR

Although consumer personality research has been conducted for more than two decades, the results of this research have been very uneven.[15] Some studies have found that personality traits have added little to our understanding of consumer behavior, while other studies, more recent ones, have been more encouraging.

To demonstrate how personality tests might be effectively used by marketers, we will now review some of these studies.

Disappointing Consumer Personality Research

As a group, those consumer studies that have *not* revealed a relationship between personality and consumer behavior have tended to possess one or more of the following *limiting* qualities: (1) they were based on convenient multitrait rather than specifically selected single-trait personality tests, (2) they employed personality tests designed for diagnosis of social adjustment problems rather than identifying the range of normal-healthy behavior, (3) they had no *a priori* hypotheses that proposed a relationship between the traits under study and specific consumer behavior, (4) they focused on single brand choices rather than on more general product category usage patterns, (5) they focused on consumers' brand choice rather than on the dimensions of the decision process leading to the choice, and (6) they assumed that the personality-consumer behavior relationship is consistent across situations rather than influenced by the particular situation.

The most frequently noted of these various limitations has been the consumer researchers' tendency to use several popular multitrait personality tests simply because they are easy to administer and score and because the researchers hope to find some chance relationship between the traits they measured and specific consumer behavior. This is in contrast to selecting a particular personality test because of a logical potential relationship between the traits measured and the consumer behavior being studied.

The earliest and most controversial application of a standard multitrait personality inventory examined two groups of consumers: those who owned 1955–58 Fords and those who owned comparable year Chevrolets.[16] The objective of the study was to determine the extent to which personality traits could distinguish between the owners of these two makes of cars. The study employed eleven of the fifteen traits measured by the Edwards Personal Preference Schedule (EPPS). Table 4-2 lists and briefly defines these traits and indicates the ones selected for the Ford-Chevrolet study.

Generally, the results revealed that the personality traits measured did not discriminate between the owners of the two types of cars.[17] However, when the data were reanalyzed on the basis of specific hypotheses concerning the relationship of certain personality traits to ownership of one or the other make of car, the results revealed some improvement in the ability of the EPPS to differentiate between Ford and Chevrolet owners.[18] Most importantly, the reanalysis underscored the need to justify the measurement of specific personality traits by hypothesizing how each trait relates to the consumer behavior under investigation.

Other studies have used multitrait personality tests in attempts to explain such consumer-related activities as the ownership of different types of cars (convertibles, standards, and compacts), the purchase and use of various convenience goods, the purchase of store brands versus national brands, and usage of specific types of banking institutions.[19] Like the original Ford-Chevrolet study, the results of these studies have typically been disappointing.[20] In summary, it appears that the inability of much personality research to find

TABLE 4-2   A Summary of Personality Traits Measured by the Edwards Personal Preference Schedule

*1. *Achievement:* To do one's best, accomplish tasks of great significance, do things better than others, be successful, be a recognized authority.

*2. *Deference:* To get suggestions, follow instructions, do what is expected, accept leadership of others, conform to custom, let others make decisions.

 3. *Order:* To have work neat and organized, make plans before starting, keep files, have things arranged to run smoothly, have things organized.

*4. *Exhibition:* To say clever things, tell amusing jokes and stories, talk about personal achievements, have others notice and comment on one's appearance, be the center of attention.

*5. *Autonomy:* To be able to come and go as desired, say what one thinks, be independent in making decisions, feel free to do what one wants, avoid conformity, avoid responsibilities and obligations.

*6. *Affiliation:* To be loyal to friends, do things for friends, form new friendships, make many friends, form strong attachments, participate in friendly groups.

*7. *Intraception:* To analyze one's motives and feelings, observe and understand others, analyze the motives of others, predict their acts, put one's self in another's place.

 8. *Succorance:* To be helped by others, seek encouragement, have others feel sorry when sick, have others be sympathetic about personal problems.

*9. *Dominance:* To be a leader, argue for one's point of view, make group decisions, settle arguments, persuade and influence others, supervise others.

*10. *Abasement:* To feel guilty when wrong, accept blame, feel need for punishment, feel timid in presence of superiors, feel inferior, feel depressed about inability to handle situations.

 11. *Nurturance:* To help friends in trouble, treat others with kindness, forgive others, do small favors, be generous, show affection, receive confidence.

*12. *Change:* To do new and different things, travel, meet new people, try new things, eat in new places, live in different places, try new fads and fashions.

 13. *Endurance:* To keep at a job until finished, work hard at a task, keep at a problem until solved, finish one job before starting others, stay up late working to get a job done.

*14. *Heterosexuality:* To go out with opposite sex, be in love, kiss, discuss sex, become sexually excited, read books about sex.

*15. *Aggression:* To tell others what one thinks of them, criticize others publicly, make fun of others, tell others off, get revenge, blame others.

*The eleven traits used in the Ford-Chevrolet study.

significant relationships between personality and consumer behavior is due to the fact that many researchers indiscriminantly use all of the scales included in the standard multitrait personality test they employ, without specifying how each trait is expected to relate to the specific consumer behavior under study.

Promising Studies in Consumer Personality Research

The persistent efforts of both marketing practitioners and consumer researchers to demonstrate that personality is an inherently useful tool for segmenting consumer markets have recently paid off in some important refinements to consumer personality research.

Personality and
Consumer Behavior

For instance, evidence suggests that other consumer behavior variables, such as demographic factors (age, sex, education, income) or the type or amount of risk perceived, can be used to help crystallize the relationship between personality and consumer behavior.[21] To illustrate, marketers may find that no significant relationship exists between consumers' purchase of their new frozen vegetables and selected personality traits. However, if they were to divide the sample of consumers into "low" and "high" income groups, and then separately examine each income group for a relationship between selected personality traits and the purchase of the new product, they might find that significant personality profiles emerge. In such instances, the additional consumer behavior variables would serve as "filters" to purify the relationship between personality and consumer behavior.

Another promising approach to consumer personality research involves the use of carefully selected single-trait personality tests (tests that measure just one trait, such as self-confidence) rather than multitrait inventories. In addition, there has recently been some effort to develop personality scales specifically designed for the study of consumer behavior. Some examples of such tailor-made personality tests are a test that measures Horney's compliant-aggressive-detached personality types (see the discussion earlier in this chapter); a test that measures self-actualization (derived from Maslow's need hierarchy described in Chapter 3); a test that taps various aspects of time that might influence consumer behavior (i.e., focus, activity, structure, and tenacity); a test that measures consumer estheticism and practicality (how individuals differ in response to appeals of appearance versus performance of things and products); and tests that measure consumer innovativeness (how receptive a person is to new experiences) and consumer venturesomeness (how attracted a person is to novel things and products).[22]

The more careful selection and application of available personality tests, and the development of new consumer-specific personality tests, are two promising steps designed to make personality a more useful consumer behavior variable. In addition, we have recently begun to appreciate that it is more realistic to expect personality to be linked to how consumers make their choices, or to the purchase or consumption of a broad product category (rather than a specific brand), especially if the particular purchase or consumption situation is taken into consideration.

PERSONALITY AND MARKET SEGMENTATION

Marketers are interested in understanding how consumers' personalities influence consumption behavior because such knowledge enables them to segment consumers and to select one or more target market segments that will respond favorably to their promotional strategies. This section examines a number of specific types of consumer behavior in which the influence of personality characteristics appears to be particularly promising for market segmentation.

Personality and Brand Usage

Consumer researchers have apparently had relatively little success when it comes to using personality traits to predict consumers' brand choices. As already noted, it might be grossly unrealistic to expect personality traits that are typically designed to capture broad dimensions of individual behavior to account for the purchase or usage of a single brand (e.g., Maybelline eye shadow) or even a single product category (e.g., eye shadow or eye cosmetics in general). Instead it would seem more reasonable to expect personality to reflect the usage of a broad product category (the use of cosmetics in general), or better yet to reflect still more general dimensions of behavior—such as personal care or grooming patterns. Supporting this view, recent consumer research suggests that carefully selected personality scales are more closely associated with people's preference for entire sets of new products, or consistent consumer strategies (an established approach to dealing with perceived risk), rather than their preferences for any particular brand within a given product category.[23]

However, some marketers of well-known brands have evidently segmented their markets successfully on the basis of specific personality traits.[24] Since personality segmentation is obviously of important competitive value, such marketers have been somewhat reluctant to openly discuss what they have discovered concerning the influence of personality on brand choice.

Fortunately, several advertising agencies and consumer goods firms have been willing to disclose certain aspects of their research linking personality traits to consumer brand choice. For example, the director of research for a leading advertising agency has reported the successful development of market segmentation strategies based on personality traits for specific brands in such product categories as women's cosmetic products, cigarettes, insurance, and liquor.[25] Table 4-3 lists the personality traits that were found to be helpful in segmenting the women's cosmetic market. A clinical psychologist employed by the advertising agency selects the initial personality traits that could logically be expected to influence brand choice decisions. Pilot test studies are then undertaken to eliminate those traits that do not appear to contribute to an understanding of consumer differences. In the final phase of the personality segmentation research, personality scales that have been found to be related to product and brand purchase behavior are used to develop profiles of specific brand usage segments.

PERSONALITY AND BEER CONSUMPTION

Anheuser-Busch, a leading marketer of beer, has sponsored consumer behavior research designed to segment beer and other alcoholic beverage drinkers into specific drinker-personality types.[26] This research effort represents a good case history of the successful application of personality theory as a market segmentation tool.

An extensive amount of exploratory research identified four distinct types of alcoholic beverage drinkers with correspondingly unique personality types. Table 4-4 presents a simplified summary of these four drinker-personality types.

TABLE 4-3   Personality Scales Found Useful in the Segmentation of the Women's Cosmetic Market

SCALE	DESCRIPTION
Narcissism—	Tendency to be preoccupied with the details of one's personal appearance
Appearance Conscious—	Emphasis on the social importance of looking properly groomed
Exhibitionism—	Tendency toward self-display and attention seeking
Impulsive—	Tendency to act in a carefree, impetuous and unreflective manner
Order—	Tendency to be compulsively neat, and live by rules and schedules
Fantasied Achievement—	Measure of narcissistic aspiration for distinction and personal recognition
Capacity for Status—	Measure of the personal qualities and attributes that underline and lead to status
Dominant—	Need to be superior to others by being in control and in the forefront
Sociable—	Need for informal, friendly, agreeable relationship with others
Active—	Need to be on the go, doing things, achieving goals set out for oneself
Cheerful—	Tendency to feel bright, cheerful and optimistic about life
Deference—	Tendency to submit to opinions and preferences of others perceived as superior
Subjective—	Tendency toward naive, superstitious and generally immature thinking

Source: Shirley Young "The Dynamics of Measuring Unchange," in Russell I. Haley, ed., Attitude Research in Transition (Chicago: American Marketing Association, 1972), 62.

Employing this classification scheme, university researchers have been able to identify specific advertising messages and media exposure patterns that effectively reach the specific drinker-personality types that constitute the prime market for Budweiser, Michelob, and Busch (three brands produced by Anheuser-Busch). Applying this information about drinker-personality types and their susceptibility to specific advertising messages, Anheuser-Busch has been able to boost the sales of Michelob beer by successfully appealing to the drinkers in a large drinker-personality segment. The Michelob ad in Figure 4-2 on page 99 appears to be appealing to the social drinker.

Further research indicated which drinker-personality types were most likely to be brand switchers and which were most likely to be brand loyal. Such insights are invaluable to marketers introducing a new brand, entering a new market, or trying to combat the advances of competitive brands.

This research project, which has been ongoing since 1968, exemplifies the fact that a marketer who is willing to expend the funds for creative personality research can reap handsome rewards.

TABLE 4-4   Drinker Personality Characteristics

TYPE OF DRINKER	PERSONALITY TYPE	DRINKING PATTERN
social drinker	Driven by his own needs, particularly to achieve, and attempts to manipulate others to get what he wants. Driven by a desire to get ahead. Usually a younger person.	Controlled drinker who may sometimes become high or drunk but is unlikely to be an alcoholic. Drinks primarily on the weekends, holidays, and vacations, usually in a social setting with friends. Drinking is seen as a way to gain social acceptance.
reparative drinker	Sensitive and responsive to the needs of others and adapts to their needs by sacrificing his own aspirations. Usually middle-aged.	Controlled drinker who infrequently becomes high or drunk. Drinks primarily at the end of the workday, usually with a few close friends. Views drinking as a reward for sacrifices made for others.
oceanic drinker	Sensitive to the needs of others. Often a failure who blames himself for his nonachievement.	Drinks heavily, especially when under pressure to achieve. At times shows a lack of control over his drinking and is likely to become high, drunk, and even alcoholic. Drinking is a form of escape.
indulgent drinker	Generally insensitive to others and places the blame for his failures on others' lack of sensitivity to him.	Like the oceanic drinker, he drinks heavily, often becomes high, drunk, or alcoholic. Drinks as a form of escape.

Source: Adapted from Russell L. Ackoff and James R. Emshoff, "Advertising Research at Anheuser-Busch, Inc. (1968–74)," Sloan Management Review, 16, No. 3 (Spring 1975), 1–15.

Consumer-Innovators

Marketing practitioners must learn all they can about consumers who are willing to try new products or brands, for the market response of such innovators is often crucial to the ultimate success of a new product.

We will now examine several personality traits that have proved useful in differentiating between consumer-innovators and noninnovators. (Chapter 17 examines more of the distinguishing characteristics of these two groups.)

 DOGMATISM

Dogmatism is a personality trait that measures the amount of rigidity a person displays toward the unfamiliar and toward information that is contrary to his or her own established beliefs.[27] A person who is highly dogmatic approaches the unfamiliar defensively and with considerable discomfort and uncertainty. On the other end of the spectrum, the person who is low in dogmatism will readily consider the unfamiliar or opposing beliefs.

FIGURE 4-2   Advertisement That Appeals to
the Social Drinker

*"If it feels like a weekend,
it must be Michelob."*

**Put a little
weekend
in your week.**

Courtesy of Anheuser-Busch, Inc.

In two closely parallel experiments, subjects who were low in dogmatism
(open-minded) were found to be significantly more likely to prefer innovative
products to established or traditional alternatives.[28] In contrast, highly dogmatic
subjects (close-minded) were more likely to choose established rather than
innovative product alternatives. A third study found that early patrons of self-
service gas stations (then highly innovative) were significantly less dogmatic than
customers of traditional full-service stations.[29]

An interesting recent extension of this research found that the relationship
between dogmatism and intended innovative behavior was influenced by
situational factors.[30] Specifically, if subjects were thinking in terms of a purchase
for personal use, the results were similar to those of earlier research (i.e., low
dogmatic consumers are more willing to accept innovative products than highly
dogmatic consumers). However, if the purchase was slated as a gift, the results
were reversed; that is, the highly dogmatic consumers indicated a greater
willingness to purchase an innovative product alternative than the low dogmatic
consumers.

By way of explanation, it seems that when contemplating a gift, highly dogmatic consumers are more "anxious" than low dogmatic consumers to portray to gift recipients an image of being more venturesome than they would be if they were purchasing for their own consumption. If confirmed by future research, these findings suggest that marketers of novel new products, especially those products that are likely to be gifts, should realize that purchasing for personal or gift purposes may present very different consumer-related situations.

Research has suggested that the promotional appeal employed to present the information about a new or unfamiliar product is extremely relevant to how low and highly dogmatic consumers are likely to respond. For instance, it has been noted that highly dogmatic consumers may be more willing to accept new products than low dogmatic consumers *if* the products are presented in an authoritative manner (e.g., by an admired celebrity, by a recognized expert, or in the context of a reassuring and ego-boosting message).[31] In contrast, low dogmatic consumer-innovators may be more receptive to messages that stress factual differences and product benefits.[32] For this reason, marketers of a new portable videotape recorder might be wise to emphasize in their promotional campaign targeted at gadget-oriented consumers the reasons why the recorder will technically be as good as or better than competitive products. However, to reach the more resistant consumers, the marketers might alter the promotional approach and employ a celebrity, since more resistant or highly dogmatic consumers are more likely to respond favorably to such celebrity-testimonial appeals.

SOCIAL CHARACTER

The personality trait known as social character has its origin in sociological research, which focuses on the identification and classification of societies into distinct social-cultural types.[33] However, as it is used in consumer psychology, social character is a personality trait that ranges on a continuum from *inner-directedness* to *other-directedness*. Available evidence indicates that inner-directed consumers tend to rely on their own "inner" values or standards in evaluating new products and are more likely to be consumer-innovators. Conversely, other-directed consumers tend to look to others for direction on what is right or wrong; thus they are less likely to be consumer-innovators.[34]

Research on innovativeness and social character has found that when new food products were ranked in terms of how much they differed from more traditional alternatives, the more novel the product, the more likely it was to be purchased by inner-directed consumers, and the less likely it was to be purchased by other-directed consumers.[35]

A study that compared the first purchasers of the Ford Maverick (when it was introduced in April 1969) with later purchasers of the same car and concurrent purchasers of an already established small car found that the consumer-innovators who first purchased the Maverick were significantly more inner-directed than later purchasers of Mavericks and concurrent purchasers of the established car.[36] These findings strongly support the notion that innovators tend to have inner-directed personalities, while later adopters have other-directed personalities.

Available evidence also suggests that inner- and other-directed consumers are likely to have different preferences in terms of promotional messages.[37] Specifically, inner-directed people seem to prefer ads that stress product features and personal benefits (enabling them to use their own values and standards in evaluating products), while other-directed people seem to prefer ads that feature a social environment or social acceptance (in keeping with their tendency to look to others for direction).

Related research has focused directly on people's reaction to the product being advertised, rather than their preference for either objective or social promotional appeals.[38] These findings offer some confirmation that other-directed individuals are generally more easily influenced because of their natural inclination to go beyond the content of an ad and to think in terms of the potential social approval of a possible purchase.

For marketing practitioners, this research suggests that while consumers tend to respond favorably to promotional themes that are consistent with their personalities, other-directed consumers seem to be more easily persuaded by advertisements regardless of their content appeal.

CATEGORY WIDTH

Another personality trait that has been found to discriminate between innovative and noninnovative consumers is *category width*. This trait seems to tap an important dimension of a person's risk-handling strategy. Research has shown that people handle risky decisions differently.[39] Some people tend to have a tolerance for error; that is, they are willing to accept the possibility of poor or negative outcomes in order to maximize the number of satisfying or positive alternatives from which to choose. Other people handle risk in the opposite way; that is, they have a low tolerance for error and prefer to forgo satisfying or positive alternatives so that they might minimize exposure to poor or negative alternatives. As measured by the category-width scale, individuals who have a high tolerance for error are called "broad categorizers," while individuals with a low tolerance for error are called "narrow categorizers."

The first use of the category-width scale in consumer behavior research explored its relationship to individuals' perceived willingness to try new products.[40] The results found that student subjects who were broad categorizers were willing to try qualitatively different brands (innovations), while those who were narrow categorizers tended to choose established or familiar alternatives (noninnovations). These findings were substantiated in later research among actual consumers.[41]

Another study found that homemakers who were broad categorizers were more likely to have purchased genuinely new products (e.g., nonrefrigerated main dishes), while those who were narrow categorizers were more likely to have purchased superficially new products (e.g., lime-scented dishwashing detergent).[42] For the marketer, this study indicates that the degree of newness inherent in a product may influence consumers differently, depending upon their personalities. That is, broad categorizers may be more willing to purchase genuinely new or novel products, while narrow categorizers may be more receptive to superficially new products. Thus it would seem that marketing practitioners should carefully consider the *degree* of newness inherent in their new product when they design their marketing strategy.

OPTIMUM STIMULATION LEVEL

Many of us have observed that some people seem to prefer a simple, uncluttered, and calm existence; whereas others seem to prefer an environment crammed with novel, complex, and unusual experiences. Recent consumer researchers have begun to examine how such variations (called optimum stimulation levels) may be influenced by selected personality traits, and how in turn specific stimulation levels may be related to consumer behavior.[43] So far, given only a minimum of research, it seems that consumers with a high optimum stimulation level (OSL) are more likely to seek out risky and novel products than consumers with a low OSL. If these findings are verified by future research, it is likely that we will consider segmenting the market for certain new products in terms of consumers' OSL; that is, high OSL consumers might be expected to respond favorably to products and promotional campaigns that stress *more,* rather than *less,* risk (or novelty).

The research reported on here indicates that the consumer-innovator differs from the noninnovator in terms of personality orientation. A knowledge of these personality differences should enable marketers to segment their market for new products and to design distinct promotional strategies for both consumer-innovators and later adopters.

The Acceptance of Foreign-Made Products

Several consumer studies suggest that personality characteristics may be useful in distinguishing between consumer segments that are likely to be receptive to foreign-made products and those that are not.

Specifically, evidence indicates that American consumers who purchase foreign compact automobiles are less conservative and less dogmatic than purchasers of American-made compact cars.[44] Supporting this conclusion, another personality study found that highly dogmatic consumers were significantly more likely to rate favorably products manufactured in countries perceived to be similar to the United States (e.g., England and West Germany) than those manufactured in countries that were rated dissimilar.[45] The opposite was also true: Low dogmatic consumers were more accepting of products manufactured in countries judged dissimilar to the United States. This study also found that highly dogmatic consumers have a more favorable image of products manufactured in the United States than low dogmatic consumers.

Dogmatism has also been found to be associated with foreign visitors' general acceptance of "American" products. Basically, the personality differences of Nigerian students seem to influence their acceptance of products unfamiliar to them prior to their arrival in the United States. Those Nigerian students who scored low on the dogmatism scale were found to be more willing to accept unfamiliar American products than those scoring high on dogmatism.[46]

These studies suggest that the low dogmatic consumer should be the prime market segment for marketers of foreign-made products. Moreover, in the case of American consumers, it would seem wise for promotional appeals to stress the distinctive features and benefits of these products over available American alternatives. On the other hand, domestic marketers wishing to impede inroads of foreign products should stress a "nationalistic" theme in their promotional appeals (e.g., "Made in America"), for such appeals are likely to attract the highly dogmatic consumer. Figure 4-3 shows one of the initial ads for the Plymouth Reliant. Both the headline and the subheadline work together to emphasize that this *American* car is capable of providing sufficient fuel economy.

Personality and Store Choice

Personality also influences the choice of stores in which the consumer decides to shop. The consumer's self-confidence has been found to be associated with the type of retailer from which he or she purchases certain kinds of merchandise. For instance, female clothing shoppers who scored high in self-confidence were found to prefer discount stores as a place to buy their clothing, while shoppers with less self-confidence tended to favor the more traditional neighborhood retailer.[47] Another study reports that consumers who purchased expensive audio equipment (record players, tape players, tuners, and amplifiers) from an audio equipment specialty store were more self-confident than consumers who purchased from a traditional department store.[48]

The findings of these two studies suggest that the newer types of retailing establishments (e.g., the clothing discounter and the audio equipment specialty store) tend to attract a more self-confident type of customer than the older types of retail establishments. Therefore it would appear that new types of retailers should try to reach a more self-confident market segment by appealing to the consumer's ability to recognize and properly evaluate unlabeled or specialty merchandise. More traditional retailers should attempt to reassure their less-confident customers that they will stand behind them and assist them in their shopping tasks.

Evidence indicates that shoppers' personalities may even influence the kind of salesperson they prefer to have serve them. Specifically, "dependent" shoppers seem to prefer an aggressive salesperson who makes suggestions and takes the initiative, while "independent" shoppers prefer a less-aggressive salesperson.[49]

Ecologically and Socially Concerned Consumers

With increasing recognition that our environment and natural resources are in danger, there has in recent years been a mounting interest among marketers and government policy makers to identify those consumers who are most likely to respond to socially conscious appeals. A market segment of socially conscious

FIGURE 4-3   Advertisement Employing the Theme "Buy American"

THE [K] CARS ARE HERE
PLYMOUTH RELIANT-K

THE
AMERICAN WAY
TO BEAT THE PUMP

consumers would be a prime target for new ecologically oriented products or services and would provide the support needed for public policies designed to protect the environment. The available evidence suggests that certain demographic, psychological, and social characteristics distinguish the socially concerned consumer from the rest of society. Of particular interest to our present discussion, personality traits have been found to be useful in the development of a profile of the socially responsive consumer.[50]

In examining consumer social consciousness, researchers have found it fruitful to focus on ecologically related consumer attitudes and behavior. For example, studies have explored the characteristics of consumers who use recycling facilities, those who purchase low-lead or lead-free gasoline, beverages in returnable bottles, recycled paper products, or low-polluting washing machine detergents.[51]

Consumers who used the facilities of a local recycling plant were found to be less dogmatic, less conservative, and less status conscious, and more cosmopolitan (i.e., a broader general outlook), more isolated or alienated from society, and more likely to feel that they had some control over their personal lives and environment (i.e., personal competence) than those consumers who did not use such facilities.[52] Related research tends to substantiate this personality profile of the ecologically concerned consumer. In particular, a recent profile of socially and ecologically concerned consumers reveals them to be less dogmatic, and generally more liberal and secure in their thinking. The research also suggests that such "conserving consumers" are more likely to be especially receptive to functional rather than stylistic attributes or products, and more conservative when it comes to their consumption behavior.[53]

Taken as a whole, the ecologically concerned consumer appears to be a *self-actualizer*, one who is able to constructively deal with feelings of alienation through a belief that his or her actions can affect change in his or her personal life and environment.[54] A study that employed a tailor-made personality scale to measure self-actualization found that ecologically concerned consumers scored significantly higher on the self-actualization test than did those who were less ecologically concerned.[55]

The research evidence suggests that ecologically responsible consumers do represent a distinct market segment. In communicating with this market segment, marketers would be wise to stress the environmental benefits of their products, since such promotional appeals would be consistent with the personality characteristics of the ecologically concerned consumer.

summary

Personality can be described as the psychological characteristics that both determine and reflect how a person will respond to his or her environment. Although personality tends to be consistent and enduring, it has been known to change abruptly in response to major life events, as well as gradually over time.

Three theories of personality are prominent in the study of consumer behavior: psychoanalytic theory, neo-Freudian theory, and trait theory. Freud's psychoanalytic theory provided the foundation for the study of motivational research, which operates on the premise that human drives are largely unconscious in nature and serve to motivate many consumer actions. Neo-Freudian theory tends to emphasize the fundamental role of social relationships in the formation and development of personality. Alfred Adler viewed human beings as seeking to overcome feelings of inferiority. Harry Stack Sullivan believed that people attempt to establish significant and rewarding relationships with others. Karen Horney saw individuals as trying to overcome feelings of anxiety and categorized them as compliant, aggressive, or detached personality types. Both Freudian theory and neo-Freudian theory use qualitative measures such as observation, self-report, and projective techniques to identify and measure personality characteristics.

Trait theory is a major departure from the qualitative or subjective approach to personality measurement. It postulates that individuals possess innate psychological traits (e.g., self-confidence, aggression, responsibility, curiosity) to a greater or lesser degree, and that these traits can be measured by specially designed scales or inventories. Because they are simple to use and to score and can be self-administered, personality inventories are the preferred method of many researchers for the assessment of consumer personality.

Results of consumer personality research have been somewhat uneven. Findings suggest that to improve matters, consumer researchers might (1) use single-trait tests based on prior hypotheses, (2) examine the relationship between personality and a broad product category (rather than a specific brand), and (3) consider the specific purchase or usage situation.

The identification of personality variables (e.g., dogmatism, social character, and category width) that appears to be logically linked to product usage behavior is likely to improve marketers' ability to segment their markets on the basis of personality characteristics. Thus they can either design specific products that will appeal to certain personality types or design promotional strategies that will appeal to the personality characteristics of their existing target audiences.

discussion questions

1. Contrast the major distinctive characteristics of the following personality theories:
   a. Freudian theory
   b. Neo-Freudian theory
   c. Trait theory
2. How would you explain the fact that no two individuals have identical personalities, yet personality is used in consumer research to identify distinct market segments—each consisting of many consumers?
3. Horney classified individuals into three personality groups: compliant individuals, aggressive individuals, and detached individuals. Choose a separate magazine

advertisement that seems to be directed to each of the personality types. For each advertisement, indicate why you feel it will appeal to the specific personality type.

4. In terms of the study of consumer behavior, describe several advantages that trait-theory personality tests have over the Freudian personality measurement approach employed by motivational researchers.

5. Why is it useful to state a specific hypothesis that suggests the likely relationship between a personality trait and some particular type of consumer behavior?

6. Find a print advertisement for one of Anheuser-Busch's beers (Budweiser, Busch, or Michelob). Compare the contents of the ad with the drinker and personality profile described in Table 4-4. Which drinker-personality type(s) does the ad appeal to and why?

 7. Describe the type of promotional message that would seem most suitable for individuals with the following personality characteristics:
   a. Low dogmatic consumers
   b. High dogmatic consumers
   c. Inner-directed consumers
   d. Other-directed consumers

8. How would you expect consumers' optimum stimulation levels to influence their choice of home furnishings?

endnotes

1. E. Earl Baughman and George Schlager Welsh, *Personality: A Behavioral Science* (Englewood Cliffs, N.J.: Prentice-Hall, 1962), 22.

2. For a more-detailed examination of these and other theories of personality, see Calvin S. Hall and Gardner Lindzey, *Theories of Personality* (New York: John Wiley, 1957).

3. David Krech, Richard S. Cruchfield, and Norman Livson, *Elements of Psychology*, 2nd ed. (New York: Knopf, 1969), 745.

4. Ibid., 746.

5. William D. Wells and Arthur D. Beard, "Personality and Consumer Behavior," in Scott Ward and Thomas S. Robertson, eds., *Consumer Behavior: Theoretical Sources* (Englewood Cliffs, N.J.: Prentice-Hall, 1973), 146.

6. Ernest Dichter, *Handbook of Consumer Motivations* (New York: McGraw-Hill, 1964), 58.

7. For example, see Karen Horney, *The Neurotic Personality of Our Time* (New York: Norton, 1937).

8. Joel B. Cohen, "An Interpersonal Orientation to the Study of Consumer Behavior," *Journal of Marketing Research,* 6 (August 1967), 270–78.

9. Arch G. Woodside and Ruth Andress, "CAD Eight Years Later," *Journal of the Academy of Marketing Science,* 3 (Summer–Fall 1975), 309–13.

10. Jon P. Noerager, "An Assessment of CAD—A Personality Instrument Developed Specifically for Marketing Research," *Journal of Marketing Research,* 16 (February 1979), 53–59.

11. J.P. Guilford, *Personality* (New York: McGraw-Hill, 1959), 6.

12. Milton Rokeach, *The Open and Closed Mind* (New York: Basic Books, 1960).

13. H.G. Gough, *Manual for the California Psychological Inventory* (Palo Alto, Calif.: Consulting Psychological Press, 1964).

14. For a more-detailed discussion of personality scale development, see Jum C. Nunnally, Jr., *Tests and Measurements: Assessment and Prediction* (New York: McGraw-Hill, 1959); and George Brooker, "On Selecting an Appropriate Measure of Reliability," in Neil Beckwith et al., eds., *1979 Educators' Conference Proceedings* (Chicago: American Marketing Association, 1979), 56–59.

15. Harold H. Kassarjian, "Personality and Consumer Behavior: A Review," *Journal of Marketing Research,* 8 (November 1971), 409–18.

16. Franklin B. Evans, "Psychological and Objective Factors in the Prediction of Brand Choice: Ford versus Chevrolet," *Journal of Business,* 32 (October 1959), 340–69.

17. Ibid.

18. Jacob Jacoby, "Personality and Consumer Behavior: How *Not* to Find Relationships" (Purdue Papers in Consumer Psychology, Paper No. 102, 1969).

19. Ralph Westfall, "Psychological Factors in Predicting Product Choice," *Journal of Marketing,* 26 (April 1962), 34–40; Ronald E. Frank, "Market Segmentation Research: Findings and Implications," in F.M. Bass, C.W. King, and Edgar A. Pessemier, eds., *Applications of the Sciences in Marketing Management* (New York: John Wiley, 1968), 49–61; John G. Myers, "Determination of Private Brand Attitudes," *Journal of Marketing Research,* 4 (February 1967), 73–81; and Henry J. Claycamp, "Characteristics of Owners of Thrift Deposits in Commercial Banks and Savings and Loan Associations," *Journal of Marketing Research,* 2 (May 1965), 163–70.

20. For a detailed review, see Wells and Beard, "Personality and Consumer Behavior," 178–90.

21. For example, see Robert P. Brody and Scott M. Cunningham, "Personality Variables and the Consumer Decision Process," *Journal of Marketing Research,* 5 (February 1968), 50–57; Joseph N. Fry, "Personality Variables and Cigarette Brand Choice," *Journal of Marketing Research,* 8 (August 1971), 298–304; and Robert A. Peterson, "Moderating the Personality—Product Usage Relationships," in Ronald C. Curhan, ed., *1974 Combined Proceedings* (Chicago: American Marketing Association, 1975), 109–12.

22. George Brooker, "An Instrument to Measure Consumer Self-Actualization," in Mary Jane Schlinger, ed., *Advances in Consumer Research* (Association for Consumer Research, 1975), II, 563–75; Cohen, "An Interpersonal Orientation"; Marvin E. Goldberg, "Identifying Relevant Psychographic Segments: How Specifying Product Functions Can Help," *Journal of Consumer Research,* 3 (December 1976), 163–69; Clark Leavitt and John Walton, "Development of a Scale for Innovativeness," in Schlinger, *Advances in Consumer Research,* II, 543–54; and Robert B. Settle, Pamela L. Alreck, and John W. Glasheen, "Individual Time Orientation and Consumer Life Style," in H. Keith Hunt, ed., *Advances in Consumer Research* (Ann Arbor, Mich.: Association for Consumer Research, 1978), V, 315–19.

23. Raymond L. Horton, "Some Relationships between Personality and Consumer Decision Making," *Journal of Marketing Research,* 16 (May 1979), 223–46.

24. For example, see Shirley Young, "The Dynamics of Measuring Unchange," in Russell I. Haley, ed., *Attitude Research in Transition* (Chicago: American Marketing Association, 1972), 61–82.

25. Ibid., 63.

26. Russell L. Ackoff and James Emshoff, "Advertising Research at Anheuser-Busch, Inc. (1968–74)," *Sloan Management Review,* 16 (Spring 1975), 1–15.

27. Rokeach, The Open and Closed Mind.

28. Jacob Jacoby, "Personality and Innovation Proneness," *Journal of Marketing Research,* 8 (May 1971), 244–47; and Kenneth A. Coney, "Dogmatism and Innovation: A Replication," *Journal of Marketing Research,* 9 (November 1972), 453–55.

29. J.M. McClurg and I.R. Andrews, "A Consumer Profile Analysis of the Self-Service Gasoline Customer," *Journal of Applied Psychology,* 59 (February 1974), 119–21.

30. Kenneth A. Coney and Robert Harman, "Dogmatism and Innovation: A Situational

Perspective," in William L. Wilkie, ed., *Advances in Consumer Research* (Ann Arbor, Mich.: Association for Consumer Research, 1979), VI, 118–21.

31. Brian Blake, Robert Perloff, and Richard Heslin, "Dogmatism and Acceptance of New Products," *Journal of Marketing Research*, 7 (November 1970), 483–86; and Michael B. Mazis and Timothy W. Sweeney, "Novelty and Personality with Risk as a Moderating Variable," in Boris W. Becker and Helmut Becker, eds., *1972 Combined Proceedings* (Chicago: American Marketing Association, 1973), 406–11.

32. Jacoby, "Personality and Innovation Proneness," 246.

33. David Riesman, Nathan Glazer, and Reuel Denny, *The Lonely Crowd* (New Haven, Conn.: Yale University Press, 1950).

34. James H. Donnelly, Jr., "Social Character and Acceptance of New Products," *Journal of Marketing Research*, 7 (February 1970), 111–13; James H. Donnelly, Jr., and John M. Ivancevich, "A Methodology for Identifying Innovator Characteristics of New Brand Purchasers," *Journal of Marketing Research*, 11 (August 1974), 331–34; and John Jay Painter and Max L. Pinegar, "Post-High Teens and Fashion Innovation," *Journal of Marketing Research*, 8 (August 1971), 368–69.

35. Donnelly, "Social Character," 112.

36. Donnelly and Ivancevich, "Methodology for Identifying Innovator Characteristics."

37. Harold H. Kassarjian, "Social Character and Differential Preference for Mass Communication," *Journal of Marketing Research*, 11 (May 1965), 146–53; and Robert B. Settle and Richard Mizerski, "Differential Response to Objective and Social Information in Advertisements," in Thomas V. Greer, ed., *1973 Combined Proceedings* (Chicago: American Marketing Association, 1974), 250–55.

38. Richard W. Mizerski and Robert B. Settle, "The Influence of Social Character on Preference for Social versus Objective Information in Advertising," *Journal of Marketing Research*, 16 (November 1979), 552–58.

39. Thomas F. Pettigrew, "The Measurement and Correlates of Category Width as a Cognitive Variable," *Journal of Personality*, 26 (December 1956), 532–44.

40. Donald I. Popielarz, "An Exploration of Perceived Risk and Willingness to Try New Products," *Journal of Marketing Research*, 4 (November 1967), 368–72.

41. James H. Donnelly, Jr., Michael J. Etzel, and Scott Roeth, "The Relationship between Consumers' Category Width and Trial of New Products," *Journal of Applied Psychology*, 57 (May 1973), 335–38; James H. Donnelly, Jr., and Michael J. Etzel, "Degree of Product Newness and Early Trial," *Journal of Marketing Research*, 10 (August 1973), 295–300; and Leon G. Schiffman, "Perceived Risk in New Product Trial by Elderly Consumers," *Journal of Marketing Research*, 9 (February 1972), 106–8.

42. Donnelly and Etzel, "Degree of Product Newness," 299.

43. P.S. Raju, "Optimum Stimulation Level: Its Relationship to Personality, Demographics, and Exploratory Behavior," *Journal of Consumer Research*, 7 (December 1980), 272–82.

44. William H. Cunningham and J.E. Crissy, "Market Segmentation by Motivation and Attitude," *Journal of Marketing Research*, 9 (February 1972), 100–102.

45. Richard C. Tongberg, "An Empirical Study of the Relationship between Dogmatism and Attitudes toward Foreign Products," in Greer, *1973 Combined Proceedings*, 87–91.

46. Leon G. Schiffman, William R. Dillon, and Festus E. Ngumah, "The Influence of Subcultural and Personality Factors on Consumer Acculturation," *Journal of International Business Studies*, 12 (Fall 1981), 137–143.

47. H. Lawrence Issacson, "Store Choice" (Doctoral dissertation, Graduate School of Business Administration, Harvard University, 1964), 85–89.

48. Joseph F. Dash, Leon G. Schiffman, and Conrad Berenson, "Risk and Personality-Related Dimensions of Store Choice," *Journal of Marketing*, 40 (January 1976), 36.

49. James E. Stafford and Thomas V. Greer, "Consumer Preference for Types of Salesmen: A Study of Independence-Dependence Characteristics," *Journal of Retailing*, 41 (Summer 1965), 27–33.

50. W. Thomas Anderson, Jr., and William H. Cunningham, "The Socially Conscious Consumer," *Journal of Marketing*, 36 (July 1972), 23–31; and W. Thomas Anderson, Jr., Karl E. Henion, and Eli P. Cox III, "Socially vs. Ecologically Responsible Consumers," in Curhan, *1974 Combined Proceedings*, 304–10.

51. Thomas C. Kinnear, James R. Taylor, and Sadrundin A. Ahmed, "Ecologically Concerned Consumers: Who Are They?" *Journal of Marketing*, 38 (April 1974), 20–24; Frederick E. Webster, Jr., "Determining the Characteristics of the Socially Conscious Consumer," *Journal of Consumer Research*, 2 (December 1975), 188–96; and George Brooker, "The Self-Actualizing Socially Conscious Consumer," *Journal of Consumer Research*, 3 (September 1976), 107–12.

52. Anderson, Henion, and Cox, "Socially vs. Ecologically," 308.

53. Michael A Belch, "Identifying the Socially and Ecologically Concerned Segment through Life-Style Research: Initial Findings," in Karl E. Henion and Thomas C. Kinnear, eds., *The Conserver Society* (Chicago: American Marketing Association, 1979), 69–81.

54. Anderson, Henion, and Cox, "Socially vs. Ecologically," 310.

55. Brooker, "The Self-Actualizing," 109.

FIVE

Consumer Psychographics

introduction

PSYCHOGRAPHIC research has caught the imagination of many marketers since reports of its application to segmentation strategy first appeared in the late 1960s. Indeed, the following partial roster of well-known products and brands that have benefited from psychographic studies indicates its popularity: Schlitz beer, Lava soap, Union 76 gasoline, Kentucky Fried Chicken, Dewar's White Label Scotch, Nescafé and Taster's Choice coffees, Chevrolet Vega, Colgate-Palmolive's Irish Spring bar soap, Sony Betamax videotape player, Jack Daniel's whiskey, Peter Paul's Mounds and Almond Joy, and Tums.

In Chapter 2 we briefly discussed psychographic, or lifestyle, analysis and showed how it has proved to be a useful segmentation approach. In the present chapter our discussion of psychographics identifies different forms of psychographics, considers how psychographic inventories are constructed, and, most important, presents a wide range of real-world illustrations and applications of this highly pragmatic segmentation tool.

WHAT IS PSYCHOGRAPHICS?

Psychographics, also commonly referred to as *lifestyle analysis* or *AIO research* (i.e., activities, interests, and opinions), is an especially exciting consumer segmentation approach because it has been so heartily embraced by both marketing practitioners and academic consumer researchers. The appeal of psychographics lies in the frequently vivid and practical profiles of consumer segments that it has made possible.

In its most common form, psychographics can be thought of as consisting of a battery of statements designed to capture relevant aspects of a consumer's personality, buying motives, interests, attitudes, beliefs, and values. Other more product-specific forms of psychographics have consumers respond to selective statements about products, services, brands, or specific consumption situations.

We will examine the different types of psychographics and illustrate their

Why is it that, in spite of all the mirrors in the world, no one really knows what he looks like?

SCHOPENHAUER, Further Psychological Observations

applications later in this chapter. First, in order to gain a sharper picture of what psychographics is, we will compare it with both consumer demographics and motivational research, two other aspects of consumer behavior that have a bearing on the development of psychographics.

PSYCHOGRAPHICS VERSUS DEMOGRAPHICS

Psychographic and demographic profiles are often portrayed as competitive segmentation approaches, as if marketers could only choose one. They are, however, highly complementary approaches and are best conceived as working together.[1]

As we noted in Chapter 2, demographics consists of objective and somewhat easily measured characteristics of a population, such as age, income, education, sex, and marital status. Psychographics, on the other hand, tends to include relatively intangible variables, such as motives, interests, attitudes, and values; but these variables add vitality to consumer profiles that cannot usually be captured by demographics. Tables 5-1 and 5-2 (on pages 114 and 115) reflect the very different types of information that marketers are able to gain from demographic and psychographic profiles of consumer segments.

Specifically, Table 5-1 reveals that heavy shotgun shell buyers differ from nonbuyers in terms of demographic characteristics; that is, they are younger, have lower incomes and less education, and are typically drawn from blue-collar occupations. They are also concentrated in rural areas (where hunting is more common), particularly in the southern sections of the United States.

Such insights are invaluable when it comes to indicating which portion of the population is the key target market for ammunition and where they are located. Moreover, the demographic profile can be contrasted with the available demographics of various advertising media, allowing a firm selling ammunition to make reasonably good decisions as to where to spend its advertising budget.

However, the demographic profile does not precisely indicate what an ad ought to say (or show) and what psychological characteristics best explain the buyer of ammunition. By scanning Table 5-2 we can see that hunters are usually outdoor types and that they are attracted to violence and adventure. They can also be characterized as risk avoiders, self-indulgent, and pleasure seeking.

While this additional information does not locate the target market, it does—like the consumer demographics—let us know quite a bit about them. By combining the knowledge gained from demographics and psychographics, the marketer is provided with some powerful information about a potential target market. Also, we can see that our understanding of the ammunition buyer would not be complete without both types of information. This has led a well-known consumer researcher to say that "...psychographic information can put flesh on demographic bones."[2]

	PERCENT WHO SPEND $11+ PER YEAR ON SHOTGUN AMMUNITION (141)	PERCENT WHO DON'T BUY (395)
age		
Under 25	9	5
25–34	33	15
35–44	27	22
45–54	18	22
55+	13	36
occupation		
Professional	6	15
Managerial	23	23
Clerical-Sales	9	17
Craftsman	50	35
income		
Under $6,000	26	19
$6,000–$10,000	39	36
$10,000–$15,000	24	27
$15,000+	11	18
population density		
Rural	34	12
2,500–50,000	11	11
50,000–500,000	16	15
500,000–2 million	21	27
2 million+	13	19
geographic division		
New England–Mid-Atlantic	21	33
Central (N, W)	22	30
South Atlantic	23	12
E. South Central	10	3
W. South Central	10	5
Mountain	6	3
Pacific	9	15

Source: William D. Wells, "Psychographics: A Critical Review," *Journal of Marketing Research*, 12 (May 1975), 197.

PSYCHOGRAPHICS VERSUS MOTIVATIONAL RESEARCH

In Chapter 3 we discussed motivational research and considered its various strengths and limitations. Like motivational research, psychographic research provides the marketer with a comprehensive profile of the consumer. Unlike motivational research, with its typically qualitative portrayal of the consumer characteristics under study, psychographic research initially produces quantified insights that are normally presented in the form of tables. In this respect, psychographic measures are somewhat similar to the measurement of personality traits, in that they require the use of self-administered questionnaires or "inventories" consisting of statements or questions concerning the respondent's

TABLE 5-2   Psychographic Profile of the Heavy User of Shotgun Ammunition

BASE	PERCENT WHO SPEND $11+ PER YEAR ON SHOTGUN AMMUNITION (141)	PERCENT WHO DON'T BUY (395)
I like hunting	88	7
I like fishing	68	26
I like to go camping	57	21
I love the out-of-doors	90	65
A cabin by a quiet lake is a great place to spend the summer	49	34
I like to work outdoors	67	40
I am good at fixing mechanical things	47	27
I often do a lot of repair work on my own car	36	12
I like war stories	50	32
I would do better than average in a fist fight	38	16
I would like to be a professional football player	28	18
I would like to be a policeman	22	8
There is too much violence on television	35	45
There should be a gun in every home	56	10
I like danger	19	8
I would like to own my own airplane	35	13
I like to play poker	50	26
I smoke too much	39	24
I love to eat	49	34
I spend money on myself that I should spend on the family	44	26
If given a chance, most men would cheat on their wives	33	14
I read the newspaper every day	51	72

Source: William D. Wells, "Psychographics: A Critical Review," *Journal of Marketing Research*, 12 (May 1975), 198.

needs, perceptions, attitudes, beliefs, values, interests, activities, tastes, and problems. It is this blending of the desirable characteristics of both motivational research and standard paper-and-pencil personality tests that gives psychographic measurement a distinctive appeal as a consumer behavior research tool.

While psychographic research initially generates quantitative results, these results can relatively easily be transformed from their tabular form to verbal profiles that are similar to the qualitative profiles usually associated with motivational research.

For instance, starting with an abundance of psychographic tabular data, consumer researchers at a major advertising agency were able to convert their tables into descriptive verbal profiles of various market segments.[3] Table 5-3 describes (and assigns vivid names to) the profiles of the five major psycho-

TABLE 5-3   Five Major Psychographic Segments of the Female Population

thelma, the old-fashioned traditionalist (25%)

This lady has lived a "good" life—she has been a devoted wife, a doting mother, and a conscientious housewife. She has lived her life by these traditional values and she cherishes them to this day. She does not condone contemporary sexual activities or political liberalism, nor can she sympathize with the women's libbers. Even today, when most of her children have left home, her life is centered around the kitchen. Her one abiding interest outside the household is the church which she attends every week. She lacks higher education and hence has little appreciation for the arts or cultural activities. Her spare time is spent watching TV, which is her prime source of entertainment and information.

mildred, the militant mother (20%)

Mildred married young and had children before she was quite ready to raise a family. Now she is unhappy. She is having trouble making ends meet on her blue-collar husband's income. She is frustrated and she vents her frustrations by rebelling against the system. She finds escape from her unhappy world in soap operas and movies. Television provides an ideal medium for her to live out her fantasies. She watches TV all through the day and into late night. She likes heavy rock and probably soul music, and she doesn't read much except escapist magazines such as True Story.

candice, the chic suburbanite (20%)

Candice is an urbane woman. She is well educated and genteel. She is a prime mover in her community, active in club affairs and working on community projects. Socializing is an important part of her life. She is a doer, interested in sports and the outdoors, politics and current affairs. Her life is hectic and lived at a fast clip. She is a voracious reader, and there are few magazines she doesn't read. However, TV does relatively poorly in competing for her attention—it is too inane for her.

cathy, the contented housewife (18%)

Cathy epitomizes simplicity. Her life is untangled. She is married to a worker in the middle of the socioeconomic scale, and they, along with their several preteen children, live in a small town. She is devoted to her family and faithfully serves them as mother, housewife, and cook. There is a certain tranquility in her life. She enjoys a relaxed pace and avoids anything that might disturb her equilibrium. She doesn't like news or news-type programs on TV but enjoys the wholesome family entertainment provided by Walt Disney, The Waltons, and Happy Days.

eleanor, the elegant socialite (17%)

Eleanor is a woman with style. She lives in the city because that is where she wants to be. She likes the economic and social aspects of big city living and takes advantage of the city in terms of her career and leisure time activities. She is a self-confident on-the-go woman, not a homebody. She is fashion-conscious and dresses well. She is a woman with panache. She is financially secure; as a result she is not a careful shopper. She shops for quality and style, not price. She is a cosmopolitan woman who has traveled abroad or wants to.

Source: Sunil Mehrota and William D. Wells, "Psychographics and Buyer Behavior: Theory and Recent Empirical Findings," in Arch G. Woodside et al., eds., *Consumer and Industrial Buying Behavior* (New York: North-Holland, 1977), 54.

graphic segments that these researchers created from their mountains of data. To make these distilled profiles even more useful for segmenting the markets for specific products, the researchers then portrayed the five female segments in terms of an index of their product usage (see Table 5-4) and their media habits (see Table 5-5).

Combining these various pieces of consumer insights, we can see, for example, that Thelma ("the old-fashioned traditionalist"), as a stereotype of a particular market segment, is most likely to color her hair, but least likely to use eye makeup. Moreover, when it comes to listening to the radio, she is a country and western fan; and her magazine tastes lean toward the *Reader's Digest*. Such information would be quite useful to a firm like Clairol if it wished to reach the Thelmas of the world.

TABLE 5-4   An Index of Cosmetic Produce-Usage for the Five Female Psychographic Segments

	THELMA	ELEANOR	CANDICE	CATHY	MILDRED
I often wear very expensive cologne	79	175	111	80	82
Lipstick	100	156	111	100	81
Hair spray	114	150	92	100	72
Nail polish	76	142	100	88	142
Hair coloring	200	142	150	65	15
Eye makeup	31	135	115	104	127
Wig	80	124	100	106	103
Breath freshener	132	139	86	82	93
Medicated face makeup	70	106	94	106	140
Cleansing face cream or lotion	96	129	107	82	121
Suntan lotion	35	126	126	118	140
Hand lotion	100	99	108	100	95
Shampoo	90	92	107	106	111

Source: Sunil Mehrota and William D. Wells, "Psychographics and Buyer Behavior: Theory and Recent Empirical Findings," in Arch G. Woodside et al., eds., *Consumer and Industrial Buying Behavior* (New York: North-Holland, 1977), 57.

TABLE 5-5   An Index of Media Habits for the Five Female Psychographic Segments

	THELMA	ELEANOR	CANDICE	CATHY	MILDRED
Heavy rock	14	71	92	86	257
Popular music	65	92	98	112	143
Middle-of-the-road music	79	102	130	100	98
Country and western	112	89	81	115	102
Classical/semiclassical	90	97	162	67	79
Time	64	100	206	53	92
Newsweek	60	113	180	67	73
US News and World Report	90	100	172	73	45
People	46	115	154	85	115
Cosmopolitan	43	150	121	64	136
Vogue	50	167	167	33	83
Glamour	40	130	130	80	120
Playboy	21	129	121	100	171
True Story	83	50	33	133	233
Redbook	83	93	113	103	113
TV Guide	76	103	84	108	137
Parents	60	70	130	120	180
Family Circle	93	100	115	171	85
Better Homes and Gardens	92	106	129	90	86
House and Garden	83	117	133	78	100
American Home	86	114	124	81	100
Good Housekeeping	86	104	120	104	88
Ladies' Home Journal	95	115	117	102	80
McCall's	95	114	116	93	86
Reader's Digest	106	100	110	100	82
Morning newspaper	107	115	144	78	60
Evening newspaper	100	105	105	113	79
Sunday newspaper	100	112	118	100	76

Source: Sunil Mehrota and William D. Wells, "Psychographics and Buyer Behavior: Theory and Recent Empirical Findings," in Arch G. Woodside et al., eds., *Consumer and Industrial Buying Behavior* (New York: North-Holland, 1977), 58.

As previously noted, psychographic variables are often referred to as AIOs, for much psychographic research focuses on the measurement of activities, interests, and opinions:[4]

Activities: How a consumer (or a family) spends time
Interests: A consumer's (or a family's) preferences and priorities
Opinions: How a consumer feels about a wide variety of events or things

Table 5-6 lists the general elements often included within each of these major dimensions of psychographic analysis.

Psychographic, or AIO, inventories usually require consumers to evaluate their personal or their family's stand in relation to a wide variety of statements, such as the following:

PERSONAL STATEMENTS
"I wish I had more good neighbors."
"I budget my money very carefully."
"I avoid joining clubs and other organizations."
"I have a first-aid kit in my car."
"I find that I'm always buying new gadgets."

FAMILY STATEMENTS
"The father should be the boss in the house."
"We try to go on at least one vacation a year as a family."
"Our family watches too much TV."
"We always try to eat dinner as a family."
"We will probably move during the next three years."

Another popular form of psychographic variable concentrates on determining the time spent by an individual or family on various activities and interests. Table 5-7 lists some of the lifestyle activities and interests that this time-oriented approach is designed to capture.

General and Product-Specific Statements

In addition to reflecting either personal or family activities, interests, and opinions, psychographic statements can be designed to be either general or product-specific.[5] Indeed, in carrying out a psychographic study of a specific product category, a consumer researcher would frequently include both general and product-specific statements.

TABLE 5-6   AIO Studies Encompass a Wide Variety of Variables

ACTIVITIES	INTERESTS	OPINIONS
Work	Family	Themselves
Hobbies	Home	Social issues
Social events	Job	Politics
Vacation	Community	Business
Entertainment	Recreation	Economics
Club membership	Fashion	Education
Community	Food	Products
Shopping	Media	Future
Sports	Achievement	Culture

Source: Joseph T. Plummer, "The Concept and Application of Life Style Segmentation," *Journal of Marketing*, 38 (January 1974), 34.

For example, a study aimed at examining the consumption of inexpensive domestic wines might include such general statements as "I dress to please myself, not other people," or "I read labels so as to avoid foreign-made products." It might also include such product-specific statements as "I'm of the opinion that white wine goes with everything," or "When guests come over, the first thing I do is serve wine," or "When I have a choice, I will always buy a domestic wine." Both types of statements supply valuable insights regarding

TABLE 5-7   Time Spent on Specific Activities and Interests

For each of the following activity or interest areas, please place an "X" in the box that best indicates how often you have engaged in the activity during the past 12 months.

	0 TIMES	1–2 TIMES	3–4 TIMES	5 OR MORE TIMES
Went to a library	☐	☐	☐	☐
Went to a gym or health club	☐	☐	☐	☐
Had food sent in	☐	☐	☐	☐
Went to a basketball game	☐	☐	☐	☐
Wrote a letter to a friend	☐	☐	☐	☐
Attended a concert	☐	☐	☐	☐
Went on a vacation	☐	☐	☐	☐
Went shopping for clothing	☐	☐	☐	☐
Attended an art museum	☐	☐	☐	☐
Played bridge	☐	☐	☐	☐

consumers' attitudes; however, the product-specific statements pertain directly to the product and its use, while the general statements focus on broader perceptions, preferences, or "style of life" matters.

The range of psychographic statements can actually be thought of as existing on a continuum, with very general lifestyle statements at one end of the spectrum and very product- or brand-specific attitudinal and behavioral statements at the other end.[6] The simple schematic in Figure 5-1 characterizes the range of psychographic statements on a "general" to "specific" continuum. In setting out a segmentation study for a particular brand or product category, a consumer researcher would probably be wise to consider constructing psychographic statements that span the full range of this continuum.

CONSTRUCTING A PSYCHOGRAPHIC INVENTORY

In constructing an inventory of psychographic items or statements, consumer researchers should first review available market research studies that might be of help in isolating psychographic variables. Motivational research studies are a particularly good source, for they tend to include consumers' reflections on their experiences and needs. Based upon such a review, psychographic statements are prepared which reflect the range of activities, interests, and opinions that the researcher wishes to evaluate. Table 5-8 lists several psychographic categories

FIGURE 5-1   **A General/Product-Specific Psychographic Continuum** Source: Adapted from Michel A. Zins, "An Exploration of the Relationship between General and Specific Psychographic Profiles," in Kenneth Bernhardt, ed., *Marketing: 1776–1976 and Beyond* (Chicago: American Marketing Association, 1976), 508.

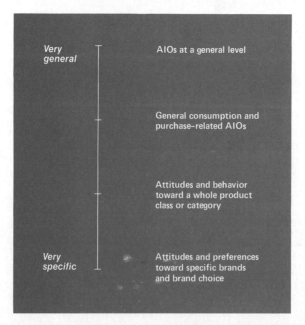

Very general — AIOs at a general level

General consumption and purchase-related AIOs

Attitudes and behavior toward a whole product class or category

Very specific — Attitudes and preferences toward specific brands and brand choice

TABLE 5-8   A Sample of Psychographic Categories
and Corresponding Statements

PSYCHOGRAPHIC CATEGORY	SAMPLE ITEMS
Time consciousness	It takes too much time to shop out of town. I always shop where it saves me time.
Gregarious community work	I like to work on community projects. I have personally worked on projects to better our town.
Attitudes toward local shopping conditions	Local prices are out of line with other towns. Local stores are attractive places to shop.
Shopping center orientation	I enjoy going to big shopping centers. I prefer shopping centers over downtown shopping areas.
Price consciousness	I shop a lot for specials. A person can save a lot of money by shopping around for bargains.
Venturesomeness	When I see a new brand on the shelf, I often buy it just to see what it is like. I enjoy doing new things.
Self-confidence	I think I have a lot of personal ability. I like to be considered a leader.

Source: Adapted from Fred D. Reynolds, "An Analysis of Catalog Buying Behavior," *Journal of Marketing*, 38 (July 1974), 49.

and corresponding statements employed in a study designed to identify consumers with different degrees of commitment to in-home catalog shopping.

In constructing a psychographic instrument, it is important to determine whether consumers will understand the meaning of each of the items as the marketer intended them to be interpreted or whether a variety of different interpretations are possible—which may produce invalid results. It is also necessary to attempt to avoid including items that lead consumers to report a socially acceptable response when it really does not reflect their true feelings or likely actions. Actually, everything said about the construction of reliable (i.e., does it provide consistent results?) and valid (i.e., do different scores reflect true differences between people?) personality scales in Chapter 4 is also true of the construction of a psychographic instrument.

Finally, in responding to a psychographic inventory, consumers are often asked to rate the extent of their "agreement" or "disagreement" with such statements. Table 5-9 presents a portion of a psychographic inventory used by the American Telephone and Telegraph Company to study various aspects of consumers' telephone behavior.

APPLICATIONS OF PSYCHOGRAPHIC ANALYSIS

Psychographic analysis is particularly useful in three closely related areas of marketing strategy: (1) segmenting markets, (2) positioning and repositioning products, and (3) developing specific promotional campaigns.

TABLE 5-9   A Portion of an Actual Psychographic Inventory

Understanding what the telephone means to you, how you use it and how it fits into your life is important to us in planning for your telephone needs. Each of the following statements is about telephones or how they fit into your life. Please read each statement and then put an "X" in the box which best indicates how strongly you agree or disagree with the statement in terms of your home phone. For example, if you "strongly agree" with a statement you would put an "X" in the "+3" box($\boxed{X}$). If you "somewhat disagree" you would put an "X" in the "−2" box ($\boxed{X}$). If you neither agree nor disagree, you would put an "X" in the "0" box ($\boxed{X}$). *Please disregard the small black numbers beside the boxes. They are for office use only.*

	COMPLETELY AGREE			NEITHER AGREE NOR DISAGREE	COMPLETELY DISAGREE			
I spend a lot of time talking on the telephone	+3 ¹	+2 ²	+1 ³	0 ⁴	−1 ⁵	−2 ⁶	−3 ⁷	31
People who have stylish telephones are lucky because they can afford them	+3 ¹	+2 ²	+1 ³	0 ⁴	−1 ⁵	−2 ⁶	−3 ⁷	32
We live a long way from our friends and relatives	+3 ¹	+2 ²	+1 ³	0 ⁴	−1 ⁵	−2 ⁶	−3 ⁷	33
Those who know me would consider me to be thrifty	+3 ¹	+2 ²	+1 ³	0 ⁴	−1 ⁵	−2 ⁶	−3 ⁷	34
I need several telephones in my home because of my work/business	+3 ¹	+2 ²	+1 ³	0 ⁴	−1 ⁵	−2 ⁶	−3 ⁷	35
I am influential in my neighborhood	+3 ¹	+2 ²	+1 ³	0 ⁴	−1 ⁵	−2 ⁶	−3 ⁷	36
Pushbutton telephones probably break down a lot	+3 ¹	+2 ²	+1 ³	0 ⁴	−1 ⁵	−2 ⁶	−3 ⁷	37
I prefer to have several telephones in my home as a convenience	+3 ¹	+2 ²	+1 ³	0 ⁴	−1 ⁵	−2 ⁶	−3 ⁷	38
For me the telephone is a means of avoiding seeing some people	+3 ¹	+2 ²	+1 ³	0 ⁴	−1 ⁵	−2 ⁶	−3 ⁷	39
I prefer colored appliances	+3 ¹	+2 ²	+1 ³	0 ⁴	−1 ⁵	−2 ⁶	−3 ⁷	40
My home is an open house, with friends and neighbors always visiting	+3 ¹	+2 ²	+1 ³	0 ⁴	−1 ⁵	−2 ⁶	−3 ⁷	41
I prefer pushbutton phones even though they are more expensive	+3 ¹	+2 ²	+1 ³	0 ⁴	−1 ⁵	−2 ⁶	−3 ⁷	42
When I must choose between the two, I usually dress for fashion, not comfort	+3 ¹	+2 ²	+1 ³	0 ⁴	−1 ⁵	−2 ⁶	−3 ⁷	43

Source: Joseph N. Spiers, "Getting More from Market Research," *Industry Week,* December 1, 1975, 34. Also, courtesy of the American Telephone and Telegraph Company.

Market Segmentation

Psychographic research is an efficient way of identifying aspects of the psychological and social-cultural characteristics of specific target markets. For example, the psychographic profile in Table 5-10 compares drivers who have not had any automobile accidents during a five-year period with drivers who have had at least two accidents. The findings reveal that accident-prone drivers are risk takers and are more-pressured individuals and impulsive consumers than those drivers who did not have any accidents. Also, while they seem to have more money problems, accident-prone drivers are generally more optimistic

TABLE 5-10   A Brief Psychographic Profile of the Accident-Prone Driver (in percentages)

	NUMBER OF ACCIDENTS IN PAST FIVE YEARS	
	two or more	none
risk taker		
I don't like to take chances (disagree).	42	31
I am the kind of person who will try anything once.	64	53
restless		
I would probably be content to live in the same town the rest of my life (disagree).	40	28
We will probably move at least once in the next five years.	50	32
pressured		
I work under a great deal of pressure most of the time.	69	57
impulse buyer		
I am an impulse buyer.	47	35
When I see a brand somewhat different from the usual, I investigate it.	73	63
money problems		
Our family is too heavily in debt today.	36	25
Worrying about money.	52	30
optimistic		
My greatest achievements are ahead of me.	78	61
Five years from now our family income will probably be a lot higher than it is now.	81	60
cosmopolitan		
I like to think I am a bit of a swinger.	46	28
I would like to spend a year in London or Paris.	41	30
interested in movies		
I like to watch disaster movies.	47	32
Attended an x-rated movie.	19	9
less conservative		
Communism is the greatest peril in the world today.	48	59
U.S. would be better off if there were no hippies.	46	60
Unions have too much power in America today.	67	77
Most big companies are just out for themselves.	77	67

Source: Sunil Mehrota and William D. Wells, "Psychographic and Buyer Behavior: Theory and Recent Empirical Findings," in Arch G. Woodside et al., eds., *Consumer and Industrial Buying Behavior* (New York, North-Holland, 1977), 60.

about the future, more cosmopolitan in their interests, and more adventurous and less conservative in their lifestyles.[7]

Armed with such a portrayal of the accident-prone driver, automobile insurance companies and governmental highway safety agencies might be in a better position to develop public service promotional appeals that more effectively stimulate particular segments of the driving public to be cautious when on the road.

Psychographic research has also been employed to compare "heavy" moviegoers (those who have gone to the movies at least nine times in the preceding year) with nonmoviegoers (those who have not gone to the movies in the preceding year). The study produced the following behavioral profile of "heavy" moviegoers as compared with nonmoviegoers:[8]

1. Heavy moviegoers are more ambitious, more optimistic, and more self-confident.
2. Heavy moviegoers have a richer fantasy life.
3. Heavy moviegoers are more active and more socially oriented.
4. Heavy moviegoers have more "swinging" interests.
5. Heavy moviegoers are more inclined toward new and sporty possessions.
6. Heavy moviegoers have more "contemporary" values.

A portion of the AIO inventory from which this summary characterization was drawn is presented in Table 5-11.

Psychographics has also successfully been applied in a variety of retail settings. Most specifically, it has proved useful in segmenting consumers into various retail shopper categories.[9] For instance, Table 5-12 shows the results of a study that compares recreational shoppers (those consumers who enjoy shopping and consider it a leisure-time activity) with economic shoppers (those who basically are neutral to or dislike shopping and view it from a strictly time- or money-saving perspective). The results indicate that recreational shoppers tend to exhibit the following preferences and characteristics as compared with economic shoppers:[10]

TABLE 5-11   A Partial Psychographic Comparison of "Heavy" Moviegoers and Nonmoviegoers

	PERCENTAGE AGREEMENT	
	non-moviegoers	"heavy" moviegoers
My greatest achievements are still ahead of me.	49	80
Five years from now the family income will probably be a lot higher than it is now.	63	88
I'd like to spend a year in London or Paris.	19	42
I like to be considered a leader.	60	82
I don't like to take a chance.	71	51
I like parties where there is lots of music and talk.	37	65
I always have the car radio on when I drive.	49	82
"Playboy" is one of my favorite magazines.	13	48
I think I'm a bit of a swinger.	13	33
I like sports cars.	29	58
Liquor is a curse on American life.	59	36
A woman should not smoke in public.	62	36
If Americans were more religious, this would be a better country.	83	63

Source: Glen Homan, Robert Cecil, and William Wells, "An Analysis of Moviegoers By Life Style Segments," in Mary Jane Schlinger, ed., *Advances in Consumer Research*, 2 (Association for Consumer Research, 1975), 219.

1. They spend more time shopping, and they prefer enclosed shopping malls and department stores.
2. They attach greater importance to stores featuring quality products, a wide selection of merchandise, and a pleasant decor.
3. They are more likely to be impulse shoppers.
4. They have greater exposure to retail-oriented mass media.
5. They enjoy outdoor activities, and they are more inclined to entertain guests in their home.

This research strongly suggests that recreational shoppers are an especially profitable consumer segment and that they should be actively pursued by the operators of enclosed shopping malls, and particularly by department stores that seem to be in the best position to satisfy their needs.

TABLE 5-12   A Psychographic Comparison of Recreational Shoppers and Economic Shoppers

VARIABLE		PERCENTAGE OF RECREA-TIONAL SHOPPERS	PERCENTAGE OF ECO-NOMIC SHOPPERS
Spend at least one hour per shopping trip		97	76
Usually shop at:	Closed shopping mall	83	67
	Open shopping center	12	23
	Downtown	5	6
Type of store shopped at:	Department	72	52
	Discount	11	16
	Specialty	17	32
Consider quality of merchandise to be important		68	60
Consider variety of merchandise to be important		59	42
Consider store decor to be important		35	19
Usually have an idea of what I am going to buy		90	100
Continue to shop after making a purchase		73	37
Usually buy what I would like to have		45	23
Usually buy products that I like but don't need immediately		20	6
Enjoy watching TV		67	52
Enjoy hiking		60	40
Enjoy cooking		35	50
Enjoy camping		65	35
Enjoy sewing		11	31
Enjoy attending sports events		84	70
Enjoy entertaining guests at home		87	73
Daily reading of local newspaper		70	30
Three or more hours of TV viewing		12	4

Source: Adapted from Danny N. Bellenger and Pradeep K. Korgaonkar, Profiling the Recreational Shopper," *Journal of Retailing*, 56 (Fall 1980), 84–85.

Product Positioning and Repositioning

If a company is not certain which one of a number of alternative consumer segments should be the target for a new-product concept, it can use psychographic analysis to identify those consumers who seem to be least satisfied with existing products, and thus more likely to respond to a new product. On the basis of its findings, the company can design a product and marketing strategy that specifically appeals to this market.

An interesting new-product application of psychographic positioning relates to General Foods' line of Cycle canned dog foods.[11] Originally General Foods, although a leading marketer of dog foods, did not market canned dog foods. To gain a foothold in this important submarket, it undertook a rather exhaustive research program that examined various social-cultural changes that might be expected to influence dog ownership and dog care.[12] An important part of this research focused on the identification of major dog owner segments. Specifically, it found that there were five psychographic dog owner types, each with a unique set of needs or motives when it came to the ownership or care of dogs. Table 5-13 (on pages 128–29) summarizes the main characteristics of the key dog owner segments and reveals some important information about their pet-feeding attitudes and behavior.

Based upon this and other research, General Foods eventually launched its Cycle canned dog foods. Figure 5-2 shows an early advertisement for the product line.

For existing products, especially those with declining sales, psychographic research can be employed to identify the psychographic characteristics of the present market and of competitors' markets, so that a campaign can be designed to appeal to the more promising market segments, even if it means repositioning the product. For instance, an advertising agency was requested by a client who produced a heavy-duty hand soap to reposition the product to appeal to new market segments, since the traditional audience for the product (men who used it after completing dirty jobs around the house or shop) was felt to be too restrictive in size. A psychographic study of female users of heavy-duty hand soap produced the following profile:[13]

1. Her interests and activities are centered on her home and her children.
2. She influences others and sees herself as an expert on products.
3. She needs to live within a limited income.
4. Many of her ideas and values are traditionally blue-collar.
5. She has a strong predisposition for deep-down cleanliness.

The AIO statements from which this profile was drawn are listed in Table 5-14 on page 130. The findings provided valuable insights for repositioning the product to a female audience.

Promotional Campaigns

Psychographic analysis has been widely used in the development of advertising campaigns to answer three questions: (1) Whom should we aim our advertising at? (2) What should we say? and (3) Where should we say it? In the past, copywriters tended to rely on their own intuition or on small-scale motivational

Advertisement for CYCLE® dog food reproduced with permission of General Foods Corporation, White Plains, New York.

research studies as a guide for the creation of copy. However, psychographic profiles provide the opportunity to create advertising copy based on more objective, large-scale research studies.[14]

Mass media also develops psychographic (and demographic) profiles of their audiences. (Table 5-15 on page 130 presents a brief comparison of "heavy" *Playboy* and "heavy" *Reader's Digest* readers.) By offering media buyers psychographic studies of their audiences, in addition to the traditional demographic profiles, mass-media publishers and broadcasters make it possible for advertisers to select media that have audiences most closely resembling their own target audiences.

TABLE 5-13 A Profile of Five Key Psychographic Segments of the Dog Food Market

NAME	FUNCTIONALIST	FAMILY MUTT	BABY SUBSTITUTE	NUTRITIONALISTS	MIDDLE OF ROAD
size:					
% of Dog Owners	40%	25%	10%	13%	12%
% of Commercial Dog Food Feedings	55%	20%	5%	10%	10%
demography: (Note these are tendencies based upon a given group's profile relative to the other groups)	Multiple dog ownership; Children present; lower income/C, D counties	Own one dog; Average size; Children present; lower income/C, D counties	Own one very small, older dog; Kids not present; higher income, urban	Multiple dog ownership; largest dogs; low probability of kids; Eastern, urban, higher income	No distinctive characteristics
attitudes: (Note these are tendencies based upon a given group's profile relative to other groups)	Dogs outdoor/hearty; eat anything, no bother; Little attachment to dog; Interested in ownership benefits; Average interest in nutrition; Housewife not involved with dog.	Little interest in dog; Dog playful, no bother; Below average menu acceptance; Interest in owner-benefits; Least interest in nutrition; Housewife not involved, dog is for kids.	Dog fragile, indoor animal; above average attachment to dog; Heavily involved in choice of food; Dog finicky eater, great desire to prepare what dog wants.	Very personally attached to dog; Dog belongs to housewife; Most interested in nutrition; Least interested in cost, food flexibility; Virile dog.	

	Segment 1	Segment 2	Segment 3	Segment 4	Segment 5
types used:	Basically meal feeders—very little use of other types.	Heavy meal usage but also atypically high use of low priced canned.	High degree of canned use, relatively little of meal; High relative use of soft-moist and biscuits.	Most feedings meal—relatively strong high priced canned and biscuit use.	Feed meal and canned to about same extent; High relative use of soft-moist.

% of total feedings given to each type	Soft-Moist 2.0%
	Meal 88.2
	Canned 8.9
	  High 1.2
	  Parity 1.8
	  Economy 5.9
	Biscuits 0.9
		Soft-Moist 6.4%
		Meal 63.7
		Canned 28.4
		  High 3.2
		  Parity 8.2
		  Economy 17.0
		Biscuits 1.5
			Soft-Moist 7.8%
			Meal 59.0
			Canned 27.1
			  High 10.2
			  Parity 7.4
			  Economy 9.5
			Biscuits 6.1
				Soft-Moist 25.4%
				Meal 22.7
				Canned 44.9
				  High 14.9
				  Parity 16.9
				  Economy 13.1
				Biscuits 7.0
					Soft-Moist 41.0%
					Meal 43.7
					Canned 37.7
					  High 6.7
					  Parity 12.5
					  Economy 18.5
					Biscuits 4.6

location: post region	Stronger than average in Central & South; very weak in West.	Stronger than average in East; very weak in West.	Stronger than average in West; relatively weak in East.	Very strong in South & East; very weak in West.	Stronger than average in East and Central; Western South.

Source: F. Stewart DeBruicker and Scott Ward, *Cases in Consumer Behavior* (Englewood Cliffs, N.J.: Prentice-Hall, 1980), 28.

TABLE 5-14   A Comparison of "Users" and "Nonusers" of Heavy-Duty Hand Soap

	PERCENTAGE AGREEMENT	
	nonusers	users
home-oriented		
I must admit I really don't like household chores.	44	29
I always make my cakes from scratch.	17	48
I try to arrange my home for my children's convenience.	31	44
When making important family decisions, consideration of the children should come first.	40	50
she is a "gatekeeper" and knowledgeable shopper		
I like to go grocery shopping.	44	65
People come to me more often than I go to them for information about brands.	24	35
budget-conscious		
I shop a lot for "specials."	41	52
When I think of bad health, I think of doctor bills.	42	53
traditional blue-collar values		
Women should not use false eyelashes.	20	49
A woman should not chew gum.	37	21
Clothing should be dried in the fresh air and sunshine.	34	49
There should be a gun in every home.	22	38
compulsive concern with cleanliness		
You have to use disinfectants to get your house really clean.	35	58
I am uncomfortable when my house is not completely clean.	51	64
Everyone should use a mouthwash.	44	63

Source: Adapted from Joseph T. Plummer, "Life Style and Advertising: Case Studies," *Combined Proceedings* (Chicago: American Marketing Association, 1972), 294–95.

TABLE 5-15   A Psychographic Comparison of *Playboy* and *Reader's Digest* Readers

	PERCENT WHO DEFINITELY AGREED AMONG	
	heavy *Playboy* readers	heavy *Reader's Digest* readers
My greatest achievements are still ahead of me.	50	26
I go to church regularly.	18	40
Movies should be censored.	14	40
Most men would cheat on their wives if the right opportunity came along.	27	12

Source: Douglas J. Tigert, "Life Style Analysis as a Basis for Media Selection," in William D. Wells, ed., *Life Style and Psychographics* (Chicago: American Marketing Association, 1974), 179.

In the opening paragraph of this chapter we identified over a dozen products that have evidently benefited from research that included psychographic measures that provided valuable insights for the formulation of marketing and promotional strategies. To these known examples, undoubtedly numerous additional unpublicized cases exist where psychographic analysis has also been employed to enrich a firm's understanding of its target markets.[15]

At the present time, the outlook for psychographic research, especially pragmatic research sponsored by firms for their products and services, continues to be bright.

summary

During the past two decades psychographic, lifestyle, or AIO research has become an important basis for market segmentation and related marketing strategy efforts. Its popularity with both marketing practitioners and academic researchers seems to lie in the vivid and actionable consumer profiles that have frequently been produced from psychographic instruments.

In its more general form, a psychographic instrument can be conceived of as a battery of statements designed to capture relevant aspects of a consumer's personality, buying motives, interests, attitudes, beliefs, and values. In contrast, other more product-specific forms of psychographics have consumers respond to selective statements about products, services, brands, or specific consumption situations. Both of these forms of psychographics are useful because they tap different dimensions of a consumer's psychological and social nature.

Psychographics seemed to come into existence as an answer to marketers' search for a quantitative researcher approach (i.e., one producing numerical responses that could easily be computer analyzed) that would provide many of the dramatic insights of motivational research and resemble personality measures in their form. Still further, as a survey research tool, psychographic profiles are complementary to traditional demographic profiles of consumers. While demographic variables help marketers "locate" their target market of consumers, psychographic variables help them acquire a picture of the "inner consumer"; that is, to know what consumers are feeling and what ought to be stressed in the firm's marketing campaign.

In constructing psychographic instruments, researchers strive to capture *activities* (i.e., how a consumer or a family spends time), *interests* (i.e., how a consumer's or a family's preferences and priorities are determined), and *opinions* (i.e., how a consumer feels about a wide variety of events or things). Several steps suggest themselves when it comes to constructing psychographic instruments: (1) review existing market research studies that might aid in the identification of psychographic items; (2) prepare psychographic statements that reflect the full range of activities, interests, and opinions that the marketer wishes to assess; (3) select an appropriate rating scale (often an "agree-disagree" scale); (4) evaluate the instrument for clarity and socially acceptable responses; and (5) test the instrument to determine its reliability and validity.

The strongest endorsement for the application of psychographic research has been its widescale employment by both practitioner and academic consumer researchers. Most important, as a real-world research tool, psychographics has proved useful in three closely related areas of marketing strategy: segmenting markets, positioning and repositioning products, and designing promotional campaigns.

discussion questions

1. A media buyer for a local beverage distributor has relied entirely on demographic profiles to identify magazines and TV shows in which to place the company's advertising. Describe several benefits that the company might receive by using psychographic profiles to identify target audiences.

2. When is consumer demographic information likely to be more useful than psychographic information?

3. Using shampoo as an example, describe why demographics and psychographics are both desirable types of consumer information for marketers to have about their target markets.

4. In response to a request from a firearms manufacturer, review the data in Tables 5-1 and 5-2 and make suggestions as to the distribution, promotion, and pricing strategy that the firm might employ with regard to its line of shotgun ammunition.

5. What are the main advantages and disadvantages of presenting demographic/psychographic profiles in the descriptive narrative form shown in Table 5-3 rather than in the usual tabular form?

6. Why is it important that psychographic items be both reliable and valid?

7. If you were the owner of a sporting goods store located in a large shopping mall, how might you use the comparison of recreational and economic shoppers in Table 5-12?

8. The president of a fast-food chain has asked you to prepare a psychographic profile of families living in a number of communities surrounding a new location he is considering. Construct a 10-question psychographic questionnaire that would seem appropriate for segmenting families in terms of their dining-out preferences.

endnotes

1. A. Marvin Roscoe, Jr., Arthur Le Claire, Jr., and Leon G. Schiffman, "Theory and Management Applications of Demographics in Buyer Behavior," in Arch G. Woodside et al., eds. *Consumer and Industrial Buying Behavior* (New York: North-Holland, 1977), 70–71.

2. William D. Wells, "Psychographics: A Critical Review," *Journal of Marketing Research*, 2 (May 1975), 198.

3. Sunil Mehrota and William D. Wells, "Psychographics and Buyer Behavior: Theory and Recent Empirical Findings," in Woodside et al., *Consumer and Industrial Buying Behavior,* 52–57.

4. William D. Wells and Douglas J. Tigert, "Activities, Interests and Opinions," *Journal of Advertising Research,* 11 (August 1971), 27–35; and Joseph T. Plummer, "The Concept of Life Style Segmentation," *Journal of Marketing,* 38 (January 1974), 33–37.

5. Stuart Van Auken, "General versus Product-Specific Life Style Segmentation," *Journal of Advertising,* 7 (Fall 1978), 31–35; and Michel A. Zins, "An Exploration of the Relationship between General and Specific Psychographic Profiles," in Kenneth Bernhardt, ed., *Marketing: 1776–1976 and Beyond* (Chicago: American Marketing Association, 1976), 507–11.

6. Zins, "Relationship between General and Specific Psychographics," 508.

7. Mehrota and Wells, "Psychographics and Buyer Behavior," 57.

8. Glen Homan, Robert Cecil, and William Wells, "An Analysis of Moviegoers by Life Style Segments," in Mary Jane Schlinger, ed., *Advances in Consumer Research,* 2 (Association for Consumer Research, 1975), 219.

9. William R. Darden and William D. Perreault, Jr., "Identifying Interurban Shoppers: Multiproduct Purchase Patterns and Segmentation Profiles," *Journal of Marketing Research,* 13 (February 1976), 51–60; and William R. Darden and Dub Ashton, "Psychographic Profiles of Patronage Preference Groups," *Journal of Retailing,* 50 (Winter 1974–75), 99–112.

10. Danny N. Bellenger and Pradeep K. Korgaonkar, "Profiling the Recreational Shopper," *Journal of Retailing,* 56 (Fall 1980), 83–92.

11. Peter W. Bernstein, "Psychographics Is Still an Issue on Madison Avenue," *Fortune,* January 1978, 80.

12. F. Stewart DeBruicker and Scott Ward, *Cases in Consumer Behavior* (Englewood Cliffs, N.J.: Prentice-Hall, 1980), 11–33.

13. Joseph T. Plummer, "Life Style and Advertising: Case Studies," in Fred C. Allvine, ed., *1971 Combined Proceedings* (Chicago: American Marketing Association, 1972), 294–95.

14. See, for example, William O. Bearden, Jesse E. Teel, Jr., and Richard M. Durand, "Media Usage, Psychographic, and Demographic Dimensions of Retail Shoppers," *Journal of Retailing,* 54 (Spring 1978), 65–74; and William D. Wells and Stephen C. Cosmas, "Life Styles," in *Selected Aspects of Consumer Behavior* (Washington, D.C.: Government Printing Office, 1977), 299–316.

15. See William D. Wells, ed., *Life Style and Psychographics* (Chicago: American Marketing Association, 1974); and Thomas C. Kinnear and James R. Taylor, "Psychographics: Some Additional Findings," *Journal of Marketing Research,* 13 (November 1976), 422–25.

SIX

The Consumer as a Perceiver

introduction

As individuals, we tend to see the world and all its varied happenings in our own special ways. Four people can view the same event at the same time, and each will report in total honesty a story different from all the others. For example, the classic Japanese film *Rashomon*—shown frequently on late night television—tells the story of the abduction and rape of a woodcutter's wife and the murder of her husband, first from the point of view of the bandit, then the wife, then the husband, and finally a hidden bystander. Each story varied because each participant perceived the events that occurred in a different way. Hard to believe? Not really. For each individual, reality is a totally personal phenomenon, based on that person's needs, wants, values, and personal experiences.

Reality to an individual is merely that individual's perception of what is "out there"—of what has taken place. Individuals act and react on the basis of their perceptions, not on the basis of objective reality (i.e., reality as recorded by a camera). Thus, consumers' perceptions are much more important to the marketer than their knowledge of objective reality. For, if one thinks about it, it's not what actually *is* so, but what consumers *think* is so, that affects their actions, their buying habits, their leisure habits, and so forth. And because individuals make decisions and take actions based on what they *perceive* to be reality, it is important that marketers understand the whole notion of perception and its related concepts so that they can more readily determine what influences consumers to buy.

This chapter examines the psychological and physiological bases of human perception and discusses the principles that control our reception and interpretation of the world we see. Knowledge of these principles of perception enables astute marketers to develop strategies that have a good chance of being seen and remembered by their target consumers.

> *Every man takes the limits of his own field of vision for the limits of the world.*
>
> *SCHOPENHAUER:*
>
> *"Further Psychological Observation," Parerga and Paralipomena (1851)*

Perception can be described as "how we see the world around us." Two individuals may be subject to the same stimuli under apparently the same conditions, but how they recognize them, select them, organize them, and interpret them is a highly individual process, based on each person's own needs, values, expectations, and the like. The influence that each of these variables plays in the perceptual process, and its relevance to marketing, will be examined in some detail. First, however, we will examine some of the basic concepts that underlie the perceptual process. These will be discussed within the framework of consumer behavior.

Perception can be defined as *the process by which an individual selects, organizes, and interprets stimuli into a meaningful and coherent picture of the world.* A *stimulus* is any unit of input to any of the senses. Examples of stimuli (i.e., *sensory inputs*) include products, packages, brand names, advertisements, and commercials. *Sensory receptors* are the human organs (the eyes, ears, nose, mouth, and skin) that receive sensory inputs. Their sensory functions are to see, hear, smell, taste, and feel. All of these functions are called into play—either singly or in combination—in the evaluation and use of most consumer products. The study of perception is largely the study of what we subconsciously add to or subtract from our raw sensory inputs to produce our private picture of the world.

Sensation

Sensation is the immediate and direct response of the sensory organs to simple stimuli (an advertisement, a package, a brand name). Human sensitivity refers to the experience of sensation. Sensitivity to stimuli varies with the quality of an individual's *sensory receptors* (e.g., eyesight or hearing) and the amount or intensity of the stimuli to which he or she is exposed. For example, a blind person may have a more highly developed sense of hearing than the average sighted person and may be able to hear sounds that the average person cannot.

Sensation itself depends on energy change or differentiation of input. A perfectly bland or unchanging environment—regardless of the strength of the sensory input—provides little or no sensation at all. Thus a person who lives on a busy street in midtown Manhattan would probably receive little or no sensation from the inputs of such noisy stimuli as horns honking, tires screeching, or fire engines clanging, since such sounds tend to be the rule in New York City. One more or one less horn honking would never be noticed. In situations where there is a great deal of sensory input, the senses do not detect small intensities or differences in input.

As the sensory input *decreases*, however, the ability to detect changes in input or intensity *increases,* to the point where we attain our maximum sensitivity under conditions of minimal stimulation. This accounts for the statement "It was so quiet I could hear a pin drop." It also accounts for the increased attention given to a commercial that appears alone during a program break, or the attention given to a black-and-white advertisement in a magazine full of four-color advertisements. This ability of the human organism to accommodate itself to varying levels of sensitivity as external conditions vary not only provides more sensitivity when it is needed but also serves to protect us from damaging, disruptive, or irrelevant bombardment when the input level is high.

THE ABSOLUTE THRESHOLD

The lowest level at which an individual can experience a sensation is called the *absolute threshold*. The point at which a person can detect a difference between "something" and "nothing" is that person's absolute threshold for that stimulus. To illustrate, the distance at which a driver can note a specific billboard on the highway is that individual's absolute threshold. Two people riding together may first spot the billboard at different times (i.e., at different distances); thus they appear to have different absolute thresholds.

Under conditions of constant stimulation, such as driving through a "corridor" of billboards, the absolute threshold increases (that is, the senses tend to become increasingly dulled). After an hour of driving through billboards, it is doubtful that any one billboard will make an impression. Hence we often speak of "getting used to" a hot bath, a cold shower, the bright sun, or even the odor in a locker room. In the field of perception, the term *adaptation* refers specifically to "getting used to" certain sensations, becoming accommodated to a certain level of stimulation. It is because of adaptation that advertisers tend to change their advertising campaigns regularly. They are concerned that consumers will get so used to their current print ads and commercials that they will no longer "see" them; that is, the ads will no longer provide a sufficient sensory input to be noted.

Package designers try to determine consumers' absolute thresholds to make sure that their new-product designs exceed this level, so that new products will stand out from the competition on retailers' shelves.

THE DIFFERENTIAL THRESHOLD

The minimal difference that can be detected between two stimuli is called the *differential threshold,* or the *j.n.d.* (for *just noticeable difference*). A nineteenth-century German scientist named Ernst Weber discovered that the just noticeable difference between two stimuli was not an absolute amount, but an amount relative to the intensity of the first stimulus. Weber's law, as it has come to be known, states that the stronger the initial stimulus, the greater the additional intensity needed for the second stimulus to be perceived as different. For example, if the price of an automobile were increased by twenty dollars, it would probably not be noticed (that is, the increment would fall below the *j.n.d.*); it may take an increase of two hundred dollars or more before a differential in price would be noticed. However, a twenty-cent increase in the price of gasoline would be very quickly noticed by consumers because it is a significant percentage of the base cost of the gasoline.

According to Weber's law, an additional level of stimulus equivalent to a *j.n.d.* must be added for the majority of people to perceive a difference between the resulting stimulus and the initial stimulus.

Let us say that a manufacturer of silver polish wishes to improve the product sufficiently to claim that it retards tarnish longer than the leading competitor's. In a series of experiments, the company has determined that the *j.n.d.* for its present polish, which now gives a shine that lasts about twenty days, is five days. According to Weber's law, the *j.n.d* is

$$\frac{dI}{I} = k,$$

where k is the constant ratio, I is the initial stimulus, and dI is the just noticeable difference. In this case,

$$\frac{dI}{I} = \frac{5}{20} = \frac{1}{4}$$

That is, the shine given by the improved silver polish must last at least one-fourth longer than that of the present polish for it to be perceived by the majority of users as improved. By finding this *j.n.d* of five days, the company has isolated the minimum amount of time necessary to make its claim of "lasts longer" believable to the majority of consumers.

If the company had decided to make the silver polish effective for forty days, it would have sacrificed a good deal of purchase frequency. If it had decided to make the polish effective for twenty-three days (just three extra days of product life), its claim of "lasts longer" would not be perceived as true by most consumers. Making the product improvement just equal to the *j.n.d.* thus becomes the most efficient decision that management could make.

The *j.n.d.* has other uses as well. For example, retailers have long made use of a general rule of thumb that markdowns of merchandise must amount to at least 20 percent of the old price, since a smaller amount often goes unnoticed by consumers.[1] They recognize that the *just noticeable difference* is not an absolute amount, but rather a relative amount contingent upon the level of the initial price. For the same reason, the Federal Trade Commission monitors the size of the printed warnings in cigarette advertisements to ensure that they appear in a type size sufficiently large in relation to the size of the ad to be perceived and read.[2]

Weber's law is concerned with comparisons between two stimuli. It holds for all the senses and for almost all intensities. In the case of vision and hearing, it is operable in more than 99.9 percent of the usable stimulus range (the broad normal range of intensities).[3]

MARKETING APPLICATIONS OF THE J.N.D.

Weber's law has important applications to marketing. Manufacturers and marketers endeavor to determine the relevant *j.n.d.* for their products for two very different reasons: (1) so that reductions in product size, increases in product price, or changes in packaging *are not* readily discernible to the public; and (2) so that product improvements *are* readily discernible to the public without being wastefully extravagant. For example, because of rising costs, many manufacturers are faced with the choice of increasing their prices or reducing the quantity or the quality of the product offered at the existing price. Hershey has done both. Over the past twenty-five years, it has increased the price of its chocolate bar four times and altered its weight fifteen times. Because a candy bar is so inexpensive to begin with, price increases are very noticeable, so decreasing the size of the bar to just under the *j.n.d* has been the preferred strategy.[4]

Manufacturers who choose to reduce the quality of their products also try to ensure that product changes remain just under the point of noticeable difference. For example, when the price of coffee beans goes up, coffee processors often downgrade their quality by using inferior beans, up to but not including the *j.n.d.*—the point at which the consumer will notice a difference in taste.

Another type of problem faced by many marketers is the need to update their existing packaging without losing the ready recognition of consumers who have been exposed to years of cumulative advertising impact. In such cases, marketers usually make a number of small changes, each one carefully designed to fall below the *j.n.d.* so that consumers will not perceive the difference. For example, the familiar Crackerjack package which we have all known as children has undergone some fifteen to twenty changes in small increments over the years without alerting consumers that changes have been made.

The Campbell Soup Company has been one of the most subtle of all marketers in changing its package. An alteration here, a slight typographic change there, refinement of its logotype, have all combined to keep the product looking up-to-date without losing any of the valuable Campbell image. Campbell is still one of the most widely recognized packages in the world today.[5]

Another interesting example is Ivory soap, which was introduced in 1879. The subtle packaging changes Ivory experienced over the years were each small enough to avoid notice, but they managed to retain a contemporary look (see Figure 6-1). The latest Ivory package is considerably different from the original, but the changes made each step of the way were so skillfully designed that the transition has been hardly noticeable to the consumer. Marketers also use the *j.n.d.* to determine the ideal level of distribution of goods or services, the optimum ratio of copy to headline in print ads, and the frequency with which ads must be repeated to have maximum effect.[6]

The examples given above are concerned with changes that marketers do not want consumers to perceive. When it comes to product improvements, however, marketers very much want to meet or exceed the consumer's differential threshold; that is, they want consumers to readily perceive the improvement made to the original product. One well-known marketing authority has suggested that marketers use the *j.n.d.* to determine the amount of improvement they should plan to make in their products.[7] Less than the *j.n.d.* is wasted because it will not be perceived; more than that may be wasteful because it will reduce the level of repeat sales.

Subliminal Perception

In Chapter 3 we spoke of people being motivated "below their level of conscious awareness." People are also *stimulated* below their level of conscious awareness; that is, they can perceive stimuli without being consciously aware of the stimuli in

FIGURE 6-1   Sequential Changes in Packaging That Fall Below the J.N.D.

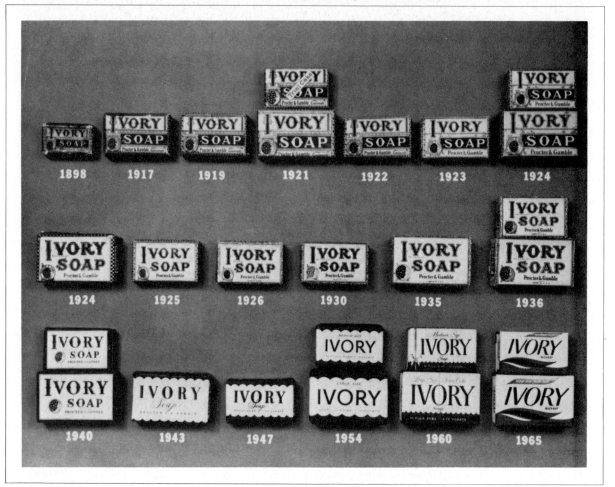

question. The threshold for conscious awareness or conscious recognition appears to be higher than the absolute threshold for effective perception. Thus stimuli that are too weak or too brief to be consciously seen or heard may nevertheless be strong enough to be perceived by one or more receptor cells. This process is called "subliminal perception" because the stimulus is *beneath* the threshold, or "limen," of awareness, though obviously not beneath the absolute thresholds of the receptors involved. (Perception of stimuli that are *above* the level of conscious awareness is called "supraliminal perception.")

Subliminal perception created a great furor in the 1950s when it was reported that advertisers could expose consumers to subliminal advertising messages that they were not aware of receiving. Researchers thought these messages could persuade people to buy goods or act in ways that would benefit the advertiser without being aware of why they did so. The effectiveness of such subliminal advertising was reportedly tested in a drive-in movie in New Jersey, where popcorn and Coca-Cola ads were flashed on the screen during the showing of the movie so rapidly that viewers were not consciously aware of having seen them. It was reported that during the six-week test period, popcorn sales increased 58 percent and Coca-Cola sales increased 18 percent.[8] However, since no scientific controls were used in the so-called experiment, the results have been called into question. Furthermore, no one has been able to replicate the results with consumers.

One researcher who conducted several experiments designed to test the effectiveness of subliminal stimulation did find that while the simple subliminal stimulus COKE served to arouse thirst in subjects, the subliminal command to DRINK COKE did not have any greater effect nor did it have any behavioral consequences.[9] In another experiment, he found that subliminal stimuli associating a brand name with a sexy girl did not significantly affect recall or choice of the product by either sex.[10]

Although researchers have been unable to demonstrate that subliminal messages have any effect on consumer behavior, they have recently shown that subliminal messages can have some interesting psychological effects. It has been demonstrated, for example, that the degree of depression that a "depressive" individual experiences can be increased by exposure to subliminal messages. Similarly, such exposure can increase pathological behavior in schizophrenics and homosexual feelings in homosexuals.[11] One advertising researcher has concluded from these experiments that the reason a subliminal perceptual effect has not been demonstrated in a marketing context is that subliminal stimuli have not been directed at individuals who might be particularly susceptible to them. For example, the message "Choose Revlon" might influence people who are especially motivated by social needs, but it would have little effect on the balance of viewers.[12]

One experiment that lends support to this theory was conducted by a behavioral scientist in six large department stores. By playing a subliminal message ("I am honest; I won't steal; stealing is dishonest") just below the perceptible level on the Muzak sound track, he was reportedly able to produce a 37.5 percent decline in shoplifting in a nine-month period.[13]

Interest in the whole topic of subliminal perception has been reawakened by the charge that even though subliminal messages may not work, *subliminal embeds* may have the desired effect. Embeds are still pictures, not word messages, planted in print ads. One critic of the technique alleges, for example, that liquor advertisers have sought to increase the subconscious appeal of their products by embedding sexually suggestive symbols in ice cubes floating in a pictured drink.[14] A researcher who tested the effectiveness of embeds found no significant influence on brand recall.[15] He admitted, however, that recall—which relies on subjects verbally recollecting a visual experience—may be an invalid measure of whether an ad has had an impact. Advertisements may do their job by merely evoking recognition—the intuitive "oh, yes" that people experience on seeing a brand after being exposed to it in an ad.[16]

Because of the questions raised by recent research, it is impossible to close the book entirely on the effectiveness of subliminal stimuli on consumer behavior. A need for further research in this area is strongly indicated.

The preceding section explained how the individual receives sensations from stimuli in the outside environment, and how the human organism adapts to the level and intensity of sensory input. We now come to one of the major principles of perception: Raw sensory input by itself does not produce or explain the coherent picture of the world that most adults possess.

The human being is constantly being bombarded with stimuli during every minute and every hour of every day. The sensory world is made up of an almost infinite number of discrete sensations, which are constantly, though perhaps minutely, changing. According to the principles of sensation, such heavy intensity of stimuli should serve to "turn off" most individuals, as the body protects itself from the heavy bombardment to which it is subjected. Otherwise the billions of different stimuli to which we are constantly exposed might serve to totally confuse us and keep us perpetually disoriented in a constantly changing environment. However, neither of these alternatives tends to occur, because perception is not a function of sensory input alone; rather, it is the result of two different kinds of inputs which interact to form the personal pictures, the perceptions, that each individual experiences.

One type of input is physical stimuli from the outside environment; the other type of input is provided by individuals themselves in the form of certain predispositions, such as expectations, motives, and learning based on previous experience. The combination of these two very different kinds of inputs produces for each of us a very private, very personal picture of the world. Because each individual is a unique entity, with unique experiences, wants, needs, wishes, and expectations, it follows that each individual's perceptions are also unique. This explains why no two people see the world in precisely the same way.

Individuals are very selective in terms of which stimuli they "recognize"; they organize the stimuli they do recognize according to some widely held subconscious principles; and they give meaning to such stimuli (i.e., they interpret them) very subjectively in accordance with their own needs, expectations, and experiences. Let us examine in more detail each of these three aspects of perception: selection, organization, and interpretation of stimuli.

Perceptual Selection

Consumers subconsciously exercise a great deal of selectivity regarding what aspects of the environment—what stimuli—they will perceive. An individual may look at some things, ignore others, and turn away from still others. In total, people actually receive—or perceive—only a small fraction of the stimuli to which they are exposed. Consider, for example, a woman in a supermarket. She is exposed to literally thousands of products of different colors, sizes, and shapes; to perhaps a hundred people (looking, walking, searching, talking); to smells (from fruit, from meat, from disinfectant, from people); to sounds within the store (cash registers ringing, shopping carts rolling, air conditioners humming, and clerks sweeping, mopping aisles, stocking shelves); and to sounds from outside the store (planes passing, cars honking, tires screeching, children shouting, car doors slamming). Yet she manages on a regular basis to visit her local supermarket, select the items she needs, pay for them, and leave, all within a relatively brief time, without losing her sanity or her personal orientation to the world around her. This is because she exercises selectivity in perception. Which stimuli get selected depends on two major factors in addition to the nature of the stimulus itself: the consumer's previous experience as it affects her expectations (what she is prepared or "set" to see) and her motives at the time (her needs, desires, interests, and so on). Each of these factors can serve to increase or decrease the probability that the stimulus will be perceived, and each can affect the consumer's selective exposure to and selective awareness of the stimulus itself.

NATURE OF THE STIMULUS

Marketing stimuli include an enormous number of variables, all of which affect the consumer's perception, such as the nature of the product, its physical attributes, the package design, the brand name, the advertisements and commercials (including copy claims, choice and sex of model, positioning of model, size of ad, and typography), the position of the ad or time of the commercial, and the editorial environment.

In general, contrast is one of the most attention-compelling attributes of a stimulus.[17] Advertisers often use extreme attention-getting devices to achieve maximum contrast and thus penetrate the consumer's perceptual screen. The chairman of the board of a major advertising agency once complained that his competitors were using "exotic locales, bizarre plots and overstated characterizations to a degree that is reducing the airwaves to an absolute babble."[18] Actually, advertising does not have to be "way out" to achieve a high degree of differentiation; it simply has to contrast with the environment in which it is run. The use of lots of white space in a newspaper advertisement, the absence of sound in a commercial's opening scene, a sixty-second commercial among a string of twenty-second spots—all of these offer sufficient contrast from their environment to achieve differentiation and merit the consumer's attention.

An opposite tack, but one that has been used effectively in TV commercials, is to make the commercial seem so close to the story line of a program that viewers are unaware that they are watching an ad until they are well into it. During the television coverage of the marriage of Prince Charles to Lady Diana, for example, a commercial filmed in a great English mansion, complete with liveried footmen, led the unsuspecting viewer into a sales pitch for the "Royal" line of photocopiers. In the case of children's programming, the Federal Trade Commission has severely limited the use of this technique. TV stars or cartoon characters are prohibited from promoting products during children's shows in which they appear.

With respect to packaging, astute marketers usually try to differentiate their packaging sufficiently to ensure rapid consumer perception. Since the average package on the supermarket shelf has about one-tenth of a second to make an impression on the consumer, it is important that every aspect of the package—its name, shape, color, label, and copy—provide sufficient sensory stimulation to be noted and remembered. A survey designed to test whether consumers could recognize a number of well-known packages with their brand names concealed found that many packages do not achieve the recognition their marketers assume.[19] Figure 6-2 shows the packages tested in the study; Table 6-1 lists the recognition scores received. The packages with low recognition scores obviously do not provide sufficient sensory input to the consumer to be readily perceived and remembered.

EXPECTATIONS

People usually see what they expect to see, and what they expect to see is usually based on familiarity, on previous experience, or on preconditioned "set." A number of interesting experiments have supported this notion. For example,

TABLE 6-1   Recognition Scores of Well-Known Packaged Goods

PRODUCT	RECOGNITION
rice	
Minute Rice	62%
River	—
Carolina	63%
Uncle Ben's	72%
bathroom tissue	
Waldorf (top row)	20%
Charmin (top row)	97%
Hudson (top row)	20%
Lady Scott (bottom row)	42%
Soft-Weve (bottom row)	—
freeze-dried coffee	
Brown Gold	11%
Taster's Choice	92%
Maxim	51%
Martinson's	9%
Yuban	72%
liquid cleaners	
Top Job	29%
Lysol	18%
Mr. Clean	68%
Lestoil	30%
Janitor in a Drum	87%
liquid dishwashers	
Palmolive	52%
Joy	51%
Dove	50%
Ivory	39%
Ajax	—
Lux	31%
salad oils	
Kraft	—
Mazola	63%
Wesson	55%
Crisco	64%

Source: Reprinted with permission from the August 21, 1972 issue of Advertising Age. Copyright 1972 by Crain Communication Inc. Also, courtesy of Lippincott & Margulies, Inc.

FIGURE 6-2   Well-Known Packaged Goods Tested for Recognition

Reprinted with permission from the August 21, 1972 issue of Advertising Age. Copyright 1972 by Crain Communication Inc. Also, courtesy of Lippincott & Margulies, Inc.

one researcher had a "guest speaker" give the same prepared lecture to two different college classes. He preconditioned the students in the first class by telling them in advance of the lecture that the speaker was an expert in his field but "cold" in nature; the second class was told that the speaker was an expert and "warm" in nature. Questionnaires completed after each lecture showed that the students who were "set" to hear a cold lecturer did indeed find him cold; those who anticipated a warm lecturer found him to be warm. Furthermore, there was more interaction and participation in the classroom discussion from those students who expected the lecturer to be warm than from those who expected him to be cold.[20]

In a marketing context, people tend to perceive products and product attributes according to their own expectations. A man who has been told by his friends that a new brand of Scotch has a bitter taste will probably perceive the taste to be bitter; a teenager who attends a horror movie that has been billed as terrifying will probably find it so.

On the other hand, stimuli that conflict sharply with expectations often receive more attention than those that conform to expectations. In other words, novelty tends to promote perception. An advertisement for bathing suits by Cole of California showed a lineup of pretty girls on a beach wearing a variety of bathing suit styles. However, the girl on the end wore no suit at all. Research showed that many readers simply glanced at the advertisement and started to turn the page but then did a double take when they realized what they had seen and turned back to look at the ad more closely. Thus the ad ended up receiving much more attention than it otherwise would have, simply because of the inclusion of an element that surprised readers.

Advertisers of sheets and blankets have discovered that showing a male model in bed instead of the traditional female model improves readership. After running a series of ads for its sheets which featured a male model, J.P. Stevens reported receiving a number of approving letters from consumers, one of which said: "For ten years as a housewife, I have never noticed an ad for sheets that particularly caught my attention—until this one."[21]

For years certain advertisers have used blatant sexuality in advertisements for products to which sex was not relevant because they knew such advertisements attracted a high degree of attention; however, such ads often defeated their own purpose because readers tended to remember the sex (e.g., the girl), but not the product or brand.[22] Still, advertisers continue to use sex appeal in ads. Because it has become so commonplace, critics contend that advertisers have had to increase the shock value of their presentations to achieve any impact. Some consumer resistance has developed. For example, in some cities, consumers forced the cancellation of television commercials for jeans that featured very young models in sexually suggestive poses.

MOTIVES

People tend to perceive things they need or want; the stronger the need, the greater the tendency to ignore unrelated stimuli in the environment. A man who wants to replace his lawnmower will carefully note every advertisement for lawnmowers in his local newspaper; one who has no need of a new lawnmower will rarely notice such advertisements. In general, there is a heightened awareness of stimuli that are relevant to one's needs and interests, and a decreased awareness of stimuli that are irrelevant to those needs.

An individual's perceptual process simply attunes itself more closely to those elements of the environment that are important to that person. Someone who is hungry looks for, and more readily perceives, restaurant signs; a sexually repressed person perceives sexual symbolism where none may exist.

Marketing managers recognize the efficiency of targeting their products to the perceived needs of consumers. In this way, they help to ensure that their products will be perceived by potential prospects. The identification of perceived consumer needs has a number of different applications. For example, marketers can determine through marketing research what consumers consider to be the ideal attributes of the product category, or what consumers perceive their needs to be in relation to the product category. The marketer can then segment the market on the basis of these needs into a number of smaller market segments, each composed of individuals with similar perceived needs in connection with the product category. The marketer is now able to develop different marketing strategies for each segment which stress how the product can fulfill the perceived needs of that segment. In this way, the marketer can vary the product advertising to specific market segments so that consumers in each segment will perceive the product as meeting their own specific needs, wants, and interests.

RELATED CONCEPTS

As the preceding discussion illustrates, the consumer's "selection" of stimuli from the environment is based on the interaction of expectations and motives with the stimulus itself. These factors give rise to a number of important concepts concerning perception.

SELECTIVE EXPOSURE.   Consumers actively seek out messages that are pleasant or with which they are sympathetic, and they actively avoid painful or threatening ones. Thus heavy smokers avoid articles that link cigarette smoking to cancer and note (and quote) the relatively few that deny the relationship. Consumers also selectively expose themselves to advertisements that reassure them of the wisdom of their purchase decisions.

SELECTIVE ATTENTION.   Consumers have a heightened awareness of stimuli that meet their needs or their interests and a depressed awareness of stimuli irrelevant to their needs. Thus they are likely to note ads for products that meet their needs or for stores with which they are familiar and disregard those in which they have no interest.[23] While estimates of the number of advertisements the average consumer is exposed to each day vary widely (from about three hundred to fifteen hundred exposures per day), daily exposure to magazines, newspapers, television, radio, billboards, direct mail, transit advertising, and the like, is undoubtedly far above the five hundred mark.[24] *Exposure*, however, is not equivalent to *perception*.

People also vary in the kind of information in which they are interested and in the form of message and type of medium they prefer. Some people are more interested in price, some in appearance, and some in social acceptability.[25] Some people like complex, sophisticated messages; others like simple graphics. Consumers, therefore, exercise a great deal of selectivity in terms of the attention they give to commercial stimuli.

PERCEPTUAL DEFENSE. Consumers subconsciously screen out stimuli that for them are important *not* to see, even though exposure has already taken place. Thus, threatening or otherwise damaging stimuli are less likely to achieve awareness than neutral stimuli at the same level of exposure.[26] Furthermore, individuals may distort information that is not consistent with their needs, values, and beliefs.[27] For example, a consumer may "hear" that a set of dishes she loves is dishwasher safe (even though the salesclerk has clearly warned her it is not), because the dishes match her dining-room rug so perfectly. This is another example of people hearing what they want to hear rather than what has actually been said.

PERCEPTUAL BLOCKING. Consumers protect themselves from bombardment of stimuli by simply "tuning out"—blocking such stimuli from achieving conscious awareness. For example, tests have shown that enormous amounts of advertising are being screened out by consumers, though there are suggestions that this problem may be more severe for television than for print.[28] Various hypotheses have been offered to explain why television advertising-recall scores are falling, such as the greater amount of time allotted for commercials, the use of shorter commercials (and thus the increased number of advertising messages aired within the same period of time), the larger number of commercials that are strung together back-to-back, the larger number of advertisers, and the larger number of products being advertised.

In addition to the sheer number of television ads, they may be less well remembered because consumers tend to view the medium as less informative and truthful than print media.[29]

Perceptual Organization

People do not experience the numerous stimuli that they select from the environment as separate and discrete sensations; rather, they tend to organize them into groups and perceive them as unified wholes. Thus the perceived characteristics of even the simplest stimulus are viewed as a function of the whole to which the stimulus appears to belong. This method of organization simplifies life considerably for the individual.

The specific principles underlying perceptual organization are often referred to by the name given the school of psychologists who first developed and stressed "Gestalt" psychology. (*Gestalt* in German means "pattern" or "configuration.") Three of the most basic principles of organization center on figure and ground relationships, grouping, and closure.

FIGURE AND GROUND

We noted earlier that to be noticed, stimuli must contrast with their environment. A sound must be louder or softer, a color brighter or paler. The simplest visual illustration consists of a figure on a ground (i.e., background). The figure is usually perceived clearly because, in contrast to its ground, it appears to be well defined, solid, and in the forefront. The ground, however, is usually perceived as indefinite, hazy, and continuous. The common line that separates the figure and the ground is perceived as belonging to the figure rather than to the ground, which helps give the figure greater definition. Consider the stimulus of music. People can either "bathe" in music or listen to music. In the first case, music is simply ground to other activities; in the second, it is figure. Figure is more clearly perceived because it appears to be dominant; by contrast, ground appears to be subordinate and therefore unimportant.

People have a tendency to organize their perceptions into figure and ground relationships. However, learning affects which stimuli will be perceived as figure and which as ground. We are all familiar with reversible figure-ground patterns, such as the picture of the woman in Figure 6-3. How old would you say she was? Look again, very carefully. Depending on how you perceived figure and how you perceived ground, she can be either in her early twenties or her late seventies.

FIGURE 6-3   Figure-Ground Reversal

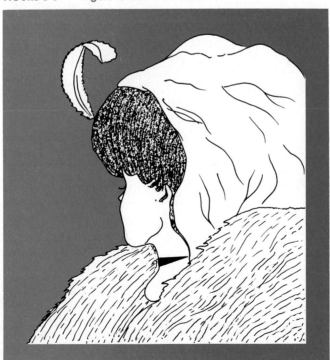

Like perceptual selection, perceptual organization is affected by motives and by expectations based on experience. For example, how a reversible figure-ground pattern will be seen can be influenced by prior pleasant or painful associations with one or the other element in isolation.

The consumer's own physical state can also affect how he or she perceives reversible figure-ground illustrations. For example, after a particularly strenuous week, the thirty-five-year-old secretary of one of the authors happened to note with surprise the picture of the old woman shown in Figure 6-3. It took a great deal of concentrated effort for her to recognize it as the reversal of the picture of the smartly dressed young woman that she had been used to seeing on the author's desk.

Advertisers have to plan their advertisements carefully to make sure that the stimulus they want noted is seen as figure and not as ground. The musical background must not overwhelm the jingle; the background of an advertisement must not detract from the product. Some print advertisers often silhouette their products against a white background to make sure that the features they want noted are clearly perceived. Others use reverse lettering (white letters on a black background) to achieve contrast; however, they must be careful to avoid the problem of figure-ground reversal.

Marketers sometimes make the mistake of running advertisements that confuse the consumer because there is no clear indication of which is figure and which is ground. A steel company that produces the steel for a variety of products, including bedsprings, once ran an ad that showed a sexy-looking girl bouncing up and down on a bed. Many critics wondered aloud just what it was the sponsor was selling—i.e., which was figure and which was ground.

We also tend to structure the social environment into figure and ground, much as we do the impersonal environment. We see the world clearly as "us" and "them," as "good guys" and "bad guys," as friends and enemies. Politicians and reporters have often structured the world into the "free world" and the "Communist world," ignoring many of the other differences between nations and governments and people.[30]

GROUPING

Individuals tend to group stimuli automatically so that they form a unified picture or impression. Experiments have shown that the perception of stimuli as groups or "chunks" of information, rather than as discrete bits of information, facilitates their memory and recall.[31] For example, most of us can remember and repeat our social security numbers because we automatically group them into three chunks rather than nine separate numbers. When the telephone company introduced the idea of all-digit telephone numbers, consumers objected strenuously on the grounds that they would not be able to recall or repeat so many numbers. However, because we automatically group telephone numbers into just two chunks (or three, with the area code), the problems that were anticipated never occurred. The same objection was raised to the notion of adding four more digits to the ZIP code, and the same experience will no doubt prevail.

Grouping can be used advantageously by marketers to imply certain desired meanings in connection with their products. For example, an advertisement for tea may show a young man and woman sipping tea in a well-furnished room before a blazing hearth. The grouping of stimuli by proximity leads the consumer to associate the drinking of tea with romance, fine living, and winter warmth.

CLOSURE

Individuals have a need for closure. They express this need by organizing their perceptions so that they form a complete picture. If the pattern of stimuli to which they are exposed is incomplete, they tend to perceive it, nevertheless, as complete; that is, they consciously or subconsciously fill in the missing pieces. Thus a circle that has a section of its periphery missing will nevertheless usually be perceived as whole. The need for closure is also seen in the tension that an individual experiences when a task is incomplete, and the satisfaction and relief that come upon its completion. A classic study reported in 1972 found that incomplete tasks are better remembered than complete tasks.[32] One explanation for this phenomenon is that the person who begins a task develops a need to complete it. If he or she is prevented from doing so, a state of tension is created which manifests itself in improved memory for the uncompleted task. One researcher extended this theory to advertising messages and suggested that hearing the beginning of a message leads to the development of a need to hear the rest of it—"rather like waiting for the second shoe to drop."[33] The resulting tension leads to improvement in memory for that part of the message that has already been heard.

The need for closure has some interesting implications for marketers. The presentation of an incomplete advertising message "begs" for completion by consumers, and the very act of completion serves to involve them more deeply in the message itself. Thus an incomplete ad tends to be perceived more readily than a complete one. Clever marketers have tried to exploit this phenomenon by constructing commercials that are deliberately "interrupted" before their expected finish. For example, Salem cigarettes very successfully ran a commercial that featured a catchy musical jingle that went: "You can take Salem out of the country, *but,* you can't take the country out of Salem." After repeating the jingle a number of times, the commercial ceased abruptly on a high note after the "*but.*" Due to their needs for closure, for completion, listeners invariably completed the jingle themselves, either aloud or silently: ". . . you can't take the country out of Salem." Such close involvement with the commercial served to increase its overall impact on the consumer.

In a related vein, advertisers have discovered that they can use the soundtrack of a frequently shown television commercial on radio with excellent results. Consumers who are familiar with the TV commercial perceive the audio part alone as incomplete; in their need for completion, they mentally play back the visual content as well.

In summary, it is clear that perceptions are not equivalent to the raw sensory input of discrete stimuli or the sum total of discrete stimuli. Rather, people tend to add to or subtract from the stimuli to which they are exposed according to their own expectations and motives, using generalized principles of organization based on Gestalt theory.

Perceptual Interpretation

The preceding discussion has emphasized that perception is a personal phenomenon. People exercise selectivity in terms of which stimuli they perceive, and they organize these stimuli on the basis of certain psychological principles. The interpretation of stimuli is also uniquely individual, since it is based upon what individuals expect to see in light of their previous experience, on the number of plausible explanations they can envision, and on their motives and interests at the time of perception.

Stimuli are often highly ambiguous. Some stimuli are weak because of such factors as poor visibility, brief exposure, high noise level, and constant fluctuation. Even stimuli that are strong tend to fluctuate dramatically because of such factors as different angles of viewing, varying distances, and changing levels of illumination.

The consumer usually attributes the sensory input received to sources that he or she considers most likely to have caused the specific pattern of stimuli. Past experience and social interaction with other people may help to form certain expectations which provide categories or alternatives that the individual can use in interpreting stimuli.[34] The narrower the individual's experience, the more limited is the access to alternative categories.

When stimuli are highly ambiguous, an individual will usually interpret them in such a way that they serve to fulfill his or her own needs, wishes, interests, and so on. It is this principle that provides the rationale for the projective tests discussed in Chapter 3. Such tests provide ambiguous stimuli (such as incomplete sentences, unclear pictures, untitled cartoons, and inkblots) to respondents who are asked to interpret them. How a person describes a vague illustration, what meaning that individual ascribes to an inkblot, is a reflection not of the stimulus itself, but of his or her own needs, wants, and desires. Thus, through the interpretation of ambiguous stimuli, respondents reveal a great deal about themselves.

How close a person's interpretations are to reality, then, depends on the clarity of the stimulus, the past experiences of the perceiver, and his or her motives and interests at the time of perception.

DISTORTING INFLUENCES ON PERCEPTION

The individual is also subject to a number of influences that tend to distort perception, some of which are discussed below.

PHYSICAL APPEARANCES.   People tend to attribute the qualities they associate with certain people to others who may resemble them, whether or not they consciously recognize the similarity. For this reason, the selection of models for advertisements and for television commercials can be a key element in their ultimate persuasibility. For example, baking advice given by a woman who looks like somebody's kindly old grandmother is likely to be perceived as very helpful.

STEREOTYPES. Individuals tend to carry "pictures in their minds" of the meaning of various kinds of stimuli. These stereotypes serve as expectations of what specific situations or people or events will be like and are important determinants of how such stimuli are subsequently perceived. For example, an ad headlined "First Date" which shows a young man ringing a front doorbell will set up a whole chain of expectations and interpretations based on stereotypical movies, TV shows, and books.

HALO EFFECT. A generalized impression that may be favorable or unfavorable is extended to the interpretation of nonrelevant stimuli. This effect tends to be more pronounced when the perceiver is interpreting stimuli with which he or she has had little experience. Marketers take advantage of the halo effect when they extend a brand name associated with one line of products to another. Bic, playing on the reputation it had gained in marketing inexpensive, reliable, disposable pens under the Bic name, put out a line of disposable razors under the same Bic name, with a great deal of success.

RESPECTED SOURCES. We tend to give added perceptual weight to advice coming from sources we respect. Marketers often use celebrities or known experts to give testimonials for their products or to act as company spokespersons to ensure that their products will be well perceived.

IRRELEVANT CUES. When required to form a difficult perceptual judgment, consumers often respond to irrelevant stimuli. For example, many high-priced automobiles are sold on the basis of color, a luxury option like retractable headlights or type of upholstery, rather than on the basis of mechanical or technical superiority.

FIRST IMPRESSIONS. First impressions tend to be lasting, yet in forming such impressions the perceiver does not yet know which stimuli are relevant, important, or predictive of later behavior. For this reason, introducing a new product before it has been perfected may prove fatal to the product because subsequent information about its superiority, though true, will often be negated by memory of its early failure.

JUMPING TO CONCLUSIONS. Many people tend to jump to conclusions before examining all the relevant evidence. For example, the consumer may perceive just the beginning of a commercial message and draw conclusions regarding the product or service being advertised on the basis of such limited information. For this reason, copywriters should be careful not to save their most persuasive arguments for last.

The reader may well ask how "realistic" perception can be, given the many subjective influences on perceptual interpretations. It is therefore somewhat reassuring to remember that previous experiences usually serve to resolve stimulus ambiguity in a realistic way and help in its interpretation. It is only in situations of unusual or changing stimuli conditions that expectations may lead to wrong interpretations.

Consumers have a number of enduring perceptions, or images, which are particularly relevant to the study of consumer behavior. These include the image they hold of themselves and their perceived image of products and product categories, of retail stores, and of producers.

Self-Image

Each individual has a perceived image of himself or herself as a certain kind of person, with certain traits, habits, possessions, relationships, and ways of behaving. As with other types of perceptions, the individual's self-image is unique, a product of that person's own background and experience. The individual develops a perceived self-image through interactions with other people: parents to begin with, then other individuals or groups with whom he or she relates over the years.

Products and other objects have symbolic value for individuals, who evaluate them on the basis of their consistency (i.e., congruence) with their personal pictures of themselves. Some products seem to agree with the individual's self-image; others seem totally alien. Consumers attempt to preserve or enhance their self-image by buying products that they believe are congruent with that self-image and avoiding products that are not. These strategies have been the subject of a number of consumer studies.[35]

Research indicates that consumers tend to shop in stores that have an image consistent with their own self-image. Thus, in New York, upper-class shoppers have said they prefer Bloomingdale's because of its "modern, sophisticated, extravagant" aura.[36]

Several researchers have explored the notion that individuals' *ideal self-concept* (that is, how they would like to perceive themselves) is more relevant to consumption behavior than *actual self-concept* (how they do in fact perceive themselves).[37] There is no evidence as yet that this distinction is relevant to product choice.[38] However, researchers have distinguished an intermediate concept, *expected self-concept* (how individuals expect to see themselves at some specified future time). They have concluded that as self-concept changes from actual self-image to some future or expected self-image, product preferences also change, and that expected self-concept may be more valuable than ideal self-concept as a guide for designing and promoting products.[39]

The concept of self-image has strategy implications for marketers. For example, marketers can segment their markets on the basis of relevant consumer self-images and position their products or stores as symbols of such self-images. Such a marketing strategy is in complete agreement with the classical marketing concept, in that the marketer first determines the needs of a consumer (both in respect to the product segment category and in respect to an appropriate symbol of self-image) and then proceeds to develop and market a product that will meet both criteria.

Product Image

The way the product is perceived is probably more important to its ultimate marketing success than are its actual product characteristics. For example, taste tests reveal that most beer drinkers cannot discriminate between beer tastes, but many brand-loyal beer drinkers insist that their brand of beer has a superior taste.[40] In such cases, it is clear that the *image* of the product prevails, since taste tests do not support any other conclusion.

PRODUCT POSITIONING

Marketers try to "position" their brands so that they are perceived by specific market segments as fulfilling certain needs or possessing certain attributes. The product's positioning is especially important in relation to other brands in the same product category. For example, a toothpaste manufacturer may position its product as a mouth deodorant because research has revealed that this niche is not being occupied by competing brands. In effect, the manufacturer seeks to carve out a market segment of toothpaste users who are more interested in the mouthwash characteristics of toothpaste than they are, for example, in decay prevention, teeth whiteners, or sex appeal.

The technique of perceptual mapping helps marketers to determine just how their products appear to consumers in relation to competitive brands on one or more product characteristics. It enables them to see gaps in the positioning of all brands in the product class, and to identify areas in which consumer needs are not being adequately met. The manufacturer of luxury car *A* (see Figure 6-4) may discover that consumers now perceive its car to be very

FIGURE 6-4   A Consumers' Perceptual Map of Automobile Characteristics Facilitates Product Positioning

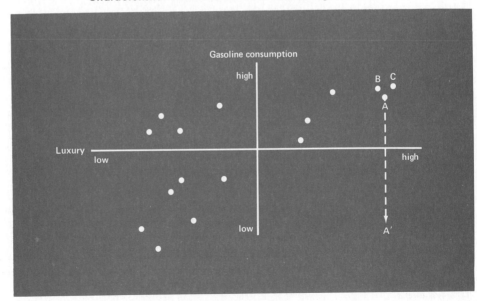

similar to luxury cars *B* and *C;* at the same time, it may note that consumers do not perceive any luxury car to have good gas mileage. To carve out a new market segment consisting of luxury owners who are interested in low gas consumption, the manufacturer may decide to reposition the car's image from point *A* to point *A'* (i.e., as a low-gas-consumption luxury car). This could be accomplished through a promotional campaign directed to the luxury car market which stresses both luxury and good gas mileage. Of course, such a campaign could not succeed unless the car actually does have low gas consumption.

UNFAVORABLE PRODUCT IMAGES

Sometimes product categories develop unfavorable images that inhibit their success in the marketplace. These images may result from early unfavorable trial of a product, or simply from human resistance to change. Unfortunately, many unfavorable product images tend to persist. For this reason, marketers should resist the temptation of introducing a new product prematurely; that is, before it has been totally perfected. (Remember, first impressions tend to be lasting.)

Sometimes unfavorable product images may be totally unwarranted. For example, some people claim that decaffeinated coffee is inferior in taste to regular coffee. In blind taste tests, however, consumers have not been able to differentiate between the two.[41]

EVOKED SET

The specific brands that a consumer will consider in making a purchase choice in a particular product category are known as the "evoked set." A consumer's evoked set is distinguished from his or her *inept set,* consisting of brands that the consumer excludes from purchase consideration, and the *inert set,* consisting of brands that the consumer is indifferent toward because they are not perceived as having any particular advantages.[42] Regardless of the total number of brands in a product category, a consumer's evoked set tends to be quite small. A study concerning such large product categories as toothpaste and laundry detergent revealed an average evoked set of only three brands and five brands, respectively.[43] This is not surprising, since research indicates that most people have a span of recall limited to approximately seven items.[44]

Among those brands with which the consumer is familiar, there are acceptable brands, unacceptable brands, and overlooked (or forgotten) brands. The evoked set consists of the small number of brands that the consumer is familiar with, remembers, and finds acceptable. Figure 6-5 presents a simple model of the evoked set as a subset of all available brands in a product category. As the figure indicates, it is essential that a product be part of a consumer's evoked set if it is to be considered at all. The four terminal positions in the model which do *not* end in purchase (labeled 1, 2, 3, and 4) would appear to have perceptual problems. For example: (1) Brands may be *unknown* because of consumers' selective exposure to advertising media and their selective perception of advertising stimuli. (2) Brands may be *unacceptable* because of poor or inappropriate positioning in either advertising or product characteristics, or both. (3) Brands may be *overlooked* because they have not been clearly positioned

FIGURE 6-5 The Evoked Set as a Subset of All Brands in a Product Class

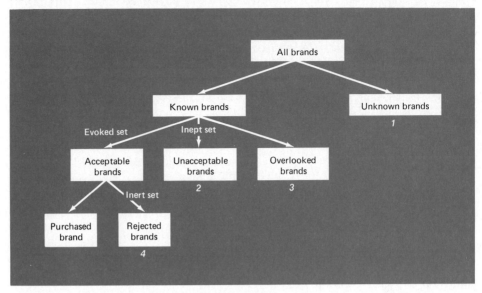

or sharply targeted at the consumer market segment under study. (4) Brands may be *rejected* because they are perceived by consumers as unable to satisfy their perceived needs as completely as the brand they select.

In each of these instances, the implication for marketers is that promotional techniques should be designed to impart a more favorable, perhaps more relevant, product image to the target consumer. This may sometimes require a change in product attributes as well.

PERCEIVED QUALITY

Consumers often judge the quality of a product on the basis of a variety of informational cues which they associate with the product. Some of these cues are intrinsic to (inherent in) the product, such as specific product characteristics; others are extrinsic to (external to) the product, such as price, store image, brand image, and promotional message.[45] Either singly or in composite, such cues provide the basis for perceptions concerning product quality.

INTRINSIC CUES.   Cues that are intrinsic concern physical characteristics of the product itself, such as size, color, flavor, or aroma. In some cases, consumers use physical characteristics to judge product quality. For example, research has found that consumers judge the flavor of ice cream, the mildness of dishwashing detergent, and the quality of shirts by color cues.[46]

Consumers like to believe that they base their product quality evaluations on intrinsic cues, because they can justify resulting product decisions (either positive or negative) on the basis of "rational" or "objective" product choice. More often than not, however, the physical characteristic they select to judge quality has no intrinsic relation to the product's quality. Thus, though many consumers claim they buy a brand because of its superior taste, they are often unable to identify that brand in blind taste tests.

In one study, Budweiser-loyal beer drinkers were asked to sample two beers: first Budweiser, and then a second brand of beer which they had professed to dislike. The subjects could not bring themselves to finish the second beer because of its "skunky" and "terrible" taste. In actuality, both samples of beer were Budweiser. In this situation, perception of taste was clearly based on the product images, not on actual taste differences.[47] In another study, housewives were asked to evaluate the tastes of two different beverages successively, which were identified as Coke and Diet Coke.[48] The housewives were enthusiastic about the Coke but complained about the bitter aftertaste of Diet Coke. Both samples, however, actually contained the same beverage—regular Coke. Because some of the early diet beverages did have a bitter aftertaste, many consumers simply attributed that characteristic to all diet sodas and thus "tasted" (perceived) what they expected to taste. Other consumers may not have wished to identify with a product designed for overweight people because of its lack of congruence with their own self-images.

EXTRINSIC CUES. In the absence of actual experience with a product, consumers often "evaluate" quality on the basis of factors quite external to the product itself, such as its price, the image of the store(s) that carries it, or the image (that is, the reputation) of the manufacturer who produces it.

1. PRICE-QUALITY RELATIONSHIP. A number of research studies support the view that consumers rely on price as an indicator of product quality. Several studies have shown that consumers attribute differential qualities to identical products that carry different price labels. For example, one study reported that subjects ranked the quality of three samples of unlabeled beer in a direct relationship to the prices they carried: The high-priced beer was ranked first in quality, the medium-priced beer second, and the low-priced beer as lowest in quality, despite the fact that all three beer samples were actually the same brand.[49] Another study found that housewives rated high-priced panty hose as better in quality than medium-priced or low-priced panty hose, even though the three samples were of identical quality.[50]

How closely are price and quality actually related across product lines? One researcher found such a relationship for only 51 percent of the products he analyzed. For 14 percent of the products, the higher prices were actually associated with poorer-quality products. Some of the items that showed no relation between price and quality are listed in Table 6-2.[51]

If price and quality are so tenuously related, why do consumers continue to use price as a guide to product selection? The answer seems to be that they use price as a surrogate indicator if they have little other information to go by, or if they have little confidence in their own ability to make the choice on other grounds. When brand names are known, or experience with a product is great, price declines as a factor in product selection.[52]

When these conditions do not hold (as, for example, when a new product is introduced), marketers can take advantage of the assumed price-quality relationship. Some marketers have successfully used the price-quality relationship to

TABLE 6-2   Items Showing No Relation of Price to Quality

PRODUCT	MEAN PRICE OF TOP QUARTER IN QUALITY	MEAN PRICE OF BOTTOM QUARTER IN QUALITY
Sweepers	$ 16	$ 17
Blenders	28	41
Electric hairdryers	21	23
Loudspeakers	62	67
8-track tape decks	51	71
Slow cookers	11	20
19″ black-and-white TVs	149	163
Microwave ovens	352	406
Chain saws	145	159
Electric blankets	20	29

Source: Selected from tables compiled by George B. Sproles, "New Evidence on Price and Product Quality," *Journal of Consumer Affairs*, Summer 1977, 69–73.

position their products as the top quality offering in their product category. For example, Chock Full O'Nuts coffee was introduced as a high-priced coffee that was "worth the difference" in cost because of its allegedly "superior" flavor and taste.

2. STORE IMAGE.   Retail stores have images of their own, which serve to influence the perceived quality of products they carry as well as the decisions of consumers as to where to shop. For example, retail stores may have a high-fashion image, a low-price image, a wide-selection image, or a good-service image. The type of product the consumer wishes to buy will influence his or her selection of retail outlet; conversely, the consumer's evaluation of a product will be influenced by the knowledge of where it was bought. A consumer wishing to buy an elegant dress for a special occasion may go to a store with an elegant, high-fashion image, such as Bergdorf Goodman in New York. Regardless of what she actually pays for the dress she selects (regular price or marked-down price), she will probably perceive its quality to be high. However, she may perceive the quality of the same dress to be much lower if she buys it in a discount store with a low-price image.

Most studies of the effects of extrinsic cues on perceived product quality have focused on just one variable—price or store image. However, where a second extrinsic cue is available, it is likely that perceived quality will be a function of the interaction of both cues on the consumer. To test this hypothesis, four identical samples of carpet—cut from the same bolt—were given to female subjects, who were asked to rate their quality on a scale ranging from very low to very high.[53] Each carpet sample was labeled with a price and the name of a store, as follows: (1) high-image store, high price; (2) high-image store, low price; (3) low-image store, high price; and (4) low-image store, low price. The researchers discovered that the samples with the high price were perceived to be of significantly better quality than the samples with the low price; similarly, the samples from the prestige store had a somewhat better perceived image than the samples from the low-prestige store. In addition, the researchers found that the interactive effects of both price and store image significantly altered the subjects' perceptions of product quality from the perceptions achieved by either cue alone.

3. MANUFACTURER'S IMAGE. Consumer imagery extends beyond perceived price and store image to the producers themselves. Manufacturers who enjoy a favorable image generally find that their new products are accepted more readily than those of manufacturers who have a less-favorable or a "neutral" image. Obviously, consumers have greater confidence that they will not be disappointed in a major name-brand product.

Advertising has an important role in establishing a favorable brand image. Studies have shown, for example, that advertised brands of both peanut butter and cat food were perceived as higher in quality than nonadvertised brands, and that people expressed a greater willingness to buy the advertised than the unadvertised brands.[54] Buying well-known brands is a consumer purchasing strategy that will be discussed later in the chapter.

PERCEIVED RISK

Consumers must constantly make decisions regarding what products or services to buy and where to buy them. Because the outcomes (or consequences) of such decisions are often uncertain, the consumer faces some degree of "risk" in making a purchase decision. The concept of *perceived risk* has been defined as follows: "Consumer behavior involves risk in the sense that any action of a consumer will produce consequences which he cannot anticipate with anything approximating certainty."[55] This definition highlights two relevant dimensions of perceived risk: *uncertainty* and *consequences*.

The degree of risk that consumers perceive and their own tolerance for risk-taking serve to influence their purchase strategies. It should be stressed that consumers are influenced only by risk that they *perceive,* whether or not such risk actually exists. Risk that is not perceived—no matter how real or how dangerous—will not influence consumer behavior. Furthermore, the amount of money involved in the purchase is not directly related to the amount of risk perceived. Selecting the right mouthwash may present as great a risk to a consumer as selecting a new television set.

Why Consumers Perceive Risk

In making product decisions, consumers perceive risk because they may have had little or no experience with the product or product category they are considering—either because they have never used it or because it is new on the market. Or they may have had an unsatisfactory experience with other brands and are somewhat concerned about making a similar mistake. Their financial resources may be very limited, so that they may recognize that their selection of one product requires them to forgo purchase of another. Finally, they may feel that they have very limited knowledge on which to base a decision or may lack self-confidence in their ability to make the "right" decision.

Types of Risk

The major types of risk that consumers perceive in making product decisions include the following: functional risk, physical risk, financial risk, social risk, and psychological risk.

1. FUNCTIONAL RISK. The risk that the product will not perform as expected. ("Will the dishwasher really clean my dishes *and* my pots?")

2. PHYSICAL RISK. The risk to self and to others which the product may pose. ("Is a microwave oven really safe or does it emit harmful radiation?")

3. FINANCIAL RISK. The risk that the product will not be worth its cost either in time or in money. ("Will graduate school really help me get a better job?")

4. SOCIAL RISK. The risk that a poor product choice may result in embarrassment before others. ("Will that new deodorant really suppress perspiration odor?")

5. PSYCHOLOGICAL RISK. The risk that a poor product choice will bruise the consumer's ego. ("Will I really be happy in this house?")

Table 6-3 lists the specific types of uncertainty that the consumer faces in making product choices. These are categorized by the types of perceived risk listed above.

The Perception of Risk Varies

Studies show that the perception of risk by the consumer varies, depending on the person, the product, the situation, and the culture.

RISK PERCEPTION VARIES BY CONSUMER

The *amount* of risk perceived depends on the consumer. Some consumers tend to perceive high degrees of risk in various consumption situations; others tend to perceive little risk.[56] High-risk perceivers have been described as "narrow categorizers," since they limit their product choices to a few safe alternatives.[57] They would rather exclude some perfectly good alternatives than chance a poor selection. Low-risk perceivers have been described as "broad categorizers," since they tend to make their choices from a much wider range of alternatives.[58] They would rather risk a poor selection than limit the number of alternatives from which they can choose.

The *kind* of risk perceived also depends on the consumer. For example, a study of the acceptance of a new product found that low-risk perceivers reported perceiving only one risk in buying the new product (inconvenience—a functional risk), while high-risk perceivers perceived two major risks (wasting money—a financial risk, and their spouses' disapproval—a social risk).[59] Along

TABLE 6-3   Types of Uncertainty Faced by Consumers Making Product Decisions

TYPE OF RISK	TYPE OF UNCERTAINTY
Functional	1. Will it do what it's supposed to do? 2. Will it last? 3. Will it work as well as or better than competitive products?
Physical	1. Is it safe to use? 2. Does it pose any physical threat to others? 3. Does it pose any danger to the environment?
Financial	1. Is it the best use of my limited funds? 2. Is it worth the money (or time or effort) it costs? 3. Am I paying the best price for it?
Social	1. Will my family and friends approve? 2. Will it please others whose opinions are important to me? 3. Is it similar to products used by groups with whom I identify?
Psychological	1. Will I feel good using it? 2. Will it impress others? 3. Do I deserve it?

these lines, other consumer researchers have suggested that the importance of perceived negative consequences of a specific purchase decision may vary by individual and thus may be a relevant variable upon which to segment markets.[60]

RISK PERCEPTION VARIES BY PRODUCT CATEGORY

An individual's perception of risk varies with product categories. For example, purchasers of headache remedies were found to perceive a higher degree of risk than did purchasers of dry spaghetti.[61] Similarly, consumers were found to perceive a higher degree of risk in the purchase of color television sets than in the purchase of golf clubs.[62]

Some researchers have suggested that it is possible to classify products on the basis of type and intensity of risk. For example, color television sets would be classified as high-risk products because they engender more different types of perceived risk and potentially greater losses than products classified as medium-risk products, such as lawn furniture, or as low-risk products, such as personal stationery.[63]

RISK PERCEPTION VARIES WITH THE SHOPPING SITUATION

Researchers have found that the degree of risk perceived by the consumer is affected by the shopping situation. For example, consumers were found to perceive a higher degree of risk in shopping by telephone than in shopping in person.[64] Similarly, consumers were found to perceive a significantly greater risk in ordering products by mail than in buying the same products in person.[65]

RISK PERCEPTION VARIES BY CULTURE

Not all people around the world exhibit the same level of risk perception. Research shows, for example, that risk is a less important determinant of consumer behavior in Mexico than in the United States.[66] In general, marketers who do business in several countries would be well advised not to generalize the results of consumer behavior studies done in one country to other countries without further research.

How Consumers Handle Risk

Consumers characteristically develop their own unique strategies for reducing perceived risk. These risk-reduction strategies enable them to act with increased confidence in making product decisions, even though the consequences of such decisions are still somewhat uncertain. Some of the more common risk-reduction strategies are listed in Table 6-4 and discussed below.

CONSUMERS SEEK INFORMATION

Consumers seek information about the product and the product class through word-of-mouth communication (from friends and family, from people whose opinions are valued, from stores and from salespeople) and from mass-media communications (such as newspapers and magazines, consumer reports, testimonials and endorsements).

This strategy is straightforward and logical, since the more information the consumer has regarding the product and the product category, the more predictable the probable consequences, and thus the lower the perceived risk. One researcher reported that high-risk perceivers were more likely than low-risk perceivers to have engaged in product-related conversations during the past six

TABLE 6-4   Types of Risk-Reduction Strategies

1. Information Seeking
   —Informal sources (friends, family, opinion leaders, etc.)
   —Formal sources (stores, salespeople, advertisements, endorsements, editorials, consumer reports, etc.)
2. Brand Loyalty
3. Major Brand Image
4. Store Image
5. Most Expensive Model
6. Reassurance
   —Money-back guarantees
   —Warranties
   —Government and private laboratory tests
   —Prepurchase trial (ten-day trial, free samples, etc.)

months for two out of three products studied.[67] Furthermore, high- and medium-risk perceivers were more likely than low-risk perceivers to seek information when they initiated a product-related conversation.

High-risk perceivers are also more likely to act upon the advice they seek than are low-risk perceivers. Research has found, for example, that high-risk perceivers are more affected by both favorable and unfavorable information than low-risk perceivers.[68]

Since consumers tend to seek out information, especially from those who are already product users, astute marketers can try to influence word-of-mouth communications in their ads. For example, ads showing group discussions of possible product risks and the overriding rewards, by people representing the target market, may reassure high-risk perceivers to buy the product. Zenith used this strategy in introducing color television. To allay doubts about the risks involved (relatively high price and uncertainty about the quality), ads showed informal peer group discussions of the product in which the messages were "I've bought one," "Everyone's buying Zenith," and "It's handcrafted." The strategy proved successful.[69]

CONSUMERS ARE BRAND LOYAL

Consumers can avoid risk by remaining loyal to a brand with which they have been satisfied instead of purchasing new or untried products. A study of the acceptance of a new food product revealed that high-risk perceivers were more likely to be loyal to their old brands and less likely to purchase the new product.[70] A study of consumers of headache remedies found that a significantly greater number of high-risk perceivers were brand loyal as compared with low-risk perceivers.[71]

CONSUMERS SELECT BY BRAND IMAGE

If consumers have had no experience with a product, they tend to "trust" a favored or well-known brand name. Consumers often think well-known brands are better and are worth buying for the assurance offered of quality, dependability, performance, and service. Marketers' promotional efforts supplement the perceived quality of their products in helping to build and sustain a favorable brand image.

CONSUMERS RELY ON STORE IMAGE

If consumers have no other information about a product, they will trust the judgment of the merchandise buyers of a reputable store and will depend on them to have made careful decisions in selecting products for that store. Store image also imparts the implication of product testing and the assurance of service, return privileges, and adjustments in case of dissatisfaction.

CONSUMERS BUY THE MOST EXPENSIVE MODEL

When in doubt, consumers may feel that the most expensive model is probably the best in terms of quality; i.e., they equate price with quality. (The price-quality relationship was discussed earlier in this chapter.)

Consumers who are uncertain about the wisdom of a product choice seek reassurance through money-back guarantees, government and private laboratory test results, warranties, and prepurchase trial (such as free samples or limited free trials).

Of the risk-reduction strategies listed above, one researcher found that the most-favored strategies were brand loyalty and brand image.[72] The least-favored strategies were buying the most expensive model, private laboratory tests, money-back guarantees, and endorsements. These findings suggest that marketers should first determine the kinds of risks perceived by potential customers and then create a mix of "risk relievers" tailored to their target markets.

The concept of perceived risk has major implications for the introduction of new products. Since high-risk perceivers are less likely to purchase new products than low-risk perceivers, it is important to provide such consumers with acceptable risk-reduction strategies, such as distribution through reputable retail outlets, informative advertising, publicity stories in the media, impartial test results, free samples, and money-back guarantees. And, of course, as will be discussed in Chapter 16, it is most important to reach the influentials—the opinion leaders—from whom product advice and information are actively sought and acted upon by others.

summary

Perception is the process by which individuals select, organize, and interpret stimuli into a meaningful and coherent picture of the world. It has strategy implications for marketers because consumers make decisions based upon what they perceive, rather than on the basis of objective reality.

The lowest level at which an individual can perceive a specific stimulus is called the *absolute threshold.* The minimal difference that he or she can perceive between two stimuli is called the *differential threshold,* or *just noticeable difference* (*j.n.d.*)

Most stimuli are perceived *above* the level of the consumer's conscious awareness; however, weak stimuli can be perceived *below* the level of conscious awareness (i.e., subliminally). No research shows conclusively that subliminal stimuli have an effect on consumer buying decisions, though the psychological effects of such stimuli have been demonstrated.

Consumers' selection of stimuli from the environment is based on the interaction of their expectations and motives with the stimulus itself. The principle of selective perception includes the following concepts: selective exposure, selective attention, perceptual defense, and perceptual blocking. People usually perceive things they need or want, and they block the perception of unfavorable or painful stimuli.

The interpretation of stimuli is highly subjective and is based upon what the consumer expects to see in light of previous experience, on the number of plausible explanations he or she can envision, on motives and interests at the time of perception, and on the clarity of the stimulus itself. Influences that tend to distort objective interpretation include physical appearances, stereotypes, halo effects, respected sources, irrelevant cues, first impressions, and the tendency to jump to conclusions.

Each individual has a perceived self-image as a certain kind of person, with certain traits, habits, possessions, relationships, and ways of behaving. The consumer attempts to preserve or enhance that self-image by buying products or shopping at stores believed to be consistent with self-image and by avoiding products and stores that are not.

Products also have images (i.e., symbolic meanings) for the consumer. The way the product is perceived is probably more important to its ultimate success than are its actual product characteristics. Products that are perceived favorably obviously have a better chance of being purchased than those that are not. The brands that a consumer considers in making a purchase choice in a particular product category are known as the *evoked set*.

In the absence of more objective information, consumers often judge the quality of a product on the basis of cues that are *intrinsic* to the product (e.g., flavor) or *extrinsic* to the product (e.g., price, store image, or brand image).

Consumers often perceive risk in making product selections because of uncertainty as to the consequences of their product decisions. The most frequent types of risk that consumers perceive are functional risk, physical risk, financial risk, social risk, and psychological risk. Studies show that the perception of risk by the consumer varies with the individual, the product, the shopping situation, and the culture.

People characteristically develop their own strategies for reducing or handling risk. Some of these strategies include seeking added information through word-of-mouth and through the media, being loyal to brands with which they have previously been satisfied, buying products that carry major brand names, buying from stores that have a favorable image, buying the most expensive model, and seeking reassurances in the form of money-back guarantees, warranties, laboratory test results, and prepurchase trial.

The concept of perceived risk has important implications for marketers, who can facilitate the introduction and acceptance of new products by providing consumers with an optimal number of acceptable risk-reduction strategies.

discussion questions

1. Give two examples of how marketers of consumer detergents can apply their knowledge of differential threshold in a period of rising prices and increasing competition.
2. An advertising agency has submitted a proposed promotional campaign based on subliminal advertising to the marketer of an established line of male fragrances. As vice-president of marketing of this company, how would you evaluate the prospects of this new campaign?

3. As a market researcher for an automobile manufacturer, you are attempting to segment the market in terms of consumer self-images. Would you want to determine actual, ideal, or expected self-image? Discuss.

4. Find three different wine advertisements that you believe are directed to different market segments. In each case, has the marketer effectively positioned the product to communicate a specific image? Discuss.

5. Choose two product advertisements from different product categories. List the possible risks the consumer may perceive in purchasing these products. Have the marketers incorporated any risk-reduction strategies in their advertisements? Discuss.

6. Recently the management of a well-known quality cosmetic company decided to add shampoo to its product line. From your knowledge of perceived risk, outline a strategy to reduce consumers' perceived risk in the new shampoo introduction.

7. Discuss the relationship of (a) extrinsic cues and (b) intrinsic cues in the perception of product quality of a line of ready-made draperies.

8. Mrs. Brown spent the hour from 1:00 P.M. to 2:00 P.M. ironing while she watched her favorite soap operas. Yet, when questioned by a television researcher two hours later, she could not recall even one commercial that she had seen, though she could repeat the story line of both TV shows in detail. How can you explain her apparent forgetfulness?

endnotes

1. Richard Lee Miller, "Dr. Weber and the Consumer," *Journal of Marketing*, 26 (January 1962), 57–61.

2. John Revett, "FTC Threatens Big Fines for Undersized Cigarette Warnings," *Advertising Age*, March 17, 1975, 1, 74.

3. Bernard Berelson and Gary A. Steiner, *Human Behavior: An Inventory of Scientific Findings* (New York: Harcourt, Brace & World, 1964), 87–130.

4. "Consumers Find Firms Are Paring Quantities to Avoid Price Rises," *Wall Street Journal*, February 15, 1977, 1, 21.

5. Walter P. Margulies, "Design Changes Reflect Switches in Consumer Retail Graphics," *Advertising Age*, February 14, 1972, 41.

6. Stewart Henderson Britt and Victoria M. Nelson, "The Marketing Importance of the 'Just Noticeable Difference,'" *Business Horizons*, 14 (August 1976), 38–40.

7. Stewart Henderson Britt, "How Weber's Law Can Be Applied to Marketing," *Business Horizons*, 13 (February 1975), 21–29.

8. H. Brean, "What Hidden Sell Is All About," *Life*, March 31, 1958, 104–14.

9. Del Hawkins, "The Effects of Subliminal Stimulation on Drive Level and Brand Preference," *Journal of Marketing Research*, 7 (August 1970), 322–26.

10. Ibid.

11. L.H. Silverman, "Psychoanalytic Theory: The Reports of My Death Are Greatly Exaggerated," *American Psychologist*, 31 (September 1976), 621–37.

12. Joel Saegert, "Another Look at Subliminal Perception," *Journal of Advertising Research*, 19 (February 1979), 55–57.

13. "Mind Benders," *Money*, 7 (September 1978), 24.

14. Wilson Bryan Key, *Subliminal Seduction* (New York: New American Library, 1973).

15. J. Steven Kelly, "Subliminal Embeds in Print Advertising: A Challenge to Advertising Ethics," *Journal of Advertising*, 8 (Summer 1979), 43–46.

16. For an extended discussion of the difference between recall and recognition and their importance for advertisers, see Herbert E. Krugman, "Memory without Recall, Exposure without Perception," *Journal of Advertising Research*, 17 (August 1977), 7–12.

17. Berelson and Steiner, *Human Behavior*, 95.

18. Russell I. Haley, "Beyond Benefit Segmentation," *Journal of Advertising Research*, 11 (August 1971), 5.

19. Walter P. Margulies, "How Many Brands Can You Spot with Names Off Packages?" *Advertising Age*, August 21, 1972, 37.

20. H.H. Kelley, "The Warm-Cold Variable in First Impressions of Persons," *Journal of Personality*, 18 (1950), 431–39.

21. "Man-in-Bed Ads Score Well with Women, Stevenson Says," *Advertising Age*, February 26, 1973, 136.

22. Anne Anastasi, *Fields of Applied Psychology* (New York: McGraw-Hill, 1964); and M. Wayne Alexander and Bed Judd, Jr., "Do Nudes in Ads Enhance Brand Recall?" *Journal of Advertising Research*, 18 (February 1978), 47–50.

23. Wolfgang Schaefer, "Selective Perception in Operation," *Journal of Advertising Research*, 19 (February 1979), 59–60.

24. Stewart Henderson Britt, Stephen C. Adams, and Allan S. Miller, "How Many Advertising Exposures per Day?" *Journal of Advertising Research*, 12 (December 1972), 3–9.

25. Raymond Bauer and Stephen Greyser, *What Americans Think of Advertising* (New York: Dow Jones-Irwin, 1969).

26. Berelson and Steiner, *Human Behavior*, 102–3.

27. Ibid.

28. Haley, "Beyond Benefit Segmentation," 5.

29. Ernest F. Larkin, "Consumer Perceptions of the Media and Their Advertising Content," *Journal of Advertising*, 8 (Spring 1979), 5–7.

30. Ernest R. Hilgard, *Introduction to Psychology*, 3rd ed. (New York: Harcourt, Brace & World, 1962), 552–53.

31. George A. Miller, "The Magical Number Seven, Plus or Minus Two: Some Limits on Our Capacity for Processing Information," *Psychological Review*, 63 (March 1956), 81–97.

32. James T. Heimbach and Jacob Jacoby, "The Zeigarnik Effect in Advertising," in M. Venkatesan, ed., *Proceedings of the Third Annual Conference* (Association for Consumer Research, 1972), 746–58.

33. Ibid.

34. Jerome Bruner, "Social Psychology and Perception," in E. Maccoby, T. Newcomb, and E. Hartley, eds., *Readings in Social Psychology*, 3rd ed. (New York: Holt, Rinehart & Winston, 1958), 85–94.

35. For example, see Ira J. Dolich, "Congruence Relationships between Self Images and Product Brands," *Journal of Marketing Research*, 6 (February 1969), 80–84; B. Curtis Hamm and Edward W. Cundiff, "Self-Actualization and Product Perception," *Journal of Marketing Research*, 6 (November 1969), 470–73; and Edward L. Grubb and Gregg Hupp, "Perception of Self, Generalized Stereotypes and Brand Selection," *Journal of Marketing Research*, 5 (February 1968), 58–61.

36. Irving Burstiner, "A Three-Way Mirror," *Journal of Retailing*, 50 (Spring 1974), 24–36. See also Danny N. Begginger, Earle Steinberg, and Wilbur W. Stanton, "The Congruence of Store Image and Self Image," *Journal of Retailing*, 52 (Spring 1976), 17–32; and Bruce L. Stern, Ronald F. Bush, and Joseph F. Hair, Jr., "The Self-Image/Store Image Matching Process: An Empirical Test," *Journal of Business*, 50 (January 1977), 63–69.

37. See, for example, E. Laird Landon, Jr., "Self-Concept, Ideal Self-Concept, and Consumer Purchase Intentions," *Journal of Consumer Research,* 1 (September 1974), 44–51.

38. Ivan Ross, "Self-Concept and Brand Preference," *Journal of Business,* 44 (January 1971), 38–50.

39. Humberto S. Tapia, Terrence V. O'Brien, and George W. Summers, "Self-Concept in Consumer Motivation," *Proceedings of the American Marketing Association,* 37 (Chicago: American Marketing Association, 1975), 225–27; and Terrence V. O'Brien, Humberto S. Tapia, and Thomas L. Brown, "The Self-Concept in Buyer Behavior," *Business Horizons,* 20 (October 1977), 65–71.

40. For example, see Ralph L. Allison and Kenneth P. Uhl, "Influence of Beer Brand Identification on Taste Perception," *Journal of Marketing Research,* August 1964, 36–39.

41. Charles E. Overholser and John M. Kline, "Advertising Strategy from Consumer Research," *Journal of Advertising Research,* 11 (October 1971), 3–10.

42. Chem L. Narayana and Rom J. Markin, "Consumer Behavior and Product Performance: An Alternative Conceptualization," *Journal of Marketing,* 39 (October 1975), 2.

43. Lance P. Jarvis and James B. Wilcox, "Evoked Set Size—Some Theoretical Foundations and Empirical Evidence," in Thomas V. Greer, ed., 1973 *Combined Proceedings* (Chicago: American Marketing Association, 1974), 326–40.

44. Miller, "Magical Number Seven," 82.

45. George J. Szybillo and Jacob Jacoby, "Intrinsic versus Extrinsic Cues as Determinants of Perceived Product Quality," *Journal of Applied Psychology,* 59 (February 1974), 74–77.

46. Donald F. Cox, "The Measurement of Information Value: A Study in Consumer Decision Making," in *Emerging Concepts in Marketing* (Chicago: American Marketing Association, 1962), 414–17; and David M. Gardner, "An Experimental Investigation on the Price-Quality Relationship," *Journal of Retailing,* 46 (Fall 1970), 39–40.

47. David M. Stander, "Testing New Product Ideas in an 'Archie Bunker' World," *Marketing News,* November 15, 1973, 1, 4, 5, and 10.

48. Ibid.

49. J. Douglas McConnell, "Effect of Pricing on Perception of Product Quality," *Journal of Applied Psychology,* 52 (1968), 331–34.

50. Barry Berman, "The Influence of Socioeconomic and Attitudinal Variables on the Price-Quality Relationship" (Doctoral dissertation, City University of New York, 1973).

51. George B. Sproles, "New Evidence on Price and Product Quality," *Journal of Consumer Affairs,* 11 (Summer 1977), 63–67.

52. Robert A. Peterson, "Consumer Perceptions as a Function of Product Color, Price and Nutrition Labeling," in William D. Perreault, Jr., ed. *Advances in Consumer Research* (Atlanta: Association for Consumer Research, 1977), 61–63.

53. Ben M. Enis and James E. Stafford, "Consumer's Perception of Product Quality as a Function of Various Informational Inputs," in Phillip R. McDonald, ed., *Marketing Involvement in Society and the Economy* (Chicago: American Marketing Association, 1969), 340–44.

54. Arch G. Woodside and James L. Taylor, "Consumer Purchase Intentions and Perceptions of Product Quality and National Advertising," *Journal of Advertising,* 7 (Winter 1978), 48–51; and Leonard N. Reid and Lauranne Buchanan, "A Shopping List Experiment of the Impact of Advertising on Brand Images," *Journal of Advertising,* 8 (September 1979), 26–28.

55. Raymond A. Bauer, "Consumer Behavior as Risk Taking," in Robert S. Hancock, ed., *Dynamic Marketing for a Changing World* (Chicago: American Marketing Association, 1960), 87.

56. For example, see Johan Arndt, "Role of Product-Related Conversations in the Diffusion of a New Product," *Journal of Marketing Research*, 4 (August 1967), 291–95; Leon G. Schiffman, "Perceived Risk in New Product Trial by Elderly Consumers," *Journal of Marketing Research*, 9 (February 1972), 106–8; and James R. Bettman, "Perceived Risk and Its Components: A Model and Empirical Test," *Journal of Marketing Research*, 10 (May 1973), 184–90.

57. Thomas F. Pettigrew, "The Measurement and Correlates of Category Width as a Cognitive Variable," *Journal of Personality*, 26 (December 1968), 532.

58. Ibid.

59. Johan Arndt, "Perceived Risk, Sociometric Integration and Word of Mouth in the Adoption of a New Food Product," in Donald F. Cox, ed., *Risk Taking and Information Handling in Consumer Behavior* (Boston: Division of Research, Graduate School of Business, Harvard University, 1967), 303.

60. J. Paul Peter and Michael J. Ryan, "An Investigation of Perceived Risk at the Brand Level," *Journal of Marketing Research*, 13 (May 1976), 184–88.

61. Scott Cunningham, "Major Dimensions of Perceived Risk," in Cox, *Risk Taking and Information Handling*, 87.

62. Michael Perry and B. Curtis Hamm, "Canonical Analysis of Relations between Socioeconomic Risk and Personal Influence in Purchase Decisions," *Journal of Marketing Research*, 6 (August 1969), 352.

63. "Investigation of the Role of Product Characteristics in Risk Perception," *Review of Business and Economic Research*, 13 (Fall 1977), 19–34.

64. Donald F. Cox and Stuart V. Rich, "Perceived Risk and Consumer Decision Making: The Case of Telephone Shopping," in Cox, *Risk Taking and Information Handling*, 504.

65. Homer E. Spence, James F. Engel, and Roger D. Blackwell, "Perceived Risk in Mail-Order and Retail Store Buying," *Journal of Marketing Research*, 7 (August 1970), 364–69.

66. Robert J. Hoover, Robert T. Green, and Joel Saegert, "A Cross National Study of Perceived Risk," *Journal of Marketing*, 42 (July 1978), 102–8.

67. Scott M. Cunningham, "Perceived Risk as a Factor in Informal Consumer Communication," in Cox, *Risk Taking and Information Handling*, 274.

68. Arndt, "Perceived Risk, Sociometric Integration," 315.

69. Arch G. Woodside and M. Wayne DeLozier, "Effects of Word-of-Mouth Advertising on Consumer Risk-Taking," *Journal of Advertising*, 5 (Fall 1976), 12–16.

70. Arndt, "Role of Product-Related Conversations," 294.

71. Scott M. Cunningham, "Perceived Risk and Brand Loyalty," in Cox, *Risk Taking and Information Handling*, 513.

72. Ted Roselius, "Consumer Rankings of Risk Reduction Methods, *Journal of Marketing*, 35 (January 1971), 61.

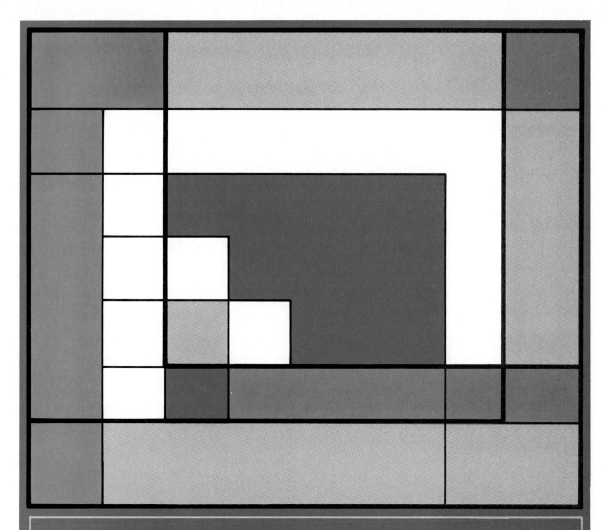

SEVEN

The Consumer
as a Learner

L EARNING is a human activity that is as natural as breathing. Studies show that learning begins even before we leave our mother's womb. Before we die, we will have collected enough information through learning to fill an average-sized library.

Despite the fact that learning is all-pervasive in our lives, psychologists do not agree on how learning takes place. Indeed, at the present time, there is a sharp schism among learning theorists who are divided into two camps: the behaviorists, who believe that all learning is a result of stimulus and response, and the cognitive scientists, who view learning as a function of purely mental processes that operate like computers in processing information.

How individuals learn is a subject of immense importance to marketers, who want consumers to learn about goods and services and new ways of behaving that will satisfy not only the consumers' needs but the marketers' objectives. In this chapter we will examine both general categories of learning theory—behavioral theory and cognitive theory (see Figure 7-1). Though both theories differ markedly in a number of essentials, each theory offers insights to marketers on how to shape their messages to consumers to bring about desired purchase behavior. At the end of the chapter, we will show how both theories lend themselves to understanding an important type of learned consumer behavior—brand loyalty.

WHAT IS LEARNING?

Since psychologists disagree on how individuals learn, it is difficult to come up with a generally acceptable definition. From a marketing perspective, however, *consumer learning* is *the process by which individuals acquire the purchase and consumption knowledge and experience they apply to future related behavior.* Several points in this definition are worth noting.

I am always ready to learn, although I do not always like being taught.

WINSTON CHURCHILL

FIGURE 7-1 Learning Behavior—Behavioral or Cognitive?

©1982 United Feature Syndicate. Reprinted with permission.

First, consumer learning is a *process;* that is, it continually evolves and changes as a result of newly acquired knowledge (which may be gained from reading or observation or thinking) or from actual experience. Both newly acquired *knowledge* and *experience* serve as feedback to the individual and are the bases upon which he or she acts, sustains, or modifies behavior in similar situations in the future. The definition makes clear that learning results from acquired knowledge or experience. This qualification distinguishes learning from instinctive behavior, such as sucking in infants.

The role of experience in learning does not mean that all learning is deliberately sought. Some learning may be *intentional*—that is, it may be acquired as the result of a careful search for information. But much learning is *incidental*, secured without much effort. Ads often induce learning in consumers (of brand names, for example), even though the consumer's attention is elsewhere (on a magazine article instead of the advertisement on the facing page).[1]

Basic Principles of Learning

The term *learning* encompasses the total range of learning, from simple conditioned responses to the learning of concepts and complex problem solving. Some psychologists would deny that "higher learning" is different from simple learned responses. But most learning theorists recognize the existence of different types of learning and explain the differences among them through the use of distinctive models of learning.

Despite their disagreements, learning theorists in general agree that in order for learning to occur, certain basic elements must be present. The elements included in most learning theories are *motivation, cues* (i.e., stimuli), *response*, and *reinforcement*. Some theorists would deny that all of these are equally important. Some would add other elements, and others would subtract one or more of those listed. These concepts are discussed here because they will recur in the theories discussed later in this chapter.

MOTIVATION

The concept of motivation introduced in Chapter 3 is an important one in learning theory. Remember, motivation is based on needs and goals. Motivation thus acts as a spur to learning, with needs and goals serving as stimuli to learning. For example, men and women who want to become good tennis players are motivated to learn all they can about tennis and to practice whenever they can. They may seek information concerning the prices and quality and characteristics of tennis racquets if they "learn" that a good racquet is instrumental to playing a good game. Conversely, individuals who are not interested in tennis will simply ignore all information related to the game. The goal object (proficiency in tennis) simply has no relevance. Uncovering consumer motives is one of the prime tasks of marketers, who then set about teaching "motivated" consumer segments why their product will best fulfill the consumer's needs.

CUES

If motives serve to stimulate learning, *cues* are the stimuli that give direction to those motives. An advertisement for a tennis camp may serve as a cue for tennis buffs who may suddenly "recognize" that attending a tennis camp is a concentrated method to improve their game while taking a vacation. The ad is the cue, or stimulus, that suggests a specific way to satisfy a salient motive. In the marketplace, price, styling, packaging, advertising, and displays all serve as cues to help consumers fulfill their needs in product-specific ways.

Cues serve to direct consumer drives when they are consistent with consumer expectations. Marketers must be careful to provide cues that do not upset those expectations. A liquor manufacturer's attempt to market a white whiskey, Frost 8/80, met with total failure because people could not accept a whiskey that looked like vodka.[2]

Consumers expect high-fashion stores to carry designer clothes at high prices. Thus a high-fashion designer should distribute his or her clothes only through exclusive stores and advertise in quality fashion magazines. Each aspect of the marketing mix must reinforce the others if cues are to serve as the stimuli that guide consumer actions in the direction desired by the marketer.

RESPONSE

How an individual reacts to a drive or cue constitutes his or her *response*. Learning can occur even if responses are not overt. The carpet manufacturer who provides consistent cues to a consumer may not always succeed in stimulating a purchase, even if that individual is motivated to buy. Instead, the manufacturer may succeed only in forming a favorable image of the carpet in the consumer's mind—that is, evoking a tendency to respond by buying.

A response is not tied to a need in a one-to-one fashion. Indeed, as Chapter 3 pointed out, a need or motive may evoke a whole variety of responses. For example, there are many ways to respond to the need for physical exercise or prowess besides tennis playing. Cues provide some direction, but there are many cues competing for the consumer's attention. Which response he or she will make depends heavily on previous learning. That, in turn, may depend on which responses were reinforced in the past.

REINFORCEMENT

Reinforcement increases the likelihood that a specific response will occur in the future as the result of particular cues or stimuli. If a college student finds that he is able to ward off or avert the beginnings of a cold by taking some advertised vitamin C tablets, he is more likely to take vitamin C tablets at the next sign of a cold. Clearly, through reinforcement, learning has taken place because he recognizes that vitamin C tablets have lived up to his expectations in the past. On the other hand, if the vitamin C tablets did not help him the first time, he would be less likely to use them again, despite advertising or store display cues for the product.

Reinforcement is a controversial concept in learning theory. Some theorists believe that an explicit reward is not necessary for a response to become part of learned behavior. But many marketers intuitively find that reinforcement serves to teach their customers a desired behavior. For example, telephone companies that give cash discounts to customers who pay their bills promptly are acting to reinforce prompt payment in the future.

With the basic principles outlined above, we can now discuss some well-known theories or models of how learning occurs.

Behavioral learning theories are sometimes referred to as stimulus-response theories because they are based on the premise that learning takes place as the result of observable responses to external stimuli. If a person acts (i.e., responds) in a predictable way to a known stimulus, he or she is said to have "learned." Two behavioral theories with great relevance to marketing are *classical conditioning* and *instrumental conditioning*.

Classical Conditioning

In everyday speech, the word *conditioned* has come to mean a kind of knee-jerk or automatic response to a situation built up through repeated exposure. If you get a headache every time you think of taking an exam, your reaction may be conditioned from years of "all-nighters" when long hours of study for an exam resulted in headaches based on lack of sleep. Ivan Pavlov, a Russian physiologist, was the first to describe conditioning and to propose it as a general model of how learning occurs. According to Pavlovian theory, *conditioned learning* results when a stimulus that is paired with another stimulus that elicits a known response serves to produce the same response by itself.

Pavlov demonstrated what he meant by conditioned learning in his studies with dogs. The dogs were hungry and highly motivated. In his experiments, Pavlov sounded a tone and immediately followed it by applying a meat paste to the dogs' tongues, which caused salivation. Learning or conditioning occurred when, after a sufficient number of repetitions of the tone, followed almost immediately by the food, the tone alone caused salivation. The tone had been "learned" to be an indicator of the rewards of the meat paste. In Pavlov's terms, the dogs learned to make the response of salivating by associating an *unconditioned stimulus* (known to cause the response) with a *conditioned stimulus*, which acquired the capacity to elicit the response because of repeated pairing.

An analogous situation would be one where the smells of dinner cooking would cause your mouth to water. If you usually listened to the six o'clock news while waiting for dinner to be served, you would tend to associate the six o'clock news with dinner; so that eventually the sounds of the six o'clock news alone would cause your mouth to water, even if dinner was not being prepared and even if you were not hungry. Figure 7-2 diagrams this basic relationship.

A great deal of advertising fits the model of conditioned learning. For example, commercials for Nestea, which invite viewers to "take the Nestea plunge," try to condition the audience to associate a plunge into a pool with the sipping of iced tea. The response—cool refreshment—is the same, the ads imply.

There are three basic concepts to conditioned learning: *repetition, stimulus generalization,* and *stimulus discrimination.* Each of these concepts is important to an understanding of consumer behavior.

FIGURE 7-2   Classical Conditioning

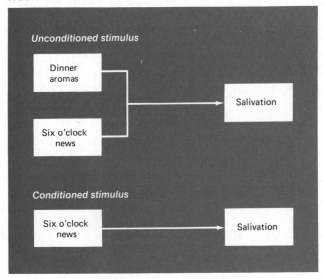

REPETITION

Just as dogs may learn to salivate at the sound of a bell after repeated trials, so too consumers may learn a message that a marketer wants to impart by repeated exposure to the same message through advertising. Evidence of the efficiency of sheer repetition to impart a message is plentiful.[3] One experiment tested the effects of various levels of exposure to magazine ads on consumers' familiarity with the brand name, willingness to buy, and belief in the brand claim. Copies of a magazine were sent to participants on two separate days. Some of the participants received copies with no ads for the brands being tested, others received copies containing the relevant ads on only one day, and still others saw the ads on both days. For those who were exposed to the ads on both days, brand familiarity and willingness to buy doubled, and belief in the brand claim tripled.[4]

Some researchers believe that repetition works by increasing the strength of the association and by slowing the process of forgetting, which is seen as a process of decay. Apparently there is a limit to the amount of repetition that will aid retention. The evidence suggests that some *overlearning*, or repetition beyond what is necessary to learn, aids retention.[5] But with exposure beyond a certain point, an individual can become satiated, and attention and retention can decline.

Three researchers demonstrated this phenomenon by inducing in subjects 100 percent learning (after seven exposures to an ad), 200 percent learning (after fourteen exposures), and 300 percent learning (after twenty-one exposures). More retention resulted from 200 percent learning than from 300 percent, as measured after a lapse of twenty-eight days. Apparently, at the higher number of exposures, boredom set in, leading to inattention and negative reactions. It has been suggested that this effect, known as *advertising wearout,* can be decreased by varying the advertising message.[6] For example, Jello Pudding has varied advertising messages that associate the dessert with fun for children by showing comedian Bill Cosby as the object of different jokes children play while eating the dessert. Other techniques to achieve variety include stressing different benefits or using a number of different advertising spokespersons.

Though the principle of repetition is well established in advertising circles, not everyone agrees on the effectiveness of massive doses. In fact, one researcher maintains that the optimum number of exposures to an advertisement is just three—one to make consumers aware of the product, a second to show consumers the relevance of the product, and a third to remind them of its benefits. According to this *three-hit theory,* all other ad repetitions are wasted effort.[7] However, some researchers suggest that an average frequency of eleven to twelve exposures is needed to increase the probability that consumers will actually receive three exposures.[8]

If the three-hit theory is correct, repetition may be important, not so much to maintain the association in the consumer's mind as to ensure that the proper association is made when the consumer is motivated to see the connection. Generally, classical conditioning theorists tend to deny the importance of inner processes such as motivation and to stress the automatic nature of paired associations. Controversy over the role of repetition continues today because of this basic disagreement.

STIMULUS GENERALIZATION

According to classical conditioning theorists, learning depends not only on repetition but also on the ability of individuals to generalize. Pavlov noted, for example, that a dog could learn to salivate not only to the tone of a bell but also to the similar sound of jangling keys. If we were not capable of *stimulus generalization,* that is, of making the same response to a slightly different stimulus, not much learning would occur.

Stimulus generalization explains why imitative "me too" products usually crowd onto the market immediately after the introduction of an innovative product. For example, when Tic-Tac, the pellet-shaped mint in a clear plastic package, was introduced, it was followed almost immediately by Dynamints and Mighty Mints, candies with a similar taste, configuration, and packaging.[9]

Family branding, the practice of marketing a whole line of company products under the same brand name, capitalizes on the consumer's ability to generalize favorable brand associations from one product to the next. Figure 7-3 shows Jordache, best known for its line of jeans, using a family branding strategy to introduce other items of apparel.

Another marketing strategy that works on the principle of stimulus generalization is *product line extension,* the practice of adding related products to an already established brand. Clairol, which originally specialized in hair dyes, has extended its line to all kinds of beauty-care appliances—from hair dryers to facial machines. The key to the success of this type of strategy is to remain within the limits of the consumer's ability to generalize. Kool-Aid failed with a line of

FIGURE 7-3 An Attempt to Develop Stimulus Generalization

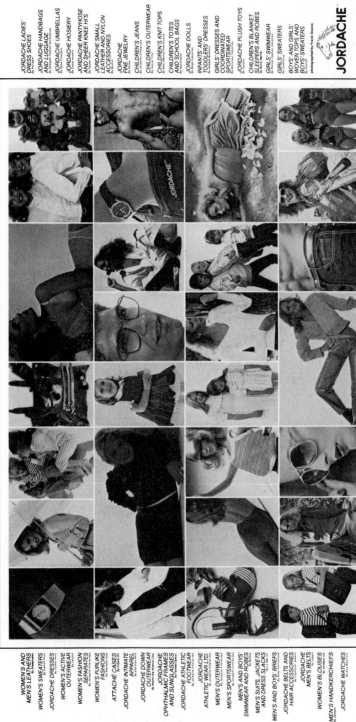

THE LOOK THAT KEEPS 'EM LOOKING

AND YOU THOUGHT WE ONLY MADE JEANS

party cups, as did Arm & Hammer with a deodorant, because they exceeded those limits.[10]

STIMULUS DISCRIMINATION

Stimulus discrimination is the opposite of stimulus generalization, and it results in the selection of a specific stimulus from among similar stimuli. The consumer's ability to discriminate among stimuli is the basis for the marketing strategy known as *positioning*, which seeks to establish a clear niche for a brand in the consumer's mind. (See Chapter 6.) For example, the makers of Seven-Up were able to win a major share of the market from Coke and Pepsi by positioning their product as the "Uncola."[11]

Imitators want consumers to generalize their experience, but market leaders want to retain the top spot by convincing consumers to discriminate. It is often quite difficult to unseat a brand leader once stimulus discrimination has occurred. For example, when National Cash Register challenged IBM with a heavy media campaign that stressed the slogan "NCR Means Computers," it failed, presumably because consumers simply did not believe the claim. One explanation is that the leader is usually first on the market and has had a longer period to teach consumers (through advertising and selling) to associate the brand name with the product. The longer the period of learning, the more likely the consumer is to discriminate, and the less likely to generalize the stimulus.[12]

For marketers who do enter the field late, the best strategy is to capture a unique position in the consumer's mind by highlighting some special product feature or by offering a unique price, distribution, or promotional strategy. Hewlett-Packard has survived in the highly competitive pocket calculator market by offering models that have more functions than those of competing brands. American Express has retained a significant share of the credit-card market with its innovative ad campaign that features celebrities whose names are better known than their faces. In both cases, success resulted from the unique pairing of a brand-name cue with an already established stimulus-response condition.

EVALUATION OF CLASSICAL CONDITIONING

The principles of classical conditioning provide the theoretical underpinnings for many marketing applications. Repetition, stimulus generalization, and stimulus discrimination are useful concepts in explaining how consumers learn to behave in the marketplace. However, they do not explain all the activities classified as consumer learning.

Classical conditioning assumes that learners are passive subjects to whom stimuli are administered and whose responses are inevitable after a number of trials. While some of our purchase behavior—for example, the purchase of low-involvement products such as branded convenience goods—tends to be spontaneous and may have been shaped to some extent by repeated advertising messages, other purchase behavior results from a more active search for and evaluation of product information. Our judgment of which product is best often rests on the rewards we experience from making specific purchases—in other words, from *instrumental conditioning*.

Instrumental Conditioning

The name most closely associated with instrumental conditioning is that of an American psychologist, B. F. Skinner. According to Skinner, most learning takes place in an effort to control the environment (that is, to obtain favorable outcomes). Control is gained by means of a trial-and-error process during which one behavior of the individual results in a more favorable response than other behaviors. The reward provides reinforcement to the behavior associated with the favorable response; that is, it is *instrumental* in teaching the individual a specific behavior that gives him or her more control.

Like Pavlov, Skinner developed his model of learning by working with animals. Such animals as rats or pigeons received rewards in his "Skinner Box" if they made appropriate movements and depressed levers or pecked keys to receive the food reinforcement. Skinner and his many followers have been able to do amazing things with this simple apparatus, including teaching pigeons to play Ping-Pong, to cha-cha, and even to act as the guiding system in a missile. In a marketing context, the consumer who tries several brands and styles of jeans before finding a style that fits her figure may be said to have engaged in instrumental learning. Presumably, the brand that fits best is the one she will continue to buy. This model of instrumental conditioning is presented in Figure 7-4.

Note the differences between classical and instrumental conditioning, as summarized in Table 7-1. Although the experimenter controls the reward in instrumental conditioning, it is the subject's action that causes the reward to happen. This situation differs from classical conditioning, where the subject's response (e.g., salivation) is involuntary. Another difference is that the "learned" response in instrumental conditioning is the result of trial-and-error among several behaviors, rather than a paired response to a specific stimulus. The subject tries a number of stimuli, and the one that yields the most rewarding response is the one that is "learned." Finally, while classical conditioning is useful

FIGURE 7-4   A Model of Instrumental Conditioning

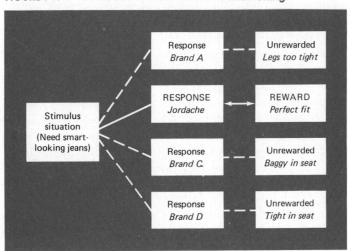

TABLE 7-1   Classical and Instrumental Conditioning Compared

	CLASSICAL	INSTRUMENTAL
1. Cause of response	Association of a conditioned with an unconditioned stimulus	Association of a reward with a specific response
2. Type of response	Automatic, involuntary	Deliberate, to obtain reward
3. Type of learning	Simple behaviors, attitudes, and feelings	Relatively complex, goal-directed behavior

in explaining how we learn very simple kinds of behaviors or feelings, instrumental conditioning is more helpful in explaining complex, goal-directed activities, such as those we would find with high-involvement products.[13]

Marketers are interested in instrumental learning theory because it seems to describe better than classical conditioning how consumers learn about goods that involve a great deal of prepurchase search for information. The purchase of a car (a high-involvement product) involves more than learning a simple association of brand name with a need for transportation. Marketers have to convince consumers that ownership of a particular automobile will give them specific rewards. In accomplishing this, repetition and discrimination are important, but even more so may be the form, amount, and timing of reinforcement provided.

POSITIVE AND NEGATIVE REINFORCEMENT

Skinner distinguished two types of reinforcement or rewards that influence the chances of a response being repeated. The first type, *positive reinforcement,* consists of events that strengthen the likelihood of a specific response. Giving food to pigeons that depress a bar is an example of positive reinforcement and is likely to result in a repetition of the pigeons' behavior in order to get more food.

Negative reinforcement is an unpleasant or negative outcome that serves to discourage a specific response. For example, an animal can be taught to avoid pressing a bar that results in an electric shock. Parents sometimes use negative reinforcement to stop a child from thumb-sucking by applying an unpleasant-tasting substance to the thumb. Instead of giving solace or comfort to the child, thumb-sucking becomes a distasteful experience to be avoided.

Marketers make use of both positive and negative reinforcement to encourage consumers to buy their products. The most effective way for a marketer to encourage consumers to repeat specific buying behavior is to maintain high product quality over time. But there are other, more overt, ways to use positive reinforcement. One jewelry store in Texas, for example, conducted an experiment in reinforcement by telephoning customers to thank them for their business. The result was a 27 percent increase in sales over those of the same month in the previous year.[14]

Marketers also sometimes use negative reinforcement. Fear appeals in ad messages are an example (see Chapter 10). Life insurance commercials that inform husbands that in the event of sudden death they can avoid leaving their wives as penniless widows rely on negative reinforcement. Since not buying a policy may result in the dreaded consequences, the company encourages a positive response (purchase of a policy) in order to avoid the threat.

Either positive or negative reinforcement can be used to elicit a desired response. When a learned response is no longer reinforced, it diminishes to the point of *extinction;* that is, to the point where it no longer occurs. Individuals may never totally forget a behavior once it is learned, but they may engage in the behavior less and less frequently.

MASSED OR DISTRIBUTED LEARNING

Another important influence on consumer learning is *timing.* Should a learning schedule be spread out over a period of time (*distributed*) or should it be "bunched up" all at once (*massed*)? The question is an important one for advertisers planning a media schedule.

Research seems to indicate that massed advertising produces more initial learning than does distributed advertising. However, learning usually persists longer with a more spread-out schedule.[15]

Unaided recall is the research technique used to measure the influence of timing on learning schedules. The researcher asks consumers (who acknowledge that they have read a certain periodical) to describe any ads they remember seeing in the magazine. Their ability to recall the ads, and the accuracy with which they do so, serves to measure the efficiency of the learning schedule. In unaided recall tests, the consumers are given no clues as to the type of advertisements they are being asked to recall. In contrast, there are *aided recall* tests, in which consumers may be told the product class of the advertisement to be recalled, and *recognition* tests, in which the consumer is shown a specific advertisement and is asked whether he or she has seen it. Each of the aided or unaided recall tests can vary a great deal in terms of what the researcher's criteria are for a "correct" response.

A recent study examined unaided recall for five different schedules of television advertising (13 weeks, 100 rating points; 26 weeks, 50 rating points; 52 weeks, 25 rating points; 6–7 weeks, 100 rating points; every 4 weeks, 100 rating points). "Rating points" refer to the intensity of advertising during the period. The highest level of recall (24 percent) was achieved with the thirteen-week schedule. (See Figure 7-5.) But after a year's time, the schedule that produced the most recall (8 percent) was the one stretched out over fifty-two weeks.[16] The conclusion seems to be that if advertisers want an immediate impact (e.g., to introduce a new product or to counter a competitor's blitz campaign), they should use a massed schedule. However, when the goal is long-lasting repeat buying on a regular basis, a distributed schedule is preferable. Automobile manufacturers usually use a combination of the two: They use concentrated

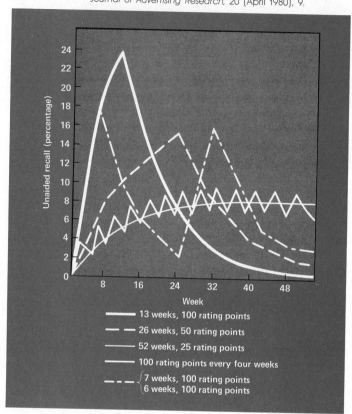

FIGURE 7-5 **Advertising Effects of Massed and Distributed Reinforcement** Source: Herbert A. Zielske and Walter A. Henry, "Remembering and Forgetting Television Ads," *Journal of Advertising Research*, 20 (April 1980), 9.

Legend:
— 13 weeks, 100 rating points
— — 26 weeks, 50 rating points
— 52 weeks, 25 rating points
— 100 rating points every four weeks
— — { 7 weeks, 100 rating points
       6 weeks, 100 rating points

advertising during the first few weeks of a new-style introduction and then distributed advertising over the rest of the product year.

EVALUATION OF INSTRUMENTAL CONDITIONING

Instrumental learning theorists believe that learning occurs through a trial-and-error process, with habits formed as a result of rewards given for certain responses or behaviors. This model of learning applies to many situations in which consumers learn about products, services, and stores. For example, we learn which stores have the clothing we want by shopping in a number of stores, looking for the colors, sizes, and styles we prefer at the prices we can afford. When we find a store that carries clothing that meets our requirements, we tend to frequent that store to the exclusion of others. Every time we purchase a suit or a dress we like at a price we want to pay, our store loyalty behavior is rewarded (i.e., reinforced) and is more likely to be repeated.

Critics of instrumental learning theory point out, however, that a considerable amount of learning takes place in the absence of direct rewards, either positive or negative. We do not have to be burned to know that fire is harmful. Children, in fact, learn a great deal through a process that psychologists call "modeling." They observe the behavior of others, remember it, and imitate it.[17] Instrumental theorists argue that children learn in this way because they can see the reward and therefore imitate the behavior that leads to it. But critics maintain that instrumentalists confuse learning and performance (i.e., behavior). Children, and adults for that matter, learn a great deal that they do not act upon. Moreover, they learn merely for the sake of learning, not for the sake of rewards. Learning as a function of thinking, of mental processes, is known as *cognitive theory*.

COGNITIVE LEARNING THEORY

Not all learning takes place as a result of repeated trials. A considerable amount of learning takes place as the result of consumer thinking and problem solving. Sudden learning is also a reality. When confronted with a problem, we sometimes see the solution instantly. For instrumental theorists, who do not acknowledge the reality of mental processes, sudden learning is inexplicable. Indeed, some instrumental theorists would deny that the mind has anything to do with learned behavior. For example, B. F. Skinner has said that efforts to explain human behavior in terms of what goes on in the mind are akin to primitive animism—the belief that spirits dwell in material objects!

Cognitive learning theory holds that the kind of learning most characteristic of human beings is problem solving, which enables individuals to gain some control over their environment. Unlike instrumental learning theory, cognitive theory holds that such problem solving involves mental processing. Instead of stressing the importance of repetition or the association of rewards with a specific response, cognitive theorists emphasize the role of motivation and mental manipulation in arriving at a desired response.

Cognitive science is a relatively new discipline comprising an amalgam of other areas, including psychology, psycholinguistics, computer science, psychobiology, anthropology, and philosophy. It is concerned with discovering how individuals think and how they learn. In contrast to the behaviorist view of human behavior as simply another form of animal behavior, cognitive scientists hold that the human mind is a highly complex mechanism capable of creative problem solving, not just in response to a need or in hope of a reward, but sometimes for the sheer joy of finding solutions to complex problems.

Cognitive theorists believe that it is impossible to understand human behavior without knowing how the mind functions. They believe that although the mind's processes cannot be directly observed, the nature of the mind's machinery can be deduced from what happens to information fed into it. The relatively new fields of information theory and computer science have provided a unified direction of inquiry to cognitive scientists, who recognize that, like the computer, the human mind is also engaged in *information processing* of data that it receives as input.

Information Processing

Just as a computer has peripheral devices that work on data before they are processed by a central device, so the mind is thought to be composed of mechanisms that process information in stages. The processing involves perception, learning, and memory, but it is with memory that information-processing theorists are chiefly concerned. Their focus is on how information gets stored in memory and how it is retrieved.

THE STRUCTURE OF MEMORY

Information processing occurs in stages. Consequently, according to one widely accepted view, there must be separate "storehouses" where information can be kept temporarily while waiting to be further processed. In this model, there are actually three separate storage units: a sensory store, a short-term store, and a long-term store.[18]

SENSORY STORE.   All data come to us through our senses. There is evidence that the image of a sensory input lasts for a second or less in the mind's sensory store. For example, after staring at a TV image for a few seconds and then looking away, we retain an after-image. That after-image, though very short-lived, is packed with more information than we tend to use and process further. As noted in Chapter 6, we unconsciously block out a great deal of information. For marketers, this means that although it is relatively easy to get information into the consumer's sensory store, it is difficult to make a lasting impression.

SHORT-TERM STORE.   The short-term store is the stage of real memory in which information is processed and held for just a brief period. Anyone who has ever looked up a number in a telephone book, only to forget it right before dialing, knows how briefly information lasts in this storage unit. Information in the short-term store which undergoes the process known as *rehearsal* is then transferred into the long-term store. The transfer process takes from two to ten seconds. If information is not rehearsed and transferred, it is lost within about thirty seconds or less. The amount of information that can be held in the short-term store is also limited. Originally it was thought that this store could hold about seven items, or chunks, of information (such as numbers),[19] but more recent research indicates that four or five items is more likely.

LONG-TERM STORE.   In contrast to the short-term store, where information lasts only a few seconds, the long-term store retains information for relatively extended periods of time. Although it is possible to forget something within a few minutes after the information has reached long-term storage, it is more common for data in that bank to last for days, weeks, and even years. Almost all of us, for example, can remember the name of our first-grade teacher.

It is somewhat misleading to refer to the long-term store as a bank, because information does not just sit there waiting to be retrieved. In the long-term store, information is constantly being organized and reorganized as new links between chunks of information are forged. In fact, many information-processing theorists consider the long-term store to be like a network, consisting of nodes, or concepts, with links between the concepts.[20] Consider the concept we have of a single product—wine. We know that various wines share certain attributes (red or white, sweet or dry, expensive or inexpensive, etc.). We link the wines we have experienced by means of these attributes (e.g., Blue Nun is more expensive than Ripple and less expensive than French champagne). As we gain more knowledge of wines, we expand our network of relationships. The methods by which information enters into the long-term store and is processed are the most relevant aspects of information processing for consumer behavior.

MEMORY PROCESSES

Four processes are key to understanding memory: *rehearsal, encoding, storage*, and *retrieval*.

REHEARSAL. How much information is available for delivery from the short-term store to the long-term store depends on the amount of rehearsal an individual gives to it. One definition of *rehearsal* is that it is the "silent, mental repetition of material."[21] In this view, we need rehearsal to amplify the weak signal that comes from the sensory store. Another view of rehearsal is that it involves relating new data to old to make the material meaningful. For example, we may remember the price of a product, not by repetition, but by relating it to the price of a similar product.[22]

Failure to rehearse an input, either by repeating it or by relating it to other data, can cause fading and eventual loss of the information. Information can also be lost because of competition for attention. If, for example, the short-term store must pay attention to more than one input from the sensory store at the same time, short-term capacity can be reduced to two or three pieces of information.[23]

Since short-term memory is so limited in capacity, marketers must be certain that the information they convey to consumers is simple enough to be absorbed without much loss. This is particularly important if the time available to convey a message is limited. One researcher has suggested that only two or three bits of information can be conveyed in a fifteen-second commercial if the goal is later recall.[24]

ENCODING. The purpose of rehearsal is to hold information in the short-term storage unit long enough for encoding to take place. *Encoding* is the process by which we select and assign a word or visual image to represent a perceived object.[25] Marketers, for example, help consumers encode brands by using brand symbols. Borden revived the symbol of Elsie the Cow for its dairy products because it was shown that the image generated high consumer recognition.[26] A memorable brand name, such as Smucker's, can also aid the consumer's encoding process.

Besides being able to code information with the aid of words and symbols, we are able to recode what we have already encoded to include larger amounts of information. This purely human ability to group objects or events together into categories is called *chunking*. Those individuals new to a typewriter keyboard must type letter by letter. Those with more experience type in chunks of whole words or phrases. It is important for marketers to discover the groupings or chunks of information that consumers can handle. Recall may be hampered if the chunks offered in an advertisement do not match those in the consumer's frame of reference. The degree of prior knowledge is an important consideration.[27] The amount and type of information given in an automobile ad in a specialty magazine such as *Road and Track* can be much more detailed than that in a general-interest magazine such as *Time*. The experts can take in more complex chunks of information.

STORAGE. *Storage* is the process by which we organize and reorganize the information in long-term memory received from the short-term store. One theory of storage is that it actually consists of two processes. In one process, information is organized *episodically*, that is, by the order in which it was acquired in the past. In the other process, information is stored *semantically*, according to significant concepts.[28] Thus we may remember having gone to a movie last Saturday because of our ability to store data episodically, and we may remember the plot, the stars, and the director because of our ability to store data semantically.

In the past, most research in consumer behavior concentrated on episodic memory. For example, recall is used by advertisers as a measure of episodic storage.[29] More recently, however, researchers have explored the way semantic storage operates. Many theorists now believe that memories stored semantically are organized into frameworks by which we integrate new data with previous experience. For information about a new brand of toothpaste to enter our memory, we would have to relate it to our previous experience with toothpastes in terms of taste, cavity prevention, whitening, and breath-freshening qualities.

One related finding is that the more experience a consumer has with a product category, the greater his or her ability to make use of product information.[30] A woman who has had no experience with perfume is easily confused by product information about a new fragrance, since she has no prior product knowledge to which to relate it. The moderately knowledgeable perfume buyer will seek out more information about new brands and is able to make use of that information by establishing comparisons with other product information she now has "in storage." With the accumulation of very great knowledge, her search for more information may cease.

Researchers have also sought to distinguish less-knowledgeable consumers from more-knowledgeable ones by differentiating the product comparisons and judgments they are able to make. Table 7-2 summarizes the levels of knowledge consumers display, as inferred from their statements about products and brands. The not-so-knowledgeable consumer at Level 5 is only able to make simple statements about a product's attributes (e.g., the economy of small cars). The highly knowledgeable consumer at Level 1 is able to compare several brands and many different attributes and come up with a statement of brand preference. To make this judgment, he or she would have to pass through the other levels of knowledge summarized in the table. People at the intermediate levels are most likely to seek out product information and to use it because they have a framework of knowledge within which to place new information.[31]

Just as advertisers must try to judge the complexity of the frameworks of

TABLE 7-2   Levels of Knowledge Consumers Display

DESCRIPTION	SAMPLE STATEMENT
1. Best brand	"Of all the cars available, Fiat is the best."
2. Whole brand or attribute rankings or comparisons	"I like Fiats better than Cadillacs."
3. Whole brand or attribute evaluations	"I have always liked Fiats a lot."
4. Single pair comparisons or rankings	"Fiats are cheaper than Cadillacs."
5. Single brand-attribute evaluation	"Small cars are economical."

Source: Adapted from J. Edward Russo and Eric J. Johnson, "What Do Consumers Know about Familiar Products?" in Jerry C. Olson, ed., *Advances in Consumer Research* (Ann Arbor, Mich.: Association for Consumer Research, 1980), VII, 418.

knowledge possessed by their target audiences, so, too, must public policy–makers. In the past, they have not always done so. For example, legislation has been passed requiring marketers to include certain nutritional information on packages. In enacting such laws, however, no studies were made of the level of information consumers already possessed concerning nutrition. As a result, researchers have found that most consumers neither use nor comprehend nutritional labels since they lack the proper framework of knowledge.[32] (Chapter 20 discusses the issue of nutritional labeling.)

RETRIEVAL.   *Retrieval* is the process by which we recover information from long-term storage. Most people have had the experience of not being able to recollect something with which they are quite familiar. Information-processing theorists look upon such forgetting as a failure of the retrieval system.

We may fail to retrieve stored information for several reasons. One is that the *context* in which we are trying to remember is different from the context in which we learned the information in the first place. We may not recognize an old schoolmate who shows up in the new city to which we have moved, because the context in which we knew him was different. Since context is so important to retrieval, advertisers can do several things to provide contextual clues. For example, showing a close-up of the product in ads can make it more easily recognizable in stores. Reproducing within a commercial the actual situation in which product selection takes place can also help.

Another major reason for the failure to retrieve information is *interference*. There are actually two kinds of interference. *New learning* may interfere with the retrieval of already stored material. In the case of Tic-Tacs mentioned earlier, the appearance of similar products on the market caused consumer confusion to set in, and Tic-Tacs lost sales. On the other hand, *old learning* may also interfere with the recall (retrieval) of recently learned material. This kind of interference probably accounted for the previously discussed failure of National Cash Register to gain a foothold in the computer market against IBM. The latter was already too well established in the consumer's mind.

FIGURE 7-6   Information-Processing Stores and Processes

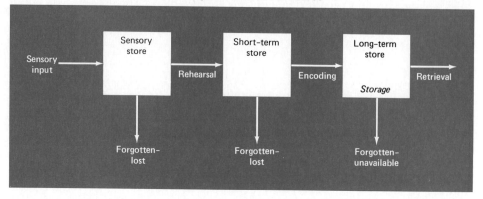

Advertisers who anticipate the effects of interference on retrieval can prevent it. With both kinds of interference, the problem is the similarity of old and new information. Advertising that creates a distinctive brand image can help consumers better retain the message. Figure 7-6 depicts the relationships of the memory stores and processes described in this model of consumer information processing.

Another View of Information Processing

The model of information processing discussed thus far looks at memory as a set of separate processing units that carry on distinct operations. Some theorists dispute the existence of such separate compartments. They point out that the encoding process of the short-term store could not take place without interaction with the long-term store. If the storehouses of memory cannot be kept separate, they say, the model is questionable.

An alternative view holds that memory is a single entity, but that memories can be distinguished by the degree or *level of processing* to which they have been subjected.[33] Very short lived memories receive only a superficial kind of sensory processing. We may remember a phone number only by the sound of the numerals, and since it may have no other meaning for us, we quickly lose it. At deeper levels of semantic processing, we start attaching meanings. According to this theory, there are degrees or depths of meaningfulness to which information is processed. A phone number may become more meaningful to us if we make up a single mnemonic device to remember it; it may become even more meaningful if we become friends with the person to whom it belongs.

The levels-of-processing theory seems to say that the more involving the information is, the better it will be understood and the longer it will be retained. Information concerning high-involvement products will receive deeper processing than information concerning low-involvement products and will thus be better remembered. Advertising research has shown that low-involvement ads do indeed produce less recall.[34] The problem for marketers, then, is to create greater product involvement among consumers; this should provoke them into processing their messages at deeper levels.

Some advertising research has been designed to produce more consumer involvement. In one study, a magazine containing nothing but ads was mailed to a sampling of housewives. Opposite each ad was a questionnaire to test the housewives' understanding of the ads. Participants were encouraged to fill out and mail in the questionnaires by the promise of free trading stamps. A panel was then selected from among the respondents, and their purchasing habits were tracked. The participants increased their purchases of many of the advertised products noticeably. Apparently the technique succeeded in getting consumers to do deep processing of the ads.[35]

Evaluation of Information Processing

A great deal of research in consumer behavior now relies on the model of learning and memory provided by information processing.[36] The fact that theorists in the field are divided in their view of the structure of memory indicates that the field is relatively new and is still questioning basic concepts. The models presented here may in fact be compatible if the memory stores are looked upon, not as separate units, but as stages in processing.

The new emphasis in marketing circles on the consumer as an information processor has provoked some criticism from those who would like to see less emphasis on mental phenomena and more on the physiological bases for consumer behavior. *Activation research,* which seeks to measure consumer brain activity in response to marketing stimuli, has been offered as an alternative to information processing.[37] Those who favor this approach dispute how much conscious control consumers actually have on the processing of product information. They believe that much of consumer behavior is biologically determined.

The criticism of activation researchers revives the longstanding dispute among learning theorists about the relative importance of behavioral versus mental processes—the old "nature versus nurture" argument about whether the mind comes equipped with innate ideas or inherited tendencies to think and behave in specific ways, or whether the mind is a blank slate at birth and comes to think only in ways that have been "written" upon it by experience and training. Recent research suggests that learning is the product of an interaction between nature and nurture; each is essential, but neither is wholly controlling.

It would appear that knowledge of both types of learning theory is relevant to a full understanding of how consumers learn about the goods and services they purchase. Furthermore, both approaches contribute to an understanding of what marketers know about *brand loyalty.*

BRAND LOYALTY

Brand loyalty has been the subject of many studies. A basic issue among researchers has been whether to define the concept in terms of consumers' *behavior* or consumers' *attitudes.* Those who favor more traditional theories of learning (classical and instrumental conditioning) tend to define it in terms of behavior. Thus, according to one researcher, a consumer can be considered brand loyal if he or she has made three successive purchases of the same brand.[38] A similar definition suggests that brand loyalty can be measured by the proportion of total product purchases a household devotes to the brand most frequently purchased. [39]

From the viewpoint of other learning theorists, such definitions lack precision. As one researcher notes, they do not distinguish between the "real" brand-loyal buyer who is intentionally faithful and the spurious brand-loyal buyer who repeats a brand purchase because it is the only one available, or because it is displayed more prominently than other brands. He suggests that loyalty must be measured both by attitudes toward a brand and purchase consistency.[40]

Most marketers today accept both measures of brand loyalty. They are interested in actual consumer purchasing patterns, but they also want to know about consumer beliefs and opinions concerning various brands. Bringing about a highly consistent pattern of purchase behavior is the ultimate goal of a marketer's strategy. Discovering how consumers learn about brands and become attached to certain brands aids in achieving this goal.

Learning Brand Loyalty

Just as the general models of learning differ significantly, so, too, do views on how brand loyalty is established. Those who favor the theory of instrumental conditioning, for example, think brand loyalty results from an initial product trial that leads to satisfaction and therefore reinforcement. This, in turn, generates repeat purchase behavior. Those who adhere to the information-processing theory, on the other hand, emphasize the role of mental processes in the building of brand loyalty. As a consumer accumulates more and more information through experience, he or she moves from a knowledge of simple product attributes to comparisons and rankings of brands, and eventually to a strong brand preference and repeat purchasing.

Both interpretations of the development of brand loyalty have merit; which is superior cannot be resolved here. What is clear from consumer research is that a great deal of brand loyalty develops quite early in life within the family. One study comparing middle-school children with high-school students found that both groups scored high on the ability to express brand preferences, although the older group had significantly more brand preferences.[41]

What children learn is apparently quite lasting. A study of fifteen products was conducted among children in grades 3 through 11 in 1941. A follow-up study was conducted among many of the same group in 1961 to determine the degree of consistency of preference for and use of certain brands. The results showed that about a quarter of the subjects who responded preferred the same brands they did twenty years earlier, and most of those still used the same brands they used then.[42] Although people do change over time, at least some of their preferences and buying habits are very stable.

Brand Switching

Not all consumers are brand loyal. Some engage in brand switching because they become dissatisfied or bored with a product. Moreover, in a number of product categories, brand loyalty is very rare. Few individuals are absolutely loyal to one brand of cereal or dishwashing liquid. Brand switching is common in those categories, perhaps because they are low-involvement products.

Marketers have tried to influence brand switching by offering special deals (e.g., coupons or cents-off offers). Most research suggests that deals do induce consumers to switch brands. However, after the special offer ends, switching recurs. No new brand loyalty has been established.[43]

More recent research suggests that the kind of deal offered may influence the final outcome. Coupons distributed through the media are the least successful in inducing repeat purchases after the deal is withdrawn. Cents-off offers and coupons distributed in packages result in relatively more repeat purchases after withdrawal, and package coupons have the added benefit of reinforcing brand loyalty among those who are already purchasers.[44]

Brand loyalty is only one instance of consumer learning, although it is a goal to which most marketers aspire.

summary

Consumer learning is the process by which individuals acquire the purchase and consumption knowledge and experience they apply to future related behavior. While some learning is intentional, much learning appears to be incidental. Basic elements that contribute to an understanding of learning are motivation, cues, response, and reinforcement. Motivation (that is, an individual's needs and goals) acts as a stimulus to learning. Cues give direction to those motives and help consumers fulfill their needs in product-specific ways. An individual's response to a drive or stimulus (cue) often depends on previous learning, which in turn is often the result of the type and degree of reinforcement received. Reinforcement increases the likelihood that a specific response will occur in the future as the result of particular cues.

There are two widely divergent theories of how individuals learn: behavioral theories and cognitive theories. Both kinds of theory contribute to an understanding of consumer behavior. Traditional behavioral theories include classical conditioning and instrumental conditioning. Three principles of classical conditioning provide the theoretical underpinnings for many marketing applications: repetition, stimulus generalization, and stimulus discrimination. Instrumental learning theorists believe that learning occurs through a trial-and-error process that associates a reward with a certain behavior. Both positive and negative reinforcement can be used to affect the likelihood of eliciting the desired response (behavior). The timing of learning schedules influences how long the learned material is retained. Massed learning produces more initial learning than distributed learning; however, learning usually persists longer with distributed (that is, spread out) schedules.

Cognitive learning theory holds that the kind of learning most characteristic of humans is problem solving, which involves mental processes rather than the purely behavioral components of learning stressed by the classical or instrumental theorists. Cognitive theorists are chiefly concerned with how information is processed by the human mind, and they draw an analogy with information processing by computers. A very simple model of the structure and operation of memory suggests the existence of three separate storage units: a sensory store, a short-term store, and a long-term store. The processes of memory include rehearsal, encoding, storage, and retrieval. Another model of information processing, called the levels-of-processing theory, suggests that the more involving the information is, the better it will be understood and the longer it will be retained.

For marketers, the purpose of understanding consumer learning theory is to teach the consumer that their brand is best so that they can develop brand loyalty. A basic issue among researchers is whether to define brand loyalty in terms of consumers' behavior (whether or not they buy the brand) or consumers' attitudes toward the brand (do they think of it favorably?). It has been suggested that the basic elements of learning theory can be used to promote brand loyalty by motivating consumers, by facilitating product trial, by repetition of promotional appeals, and by reinforcement.

discussion questions

1. Which of the following consumer behaviors demonstrate real learning as opposed to mere behavior? Why or why not?
   a. Buying the "store brand" of canned peas when it is the only one available.
   b. Recommending a brand you have used for years.
   c. Telling a friend about a funny television commercial but forgetting the brand name.

2. When a person is in a supermarket, his or her ultimate actions are affected by the types of learning discussed in this chapter. Give an example of how each may have affected your shopping behavior during your last trip to a supermarket.

3. How might classical conditioning affect our responses to certain kinds of food?

4. In what ways can brand-purchasing behavior be affected by *both* stimulus generalization and stimulus discrimination?

5. Kraft Foods uses family branding, but Procter and Gamble (Crest, Duncan Hines, Charmin, Tide) does not. Yet both companies are successful. Describe in "learning terms" the conditions under which family branding is a good policy and those under which it is not. What do you think are the reasons for the difference in family-branding policy between Kraft and P&G?

6. List the learning factors that affect the rate at which we will forget a brand name. (Hint: There are many more than three.)

7. Assume that you are advising the brand manager of Royal Crown Cola. Using your knowledge of brand loyalty, outline the strategies he or she might use for capturing a greater market share from the leaders, Pepsi and Coke.

8. Discuss the basic differences between behavioral theories of learning and cognitive theories of learning. Which of these learning theories do you think is more applicable to consumer behavior? Why?

endnotes

1. Stewart Henderson Britt, "Applying Learning Principles to Marketing," *MSU Business Topics*, 23 (Spring 1975), 5–6.
2. Robert F. Hartley, *Marketing Mistakes* (Columbus, Ohio: Grid, 1976), 81–95.
3. For a summary article on the effects of repetition on consumer behavior, see Alan G. Sawyer, "The Effects of Repetition: Conclusions and Suggestions from Experimental Laboratory Research," in G. David Hughes and Michael L. Ray, eds., *Buyer/Consumer Information Processing* (Chapel Hill: University of North Carolina Press, 1974), 190–219.
4. Politz Media Studies, *The Rochester Study* (New York: Saturday Evening Post, 1960). For subsequent similar studies, see also D.B. Lucas and S.H. Britt, *Measuring Advertising Effectiveness* (New York: McGraw-Hill, 1963); and A.W. Hubbard, *A Study of Advertising Effects in "Modern Medicine"* (New York: Modern Medicine, 1970).
5. W.L. Kruger, "The Effects of Overlearning on Retention," *Journal of Experimental Psychology*, 12 (1929), 71–78; and "Further Studies in Overlearning," *Journal of Experimental Psychology*, 13 (1930), 152–63. See also L. Postman, "Retention as a Function of Overlearning," *Science*, 135 (1962), 656–67.
6. C.S. Craig, B. Sternthal, and K. Olshan, "The Effect of Overlearning on Retention," *Journal of General Psychology*, 87 (1972), 85–94; and C.S. Craig, B. Sternthal, and C. Leavitt, "Advertising Wearout: An Experimental Analysis," *Journal of Advertising Research*, 16 (November 1976), 365–72.
7. Herbert Krugman, "What Makes Advertising Effective?" *Harvard Business Review*, 53 (March–April 1975), 96–103.
8. Howard Kamin, "Advertising Reach and Frequency," *Journal of Advertising Research*, 18 (February 1978), 21–25.
9. George Miaoulis and Nancy D'Amato, "Consumer Confusion and Trademark Infringement," *Journal of Marketing*, 42 (April 1978), 48–55.
10. Bernice Kanner, "DFS Develops System to Find New Extension," *Advertising Age*, November 19, 1979, 20. See also Herbert Zeltner, "Product Line Extensions Can Spur Profitable New Volume," *Advertising Age*, April 26, 1976, 60, 62.
11. For other examples of positioning, see the series of articles by Jack Trout and Al Ries in *Advertising Age*, April 24, May 1, and May 8, 1972.
12. B.R. Hergenhahn, *An Introduction to Theories of Learning* (Englewood Cliffs, N.J.: Prentice-Hall, 1976), 170.
13. These and other differences are treated at greater length in Henry R. Ellis, *Fundamentals of Human Learning and Cognition* (Dubuque, Iowa: William C. Brown Co., 1972), 13–15.
14. J. Ronald Carey, Steven H. Clicque, Barbara A. Leighton, and Frank Milton, "A Test of Positive Reinforcement of Customers," *Journal of Marketing*, 40 (October 1976), 98–100.
15. See H.A. Zielske, "The Remembering and Forgetting of Advertising," *Journal of Marketing*, 23 (January 1959), 231–43; and E.C. Strong, "The Effects of Repetition of Advertising: A Field Study" (Ph.D. dissertation, Stanford University, 1972).

16. H.A. Zielske and Walter A. Henry, "Remembering and Forgetting Television Ads," *Journal of Advertising Research,* 20 (April 1980), 7–13.

17. The chief advocate of modeling, or social learning theory, is Albert Bandura. See his *Social Learning Theory* (Englewood Cliffs, N.J.: Prentice-Hall, 1977). Social learning theory has become particularly important in explaining how children learn from television, including TV advertising. See Elzora Dalrymple, "Learning Theory: Children and Television," in Barbara J. Redman, *Consumer Behavior: Theory and Applications* (Westport, Conn.: AVI Publishing Co., 1979), 164–76.

18. R.C. Atkinson and R.M. Shiffrin, "Human Memory: A Proposed System and Its Central Processes," in E.W. Spence and J.T. Spence, eds., *The Psychology of Learning and Motivation* (New York: Academic Press, 1968), Vol. II.

19. See George A. Miller, "The Magical Number Seven, Plus or Minus Two: Some Limits on Our Capacity for Processing Information," *Psychological Review,* 63 (1956), 81–97; and Herbert A. Simon, "How Big Is a Chunk?" *Science,* 183 (February 1974), 482–88.

20. See, for example, Nicoll Frijda, "Simulation of Human Long-Term Memory," *Psychological Bulletin,* 77 (January 1972), 1–31.

21. Peter H. Lindsay and Donald A. Norman, *Human Information Processing: An Introduction to Psychology* (New York: Academic Press, 1972), 340.

22. For a review of the literature on rehearsal and some of the other processes discussed here, see James R. Bettman, "Memory Factors in Consumer Choice: A Review," *Journal of Marketing,* 43 (Spring 1979), esp. 39–42.

23. Nancy C. Waugh and Donald A. Norman, "Primary Memory," *Psychological Review,* 72 (1965), 89–104.

24. Bettman, "Memory Factors in Consumer Choice," 50.

25. Jerry C. Olson, "Theories of Information Encoding and Storage: Implications for Consumer Research," in Andrew B. Mitchell, ed., *The Effects of Information on Consumer and Market Behavior* (Chicago: American Marketing Association, 1978), 51.

26. Sam Harper, "Elsie Moo-ves Back into Ad Limelight," *Marketing News,* November 19, 1979, 1.

27. Bettman, "Memory Factors in Consumer Choice," 50.

28. Endel Tulvig, "Episodic and Semantic Memory," in Endel Tulvig and W. Donaldson, eds., *Organization of Memory* (New York: Academic Press, 1972), 381–403.

29. Olson, "Theories of Information Encoding and Storage," 54.

30. Eric J. Johnson and J. Edward Russo, "Product Familiarity and the Learning of New Information" (Unpublished paper, 1980).

31. J. Edward Russo and Eric J. Johnson, "What Do Consumers Know about Familiar Products?" in Jerry C. Olson, ed., *Advances in Consumer Research* (Ann Arbor, Mich.: Association for Consumer Research, 1980), VII, 418.

32. Jacob Jacoby, Robert W. Chestmist, and William Silberman, "Consumer Uses and Comprehension of Nutrition Information," *Journal of Consumer Research,* 4 (September 1977), 119–28.

33. The levels-of-processing theory was originated by Fergus I.M. Craik and Robert S. Lockhard in "Levels of Processing: A Framework for Memory Research," *Journal of Verbal Learning and Verbal Behavior,* 11 (December 1972), 671–84. For further discussion of the theory, see Joel Saegert and Robert J. Hoover, "Learning Theory and Marketing: An Update," in Kenneth L. Bernhardt, ed., *1976 Educators' Proceedings* (Chicago: American Marketing Association, 1976), 513; and Bettman, Memory Factors in Consumer Choice," 38–39.

34. H.E. Krugman, "The Impact of Television Advertising: Learning without Involvement," *Public Opinion Quarterly*, 29 (1965), 349–65.

35. "Reinforcing the Impact of TV Commercials," *Business Week*, July 18, 1977, 40–41.

36. For an extensive bibliography, see Bettman, "Memory Factors in Consumer Choice," 51–53.

37. Werner Kroeber-Riel, "Activation Research: Psychobiological Approaches in Consumer Research," *Journal of Consumer Research*, 5 (March 1979), 240–50.

38. W.T. Tucker, "The Development of Brand Loyalty," *Journal of Marketing Research*, 1 (August 1964), 33.

39. Ross Cunningham, "Brand Loyalty—What, Where, How Much," *Harvard Business Review*, 34 (January–February 1956), 116.

40. George S. Day, "A Two-Dimensional Concept of Brand Loyalty," *Journal of Advertising Research*, 9 (September 1969), 30.

41. Roy L. Moore and Lowndes F. Stephens, "Some Communication and Demographic Determinants of Adolescent Consumer Learning," *Journal of Consumer Research*, 2 (September 1975), 85.

42. Lester Guest, "Brand Loyalty Revisited: A Twenty-Year Report," *Journal of Applied Psychology*, 48 (1964), 97.

43. W. Massy and R. Frank, "Short-Term Price and Dealing Effects in Selected Market Segments," *Journal of Marketing Research*, 2 (May 1965), 175–85; D. Montgomery, "Consumer Characteristics Associated with Dealing: An Empirical Example," *Journal of Marketing Research*, 8 (February 1971), 118–20; and F. Webster, "The Deal-Prone Consumer," *Journal of Marketing Research*, 2 (May 1965), 186–89.

44. Joe A. Dodson, Alice M. Tybout, and Brian Sternthal, "Impact of Deals and Deal Retraction on Brand Switching," *Journal of Marketing Research*, 15 (February 1978), 72–81.

EIGHT

The Nature
of Consumer Attitudes

introduction

EVERY time consumers are asked whether they *like* or *dislike* a product, a service, an advertising theme, or a particular retailer, they are being asked to express their attitudes. Within the realm of consumer behavior, attitude research has been employed to study a wide range of critical marketing strategy questions. For example, attitude research is commonly undertaken to (1) ascertain the likelihood that consumers will accept a proposed new-product idea, (2) gauge why a firm's target audience has not reacted more favorably to its revised promotional theme, and (3) learn how target customers are likely to react to a proposed change in the firm's packaging and label.

In fact, it is difficult to imagine any consumer research project that does not measure some aspect of consumer attitudes. As an outgrowth of this pervasive interest in consumer attitudes, it is not surprising that attitudes have received much attention in the consumer behavior literature.

In this chapter we will discuss the reasons why attitude research has had such a pervasive impact on consumer behavior. We will also discuss the properties that have made attitudes so attractive to consumer researchers, as well as some of the common frustrations encountered in conducting attitude research. Particular attention will be given to a number of important models relating to the structure and composition of attitudes. Finally, we will review the approaches frequently employed to measure consumer attitudes. In Chapter 9 we will continue our discussion of attitudes by focusing on the central topics of attitude formation and attitude change, and a number of related issues.

WHAT ARE ATTITUDES?

As the opening sentence of this chapter implies, attitudes are an expression of inner feelings that reflect whether a person is favorably or unfavorably predisposed to some "object" (e.g., a brand, a service, a retail establishment). As an outcome of some psychological process, attitudes are not directly observable but must be inferred from what people say or from their behavior. Thus

In your heart you know he's right.

POLITICAL BILLBOARD (1964)

consumer researchers tend to assess attitudes by asking questions or inferring attitudes from behavior. To illustrate, if a researcher determines from questioning a consumer that the individual has consistently bought Close-Up toothpaste and recommends it to friends, the researcher would be likely to infer a positive attitude toward Close-Up.

This illustration suggests that a whole universe of consumer behaviors—consistent purchase, recommendations to others, top rankings, beliefs, evaluations, and intentions—are related to attitudes. What, then, are attitudes? According to one popular definition, an *attitude* is *"a learned predisposition to respond in a consistently favorable or unfavorable manner with respect to a given object."*[1] Each part of this definition is an important property of an attitude and is critical for understanding the role that attitudes play in the examination of consumer behavior.

The Attitude "Object"

The word *object* in our adopted definition of attitude is designed to be interpreted broadly. Any of the many more specific concepts might be substituted in its place—e.g., issues, actions, behavior, practices, persons, or events. In consumer behavior, we would be inclined to substitute consumer- or marketing-related concepts, such as product category, brand, service, advertisement, price, or retailer. In actual attitude research, we might even be more specific. For example, if we were interested in ascertaining shoppers' attitudes toward a number of major mass merchandisers, our "object" would include Sears, Montgomery Ward, J.C. Penney, and K Mart; whereas if we were examining children's attitudes toward a number of major brands of toothpaste, our "object" would include Crest, Aqua-fresh, Colgate, and Aim.

Attitudes Are a Learned Predisposition

There is general agreement that attitudes are learned. This means that attitudes relevant to purchase behavior are formed as an outgrowth of direct experience with the product, and/or the information acquired from others and exposure to mass media (e.g., advertising). Closely related to the idea that attitudes are learned is the realization that they are not behavior itself, but rather they reflect either a favorable or an unfavorable evaluation of the attitude object. Also, as a predisposition, attitudes might have a motivational quality; that is, they might propel the consumer toward a particular behavior.

Attitudes Have Consistency

Another characteristic of an attitude is that it is relatively *consistent* with the behavior that it reflects. However, we should avoid confusing *consistency* and *permanency*. Attitudes are not necessarily permanent; they do change (we will explore attitude change in the next chapter).

It is important to illustrate what we mean by consistency. Normally we expect consumer attitudes to correspond with behavior; that is, if a segment of consumers report that they especially like Dannon Yogurt, we expect that they will buy Dannon Yogurt. Similarly, if these consumers are not particularly fond of Yoplait Yogurt, we do *not* expect that this brand will be bought by these consumers. Thus, when consumers are free to act as they desire, we anticipate that their actions will be consistent with their attitudes. However, circumstances are not always uniform. Therefore we must consider the influence of the *situation* on consumer attitudes and behavior.

Attitudes Occur Within a Situation

It is not immediately evident from our definition of attitudes that they occur within and are affected by a situation. What are situations? *Situations* are events or circumstances that, at a point in time, influence the relationship between attitudes and behavior. Specifically, a situation can cause consumers to behave in a manner seemingly inconsistent with their attitudes. For instance, let us assume that a consumer purchases a six-pack of a different brand of soft drink each time his or her inventory runs low. Although the brand switching may indicate a negative attitude or dissatisfaction, it may alternatively have been influenced by a specific event or situation. That is, although the consumer may have a strong preference for Coca-Cola, it is possible that he or she is on a tight budget and, therefore, is responding by purchasing any brand on "special" at the supermarket or any brand for which a cents-off coupon appears in the local newspaper.

The opposite is also true. For instance, if a consumer purchases a six-pack of Tab each time his or her supply runs low, we may mistakenly conclude that the consumer has a generally favorable attitude toward Tab. On the contrary, the consumer may dislike the taste of Tab but may be on a diet and therefore have a specifically favorable attitude toward Tab as a means of losing a couple of pounds.

In a similar vein, individuals can have different attitudes toward a particular behavior; each corresponding to a particular situation. To illustrate, a man may feel that it is suitable to eat lunch at McDonald's but may not consider it acceptable for dinner. In this case, McDonald's has its "time and place," which functions as a boundary indicating those situations when McDonald's is acceptable. However, if the individual is coming home late one night, feels exhausted and hungry, and spots a McDonald's, he may just decide to have "dinner" there. Why? Because it is late, he is tired and hungry, and McDonald's is convenient. Has he changed his attitude? Probably not.

The lesson to be gained from each of these cases is that unless we consider the situation when measuring attitudes, we can misinterpret the relationship between attitudes and behavior.

In recent years, increased attention has been given to how consumer behavior is influenced by the *situation* in which it is likely to occur.[2] As part of this research, a number of studies have reported that consumer attitudes may vary from situation to situation.[3] For instance, one study examined whether consumer preferences for different fast-food chains operating in a midwestern city (e.g., Arby's, Burger King, McDonald's, and Wendy's) varied in terms of four eating occasions or situations (i.e., lunch on a weekday, snack during a shopping trip, evening meal when rushed for time, and evening meal with family when not rushed for time).[4] The results revealed that there are some distinct differences in consumer preferences for the various fast-food restaurants depending upon the anticipated eating situation. McDonald's, for example, was the front-runner across all four of the eating situations, whereas Wendy's was found to be at its strongest with consumers who were seeking a place to have the evening dinner with the family when not in a rush. For Wendy's, the findings suggest that it might emphasize building consumer acceptance that Wendy's is a nice place to take the family for a leisurely (and inexpensive) dinner.

STRUCTURAL MODELS OF ATTITUDES

Now that we have defined what attitudes are, *and* elaborated on their basic properties, it is appropriate that we examine several important attitude models. Specifically, we will consider the following structural models of an attitude: (1) the tricomponent attitude model, (2) single-component attitude models, and (3) multiattribute attitude models. Each of the models provides a somewhat different perspective as to the number of component parts of an attitude, or how those parts are arranged or interrelated.

Tricomponent Attitude Model

Motivated by a desire to understand the attitude-behavior relationship, behavioral scientists, especially social psychologists, have endeavored to construct models that capture the underlying dimensions of an attitude.[5] To this end, the focus has been on more precisely specifying the composition of an attitude and thereby to better explain or predict behavior.

Attitudes are frequently portrayed as consisting of three major components: (1) a cognitive component, (2) an affective component, and (3) a conative component (see Figure 8-1). We will briefly define each of these components and then consider various ways in which they have been organized or arranged.

THE COGNITIVE COMPONENT

The first component of the tricomponent attitude model consists of a person's knowledge and perceptions that are acquired by a combination of direct experience with the attitude-object, and related information secured from various sources. This knowledge and resulting perceptions frequently take the form of *beliefs;* that is, the attitude-object possesses various attributes, or beliefs, that specific behavior will lead to specific outcomes.

While capturing only a portion of a consumer's belief system toward two brands of mouthwash, Figure 8-2 illustrates just how complex a consumer's belief system can be. It is interesting that, with the exception of the attribute "dentist," the same basic attributes for both brands are included in the consumer's belief system. However, the beliefs about several of the attributes are different. For instance, the consumer sees Scope as tasting "sweet like a soft

FIGURE 8-1   A Simple Representation of the Tricomponent Attitude Model

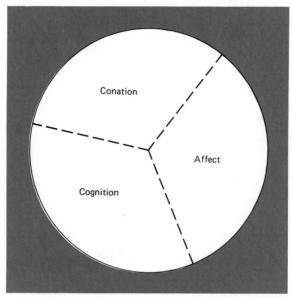

FIGURE 8-2   A Consumer's Belief System for Two Different Brands of Mouthwash

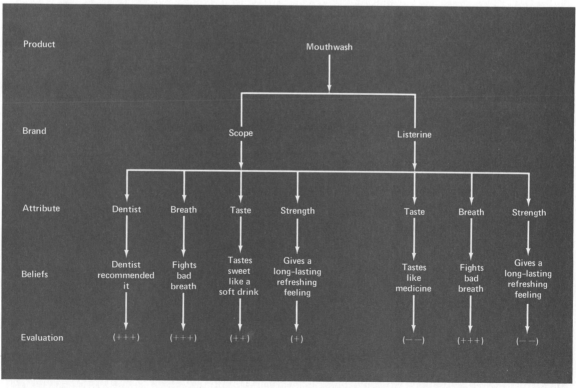

drink;" whereas Listerine is perceived as tasting "like medicine." Also, the consumer does not necessarily evaluate the same basic belief the same for each brand. For example, with regard to the *long-lasting quality,* Scope is evaluated positively, whereas Listerine is evaluated negatively.

Such insights are useful in positioning a particular brand against competing brands (see the discussion of perceptual mapping in Chapter 6 for more detail on this topic).

THE AFFECTIVE COMPONENT

A consumer's emotions or feelings with respect to a particular product or brand constitute the affective component of an attitude.

These emotions and feelings are primarily *evaluative* in nature. They capture an individual's *overall* assessment of the attitude-object; that is, the extent to which the individual rates the attitude-object as favorable or unfavorable.

Since the affective component assesses overall feelings about the attitude-object, it has frequently been considered the essential aspect of an attitude. Indeed, as we will discuss later, some researchers *treat the affective component as being the attitude itself,* and the two other components as serving some related or supportive functions.[6]

THE CONATIVE COMPONENT

Conation, the final component of the tricomponent attitude model, is concerned with the *likelihood* or *tendency* that an individual will undertake a specific action or behave in a particular way with regard to the attitude-object. Also, according to some interpretations, the conative component may include the actual behavior itself.

In marketing and consumer research, the conative component is frequently treated as an expression of the consumer's *intention to buy.* Therefore a variety of buyer-intention scales are employed to assess the likelihood of purchasing or behaving in a certain way.

Single-Component Attitude Models

In contrast to the tricomponent perspective, researchers subscribing to a single-component attitude model treat the affective, or feeling, component by itself as being the attitude.[7]

Following this viewpoint, a consumer's attitude toward various brands of 35-mm cameras would be equal to the individual's overall evaluation of the comparative merit (e.g., "good" versus "bad," "positive" versus "negative," "favorable" versus "unfavorable" assessments) of those brands being considered (frequently known as the consumer's evoked set; see Chapter 6).

The single-component attitude model is especially popular with marketing researchers who want to save time and space by including a single evaluative scale on a questionnaire.[8] However, although it is uncomplicated, the single-component model fails to provide useful insights as to what influences or explains a consumer's evaluative rating. To illustrate, two consumers may possess the same positive attitude (i.e., the same level of affect) toward Aqua-fresh toothpaste with quite different salient beliefs; that is, one may like it because of its fresh taste, whereas the other may like it because it helps whiten teeth. Unless the researcher were to measure each consumer's beliefs and evaluations about each attribute of Aqua-fresh, all that would be known is that they possess the same basic level of affect toward Aqua-fresh. Thus we would be left in the dark as to the underlying knowledge and beliefs that the consumers are likely to bring to bear in arriving at their overall assessment. Moreover, we would not be provided with any relevant insights as to the relationship between the evaluation and the consumer's intention to buy.

To overcome the shortcomings of the single-component attitude model, a number of attitude researchers have suggested a compromise between the broadly conceived tricomponent attitude model and the too narrowly focused single-component model. The resulting *modified single-component attitude models,* while still considering affect to be the attitude, include cognition and conation as interrelated and important factors that flow into and flow out of the affective component (see Figure 8-3). In a sense, the modified model is a *rearrangement* of the tricomponent model—with the distinction being that the affect component is treated as being the attitude, and the two other components are somewhat downgraded to "supporting roles."

We will now consider a number of modified single-component attitude models under their popular label of "multiattribute attitude models."

Multiattribute Attitude Models

Given that multiattribute attitude models examine consumer attitudes in terms of selected product attributes or beliefs, they are particularly appealing to both consumer researchers and marketing practitioners.[9] While there are many variations of this type of attitude model, those proposed by Fishbein and his

FIGURE 8-3   **A Modified Single-Component Attitude Model**   Source: Adapted from Richard J. Lutz, "The Role of Attitude Theory in Marketing," in Harold H. Kassarjian and Thomas S. Robertson, eds., *Perspectives in Consumer Behavior,* 3rd ed. (Glenview, Ill.: Scott, Foresman, 1981), 235.

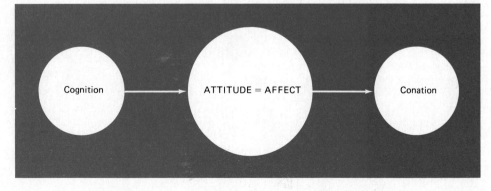

associates have stimulated the greatest amount of research interest.[10] We have selected three Fishbein models to be considered here because of their potential merit in applied consumer behavior research: (1) the attitude-toward-object model, (2) the attitude-toward-behavior model, and (3) the theory of reasoned action model.

THE ATTITUDE-TOWARD-OBJECT MODEL

The attitude-toward-object model has received widescale attention in consumer behavior.[11] Its attraction stems from the fact that it is especially suitable for measuring attitudes toward a *product* or specific *brands* (i.e., the object). In accordance with this model, a consumer's attitude is defined as being a function of the presence (or absence) *and* evaluation of a number of product-specific beliefs or product attributes possibly possessed by a product or specific brands of a product. Following from this, consumers will generally have favorable attitudes toward those brands they assess as having an adequate level of positive attributes, and unfavorable attitudes toward those brands they feel have an inadequate level of desired attributes or too many negative attributes. Table 8-1 lists two different belief systems (one favorable and other unfavorable) for two different consumers.

The Fishbein attitude-toward-object model is usually depicted in the form of the following equation:[12]

$$\text{Attitude}_0 = \sum_{i=1}^{n} b_i e_i$$

where Attitude_0 is a separately assessed overall measure of affect for or against the attitude-object (e.g., a product, a brand, a service, a retail establishment); b_i is the *strength* of the belief that the attitude-object contains the ith attribute (e.g., the likelihood that Duncan Hines cake mix tastes "homemade"); e_i is the evaluative dimension associated with the ith attribute (e.g., how good or bad is the quality of being "homemade"); and Σ indicates that there are n salient attributes over which the b_i and e_i combinations are summated.

Before moving on to the next model proposed by Fishbein and his colleagues, it should be pointed out that numerous modified versions of the

TABLE 8-1   Two Hypothetical Belief Systems Concerning Nikon Cameras

consumer 1 (mainly negative)	consumer 2 (mainly positive)
Nikons are expensive.	Nikons are high quality
Nikons are too complex.	Nikons are dependable.
Nikons are used by professionals.	Nikons are used by professionals.
Nikons are high quality.	Nikons have the best lenses.

Source: Inspired by Icek Ajzen and Martin Fishbein, *Understanding Attitudes and Predicting Social Behavior* (Englewood Cliffs, N.J.: Prentice-Hall, 1980), 63.

Fishbein attitude-toward-object model have been suggested in the consumer behavior and marketing literature.[13] These models, which have been referred to as "ad hoc" or "intuitive," frequently examine the relationship between some overall evaluation of a brand (e.g., preference, affect, intention, or brand choice) and a combination of consumers' beliefs as to the brand's possession of specific product attributes and the importance attached to these attributes. As a group, these intuitive models have been criticized for not faithfully testing the attitude models that were borrowed from social psychology.[14]

THE ATTITUDE-TOWARD-BEHAVIOR MODEL

Consumer researchers are paying more and more attention to the Fishbein attitude-toward-behavior model.[15] The focus of this second model is the individual's attitude toward *behaving or acting with respect to an object, rather than the attitude toward the object itself.*

The attitude-toward-behavior model is now favored by Fishbein and his associates, for they believe that it corresponds more closely with actual behavior than the attitude-toward-object model.[16] For instance, knowing a consumer's attitude about the act of *purchasing* a $10,000 Rolex watch (i.e., attitude toward the behavior) is more revealing about the potential act of purchasing than simply knowing the consumer's attitude toward the watch (i.e., attitude toward the object). This seems logical, for a consumer might have a positive attitude toward the $10,000 watch, but a negative attitude as to the prospects of purchasing such an expensive watch.

The attitude-toward-behavior model is depicted by the following equation:[17]

$$\text{Attitude}_{\text{(beh)}} = \sum_{i=1}^{n} b_i e_i$$

where Attitude$_{\text{(beh)}}$ is a separately assessed overall measure of affect for or against carrying out a specific action or behavior (e.g., buying, preparing, or serving a Duncan Hines cake); b_i is the *strength* of the belief that an ith specific action will lead to a specific outcome (e.g., that the preparation of a Duncan Hines cake will indeed taste "homemade"); e_i is an evaluation of the ith outcome (e.g., the "favorableness" of a cake's tasting "homemade"); and Σ indicates that there are n salient outcomes over which the b_i and e_i combinations are summated.[18]

THEORY OF REASONED ACTION MODEL

The theory of reasoned action builds on the earlier research conducted by Fishbein and his associates.[19] It represents a comprehensive and integrated arrangement of attitude components into a structure that is designed to lead to both better prediction and better explanation of behavior. Like the basic tricomponent attitude model that we have already reviewed, the theory of reasoned action incorporates a cognitive component, an affective component, and a conative component, which are arranged in a pattern different from that of the tricomponent model.

Figure 8-4 sets out the theory of reasoned action (examine it carefully). Working backward from behavior (e.g., the act of purchasing a particular product or brand), the model suggests that the best predictor of behavior is intention to act. Thus, if consumer researchers were solely interested in predicting behavior, they would directly measure intention (i.e., use an intention-to-act scale). However, if they were also interested in understanding the underlying factors that contribute to intention to act in a particular consumer situation, they would look behind intention and consider the factors that lead to intention; that is, a consumer's attitude-toward-behavior and the subjective norm.

Continuing with the same basic logic, attitude-toward-behavior can be directly measured as *affect* (i.e., a measure of overall favorability toward the act of purchasing a product or brand). Further, as with intention, we can get behind the attitude to its underlying dimensions (see our discussion of the attitude-toward-behavior model).

In accordance with this expanded model, if we wish to understand intention we must also measure an individual's subjective norm that influences

FIGURE 8-4   A Simplified Version of the Theory of Reasoned Action
Source: Adapted from Icek Ajzen and Martin Fishbein, *Understanding Attitudes and Predicting Social Behavior* (Englewood Cliffs, N.J.: Prentice-Hall, 1980), 84.

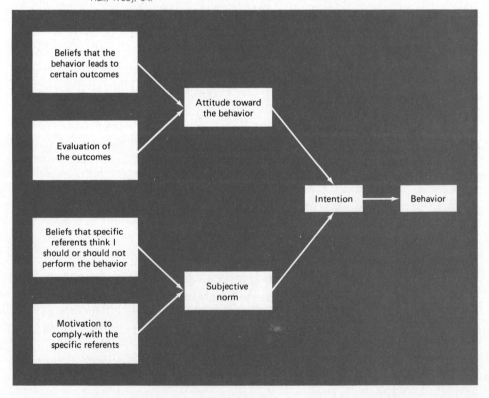

intention to act. A subjective norm can be measured directly by assessing a consumer's feelings as to what relevant others (family, friends, roommates, co-workers) would think of the action being contemplated; that is, Would they look favorably or unfavorably on the anticipated action?

Within a consumer behavior context, if a college student were considering purchasing microstereo equipment for his dormitory room and stopped to ask himself what his parents or his roommate would think of such behavior (i.e., approve or disapprove), such a reflection would constitute the subjective norm.

Still further, as with an attitude, consumer researchers can get behind the subjective norm to the underlying factors that are likely to produce it. They would accomplish this by assessing those *normative beliefs* that the individual attributes to relevant others, as well as the individual's motivation to comply with each of the relevant others. For instance, consider the student who is contemplating the purchase of microstereo equipment. To understand what precipitates his subjective norm about the anticipated purchase, we would have to determine who are his relevant others (e.g., parents and roommate); his belief as to how each would respond to his purchasing the equipment (e.g., "Mom and Dad would consider the purchase to be unwarranted, but my roommate would love it"); and finally, his motivation to comply with his parents and roommate.

The above discussion and examples suggest that the theory of reasoned action is a series of interrelated attitude components (i.e., beliefs precede attitude and normative beliefs precede subjective norms; then attitudes and subjective norms precede intention; and intention precedes actual behavior).

Consistent with the theory of reasoned action, an attitude is not as strongly or as directly linked to behavior, as intention is linked to behavior. In part, this framework flows from the observation that intention is usually more highly associated with behavior than is the link between attitude and behavior.

It is possible to ask, Why study attitudes at all if intention is ultimately a better predictor of behavior? The answer is, Although intention may be a better predictor, it does *not* provide an adequate explanation of behavior. Thus, if marketers desire (which they often do) to understand *why* consumers are acting as they do, then they require something more than a basically mechanical measure of what the consumers are expected to do (i.e., buying intention). Similarly, a measure of *affect* may do just fine in terms of predicting an attitude; however, marketers usually desire to know what the underlying or salient attributes or beliefs are that produce the specific attitude.

THE MEASUREMENT OF ATTITUDES

Now that we have explored the structure of various attitude models, let us briefly examine a number of major attitude measurement approaches. The measurement of attitudes is an important topic, one that marketing and consumer researchers recognize as influencing their ability to predict consumer behavior accurately.

In our discussion of attitude measurement, we will consider three important research approaches that are frequently employed to gauge consumers' attitudes: (1) observation of behavior, (2) qualitative research methods, and (3) self-report attitude scales.

Observation of Behavior

Since we cannot get inside consumers' heads to observe their attitudes directly, we must rely on *indirect* measures of attitudes. One such measurement approach is to observe consumers' behavior and to infer from their behavior their attitudes.

This practice of inferring attitudes from behavior is going on constantly, not only by professional researchers but by each of us in the course of our daily lives. For instance, if you were to observe that the person ahead of you on the supermarket checkout line was buying five boxes of a breakfast cereal, you might conclude that several members of the shopper's family probably liked the brand.

In much the same way as you might informally observe and draw conclusions from others' behavior, so too do professional researchers observe behavior. However, the difference is that they are *trained observers* and they are scrutinizing consumer behavior in order to draw conclusions that will become part of a research report.

Although observational research is quite useful (e.g., when consumers are observed in the act of shopping in a supermarket or some other type of retail establishment), drawing conclusions as to consumers' attitudes from their behavior is often difficult and almost always quite subjective. For instance, the shopper who was observed purchasing five boxes of breakfast cereal might have done so in order to take advantage of the store's special low price, rather than because family members especially liked the brand.

It is difficult for an observer, even a highly trained one, to be particularly confident when inferring attitudes from a single action, in a single situation. However, if the researcher were able to observe the same behavior at different points in time (e.g., see the same shopper purchase the same brand of cereal on other trips to the supermarket), or see the shopper purchase the cereal under different circumstances (e.g., when the brand was *not* on store special), then the researcher might be more confident that the behavior reflected a positive attitude. Since researchers seldom have the opportunity to observe the same consumers repeatedly, it is common practice to employ observations as a supplement to other research approaches.

Qualitative Research Methods

Attitude researchers have found qualitative research methods, especially depth interviews and focus group sessions, to be quite useful in getting a handle on the nature of consumers' attitudes.

While these two research methods differ in composition (i.e., depth interviews question one person at a time, whereas focus group sessions question about eight to ten participants and are designed to take advantage of group dynamics), they both are closely associated with motivational research (see Chapter 3) and have their roots in the psychoanalytic and clinical aspects of psychology. In particular, they both stress open-ended and free-response types of questioning that attempt to stimulate respondents to reveal their inner thoughts or beliefs.

Specifically, these two methods are regularly employed in the early stage of attitude research to pinpoint the relevant product-related beliefs or attributes. To illustrate, let us assume that, as a result of a number of focus group sessions, a leading marketer of clock-radios notices that sleepy users are more interested in the ease of setting and resetting the clock-radio's timer than in the audio quality of the radio.

As the illustration implies, depth interviews and focus groups, consisting of potential product users, are frequently held to determine which product or brand attributes consumers are likely to use in judging alternative brands. Table 8-2 lists a sample of product attributes associated with four different product categories. Such lists of attributes are often developed as an outcome of depth interviews or focus group sessions, or some related form of qualitative research.

Self-Report Attitude Scales

The most common way of assessing consumers' attitudes is through the administration of a questionnaire containing attitude scales.[20]

While a great many attitude-scaling procedures have been proposed, a recent survey reveals that the three most popular scaling procedures are (1) Likert scales, (2) semantic differential scales, and (3) rank-order scales.[21] We will briefly examine each of these three attitude scales, along with the Lampert Pollimeter—an interesting new scaling device that seems especially suitable for measuring consumer attitudes.

LIKERT SCALES

The Likert scale is by far the most popular form of attitude scaling. It enjoys this status because it is easy for researchers to prepare and uncomplicated for consumers to respond to. Likert scales can be recognized by their characteristic "agreement" scale, which provides respondents with the opportunity to reveal their degree of agreement or disagreement with a series of statements that are prepared to fully describe the attitude-object under investigation. Figure 8-5 on Page 213 presents a sample of Likert scales as they might be employed in a consumer attitude survey for a proposed skin-care product.

A principal attraction of Likert scales is that they give researchers the option of either treating the response to each attitude statement as a separate scale or combining the responses of those items that pertain to the same basic attitude dimension into a composite or weighted attitude score. It is because of this feature that Likert scales are frequently referred to as *summated scales*.

SEMANTIC DIFFERENTIAL SCALES

Similar to the Likert scale, the semantic differential scale is relatively easy to construct and administer. The scale typically consists of a series of bipolar antonyms (adjectives or phrases, e.g., good-bad, liberal-conservative, like-dislike, sweet-sour, high priced-low priced, slow service-fast service), which when anchored at the ends of a 5-point or 7-point scale provide respondents with an opportunity to evaluate a concept (e.g., United Airlines, 7-Eleven stores, Audi 5000 Turbo, Blue Diamond almonds, and All-Temperature Cheer). The major

TABLE 8-2   Examples of Product Attributes Associated with Four Different Product Categories

mouthwash:
- effective against colds and sore throats
- gives long-lasting protection
- effective for killing germs
- recommended by dentists
- effective against bad breath
- leaves mouth feeling refreshed
- not too strong tasting
- effective for relief of gum trouble
- leaves no unpleasant after-taste
- pleasant flavor

juice drinks:
- convenient
- children can drink as much as they like
- excellent source of Vitamin C
- great wake-up taste
- cost-per-serving
- nutritional
- high fresh-fruit content
- appealing taste
- uniquely suitable for children
- significant contribution to diet

household disinfectant:
- kills flu virus
- prevents spread of colds
- eliminates significant number of germs and viruses
- medically beneficial in reducing spread of colds
- kills germs on environmental surfaces
- reduces incidence of colds
- eliminates odor
- kills germs that cause illnesses
- protects your family
- kills viruses and germs in the air

washing machines:
- variable wash and spin speeds
- wash water temperature control
- frequency of repair record
- variable fill levels
- rinse-water temperature control
- detergent requirements
- availability of repair service
- guarantee
- price
- maximum load capacity

Source: Winifred A. Adams, "Evaluation of an Expectancy Screening Model for Federal Trade Commission Reviews of Advertising Deception," in John C. Maloney and Bernard Silverman, eds., *Attitude Research Plays for High Stakes* (Chicago: American Marketing Association, 1979), 357.

FIGURE 8-5　　An Application of Likert Scales to Gauge Consumer
　　　　　　　　Attitudes Toward a Proposed Skin-Care Product

Instruction:

Please place an "X" in the space which best indicates how strongly you agree or disagree with each of
the following statements about your trial of the skin care product.

	Strongly agree	Agree	Neither agree nor disagree	Disagree	Strongly disagree
The product has an especially fresh scent	_____	_____	_____	_____	_____
This skin cream has not improved how my skin feels	_____	_____	_____	_____	_____
I would recommend this product to my friends	_____	_____	_____	_____	_____
I prefer my regular skin-care product	_____	_____	_____	_____	_____
My skin looks better since I have been using this product	_____	_____	_____	_____	_____
I wouldn't purchase this product if it were available for sale	_____	_____	_____	_____	_____
My face feels cleaner since I started using the product	_____	_____	_____	_____	_____
The product feels more greasy than my regular product	_____	_____	_____	_____	_____

　　　　Continued . . . . .

feature of the semantic differential is that it lends itself to the creation of profiles
of consumers' attitudes that can be depicted in graphic form.

A popular application of the semantic differential scaling procedure has
been in the examination of shoppers' attitudes toward competitive retail
establishments. Such studies are frequently referred to as *store image studies.*
Figure 8-6 presents a semantic differential instrument used in an actual store
image study. The findings that are superimposed on the instrument in graphic

FIGURE 8-6   An Example of the Image Profiles That Can Be Constructed
with Semantic Differential Scales   Source: G.H.G. McDougall and
J.N. Fry, "Combining Two Methods of Image Measurement," *Journal of
Retailing*, 50 (Winter 1974–75), 60.

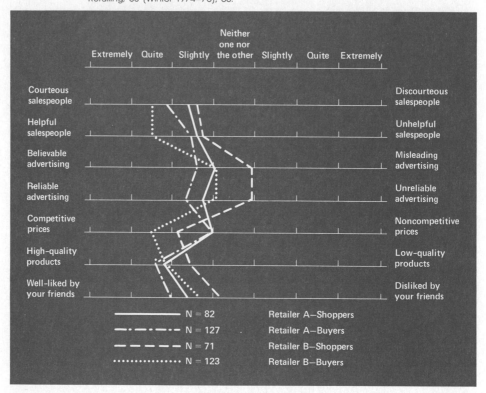

form have been partitioned into two groups ("shoppers" and "buyers") for each
of the two types of stores being contrasted (Retailer A—a traditional full-line
department store, and Retailer B—a promotional furniture and appliance
store.)[22]

RANK-ORDER SCALES

As its name implies, a rank-order scale has subjects *rank* a set of attitude-objects
(e.g., brands of frozen vegetables) in terms of some criterion (e.g., fresh taste).
Rank-order scaling procedures are especially suitable in attitude measurement
because they allow consumers to evaluate alternative brands, and thus they are
an important way of assessing brand preference or brand choice.

Figure 8-7 shows how the rank-order scale is utilized in consumer attitude
research.

THE LAMPERT POLLIMETER

The Lampert Pollimeter is a simple scaling device embodying a number of
characteristics that make it a useful tool for attitude research.[23] It looks and

FIGURE 8-7   Examples of Rank-Order Scales Used in Attitude Research

A. Rank the following motel/hotels from 1st to 6th in terms of the quality of the food served.

_____ Holiday Inn

_____ Howard Johnson

_____ Hyatt

_____ Marriott

_____ Quality Inn

_____ Ramada Inn

B. We're interested in knowing how much you enjoy each of the following *four* types of TV programs. Please rank them from "1" to "4," where a "1" means that you enjoy it most and a "4" means that you enjoy it least.

_____ Police or Detective Stories

_____ Sports

_____ Western Drama

_____ Game Shows

C. The following are six brands of French salad-dressing. We are interested in learning your preference for each of these brands. Place a "1" alongside the brand that you would be most likely to buy, a "2" alongside the brand that you would be next most likely to buy. Continue doing this untiil you have ranked all six brands.

_____ Good Seasons

_____ Wish-Bone

_____ Kraft Creamy

_____ Walden Farms Creamy

_____ Seven Seas Creamy

_____ Girard's Original

operates like a common slide rule (see Figure 8-8). The Pollimeter enables subjects to express their attitude toward an object by adjusting a two-colored bar that reveals *direction* ("positive" or "negative") and *degree* (the portion of either color that is showing).

As the bottom part of Figure 8-8 indicates, the back of the Lampert Pollimeter contains a precise numerical equivalent of the subject's visual-color rating. This feature means that although subjects avoid numbers and express their attitudes in terms of a visual scale, the researcher is provided with a numerical response that can easily be statistically analyzed.

**The Nature of
Consumer Attitudes**

215

FIGURE 8-8 **A Diagrammatic Representation of the Lampert Pollimeter***
Source: Schlomo I. Lampert, "A New Scale for Consumer Research,"
Journal of Advertising Research (April 1981), 24.

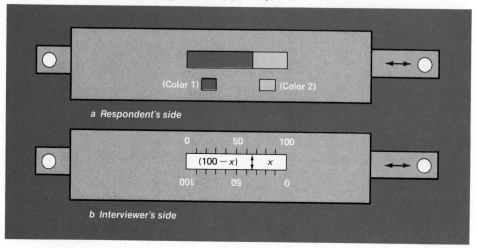

a Respondent's side

b Interviewer's side

summary

An *attitude* has been defined as *a learned predisposition to respond in a consistently favorable or unfavorable manner with respect to a given object* (e.g., a product category, a brand, a service, an advertisement, or a retail establishment). Each property of this definition is critical for understanding why and how attitudes are relevant in consumer behavior and marketing.

Of considerable importance in understanding the role of attitudes in consumer behavior is an appreciation of the structure and composition of an attitude. Three broad categories of attitude models have received attention: (1) the tricomponent attitude model, (2) single-component attitude models, and (3) multiattribute attitude models.

The tricomponent model of attitudes consists of three parts: a *cognitive* component, an *affective* component, and a *conative* component. The cognitive component captures a consumer's knowledge and perceptions, frequently in the form of *beliefs,* about products and services. In contrast, the affective component concentrates on a consumer's emotions or feelings with respect to a particular product or service. Evaluative in nature, the affective component ascertains an individual's *overall assessment* of the attitude-object in terms of some kind of rating of *favorableness.* Finally, the conative component is concerned with the *likelihood* or *tendency* that a consumer will act in a specific fashion with respect to the attitude-object. In marketing and consumer behavior, the conative component is frequently measured in terms of a consumer's *intention to buy.*

Single-component attitude models depict an attitude as consisting of just one overall affective, or feeling, component. In this case, the cognitive and conative components either are ignored or play a more supportive secondary role. As popular extensions of single-component attitude models, *multiattribute attitude models* have received much attention from consumer researchers. As a group, these models examine consumer beliefs about specific product attributes (e.g., product or brand features or benefits). In particular, three multiattribute models (i.e., attitude-toward-object, attitude-toward-behavior, and the theory of reasoned action), each proposed by Fishbein and his associates, tend to represent the present "state of the art" in applying attitude models to consumer behavior problems.

The measurement of attitudes is accomplished by observation of behavior and inferring of attitudes, qualitative research methods (especially focus group sessions and depth interviews), and a variety of self-report attitude scales (most notably: Likert scales, semantic differential scales, and rank-order scales).

discussion questions

1. Explain how situational factors are likely to influence the degree of consistency between a person's attitudes and his or her behavior.
2. Based upon your personal knowledge and experience with two well-known brands of soft drinks, construct a consumer belief-system chart resembling the one for mouthwash in Figure 8-2.
3. Since attitudes are learned predispositions to respond, why don't marketers and consumer researchers just measure purchasing behavior and forget attitudes?
4. From a marketing practitioner's point of view, briefly state the strengths and weaknesses of the basic single-component attitude model.
5. Explain a person's possible attitude toward eating at a fast-food establishment in terms of the tricomponent attitude model.
6. In terms of assessing shoppers' attitudes toward a local department store, what would be the specific benefits of the attitude-toward-object and the attitude-toward-behavior models discussed in this chapter?
7. Why would a researcher employ focus group sessions to explain potential consumers' attitudes toward a new inexpensive home computer?
8. What are the potential limitations of attempting to ascertain consumers' attitudes from observing their behavior?

endnotes

1. Martin Fishbein and Icek Ajzen, *Belief, Attitude, Intention and Behavior* (Reading, Mass.: Addison-Wesley, 1975), 6.
2. Russel R. Belk, "Situational Variables and Consumer Behavior," *Journal of Consumer Research,* 2 (December 1975), 157–63; and Pradeep Kakkar and Richard J. Lutz, "Situational Influence on Consumer Behavior: A Review," in Harold H. Kassarjian and Thomas S. Robertson, eds., *Perspectives in Consumer Behavior*, 3rd ed. (Glenview, Ill.: Scott, Foresman, 1981), 204–15.
3. For example, see William O. Bearden and Arch G. Woodside, "Situational Influence on Consumer Purchase Intentions," in Arch G. Woodside et al., eds., *Consumer and Industrial Buying Behavior* (New York: North-Holland, 1977), 167–77.

4. Kenneth E. Miller and James L. Ginter, "An Investigation of Situational Variations in Brand Choice Behavior and Attitude," *Journal of Marketing Research,* 16 (February 1979), 111–23.

5. George S. Day, "Theories of Attitude Structure and Change," in Scott Ward and Thomas S. Robertson, eds., *Consumer Behavior: Theoretical Sources* (Englewood Cliffs, N.J.: Prentice-Hall, 1973), 303–53; and Richard J. Lutz, "The Role of Attitude Theory in Marketing," in Kassarjian and Robertson, *Perspectives in Consumer Behavior,* 233–250.

6. Fishbein and Ajzen, *Belief, Attitude, Intention and Behavior,* 12.

7. Lutz, "Role of Attitude Theory," 234.

8. Russel I. Haley and Peter B. Case, "Testing Thirteen Attitude Scales for Agreement and Brand Discrimination," *Journal of Marketing,* 43 (Fall 1979), 21–30.

9. Richard J. Lutz and James R. Bettman, "Multi-Attribute Models in Marketing: A Bicentennial Review," in Woodside et al., *Consumer and Industrial Buying Behavior,* 137–49.

10. Icek Ajzen and Martin Fishbein, *Understanding Attitudes and Predicting Social Behavior* (Englewood Cliffs, N.J.: Prentice-Hall, 1980); and Fishbein and Ajzen, *Belief, Attitude, Intention and Behavior.*

11. Martin Fishbein, "An Investigation of the Relationships between Beliefs about an Object and the Attitude toward the Object," *Human Relations,* 16 (1963), 233–40; and Martin Fishbein, "A Behavioral Theory Approach to the Relations between Beliefs about an Object and the Attitude toward the Object," in Martin Fishbein, ed., *Readings in Attitude Theory and Measurement* (New York: John Wiley, 1967), 389–400.

12. Fishbein and Ajzen, *Belief, Attitude, Intention and Behavior,* 223.

13. For excellent reviews, see William L. Wilkie and Edgar A. Pessemier, "Issues in Marketing's Use of Multi-Attribute Attitude Models," *Journal of Marketing Research,* 10 (November 1973), 428–41; and Lutz and Bettman, "Multi-Attribute Models in Marketing," 137–49.

14. Ibid.

15. Ajzen and Fishbein, *Understanding Attitudes,* 62–73.

16. Ibid., 159–61.

17. Ibid., 62–73.

18. For marketing applications, see Michael J. Ryan and Michael J. Etzel, "The Nature of Salient Outcomes and Referents in the Extended Model," in Beverlee B. Anderson, ed., *Advances in Consumer Research* (Atlanta: Association for Consumer Research, 1976), III, 485–90; Michael J. Ryan and E.H. Bonfield, "Fishbein's Intentions Model: A Twist of External and Pragmatic Validity, *Journal of Marketing,* 44 (Spring 1980), 82–95; and Paul R. Warshaw, "A New Model for Predicting Behavioral Intentions: An Alternative to Fishbein," *Journal of Marketing Research,* 17 (May 1980), 153–72.

19. Ajzen and Fishbein, *Understanding Attitudes,* 1–78.

20. For a review of various attitude scales, see Haley and Case, "Testing Thirteen Attitude Scales for Agreement and Brand Discrimination," 20–32.

21. E.H. Bonfield, "A Comment on the State of Attitude Measurement in Consumer Research: A Polemic," in William L. Wilkie, ed, *Advances in Consumer Research* (Ann Arbor, Mich.: Association for Consumer Research, 1979), VI, 238–44.

22. G.H.G. McDougall and J.N. Fry, "Combining Two Methods of Image Measurement," *Journal of Retailing,* 50 (Winter 1974–75), 53–61.

23. Shlomo I. Lampert, "The Attitude Pollimeter: A New Attitude Scaling Device," *Journal of Marketing Research,* 16 (November 1979), 578–82; and Shlomo I. Lampert, "A New Scale for Consumer Research," *Journal of Advertising Research,* 21 (April 1981), 23–29.

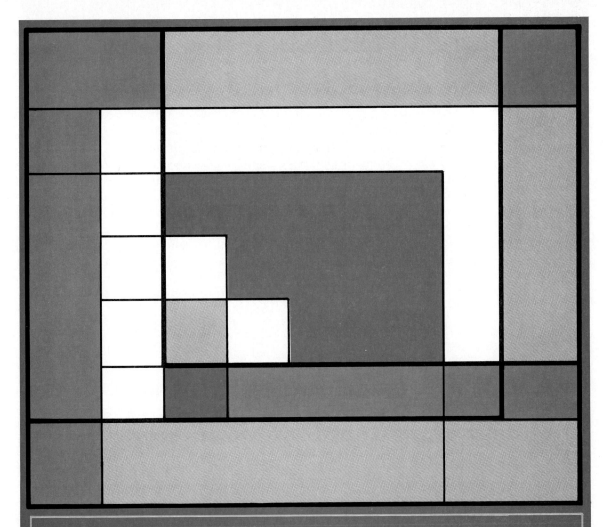

NINE

Consumer Attitude
Formation and Change

introduction

THIS chapter continues our discussion of attitudes that began in Chapter 8. While the preceding chapter defined what we mean by an attitude and explored its various properties—including an examination of a number of attitude models and how attitudes are commonly measured—the present chapter focuses on the important topics of *attitude formation* and *attitude change*. Moreover, as an outgrowth of our exploration of attitude change, we will consider cognitive dissonance theory and attribution theory, two different perspectives on how attitude change follows from behavior. The chapter concludes with a brief discussion of consumer involvement theory, which provides a useful framework as to when attitudes are likely to precede or follow from behavior.

ATTITUDE FORMATION

How does a young woman form her initial attitudes toward using cosmetics in general, and Cover Girl makeup in particular? How do family members and friends, admired sports celebrities, and mass-media advertising influence the establishment of attitudes? Why do some attitudes seem to be maintained indefinitely (e.g., a positive attitude toward a particular political party)? The answers to such questions are important to marketers, for unless they have some idea as to how attitudes are formed, they are unlikely to be able to either understand or affect consumers' attitudes or behavior.

Our examination of attitude formation is divided into the three areas: (1) the learning of attitudes, (2) the sources of influence in attitude formation, and (3) the impact of personality factors on attitude formation.

A Man bears beliefs as a tree bears apples.

EMERSON

Worship

Learning of Attitudes

When we speak of the formation of an attitude, we are referring to the shift from having *no* attitude toward a given object to having *some* attitude toward it.[1] To understand this shift, or attitude formation, requires that we appreciate the various basic learning processes involved. We will briefly focus on how attitudes are learned by considering how the following four learning theories or processes (described in detail in Chapter 6) relate to attitude formation: (1) classical conditioning, (2) instrumental conditioning, (3) cognitive learning theory, and (4) information-processing theory.

CLASSICAL CONDITIONING

An originally neutral stimulus, such as the brand name for a new product, can produce a favorable or unfavorable attitude if it is repeatedly followed by or associated with a reward or punishment. The idea of family branding is based on this form of attitude learning; by giving a new brand the same name as an established one, the marketer is counting on having the favorable attitude already associated with the established brand name extended to the new product.

Similarly, marketers who associate their new products with well-known and respected celebrities are trying to create a positive bond between the celebrity that already enjoys a positive attitude and the "neutral" new product. They hope to transfer recognition and goodwill from the celebrity to their product so that potential consumers will more quickly acquire a positive attitude toward the new product.

INSTRUMENTAL CONDITIONING

Consumers can purchase a brand *without* having an attitude toward it. They may buy a brand, for instance, because it is the only one of its kind left on a store's shelf; or they may make a trial purchase of a new brand from a product category that they feel does not warrant any further initial information than an awareness of its existence. If they find the brand satisfactory, they may eventually develop a favorable attitude toward the brand because the brand rewards them by providing satisfaction.

COGNITIVE LEARNING THEORY

In those situations where consumers are quite involved in a purchase decision—cognitions—knowledge and beliefs are likely to be a major input in the formation of attitudes. To illustrate, if a shopper who is interested in a new 10-speed bike learns that a lug frame and a precision derailleur (gear changer) are two essential attributes of a fine-quality 10-speed bike, and that a certain brand of bike exclusively uses a highly durable lug frame and a precision derailleur, then the shopper could be expected to form a positive attitude toward that brand of bike. Generally speaking, the more information (up to a point) an individual has about a product or service, the more likely he or she is to have an attitude toward it—either positive or negative.

INFORMATION PROCESSING

As an outgrowth of cognitive learning theory, the focus of the information-processing framework centers on the *limits* of consumers' abilities or interests to process purchase-related information. It is sufficient for us to point out here that consumers often take advantage of only a relatively small portion of the information available to them. Recent experimental research supports this contention by suggesting that the summation of the three most important beliefs dominates when it comes to the formation of attitudes toward a fictitious imported car called the "Vendome," and that less-important beliefs provide little additional information.[2]

Sources of Influence in Attitude Formation

Although learning theories tell us how attitudes may be established, a recognition of the sources from which consumers gain their information, advice, and influence is also important. The following are the principal sources that affect the formation of consumers' attitudes.

DIRECT AND PAST EXPERIENCE

The primary means by which attitudes are formed toward goods and services are through the direct experience of trying and evaluating them. Recognizing the importance of direct experience, marketers frequently attempt to stimulate trial of new products by offering cents-off coupons or even free-trial samples. Their objective is to get consumers to *experience* the new product and then to evaluate it. If a product proves satisfactory, it is then likely that the consumers will form positive attitudes and possibly purchase the product when they again have need of it at some future time.

PERSONAL INFLUENCE

As we come in contact with others, especially our family, close friends, and admired individuals (e.g., a respected teacher), we acquire attitudes that influence our lives. Our family is an extremely important source of influence when it comes to the establishment of attitudes, for it is our family that provides us with many of our basic values and a wide range of less-central beliefs. For instance, young children who are exposed to sweet foods and candy as part of their daily diet will probably, as adults, retain a taste for (or positive attitude toward) sweet foods.

EXPOSURE TO MASS MEDIA

It seems inevitable that in a world where people have easy access to newspapers and an almost infinite variety of general and special-interest magazines, and where so many people spend so much time watching television, that mass-media advertising would be an important source of information and influence our attitudes.

Personality Factors

In addition to the critical role that learning theory plays in the understanding of attitude formation and the recognition that various sources of information influence consumer attitudes, it is also important to realize that what any particular consumer finds rewarding depends to some extent on his or her personality. Introverted individuals, for instance, are likely to express their introversion with negative attitudes toward flashy cars, dancing classes, group tours, and public activities. Similarly, the attitudes of people with other personality and motivational configurations can also be predicted. Many attitudes toward new products and new-consumption situations are influenced by personality factors.

ATTITUDE CHANGE

As we begin our discussion of attitude change, it is important to recognize that what we have said about attitude formation is also basically true of attitude change. That is, attitude changes are learned, they are influenced by personal experience and other sources of information, and personality affects both the receptivity and the speed with which attitudes are likely to be altered.

Strategies of Attitude Change

Altering consumer attitudes is a key strategy consideration for most marketers. If marketers are in the fortunate position of having their brand possess the lion's share of the market, the overriding goal is likely to be to *fortify* the existing positive attitudes of their customers so that they will not succumb to the efforts of competitors and defect in favor of the competitors' brands. For instance, in product categories like gelatin dessert, where Jell-O brand has dominated for years, or ketchup, where Heinz has dominated, most competitors take aim at these market leaders when developing their own marketing strategies.

To understand the dynamics of attitude change, we will now examine a variety of attitude change strategies that can be assigned to the following five categories: (1) changing the basic motivational function, (2) associating the product with a specific group or event, (3) relating to conflicting attitudes, (4) altering components of the multiattribute model, and (5) changing beliefs about competitors' brands.

CHANGING THE BASIC MOTIVATIONAL FUNCTION

One way of changing attitudes toward a product or brand is to make new needs prominent. One attitude-change theory that demonstrates how changing the basic motivations can change attitudes is known as the *functional approach*.[3] With

Courtesy of Celestial Seasonings

this approach, we classify attitudes in terms of four functions: the utilitarian function, the ego-defensive function, the value-expressive function, and the knowledge function.

THE UTILITARIAN FUNCTION.   We hold certain brand attitudes partly because of the brand's utility. If a product has helped us in the past, even in a small way, our attitude toward it tends to be favorable. One way of changing attitudes in favor of a product is by showing people that it can solve a utilitarian goal that they may not have considered. To illustrate, while teas normally contain caffeine, which is a stimulant, the advertisement for Sleepytime Herb Tea in Figure 9-1 stresses that this tea contains no caffeine. Even the name portrays the message that the product will help the consumer relax and become sleepy.

THE EGO-DEFENSIVE FUNCTION.   We want to protect our self-concept from inner feelings of doubt. Cosmetics and personal-hygiene products, by acknowledging this need, make themselves seem much more relevant and heighten the possibility of a favorable attitude toward these products by offering reassurance to the consumer's self-concept. Denim Cologne and After Shave applies the ego-defensive function in a magazine ad that states: "For the man who doesn't have to try too hard" (see Figure 9-2).

THE VALUE-EXPRESSIVE FUNCTION.   Attitudes are one expression of our more general values, lifestyle, and outlook. If a consumer segment generally holds a high evaluation of being "in fashion," and high-fashion clothing and accessories are treated as symbols of that lifestyle, then attitudes toward fashion and fashionable clothing will reflect the positive attitudes that this segment has toward the values that being in fashion represent. If a consumer segment holds a low evaluation of the "fashionable life," however, high-fashion clothing will take on the negative attitudes that this segment has toward the lifestyle that faddish fashions symbolize. The Kretschmer wheat germ advertisement in Figure 9-3 is a wholehearted appeal to a lifestyle that values nutrition, good health, and physical fitness.

FIGURE 9-2   Advertisement Appealing to the Ego-Defensive Function

FIGURE 9-3   Advertisement Applying to a Value-Expressive Function

Courtesy of International Multifood Corporation

THE KNOWLEDGE FUNCTION.   We have a strong need to know and under-stand the people and things that we come in contact with, especially if we think they might influence our behavior. The "need to know," a cognitive need, is important to marketers if they are going to position their products properly. Indeed, most product and brand "positionings" are attempts to satisfy consum-ers' need to know and increase positive attitudes toward the brand by clarifying its advantages over competitive brands. For instance, ads for Shield, an extra-strength deodorant soap, point out that it was more effective against odor than the leading deodorant soap (see Figure 9-4). The inclusion of a graph that contrasts the effectiveness of Shield with that of its major competitor appeals to the knowledge function and is designed to positively influence consumer attitudes toward Shield.

There is one consumer-oriented study that applies the four-function framework to explore attitudes toward playing tennis.[4] The findings reveal that it is a useful framework and suggest that different consumers may indeed like or dislike the same product or service for different reasons. For instance, although

FIGURE 9-4   Advertisement Appealing to the Knowledge Function

Courtesy of Lever Brothers

two consumers might both have especially positive attitudes toward a particular brand of tennis racquet, one may be responding to the fact that the racquet provides greater control (a utilitarian function), whereas the other may be reacting to the masculine image created by the sports celebrities frequently used in the brand's advertising (an ego-defensive function).

ASSOCIATING THE PRODUCT WITH A GROUP OR EVENT

Attitudes are related, at least in part, to certain groups or social events. It is possible to alter attitudes toward products, services, and brands by pointing out their relationships to particular social groups and events. For instance, the Cutty Sark advertisement in Figure 9-5 salutes the accomplishments of Ted Turner in business and sports (and his wisdom in selecting Cutty Sark Scotch).

RELATING TO CONFLICTING ATTITUDES

Attitude-change strategies can also be designed to take advantage of actual or potential conflict between attitudes. Specifically, if consumers can be made to see that their brand attitude is in conflict with some other more basic attitudes, they may be "forced" to change their evaluation of the brand.

A simple theoretical notion—balance theory—shows how this attitude-change approach works.[5] It assumes that individuals attempt to avoid inconsistency and, instead, seek consistency, balance, or harmony. Specifically, balance theory proposes that consumers alter their attitudes in such a way as to place their attitudes in balance. The theory can be thought of as a *triangular* relationship between an individual consumer and two attitudes that are in conflict. Let us take the fictitious case of a consumer (call him Robert Rugoff) and his negative attitude toward Head and Shoulders (the leading brand of shampoo that stresses its dandruff-fighting ability). Within the context of balance theory, the key relationships are Robert and Head and Shoulders Shampoo, (2) Robert and some other person, and (3) the other person and Head and Shoulders. Again, assuming that Robert now has a negative attitude toward Head and Shoulders Shampoo, let us look at the four possible balance relationships that may exist:

1. *Admired friends dislike Head and Shoulders (see Figure 9-6a).* If Robert's friends dislike Head and Shoulders, this kind of relationship will maintain his own negative feelings toward the brand. Since the friends are admired, their attitudes are likely to reinforce his own negative attitude.

2. *Disliked dermatologists like Head and Shoulders (see Figure 9-6b).* If Robert believes that dermatologists are overly concerned with the dandruff control aspects of shampoo, their endorsement of Head and Shoulders as effective dandruff-controlling shampoo may serve to maintain Robert's negative feelings toward the brand.

3. *Disliked TV endorser rejects Head and Shoulders (see Figure 9-6c).* Some commercials show a rather bumbling individual foolishly avoiding the advertised brand. If this depiction is accepted by the viewers, they may change their attitude in favor of the product in order to avoid identifying with the endorser. Unfortunately, however, this individual might merely be rejected as unrealistic, and no change would occur.

4. *Admired personality recommends Head and Shoulders (see Figure 9-6d).* This situation probably presents the strongest one for change. If Robert is exposed to a strong

FIGURE 9-5   Advertising Tying the Product to a Special Event

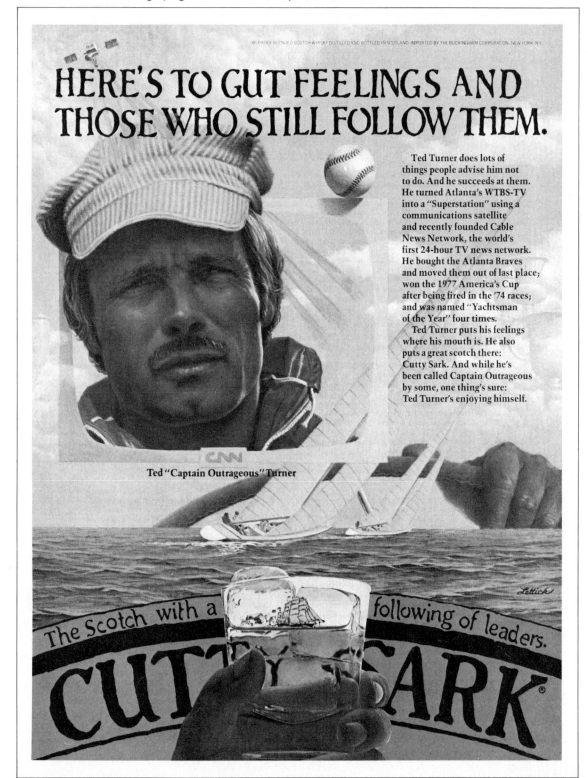

FIGURE 9-6
Alternative Attitude-Conflict States According to Balance Theory Source: Adapted from Richard J. Lutz, "The Role of Attitude Theory in Marketing," in Harold H. Kassarjian and Thomas S. Robertson, eds., *Perspectives in Consumer Behavior*, 3rd ed. (Glenview, Ill.: Scott, Foresman, 1981), 236–37.

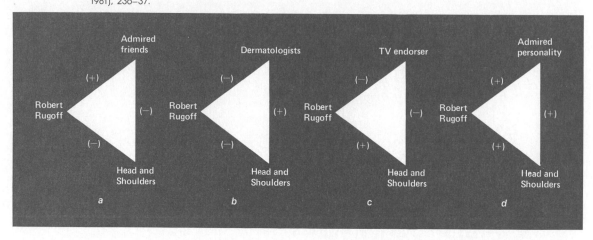

endorsement by an idol who points out that the dandruff-control superiority of Head and Shoulders is the best assurance of healthy hair and social acceptance, the negative attitude toward Head and Shoulders is likely to be reevaluated and possibly changed.

The key to changing attitudes by relating them to other attitudes is to choose other attitudes that are very strong and clearly conflicting with the one the marketer wishes to change. For instance, if consumers really respect a particular medium (e.g., The *Wall Street Journal*), they may reevaluate their negative attitude toward a particular product that advertises in the medium. Similarly, if the endorsement of an admired person is both strong and in conflict with one's preexisting views, it may effect an attitude change.

ALTERING COMPONENTS OF THE MULTIATTRIBUTE MODEL

In Chapter 8 we discussed a number of multiattribute attitude models. These models have important implications for attitude-change strategies. Keeping our illustrations as simple as possible, we will employ the popular Fishbein attitude-toward-object model. Specifically, we will consider the following strategies for carrying out programs of attitude change: (1) changing the relative evaluation of attributes (e_i), (2) changing brand beliefs (b_i), (3) adding an attribute (combined $b_i e_i$), and (4) changing the overall brand rating (A_o).[6]

CHANGING THE RELATIVE EVALUATION OF ATTRIBUTES.   The market for many product categories is structured so that different consumer segments are attracted to brands that offer different features or benefits. For instance, within a product category such as toothpaste there are brands like Crest that stress their decay-preventive ingredients, and brands like Close-Up that stress their whitening and brightening ability. These two different types of toothpaste have historically appealed to different portions of the overall toothpaste market (i.e., decay-preventive toothpastes have attracted growing families, whereas whiten-brighten toothpastes have been favored by young singles). Similarly, when it comes to coffee their are a number of major divisions, one being between regular ground coffee and instant coffee, and the other being between regular coffee and decaffeinated coffee.

In more general terms, when a product category is naturally divided with respect to distinct product features or promised benefits that appeal to a particular segment of consumers, there is usually an opportunity to attempt to "cross over" and convince consumers preferring one type of the product (e.g., regular coffee) to shift their attitudes toward another type of the product (e.g., decaffeinated coffee), and vice versa.

Such a strategy is paramount to *altering the relative evaluation of conflicting product attributes*. Stated somewhat differently, we are talking about the upgrading of consumers' beliefs about one product attribute, and either the downgrading of some other attribute or at least convincing consumers that it is *not* really in conflict with the upgraded attribute. Since the attributes slated for change are usually important and distinctive, it is likely that if consumers' evaluation of one attribute can be upgraded, then it follows that there may be a shift in overall attitude or even intention to buy.

CHANGING BRAND BELIEFS. A second cognitive-oriented strategy for changing attitudes concentrates on changing beliefs or perceptions about the brand itself. This is by far the most common form of advertising appeal. Advertisers are constantly reminding us that their product has "more" or is "better" or "best" in terms of some important product attribute.

For example, Head and Shoulders might improve its brand rating by changing beliefs about the extent to which the brand "leaves hair easy to manage" and "is gentle enough to use daily." If advertising could improve perceptions on these two attributes, consumers now avoiding dandruff shampoo might have a more favorable brand attitude toward Head and Shoulders.

Two cautions are necessary here. First, in the long run a brand-attribute perception change will not work if the brand does not actually have the attribute in question. Therefore Head and Shoulders should also tell the consumer just how commonplace dandruff is and how effective Head and Shoulders is in controlling dandruff (see Figure 9-7).

Second, the changes in the relative evaluations of both the attributes and the brand-attribute beliefs must not be too drastic, because too extreme an advertising position would probably result in rejection of the whole message. This caution is based on the *assimilation-contrast* theory.[7] This consistency theory warns that marketers must be careful in trying to change attitudes by altering the relative evaluations of either attributes or brand-attribute beliefs, to avoid overkill or "overselling" their case. According to the theory, a target segment will *assimilate* (or accept) only *moderate* changes. If the change suggested by a message is too extreme, the *contrast* will likely result in the whole message being distorted and thereby being rejected as too extreme.

FIGURE 9-7   Advertisement Designed to Address Brand Beliefs

Courtesy of Procter & Gamble Company

ADDING AN ATTRIBUTE.   Another cognitive strategy consists of adding an attribute. This can be accomplished by either adding an attribute that has previously been ignored or adding an attribute that represents a technological improvement or innovation.

The first route—adding a previously ignored attribute—may be difficult to accomplish because, for most product classes, most existing attributes have been considered by consumers at one time or another. For this reason, the second route—adding an attribute based on an actual product change or technological innovation—is preferable. Thus Head and Shoulders seems to have been on the right track in its decision to introduce a version of its shampoo that contains a conditioner (again see Figure 9-7).

CHANGING THE OVERALL BRAND RATING. Still another cognitive-oriented strategy consists of attempting to directly alter consumers' overall assessment of the *brand* without attempting to improve or change their evaluation of any single brand attribute. Such a strategy frequently relies on providing some form of significant global statement that the brand is the largest selling brand, or that it is the brand all others try to imitate, or some similar claim that sets the brand apart from all of its competitors.

CHANGING BELIEFS ABOUT COMPETITORS' BRANDS

A final strategy involves changing consumer beliefs about the attributes of competitive brands or product categories. This has become a more heavily utilized strategy as the popularity of *comparative advertising* has grown. For instance, Skippy Peanut Butter has undertaken a comparative campaign that contrasts itself with eight popular sandwich foods. In the advertisement shown in Figure 9-8, Skippy® claims that ounce for ounce it provides more protein and has no cholesterol.

Once again, however, this approach must be used with caution. Some evidence suggests that this advertising approach can boomerang by giving support to competitive brands and claims.[8] Further evidence indicates that unless the audience is relatively sophisticated and highly involved with the product, it is unlikely to comprehend two-sided messages.[9] And if the audience is sophisticated and involved, its attitudes may be quite difficult to change with any kind of message. (Chapter 10 discusses comparative advertising and one-sided versus two-sided messages in greater depth.)

BEHAVIOR PRECEDING ATTITUDES

Our discussion of attitude formation and attitude change has stressed the traditional "rational" view that consumers develop their attitudes prior to actions (e.g., "Know what you are doing before you do it"). There are alternatives to this attitude-precedes-behavior perspective, which upon careful analysis are likely to be as logical and rational. We will consider two alternatives, cognitive dissonance theory and attribution theory, both of which provide a different explanation as to why behavior might be expected to precede attitudes.

Cognitive Dissonance Theory

Of all the consistency theories, cognitive dissonance has received the greatest attention in consumer behavior and marketing circles.[10] According to the theory, dissonance or discomfort occurs when a consumer receives new information concerning a belief or an attitude that is in conflict with the original belief or

**Ounce for ounce
Skippy® Peanut Butter
provides more protein
than any of these
sandwich foods:**

HOT DOG

TUNA SALAD

BOLOGNA

EGG SALAD

HAM AND CHEESE

CHICKEN SALAD

SALAMI

BLT

**SKIPPY
CREAMY
PEANUT BUTTER**

**And has no cholesterol too.
It's Hard To Beat Skippy.**

Courtesy of Best Foods Unit of CPC International, Inc.

attitude.[11] For instance, when consumers buy a product, especially an expensive one such as an automobile, the unique positive qualities of the brands *not* selected remind the consumers that they may not have selected the best brand. Although such feelings of cognitive dissonance—especially when occurring *after* a purchase (frequently referred to as *postpurchase dissonance*)—are quite natural because purchase decisions often require some amount of compromise, they are nevertheless likely to leave consumers with an uneasy feeling about their prior beliefs or actions.

Postpurchase dissonance is discussed within the context of *changes in behavior leading to changes in attitudes* because the conflicting thoughts—or dissonant information—that follow a purchase are seen as prime factors that propel consumers to marshal their psychological forces to change attitudes so that they will be consonant with the actual purchase behavior. Thus attitude change is seen as an outcome of behavior.

To illustrate how attitude change occurs within the context of postpurchase dissonance, let us once again return to our shampoo example. The thought (i.e., belief) that "All dandruff shampoos are too harsh for me to use daily" is *dissonant* with the behavior of using Head and Shoulders daily. To reduce the dissonance arising out of this conflict, the dissonant consumer can elect one or both of the following basic strategies: (1) introduce new cognitive beliefs supporting the original attitude or behavior, (2) reevaluate the conflicting beliefs to create consonance. To make the daily use of Head and Shoulders consonant with the negative statement of the daily use of a dandruff shampoo, the consumer can introduce a new supportive belief—e.g., "It's probably because of the dandruff shampoo that my hair now feels and looks so healthy." Alternatively, the consumer may reevaluate the dissonant belief and reject it—e.g., "I don't believe that dandruff shampoos are too harsh for me."

What makes postpurchase dissonance relevant to marketing strategists is the premise that dissonance propels consumers to take steps to reduce the unpleasant feelings created by the rival thoughts.

A variety of tactics are open to consumers to reduce postpurchase dissonance and fortify or change their attitudes. The consumer could rationalize the decision as being wise, seek out advertisements that support the choice (while avoiding those of dissonance-creating competitive brands), try "selling" friends on the positive features of the brand, or look to others who are satisfied owners for their reassurance.

In addition to such consumer-initiated tactics to reduce postpurchase uncertainty, a firm can also assist the consumer by including messages in its advertising aimed specifically at reinforcing consumer decisions, offering a stronger guarantee or warranty, increasing the number and effectiveness of its services, and providing detailed brochures on how to use its products correctly.

Attribution Theory

In recent years a group of loosely interrelated social psychological principles, collectively referred to as *attribution theory,* have received increasing attention in the literature of consumer behavior.[12] Basically, attribution theory attempts to explain how people assign causality to events in terms of either their own behavior or the behavior of others.[13] In other words, a person might say "I did this because..." or "He is trying to sell me this because...." In effect, the underlying question is "Why?" "Why did I do this?" "Why did he say this is the best product on the market?" The process of making inferences about one's own or about another's behavior is a major component of how individuals form and change their attitudes. Indeed, it is because attribution theory portrays attitude formation and change as an outgrowth of people's interpretation of their behavior and experiences that we are examining it here.

SELF-PERCEPTION THEORY

Of the various perspectives on attribution theory that have been proposed, individuals' inferences or judgments as to the causes of their own behavior, known as *self-perception theory,* are a good beginning point for our discussion of attribution.[14]

In terms of consumer behavior, self-perception theory suggests that attitudes come about as consumers *look at* and *make judgments from* their own behavior. Simply stated, if a man observes that he routinely purchases a Milky Way on his way home from work, he is apt to conclude from such behavior that he *likes* Milky Ways (i.e., he has a positive attitude toward Milky Ways).

INTERNAL AND EXTERNAL ATTRIBUTIONS.   Drawing inferences from our own behavior is not always as simple or as clear-cut as the candy bar example might suggest. To appreciate the complexity of self-perception theory, it is useful to distinguish between internal and external attributions. Let us assume that you have just finished baking your first cherry pie and that it is perfect. If upon tasting this "masterpiece" you think to yourself, "I'm really a naturally good baker," this statement would be an example of an *internal attribution.*[15] It is an internal attribution because you are giving yourself credit for the outcome (e.g., your ability, your skill, or your effort). That is, you are saying, "This pie is good *because* of me." On the other hand, if you were to conclude that the successful cherry pie was due to factors beyond your control (e.g., ingredients, the assistance of a friend, or just "luck"), this would be an example of an *external attribution.* Here you would be saying, "This pie is good *because* of beginner's luck."

This distinction between internal and external attributions may be of strategic marketing importance. For instance, it would generally be in the best interests of a firm such as Pillsbury (a producer of a variety of ingredients that go into baking cakes and pies) that bakers, especially inexperienced ones, internalize their successful baking experiences. If they internalize such positive experiences, it seems more likely that they will repeat the behavior and even start baking on a regular basis. Alternatively, however, if they were to externalize their success, it would be most desirable that they externalize it to a Pillsbury ingredient, rather than some secondary or incidental environmental factor such as "beginner's luck," or a friend's "foolproof" recipe.

According to the principle of *defensive attribution,* consumers are likely to personally accept credit for success (internal attributions), whereas failure is likely to be credited to others or outside events (external attributions). For this reason, it is crucial that marketers offer uniformly high-quality products that allow consumers to perceive themselves as the reason for the success—i.e., "I'm competent." Moreover, a company's advertising should serve to reassure consumers, particularly inexperienced ones, that its products will not let them down but instead will make them into "heroes."

FOOT-IN-THE-DOOR TECHNIQUE.   Consumer researchers interested in self-perception theory have focused much of their attention on determining under what circumstances the gaining of consumers' compliance with some small or simple request affects subsequent attempts to gain compliance with respect to a more substantial request.[16] This strategy, which is commonly referred to as the *foot-in-the-door technique,* is based on the premise that individuals look at their prior behavior (compliance with the minor request) and come to the conclusion that they are the kind of person who says yes to such requests (i.e., an internal attribution). If effective, such self-attribution serves to increase the likelihood that they will say yes to the more substantial request.

Applications of the foot-in-the-door technique have concentrated on how specific incentives (e.g., cents-off coupons of varying amounts) ultimately influence consumer attitudes and subsequent purchase behavior. The research has generally found that different-size incentives tend to create different degrees of internal attribution, which in turn lead to different amounts of attitude change.[17] For instance, individuals who tried the brand without any inducements, or individuals who have repeatedly bought the brand, are progressively more likely to infer increasingly positive attitudes toward the brand from their respective behavior (i.e., "I buy this brand because I like it"). In contrast, individuals who merely tried a free sample are least committed to changing their attitudes toward the brand (i.e., "I tried this brand because it was free").

Thus, contrary to what might be expected, it is not the biggest incentive that is most likely to lead to positive attitude change. If an incentive is too big, marketers run the risk that consumers might externalize the cause of their behavior to the incentive and be *less* likely to change their attitudes and *less* likely to make future purchases of the brand. Instead, what would seem most effective is a *moderate* incentive, one that is just big enough to stimulate consumers' initial purchase of the brand, but still small enough to encourage consumers to internalize their own positive usage-experience and to allow a positive attitude change to occur.

ATTRIBUTIONS TOWARD OTHERS

Although consumer researchers usually focus most of their attention on self-perception theory, they are becoming increasingly interested in extending their understanding of attributions toward *others.*[18]

Attributions toward others would seem to have a wide variety of potential applications within the realm of consumer behavior and marketing. As suggested earlier in this section, every time a person asks "Why?" about a statement or action of another family member, a friend, a salesperson, or anyone or anything, attribution theory is relevant. For example, if a husband and wife were in an appliance store contemplating the purchase of a microwave oven, the salesperson's recommendation that they purchase a particular oven that was $300 more than the one they were initially considering would logically lead to the question "Why?" If the couple conclude that the salesperson has suggested it because of its superior features, then they are likely to judge the salesperson's motives as "sincere" and will possibly purchase the more expensive model. However, if they conclude that the salesperson is only interested in the greater commission from selling the more expensive model, then they might judge the salesperson as "insincere" and be unlikely to buy the more expensive model. Indeed, they might leave and go elsewhere because they no longer trust the salesperson or the store. The consumer is really asking, "Is the salesperson trying to sell me the more expensive model because of the superiority of the model or because of the increased commission?"

The above illustration suggests that in evaluating the words or deeds of others, the consumer tries to determine if the other person's motives or skills are consistent with the consumer's best interests. If these motives or skills are judged congruent, then the consumer is more likely to respond favorably. Otherwise the consumer is likely to reject the other person's words, which potentially means the loss of a customer.

ATTRIBUTIONS TOWARD THINGS

Attributions toward *things* also have considerable appeal for consumer researchers, especially since a product or service can be thought of as a "thing."[19] It is in the area of judging product performance that consumers are most likely to form product attributions. Specifically, they are likely to try to establish the reason for a product's meeting or not meeting their expectations. In this regard, they could credit the product's success (or failure) as being due to themselves, to the product itself, to other people or situations, or some combination of these factors.[20]

HOW WE TEST OUR ATTRIBUTIONS

After making our initial attributions of a product's performance or a person's words or actions, we will often attempt to determine to our own satisfaction if the inference we made is correct. According to a leading attribution theorist, we acquire conviction about particular observations by acting like "naive scientists;" that is, we collect additional information and attempt to confirm (or disconfirm) our inferences. More precisely, it is suggested that we employ the following four criteria in attempting to confirm our inference:[21]

1. *Distinctiveness*—The consumer attributes the action to a particular person or product if it uniquely occurs when the person or product is present and does not occur in its absence.
2. *Consistency over time*—Each time the person or product is present, the consumer's reaction must be the same, or nearly so.
3. *Consistency over modality*—The reaction must be uniform even though the situation in which it occurs varies.
4. *Consensus*—The action is perceived the same way by other consumers.

A consumer behavior illustration will help reveal how we use each of these criteria in assessing our inferences about product performance and people's actions. If a gourmet cook (let us call him Ed), who prides himself on his culinary skills, observes that the consistency and texture of his dough seems better with his new Cuisinart food processor than when he prepared the dough by hand, he is likely to credit the food processor for the high-quality dough (i.e., distinctiveness). Furthermore, if Ed finds that his Cuisinart produces the same high-quality dough each time he uses it, he should be more confident about his initial observation (i.e., consistency over time). Similarly, he will also be more confident if he finds that his satisfaction with the Cuisinart extends across a wide range of other food preparations (i.e., consistency over modality). Finally, Ed will have more confidence in his perceptions to the extent that his friends who own Cuisinarts have also had similar experiences (i.e., consensus).[22]

Notice here how scientific Ed is being. Much like Ed, we go about gathering additional information from our experiences with people and things, which we use to *test* our initial inferences about them.

Clearly, attributions are quite relevant to consumers' satisfaction with a product, a salesperson, or even a retail establishment.[23] Moreover, since our attributions are closely associated with consumer satisfaction, we can expect that an attribution perspective is likely to become more popular as we increasingly look at the public policy effects of advertising substantiation, packaging legislation, sales cooling-off laws, and product liability practices.[24]

CONSUMER INVOLVEMENT AND ATTITUDE DYNAMICS

Increased attention is now being given to consumer decision making under conditions of high involvement versus consumer decision making under conditions of low involvement. A brief exploration of how consumer involvement influences the informational needs of consumer decision makers is a fitting way to conclude our examination of attitude formation and change because it serves to tie together a number of loose ends about the direction of the attitude-behavior relationship (i.e., whether attitudes precede or follow from behavior).

Involvement is a difficult variable to define. At its simplest, however, consumer involvement seems to capture the extent to which consumers are concerned with a particular purchase decision and consider it to be important to them. When consumers believe a purchase decision is important and are willing to exert effort to acquire information, we consider such concern to be indicative of *high involvement*. On the other hand, when consumers believe a purchase is unimportant or trivial, and they see little reason to secure information, we consider such concern to be indicative of *low involvement*.

A significant fact about the study of consumer involvement is that, until quite recently, high involvement was the only perspective considered when describing consumer decision making.[25] However, as an outgrowth of research on people's responses to mass media, especially television, we are now beginning to appreciate the error of neglecting low involvement—particularly given the likelihood that a significant portion, if not the majority, of all consumer decisions are probably of the "low-involvement variety."[26]

An especially useful portrayal of the differences between high involvement and low involvement is given in Figure 9-9. The four models, two high-involvement models and two low-involvement models, are formed in terms of the consumer's level of involvement (i.e., "high" and "low" involvement) and the degree to which a consumer *perceives* differences among brands (i.e., "little" or "great" differences with respect to product features or promised benefits). We will briefly review each of these four models.[27]

Active Learning Model

The active learning model as depicted in the upper-left-hand cell of Figure 9-9 is based on traditional cognitive learning theory (see Chapter 7). Within the context of this model, consumers are *active* learners or problem solvers. They are both highly involved with the potential purchase and see the brand alternatives as quite different in their benefits and ability to provide satisfaction. As a combination of high involvement and high brand differences, consumers are likely to perceive such decisions as being quite risky, and therefore the acquisition of sufficient information about each alternative is likely to be seen as a necessary prerequisite for making a choice.

FIGURE 9-9 **Four Consumer Involvement/Brand Differentiation Decision-Making Models** Source: Adapted from F. Stewart DeBruicker, "An Appraisal of Low-Involvement Consumer Information Processing," in John C. Maloney and Bernard Silverman, eds., *Attitude Research Plays for High Stakes* (Chicago: American Marketing Association, 1979), 124; which in part is based on Michael Ray, "Marketing Communication and the Hierarchy of Effects," in F.G. Kline and P. Clark, eds., *Sage Annual Reviews in Communication Research* (Beverly Hills, Calif.: 1973).

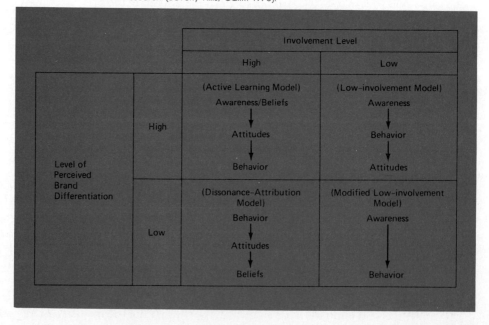

Since decisions in this category are especially important, it is not surprising that the model portrays consumers as progressing through a three-stage hierarchy—from awareness and knowledge to the formation of attitudes, and then finally on to behavior. Thus the model is a classical example of "Think before you act."

Dissonance-Attribution Model

The second high-involvement model (lower-left-hand cell of Figure 9-9) represents a decision situation that couples high consumer involvement with little or no perceived differences between the brands. In this model, behavior precedes attitudes, and attitudes precede beliefs and knowledge. The three stages of this second model correspond to the "behavior-before-attitude" that characterizes postpurchase dissonance theory and attribution theory.

Original Low-Involvement Model

The third model (upper-right-hand cell of Figure 9-9) depicts the most common characterization of a low-involvement model. The model couples low involvement in the purchase decision with the perception that there are brand differences.

In this case, the three-stage hierarchy begins with a progression from awareness to behavior, and then from behavior to attitudes. In essence, the model suggests that awareness of alternatives is likely to be sufficient information for consumers to make a purchase decision under conditions of low involvement. Following from this, attitudes are depicted as an outcome of consumers' experiences with the brand; that is, attitudes are formed as consumers establish preferences for the brand that provides them with the greatest amount of satisfaction. Such a low-involvement process is evidently a *relatively passive* learning experience.

Modified Low-Involvement Model

The fourth and final model (lower-right-hand cell of Figure 9-9), portrays a situation where consumers perceive both little involvement and little difference between the various brands. In this case, the model consists of only two stages—a brand awareness stage and behavior. In essence, *no brand-specific attitude need ever develop*. The consumer perceives the various brands to be so uniform that any preexisting attitudes toward the overall product category are sufficient for all brands, and there is no additional need to establish brand-specific attitudes. This fourth model can especially be considered a *highly passive* learning process, with little brand-level learning actually taking place.

Although some of the assumptions of the four models can be and have been questioned by various researchers, the models do represent an advancement in terms of focusing our attention on the consumer information-processing implications of models that reflect consumer involvement. Specifically, the distinction between high involvement and low involvement implies that consumers require different kinds of information depending upon the type or amount of involvement. For instance, in the case of low involvement, consumers seem willing to make a purchase with a minimum of information; therefore, what is required are messages that create awareness and repeatedly remind consumers of the product's existence. In contrast, in high-involvement situations where consumers are willing to exert effort to acquire information before acting, there may be a strong need for information. High involvement provides marketers with their real opportunity to create *persuasive* messages designed to convince the consumer to select their brand over available competitive brands.

Finally, the four models provide a useful framework for distinguishing those situations where attitudes precede or follow from behavior. More precisely, the models provide beginning support for the idea that the amount and nature of consumer involvement in a particular purchase decision, as well as the perceived degree of brand differentiation, are likely to influence which comes first: attitudes or behavior. And that implies important alternative approaches for marketers; that is, the effort to influence behavior directly is very different from influencing attitudes.

summary

How consumers' attitudes are formed and how they are changed are two closely related issues of considerable concern to marketing practitioners.

When it comes to attitude formation, it is useful to remember that attitudes are learned, and that different learning theories provide unique insights as to how attitudes may initially be formed. Attitude generation is also facilitated by direct personal experience, as well as the ideas and experiences of friends and family members, and the impressions acquired by exposure to various sources of mass media. Still further, it is likely that an individual's personality plays a major role in attitude formation.

These same factors also have an impact on attitude change; that is, attitude changes are learned, they are influenced by personal experiences and information gained from various personal and impersonal sources, and one's own personality affects both the acceptance and the speed with which attitudes are likely to be altered.

Marketing relevant strategies of attitude change can be thought of as falling into five distinct categories: (1) changing the basic motivational function, (2) associating the product with a specific group or event, (3) relating to conflicting attitudes, (4) altering components of the multiattribute model, and (5) changing beliefs about competitors' brands. Each of these strategies provides the marketing practitioner with alternative ways of carrying out a program that attempts to alter consumers' existing attitudes.

Most discussion of both attitude formation and attitude change stresses the traditional "rational" view that consumers develop their attitudes before they act. However, this may not always, or even usually, be true. Both cognitive dissonance theory and attribution theory provide alternative explanations for attitude formation and change that suggest that behavior might be expected to precede attitudes. Cognitive dissonance suggests that conflicting thoughts or dissonant information that follows a purchase decision might propel consumers to change their attitudes in order to make them consonant with their actions. On the other hand, attribution theory focuses on a variety of explanations as to how people go about assigning causality to events and form or alter attitudes as an outcome of assessing their own behavior, or the behavior of other people or things.

The level of consumer involvement (e.g., high versus low involvement) may influence the kind of information processing that a consumer finds necessary and may therefore affect the direction of the attitude-behavior relationship (i.e., whether attitudes precede or follow behavior). Additional research is needed to expand and test these notions about the sequence in which attitude and behavior occur.

discussion questions

1. Explain a recently formed attitude toward a product or service in terms of both instrumental conditioning and cognitive learning theory.
2. Describe a situation in which you felt that you had acquired an attitude toward a new product through exposure to another person who had had direct experience.
3. Find advertisements that illustrate each of the four motivational functions of attitudes.
4. Explain how a marketer of cold remedies might attempt to change consumers' attitudes toward the brand by changing the overall brand rating.
5. Why would marketers generally prefer consumers to make internal rather than external attributions?
6. How can the following attitude theory ideas help to change attitudes: (a) the functional approach, (b) the assimilation-contrast theory, (c) cognitive dissonance, and (d) the self-perception theory?
7. Have you ever experienced postpurchase dissonance? How did you get over it? In what other ways do people reduce it? How can marketers help?
8. Evaluate this statement made by John C. Maloney: "Sometimes attitudes come first, sometimes behavior is first. It's a chicken-egg problem. The only sure thing is that marketing is the chicken feed."

endnotes

1. Stuart Oskamp, *Attitudes and Opinions* (Englewood Cliffs, N.J.: Prentice-Hall, 1977), p. 120.

2. Morris B. Holbrook, "Beyond Attitude Structure: Toward the Informational Determinants of Attitude," *Journal of Marketing Research,* 15 (November 1978), 550–51; also see Morris B. Holbrook, David A. Velez, and Gerard J. Tabouret, "Attitude Structure and Search: An Integrative Model of Importance-Directed Information Processing," in Kent B. Monroe, ed., *Advances in Consumer Research* (Ann Arbor, Mich.: Association for Consumer Research, 1981), VIII, 35–41; and Jerry C. Olson, "Ideas on Integrating Attitude Theory with Information Processing Theory," in Richard W. Olshavsky, ed., *Attitude Research Enters the 80's"* (Chicago: American Marketing Association, 1980), 1–13.

3. Daniel Katz, "The Functional Approach to the Study of Attitudes," *Public Opinion Quarterly,* 24 (Summer 1960), 163–91; Richard J. Lutz, "A Functional Approach to Consumer Attitude Research," in H. Keith Hunt, ed., *Advances in Consumer Research* (Ann Arbor, Mich.: Association for Consumer Research, 1978), V, 360–69; and Richard J. Lutz, "A Functional Theory Framework for Designing and Pretesting Advertising Themes," in John C. Maloney and Bernard Silverman, eds., *Attitude Research Plays for High Stakes* (Chicago: American Marketing Association, 1979), 37–49.

4. William B. Locander and W. Austin Spivey, "A Functional Approach to Attitude Measurement," *Journal of Marketing Research,* 15 (November 1978), 576–87.

5. George S. Day, "Theories of Attitude Structure and Change," in Scott Ward and Thomas Robertson, eds., *Consumer Behavior: Theoretical Sources* (Englewood Cliffs, N.J.: Prentice-Hall, 1973), 303–53, esp. 331–33; Martin Fishbein and Icek Ajzen, *Belief, Attitude, Intention and Behavior,* (Reading, Mass.: Addison-Wesley, 1975), esp. Chap. 2; and Bobby J. Calder, "Cognitive Consistency and Consumer Behavior," in Harold H. Kassarjian and Thomas S. Robertson, eds., *Perspectives in Consumer Behavior,* 3rd ed. (Glenview, Ill.: Scott, Foresman, 1981), 258–70.

6. Richard J. Lutz, "Changing Brand Attitudes through Modification of Cognitive Structure," *Journal of Consumer Research,* 1 (March 1975), 49–59; Richard J. Lutz, "An Experimental Investigation of Causal Relations among Cognitions, Affect, and Behavioral Intention," *Journal of Consumer Research,* 3 (March 1977), 197–208; and Andrew A. Mitchell and Jerry C. Olson, "Are Product Attribute Beliefs the Only Mediator of Advertising Effects on Brand Attitude?" *Journal of Marketing Research,* 18 (August 1981), 318–32.

7. Carl I. Hovland, O.J. Harvey and Muzafer Sherif, "Assimilation and Contrast Effects in Reactions to Communication and Attitude Change," *Journal of Abnormal and Social Psychology,* 55 (July 1957), 244–52; and Rolph E. Anderson, "Consumer Dissatisfaction: The Effect of Disconfirmed Expectancy on Perceived Product Performance," *Journal of Marketing Research,* 10 (February 1973), 38–44.

8. Alan G. Sawyer, "The Effects of Repetition of Refutational and Supportive Advertising Appeals," *Journal of Marketing Research,* 10 (February 1973), 23–33; and William L. Wilkie and Paul Farris, "Comparison Advertising: Problems and Potential," *Journal of Marketing,* 39 (October 1975), 7–15.

9. Sawyer, "Effects of Repetition of Refutational and Supportive Advertising Appeals"; and Wilkie and Farris, "Comparison Advertising."

10. William H. Cummings and M. Venkatesan, "Cognitive Dissonance and Consumer Behavior: A Review of the Evidence," *Journal of Marketing Research,* 13 (August 1976), 303–8. Also see, for example, Robert J. Holloway, "An Experiment on Consumer Dissonance," *Journal of Marketing,* 31 (January 1967), 39–43; Richard N. Cardozo, "An Experimental Study of Customer Effort, Expectation, and Satisfac-

tion," *Journal of Marketing Research*, 2 (August 1965), 244–49; Robert Mittelstaedt, "A Dissonance Approach to Repeat Purchasing Behavior," *Journal of Marketing Research*, 6 (November 1969), 444–46; Shelby D. Hunt, "Post-Transaction Communication and Dissonance Reduction," *Journal of Marketing*, 34 (July 1970), 46–51; S. Oshikawa, "The Measurement of Cognitive Dissonance: Some Experimental Findings," *Journal of Marketing*, 36 (January 1972), 64–67; S. Oshikawa, "Dissonance Reduction or Artifact?" *Journal of Marketing Research*, 8 (November 1971), 514–15; and Jagdish N. Sheth, "Dissonance Reduction or Artifact? A Reply," *Journal of Marketing Research*, 8 (November 1971), 516–17.

11. Leon Festinger, *A Theory of Cognitive Dissonance* (Stanford, Calif.: Stanford University Press, 1957).

12. Richard W. Mizerski, Linda L. Golden, and Jerome B. Kernan, "The Attribution Process in Consumer Decision Making," *Journal of Consumer Research*, 6 (September 1979), 123–40.

13. Edward E. Jones et al., *Attribution: Perceiving the Causes of Behavior* (Morristown, N.J.: General Learning Press, 1972).

14. Daryl Bem, "Self Perception Theory," in Leonard Berkowitz, ed., *Advances in Experimental Social Psychology* (New York: Academic Press, 1972), VI, 2–62.

15. Jonathan L. Freedman, David O. Sears, and J. Merrill Carlsmith, *Social Psychology*, 3rd ed. (Englewood Cliffs, N.J.: Prentice-Hall, 1978), 104–5.

16. Carol A. Scott, "Self-Perception Processes in Consumer Behavior: Interpreting One's Own Experiences," in Hunt, *Advances in Consumer Research*, V, 714–20; and Carol A. Scott; "Forming Beliefs from Experience: Evidence from Self-Perception Theory," in Kassarjian and Robertson, *Perspectives in Consumer Behavior*, 296–306.

17. Carol A. Scott, "Modifying Socially-Conscious Behavior: The Foot-in-the-Door Technique," *Journal of Consumer Research*, 4 (December 1977), 156–64; Carol A. Scott, "The Effects of Trial and Incentives on Repeat Purchase Behavior," *Journal of Marketing Research*, 13 (August 1976), 263–69; and Joe A. Dodson, Alice M. Tybout, and Brian Sternthal, "Impact of Deals and Deal Retraction on Brand Switching," *Journal of Marketing Research*, 15 (February 1978), 72–81.

18. Mizerski, Golden, and Kernan, "The Attribution Process," 124–25. Also see Fritz Heider, *The Psychology of Interpersonal Relations* (New York: John Wiley, 1958); and Edward E. Jones and Keith E. Davis, "From Acts to Dispositions: The Attribution Process in Person Perception," in L. Berkowitz, ed., *Advances in Experimental Social Psychology* (New York: Academic Press, 1965), Vol. II.

19. Mizerski, Golden, and Kernan, "The Attribution Process," 126–27; and Robert E. Burnkrant, "Cue Utilization in Product Perception," in Hunt, *Advances in Consumer Research*, V, 724–29.

20. Alain Jolibert and Robert A. Peterson, "Casual Attributions of Product Failure: An Exploratory Investigation," *Journal of the Academy of Marketing Science*, 4 (Winter 1976), 446–55.

21. Harold H. Kelley, "Attribution Theory in Social Psychology," in David Levine, ed., *Nebraska Symposium on Motivation* (Lincoln: University of Nebraska Press, 1967), XV, 197.

22. Inspired by Mizerski, Golden, and Kernan, "The Attribution Process," 127.

23. S. Krishhnan and Valerie A. Valle, "Dissatisfaction Attributions and Consumer Complaint Behavior," in William L. Wilkie, ed., *Advances in Consumer Research* (Ann Arbor, Mich.: Association for Consumer Research, 1979), VI, 445–49; and Valerie Valle and Melanie Wallendorf, "Consumers' Attributions of the Cause of Their Product Satisfaction and Dissatisfaction," in Ray L. Day, ed., *Consumer Satisfaction, Dissatisfaction and Complaining Behavior* (Bloomington: Department of Marketing, School of Business, Indiana University, 1977) 26–30.

24. Linda Golden, "Attribution Theory Implications for Advertising Claim Credibility," *Journal of Marketing Research*, 14 (February 1977), 115–17; and Robert B. Settle

and Linda L. Golden, "Attribution Theory and Advertiser Credibility," *Journal of Marketing Research,* 11 (May 1974), 181–85; and Robert E. Smith and Shelby D. Hunt, "Attributional Processes and Effects in Promotional Situations," *Journal of Consumer Research,* 5 (December 1978), 149–58.

25. Harold H. Kassarjian and Waltraud M. Kassarjian, "Attitudes under Low Commitment Conditions," in John C. Maloney and Bernard Silverman, eds., *Attitude Research Plays for High Stakes* (Chicago: American Marketing Association, 1979), 3–13.

26. Herbert E. Krugman, "The Impact of Television Advertising: Learning without Involvement," *Public Opinion Quarterly,* 29 (Fall 1965), 349–56; "Brain Wave Measures of Media Involvement," *Journal of Advertising Research,* 11 (February 1971), 3–10; and "Low Involvement Theory in the Light of New Brain Research," in John C. Maloney and Bernard Silverman, eds., *Attitude Research Plays for High Stakes* (Chicago: American Marketing Association, 1979), 16–24.

27. F. Stewart DeBruicker, "An Appraisal of Low-Involvement Consumer Information Processing," in John C. Maloney and Bernard Silverman, eds., *Attitude Research Plays for High Stakes* (Chicago: American Marketing Association, 1979), 112–30; Michael Ray, "Marketing Communication and the Hierarchy of Effects," in F.G. Kline and P. Clark, eds., *Sage Annual Reviews in Communication Research* (Beverly Hills, Calif.: Sage Press, 1973); Bobby J. Calder, "When Attitudes Follow Behavior—A Self-perception/Dissonance Interpretation of Low Involvement," in John C. Maloney and Bernard Silverman, eds., *Attitude Research Plays for High Stakes* (Chicago: American Marketing Association, 1979), 25–36; Michael L. Rothschild, "Advertising Strategies for High and Low Involvement Situations," in John C. Maloney and Bernard Silverman, eds., *Attitude Research Plays for High Stakes* (Chicago: American Marketing Association, 1979), 74–94; and Robert E. Smith and William R. Swinyard, "Involvement and the Hierarchy of Effects: An Integrated Framework," in George B. Hafer, ed., *A Look Back, A Look Ahead* (Chicago: American Marketing Association, 1980), 86–98.

TEN

Communication and
Consumer Behavior

introduction

THE preceding chapters focused on individual consumers: what motivates them, how they perceive and learn, how their personality and attitudes influence their buying choices, and how these attitudes can sometimes be modified by persuasive marketing information. This chapter, which concludes Part II, explores the ways in which the consumer receives and is influenced by such marketing information. It discusses the structure and process of communication, the effects of communication sources on consumers' buying decisions, and the types of marketing messages that tend to be most persuasive.

Part III discusses consumers, not as individuals, but in the context of their social-cultural involvement with others: family, friends, and other groups to which they may belong or aspire to belong. Because communications with and from such outside influences tend to have a major impact on each individual's consumption behavior, it is important for us to understand how communication operates to influence and persuade consumers to make buying choices. In effect, communication is the bridge between individual consumers and their social-cultural world.

WHAT IS COMMUNICATION?

Everyone "knows" what communication is, yet textbooks often vary in their definitions. At a basic level, most writers agree that *communication* is *the transmission of a message from a sender to a receiver by means of a signal of some sort sent through a channel of some sort.* Figure 10-1 depicts this basic communication model.

However, the model leaves us with too many unknowns. What type of message does the sender wish to convey? Has he or she put it into a format that conveys its precise meaning? Through what medium (or what channel) is the message transmitted? Does the intended audience have access to this channel? Can the message surmount the psychological barriers that invariably surround all human receivers? Will the audience understand the message in the same way

> *Good communication is stimulating as black coffee, and just as hard to sleep after.*
>
> ANNE MORROW LINDBERGH
> "Argonauta," Gift from the Sea (1955)

FIGURE 10-1   Basic Communication Model

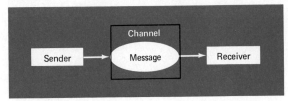

as the sender intended? And finally, how does the sender know if communication has taken place? Let us defer the answers to these questions until after we have examined the structure and process of communication. In so doing, we will explore many of the questions posed above concerning the basic communication process.

THE STRUCTURE AND PROCESS OF COMMUNICATION

There are four basic components of all communication: a *source,* a *destination,* a *medium,* and a *message.* The source is the initiator of the message. She may wish to impart a feeling, an attitude, a belief, or a fact to another person or persons. To do so, she must first find some way to encode this message so that it will accurately convey her feelings to the intended destination. She may use words, or pictures, or a facial expression, or some other kind of signal or code, but she must use some means that is familiar to the receiver if she wishes him to understand her intended meaning.

The source must then find an appropriate channel through which to transmit the message. To facilitate its delivery, the channel must have direct access to the receiver and must be relatively free of distortion and static. The receiver must be willing and ready to accept the message. After receiving it, he decodes the message within the realm of his own experience. His acknowledgment of the message, in whatever form it may take, provides *feedback* to the sender that the message was received. In communications between two people, acknowledgment may consist of a nod, a smile, a frown, or a signed contract. In an impersonal communication (e.g., an advertisement), acknowledgment may consist of a purchase, a vote, or a redeemed coupon. The basic communication model, then, should be somewhat modified, as depicted in Figure 10-2.

FIGURE 10-2   Communication Model

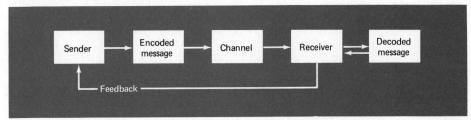

Types of Communication

There are basically two types of communication to which a consumer is exposed: *interpersonal communication* and *impersonal* (or *mass*) *communication*. Their impact and influence differ markedly.

INTERPERSONAL COMMUNICATION

Communication that occurs on a personal level between two or more people is called interpersonal communication. Such communication may take place between two people who meet on a face-to-face basis, who speak with each other on the telephone, or who correspond by mail. Interpersonal communication may be either formal or informal.

Informal communication concerning products or services is frequently called word-of-mouth communication. It differs from formal communication in that the sender does not speak in the capacity of a professional or commercial communicator (e.g., a sales representative). For example, two friends who discuss the merits of a specific product are engaging in informal communication. Alternately, each person may serve as the sender or the receiver of product information. *Formal interpersonal communication* is the kind of communication that takes place between a salesperson and a prospect, in which the salesperson serves as the sender and the prospect the receiver of product information.

Interpersonal communication tends to be effective because it enables the sender to detect almost at once the receiver's reaction to his or her message. This is particularly true of face-to-face communication, and to a lesser extent it is true of telephone communication. Mail correspondence also permits feedback, but it is obviously slower. It depends on the receiver's willingness and ability to answer, and the time required for mail transmission and delivery.

Face-to-face communication may be both *verbal* and *nonverbal*. A mother may express displeasure with her child through a frown; a customer may express his indifference to a sales pitch through a yawn. Other types of nonverbal communication include smiles, fear, quizzical expressions, finger drumming, fist clenching, and applause.[1] Table 10-1 lists other examples of nonverbal communication.

INTERPERSONAL FEEDBACK.   Both verbal and nonverbal feedback give the sender some indication of how the receiver has accepted the message and enable the sender to modify, repeat, or explain the message in greater detail. An experienced communicator is very attentive to feedback and constantly modifies messages in light of what he or she sees or hears from the audience.

Immediate feedback is the factor that makes personal selling so effective. It enables the salesperson to tailor the sales pitch to the expressed needs and the observed reactions of each prospect. Similarly, it enables a political candidate to selectively stress specific aspects of his or her platform in response to questions posed by prospective voters in face-to-face meetings. Immediate feedback in terms of inattention serves to alert the college professor to the need to awaken the interest of a dozing class; thus the professor may make a deliberately provocative statement, such as "This material will probably appear on your final exam."

TABLE 10-1　A Listing of Nonverbal Behaviors

mouth region
1. Simple smile
2. Upper smile
3. Broad smile
4. Compressed smile
5. Wry smile
6. Oblong smile
7. Lip-in smile
8. Play face
9. Grin
10. Open grin
11. Mouth corners tremble
12. Mouth corners back
13. Squared mouth
14. Mouth corners out
15. Oblong mouth
16. Intention bite
17. Lip up
18. Sneer
19. Bite lips
20. Tight lips
21. Lips in
22. Lower lip out
23. Point
24. Purse
25. Small mouth
26. Twist mouth
27. Lips forward
28. Open mouth
29. Spit
30. Kiss
31. Intention speak
32. Chew
33. Tongue between lips
34. Tongue out
35. Lick
36. Mouth corners down
37. Scowl
38. Lower lip tremble
39. Yawn
40. Basic mouth

eyebrows
41. Raise
42. Flash
43. Angry frown
44. Sad frown
45. Sad raise
46. Low frown

eyelids and eyes
47. Shut
48. Blink
49. Narrow eyes
50. Droop
51. Wink
52. Stare
53. Widen
54. Pouch
55. Tears
56. Open

gaze direction
57. Look at
58. Look away
59. Look down
60. Look up
61. Look around

additional facial
62. Grimace
63. Screwface
64. Flare
65. Twitch
66. Sweat
67. Facial reddening
68. Blanch
69. Smooth face
70. Normal face

head movement
71. Threat
72. Head forward
73. Chin out
74. Head to side
75. Head movement
76. Jerk
77. Nod
78. Shake
79. Bob
80. Chin in
81. Hang
82. Head rock
83. Evade
84. Level

hands and arms
85. Shrug
86. Sit on hands
87. Scratch
88. Caress
89. Rub
90. Pick

91. Adjust
92. Fumble
93. Tap
94. Hand flutter
95. Digit suck
96. Mouth
97. Cup
98. Teeth
99. Cover eyes
100. Face
101. Finger face
102. Offensive beating posture
103. Defensive beating posture
104. Beat
105. Incomplete beat
106. Hand on neck
107. Arm over face
108. Clap
109. Pound
110. Push gesture
111. Demonstrate
112. Show
113. Gesture
114. Flat gesture
115. Palms up
116. Akimbo
117. Fold
118. Fist
119. Link
120. Grasp
121. Hands behind back
122. Hold
123. Punch
124. Touch
125. Single

lower limb
126. Cross legs
127. Shuffle
128. Tap floor
129. Leg tremor
130. Foot
131. Foot rock
132. Circle
133. Swing

trunk
134. Slope
135. Crouch
136. Hunch

Source: Christopher R. Branigan and David A. Humphries, "Nonverbal Behavior," in N. Burton Jones, ed., *Ethological Studies of Child Behavior* (Cambridge: Cambridge University Press, 1972).

Only through feedback can the sender know if and how well the message has been received. That is why, in our model of the communication process, feedback is shown to be an integral link.

IMPERSONAL COMMUNICATION

Communication directed to a large and diffuse audience is called impersonal, or mass, communication. It operates in much the same way as interpersonal communication, even though there is no direct contact between source and receiver. The sources of mass communication are usually organizations that develop and transmit appropriate messages through specific departments or spokespersons. The destinations, or receivers, for such messages are usually a specific audience or several audiences that the organization is trying to inform, influence, or persuade. For example, the American Cancer Society may wish to persuade teenagers not to smoke, or a bank may wish to convince businesspeople to use its services, or a detergent company may wish to persuade housewives to use its soap powder.

Impersonal communication is carried by such mass-media channels as television, radio, newspapers, magazines, and billboards. Because mass-communication sources are organizations, their messages are considered formal. When such organizations are marketing organizations, their mass communications usually have commercial objectives (e.g., to persuade consumers to buy their products). Obviously, however, not all mass communications have commercial objectives. A school board may wish to persuade townspeople to support the new school budget, or the government may wish to persuade taxpayers to file their tax returns early.

IMPERSONAL FEEDBACK.   Feedback is just as important a concept in mass communication as it is in interpersonal communication. Indeed, because of the large sums of money required for mass communication, many people consider such feedback even more essential than interpersonal feedback.

The organization that initiates the communication must develop some method for determining whether its mass communications are, in fact, received by its intended audience, understood in the intended way, and successful in achieving its intended objectives. Unlike interpersonal communication feedback, mass communication feedback is rarely direct; indeed, it is usually inferential.[2] Receivers buy (or do not buy) the advertised product, renew (or do not renew) their magazine subscriptions, or vote (or do not vote) for the candidate. The sender infers how persuasive his or her message was from the resulting action (or inaction) taken by the audience.

Mass-communication feedback does not have the timeliness of interpersonal feedback; instead, it is usually somewhat delayed. Marketers rarely have the opportunity to find out immediately how effective their consumer advertising is. Since the "pipeline" from factory to consumer is fairly long, they must usually wait some time for reorders to occur in order to judge the effects of a national campaign. Retail executives are more fortunate, in that they can usually assess the effectiveness of newspaper advertisements by midday on the basis of sales activity for the advertised product.

Mass-communication sources often try to gauge the effectiveness of their messages by conducting audience research to find out which media are read, which television programs are watched, and which advertisements are remembered by their target audience. If negative feedback can be obtained fairly promptly, the source has the opportunity to modify or revise the message so that the intended communication does, in fact, take place.

Another type of feedback that companies seek from mass audiences is the degree of customer satisfaction or dissatisfaction with a product purchase. Smart marketers know that it is in their company's best interests to discover and correct any problems that occur as quickly as possible in order to retain the brand's image of reliability. Whirlpool has found an easy and relatively inexpensive way of doing this with its "Cool Line." Customers with questions or complaints can call a special toll-free number to give the company immediate feedback. This novel approach has served to increase customer satisfaction, and to decrease the company's cost of handling customer complaints.[3]

THE AUDIENCE

While marketers are primarily concerned with directing mass communications to multiple, or mass, audiences, such audiences must not be thought of as large, undifferentiated masses, but rather as hundreds or thousands or even millions of individual consumers. Since messages are received *by* individuals; they must be written and directed *to* individuals, albeit many of them. To do so successfully, the marketer must understand those personal characteristics of individuals that operate to help or hinder the acceptance of persuasive communications.

Barriers to Communication

There are many barriers to communication; some are physical, others are psychological. Among the psychological barriers that serve to filter receipt of mass communications are *selective attention, selective perception,* and *selective appeal.* These factors, discussed in detail in Chapter 6, will be reviewed briefly here.

SELECTIVE ATTENTION

Since most individuals are bombarded daily with more messages than any one person could possibly comprehend, individuals tend to give their attention selectively to those messages that are in their realm of interest or experience. For example, a woman whose youngest child has gone off to college might look for announcements of women's career seminars or employment opportunities while ignoring ads for new furniture or for camping equipment. Expectant first-time parents or grandparents might eagerly look at advertisements for baby carriages and other infant equipment, but those not interested in babies would ignore such ads. It is because of selective attention that market segmentation is such an effective marketing strategy. Marketers segment their markets on the basis of some relevant product interest or need. Prospects who are homogeneous in relation to a product interest are likely to perceive advertisements that address that interest, while those who are not interested in the product category will simply ignore them.

In summary, people seek information about topics in which they are interested or which relate to their way of life, and they ignore information concerning matters in which they have no interest. For this reason, marketers must present their persuasive communications in a context with which their target audiences can identify or which will be of general interest to them.

Related to selective attention is another communications barrier which is technically known as *noise*. In terms of communication reception, noise can be either mechanical or psychological. Static on a telephone or radio is mechanical noise, which may interfere with reception. No less a barrier to message reception is *psychological* noise, which may take the form of competing advertising messages or distracting thoughts. A viewer faced with the clutter of nine successive commercial messages during a program break may actually receive and retain nothing of what he has seen. Similarly, a woman planning her dinner menu while driving to work may be too engrossed in her thoughts to hear a radio commercial. On a more familiar level, a student daydreaming about his Saturday night date may simply not "hear" a question directed to him by his professor. He is just as much a victim of "noise"—albeit psychological noise—as the student who literally cannot hear a question because of hammering in the next room.

In all the instances mentioned, the best way for a sender to overcome noise is simply to repeat the message several times, much as the sailor does when sending an SOS over and over again to make sure it is received. (The effects of repetition on learning are discussed in Chapter 7.) Redundancy is constantly practiced by marketers who repeat the same advertisements over and over in the same medium and in supplementary media. For example, an advertising campaign usually consists of several different commercials and/or advertisements that feature the same advertising appeals presented in different contexts. The principle of redundancy is also seen in advertisements that use both illustrations and copy to emphasize the same points. A major advantage of television is that it enables the advertiser to repeat the same message both verbally and visually. Redundancy frequently occurs in interpersonal communication—not only can the sender give examples and analogies to clarify the message, but he or she can also reinforce them with facial expressions and body movements. Repeated exposure to an advertising message (redundancy of the advertising appeal) helps surmount a very real barrier to message reception and thus facilitates communication.

SELECTIVE PERCEPTION

As our discussion on perception indicated, people actually see or hear only those things in which they are specifically interested. Subconsciously, they filter out messages in which they have no interest or about which they have no expectations. A person riding in an automobile may pass fifty roadside restaurants without noticing them, but if she gets hungry, she will be able to detect a small restaurant sign some sixty yards off the road. The father of a preschooler may note and carefully read every sign and every advertisement he sees for tricycles, but once his child outgrows tricycles, he literally will not perceive such ads, even if they flood his local newspaper. A young married couple looking for a new car will see and hear and read advertisements for all cars within their relevant price range; however, they may not even notice an ad for a Rolls Royce. A similar couple, exposed to the same media but not interested in purchasing a car, would probably notice no automobile ads at all. However, if the couple had just bought a new car, they would be likely to continue to note and read selected automobile advertisements in an attempt to reassure themselves that they had made the right choice—i.e., they would try to alleviate their *postpurchase dissonance.*[4]

In general, people tend to avoid dissonant or opposing information. They seek information that agrees with their beliefs, and they avoid information that does not. Thus Democrats tend to read Democratic campaign literature, listen to Democratic political speeches, and attend Democratic political rallies. Conversely, Republicans read Republican campaign literature, listen to Republican political speeches, and attend Republican political rallies. Each side carefully avoids information furnished by the opposing party. Political campaign efforts to recruit votes through mass-communication efforts are often pointless, since such political messages are "received" only by those who intend to vote for the party anyway. The only campaign efforts that are truly worthwhile are those directed at new voters and voters who have not yet made up their minds. This latter group was especially relevant to both Reagan and Carter during the 1980 presidential race, since polls continually indicated that many people remained uncommitted throughout most of the campaign.

Even though people tend to avoid viewpoints opposite to their own, there are times when it makes sense to advertise to hostile audiences. Though it may not change the beliefs of those fully persuaded, an ad can prevent others from being infected with the same degree of hostility. This was the experience of the oil companies during the oil shortage situations of the middle and late 1970s. Chevron, Exxon, and Mobil did a great deal of advertising to explain their positions and boost their sagging company images. According to one researcher, such campaigns did indeed stop a further downward slide in public opinion polls.[5]

SELECTIVE APPEAL

A corollary of both selective attention and selective perception is the concept of selective appeal. Our discussion of motivation noted that individuals are motivated to satisfy their own needs, wants, and desires. Most of their shopping time and attention is focused on finding ways to fulfill their unique needs. Messages that address their specific problems or tell them how to fulfill their special needs generally receive their close attention; messages not related to their specific needs are usually ignored.

Thus marketers must couch their advertising messages to consumers in such a way that they clearly demonstrate that usage of a particular product or service will enable the consumer to fulfill a specific objective. Advertisements that stress the benefits to be achieved and the needs that will be fulfilled by the product are much more effective than advertisements that stress the features of the product. The latter type of ad expects the consumer to mentally convert a product feature into a consumer benefit. However, not all consumers can readily see the connection between a product feature and its ability to fulfill an unsatisfied need. For this reason, marketers must use care in selecting and depicting—in words and illustrations—appeals that clearly demonstrate that their products will satisfy the consumer's unmet need.

The Mass Audience as Individual Receivers

We stressed earlier that all communications, whether interpersonal or impersonal, are ultimately received by individuals. A mass audience is simply a great number of individual receivers, each with his or her own interests, experiences, needs, wants, desires. It is unlikely that a marketer could develop a single communications campaign that would simultaneously appeal to the specific interests of great numbers of individuals in words they all understand via media they all see. For this reason, marketers who do try to reach their total audience with a single communications effort (i.e., those who do not segment their markets) often are unsuccessful. Efforts to use "universal" appeals phrased in simple language that all can understand invariably result in advertisements to which few people will closely relate.

Clearly, all individuals are *not* unique; they have specific traits or interests or needs that are shared by many others. A market segmentation strategy enables experienced marketers to exploit this fact by dividing their total audience into a number of smaller audiences, each of which is homogeneous in relation to some characteristic pertinent to the product. The marketer can then design a specific advertising message for each market segment which will appeal directly to the common interests of all the people in the segment.[6] As a result, each individual in each market segment may feel that the advertising message received is specifically addressed to him or her in that it focuses directly on that individual's special interests or needs. Since individuals with similar interests and attitudes frequently expose themselves to the same media, the marketer can place such messages in the specific media each market segment prefers. Because it enables marketers to tailor their appeals to the specific needs of like groups of people, market segmentation overcomes some of the problems inherent in trying to communicate with mass audiences.

Multiple Audiences

All organizations—and certainly marketing organizations—recognize that their ultimate success depends on their ability to persuade many different kinds of audiences of the worthwhile nature of their products and their other endeavors. Such audiences include selling intermediaries (distributors, wholesalers, and retailers), as well as other audiences that are important to the organization's ultimate well-being.

SELLING INTERMEDIARIES

Most national manufacturers concern themselves primarily with transmitting persuasive communications to their ultimate consumers, but they must at the same time persuade the people through whom they sell their products—their *channels of distribution*—to buy and stock their products. It would be pointless to persuade final consumers to buy their products if consumers could not find such products at their local stores. Thus, in addition to advertising to the ultimate consumer (called national advertising), manufacturers usually direct advertising messages to each functional level of their distribution channels, utilizing appeals and media that are unique to that function (see Table 10-2).

For example, trade advertising is transmitted to product resellers (distributors, wholesalers, and retailers) through the relevant trade media by using appeals that are of specific interest to them, such as high profit, fast turnover, and increased store traffic. Industrial advertising is directed from one manufacturer to another manufacturer who can use the advertised product to make its own product (e.g., a thread manufacturer may advertise to clothing manufacturers). The type of appeal used in industrial advertising stresses the fact that the advertised product will enhance the second manufacturer's product (or increase profits, decrease costs, etc.). Where appropriate, manufacturers also advertise to professionals in the field in order to persuade them to recommend or prescribe or otherwise specify the advertised product to patients or clients. For example, a drug manufacturer may advertise a new product to physicians, hoping that they in turn will prescribe the product for their patients.

Retailers monopolize the nation's newspapers with retail advertising directed to the ultimate consumer. Such ads often feature products, sale prices, store services, and facilities; their prime purpose is to bring consumers into the store to do their shopping. Whether they actually buy the products or brands advertised is of little importance to the retailer, so long as they make their purchases at the retailer's store.

The marketer also tries to reach other intermediaries (designers, salespeople, manufacturers, etc.) in the hope that each of these receivers will favorably affect the ultimate reception of the product by the end-user.

TABLE 10-2 Types of Mass-Communication Efforts Initiated by Manufacturers and Selling Intermediaries

SOURCE	AUDIENCE	TYPE OF ADVERTISING	TYPICAL APPEALS	TYPICAL MESSAGE
Manufacturer	Wholesalers Retailers	Trade	Assortment, profit, turnover, store traffic, etc.	"Stock and display my product."
Manufacturer	Consumers	National	Convenience, personal benefits	"Buy my product anywhere."
Manufacturer	Other manufacturers	Industrial	Product improvement, cost savings, profits, etc.	"Use my product to make your product."
Manufacturer	Professionals	Professional	Satisfied clients, relieved patients	"Recommend or prescribe my product."
Wholesaler	Retailers	Trade	Large assortment, delivery, service	"Buy your stock from me."
Retailer	Consumers	Local or retail	Convenience, service, price	"Shop and buy all your needs at my store."

TABLE 10-3 Audiences Outside the Channel of Distribution with Which Favorable Communications Must Be Maintained

AUDIENCE	COMMUNICATIONS OBJECTIVES
Suppliers	Obtain credit, prompt delivery
Customers	Encourage sales, profits
Government	Discourage unfavorable or restrictive legislation; encourage favorable legislation
Stockholders	Encourage stock purchases and reduce trading of company's stock
Community	Receive local support for building programs; attract labor pool; etc.
Employees	Motivate workers; improve product quality and production
Financial community	Raise short- and long-term capital at favorable rates when needed

OTHER AUDIENCES

Wise managers are very much aware of the influence that many outside publics have on the ultimate success of their organizations. Table 10-3 lists some of these publics and the reasons why their good favor is important. For example, suppliers who think well of a firm will advance it credit and give prompt delivery of materials in short supply. Stockholders who are impressed with a company and its prospects will buy and retain its stocks. Employees who are convinced they are working for a fine organization will be loyal, hardworking, and highly motivated. The financial community will readily advance short- and long-term funds for operations and expansions.

To maintain favorable communications with all of their publics, most large organizations employ public relations counselors or establish their own public relations departments to provide favorable information about the company or to suppress unfavorable information. A good public relations person will develop a close working relationship with editors and program directors of all the relevant media in order to facilitate editorial placement of desired messages. The greater credibility of editorial vehicles as compared with paid messages (advertisements) is discussed in greater detail in the next section.

THE SOURCE

The source of a communication—the initiator of the message—is not only an integral component of the communications process itself but also a vital influence on the impact of the message.

Classification of Sources
of Consumer Communications

We have already noted that there are basically two types of communication: interpersonal and mass communication. Sources of *interpersonal* communication may be either formal or informal. Informal sources include friends, family, neighbors, fellow employees, and the like, who speak with the receiver regularly or irregularly and may, in the course of conversation, impart product or service information. (Chapter 11 discusses the effects of such informal interpersonal influences.) Formal interpersonal sources include representatives of formal organizations, such as salespeople, company spokespersons, or political candidates, who are compensated in one form or another for influencing or persuading consumers to act in a prescribed way.

Impersonal sources of consumer communications are usually organizations—either commercial or noncommercial (nonprofit)—such as manufacturers, service companies, institutions, charities, and government and political groups, who want to promote an idea, a product, a service, or an organizational image to the consumer. Such organizations generally appoint a specific department or person to create and transmit approved messages to desired audiences. These communications are usually encoded in paid advertising messages and transmitted via impersonal or mass media such as television, radio, newspapers, magazines, and billboards. In addition, they sometimes use such personal media as direct mail or sales promotion techniques (e.g., coupon or sample distribution) to transmit intended messages.

Sometimes a medium itself will be the source or initiator of product-related messages. This is particularly true of media with independent editorial departments, which can take specific stands on issues, ideas, and products and impart their views to their audiences. Included among such media are specialized rating publications, such as *Consumer Reports*. To avoid jeopardizing their reputation for impartial evaluations, these publications do not accept advertising.

Very often an organization's public relations department will encode a desired message within a newsworthy story format and transmit it via the editorial sections of mass media. The ensuing story is called *publicity* and differs from advertising only in that it appears in space or time that has not been bought by the sender. Since creation of the story events and subtle placement of the message may cost the sender considerably more in terms of money and trouble than a paid advertisement, cost savings are obviously not the basic motivation for publicity stories. The prime reason why companies prefer publicity is the increased credibility with which receivers regard editorial sources as compared with commercial sources of product communications.

Figure 10-3 depicts the various kinds of communications sources for consumer messages and the vehicles they use to transmit these messages. Among the most effective vehicles used by impersonal sources are formal interpersonal vehicles, such as sales representatives or other company spokespeople, who interact on a personal basis with individual receivers.

Table 10-4 reports the findings of research undertaken to determine the relative importance of various communications sources in the purchase decision

FIGURE 10-3   Sources of Consumer Communications and Related Message Vehicles

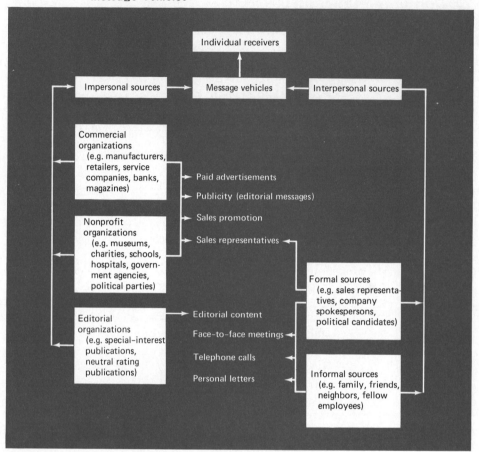

process. Women respondents were asked the following questions concerning purchases of small appliances, clothing, and food items: (1) Could you tell me how this product came to your attention for the *very first time?* (2) How *else* did you hear about this product before you bought it? (3) Which one of these ways was your *most important* source of information on your decision to buy this product?[7] As the table indicates, informal interpersonal sources were most influential in the purchase decision process for each of the product categories under study. In the case of clothing purchases, sales promotion (such as displays) also played a very important part. For small appliances and food, neutral sources such as editorials and consumer rating services had surprisingly little influence.

Table 10-5 presents the results of a study in which women were asked to name the sources of information that influenced them to purchase (1) a man's shirt and (2) a television set in a specific retail store.[8] It is interesting to note that previous experience with the store ranked first and second, respectively, while information from *Consumer Reports* or other neutral rating sources ranked sixth. Impersonal sources such as advertisements were clearly more influential for a

TABLE 10-4 Relative Importance of Message Sources in the Purchase Decision Process

SOURCE	SMALL APPLIANCES			CLOTHING			FOOD		
	first	else	most important	first	else	most important	first	else	most important
commercial sources									
Advertising	48%	23%	8%	35%	27%	16%	45%	25%	19%
Salesmen	1	1	1	4	1	6	0	0	0
Sales promotion*	9	7	9	19	14	32	26	16	27
interpersonal sources									
Friends, neighbors, relatives†	23	41	53	27	29	33	16	19	29
Immediate family	8	7	11	2	4	0	12	12	21
Professional advice	6	8	13	0	0	0	1	0	0
editorial and news sources††	1	0	1	6	6	6	0	0	1
No Mentions	4	13	4	7	19	7	0	28	3
Total (N = 99)	100%	100%	100%	100%	100%	100%	100%	100%	100%

*Includes sampling, displays, in-store promotions, packaging.
†Includes actual discussions as well as noticing the item, or trying the item (e.g., in the home of a friend).
††Includes Consumer Reports.

Source: From Innovative Behavior and Communication, by Thomas S. Robertson. Copyright © 1971 by Holt, Rinehart and Winston, Inc. Reprinted by permission of Holt, Rinehart and Winston.

high-priced technical product like a television set, while interpersonal sources such as friends were more influential for an inexpensive utilitarian item like a shirt.

According to recent research, it may even be possible to segment markets on the basis of the sources of information used in making purchase decisions. A study of major appliance buyers distinguished four segments of buyers on the basis of the number of stores visited and the types of information sources used: (1) *objective shoppers,* who rely mainly on neutral sources of information; (2) *personal advice seekers,* who rely mainly on personal sources; (3) *store intense*

TABLE 10-5 Rank Order of Information Sources Influencing Selection of a Retail Outlet When Shopping for Men's Shirts and Television Sets

INFORMATION SOURCE	MEN'S SHIRTS	TELEVISION SETS
Previous Experience	1	2
Suggestion of Friends	2	5
Window Display	3	4
Newspaper Advertisements	4	1
Radio/TV Advertisements	5	3
Consumer Reports or other Services	6	6

Source: Ben M. Enis and Gordon W. Paul "Store Loyalty as a Basis for Market Segmentation," *Journal of Retailing,* 46 (Fall 1970), 46.

shoppers, who rely heavily on physical visits to stores as well as on personal advice; and (4) *moderate shoppers,* who seek more neutral sources of information and who rely less on store visits than do store intense shoppers. A different marketing strategy would be necessary to reach each segment. For example, ads stressing objective information would be most appropriate for objective shoppers, whereas advice from trained sales personnel would be most effective with personal advice seekers.[9]

The Credibility of Communication Sources

The source of the communication—his or her perceived honesty and objectivity—has an enormous influence on whether or not the communication is accepted by the receiver. If the source is well respected and highly thought of by the intended audience, the message is much more likely to be believed. Conversely, messages from a source who is considered unreliable or untrustworthy will be received with skepticism and ultimately rejected.

Research shows that the credibility of the source is a vital element in the ultimate persuasibility of the message.[10] Credibility is built upon a number of factors, the most important of which is the perceived intentions of the source. The receiver asks himself or herself: "Just what does he (or she) stand to gain if I do what is suggested?" If the receiver perceives any type of personal gain for the sender as a result of the proposed action or advice, the message may become suspect: "He (or she) wants me to buy that product just to earn a commission." Any prospect of personal gain for the sender immediately casts a veil of doubt upon that individual's objectivity.

One of the major reasons why informal sources such as friends, neighbors, and relatives have such a strong influence on a receiver's behavior is simply that they are perceived as having no "ax to grind." Since they apparently have nothing to gain from a product transaction they recommend, their advice is considered totally objective, and their intentions are perceived to be in the best interests of the receiver.

Interestingly enough, such informal sources, called opinion leaders, often do profit—psychologically if not tangibly—by providing product information to others. A person may obtain a great deal of ego satisfaction by providing solicited as well as unsolicited information and advice to friends. As Chapter 16 points out, this ego gratification may actually improve the quality of the information provided, since the opinion leader will deliberately seek out impartial information in order to enhance his or her own position as "expert" on a particular product category.[11] The fact that the opinion leader does not receive material gain from the action recommended increases his or her credibility with the receiver and improves the likelihood that the advice will be seriously considered.

Experienced marketers try to utilize the phenomenon of opinion leadership by targeting their mass communications to opinion leaders, hoping that they, in turn, will pass these communications on to the rest of the population.

Even with informal sources, intentions are not always what they appear to be. Individuals who experience postpurchase dissonance often try to alleviate their uncertainty by convincing others to make a similar purchase choice. Each time they persuade a friend or an acquaintance to make the same brand selection, they are somewhat reassured that their own product choice was a wise one. The receiver, on the other hand, regards product advice from "the man who owns one" as totally objective, since the source had obviously conducted his own information search and is also able to speak from actual experience. Thus the increased credibility accorded the informal source may not really be warranted, despite the aura of perceived objectivity.

Neutral or editorial sources have greater credibility than commercial sources because of the likelihood that they are more objective in their product assessments. That is why publicity is so valuable to a manufacturer; citations of a product in an editorial context, rather than in a paid advertisement, give the reader much more confidence in the message.

MULTIPLICITY OF PERCEIVED SOURCES

Where the intentions of the source are clearly profit making, then reputation, expertise, and knowledge become important factors in message credibility. The credibility of commercial messages is often based on the composite evaluation of the reputations of (1) the initiator (the organization that approves and pays for the advertising message), (2) the retail outlet that carries the product, (3) the medium that carries the message, and (4) the company spokesperson (the actor or sales representative who delivers the message).

THE MESSAGE INITIATOR.   Initiators of commercial messages include manufacturers, service companies, commercial institutions, and retailers. Since their intentions are clearly to make a profit, their credibility is based on such factors as past performance, the kind and quality of service they are known to render, the quality and image of other products they manufacture, the type of retail outlets through which they sell, and their position in the community (e.g., their stand on such issues as social responsibility or equal employment).

Firms with well-established reputations generally have an easier time selling their products than do firms with less-well-established reputations. This was demonstrated in an experiment in which the researcher showed a group of subjects two films of sales presentations. One film showed a poor sales presentation by a representative from a well-known company; the other showed a good sales presentation by a representative from an unknown company. The group preferred the products of the well-known company, even though they found the sales presentation less convincing.[12]

The ability of a quality image to invoke credibility is one of the reasons for the growth of "family" brands. Manufacturers with favorable brand images prefer to give their new products the existing brand name in order to obtain ready acceptance from consumers. A study conducted among housewives in four cities across the nation concluded that a new product has a much better chance for acceptance if it comes in under an existing brand name.[13]

Besides allowing a company to market new products with less risk, a quality image permits a company to experiment more freely in many areas of marketing than would otherwise be considered prudent. The long-established manufacturer can open new retail outlets, try new price levels, or experiment with innovative promotional techniques with confidence that the company's good image will carry over.[14] Because a manufacturer with a good reputation generally has high credibility among consumers, many companies spend a sizable part of their advertising budget on *institutional* advertising, which is designed to promote a favorable company image rather than to promote specific products.

THE RETAILER AS A PERCEIVED SOURCE.   The reputation of the retailer who sells the product also has a major influence on credibility. Products sold by well-known quality stores seem to carry the added endorsement (and implicit guarantee) of the store itself: "If Macy's carries it, it must be good." The aura of credibility generated by reputable retail advertising reinforces the manufacturer's message as well. A product carried in a quality store such as Saks Fifth Avenue is usually perceived as being of better quality than one carried by a mass merchandiser; therefore a message concerning its attributes is more readily believed. That is why so many national advertisements (i.e., manufacturer-initiated ads) carry the line "Sold at better stores everywhere."

THE MEDIUM AS A PERCEIVED SOURCE.   The reputation of the medium that carries the advertisement affects the credibility of the message. Marshall McLuhan underscored this fact in his book *The Medium Is the Message.*[15] The image of a prestige magazine like the *New Yorker* confers added status on the products whose advertisements it carries. The reputation of the medium in terms of honesty or objectivity also affects the credibility of the advertising. Consumers often think that a medium they respect would not accept advertising for products it did not "know" were good. For example, the *Good Housekeeping* "Seal of Approval" carries a lot of weight with some consumers. For this reason, manufacturers are often happy to avail themselves of the merchandising services offered by some media, and purchase and distribute supplementary promotional material, such as counter cards and product hangtags that say, for example, "As Advertised in *Vogue* Magazine."

THE SPOKESPERSON AS A PERCEIVED SOURCE.   People sometimes regard the person who gives the product message as the source (or initiator) of the message. Thus the "pitchman"—whether he or she appears personally or in an advertisement—has a major influence on message credibility. In interpersonal communication, a salesperson who engenders confidence, and who gives the impression of honesty and integrity, is generally more successful in persuading a prospect than one who does not have these characteristics. Such confidence or credibility is created in diverse ways. A salesperson who "looks you in the eye" may appear more honest than one who evades direct eye contact. For many products, a sales representative who dresses well and drives an expensive, late-model car may have more credibility than one without such outward signs of success (and inferred representation of a best-selling product). For some products, however, a salesperson may achieve more credibility by dressing in the role of expert. For example, a man selling home improvements may achieve more credibility by looking like someone who has just climbed off a roof or out of a basement than by looking like a stockbroker.

In impersonal communication, the reputation or expertise of the advertising spokesperson may strongly influence the credibility of the message. That accounts for the popularity and effectiveness of testimonials as a promotional technique. In general, three types of individuals are used in testimonials: the celebrity, the professional (or recognized) expert, and the typical consumer.[16]

Experts are particularly sought after for testimonials. If a known or reputed expert in a specific field endorses a related product, consumers are usually ready to follow his or her advice, even though the endorsement is clearly profit-motivated. This is true of testimonials given by recognized experts as well as of testimonials given by unknown but stereotypical actors with inferred or implied expertise. White-coated actors who look like doctors have been able to successfully persuade viewers to buy over-the-counter drugs, despite the fact that the audience was warned that the commercial was a staged presentation.

Karl Malden, well known for his roles as a police officer in films and on TV, has lent some of that air to his role as a spokesperson for American Express traveler's checks. His warning "Don't leave home without them" has an air of believability about it because viewers associate him with crime prevention.[17]

Marketers who use a testimonial strategy should recognize that the potential success of their advertising rests on the credibility of the spokespeople they use. If celebrities are used, they should have some obvious knowledge about the product or recognized expertise in the product category. Guidelines used by the Federal Trade Commission require endorsers to have the experience, special competence, or expertise to form the judgment expressed by their endorsement. Persuasive endorsements by nonusers are considered deceptive advertising.

Advertisers who use testimonials must take care that the specific wording of the endorsement be within the recognized competence of the spokesperson. A movie actress can believably endorse a face cream with comments about its overall skin coverage or smoothing effects; however, a recitation of its chemical properties is beyond her expected knowledge and expertise and thus reduces, not enhances, message credibility. A TV campaign by Ace Hardware featured the actress Suzanne Somers endorsing its chain of stores. Since few people can envision sex symbol Somers as ever having been inside a hardware store, much less lifting a wrench, the commercials lacked credibility.

EXPERIENCE AFFECTS MESSAGE CREDIBILITY

The consumer's own experience with the product or the retail channel acts to affirm or deny the credibility of the message. A product or a store that lives up to its advertised claims increases the credibility with which future claims are received. Research suggests that fulfilled product expectations tend to increase the credibility accorded future messages by the same advertiser, while unfulfilled product claims or disappointing products tend to reduce the credibility of future messages.[18]

HIGH-CREDIBILITY VERSUS LOW-CREDIBILITY SOURCES

A number of researchers have explored the effectiveness of persuasive messages given by high-credibility sources as opposed to those given by low-credibility sources. In one experiment, college students were divided into two groups. One group was given material attributed to a high-credibility source (J. Robert Oppenheimer, a nuclear physicist), while the other group was given material attributed to a low-credibility source (the Communist newspaper *Pravda*). The results showed that the group exposed to the high-credibility source was more persuaded than the one exposed to the low-credibility source. Though the message content was identical, students consistently rated material attributed to the highly credible source as "more fair."[19]

Though high-credibility sources are generally more persuasive, their persuasiveness diminishes under certain conditions. Time, the nature of the message, and audience characteristics affect the persuasiveness of highly credible sources.

THE "SLEEPER EFFECT." The persuasive effect of high-credibility sources does not endure over time. In the experiment mentioned above, when the subjects were tested four weeks later, the percentage of those exposed to the high-credibility source who had been persuaded (i.e., who had changed their opinions) decreased, while the percentage of those exposed to the low-credibility source who had changed their opinions actually increased. In other words, both the positive and the negative credibility effects of the sources of the communications tended to disappear after several weeks. These findings were supported and extended by the results of a later experiment, which showed that a high-credibility source was initially more influential than a low-credibility source in persuading an audience.[20] However, remeasurement three weeks later revealed that effects of both persuasive messages were somewhat similar. This phenomenon has been termed the "sleeper effect."[21]

What happens if, after a period of time has elapsed since the presentation of material, the sources as well as the material are reintroduced to the audience? Does the sleeper effect occur? The answer is no. Researchers have found that reintroduction jogs the audience's memory and the original effect holds—that is, the high-credibility source remains more persuasive than the low-credibility source.[22] The implication for marketers who utilize high-credibility sources is that they must repeat the message by the source frequently to obtain and retain the desired effect.

NATURE OF THE MESSAGE. The kind of message presented can cancel the effectiveness of a high-credibility source and diminish the lack of persuasiveness of a low-credibility source. If an audience perceives a message to be incompatible with its source, a high-credibility source will be no more believable than a low-credibility source.[23] Similarly, if the arguments used are unfamiliar to the audience, the high-credibility source induces about the same amount of opinion change as the low-credibility source.[24]

AUDIENCE CHARACTERISTICS. The initial opinion that an audience holds prior to receiving the message can affect the persuasiveness of both high- and low-credibility sources. When the audience is favorably predisposed to the message prior to its presentation, moderately credible sources produce more attitude change than highly credible sources. However, when the audience is opposed to the communicator's position, the high-credibility source is more effective than the less-credible source.[25]

Evidently, research suggests that marketers must exercise caution in pursuing strategies to enhance source credibility. Sometimes such strategies may be wasteful because they will have little or no effect on increasing the believability of their messages or inducing product purchases.[26]

THE MEDIUM

To receive a message, an individual must, at the very least, be exposed to the medium through which it is transmitted. If a marvelously persuasive commercial is shown on one television channel while a housewife is tuned to another channel, obviously there is no way for her to receive the message. If an advertisement runs in the *Reader's Digest,* only those people who read the magazine have any chance of seeing it and being persuaded by it. If an editorial endorsing longer hemlines appears in *Woman's Wear Daily,* only those people who see that paper have the opportunity of reading it.

There are so many different categories of media available today and so many media alternatives available within each category that individuals tend to develop their own special media habits. One cannot be exposed to all available media—there are simply too many. While it may be possible for a person to read all the newspapers in his or her hometown, the likelihood of doing so tends to decrease as the number of newspapers available increases. Since an individual can reasonably watch only one TV channel or listen to only one radio station at a time, he or she can only be exposed to one of the numerous advertising messages that are broadcast simultaneously.

It is clear that only messages that are transmitted via media to which specific individuals are exposed have any chance of reaching them directly. However, as discussed earlier, such messages do have a chance of reaching individuals *indirectly* through opinion leaders.

Media Strategy Affects Message Reception

Since individuals expose themselves selectively to various media, it is important that mass communicators discover the specific media habits of those they wish to reach. In this way they can be sure that their advertisements are run in media that are seen and read by the individuals who constitute their audience. For this reason, media strategy is one of the most critical components of advertising planning. Advertisers must determine the media habits of the buyers or the expected buyers of their products. They can do this by segmenting their audiences in terms of some relevant characteristic that enables them to develop a "consumer profile." They then try to identify the specific media that individuals who fit this profile read or view. This search is facilitated by the media themselves, which carefully study their own audiences in order to develop descriptive "audience profiles." (See Figure 10-4.) An efficient media choice is considered to be one that closely matches the advertiser's consumer profile to a medium's audience profile.

FIGURE 10-4   A Media Advertisement Targeted at Advertisers

Does he get angry when you say dumbbell?

Or does he know you know more about muscles than he does?

She's not just smart about dumbbells. Right now she's lifting weights. Working her way through the October Vogue Spot/Toning Plan.

October Vogue also tells her woman does not live by exercise alone. To feel better, look great, she has to 'Let Go!' "Not only," assures Vogue, "is relaxation not self-indulgent, it's as essential as exercise to survival."

Vogue heralds the return of the spa. And maybe even the siesta.

"Never trust those who don't like to eat."

Vogue talks healthy food. Introduces "Le Hamburger," perfectly balanced for nutrition, it's an exclusive Vogue recipe from Michael Guerard.

The care and feeding of Bordeaux wines is in October Vogue.

So is help on avoiding hidden sugar. Secret salt.

Takes the Paris Pulse.

Sixteen Paris couture pages proclaim the genius of St. Laurent. The daring of Ungaro. All photographed on Brooke Shields by Avedon.

The book women live better by.

Nothing important to women escapes Vogue. Nothing in Vogue escapes women.

Vogue prescribes. 5.2 million Vogue readers subscribe. To everything Vogue suggests. Thanks to Vogue they know what to eat. And what not. How and how much to exercise.

Healthy climate for advertisers.

75% of Vogue readers say they buy Vogue to read the ads. That means almost 4 million of the most educated, affluent, intelligent, influential women in America are eager to know what's on your mind. Got a swimming new idea for pools?

20% of Vogue families are pool owners. Ready to plunge right into your message.

How about bicycles? Tennis or golf equipment? Skis? Weights? Water skis? Fishing or boating gear? More than one hundred thousand Vogue families are hitting the water in their own boats.

Healthy incomes, too.

Vogue's 5.2 million have the millions to get what they want and go where they want. 73% of subscribers own stock. 49% own real estate, in addition to their own homes. A

whopping 94% have department store charge accounts. And last year alone 90% spent an average of $3500 on pure pleasure travel. It's a rich market that can afford the things that make it look good. And feel good. And travel far. And entertain well. And decorate to the teeth. And live gloriously.

Vogue says.

Next to Bartlett's, no book is quoted more. In the office. On the plane. At the bar. And now, even in the examining room.

VOGUE
The book women live by.

OVERLAPPING AUDIENCES

Since many media—especially those with similar editorial features and formats—have overlapping audiences, advertisers usually place their advertising messages simultaneously or sequentially in a number of similar media (media with similar audience profiles). This enables them to either reach a wider audience with the same relevant market characteristics or reach the same individuals in several media in order to give them repeated exposure to the same advertising message. For example, many women read one or more fashion magazines. A perfume manufacturer who wishes to reach fashion-conscious women may run the same advertisement simultaneously in *Vogue* and *Harper's Bazaar*. Each advertisement will reach a unique part of the desired market segment that reads only that magazine; in addition, however, each ad will reach women who read both magazines and thus they see the ad twice. As Figure 10-5 illustrates, a *Vogue* ad will reach women in the desired market segment who read *Vogue* but not *Harper's Bazaar* (subset *A*); a *Harper's Bazaar* ad will reach women who read *Harper's Bazaar* but not *Vogue* (subset *B*); the overlapping area (subset *C*) reaches women who read both magazines and therefore see the advertisement twice. By using both media, the advertiser increases the size of the market segment exposed to the advertisement and, in instances of overlapping readership, increases the exposure (and therefore the redundancy and impact) of the advertising message.

MEDIA AS PRODUCT VEHICLES

Another aspect of media strategy focuses on the product and the intended message. Advertisers must select a general media category that will enhance the message they wish to convey. Some media categories are more appropriate vehicles for certain products or messages than others. For example, a retailer who wants to advertise a clearance sale should advertise in local newspapers, since that is where consumers are accustomed to looking for sale announcements. A manufacturer who wants to present a detailed argument in favor of its sewing machines should advertise in household magazines, where readers are accustomed to reading detailed articles and stories. A marketer who wants to promote a power mower with unique cutting features would be wise to use a

FIGURE 10-5 **Unique and Overlapping Readership of Magazines with Similar Audience Profiles**

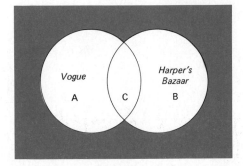

medium like television, where the mower can be demonstrated in action. Once marketers have identified the appropriate media *category,* they can then choose the specific medium in that category that reaches their intended audiences.

Which media are appropriate may also depend on the type of effect an advertiser wishes to have on a target audience. If the advertiser merely wants to stimulate brand interest or awareness, radio and television may be most effective because they are "passive" media from which the audience receives communications with minimal effort (i.e., they are low-involvement media). But if the purpose is to motivate consumers to action—that is, to buy the product— magazines and newspapers may be more effective because those media are thought to involve audiences more actively.[27]

Some evidence indicates that the same advertisement will generate different communication effects when run in different media.[28] A study of the interaction of two types of magazine vehicles (a prestige magazine like the *New Yorker* and an "expert" or special-interest magazine like *Tennis World*) and two types of copy approaches ("reason-why" and "image" copy) found that, for nonusers of the product in question, prestige magazines were more persuasive in communicating product quality and image than expert magazines. Conversely, expert magazines were more effective in delivering factual information.[29] These results give support to the notion that a media vehicle induces a "mood" of receptivity that affects the impact of a persuasive communication.

Clearly, marketers must be familiar with the characteristics of their audiences and the characteristics of media if they are to make wise media choices. To implement the most effective media strategies, however, they must also be totally familiar with the characteristics of their products. That is a prime requisite for preparing a persuasive message.

THE MESSAGE

The message is often considered the most vital component of all in the communications process. The message is the thought, idea, attitude, image or other information that the sender wishes to convey to the intended audience. In trying to encode the message in a form that will enable the audience to understand its precise meaning, the sender must clearly recognize exactly what it is that he or she is trying to say and why (what the objectives are and what the message is supposed to accomplish).

The marketer's objectives tend to vary with the audience. Objectives in communicating with consumers, for example, may be one or all of the following: (1) informing them what is for sale, (2) creating brand awareness, (3) getting them to buy the product, (4) reducing their uneasiness after the purchase is made. The marketer's objective with intermediary customers is to get them to stock the product; with other manufacturers, to get them to buy the product and use it to make their own.

Senders must also know their audiences well in terms of their education, interests, needs, and realms of experience. They must then endeavor to encode or phrase their messages in such a way that they will fall within the consumers' zones of understanding and familiarity.

Suppose a manufacturer of expensive men's leather goods wishes to sell a new line of wallets in order to increase the firm's profits. It may identify the target audience as well-to-do business executives and their gift-giving wives, and select appropriate media through which to reach this audience. To develop effective advertising appeals, it must understand the needs or objectives of the target audience in regard to wallets. Conceivably, these needs may include the following: (a) a slim case that will not cause bulges in tailored suits; (b) an ample interior that will accommodate business cards, credit cards, and money; and (c) a handsome exterior that will signify status, wealth, and good taste. The copywriter will then create a suitable advertisement that will illustrate how well the wallet fulfills these needs. If the advertisement embodies a situation, a model, and copy with which the target audience can identify, it has a good chance of being successful. If it uses an inappropriate situation (such as a shoe salesman pulling out pictures of the kiddies), it will not work.

To attract the attention and interest of their target audiences, marketers should start their advertisements with an appeal to the needs and interests of the audience, and end their advertisements with an appeal relevant to their own needs (i.e., end with an effective sales closing). Marketers have found that the most effective ads conclude by telling the audience exactly what it is they want them to do: "Visit your Chevrolet showroom today"; "Ask for it at your favorite cosmetic counter"; "Send us your order by return mail." Advertisements that do not conclude with an "action" closing tend to provoke much *less* action on the part of the consumer than those that do.

Method of Presentation

We have already demonstrated that to be effective, a message must (1) be directed to the appropriate audience, (2) use appeals that are relevant to the interests and experience of the audience, and (3) be transmitted via media to which the audience is exposed. In addition, the *manner* in which a message is presented strongly influences its impact. The method of presentation affects the readiness with which the message is received, accepted, and acted upon. The following discussion examines some well-known principles concerning message presentation.

ONE-SIDED VERSUS TWO-SIDED MESSAGES

Should marketers tell their audiences only the good points about their products or should they also tell them the bad (or the commonplace)? Should they pretend theirs is the only product of its kind, or should they acknowledge competing products? These are very real strategy questions which marketers face every day, and the answers depend on the nature of the audience and the nature of the competition.

If the audience is friendly (e.g., if it uses the advertiser's products), if it initially favors the communicator's position, or if it is not likely to hear an opposing argument, then a one-sided (*supportive*) communication that stresses only favorable information is most effective.[30] However, if the audience is critical or unfriendly (e.g., if it uses competitive products), if it is well educated, or if it is likely to hear opposing claims, then a two-sided (*refutational*) message is most effective.[31]

These findings are especially relevant in today's marketing environment, in which many competing products claim superiority over others. Less-sophisticated marketers continue to stress only positive factors about their products and pretend that competition does not exist. However, when competition does exist, and when it is likely to be vocal, such advertisers tend to lose credibility with the consumer. Some recent research suggests that claim credibility can be enhanced by actually *disclaiming* superiority in some product features in relation to a competing brand.[32]

Communication researchers not only have explored the problem of persuading audiences to take some prescribed action (e.g., to buy a product) but also have investigated ways to keep existing followers (e.g., customers) safe from outside persuasion.[33] Their findings suggest that two-sided appeals containing both pro and con arguments about the brand serve to *inoculate* consumers against arguments that may be raised by competitors. In effect, this strategy provides consumers with *counterarguments* with which to rationalize against future attacks by competing brands.

A practical illustration of two-sided advertising is seen in *comparison advertising,* a marketing strategy used by increasing numbers of marketers. In the late 1970s, for example, one out of ten TV commercials was a comparison advertisement.[34]

Comparison advertising (also called *comparative advertising*) has been defined as advertising that explicitly names or identifies one or more competitors of the advertised brand for the purpose of claiming superiority, either on an overall basis or in selected product attributes (see Figure 10-6).[35] It can be useful for product positioning, for target market selection, and for brand differentiation strategies (which stress the differential advantage of the "underdog" product over leading brands). To reinforce credibility, marketers will use and cite an independent research organization as the supplier of data used for the comparison.[36]

Although comparison advertising has been widely used, it is not without critics. Researchers dispute its effectiveness in aiding message recall. Some maintain that the message-recall effectiveness of comparative ads is somewhat higher than that of ads that do not explicitly name the competition.[37] Others maintain that though recall is better immediately afterward, it is not better twenty-four hours later, and that comparison advertising may aid recall of the competitor's brand as much as that of the advertised brand.[38]

There is also some research disputing how informative comparative ads really are. One advertising agency found that audiences perceived comparative commercials as more confusing and less believable than non-comparative commercials.[39] The reason appeared to be that the points of comparison seemed arbitrarily selected. Other more recent studies have found no major differences between comparative and noncomparative ads in increasing awareness of product features.[40]

In defense of comparison ads, research has found that consumers think them more interesting but generally less informative than noncomparative ads.[41] Comparison ads are likely to work best for lesser-known brands, since the association of an unknown brand with a market leader may help consumers

FIGURE 10-6   Comparative Advertising

A message to consumers from the Pepsi-Cola Company.

We have believed for a long time that we produce a better-tasting product than our leading competitor. But we wanted to be sure of that fact. We did not want to advertise it until we had it documented by careful, objective, independent research. We now have that documentation.

Truth in advertising is very important to us. And the truth is:

NATIONWIDE, MORE COCA-COLA DRINKERS PREFER PEPSI THAN COKE.

The better taste we always thought we had has now been confirmed by blind taste tests conducted among thousands of people in over a hundred cities and towns throughout this country. This concrete fact may explain some of the strange advertising sponsored by the Coca-Cola Company lately. Advertising like the silly blindfold commercials comparing Fresca (a sugar-free, citrus flavored drink) with Pepsi. These commercials announce that one third of the participants chose Fresca. They fail to point out that what this actually means is that *two thirds* preferred Pepsi.

Now they've come out with a series of comparative commercials in which both Pepsi and Coke are tasted side-by-side. In these, they claim that New Yorkers prefer Coke to Pepsi 2 to 1. But each product in these commercial tests is clearly identified. How can the results be valid when the only fair test must be a *blind* test, eliminating the bias of habit, which may have nothing to do with taste.

All this is Coca-Cola's attempt to answer what we call, "The Pepsi Challenge." The fact that none of these efforts constitute a real answer is not surprising. After all, how can there be a real answer when there is no real question, no question whatsoever that NATIONWIDE, MORE COCA-COLA DRINKERS PREFER PEPSI THAN COKE. (And, of course, Pepsi-Cola drinkers overwhelmingly prefer Pepsi.)

But don't take our word for it. Don't take anybody's word for it—

Let your taste decide. Take the Pepsi Challenge.

PEPSI

For a summary of these research findings, please write to P.O. Box 102, Purchase, New York 10577

Reprinted with permission of PepsiCo, Inc.

remember the unknown one. Research also indicates that they are more effective for branded convenience and specialty goods than for shopping goods.[42]

ORDER EFFECTS

Is it best to present your commercial first or last? Should you give the bad news first or last? Communication researchers have found that the order in which a message is presented affects audience receptivity.[43] For this reason, politicians and other professional communicators often jockey for position when they address an audience sequentially; they are aware that the first and last speeches are more likely to be retained in the audience's memory than those in between.[44] The media recognize the impact of order effects by according "preferred position" placement to front, back, and inside covers of magazines, which means they charge more for these positions than for inside magazine pages because of their greater visibility and recall.

Order is also important in arranging points within a message. Should the most important point be first or last? If audience interest is low, the most important point should probably be made first to get attention. However, if interest is already high, it is not necessary to pique curiosity, and so points can be arranged in order until the most important point is made at the end.

When just two competing messages are presented, one after the other, the evidence is somewhat conflicting as to which position is more effective. Some researchers have found that the material presented first produces a greater effect (the "primacy" effect), while others have found that the material presented last is more effective (the "recency" effect).[45] Further research is needed to see how audience characteristics and message characteristics influence primacy and recency effects.

When both favorable information and unfavorable information are to be presented (for example, in an annual stockholders' report), placing the favorable material first often produces greater tolerance for the unfavorable news. It also produces greater acceptance and better understanding of the total message.[46]

Copy Approach

Sometimes rational or factual appeals are more effective; sometimes nonrational or emotional ones are. It depends on the kind of audience to be reached and the product itself. In general, logical, reason-why appeals are more effective in persuading high-IQ audiences, who tend to be "turned off" by unsupported generalities, irrelevant arguments, or emotional appeals. Conversely, emotional appeals tend to be more effective in persuading people of lower intellectual achievement.[47]

FEAR APPEALS

Fear is often used as an appeal in marketing communications. Early research findings reported a negative relationship between the intensity of fear appeals and their ability to persuade. That is, strong fear appeals were found to be less effective than mild fear appeals.[48] For example, after a brief decline in cigarette smoking following the *Attorney General's Report* in 1964 linking cigarette smoking to lung cancer, cigarette consumption actually increased. A number of explanations have been offered for this phenomenon. Strong fear appeals concerning a highly relevant topic (e.g., a smoking habit) cause the individual to experience cognitive dissonance, which he or she resolves either by rejecting the habit or by rejecting the unwelcome information. Since giving up a cherished habit is difficult, consumers more readily reject the threat. This they do by a variety of techniques, including denial of the validity of the fear claims ("There still is no real proof"), the belief that they are immune to personal disaster ("It can't happen to me"), and a diffusing process that robs the claim of its true significance and thereby renders it impotent ("I play it safe by smoking only filter cigarettes").[49]

Recent research has come up with diverse findings on the relationship between the intensity of fear appeals and persuasion.[50] An analysis of such research suggests that strong fear appeals are more persuasive than mild fear appeals when source credibility is high.[51]

Fear appeals are also more effective when they pose a threat to the audience's loved ones or deal with unfamiliar topics.[52] Characteristics of the audience may also influence the persuasive effects of fear appeals. For example, individuals who can cope well and who are high in self-esteem or low in perceived vulnerability appear to be most easily persuaded by fear.[53] So are older individuals, especially blue-collar blacks or those who are more liberal politically.[54] Because of contradictory findings concerning the use of fear in persuasive communications, it seems apparent that more empirical research attention is needed before any firm principles can be formulated.

HUMOR IN ADVERTISING

Many advertisers use humor in their advertising in the implicit belief that humor will increase the acceptance and the persuasibility of their communications. Other advertisers avoid the use of humor because they fear that their product will become an object of ridicule, that consumers will laugh *at* them rather than *with* them. Reported studies on the use of humor in advertising do little to settle this controversy. Although several studies indicate that humor is persuasive (accounting for as much as 42 percent of all TV commercials), they do not show that humor is more effective than a serious version of the same appeal. The effects of humor in advertising have not been sufficiently explored to come to any definite conclusions; however, an analysis of existing research suggests some tentative generalizations:[55]

1. Humorous messages attract attention.
2. Humorous messages may impair comprehension.
3. Humor may distract the audience, thereby reducing counterargumentation and increasing persuasion, but at the same time drawing attention away from the product.[56]
4. Humorous appeals appear to be persuasive, but the persuasive effect at best is no greater than that of serious appeals.
5. Humor tends to enhance source credibility.
6. Audience characteristics may confound the effects of humor. (For example, blacks and whites in the United States do not always perceive the same things to be humorous.)[57]
7. A humorous context may increase liking for the source and create a positive mood. This may increase the persuasive effect of the message.
8. To the extent that a humorous context functions as a positive reinforcer, a persuasive communication placed in such a context may be more effective than a serious appeal.

There is some evidence that the program or editorial matter surrounding a humorous message may influence its effectiveness. In accordance with the principle of contrast, humorous commercials have been found to work best when presented in an action-adventure environment rather than in a situation-comedy environment.[58]

With so many conditions on the effectiveness of humor, perhaps the wisest policy for marketers to follow is to use it very selectively for products and audiences that seem to lend themselves strongly to this approach.

"AGONY" ADVERTISING

All of us have at one time or another been repelled by the so-called agony commercials which depict in diagrammatic detail the internal and intestinal effects of heartburn, indigestion, clogged sinus cavities, and hammer-induced headaches. Nevertheless, pharmaceutical companies continue to run such commercials with great success because they appeal to a certain segment of the population that suffers from ailments that are not visible, and which therefore evoke little sympathy from family and friends. Their complaints are legitimized by commercials with which they immediately identify. With the sponsor's credibility established ("They really understand the misery I'm going through"), the message itself is often highly persuasive in getting consumers to buy the advertised product.

ABRASIVE ADVERTISING

Studies of the "sleeper effect," discussed earlier, suggest that an individual's agreement with a persuasive communication from a low-credibility source is stronger a long time after exposure rather than immediately thereafter.[59] This has interesting implications for marketing—and helps explain the old public relations dictum: "It matters not whether they think well of you or ill of you so long as they remember your name." It suggests that the memory of an unpleasant commercial that saturates the media and antagonizes listeners or viewers may, in the end, dissipate, leaving only the brand name and the persuasive message in the minds of consumers.

AUDIENCE PARTICIPATION

Earlier we spoke about the importance of feedback in the communications process. The provision of feedback changes the communications process from one-way to two-way communication. This is important to senders in that it enables them to determine whether and how well communication has taken place. But it is also important to receivers because it enables them to participate, to be involved, to actually experience in some way the message itself. Participation by the receiver reinforces the message. An experienced communicator will ask questions and opinions of an audience to draw them into the discussion. Many professors use the participative approach in classrooms rather than the more sterile lecture format because they recognize that student participation tends to facilitate internalization of the information discussed.

Although participation is easily accomplished in interpersonal situations, it takes a great deal of ingenuity in impersonal situations. Thus it is a challenge for imaginative marketers to get consumers involved in their advertising. The counterargumentation provoked by two-sided messages may be one feasible way to do so. Two-way television, already an experimental reality, may be another.

summary

This chapter has described how the consumer receives and is influenced by marketing communications. *Communication* is defined as *the transmission of a message from a sender to a receiver by a signal of some sort sent through a channel of some sort.*

There are four basic components of all communication: a source, a destination, a medium, and a message. The source is the initiator of the message; the destination is the audience. The audience can be a single individual or many individuals—collectively called a mass audience.

There are two types of communication: interpersonal and impersonal (or mass) communication. Interpersonal communication occurs on a personal level between two or more people and may be verbal or nonverbal. In mass communication, there is no direct communication between source and receiver. Interpersonal communication takes place in person, by telephone, or by mail; mass communication uses such impersonal media as television, radio, newspapers, and magazines. In both types of communication, feedback is an essential step because it provides the sender with some notion as to if and how well the message has been received.

Barriers to communication include selective attention, selective perception, and selective appeal. Repetition or redundancy of the message is used to surmount the barrier of psychological noise.

Informal sources of interpersonal communication include friends, family, neighbors, and fellow employees. Formal interpersonal sources include organizational representatives, such as salespeople or company spokespersons. Impersonal sources of consumer communications are organizations (both commercial and noncommercial) and the media (including neutral rating publications).

The credibility of the source, a vital element in the ultimate persuasibility of a message, is often based upon his or her perceived intentions. Informal sources and neutral or editorial sources are generally considered highly objective and, therefore, highly credible. The credibility of a commercial source is usually more problematic and is based on a composite evaluation of his or her reputation, expertise, and knowledge and that of the medium, the retail channel, and the company spokespeople it uses.

Product endorsement by someone perceived to have experience or expertise with the product can be very persuasive if that person is also perceived as being highly credible. The consumer's own experience with the product also affects the credibility that he or she attributes to the source. The differential impact of high- and low-credibility sources tends to disappear over time, and the message alone remains. This has been termed the "sleeper effect." The nature of the message and characteristics of the audience also affect the impact of high- and low-credibility sources.

Marketers cannot communicate effectively with large, heterogeneous audiences by using general appeals. Instead, they usually segment their markets on the basis of some relevant product or market characteristic and transmit individually tailored messages to these segments via media to which they are exposed. In addition to ultimate consumers, a marketer's audiences include selling intermediaries and other publics that are relevant to the organization's success.

The manner in which a message is presented influences its impact. For example, one-sided messages are more effective in some situations and with some audiences; two-sided messages are more effective with others. When three or more messages are given sequentially, the first and the last tend to be the best remembered. However, when just two messages are given, in some cases the first is more effective (primacy effect) and in others the last is more effective (recency effect).

It is apparent that conflicting research reports in some areas of message presentation and inadequate research studies in others make it difficult to develop a firm set of "principles" to guide communication strategy. Future research studies will have to carefully identify the many situational variables that seem to mediate the effects of message order and message presentation in persuading consumers to buy.

discussion questions

1. List and discuss the effects of psychological barriers on the communications process. How can a marketer overcome the communications barrier known as "noise"?

2. How may a consumer use an informal communications situation to reduce postpurchase dissonance?

3. Select two advertisements with different advertising messages: one supportive and the other refutational. Explain why you believe each marketer chose that specific message strategy.

4. List and discuss the factors that influence the credibility of impersonal sources of product information.

5. Explain the differences between feedback from interpersonal communications and feedback from impersonal communications. How does the marketer obtain and use each kind of feedback?

6. You are the marketing manager for a headache remedy. Your advertising agency has just presented two different promotional strategies, one using a humorous approach and one taking an "agony" approach. Which approach would you suggest they adopt? Why?

7. Why are publicity stories often more effective than advertisements for the same product?

8. What are the advantages and disadvantages of (a) interpersonal communication and (b) impersonal communication for the marketing of consumer products?

9. For what kind of audiences would you consider using comparative advertising? Why?

endnotes

1. For a review of research on nonverbal communication and its implications for marketers, see Thomas V. Bonoma and Leonard C. Felder, "Nonverbal Communication in Marketing: Toward a Communicational Analysis," *Journal of Marketing Research,* 14 (May 1977), 169–80.

2. Wilbur Schramm, *The Process and Effects of Mass Communication* (Urbana: University of Illinois Press, 1955), 639–51.

3. Noel L. Griese, "Feedback: The Vital Link," *Public Relations Journal,* 33 (December 1977), 12–14.

4. Shelby D. Hunt, "Post Transaction Communication and Dissonance Reduction," *Journal of Marketing,* 34 (July 1970), 46–51; and Eldon M. Wirtz and Kenneth E. Miller, "The Effect of Post-purchase Communication on Consumer Satisfaction and on Consumer Recommendation of the Retailer," *Journal of Retailing,* 53 (Summer 1977), 39–46.

5. Lewis C. Winters, "Should You Advertise to Hostile Audiences?" *Journal of Advertising Research,* 17 (June 1977), 7–15.

6. Charles W. King and John O. Summers, "Attitudes and Media Exposure," *Journal of Advertising Research,* 11 (February 1971), 26–32.

7. Thomas S. Robertson, "The Effect of the Informal Group upon Member Innovative Behavior," in Robert L. King, ed., *Marketing and the New Science of Planning* (Chicago: American Marketing Association, 1968), 334–40.

8. Ben M. Enis and Gordon W. Paul, "Store Loyalty as a Basis for Market Segmentation," *Journal of Retailing,* 46 (Fall 1970), 46.

9. Robert A. Westbrook and Claes Fornell, "Patterns of Information Source Usage among Durable Goods Buyers," *Journal of Marketing Research,* 16 (August 1979), 303–12.

10. Robert B. Settle and Linda L. Golden, "Attribution Theory and Advertiser Credibility," *Journal of Marketing Research,* 11, (May 1974), 181–85.

11. Elihu Katz and Paul F. Lazarsfeld, *Personal Influence* (New York: Free Press, 1955), 309–20.

12. Theodore Leavitt, "Communications and Industrial Selling," *Journal of Marketing,* 31 (April 1967), 15–21.

13. Leo Bogart and Charles Lehmann, "What Makes a Brand Name Familiar?" *Journal of Marketing Research,* 10 (February 1973), 17–22.

14. A. Maile and A. H. Kizilbash, "A Marketing Communications Model," *Business Horizons,* 20 (December 1977), 77–84.

15. Marshall McLuhan, *The Medium Is the Message* (New York: Random House, 1967).

16. Hershey H. Friedman and Linda Friedman, "Endorser Effectiveness by Product Type," *Journal of Advertising Research,* 19 (October 1979), 63–71.

17. Bourne Morris, "Will a Personality Sell a Product Better? Pros and Cons," *Advertising Age,* February 5, 1979, 43–44.

18. See, for example, Kurt Lewin, "Psychology of Success and Failure," in T. Costello and S. Zalkind, eds. *Psychology in Administration* (Englewood Cliffs, N.J.: Prentice-Hall, 1963), 67–72.

19. Carl I. Hovland and Walter Weiss, "The Influence of Source Credibility on Communication Effectiveness," *Public Opinion Quarterly,* 15 (Winter 1951–52), 635–50.

20. Herbert C. Kelman and Carl I. Hovland, "Reinstatement of the Communication in Delayed Measurement of Opinion Change, *Journal of Abnormal and Social Psychology,* 48 (1953), 327–35.

21. Carl I. Hovland, Arthur A. Lumsdaine, and Fred D. Sheffield, *Experiments on Mass Communication* (New York: John Wiley, 1949), 182–200.

22. Kelman and Hovland, "Reinstatement of the Communication."

23. A. Eagly and J. Chaiken, "An Attribution Analysis of the Effect of Communicator Characteristics on Opinion Change: The Case of Consumer Attractiveness," *Journal of Personality and Social Psychology*, 32 (1975), 136–44.

24. James McCroskey, "A Summary of Experimental Research on the Effects of Evidence in Persuasive Communication," *Quarterly Journal of Speech*, 55 (1969), 169–76.

25. Brian Sternthal, Ruby Dholakia, and Clark Leavitt, "The Persuasive Effect of Source Credibility: Tests of Cognitive Response, *Journal of Consumer Research*, 4 (March 1978), 252–60.

26. Ruby Roy Dholakia and Brian Sternthal, "Highly Credible Sources: Persuasive Facilitators or Persuasive Liabilities?" *Journal of Consumer Research*, 3 (March 1977), 223–32.

27. William Ro Swinyard and Charles H. Patti, "The Communications Hierarchy Framework for Evaluating Copytesting Techniques," *Journal of Advertising*, 8 (Summer 1979), 29–36.

28. Charles Winick, "Three Measures of the Advertising Value of Media Context," *Journal of Advertising Research*, 2 (June 1962), 28–33.

29. David A. Aaker and Phillip K. Brown, "Evaluating Vehicle Source Effects," *Journal of Advertising Research*, 12 (August 1972), 11–16; and Gert Assmus, "An Empirical Investigation into the Perception of Vehicle Source Effects," *Journal of Advertising*, 7 (Winter 1978), 4–10.

30. Hovland, Lumsdaine, and Sheffield, *Experiments on Mass Communication*.

31. Ibid.

32. Settle and Golden, "Attribution Theory."

33. William J. McGuire, "Inducing Resistance to Persuasion: Some Contemporary Approaches," in Leonard Berkowitz, ed., *Advances in Experimental Social Psychology* (New York: Academic Press, 1964), I, 191–229; Peter L. Wright, "The Cognitive Processes Mediating Acceptance of Advertising," *Journal of Marketing Research*, 10 (February 1973), 53–62; Alan G. Sawyer, "The Effects of Repetition of Refutational and Supportive Advertising Appeals," *Journal of Marketing Research*, 10 (February 1973), 23–33; and George J. Szybillo and Richard Heslin, "Resistance to Persuasion: Innoculation Theory in a Marketing Concept," *Journal of Marketing Research*, 10 (November 1973), 396–403.

34. Aimee L. Morner, "It Pays to Knock Your Competitor," *Fortune*, February 13, 1978, 104.

35. Kanti V. Prasad, "Communications Effectiveness of Comparative Advertising: A Laboratory Analysis," *Journal of Marketing Research*, 13 (May 1976), 128–37.

36. William L. Wilkie and Paul W. Farris, "Comparison Advertising: Problems and Potential," *Journal of Marketing*, 39 (November 1975), 7–15.

37. Prasad, "Communications Effectiveness."

38. Subhash C. Jain and Edwin C. Hackleman, "How Effective Is Comparative Advertising for Stimulating Brand Recall?" *Journal of Advertising*, 7 (Summer 1978), 24.

39. "Comparative Ads Ineffective: O & M Study," *Advertising Age*, October 13, 1975, 16.

40. See Linda L. Golden, "Consumer Reaction to Comparative Advertising," in Beverlee B. Anderson, ed., *Advances in Consumer Research* (Atlanta: Association for Consumer Research, 1976), III, 63–67; and William Pride, Charles W. Lamb, and Barbara A. Pletcher, "The Informativeness of Comparative Advertisements: An Empirical Investigation," *Journal of Advertising*, 8 (Spring 1979) 29–35.

41. Terrence A. Shemp and D. C. Dyer, "The Effects of Comparative Advertising Mediated by Market Position of Sponsoring Brand," *Journal of Advertising*, 7 (Summer 1979), 13–19.

42. Jain and Hackleman, "How Effective Is Comparative Advertising?" 24–25.

43. For basic readings in this area, see Carl I. Hovland, ed., *The Order of Presentation in Persuasion* (New Haven, Conn.: Yale University Press, 1957).

44. Frederick E. Webster, Jr., *Marketing Communication* (New York: Ronald Press, 1971).

45. Ibid.

46. Scott M. Cutlip and Allen H. Center, *Effective Public Relations*, 4th ed. (Englewood Cliffs, N.J.: Prentice-Hall, 1971), 151.

47. Donald F. Cox, "Clues for Advertising Strategists: Part I," *Harvard Business Review*, September–October 1961, 160–76.

48. Irving L. Janis and Seymour Feshbach, "Effects of Fear-Arousing Communications," *Journal of Abnormal and Social Psychology*, 48 (January 1953), 78–92.

49. John R. Stuteville, "Psychic Defenses against High Fear Appeals: A Key Marketing Variable," *Journal of Marketing*, 34 (April 1970), 39–45.

50. Brian Sternthal and C. Samuel Craig, "Fear Appeals: Revisited and Revised," *Journal of Consumer Research*, 1 (December 1974), 22–34; and James C. McCrosky and David W. Wright, "A Comparison of the Effects of Punishment Oriented and Reward Oriented Messages in Persuasive Communication," *Journal of Communication*, 21 (March 1971), 83–93.

51. Gerald R. Miller and M. A. Hewgill, "Some Recent Research on Fear Arousing Message Appeals," *Speech Monographs*, 33 (1966), 377–91.

52. M. Karlins and H. I. Abelson, *Persuasion*, 2nd ed. (New York: Springer Publishing, 1970), 9–10.

53. Michael Ray and William Wilkie, "Fear: The Potential of an Appeal Neglected by Marketing," *Journal of Marketing*, 34 (January 1970), 54–62.

54. John J. Burnett and Richard L. Oliver, "Fear Appeal Effects in the Field: A Segmentation Approach," *Journal of Marketing Research*, 16 (May 1979), 190–91.

55. Brian Sternthal and C. Samuel Craig, "Humor in Advertising," *Journal of Marketing*, 37 (October 1973), 12–18.

56. P. Kelly and P. J. Salomon, "Humor in Television Advertising," *Journal of Advertising*, 4 (1975), 33–35.

57. Avraham Shama and Maureen Coughlin, "An Experimental Study of the Effectiveness of Humor in Advertising," in *1979 Educators Conference Proceedings* (Chicago: American Marketing Association, 1979), 249–52.

58. John H. Murphy, Isabella C. M. Cunningham, and Gary B. Wilcox, "The Impact of Program Environment on Recall of Humorous Television Commercials," *Journal of Advertising*, 8 (Spring 1979), 17–21.

59. For a critical review of the "sleeper effect," see Noel Capon and James Hulbert, "The Sleeper Effect—An Awakening," *Public Opinion Quarterly*, 37 (Fall 1973), 322–58.

part three

CONSUMERS IN THEIR SOCIAL AND CULTURAL SETTINGS

The five chapters that follow are designed to provide the reader with a detailed picture of the social and cultural dimensions of consumer behavior. The objectives of Part III are to (1) explain how social and cultural concepts affect the attitudes and behavior of individuals, and (2) show how these concepts can be employed by marketing practitioners to achieve their marketing objectives.

ELEVEN

Group Dynamics and Consumer Reference Groups

introduction

WITH the exception of those very few people who can be classified as hermits, people tend to be involved with others on a rather constant basis. Like almost all behavior, an individual's social involvement is often motivated by the expectation that it will help in the satisfaction of specific needs. For example, a person might join a local political club to satisfy a need for community recognition. Another person might join a singles group in an effort to find compatible friends to satisfy his or her social needs. A third person might join a food cooperative to obtain the benefits of group buying power. These are just a few of the almost infinite number of reasons why people involve themselves with others.

This chapter discusses the basic concepts of social involvement and group dynamics. It gives particular emphasis to the role that reference groups play in both directly and indirectly influencing consumer behavior. The four chapters that follow discuss other social and societal groupings that influence consumer buying processes: the family, socioeconomic classes, culture, and subculture.

WHAT IS A GROUP?

A *group* may be defined as *two or more people who interact to accomplish either individual or mutual goals.* Within the broad scope of this definition are both an intimate "group" of two neighbors who informally decide to shop together for groceries and a larger, more formal, group, such as a Parents Association, whose members are mutually concerned with the quality of education their children receive. Included in this definition, too, are more remote, one-sided, social involvements where an individual consumer looks to others for direction as to which products or services to buy, even though such others are largely unaware that they are serving as consumption models.

Every man with an idea has at least two or three followers

BROOKS ATKINSON

"January 2," Once Around the Sun (1951)

To simplify our discussion, we will consider four different types of group classification: (1) primary versus secondary groups, (2) formal versus informal groups, (3) large versus small groups, and (4) membership versus symbolic groups.

Primary versus Secondary Groups

If a person interacts on a regular basis with other individuals (i.e., with members of his or her family, with neighbors, or with co-workers whose opinions he or she values), then these individuals can be considered a *primary* group for that person. On the other hand, if a person interacts only occasionally with such others, or does not consider their opinions to be important, then these others constitute a *secondary* group for that person. From this definition, it can be seen that the critical distinctions between primary and secondary groups are (1) the importance of the groups to the individual and (2) the frequency or consistency with which the individual interacts with them.

Formal versus Informal Groups

Another useful way to classify groups is by the extent of their formality; that is, the extent to which the group structure, the members' roles, and the group's purpose are clearly defined. If a group has a highly defined structure (e.g., a formal membership list), specific roles and authority levels (e.g., a president, treasurer, and secretary), and specific goals (e.g., to support a political candidate, improve their children's education, or increase the knowledge or skills of members), then it would be classified as a *formal group*. On the other hand, if a group is more loosely defined—if it consists of several poker-playing cronies or three married couples who see each other frequently—then it is considered an *informal* group. The League of Women Voters, with elected officers and members who meet regularly to discuss topics of civic interest, would be classified as a formal group, while a group of friends who meet regularly for coffee and general conversation would be considered an informal group.

From the standpoint of consumer behavior, informal social or friendship groups are generally more important to the marketer, since their less clearly defined structures provide a more conducive environment for the exchange of information and influence about consumption-related topics.

Large versus Small Groups

It is often desirable to distinguish between groups in terms of their size or complexity. However, it is difficult to offer a precise breaking point as to when a group is considered large or small. A *large* group might be thought of as one in which a single member is not likely to know more than a few of the group's members personally or be fully aware of the specific roles or activities of more than a limited number of other group members. Examples of large groups include such complex organizations as the General Electric Company, with its numerous subordinate divisions, or the Democratic party, with its many local clubs scattered throughout the nation.

In contrast, members of a *small* group are likely to know every member personally and to be aware of every member's specific role or activities in the group. For example, each member of a local college sorority is likely to know all the other members and be aware of their duties and interests within the group.

In the realm of consumer behavior, we are principally concerned with the study of small groups, since such groups are more likely to influence the consumption behavior of group members.

Membership versus Symbolic Groups

Another useful way to classify groups is by membership versus symbolic groups. A *membership* group is a group to which a person either belongs or would qualify for membership. For example, the group of women with whom a young housewife bowls weekly or with whom she hopes to bowl when a team opening occurs would be considered, for her, a membership group.

In contrast, any group in which an individual is not likely to receive membership, despite his or her acting like a member by adopting the group's values, attitudes, and behavior, is considered a *symbolic* group. For example, professional tennis players may constitute a symbolic group for an amateur tennis buff who identifies with certain players by imitating their behavior whenever possible (e.g., in the purchase of a specific brand of tennis racquet or balls); however, the amateur does not and probably never will qualify for membership as a professional tennis player because the skill or opportunity to compete professionally is lacking. Both membership groups and symbolic groups influence consumer behavior; however, membership groups offer a more direct, and thus a more compelling, influence.

In summary, we can say that small, informal, primary membership groups are of the greatest interest to the marketing manager because they exert the greatest potential influence on consumer purchase decisions.

CONSUMER-RELEVANT GROUPS

To more fully comprehend the kind of impact that specific groups have on individuals, we will examine six basic consumer-relevant groups: (1) the family, (2) friendship groups, (3) formal social groups, (4) shopping groups, (5) consumer action groups, and (6) work groups.

The Family

An individual's family is often in the best position to influence his or her consumer decisions. The family's importance in this regard is based upon the frequency of contact that the individual has with other family members and the extent of influence that the family has had on the establishment of a wide range of values, attitudes, and behavior. (Chapter 12 examines the family's influence on consumption behavior.)

Friendship Groups

Friendship groups are typically classified as informal groups because they are usually unstructured and lack specific authority levels. In terms of relative influence, after an individual's family, it is his or her friends who are most likely to influence the individual's purchase decisions.

Seeking and maintaining friendships is a basic drive of most people. Friends fulfill a wide range of needs for the individual: They provide companionship, security, and opportunities to discuss problems that one may be reluctant to discuss with members of one's own family. Friendships are also a sign of maturity and independence, for they represent a breaking away from one's family and the forming of social ties with the outside world.

The views and opinions of friends can be an important force in influencing what products or brands a consumer will utimately select. Available research suggests that consumers are more likely to seek information from those friends that they feel have values or outlook similar to their own; and the greater the similarity, the more they are likely to trust them and to be influenced by their judgment in arriving at a purchase decision.[1]

Formal Social Groups

In contrast to the relative intimacy of friendship groups, formal social groups are more remote and serve a different function for the individual. A person joins a formal social group to fulfill such specific goals as making new friends, meeting "important" people, broadening his or her perspectives, pursuing a special interest, or promoting a specific cause. Because members of a formal social group often consume certain products together, such groups are of interest to marketers. For example, the membership list of a ski club would be of explicit interest to tour operators, travel agents, resort hotel managers, and sporting goods retailers. The membership list of a woman's club would be of interest to beauty salon managers, clothing and home furnishings retailers, and special-interest publications.

Membership in a formal social group may influence a consumer's behavior in several ways. For example, members of such groups have frequent opportunity to informally discuss products, services, or shops. Some members may copy the consumption behavior of other members whom they admire.

Because Americans are active in so many different kinds of formal social groups, this country has been called a "nation of joiners." A major research study that examined membership in formal social organizations (e.g., veterans, civic, political, fraternal, church, economic, cultural, and social associations) found that active formal social group participants tended to be married, were better educated, earned higher incomes, and had higher-status occupations than inactive members or nonmembers.[2] Such information can be helpful to marketing managers concerned with segmenting their markets for new or existing products.

Shopping Groups

Two or more people who shop together—whether for food, for clothing, or simply to pass the time—can be called a "shopping group." Such groups are often offshoots of family or friendship groups. People like to shop with others who are pleasant company or who they feel have more experience with or knowledge about a desired product or service. Shopping with others also provides an element of social fun to an often boring but necessary task. In addition, it reduces the risk that a purchase decision will be unwise or socially unacceptable. In instances where none of the members have knowledge about the product being sought, a shopping group may form for defensive reasons; members may feel more confident with a collective decision.

Very few marketing or consumer behavior studies have examined the nature of shopping groups. However, one study of the in-store behavior of shoppers revealed some differences between group and individual shopping.[3] As Table 11-1 indicates, shopping parties of at least three persons deviated more from their original purchase plans (they bought either more or less than originally planned) than did either single shoppers or two-party groups. Furthermore, two or more people shopping together were almost twice as likely

TABLE 11-1   A Comparison of Planned vs. Actual Purchases
by Size of Shopping Group

PURCHASES	SIZE OF THE SHOPPING GROUP		
	one	two	three or more
No item planned or purchased	3.7%	2.9%	0.0%
Fewer purchases than planned	15.1	12.4	31.3
Purchases as planned	58.9	41.0	26.6
More purchases than planned	22.3	43.7	42.1
Total	100.0%	100.0%	100.0%

Adapted from Donald H. Granbois, "Improving the Study of Customer In-Store Behavior," *Journal of Marketing*, 32 (October 1968), 30.

to buy more than planned than if they had shopped alone. The study also found that shopping groups tended to cover more territory in the store than individuals shopping alone, and thus they had more opportunity to see and examine merchandise and to make unplanned purchases.

A special type of shopping group is the in-home shopping group, which typically consists of a group of women who gather together in the home of a friend to attend a "party" devoted to the marketing of a specific line of products. The in-home party approach provides marketers with an opportunity to demonstrate the features of their products simultaneously to a group of potential customers. Two related advantages are (1) some of the guests may feel obliged to buy because they are guests in the home of the sponsoring hostess, and (2) early purchasers tend to create a bandwagon effect in that undecided guests often overcome a reluctance to buy when they see their friends make positive purchase decisions.

Consumer Action Groups

A new kind of consumer group has emerged in recent years in response to the consumerist movement. This type of consumer group has become increasingly visible since the 1960s and has been able to influence product design and marketing practices of both manufacturers and retailers.

Consumer action groups can be divided into two broad categories: those that organize to correct a specific consumer abuse and then disband, and those that organize to address broader, more pervasive, problem areas and operate over an extended or indefinite period of time. A group of tenants who band together to dramatize their dissatisfaction with the quality of service provided by their landlord, or a group of irate community members who unite to block the entrance of a fast-food outlet into their middle-class neighborhood, are examples of temporary, cause-specific consumer action groups. An example of a more enduring consumer action group is Action for Children's Television (A.C.T.), which was organized in the 1960s by a group of Boston mothers who were distressed by the quality of children's television programs. Today, A.C.T. is involved in a wide range of related problem areas, including the content and timing of commercials concerned with toys, breakfast cereals, and other product categories directed primarily at children.[4]

The overriding objective of many consumer interest groups is to bring sufficient pressure to bear on selected members of the business community to make them correct perceived consumer abuses. Through their collective action, a number of consumer interest groups have influenced the actions of the business community to a degree not possible by an individual consumer acting on his or her own behalf.

Work Groups

The sheer amount of time that people spend at their jobs—frequently more than thirty-five hours per week—provides ample opportunity for work groups to serve as a major influence on the consumption behavior of members.

Both the formal work group and the informal friendship/work group have the potential for influencing consumer behavior. The formal work group consists of those individuals who work together as a team. Their direct and sustained work relationship offers substantial opportunity for one or more members to influence the consumer-related attitudes and activities of other team members. Informal friendship/work groups consist of people who have become friends as a result of working for the same firm, regardless of whether or not they work together as a team. Members of informal work groups may influence the consumption behavior of other members during coffee or lunch breaks or after-hours meetings.

REFERENCE GROUPS

Reference groups are groups that serve as a frame of reference for individuals in their purchase decisions. This basic concept provides a valuable perspective for understanding the impact of other people on an individual's consumption beliefs, attitudes, and behavior. It also provides some insight into methods that can be used to effect desired changes in consumer behavior.

What Is a Reference Group?

A *reference group* is *any person or group that serves as a point of comparison (or reference) for an individual in the formation of either general or specific values, attitudes, or behavior.* The usefulness of this concept is enhanced by the fact that it does not place any restrictions on group size or membership, nor does it require that consumers identify with a tangible group (i.e., the group can be symbolic: prosperous businesspeople, rock stars, or sports heroes).[5]

Reference groups that influence general values or behavior are called *normative* reference groups. An example of a child's normative reference group is his or her immediate family, which is likely to play an important role in molding the child's general consumer values and behavior (e.g., which foods to select for good nutrition, appropriate ways to dress for specific occasions, how and where to shop, and what constitutes "good" values for his or her money).

Reference groups that serve as benchmarks for specific or narrowly defined attitudes or behavior are called *comparative* reference groups. A comparative reference group might be a neighboring family whose lifestyle appears to be both admirable and worthy of imitation (the way they maintain their home, their choice of home furnishings and cars, the number and types of vacations they take).

Both normative and comparative reference groups are important. Normative reference groups can influence the development of a basic code of behavior; comparative reference groups can influence the expression of specific consumer attitudes and behavior. It is likely that the specific influences of comparative reference groups are to some measure dependent upon the basic values and behavior patterns established early in a person's development by normative reference groups.

BROADENING THE REFERENCE GROUP CONCEPT

Like many other concepts borrowed from the behavioral sciences, the meaning of "reference group" has changed over the years. As originally employed, reference groups were narrowly defined to include only those groups with which a person interacted on a direct basis (e.g., family and close friends). However, the concept has gradually broadened to include both direct and indirect individual or group influences. Indirect reference groups consist of those individuals or groups with whom a person does *not* have direct face-to-face contact, such as movie stars, sports heroes, political leaders, or TV personalities.

Referents that a person might use in evaluating his or her own general or specific attitudes or behavior vary from an individual to a small group of people from the person's immediate family to a broader kinship, from a voluntary association to a social class, a profession, an ethnic group, a community, or even a nation.[6] As Figure 11-1 indicates, the major societal groupings that influence an individual's consumer behavior are, in order: family, friends, social class, and culture. (These important consumer reference groups are discussed more fully in Chapters 12–15).

TYPES OF REFERENCE GROUPS

Reference groups can be classified in terms of a person's membership or degree of involvement with the group and in terms of the positive or negative influences they have on his or her values, attitudes, and behavior. Table 11-2 depicts four types of reference groups that emerge from a cross-classification of these factors: (1) contactual groups, (2) aspirational groups, (3) disclaimant groups, and (4) avoidance groups.

FIGURE 11-1   Major Consumer Reference Groups

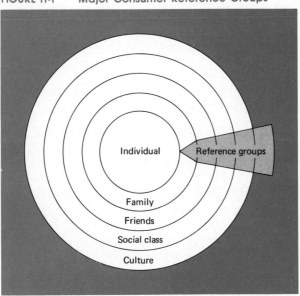

TABLE 11-2   Types of Reference Groups

	MEMBERSHIP GROUP	NONMEMBERSHIP GROUP
POSITIVE INFLUENCE	Contactual group	Aspirational group
NEGATIVE INFLUENCE	Disclaimant group	Avoidance group

A contactual group is a group in which a person holds membership or with which he or she has regular face-to-face contact and of whose values, attitudes, and standards he or she approves. Thus a contactual group has a positive influence on an individual's attitudes or behavior.

An aspirational group is a group in which a person does not hold membership or with which he or she does not have face-to-face contact but does want to be a member. Thus it serves as a positive influence on that person's attitudes or behavior.

A disclaimant group is a group in which a person holds membership or with which he or she has face-to-face contact but disapproves of the group's values, attitudes, and behavior. Thus the person intends to adopt attitudes and behavior that are in opposition to the norms of the group.

An avoidance group is a group in which a person does not hold membership or with which he or she does not have face-to-face contact and disapproves of the group's values, attitudes, and behavior. Thus he or she tends to adopt attitudes and behavior that are in opposition to those of the group.

Factors That Affect Reference Group Influence

The degree of influence that a reference group exerts on an individual's behavior usually depends on the nature of the individual and on specific social or product factors. This section discusses how and why some of these factors operate to influence consumer behavior.

INFORMATION AND EXPERIENCE

An individual who has firsthand experience with a product or service, or can easily obtain full information about it, is less likely to be influenced by the advice or example of others. On the other hand, a person who has little or no firsthand experience with a product or service, or does not expect to have access to objective information about it (i.e., he or she believes that relevant advertising may be misleading or deceptive), is more likely to seek out the advice or example of others. Research on imitative behavior provides some interesting insights on how insufficient experience or information concerning a product makes consumers more susceptible to the influence—either positive or negative—of others.[7]

For example, if a college junior wants to impress his new girlfriend, he may take her to a restaurant that he knows from experience to be good or to one that has been highly recommended by the local newspaper's "Dining-Out Guide." If he has neither personal experience nor information that he regards as valid, he may seek the advice of friends or imitate the behavior of others by taking her to a restaurant that he knows is frequented by seniors whom he admires.

GROUP DISCUSSION AND PERCEIVED RISK

Group discussion is likely to influence the individual's and the group's willingness to accept risk in purchase decisions. A study of ten groups of housewives found that subjects were more willing to accept greater risk in a purchase decision during and after a group discussion than they were initially willing as individuals.[8] These findings are consistent with what researchers have called the "risky shift" phenomenon, the tendency for individuals and groups to accept *greater* risk after group discussion.[9]

However, a more detailed analysis, which examined each product purchase situation individually, suggested that for one high-risk product, the group discussion led to a *reduced* willingness to accept risk—i.e., a conservative shift.[10] This second analysis suggests that willingness to accept risk with group discussion depends to some extent on the product category and its inherent level of risk.

This finding is supported by a study conducted among female college students, in which three categories of products judged by prior research to be "low-risk products," "medium-risk products," and "high-risk products" were examined.[11] The findings indicated a greater willingness to accept more risk for low-risk products (facial tissues and chewing gum) after group discussion, no significant shift in willingness to accept risk for medium-risk products (suntan lotion and eye shadow) after group discussion, and a movement to accept less risk after group discussion for products judged to be high in perceived risk (deodorants and cold remedies).

On the basis of these and similar studies, it would seem that a product's characteristics (its inherent perceived risk level) influence the direction of perceived risk produced by group discussion. For the marketer of a high-risk product, the results suggest that the advertising must provide sufficiently persuasive information to reduce perceived risk. Otherwise any group discussion that may naturally occur is likely to persuade consumers *not* to buy the product.

CREDIBILITY, ATTRACTIVENESS, AND POWER OF THE REFERENCE GROUP

A reference group that is perceived as credible, attractive, or powerful can induce consumer attitude and behavior change. For example, when consumers are concerned with obtaining accurate information about the performance or quality of a product or service, they are likely to be persuaded by those whom they consider to be trustworthy and knowledgeable. That is, they are more likely to be persuaded by sources with high credibility. When consumers are primarily concerned with the acceptance or approval of others whom they like, with whom they identify, or who offer them status or other benefits, they are likely to adopt their product, brand, or other behavioral characteristics.

Still further, when consumers are primarily concerned with the power that a person or group can exert over them, they might select products or services that conform to the norms of that person or group in order to avoid ridicule or punishment. However, unlike other reference groups that consumers follow either because they are credible or because they are attractive, power groups are not likely to cause attitude change. Individuals may conform to the behavior of a powerful person or group but may not experience a change in their own attitudes.

Different reference groups may influence the beliefs, attitudes and behavior of an individual at different points in time or under different circumstances. For example, the dress habits of a young secretary may vary, depending on her place and role. She may conform to the dress code of her office when at work by wearing tailored clothing and may drastically alter her mode of dress after work by wearing more conspicuous, revealing styles.

CONSPICUOUSNESS OF THE PRODUCT

The potential influence of a reference group varies according to how visually or verbally conspicuous a product is to others. A visually conspicuous product is one that can be seen and identified by others, and that will stand out and be noticed (e.g., a luxury item or novelty product). Even if a product is not visually conspicuous, it may be verbally conspicuous—it may be highly interesting or it may be easily described to others. Products that are especially conspicuous and status revealing (a new automobile, fashion clothing, and home furniture) are most likely to be purchased with some consideration being given to the reaction of relevant others. Products that are less conspicuous (canned fruits, laundry soaps) are less likely to be purchased with a reference group in mind.[12]

The success of products like the Sony Walkman (Figure 11-2 on pages 298–99) are in part aided by the fact that it is quite easy to spot a person wearing the headphones.

REFERENCE GROUP IMPACT ON PRODUCT AND BRAND CHOICE

In some cases, and for some products, reference groups may influence both a person's product category and brand (or type) choices. Such products are called "product-plus, brand-plus" items. In other cases, reference groups influence only the product category decision. Such products are called "product-plus, brand-minus" items. In still other cases, reference groups influence the brand (or type) decision. These products are called "product-minus, brand-plus" items. Finally, in some cases, reference groups influence neither the product category nor the brand decision, and these products are called "product-minus, brand-minus" items. The idea of classifying products and brands into four groups in terms of the suitability of a reference group appeal was first suggested in the mid-1950s, along with an initial classification of a small number of product

TABLE 11-3   Reference Group Influence on Product and Brand Choices

		REFERENCE GROUP INFLUENCE ON PRODUCT CATEGORY	
		weak (−)	strong (+)
REFERENCE GROUP INFLUENCE ON BRAND OR TYPE	strong (+)	*Cell 1* Magazines Furniture Clothing Instant coffee Aspirin Air conditioners Stereos Laundry detergent Microwave ovens	*Cell 2* Automobiles Color TV
	weak (−)	*Cell 3* Canned peaches Toilet soap Beer Cigarettes Small cigars	*Cell 4*

Source: Donald W. Hendon, "A New and Empirical Look at the Influence of Reference Groups on Generic Product Category and Brand Choice: Evidence from Two Nations," in *Proceedings of the Academy of International Business: Asia-Pacific Dimensions of International Business* (Honolulu: College of Business Administration, University of Hawaii, 1979), 757.

categories.[13] Table 11-3 lists the results of a recent reexamination and extension of this earlier research.[14]

Reference Groups and Consumer Conformity

Marketers are particularly interested in the ability of reference groups to change consumer attitudes and behavior (i.e., to encourage conformity). To be capable of such influence, a refence group must

1.   Inform or make the individual aware of a specific product or brand
2.   Provide the individual with the opportunity to compare his or her own thinking with the attitudes and behavior of the group
3.   Influence the individual to adopt attitudes and behavior that are consistent with the norms of the group
4.   Legitimize an individual's decision to use the same products as the group

The ability of reference groups to influence consumer conformity is demonstrated by the results of a classic experiment that was designed to compare the effects of lectures with the effects of group discussions on family food consumption habits.[15] The purpose of this study was to find the most effective method for inducing homemakers to serve such culturally undesirable cuts of meat as beef hearts, sweetbreads, and kidneys to their families during World War II. Findings indicated that group discussions were far more effective in inducing conformity than lectures in which group opinions were not aired (32 percent versus 3 percent).

Group Dynamics
and Consumer
Reference Groups

FIGURE 11-2   Advertisement Incorporating the Conspicuousness of the Product

in the streets.

The Sony Walkman

Look around. It's happening everywhere.

More and more people every day are listening to music in a revolutionary way.

The Walkman is a completely portable stereo tape machine that plays music with such power and fidelity, you won't believe you're listening to a cassette player that's just a little bigger than the cassette itself. Because the sound is much closer to that of a huge home stereo system.

You listen through tiny feather-weight headphones. And there's even a jack for a second set of headphones, in case you're in the mood to share your music with someone else.

So come into your local Sony dealer and find out what the revolution is all about. After all, the Walkman is from the people who have been revolutionizing an industry for years.

SONY
THE ONE AND ONLY

A number of more recent consumer research studies have also examined the impact of reference group influence on consumer conformity. For example, a study of male college students' responses to group pressure provides some insights on consumer conformity.[16] Three men's suits—labeled, respectively, *A, B* and *C*—were described to groups of students as being of different quality and manufacture, though they were actually of identical quality and color and manufactured by the same firm. The experiment compared the evaluations of *control groups* (in which naive subjects selected a preferred suit in private) with the evaluations of *conformity groups* (in which naive subjects made their evaluations and choices publicly after three cooperating confederates in each group all chose the same suit). The results of the experiment indicated that the naive subjects in each of the conformity groups tended to conform to the product choices of the cooperating confederates, while the naive members of the control groups, who made their choices in private, made random choices. The marketing implication of this study is that, in the absence of objective quality standards, individual consumers tend to conform to group norms; that is, to the choices of the majority.

In another consumer study, ten informal friendship groups, each consisting of four or five homemakers, were visited individually in their homes twice a week for eight weeks, and at each visit were requested to select one of four "brands" of bread.[17] Unknown to the subjects, all four brands (labeled *H, L, M,* and *P*) were identical loaves coming from the same bakery. Findings revealed that the more cohesive (close-knit) the group, the greater the likelihood that group members would select the same brand as their informal group leader. Furthermore, the greater the group leader's brand loyalty, the greater the likelihood that the other group members would be loyal to the same brand. These findings suggest that informal friendship groups positively influence member conformity.

A study of male college friendship groups offers some additional evidence on the relationship between group cohesiveness and brand choice conformity.[18] In this study, four low-cost consumer packaged goods (beer, after-shave lotion, deodorant, and cigarettes) were studied in an attempt to ascertain whether the purchase of different brands among various product categories depends on group influence. The results of the study indicated that for two of the products—beer and after-shave lotion—the more cohesive the group, the greater the brand choice conformity. No significant relationship between the extent of group cohesiveness and brand choice conformity was found in the initial analysis for either deodorants or cigarettes. However, when the share of market for each brand was accounted for, a significant relationship was found between group cohesiveness and brand choice conformity in the case of cigarettes, but not deodorants.[19] Note that for the three products where conformity was found to influence purchase choice (beer, after-shave lotion, cigarettes), the product categories tended to be more socially conspicuous than for the fourth category—deodorants. This study supports the proposition that consumer conformity is likely to vary, depending on the product category.

The research evidence reviewed underscores the fact that a consumer's selection of a product category, brand, style, or type of product is frequently influenced by the advice and information he or she obtains from others. We will complete our examination of the influence of reference groups by focusing on the applications of this concept to a firm's promotional policies.

PROMOTIONAL APPLICATIONS OF THE REFERENCE GROUP CONCEPT

Reference group appeals are used very effectively by some advertisers to segment their markets. Group situations or people with which a segment of the audience can identify are used to promote goods and services by subtly inducing the prospective consumer to identify with the illustrated user of the product. This identification may be based on admiration (e.g., of an athlete), on aspiration (e.g., of a celebrity or of a way of life), on empathy (e.g., with a person or situation), or on recognition (e.g., of a person—real or stereotypical—or of a situation). In some cases, the prospective consumer thinks, "If she uses it, it must be good. If I use it, I'll be like her." In other cases, the prospective consumer says to himself, "He's got problems I've got. What worked for him will work for me."

There are three major types of reference group appeals in common marketing usage: (1) celebrities, (2) experts, and (3) the "common man." These appeals, as well as less frequently employed appeals, are often operationalized in the guise of testimonials or endorsements. In the case of the "common man," they may be presented as "slice of life" commercials (see Chapter 10).

Celebrities

Celebrities, particularly movie stars, television personalities, and sports heroes, are a very popular type of reference group appeal. To their loyal followers and to much of the general public, celebrities represent an idealization of life that most people would like to live themselves. Advertisers spend enormous sums of money to have celebrities promote their products in the expectation that the reading or viewing audience will react positively to the celebrity's association with their product.

In Figure 11-3 Karl Malden is promoting American Express Travelers Cheques. The use of Karl Malden has frequently been praised because he is a highly recognized celebrity, one who is widely respected and liked, and because his TV role as a police officer makes him a logical spokesperson for a product that features security and peace of mind.

HOW CELEBRITIES ARE USED

A firm that decides to employ a celebrity to promote its product has a choice of using the celebrity to give a testimonial, to give an endorsement, as an actor in a

FIGURE 11-3   Advertisement Employing a Well-Known Celebrity

Introducing
the only travelers cheque with new services that protect more than just your money.

People who lose their travelers cheques often lose other things with them. Cash, credit cards, even their identification.

That's why American Express is introducing 5 exclusive services designed to give you extra vacation protection, at no extra cost. And they're available to all American Express Travelers Cheque customers who lose their travelers cheques in the U.S. or Canada.

No other travelers cheque offers even one of the following services. So if you want the best vacation protection, there's only one travelers cheque to ask for: American Express.

Only American Express will help you cancel your credit cards if they're lost with your travelers cheques. When you call the American Express Refund Center to report your loss, simply tell one of our refund operators that your credit cards are also missing. No matter what hour it is, you'll be transferred to a special operator who will assist in canceling any cards that were issued to you in the U.S. or Canada. That's all there is to it.

Only American Express will issue you a temporary ID card if all your identification is lost with your travelers cheques. Following verification, one of our Refund Center operators will direct you to an American Express Travel Service Office in the U.S. or Canada, where you can pick up your ID. It has our name and phone number on it, so you can use us as a reference wherever you go.

Only American Express will cash a check for up to $200 if you need money with your travelers cheque refund. After your U.S. or Canadian check is authorized, any of our Travel Service or Representative Offices in the U.S. or Canada will cash it for you.

Only American Express will put its Travel Service at your service 24 hours a day if you need to change travel plans because of your loss. One of our Refund Center operators will transfer you to a Travel Service Hotline operator who can help you arrange airline, car and hotel reservations.

Only American Express will send a Mailgram® for you at no charge anywhere in the U.S. or Canada, at any hour of the day or night. Just give the message you'd like to send to one of our Refund Center operators—the operator will take care of the rest. It's a service which could prove very helpful if you want to notify someone of a change in travel plans and you're having trouble reaching them on the phone.

Now we protect more than just your money.
Now we help protect your vacation.

AMERICAN EXPRESS

commercial, or as a company spokesman. These promotional roles differ as follows:[20]

1. *Testimonial*—If the celebrity has personally used the product or service and is in a position to attest to its quality, he may be asked to give a testimonial. An example would be a testimonial for a specific brand of golf ball given by a golf pro such as Arnold Palmer.

2. *Endorsement*—A celebrity who may or may not be an expert with regard to a product or service may be asked to lend his name and physical person to an advertisement for the product or service. Joe Namath's endorsement of panty hose is an example of an endorsement.

3. *Actor*—A celebrity may be asked to dramatically present the product or service as part of a character enactment, rather than as a personal testimonial or endorsement. An example of a celebrity used in this way is Jonathan Winters, the comedian.

4. *Spokesman*—A celebrity who represents a brand or company over an extended period of time, often in print, on television, and in personal appearances, can be called a company spokesman. Eventually, his appearance becomes closely associated with the brand or company. Robert Morley is a spokesman for British Airways and is closely identified with most of its advertising.

Table 11-4 gives a number of examples of each of these somewhat distinct uses of the celebrity as reference group appeals.

CREDIBILITY OF THE CELEBRITY

Of all the positive characteristics that a celebrity might contribute to a firm's advertising program (fame, talent, charisma), his or her credibility with the consumer audience is the most important. By *credibility* we mean the audience's

TABLE 11-4   How Celebrities Are Used in Reference Group Appeals

TYPES OF USE	CELEBRITY	BRAND OR COMPANY
1. Testimonial	Bjorn Borg	PreSun-Sun Products
	Bill Cosby	Jello
	Stevie Wonder	TDK Cassette Tape
2. Endorsement	Cheryl Tiegs	Olympus Camera
	Bob Hope	Texaco
	Angie Dickinson	California Avocados
	Michael Landon	Kodak
	Lynda Carter	Maybelline
	Jack Klugman	Yoplait Yogurt
	Juliet Prowse	L'eggs Pantyhose
	Orson Welles	Paul Masson Wines
3. Actor	Vivian Vance	Instant Maxwell House Coffee
	Jerry Stiller and Anne Meara	Blue Nun Wine
	Flip Wilson	Diet Seven-Up
	Jonathan Winters	Wendy's Hamburgers
4. Spokesperson	O.J. Simpson	Hertz
	Joe DiMaggio	Bowery Savings Bank
	Ed McMahon	Never Wax Vinyl Floors

perception of both the celebrity's *expertise* (how much the celebrity knows about the product area) and his or her *trustworthiness* (how honest the celebrity is about what he or she knows about the product).[21] To increase this credibility, recent evidence suggests that employing a celebrity on an exclusive basis (the celebrity does not endorse any other products) has some really positive benefits.[22] Specifically, the research reveals that when a celebrity endorses only one product, consumers are likely to perceive the product in a more favorable light and to indicate a greater intention to purchase it.

CREDIBILITY OF SPORTS CELEBRITIES

A large-scale study of sports celebrities was in part designed to identify the extent of association between three presumed celebrity characteristics (familiarity, talent, and likability) and the celebrity's credibility (would an endorsement or testimonial by the celebrity be trusted by the relevant public?)[23] Respondents were asked to rank two hundred sports personalities in terms of their familiarity, talent, and likability. Of all these attributes, "likability" was found to be most closely associated with the individual's credibility as a product endorser. Table 11-5 presents the rankings on each dimension for the first twenty-five per-

TABLE 11-5   Selected Items from a Consumers' Ranking of 200 Sports Personalities

	FAMILIARITY	TALENT	LIKABILITY	CREDIBILITY
Willie Mays	1	5	3	31
Joe Namath	2	124	143	156
Muhammad Ali	3	189	192	190
Mickey Mantle	4	8	11	2
Arnold Palmer	5	33	17	4
Howard Cosell	6	186	176	131
Yogi Berra	7	11	4	3
Joe DiMaggio	8	34	20	30
Sandy Koufax	9	4	10	5
Johnny Unitas	10	22	24	29
Joe Garagiola	11	159	32	11
Hank Aaron	12	17	18	28
Johnny Bench	13	16	2	7
Jack Nicklaus	14	37	33	16
Sugar Ray Robinson	15	30	52	67
O.J. Simpson	16	1	27	32
Joe Frazier	17	158	164	145
Wilt Chamberlain	18	167	173	150
Dizzy Dean	19	86	55	82
Lee Trevino	20	107	57	63
Curt Gowdy	21	147	88	76
Mark Spitz	22	111	181	179
Ted Williams	23	15	29	14
A.J. Foyt	24	78	67	41
Stan Musial	25	3	1	1

© 1973 by the New York Times Company. Reprinted by permission.

sonalities in terms of how well they were known. The table indicates that visibility is not highly associated with confidence in that person's endorsements. For example, Joe Namath may rank second in terms of public awareness, but he ranks 143 out of 200 in terms of likability and 156 in terms of credibility as an endorser. The evidence tends to correct the common misconception that it is the athlete's fame that contributes to his credibility.

The study also reported that four product categories especially lend themselves to sports celebrity endorsements: sporting goods, athlete's foot remedies, sportswear, and electric shavers. Four other product categories were found to be very poor candidates for sports celebrity tie-ins: pet foods, home furnishings, wine, and house paint.[24]

These findings, and those of a similar study that concentrated on movie stars and TV personalities as endorsers, confirm the notion that source credibility of a company spokesperson is based more on likableness than mere recognition or familiarity.[25]

The Expert

A second type of reference group appeal used by marketers is the expert—a person who, because of his or her occupation, special training, skill, or extensive experience, is in a unique position to help the prospective consumer evaluate the product or service that the advertisement promotes. For example, an RCA color television advertisement that features the endorsements of TV color engineers, or an AC Delco advertisement that uses a stereotypical service mechanic (an expert on automotive needs) to tell the audience about the special qualities of a Delco product, are two expert reference group appeals. Still another example is the AMF advertisement that features Arthur Ashe as an endorser of a Head racquet bearing his name (see Figure 11-4). This is a fine example of an expert appeal because in this case the expert is also a sports celebrity.

The "Common Man"

A third type of reference group appeal employs the testimonials of satisfied customers. The advantage of this "common man" appeal is that it demonstrates to the prospective customer that someone just like him, or someone he would like to be, uses and is satisfied with the product or service advertised. Experience in developing promotional appeals for public health announcements (e. g., antismoking or high-blood-pressure messages) reveal that the "common man" appeal is especially effective, for most people seem to identify with people just like them when it comes to such messages.[26]

An ad for a health insurance program that depicts six stereotypical subscribers each giving their specific reasons for satisfaction with their health insurance would be an example of a "common man" appeal. For the potential subscriber, such an ad would present various reasons for having such medical coverage. For those who are already covered, it would reassure them that they are making the correct health coverage choice.

Courtesy of AMF Inc., Head Racquet Sports Division

A promotional campaign that effectively includes the "common man" appeal has been used on a regular basis by Maytag to emphasize the dependability of its dishwashers (see Figure 11-5). Since dishwashers perform a practical or functional task, one not easily associated with glamour, the "common man" appeal seems to be ideally suited for such a product.

Many television commercials depict widely prevalent problem situations and show how a typical family or person has solved the problem by using the advertised product. These commercials are known as "slice of life" commercials because they depict situations "out of real life" with which the viewer can identify. For example, one commercial may show teenage members of a family squabbling over which television program to watch; another may show the man of the house "stealing" a light bulb from one lamp to replace one needed in another lamp. If viewers can identify with the situation, it is very likely that they will adopt the solution that worked for the family in the commercial.

In recent years, a number of advertisers have adopted the approach of "listening in" or showing a group interview in which, for example, young mothers are asked to discuss their laundry needs and evaluate the benefits of a

FIGURE 11-5   Advertisement Depicting a "Common Man" Endorsement

George, Jr., Mrs. Lang, Maryelizabeth, Mr. Lang.

"A working mother's best friend is her Maytag," writes Mrs. Lang.

Between her family and her job, who has the time to wait around for repairmen?

"Thank you for making a washer a working housewife and mother can count on," writes Mrs. Nancy Lang, Hampton Bays, New York.

"11 years ago, I purchased a Maytag. It wasn't till just this past spring that it needed its first repair."

Mrs. Lang knows from experience that Maytag Washers are

built to last longer and save you money with fewer repairs. She also knows that they can save you the hassle of waiting around for repairmen.

Mrs. Lang adds that she is also delighted with her Maytag Dryer. "As for my Maytag Dishwasher, I would be lost without it," she concludes.

Of course, we don't say al Maytags will equal that record But long life with few repairs i what we try to build into ever Maytag product.

See our washers, dryers, dish washers and disposers.

MAYTAG
THE DEPENDABILITY PEOPLE

The Maytag Company, Newton, Iowa 50208.

Courtesy of Maytag Company

new laundry soap. If the prospective consumer can identify with the laundry needs or other needs discussed by consumer-actors who are apparently just like her, it is likely that she will conform to the product wisdom expressed and buy the advertised product.

Still another "common man" approach is to use a model in an advertisement to represent the type of person the prospective consumer would like to be, or to represent a lifestyle to which the prospect may aspire. For example, the endorsement of an airline by an apparently prosperous and powerful businessman may induce a low- or middle-management executive to use that airline. The endorsement of a furniture polish by an attractive woman standing in the well-furnished living room of a beautiful home may influence an apartment dweller to buy the same polish.

Other Reference Group Appeals

A variety of other promotional strategies can creatively function as a frame of reference for consumers. During the past five years, an increasing number of firms have employed their top executive as a spokesperson in consumer ads. The popularity of this type of advertising is probably due to the success and publicity received by a number of innovative executive spokespersons. For instance, Frank Perdue has been highly effective in convincing consumers that the chickens bearing his name are superior to the typical unbranded supermarket variety. Similarly, Frank Borman (the former astronaut), in his capacity as the president of Eastern Airlines, has effectively communicated his company's eagerness to do everything possible to keep its passengers satisfied.

Just what has made these and other corporate executives successful as spokespersons has not been established. However, not unlike the celebrity, these individuals seem to be admired by the general population because of their achievements and the status that often accompanies being a business leader in the United States. A novel application of this type of appeal depicts Victor Kiam in a TV ad stating that he was so impressed with the Remington shaver that his wife had given him that he went out and bought the company (see Figure 11-6). In response to such an ad, it is likely that some consumers felt that if Kiam was really so satisfied with the product that he was willing to risk his own money by investing in the company, then the product might deserve a trial.

Respected retailers or the editorial content of selected special-interest magazines can also function as a frame of reference that influences consumers' attitudes and behavior. For instance, a loyal customer of a leading fashion-specialty store like Saks Fifth Avenue might feel that if Saks features or depicts a particular fashion as being suitable for a certain occasion, then it must be acceptable or in good taste.[27] Similarly, a regular reader of *Harper's Bazaar* might judge a particular fashion featured in the magazine as being in good taste just because it appears in its pages. In these two cases, the retailer and the magazine are functioning as a frame of reference that influences consumer behavior.

Still further, trade characters (e.g., Betty Crocker, Smokey the Bear, Tony the Tiger), as well as familiar cartoon characters (e.g., Mickey Mouse, Snoopy, Superman, Spiderman), may be useful as a kind of quasi-celebrity endorser. For instance, Figure 11-7 on page 310 shows an advertisement featuring the popular Pink Panther in a role designed to help promote the acceptance of Owens-Corning Fiberglas home insulation materials.

Finally, seals of approval and even objective product ratings can serve as a positive endorsement that encourages consumers to act favorably toward selected products. For instance, *Good Housekeeping* magazine's seal of approval is well regarded by many consumers as an indication that a particular brand is likely to function as promised. Similarly, many parents of young children look for the American Dental Association's seal of approval before selecting a brand of toothpaste. Still further, a highly rated brand by an objective rating magazine such as *Consumer Reports* can serve to "endorse" the brand.

Remington

Title: "Victor Kiam/Lady Remington"
Product: Micro Screen Shaver

Total Length: 30 Seconds

KIAM: Hello. I was a dedicated blade
shaver until my wife bought me...

this Remington Micro Screen Shaver
because it would shave as close as a
blade or your money back.

The first Micro Screen is so thin, it shaves
incredibly close.

The second even closer.

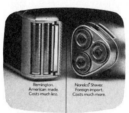

And Remington's American made--it
costs less. Norelco's imported--it costs
much more.

I was so impressed, I bought the company.

The Remington Micro Screen

shaves as close as a blade or I'll give you
your money back.

ANNCR: (VO) And the Lady Remington.
The perfect gift. Also with a money-back
guarantee.

Courtesy of Remington Products, Inc.

Benefits of the Reference Group Appeal

Advertisers use celebrities, experts, and the "common man," as well as the other
reference group appeals described here, to promote their products or services
because they believe that such appeals will give them a competitive advantage.
Reference group appeals have two principal benefits for the advertiser: They
increase brand awareness and they serve to reduce perceived risk.

Courtesy of Owens-Corning Fiberglass Corporation

INCREASE BRAND AWARENESS

The reference group appeals described above provide the advertiser with the
opportunity to gain and maintain the attention of prospective consumers with
greater ease and effectiveness than is possible with many other types of
promotional campaigns. This is particularly true of the celebrity form of
reference group appeal, where the personality employed is generally well known
to the relevant target segment. Celebrities tend to draw attention to the product

through their own popularity. This gives the advertiser a competitive advantage in gaining the audience's attention, particularly on television where there are so many brief and similar commercial announcements.

REDUCE PERCEIVED RISK

The use of one or more reference group appeals may also serve to lower the consumer's perceived risk in purchasing a specific product. The example set by the endorser or testimonial giver may demonstrate to the consumer that his or her uncertainty about the product purchase is unwarranted. Following are examples of how each of the three most popular types of reference group appeals serves to lower the consumer's perceived risk.

CELEBRITY. When consumers identify with a particular celebrity or consider the celebrity to be trustworthy, they often have the following reactions to the celebrity's endorsement or testimonial:

"She wouldn't do a commercial for that product if she didn't believe it was really good."
"An important person like him doesn't need the money, so he must be plugging the product because it really works."
"If it's good enough for him, it's good enough for me."

EXPERT. When consumers are concerned about the technical aspects of a product, they are apt to be persuaded by the comments of an acknowledged or apparent expert and have the following reactions:

"If he says it works, then it really must work."
"If an expert uses the product, it must really be good."

COMMON MAN. When consumers are worried about how the product will affect them personally, they are apt to be positively influenced by a "common man" endorsement or testimonial and have the following reactions:

"People just like me are using that new product."
"If it can help her, it's just as likely to help me."
"She has the same problem that I have; I wonder if that product will help me also?"

Government Guidelines for the Use of Testimonials and Endorsements

Because reference group appeals have been used so successfully by some firms as part of their promotional strategy, they have come under the scrutiny of the Federal Trade Commission. The FTC has issued guidelines for testimonial and endorsement advertising which have provoked a considerable amount of controversy among advertisers.[28] These guidelines are designed to protect consumers from the deceptive use of celebrities, experts, and the "common man" in advertising endorsements or testimonials. In fact, they serve to underscore the influence that reference groups have on consumer motivation.

summary

Almost all individuals regularly interact with other people who directly or indirectly influence their purchase decisions. Thus the study of groups and their impact on the individual is of great importance to marketers concerned with influencing consumer behavior. Groups may be classified according to regularity of contact (primary or secondary groups), by their structure and hierarchy (formal or informal groups), by their size or complexity (large or small groups), and by membership or aspiration (membership or symbolic groups).

Six basic types of consumer-relevant groups influence the consumption behavior of individuals: family, friendship groups, formal social groups, shopping groups, consumer action groups, and work groups.

Reference groups are groups that serve as a frame of reference for individuals in their purchase decisions. Any or all of the groups listed above can serve as reference groups. Reference groups that influence general values or behavior are called *normative* reference groups; those that influence specific attitudes are called *comparative* reference groups. The concept of consumer reference groups has been broadened to include groups with which consumers have no direct face-to-face contact, such as celebrities, political figures, social classes, and cultures.

Reference groups that are classified in terms of a person's membership and the positive or negative influences they exert on him or her include contactual groups, aspirational groups, disclaimant groups, and avoidance groups.

The credibility, attractiveness, and power of the reference group affect the degree of influence it has. In some cases, and for some products, reference groups may influence either the product category or brand choice purchase decisions, or both. Reference group appeals are used very effectively by some advertisers in promoting their goods and services because they subtly induce the prospective consumer to identify with the pictured user of the product.

The three types of reference groups most commonly used in marketing are celebrities, experts, and the "common man." *Celebrities* are used to give testimonials or endorsements, as actors, and as company spokespersons. *Experts* may be recognized experts in the product category or actors playing the part of experts (e.g., an automobile mechanic). The *common man* approach is designed to show that individuals "just like" the prospect are satisfied with the product advertised.

Reference group appeals are effective promotional strategies because they serve to increase brand awareness and reduce perceived risk among prospective consumers. Their usage is now being regulated by the Federal Trade Commission, which is showing increased interest because of the apparent effectiveness with which such appeals influence the consumers' purchase decisions.

discussion questions

1. In terms of influencing consumer behavior, what is the major difference between a primary and a secondary group?
2. Name and briefly describe three different types of groups that might influence an individual's consumer behavior. What is the importance of each of these groups for marketers in planning their marketing strategy?
3. As a marketing consultant for a large retail chain, you have been asked to evaluate a new promotional campaign. The campaign strategy is aimed at increasing "group" shopping. What recommendations would you make to the retail executive you report to?
4. In terms of consumer behavior, discuss the differences between a normative and a comparative reference group.
5. How do the following factors influence the importance of a reference group in making a consumer purchase decision?
   a. Prior experience with the product category
   b. Conspicuousness of the product
6. Select two magazine advertisements that you feel reflect reference group appeals. One should be based on an aspirational group appeal, and the other on a contactual group appeal.
7. Imagine that you are the vice-president of advertising for a large furniture manufacturer. Your advertising agency is in the process of negotiating a contract to employ this year's most valuable baseball player to promote your products. Discuss.
8. Find a magazine advertisement for a consumer product that uses the *expert* as a reference group appeal. What impact do you feel this appeal has on consumers? Explain.

endnotes

1. George P. Moschis, "Social Comparison and Informal Group Influence," *Journal of Marketing Research*, 13 (August 1976), 237–44.
2. Murray Hausknecht, *The Joiners* (New York: Bedminister Press, 1962).
3. Donald H. Granbois, "Improving the Study of Customer In-Store Behavior," *Journal of Marketing*, 32 (October 1968), 28–32.
4. "A Harsh Critic of Kids' TV," *Business Week*, May 29, 1978, 52.
5. T. Shibutani, "Reference Groups and Social Control," in Arnold Rose, ed., *Human Behavior and Social Processes* (Boston: Houghton Mifflin, 1962), 132.
6. James E. Stafford, "Reference Theory as a Conceptual Framework for Consumer Decisions," in Robert L. King, ed. *Proceedings* (Chicago: American Marketing Association, 1968), 282.
7. Solomon E. Asch, *Social Psychology* (Englewood Cliffs, N.J.: Prentice-Hall, 1952).
8. Arch G. Woodside, "Informal Group Influence on Risk Taking," *Journal of Marketing Research*, 9 (May 1972), 223–25.
9. Dean G. Pruitt, "Conclusions: Towards an Understanding of Choice Shifts in Group Discussion," *Journal of Personality and Social Psychology*, 20 (August 1971), 495–510.

10. Arch G. Woodside, "Is There a Generalized Risky Shift Phenomenon in Consumer Behavior?" *Journal of Marketing Research*, 11 (May 1974), 225–26.

11. Daniel L. Johnson and I. Robert Andrews, "Risky-Shift Phenomenon as Tested with Consumer Products as Stimuli," *Journal of Personality and Social Psychology*, 20 (August 1971), 328–85.

12. V. Parker Lessig and C. Whan Park, "Promotional Perspectives of Reference Group Influence: Advertising Implications," *Journal of Advertising*, 7 (Spring 1978), 41–47.

13. Foundation for Research on Human Behavior, *Group Influence in Marketing and Public Relations* (Ann Arbor, Mich.: The Foundation, 1956), 8–9.

14. Donald W. Hendon, "A New and Empirical Look at the Influence of Reference Groups on Generic Product Category and Brand Choice: Evidence from Two Nations," in *Proceedings of the Academy of International Business: Asia-Pacific Dimensions of International Business* (Honolulu: College of Business Administration, University of Hawaii, 1979), 752–61.

15. Kurt Lewin, "Group Decision and Social Change," in Theodore M. Newcomb and Eugene L. Hartley, eds., *Readings in Social Psychology* (New York: Henry Holt, 1947), 330–44.

16. M. Venkatesan, "Experimental Study of Consumer Behavior Conformity and Independence," *Journal of Marketing Research*, 3 (November 1966), 384–87.

17. James E. Stafford, "Effects of Group Influence on Consumer Brand Preferences," *Journal of Marketing Research*, 3 (February 1966), 68–75.

18. Robert E. Witt, "Informal Social Group Influence on Consumer Brand Choice," *Journal of Marketing Research*, 6 (November 1969), 473–76.

19. Robert E. Witt and Grady D. Bruce, "Purchase Decisions and Group Influence," *Journal of Marketing Research*, 7 (November 1970), 533–35.

20. Joseph M. Kamen, Abdul C. Azhari, and Judith R. Kragh, "What a Spokesman Does for a Sponsor," *Journal of Advertising Research*, 15 (April 1975), 17.

21. Patricia Niles Middleton, *Social Psychology and Modern Life* (New York: Knopf, 1974), 162.

22. John C. Mowen and Stephen W. Brown, "On Explaining and Predicting the Effectiveness of Celebrity Endorsers," in Kent Monroe, ed., *Advances in Consumer Research* (Ann Arbor, Mich.: Association for Consumer Research, 1981), VIII, 437–41.

23. Alan R. Nelson, "Can the Glamour and Excitement of Sports Really Carry the Ball for Your Product?" *Marketing Review*, 29 (February 1974), 21–25.

24. Ibid, p. 24.

25. Hershey H. Friedman, Michael J. Santeramo, and Anthony Traina, "Correlates of Trustworthiness for Celebrities," *Journal of the Academy of Marketing Science*, 6 (Fall 1978), 291–99.

26. "Study Identifies Qualities of Effective Health Public Service Announcements," *Marketing News*, April 3, 1981, 7.

27. Elizabeth C. Hirschman and Ronald W. Stampfl, "Roles of Retailing the Diffusion of Popular Culture: Microperspectives," *Journal of Retailing*, 56 (Spring 1980), 31–32.

28. Federal Trade Commission, *Guides Concerning Use of Endorsements and Testimonials in Advertising*, January 18, 1980, 16 CFR, Part 255.

treated as synonymous within the context of consumer behavior, and we will continue this tradition.

In the United States, as in most of Western society, three types of families dominate: the married couple, the nuclear family, and the extended family. The simplest type of family, in terms of number of members, is the *married couple*—a husband and wife. As a basic household unit, the married couple is generally most representative of younger marrieds, who have not as yet started a family, and older couples, who have already raised their children.

A husband and wife and at least one offspring constitute a *nuclear family*. This type of family is the cornerstone of family life as it now exists in the United States. Since it is composed of parents and their children, the nuclear family can properly be thought of as consisting of two generations living in the same household.

When we have a husband, wife, children, and at least one grandparent living together, we have a three-generation family, commonly called an *extended family*. This type of family, which at one time was most representative of the American family, has been declining in number as increased mobility has separated parents and their married offspring. Table 12-1 summarizes the household composition of each of these three types of families.

FUNCTIONS OF THE FAMILY

Four basic functions provided by the family are particularly relevant to a discussion of consumer behavior. These include the provision of (1) economic well-being, (2) emotional support, (3) childhood socialization, and (4) suitable lifestyles.

Economic Well-Being

Although the family in an affluent society such as the United States is no longer formed primarily to provide economic security, the satisfaction of financial needs is unquestionably a basic function of the family. Indeed there is evidence that economic wealth is strongly associated with happiness, despite the old adage that "the best things in life are free."[2]

How the family divides its responsibilities for economic well-being has

TABLE 12-1   Principal Types of American Families

TYPE OF FAMILY	COMPOSITION OF HOUSEHOLD
Married couple	Husband and wife
Nuclear family	Husband, wife, and children
Extended family	Husband, wife, children, and grandparent(s)

changed considerably during the past twenty years. For example, while the traditional roles of the husband as economic provider and the wife as child rearer and homemaker are still valid, they are no longer so rigid. As more wives seek outside employment and more husbands share household responsibilities, the traditional economic roles are becoming blurred.

The economic role of children has also changed. Today children are rarely expected to assist the family financially. Instead, they are expected to complete formal educational training and prepare themselves to be financially independent.

Emotional Support

The provision of emotional and therapeutic support to its members is an important basic function of the contemporary family. In fulfilling this function, the family attempts to assist its members in coping with personal or social problems. Unemployment of a family member, death of a close family friend, or a child who is having trouble in school are just three illustrations of an almost unlimited number of potentially emotional or tension-producing problems that require family attention.

If the family cannot provide adequate assistance when it is needed, it may turn to a professional counselor or psychologist as a logical alternative. In general terms, the selection of such professional services is not very different from other types of consumption decisions made by the family.

Childhood Socialization

The socialization of young children is a central family function. In large part, this process consists of imparting to children the basic values and modes of behavior consistent with the culture, which may include (1) personality development, (2) interpersonal competence in dealing with others, (3) appropriate dress and grooming habits, (4) proper manners and speech patterns, and (5) the selection of appropriate occupational or career skills. Within a family setting, much of this socialization is accomplished either directly, through instruction, or indirectly, as children imitate the behavior of their parents and older siblings.

Cutting across the various aspects of childhood socialization is the pertinent factor of consumer socialization. *Consumer socialization* is defined as the "...processes by which young people acquire skills, knowledge, and attitudes relevant to their functioning as consumers in the marketplace."[3] Consumer socialization has two distinct components: (1) those *directly* related to consumption, such as the acquisition of skills, knowledge, and attitudes concerned with budgeting, pricing, and brand attitudes; and (2) those *indirectly* related to consumption, such as the underlying motivations that spur a young man to purchase his first razor or a young girl to desire her first bra.[4] While both components of consumer socialization are significant, the indirect component, which emphasizes the underlying motivational factors, is of most interest to marketing executives who want to understand why people buy their products.

The socialization process is not confined to childhood but is an ongoing process extending into adulthood. For example, when a newly married couple initially sets up a household, their adjustment to living and consuming together is part of a continuing socialization process.

Suitable Lifestyles

Another important family function in terms of consumer behavior is the establishment of a suitable lifestyle (style of living) for the family. Although little is known about how families establish and alter their lifestyles, it would seem that the personal and jointly determined goals of the spouses are prominent factors. For example, the importance placed on education, the family's interest in reading, the number and types of television programs viewed, the frequency of dining out, the selection of entertainment and recreational activities, are all examples of family decisions that set the tone for the family's lifestyle.

Family lifestyle commitments greatly influence consumption patterns. For this reason, marketers should be aware of trends concerning family allocation of time, for how time is spent reflects changing family lifestyles.

FAMILY DECISION MAKING

While many marketers believe the family is the basic decision-making unit, they usually examine consumer behavior concerning their own products in terms of the one family member they believe to be the major decision maker. Although such a research approach can be justified as being simpler and less expensive than interviewing all members of the family, it may provide a distorted picture of the specific contributions of various family members to a purchase decision.[5] For instance, men's formal wear might logically be thought of as a male-dominated decision, but the wife tends to strongly influence the purchase of such items. Similarly, men's underwear is often purchased by married women who independently select such items for their husbands and unmarried sons. Because the user is not always the sole decision maker or even the buyer, marketers should try to identify the decision-making participants in the family and to direct a substantial portion of their advertising to family members who affect or select the final purchase.

As we can see, then, a very basic question for the marketer to answer is which family members are influential in making the relevant purchase decision. We will begin our discussion of this important question with an examination of family roles.

Family Role Setting

If a family is to function as a cohesive unit, roles or tasks—such as setting the dinner table, taking out the garbage, walking the dog, or dispensing family funds—must be carried out by one or more family members. We will see from our examination of the impact of cultural factors on consumer behavior (Chapters 14 and 15) that such roles or tasks are quite dynamic. As applied to family roles, for instance, research sponsored by a leading advertising agency indicates that husbands are assuming a host of nontraditional family-domestic roles. Specifically, the research reveals that 32 percent shop for food; 74 percent take out the garbage; 47 percent cook for the family; 53 percent wash the dishes; 29 percent do the laundry; 28 percent clean the bathroom; 39 percent vacuum the house; and 80 percent take care of the children (in households with children under twelve years of age).[6] Marketers need to be alert to how shifting family roles may be influencing the composition of their target market and how they need to alter their marketing strategy.

Similarly, in the context of consumer purchase decisions, roles or tasks are carried out by one or more family members. To illustrate, a family's recent purchase of a motorboat might have been subject to the following role influences: The teenage son generated initial family interest in the purchase of a boat; information from friends and mass media was gathered by the husband; the amount to be spent on the boat was determined jointly by both spouses; the selection of appropriate product features was made by parents and their teenage children; and the selection of a retail outlet and the final purchase decision were undertaken jointly by the entire family.

Since family roles vary by product category, and since different families are apt to establish somewhat different family roles for the same product decision, it is not easy to develop a marketing strategy that reflects the specific roles of family members. Through carefully conceived consumer research, however, marketers can usually uncover a pattern of decision making that describes the majority of families who are potential customers for their products.

In attempting to isolate the general consumer decision-making roles of family members, marketers seek answers to such questions as the following:

1. Which family members are most likely to *initiate interest* in the product category?
2. Which family members are most likely to *seek* out the required *information* about the product category?
3. Which family members are most likely to determine *how much will be spent* on the product?
4. Which family members are most likely to determine *specific product features* (color, size, style)?
5. Which family members are most likely to make the final decision regarding *which brand to purchase*?
6. Which family members are most likely to determine *when* the purchase will be made?
7. Which family members are most likely to determine *where* the product will be purchased?
8. Which family members are most likely to *actually purchase* the product?
9. Which family members are most likely to *use or consume* the product?

Answers to these questions provide marketers with a sound basis upon which to develop products and design promotional strategies, and aid in the selection of retail outlets for their products.

EIGHT KEY CONSUMPTION ROLES

The following classification system provides further insight into how family members interact in their various consumption-related roles:

I 1. *Influencers*—those family members who provide information and advice and thereby affect the selection of a product or service

G 2. *Gatekeepers*—those family members who control the flow of information about a product or service into the family, thereby influencing the decisions of other family members

D 3. *Deciders*—those family members who have the power to unilaterally or jointly determine whether or not to purchase a specific product or service

B 4. *Buyers*—those family members who actually make the purchase of a particular product or service

P 5. *Preparers*—those family members who transform the product into a form in which it will be consumed by other family members

U 6. *Users*—those family members who use or consume a particular product or service

m 7. *Maintainers*—those family members who service or repair the product so that it will provide continued satisfaction

D 8. *Disposers*—those family members who initiate or carry out the discontinuation or disposal of a particular product or service

[handwritten: Know these]

Quite naturally, the number and identity of the family members who fill these roles will vary from product to product. In some cases, a single family member will independently assume a number of roles; in other cases, a single role will jointly be performed by two or more family members. In still other cases, one or more of these basic roles may not be required. For example, when a housewife is shopping in a supermarket and comes upon a new salad dressing that she thinks her family might enjoy, her decision to purchase it does not directly involve the *influence* of other family members. She is the *decider,* the *buyer,* and in a sense the *gatekeeper;* however, she may or may not be the *preparer* and will not be the sole *user.*

Family Decision Making and Product Usage

In considering family consumption behavior, it is often useful to distinguish between the *decision making* that leads to the purchase and the eventual *consumption* or *use* of the product. Products might be consumed by a single family member (beer, lipstick), consumed or used *directly* by two or more family members (frozen vegetables, an automobile), or consumed *indirectly* by the entire family (paint, draperies, carpeting).[7]

DETERMINANTS OF FAMILY DECISION MAKING

Seven factors that influence a family's decision-making style are social class, lifestyle, role orientation, stage in family life cycle, perceived risk, product importance, and time constraints.[8]

SOCIAL CLASS. Both lower- and upper-class families tend to favor an autonomous or unilateral decision style, while middle-class families tend toward egalitarianism or joint decision making (see Chapter 13).

LIFESTYLE. A family's allocation of time, in terms of both work and leisure, its values and its interests, are likely to influence its decision making. Thus a family that frequently goes on vacation may make decisions differently than a family that does not.

ROLE ORIENTATION.   The more specific the roles of family members (father takes out the garbage, mother shops for groceries, teenage daughter does the dinner dishes), the more likely are family members to make autonomous decisions related to their respective roles.

FAMILY LIFE CYCLE.   The age and composition of a family tend to influence its decision-making style. Newly married and young families are more likely to make joint decisions; older families, who have had more chance to establish role specialization, are more likely to make independent or autonomous decisions.

PERCEIVED RISK.   The more risk or uncertainty that family members perceive in a particular purchase decision, the more likely it is that the decision will be made jointly. Conversely, when a product purchase is not perceived to be especially risky, it is likely that an autonomous decision will be made.

PRODUCT IMPORTANCE.   The more importance attached to a particular product's purchase, the greater the likelihood that a decision to purchase it will be jointly made.

TIME CONSTRAINTS.   The quicker a decision has to be made, the more likely that it will be an autonomous decision, since a joint decision generally requires more time.

An understanding of the relevance of these seven factors for a specific product and target market can help a marketer develop an appropriate marketing strategy.

Locus of Husband/Wife Decisions

Most husband/wife influence studies classify family consumption decisions as husband-dominated, wife-dominated, or joint decisions. To this typology, some consumer researchers have added a fourth category—the autonomic or unilateral decision. Let us consider each of these categories in turn:

> *Husband-dominated decisions*—those in which a majority of the families interviewed in a study identify the *husband* as the most influential spouse in the decision to purchase a particular product
>
> *Wife-dominated decisions*—those in which a majority of the families interviewed identify the *wife* as the most influential spouse in the decision to purchase a particular product
>
> *Joint (syncratic) decisions*—those in which a majority of the families interviewed identify the *husband* and wife as equally influential in the decision to purchase a particular product
>
> *Autonomic decisions*—those in which either the *husband or the wife*—in somewhat equal proportions—has been identified as the sole decision maker for the purchase of a particular product

Research that has examined both the extent and the nature of husband/wife influence in family decisions indicates that such influence is fluid and likely to shift, depending on the specific product or service, the specific stage in the decision-making process, and the specific product features being considered. Let us briefly review these factors and their effects on husband/wife decision making.[9]

PRODUCT OR SERVICE VARIATIONS.   Research on husband/wife decision making consistently indicates that the relative influence of a spouse depends in part on the product or service being studied. For instance, early studies revealed that the purchase of an automobile was strongly husband-dominated, while food and some financial decisions (weekly food expenditures and money management) were wife-dominated. For other products or services studied, husbands and wives tended to contribute equally (the selection of a house or apartment, vacations, and savings).[10]

A more recent large-scale study of some twenty-five hundred married men and women supports the notion that decision making varies in accordance with the specific product or service.[11] For example, husbands were found to dominate in certain areas (the purchase of automobiles and television sets), while wives were most influential in other areas (the selection of movies and television programs).

A replication of one of the pioneering studies cited above attempted to answer the basic question, Are husband/wife decision-making patterns changing? Some findings of this study follow:[12]

1. Life insurance has become a husband-dominated decision, while decisions concerning food and groceries have become more wife-dominated. These results represent an intensification of findings of the earlier study.
2. The selection of family housing and vacations are increasingly joint decisions, an intensification of the previously reported decision-making pattern.
3. Dramatic changes in the area of automobile decision making were reported. While the earlier study found that the husband strongly dominated the purchase decision, the later study showed a substantial shift toward joint decision making (45 percent of the cases in 1973 were joint decisions as compared with 25 percent in 1955). The automobile purchase decision remained a male-dominated decision in 52 percent of the households surveyed (a reduction from 70 percent in the 1955 study). The change in influence over automobile purchases undoubtedly reflects the increased activities of the wife outside of the home and the move toward two-car or multicar families.

Although this study suggests a generalized shift in the locus of family decision making, it is not clear whether the findings reflect a move toward greater *role specialization* (more husband or wife domination over specific decision categories) or greater *egalitarianism* (more joint and equal decision making). Future research might better identify role changes, particularly if a panel consisting of the same husbands and wives are interviewed annually over a five- or ten-year period.

To support the fruitfulness of panel data, additional insights into the dynamics of husband/wife decision making are provided by a study that focused on a single decision area—family financial management.[13] The research was specifically designed to identify which spouse in newly married couples undertook the principal responsibility for family money management (payment of bills and use of extra funds). The initial interview during the first year of marriage revealed that most couples shared equally in money management. However, follow-up interviews during the second year of marriage indicated a decline in joint financial decision making and a parallel increase in the money management responsibility of the wife. The results suggest that financially inexperienced newlyweds are likely to start out sharing the burdens of financial decision making; however, in a relatively short time, many young wives take the lead in this consumption-related area. For banking and other financial marketing executives, these results suggest that young married women are a particularly important target for their services.

VARIATIONS BY STAGE IN THE DECISION-MAKING PROCESS. The roles of husbands and wives often differ during the decision-making process. A study of Belgian households, for example, found that the roles of husbands and wives varied for a number of products in terms of a simple three-stage decision-making model: problem recognition, search for information, and final decision.[14] Following the same basic research design, and questioning a sample of American consumers, another researcher has explored shifts in husband/wife decision making during the same three stages of decision making.[15] Figure 12-1 (Parts A and B) plot the shifts (if any) in husband/wife decisions from Stage 1 (problem recognition) to Stage 2 (search for information), and from Stage 2 to Stage 3 (final decision) for twenty purchase items. While the results show that for the majority of items the initial decision-making pattern established in Stage 1 is continued during the two remaining stages, there are for a few items stage-to-stage shifts. For instance, the recognition of a need for a new washing machine is wife-dominated, the search for information concerning the potential purchase is largely autonomic (usually by the wife), while the final decision is jointly made by both spouses.

VARIATIONS BY PRODUCT FEATURES. An exploratory study sponsored by *Time* magazine suggests that marketers should examine husband/wife decision making in terms of specific product features.[16] For example, the study found that in the determination of brand for a potential product purchase, the husband dominated for automobiles and television sets, the wife dominated for washing machines, while the brand of dress shirts was jointly determined. Table 12-2 on page 326 presents these results and evidence pertinent to seven other purchase factors.

For the marketer, this study suggests that it is unwise to generalize about the relative influence of spouses from one product to another. Rather, the relative influence of husbands and wives should be determined uniquely for each product category.

Second, it would appear that a global measure of husband/wife influence is less insightful than an examination of their impact at specific stages of the decision-making process or in terms of specific product features.

FIGURE 12-1 **Changes in Marital Roles Over the Decision-Making Process** Source: E.H. Bonfield, "Perception of Marital Roles in Decision Processes: Replication and Extension," in H. Keith Hunt, ed., *Advances in Consumer Research* (Ann Arbor, Mich.: Association for Consumer Research, 1978), V, 302.

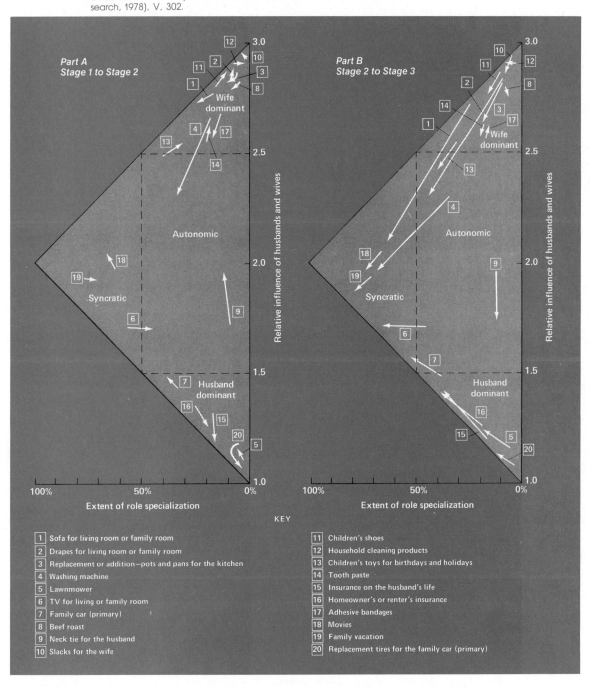

KEY

1 Sofa for living room or family room	11 Children's shoes
2 Drapes for living room or family room	12 Household cleaning products
3 Replacement or addition—pots and pans for the kitchen	13 Children's toys for birthdays and holidays
4 Washing machine	14 Tooth paste
5 Lawnmower	15 Insurance on the husband's life
6 TV for living or family room	16 Homeowner's or renter's insurance
7 Family car (primary)	17 Adhesive bandages
8 Beef roast	18 Movies
9 Neck tie for the husband	19 Family vacation
10 Slacks for the wife	20 Replacement tires for the family car (primary)

**TABLE 12-2   Relative Influence of Husband and Wife
on Selected Purchase Factors**

PURCHASE FACTORS	AUTOMOBILES	DRESS SHIRTS	TELEVISION SETS	WASHERS
Brand (make)	H	=	H	W
Performance features	H	W	H	W
Style	W	H	W	W
Size	H	H	H	W
Warranty (guarantee)	=	–	H	H
Price	H	W	H	H
Store (dealer)	H	=	W	H
Service	H	–	H	H

Key: H = Husband more influential than wife.
  W = Wife more influential than husband.
  = = Husband and wife equally influential.
  – = Not applicable to product category.

   Source: Adapted from *Family Decision Making* (New York: Time Magazine, Time Marketing Information Research Report 1428, 1967).

Reliability of Husband/Wife Decision Studies

Studies of family decision making indicate that there can be substantial disagreement between spouses as to their relative influence on consumer purchases. An evaluation of these findings suggests that such differences should not be a source of major concern to the marketing manager, since these differences tend to cancel themselves out across the entire sample of respondents.[17] However, in carrying out a large-scale study of family decision making, it might be advisable for the marketer to undertake a pilot study to determine if this generalization is true of the product category under investigation.

Children

One has only to switch on a television set, especially on a weekend morning, or thumb through the pages of a magazine like *Boy's Life*, to come to the conclusion that many advertisers are interested in reaching children. We will discuss the role of children in family decision making in terms of the family's impact on its children, and the children's impact on the family.[18]

THE FAMILY'S IMPACT ON ITS CHILDREN

As already noted, the socialization of children is a basic function of the family, and consumer socialization is an important component of this process. It is the vehicle through which the family imparts consumption-relevant knowledge, attitudes, and skills.

While the consumer socialization process is quite complex, it seems that preadolescent children tend to rely on their parents and older siblings as the major source of cues for their basic consumption learning. Adolescents and teenagers, on the other hand, are likely to shift much of their attention to the actions and behavior of friends.[19] Specifically, it might be expected that much of what preadolescents learn from their family is by way of imitation, such as imitating how an older child spends his or her money. In contrast, older children, who have already acquired the fundamentals of consumption behavior from their family, are likely to look to outside friends for models of socially acceptable consumption behavior, such as the "in" thing to wear.

Consumer socialization fulfills a unique function as a tool by which parents can influence other aspects of the socialization process. For instance, parents frequently use the promise or reward of material goods as a device to modify or control a child's behavior. Specifically, a parent may reward a child with a gift when the child does something to the parent's satisfaction, or withhold it or remove it if the child disobeys. In a sense, the use of material goods as a means of parental control over a child's behavior is intrinsic support for the importance of possessions and consumption in a society such as the United States.

CHILDREN AS INFLUENTIALS

Children are not only influenced *by* their families, in turn they also influence family consumption decisions. Young children attempt to influence family decisions as soon as they possess the basic communication skills needed to interact with other family members. Most parents, even those of very young children, can recall frequent purchase-related requests, such as "Please buy me a Barbie Doll" or "Let's eat at McDonald's." Of course, older children are likely to participate more directly in family consumption activities.

To illustrate the impact of children on family decision making, Table 12-3 lists some of the findings drawn from a study that explores the roles assumed by family members in deciding to eat out at a fast-food restaurant.[20] The study

TABLE 12-3   Family Member Participation in the Decision to Eat Out at a Fast-Food Restaurant

	HUSBAND OR WIFE ALONE	HUSBAND AND WIFE TOGETHER	CHILD/ CHILDREN	A PARENT AND CHILD	BOTH PARENTS AND CHILD	TOTAL
part a. major decision stages						
Initiate purchase	1%	6	11	27	55	100%
Provide information	3%	4	10	22	61	100%
Final decision	2%	10	4	13	71	100%
part b. dimensions of the decision						
When to go	4%	23	1	12	60	100%
What type of food	1%	9	2	13	75	100%
Which competing establishment	2%	7	2	12	77	100%
How much to spend	19%	60	—	2	19	100%

Source: Adapted from George J. Szybillo and Arlene Sosanie, "Family Decision Making: Husband, Wife and Children," in William D. Perreault, Jr., ed., *Advances in Consumer Research* (Atlanta: Association for Consumer Research, 1977), IV, 47 and 48.

confirms the common belief that children do significantly influence family decisions. More precisely, for each of the three decision stages (Part A), there is a substantial amount of child input (consisting of either a parent and child or an entire family-derived decision). Still further, Part B of Table 12-3 also reveals that children play an influential role when it comes to the family's assessment of the major dimensions of deciding to eat out; with the exception of how much to spend, which largely remains the province of the parents.

Related research indicates that the age of a child and the type of restaurant being considered affects the extent of influence that a child will have. Specifically, older children (over five years of age) were found to be more likely to share in the family's decision to eat out; and parents tended to allow children more say when the choice was to be made among inexpensive restaurants (e.g., among fast-food establishments rather than conventional restaurants).[21]

The parent-child relationship as it relates to consumer behavior can be viewed as an *influence versus yield* situation. Specifically, a child attempts to *influence* his parents to make a purchase (to *yield*). A few studies have examined the relationship between child influence and parent yielding. For example, in-store observations of purchase behavior in supermarkets indicate that children generally attempt to make their preferences known to their parents. Their efforts are strongest in areas of special interest to children (cereal, candy); however, they also occur with products of only remote interest to children (household or laundry detergents).[22]

Two other studies of the child-parent consumer relationship report conflicting results on the nature of influence and yielding. One study that focused exclusively on breakfast cereals found that the more involved the mother was with her child, the more likely she was *not* to yield, but to override the child's own choice of breakfast cereals and buy what she believed to be the best brand.[23] The researchers concluded that children's preferences for sugar-coated cereal were judged nutritionally unsound by their mothers who therefore did not yield.

The second study, which examined child-parent interaction across a number of products (including cereals), found a significant positive relationship between the number of children's influence attempts and their mothers' yielding.[24] The study also found that children's attempts to influence tend to *decrease* somewhat with age, whereas mothers' yielding requests were likely to *increase* with the child's age. These results seem to indicate that older children are more discriminating in their requests, and that parents are more willing to accede to older children's requests because they perceive them to be more mature in their judgments about purchase decisions.

There is also some evidence that teenage children significantly influence family decision making. An ongoing survey sponsored by *Co-ed* magazine (a magazine for teenage girls) indicates that an impressive number of high-school girls plan or participate in the planning of family meals, and shop for their family's food needs. The study also suggests that girls with working mothers are somewhat more involved in homemaking activities than their counterparts with nonworking mothers.[25]

College students have also been shown to exert influence over the purchase decisions of their families. In one study, college students reported that they often attempted to influence their families' decisions to purchase television sets and automobiles, and that they perceived that they did influence these purchase decisions.[26]

While a number of studies indicate that children influence family decision making, the extent and specific nature of their influence (e.g., the range of products and the extent of their influence over such decisions) is still largely undocumented.

THE FAMILY LIFE CYCLE

Behavioral scientists, particularly family sociologists, have utilized the concept of a *family life cycle* (FLC) to classify family units into significant groupings. More recently, classification by stage in the FLC has proved useful to researchers concerned with family consumption behavior and to marketers concerned with segmenting their markets. This section will describe the family life cycle and its relevance to the consumption activities of the family.

Stages of the FLC

The FLC can be considered a progression of stages through which most families pass, starting with the bachelor or unmarried state. If the individual marries, his or her resulting family unit will move through a series of stages in which the size of the family first expands with the birth of children, and then contracts as older children leave the household, and, finally, as one of the original family members dies. Ultimately, the family comes to an end when the sole survivor dies or remarries.

For consumer researchers, FLC analysis is important because it enables them to classify families into one of a number of mutually exclusive developmental stages. The FLC is a *composite* variable because it is created by systematically combining such commonly used demographic variables as:

1. Marital status (single or married)
2. Age of family members (generally head-of-household and either oldest or youngest child)
3. Size of the family (number of children)
4. Work status of the head-of-household (working or retired)

By placing families into groups based on a combination of such demographic variables, a richer picture of the family is obtained than would be possible by using any single variable. Evidence supporting this contention will be examined later in this chapter.

Table 12-4 presents, in schematic fashion, several alternative FLC models. The models differ primarily in terms of the number of stages (or substages) utilized; these in turn reflect how finely the researcher cares to examine family development. Synthesizing the various FLC models depicted in Table 12-4, we will examine the following five stages in detail and show how they lend themselves to market segmentation strategies:

Stage I: *Bachelorhood*—a young single adult not living with his or her parents
Stage II: *Honeymooners*—a young married couple
Stage III: *Parenthood*—a married couple with at least one child living at home
Stage IV: *Postparenthood*—an older married couple with no children living at home
Stage V: *Dissolution*—only one of the original spouses survives

TABLE 12-4   Alternative Family Life-Cycle Models

BROAD CATEGORIES	LANSING AND KISH (1957)*	BLOOD AND WOLFE (1958)†	FARBER (1964)‡	WELLS AND GUBAR (1966)§
Stage I: Bachelorhood	Young single		Premarital stage	Bachelor stage, not living at home
Stage II: Honeymooners	Young married couple, no children	Honeymoon stage, childless and married less than four years	Couple stage	Newly married couple, young with no children
Stage III: Parenthood	Young married couple, with youngest child under 6	Preschool stage, oldest child under 6	Preschool phase	Full nest I, youngest child under 6
	Young married couple, with youngest child 6 or over	Preadolescent stage, oldest child 6 to 12	Elementary school phase	Full nest II, youngest child 6 or over
		Adolescent stage, oldest child 13 to 18	High school phase	Full nest III, older married couples with dependent children
		Unlaunched stage, oldest child 19 or older and still living at home	College phase / Postschool phase	
Stage IV: Postparenthood	Older married couple, no children	Postparental stage	In-law phase / Grandparent phase	Empty nest I, no children at home, head in labor force
				Empty nest II, head retired
Stage V: Dissolution	Older single	Retired stage, nonemployed husband 60 or over	Widowhood and remarriage	Solitary survivor, in labor force
			End of cycle	Solitary survivor, retired

Sources: *John B. Lansing and Leslie Kish, "Family Life Cycle as an Independent Variable," *American Sociological Review,* 22 (October 1957), 512–19.
†Robert O. Blood, Jr., and Donald M. Wolfe, *Husbands and Wives* (Glencoe, Ill.: Free Press, 1960).
‡Bernard Farber, *Family: Organization and Interaction* (San Francisco: Chandler, 1964).
§William D. Wells and George Gubar, "Life Cycle Concept in Marketing Research," *Journal of Marketing Research,* (November 1966), 355–63.

STAGE I: BACHELORHOOD

The first FLC stage consists of young single men and women who have set up their own households. Although most members of this FLC stage are fully employed, many are college students who live apart from their parents.

Young single adults are apt to spend their income on apartment rent, basic home furnishings, the purchase and maintenance of automobiles, travel and entertainment, and the acquisition of stylish clothing and accessories.

Members of the bachelor stage frequently have sufficient disposable income to pursue a kind of "hedonistic" spending pattern. In most large cities, one can find travel agents, housing developments, country clubs, sports clubs, and so forth, that find this FLC stage a lucrative target market for various products and services.

It is relatively easy to reach this audience, since a number of special-interest publications cater to the "single" lifestyle. For example, *Oui* and *Penthouse* are directed to a young, sophisticated, single male audience; while *Cosmopolitan* and *Glamour* are directed to young single females.

After the fling of bachelorhood wears off, singles often turn to the serious business of finding a spouse. Here again, the individual is likely to be offered numerous services (e.g., party and dating services) designed to provide the opportunity to meet the "perfect" mate.

When the right individual is found, there is usually a period of courtship, often followed by a formal engagement. In our society, the announcement of an engagement often triggers the onslaught of marketing efforts from specialized services eager to provide the betrothed couple and their parents with a full-blown wedding—a catered affair complete with music, photographs, bridal gown, men's formal wear, wedding rings, flowers, and a honeymoon vacation. Other marketers bombard the couple with communications concerning the numerous products that are likely to be required in the establishment of a household. This market is so fertile and so eager for information that the two leading bridal magazines, *Bride's* and *Modern Bride*, are made up primarily of product and service advertisements.

STAGE II: HONEYMOONERS

The honeymoon stage starts immediately after the marriage vows are taken and generally continues up to the arrival of the couple's first child. This FLC stage serves as a period of adjustment to married life.

Since many young husbands and wives both work, they have available to them a combined income that often permits a pleasure-seeking lifestyle similar to that enjoyed by many singles. The difference is that they are now spending together.

In addition to joint pleasure seeking, there are considerable "start-up" expenditures for their apartment or home (major and minor appliances, bedroom and living-room furniture, carpeting, drapes, dishes, and a host of utensils and accessory items). During this stage, the advice and experience of other married couples are likely to be important to the newlyweds. Also important as sources of new-product information are shelter magazines, such as *Better Homes and Gardens, Apartment Ideas,* and *House Beautiful.*

STAGE III: PARENTHOOD

When young families have their first child, the honeymoon is considered over. The parenthood stage usually extends over more than a twenty-year period. Because of its long duration, it is useful to divide this stage into shorter phases: (1) the preschool phase, (2) the elementary-school phase, (3) the high-school phase, (4) the college phase, and (5) the postschool phase.

Throughout these parenthood phases, the interrelationships of family members and the structure of the family gradually changes. For example, the responsibilities of parenthood require a rather drastic recasting of the young couple's lifestyle. Income previously spent on home decorating, dining out, and vacations is now redirected to baby foods, diapers, and baby furniture. Entertainment and social activities tend to center on the home and the local community.

As children get older and become more independent, and as the family becomes financially better off (due to normal increments in the husband's earnings or the entrance of the wife into the work force), the family's lifestyle gradually becomes less restrictive and more satisfying for all concerned.

There are many magazines that cater to the information and entertainment needs of parents and children. To illustrate, *Redbook* positions itself as the "Magazine for Young Mothers," *Ladies' Home Journal* is directed to a broader age spectrum of homemakers, *Parents' Magazine* covers child rearing, health, and food topics. For children, there are many special-interest publications, such as *Humpty Dumpty,* designed for the young child just learning to read, *Scholastic Magazine,* for the elementary-school pupil, *Boy's Life,* which is aimed at the young male, and *American Girl, Seventeen, Glamour,* and *Mademoiselle,* which appeal to the fashion interest of teen and postteen girls.

STAGE IV: POSTPARENTHOOD

Since parenthood extends over many years, it is only natural to find that postparenthood—the period when all the children have left home—is traumatic for many parents who suddenly feel unneeded and somewhat alone. However, there is a bright side to the postparenthood stage—the opportunity to start things over again as a husband-wife team. For this reason, after an initial adjustment, the postparenthood stage signifies the beginning of "doing things we've always wanted to do." For the wife, who has spent most of her time rearing children, it is a time to complete her education, to get a job, to seek new interests. For the husband, it is a time to indulge in new hobbies. For both, it is the time to travel, to entertain, perhaps to refurnish their home.

Thus the spending patterns of couples in the postparenthood FLC stage are apt to change quite dramatically, especially since there is likely to be more money available. In fact, it is during this stage that the married couple is often best off financially. For this reason, families in the postparenthood stage are an important market for expensive furniture, jewelry, new automobiles, and vacations to distant places for which they did not have the time or money before.

If the older married couple are fortunate in terms of health, they will eventually retire together. If planned for adequately, retirement provides the opportunity to seek new interests and to fulfill previously less satisfied or unsatisfied needs. However, for older retired couples who do not have adequate savings or income, retirement is often very restrictive and requires the management of a household on a minimal fixed income.

Available evidence suggests that older consumers tend to consider television an important source of information and entertainment. They favor programs that provide the opportunity to "keep up with things," especially news and public affairs programs.[27] As for magazines, one would expect older consumers to continue their existing reading patterns, with the possible addition of special-interest magazines like *Modern Maturity* and *50 Plus*.

STAGE V: DISSOLUTION

Just as the postparenthood stage of the FLC is initially a difficult time, so is the loss of one's spouse. The adjustment to such a loss is largely a function of how healthy and financially solvent the survivor is, and the extent to which emotional support from loved ones is available. If the surviving spouse is still in good health, is working or has adequate savings, and lives in close proximity to understanding friends or relatives, the adjustment tends to be easier.

In terms of spending patterns, the surviving spouse might sell the family home, which may now be too large and too filled with memories, and move into a smaller, more efficient apartment, possibly within a retirement community. At this point, there is often a need for goods and services that fill the vacuum of being alone. Pleasurable and time-consuming activities, such as trips, tours, vacations, and social events with peers, become very important.

As our society becomes more enlightened in regard to the special needs of the elderly, improved social and economic services should benefit them and enable them to lead more productive and satisfying lives.

Limitations of the FLC

Conventional FLC models (see Table 12-4) generally do not include all possible life-cycle factors. This can create a classification problem for the researcher.[28] Following is a list of family factors that are usually not included in traditional FLC models:

1. Childless couples
2. Families broken up by separation or divorce
3. Older families with children younger than six
4. Widowhood at an early stage of the FLC
5. Extended families (e.g., grandparents living with married children, or newly married couples living with in-laws)
6. Mature individuals who marry late in life (e.g., when they are in their forties or fifties)
7. Unmarried mothers
8. Unmarried couples

To deal with such cases, researchers tend to elect one of the following courses of action: (1) they eliminate such respondents if they are few in number;

TABLE 12-5   Comparison of Population Distributions Across the Stages of Two Family Life Cycles, 1970*

MURPHY AND STAPLES			WELLS AND GUBAR		
stage	no. individuals or families (000's)	% total U.S. popu-lation†	stage	no. individuals or families (000's)	% total U.S. popu-lation†
1. Young single	16,626	8.2	1. Bachelor	16,626	8.2
2. Young married without children	2,958	2.9	2. Newly married couples	2,958	2.9
3. Other young					
a. Young divorced without children	277	0.1			
b. Young married with children	8,082	17.1	3. Full nest I	11,433	24.2
Infant‡					
Young (4-12 years old)‡					
Adolescent‡					
c. Young divorced with children	1,144	1.9	4. Full nest II	6,547	13.2
Infant					
Young (4-12 years old)					
Adolescent					
4. Middle-aged					
a. Middle-aged married without children	4,815	4.7			
b. Middle-aged divorced without children	593	0.3			
c. Middle-aged married with children	15,574	33.0	5. Full nest III	6,955	14.7
Young					
Adolescent					

Stage	Number	Percentage
d. Middle-aged divorced with children		
Young		
Adolescent	1,080	1.8
e. Middle-aged married without dependent children	5,627	5.5
f. Middle-aged divorced without dependent children	284	0.1
5. Older		
a. Older married	5,318	5.2
b. Older unmarried		
Divorced		
Widowed	3,510	2.0
All other§	34,952	17.2
	203,210||	

Stage	Number	Percentage
6. Empty nest I	5,627	5.5
7. Empty nest II	5,318	5.2
8. Solitary survivor—in labor force	428	0.2
9. Solitary survivor—retired	3,510	2.0
All other§	46,738	23.3
	203,210||	

†As there are single and divorced individuals in some of the stages, the numbers were calculated as a percentage of the entire population, not just the number of families. Also, the percentages of the total for families were determined by multiplying the number of families by 2.3 (average number of children per family in 1970) and adding the parents (or parent, in divorced instances) to the number. For example, the 17.1 percent in the young married with children was computed as follows:

$$\frac{8,082 \ (2.3 \ children) + 16,164 \ (parents)}{203,210} = 17.1\%$$

‡As many families have children at more than one of these age levels, it is not meaningful to compute the numbers for each of these ages independently.

§Includes all adults and children not accounted for by the family life cycle stages.

||Source: U.S. Bureau of the Census 1970. The numbers do not add to this total because of the calculations explained in Footnote†.

Source: Patrick E. Murphy and William A. Staples, "A Modernized Family Life Cycle," *Journal of Consumer Research*, 6 (June 1979), 16.

*Figures for this table were taken or derived from U.S. Bureau of the Census 1973. Tables 2 and 9.

(2) they add such respondents to the traditional life-cycle stage to which they seem to most closely conform; or (3) they establish a separate FLC stage to accommodate such respondents, particularly if there are many of them.

As a number of less-typical family groupings have grown in visibility and size, it has become less defensible to ignore them or to combine them with a more conventional FLC stage. For this reason, it is likely that consumer researchers will increasingly elect the third option of creating alternative FLC stages to account for important emerging FLC segments.[29] Supporting such a trend, Table 12-5 on pages 334–35 compares one of the more popular traditional FLC models with a refined FLC model that includes divorced and middle-aged married without-children stages. The results indicate that the "modernized" FLC model includes some 11.8 million people that go unaccounted for in the traditional model.

Even with its limitations, the traditional FLC model has demonstrated its value for market segmentation. It has provided insights into specific consumption activities that could not be obtained by using a single demographic variable. For example, evidence indicates a substantially greater decline in the proportion of home ownership for consumers in the dissolution stage (solitary survivors) than would be revealed by a census of consumers in the over-sixty-five age category. The reason for this difference between FLC analysis and age categorization is that age does *not* distinguish between households in which both the elderly husband and wife are living and those in which only one of the partners is alive.[30] Because of this, a firm renting or selling retirement housing might find that information gleaned from FLC analyses offers a more sensitive profile of its market than could be derived from age data alone.

Application of FLC Analysis by Product Category

Marketers and researchers have found that FLC analysis can provide an in-depth understanding of family consumption behavior for a variety of product categories.

RESIDENTIAL TELEPHONE USAGE

The American Telephone and Telegraph Company (AT&T) has employed FLC variables in its efforts to better serve household telephone customers. Table 12-6 presents the specific FLC model that AT&T researchers have found most clearly accounts for family telephone usage. An examination of this model indicates that AT&T has redefined some of the FLC stages listed in the prototype models in Table 12-4. Most notable among the differences are the division of (a) age of head-of-household into younger or older than fifty-five years, and (b) families into those whose youngest child is over or under twelve years. These refinements reflect the nature of residential telephone usage. A finer division of age factors is unlikely to offer greater insight into customer telephone usage.[31]

Figure 12-2 on page 338 shows the average monthly expenditures on long-distance calls for each FLC stage. Note that young marrieds spend more than singles on long-distance calls, while both of these groups spend less than the

TABLE 12-6   AT&T Family Life-Cycle Status Categories

FLC STAGE	VARIABLES EMPLOYED	DESCRIPTION OF STAGE
Younger No children	—Age of head-of-household	—Under 55 years of age
	—Size of family	—a. Single person b. Couple
Younger Young children	—Age of head-of-household	—Under 55 years of age
	—Size of family	—Three or more persons
	—Age of children	—Under 12 years of age
Younger Older children	—Age of head-of-household	—Under 55 years of age
	—Size of family	—Three or more persons
	—Age of children	—a. One child 12 years or older b. Two or more children 12 years or older
Older	—Age of head-of-household	—55 years or older
	—Employment status	—a. Employed b. Unemployed (Retired)

Source: Adapted from Richard B. Ellis, "Composite Population Descriptors: The Socio-Economic Life Cycle Grid," in Mary Jane Schlinger, ed., *Advances in Consumer Research* (Association for Consumer Research, 1974), Vol. II. Also, courtesy of the American Telephone and Telegraph Company.

average of all households studied. On the other hand, young families with and without teenage children spend more than the average, while those with teenagers spend more than those at any other stage. Finally, older couples spend about the average, while older singles spend less than the overall average. Although these results are limited to a sample of telephone users in the northeastern states, similar analyses are readily available for other geographic areas serviced by AT&T affiliate companies.[32] AT&T uses these life-cycle analyses to better understand fluctuations in family telephone expenditure patterns and equipment usage, and thus is better able to plan future telephone products and services to satisfy its customers.

FAMILY FOOD CONSUMPTION

FLC analysis has been used in a study of food purchases and other consumption activities of over four thousand urban homemakers in seven southern states.[33] One of the dimensions of food consumption explored was the "goal satisfaction" of the homemaker. Goal satisfaction was measured by asking each homemaker to evaluate such food-related activities as time spent in meal preparation, foods served, and attention given her own food preferences. On the basis of each homemaker's responses, an overall food-consumption satisfaction score was

FIGURE 12-2   **Average Monthly Long-Distance Telephone Expenditures by Family Life-Cycle Stages**   Source: A. Marvin Roscoe, Jr., and Jagdish N. Sheth, "Demographic Segmentation of Long Distance Behavior: Data Analysis and Inductive Model Building," in M. Venkatesan, ed., *Third Annual Conference of the Association for Consumer Research 1972*, 262. Also, courtesy of the American Telephone and Telegraph Company.

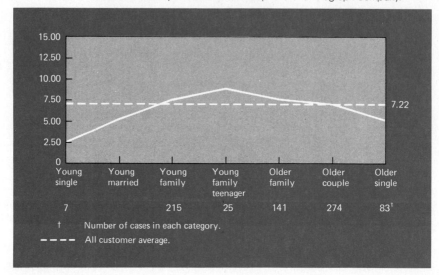

determined. Respondents were then categorized into one of the following six FLC stages based upon the age of their youngest and oldest children:[34]

Stage I: Childless young married (married less than ten years with no children)
Stage II: Expanding (youngest child less than six years old and no child sixteen or older)
Stage III: Stable (youngest child six years or older and no child at home older than age fifteen; or youngest child less than six and the oldest child older than fifteen years of age)
Stage IV: Contracting (at least one child aged sixteen years or older and no child less than six years of age)
Stage V: Postparental (childless couples with children who have all left home)
Stage VI: Childless older married (childless couples married more than ten years)

The results of this study indicated that homemakers in Stage I (childless young married) were highly satisfied in terms of food consumption, those in Stage II (expanding) were least satisfied, while those in Stage V (postparental) were most satisfied with their food consumption activities. The high degree of satisfaction expressed by the young married and postparental homemaker groups is most likely related to their more leisurely lifestyles and the relatively fewer financial pressures that exist prior to and after rearing a family. This is supported by evidence that respondents' satisfaction with food consumption is closely related to the amount of per capita income available, which was greatest for those in Stages I and V.[35] Another factor that may contribute to their satisfaction with food consumption may be that fewer compromises are required to satisfy the needs and desires of multiple family members.

Additional support for this study of homemakers' satisfaction with food consumption activities comes from a case history of an individual homemaker's perceptions of her meal preparation role over the stages of her FLC:[36]

1. As a young homemaker, she made a particular effort to intrigue her husband's appetite.
2. When she became a mother, she shifted her emphasis to the practicality of feeding a family.
3. After the children left home, she reverted to somewhat more imaginative cooking for her own pleasure and that of her husband.

These shifts in perception of food preparation activities over the FLC seem to coincide with the shifts in goal satisfaction discussed above.

ENTERTAINMENT ACTIVITIES

An exploratory study of family choice of leisure-time activities provided another opportunity to utilize the FLC concept.[37] Employing a rather simplified FLC model, families were placed into one of the following four stages: (1) under forty

TABLE 12-7   Participation in Selected Recreational Activities by Family Life-Cycle Stage

FLC STAGE	DEFINITION	ACTIVITIES WITH ABOVE-AVERAGE PARTICIPATION
Bachelor	Single, under 40, no children	Tennis, handball, swimming, baseball, soccer, volley ball, picnicking, horse riding, hiking, water skiing, biking, camping, running, and dancing
Newly Married	Young, married, no children	Tennis, handball, lake swimming, baseball, volley ball, skeet trapping, picnicking, hiking, water skiing, biking, camping, hunting, fishing, and running
Full Nest I (a)	Young, married, youngest child less than 6	Tennis, handball, swimming, soccer, volley ball, horse riding, camping, hunting, and running
Full Nest I (b)	Young, married, youngest child 6 to 13	Above average in all activities but running
Full Nest II	Older, married, dependent children 14 or older	Tennis, handball, pool swimming, baseball, soccer, skeet trapping, horse riding, hiking, water skiing, biking, camping, hunting, fishing
Empty Nest (a)	Older, married, no children at home, head working	Pool swimming
Empty Nest (b)	Older, married, no children at home, head retired	Below average on all activities
Solitary Survivor	Older, single	Below average on all activities

Source: Adapted from E. Laird Landon, Jr., and William B. Locander, "Family Life Cycle and Leisure Behavior Research," in William L. Wilkie, ed., *Advances in Consumer Research* (Ann Arbor, Mich.: Association for Consumer Research, 1979), VI, 136.

years of age without children, (2) under forty years of age with children, (3) forty years of age or older with children, and (4) forty years of age or older without children. The study found that bowling and expensive dining out were more frequently engaged in by those in later life-cycle stages, whereas attending movies, nightclubs, and school-related athletic events were activities more frequently engaged in by those in earlier FLC stages.

Table 12-7 on page 339 summarizes the findings of a more recent study that examines recreational involvement by the FLC for some eighteen different activities. The study generally indicates that those in the bachelor and newly married FLC stages were quite heavily involved in a wide variety of the activities explored. Those families constituting the Full Nest I (a) stage indicated an average level of involvement for many of the activities. This reduction in the level of recreational activity seems to reflect the concentrated attention being given to the demands of early parenthood. Therefore it is not surprising that families with older children (i.e., Full Nest I (b)) tended to report greater involvement than families with younger children (i.e., Full Nest I (a)). While selective activities remain relatively high, there is a distinct tendency for involvement levels to drop in the last four stages of the FLC.[38] Marketers offering any of a wide range of recreational products or services would benefit from an understanding of fluctuations in recreational activity over the FLC when it comes to creating their market segmentation strategy.

TABLE 12-8   An Overview of the Family Life Cycle

BACHELOR STAGE; YOUNG SINGLE PEOPLE NOT LIVING AT HOME	NEWLY MARRIED COUPLES; YOUNG, NO CHILDREN	FULL NEST I; YOUNGEST CHILD UNDER SIX	FULL NEST II; YOUNGEST CHILD SIX OR OVER
Few financial burdens. Fashion opinion leaders. Recreation oriented. Buy: Basic kitchen equipment, basic furniture, cars, equipment for the mating game, vacations.	Better off financially than they will be in near future. Highest purchase rate and highest average purchase of durables. Buy: Cars, refrigerators, stoves, sensible and durable furniture, vacations.	Home purchasing at peak. Liquid assets low. Dissatisfied with financial position and amount of money saved. Interested in new products. Like advertised products. Buy: Washers, dryers, TV, baby food, chest rubs and cough medicine, vitamins, dolls, wagons, sleds, skates.	Financial position better. Some wives work. Less influenced by advertising. Buy larger sized packages, multiple-unit deals. Buy: Many foods, cleaning materials, bicycles, music lessons, pianos.

Table 12-8 presents an overview of an FLC model that lists the consumption activities that dominate the family at each stage of the life cycle.[39] A careful examination of this model reveals the potential usefulness of FLC analyses for strategic market planning.

Marketing Implications of the FLC

FLC analysis permits marketers to segment the total universe of families into distinct, mutually exclusive markets composed of family units that are relatively homogeneous in terms of age, interests, needs, time utilization, proportionate disposable income, and so forth. Segmentation by stage in the FLC enables marketers to develop products and services to meet the very specific needs of families at each stage in their lives, and to design and implement promotional strategies with which their target audiences will identify.

THE FUTURE OF THE FAMILY

Despite widespread publicity about spiraling divorce rates and the emergence of unconventional alternatives to the traditional nuclear family (e.g., unmarried couples and open, group, or communal marriages), experts predict that the

FULL NEST III; OLDER MARRIED COUPLES, WITH DEPENDENT CHILDREN	EMPTY NEST I; OLDER MARRIED COUPLES, NO CHILDREN LIVING WITH THEM, HEAD IN LABOR FORCE	EMPTY NEST II; OLDER MARRIED COUPLES, NO CHILDREN LIVING AT HOME, HEAD RETIRED	SOLITARY SURVIVOR, IN LABOR FORCE	SOLITARY SUR-VIVOR, RETIRED
Financial position still better. More wives work. Some children get jobs. Hard to influence with advertising. High average purchase of durables. Buy: New, more tasteful furniture, auto travel, non-necessary appliances, boats, dental services, magazines.	Home ownership at peak. Most satisfied with financial position and money saved. Interested in travel, recreation, self-education. Make gifts and contributions. Not interested in new products. Buy: Vacations, luxuries, home improvements.	Drastic cut in income. Keep home. Buy: Medical appliances, medical care, products which aid health, sleep, and digestion.	Income still good but likely to sell home.	Same medical and product needs as other retired group, drastic cut in income. Special need for attention, affection, and security.

Source: William D. Wells and George Gubar, "Life Cycle Concept in Marketing Research," *Journal of Marketing Research*, 3 (November 1966), 362.

nuclear family will endure.[40] The survival of the family seems assured because of its capacity to continue to fulfill such basic functions as the provision of economic and emotional well-being to its members, child socialization, and suitable lifestyles. Moreover, as a dynamic institution, the family may become even more influential in the future as it serves to fortify its members against the strains of continued technological and social change.

Crystal ball gazing into the future of the family is not without its risks. However, consumer researchers must delve into the horizons; they must be able to predict change in order to predict how consumers will react to such change. In this spirit, Table 12-9 identifies six social-environmental trends that seem likely to influence the future of the family. It is our contention that marketers will benefit from periodic review of these and other evolving trends by asking themselves:

1. Which specific trends are most likely to influence my product or service?
2. Have there been any significant changes in the direction or intensity of the important trends, i.e., are they increasing or decreasing, and at what rate?
3. How will each important trend affect the marketing efforts for my product or service?

TABLE 12-9 Factors Affecting the Future of the Family

TREND	IMPACT
More leisure time	A shorter workweek will mean increased emphasis on family recreation and entertainment. There should also be a greater demand for products that make the use of time more rewarding and enjoyable.
More formal education	Better education will mean a more aware consumer, which should increase the demand for more reliable products. There should also be increased interest in products and services that satisfy the need for individualism.
More working married women	A higher total family income should mean less economic pressure and more money available for the purchase of products previously out of reach for the family. There should also be increased joint husband-wife decision making, a greater sharing of domestic responsibilities, and a continued preference for smaller families.
Increased life expectancy	As people live longer, the demand for products and services designed to cater to the health, recreation, and entertainment needs of an older population will increase. There should also be a greater emphasis placed on proper nutrition and diet.
Smaller-size families	Fewer children (zero population growth) will mean that parents will be able to spend more time and money on the development of each child's skills and capabilities. There will also be more discretionary income available for parents to spend on their own development, to pursue their own interests, and to improve the general standard of the family's lifestyle.
Women's movement	Husbands and wives will increasingly share household responsibilities, including joint decision making. Moreover, as an outgrowth of the women's movement, traditional sex-linked roles will continue to decline, and products that have generally been aimed at either males or females will increasingly be targeted to members of both sexes.

summary

The family is a major influence on the consumption behavior of its members; in addition, it is the prime target market for most products and product categories. As the most basic membership group, *families* are defined as two or more persons related by blood, marriage, or adoption who reside together. There are three types of families: married couples, nuclear families, and extended families. The basic functions of the family are the provision of economic and emotional support, childhood socialization, and a suitable lifestyle for its members.

The members of a family assume specific roles and tasks in their everyday functioning; such roles or tasks extend to the realm of consumer purchase decisions. Key consumer-related roles of family members include influencers, gatekeepers, deciders, buyers, preparers, users, maintainers, and disposers. A family's decision-making style is often influenced by its social class, lifestyle, role orientation, and stage in the family life cycle, and by the product importance, perceived risk, and time constraints of the purchase itself.

The majority of consumer studies classify family consumption decisions as husband-dominated, wife-dominated, joint, or autonomic decisions. The extent and nature of husband/wife influence in family decisions is dependent on the specific product or service, the stage in the decision-making process (i.e., problem recognition, information search, and final decision), and the specific product features under consideration.

Consumer socialization is an important component of the socialization process of children. It is the vehicle through which the family imparts consumer-relevant knowledge, attitudes, and skills. Children are not only influenced by their families; in turn, they also influence their family consumption decisions.

Classification of families by stage in the family life cycle provides valuable insights into family consumption behavior. These stages, which generally include bachelorhood, honeymooners, parenthood (children under six), parenthood (children over six), postparenthood, and dissolution, are an important basis of market segmentation for many products and services. Segmentation by stage in the family life cycle enables marketers to develop products and services that will meet the very specific needs of families at each stage in their lives, and to design and implement promotional strategies with which their target audiences will identify.

discussion questions

1. How does the family influence the consumer socialization of children?
2. Briefly describe a recent important purchase decision that your family made. Analyze the roles performed by various family members in terms of the following

eight consumption roles:
a. Influencers
b. Gatekeepers
c. Deciders
d. Buyers
e. Preparers
f. Users
g. maintainers
h. disposers
[Note: All of the consumption roles may not apply in a specific decision.]

3. Develop an FLC market segmentation strategy for each of the following four product categories:
a. Cosmetics
b. Food
c. Vacations
d. Housing

4. In purchasing a new TV set, how would you expect the following factors to influence the locus of decision making (i.e., husband-dominated, wife-dominated, joint, or autonomic):
a. Social class
b. Amount of perceived risk
c. Product importance
d. Time pressure

5. If you were the marketing executive in charge of convenience food products (such as frozen dinners) for a large food processor, would you spend a portion of your advertising budget to reach the teenage members of the family? Explain.

6. Select and discuss five newspaper or magazine advertisements, each of which is directed at families at a different stage of the family life cycle.

7. Suppose that you are a marketing manager for a local furniture retailer. How might a knowledge of the family life cycle help you identify appropriate market segments and establish suitable price and product lines? Explain.

8. How might the traditional family life cycle be revised so that it better accounts for changes in the structure and composition of families in the 1980s?

endnotes

1. F. Ivan Nye and Felix M. Berardo, *The Family: Its Structure and Interaction* (New York: Macmillan, 1973), 32.

2. Richard A. Easterlin, "Does Money Buy Happiness?" *Public Interest*, No. 30 (Winter 1973), 3–10.

3. Scott Ward, "Consumer Socialization," *Journal of Consumer Research*, 1 (September 1974), 2.

4. Ibid., 2–3.

5. John F. Grashof and Donald F. Dixon, "The Household: The 'Proper' Model for Research into Purchasing and Consumption Behavior," in Jerry Olson, ed., *Advances in Consumer Research* (Ann Arbor, Mich.: Association for Consumer Research, 1980), VII, 486–91.

6. Theodore Dunn, "Large Numbers of Husbands Buy Household Products, Do Housework," *Marketing News*, October 13, 1980, 1 and 3.

7. Jagdish N. Sheth, "A Theory of Family Buying Decisions," in Jagdish N. Sheth, ed., *Models of Buyer Behavior: Conceptual, Quantitative and Empirical* (New York: Harper & Row, 1974), 24.

8. Ibid., 29–30.

9. Harry L. Davis, "Decision Making within the Household," *Journal of Consumer Research,* 2 (March 1976), 241–60.

10. Elizabeth H. Wolgast, "Do Husbands or Wives Make the Purchase Decisions?" *Journal of Marketing,* 23 (October 1958), 151–58; and Harry Sharp and Paul Mott, "Consumer Decisions in the Metropolitan Family," *Journal of Marketing,* 21 (October 1956), 149–56.

11. "Who Really Makes the Decisions?" *The Bruskin Report:* A Market Research Newsletter (New Brunswick, N.J.: R.H. Bruskin Associates, September 1974), 1.

12. Isabella C.M. Cunningham and Robert T. Green, "Purchasing Roles in U.S. Family, 1955 and 1973," Journal of Marketing, 30 (October 1974), 61–64.

13. Robert Ferber and Lucy Chao Lee, "Husband-Wife Influence in Family Purchasing Behavior," *Journal of Consumer Research,* 1 (June 1974), 43–50.

14. Harry L. Davis and Benny P. Rigaux, "Perception of Marital Roles in Decision Processes," *Journal of Consumer Research,* 1 (June 1974), 51–62.

15. E.H. Bonfield, "Perception of Marital Roles in Decision Processes: Replication and Extension," in H. Keith Hunt, ed., *Advances in Consumer Research* (Ann Arbor, Mich.: Association for Consumer Research, 1978) V, 300–307.

16. *Family Decision Making* (New York: Time Magazine, Time Marketing Information Research Report 1428, 1967).

17. Harry L. Davis, "Dimensions of Marital Roles in Consumer Decision Making," *Journal of Marketing Research,* 7 (May 1970), 168–77; and Arch G. Woodside and William H. Motes, "Husband and Wife Perceptions of Marital Roles in Consumer Decision Processes for Six Products," in Neil Beckwith, et al., eds., *1979 Educators' Conference Proceedings* (Chicago: American Marketing Association, 1979), 214–19.

18. James U. McNeal, "Children as Consumers: A Review," *Journal of the Academy of Marketing Science,* 7 (Fall 1979), 346–59.

19. Ward, "Consumer Socialization," 9; Roy Moore and George P. Moschis, "Social Interaction and Social Structural Determinants in Adolescent Consumer Socialization," in Olson, *Advances in Consumer Research,* VII, 757–59; and George P. Moschis and Roy L. Moore, "Decision Making among the Young: A Socialization Perspective," *Journal of Consumer Research,* 6 (September 1979), 101–12.

20. George J. Szybillo and Arlene Sosanie, "Family Decision Making: Husband, Wife and Children," in William D. Perreault, Jr., ed., *Advances in Consumer Research* (Atlanta: Association for Consumer Research, 1977), IV, 46–49.

21. James E. Nelson, "Children as Information Sources in the Family Decision to Eat Out," in William L. Wilkie, ed., *Advances in Consumer Research* (Ann Arbor, Mich.: Association for Consumer Research, 1979), VI, 419–23; and George J. Szybillo, Arlene K. Sosanie, and Aaron Tenebein, "Should Children Be Seen But Not Heard?" *Journal of Advertising Research,* 17 (December 1977), 7–12.

22. William D. Wells and Lenard A. LoSciuto, "Direct Observation of Purchase Behavior," *Journal of Marketing Research,* 3 (August 1966), 227–33; and Charles K. Atkin, "Observation of Parent-Child Interaction in Supermarket Decision-Making," *Journal of Marketing,* 42 (October 1978), 41–45.

23. Lewis A. Berey and Richard W. Pollay, "The Influencing Role of the Child in Family Decision Making," *Journal of Marketing Research,* 5 (February 1968), 70–72.

24. Scott Ward and Daniel Wackman, "Purchase Influence Attempts and Parental Yielding," *Journal of Marketing Research,* 9 (August 1972), 316–19.

25. *Grocery Store Shopping Habits of the Young Consumer...* for Her Family, Research Report No. 2 (New York: Co-ed Magazine, published by Scholastic Magazines, Inc., 1974).

26. William D. Perreault, Jr., and Frederick A. Russ, "Student Influence on Family Purchase Decision," in Fred C. Allvine, ed., 1971 *Combined Proceedings* (Chicago: American Marketing Association, 1971); 386–89.

27. Richard H. Davis, "Television and the Older Adult," *Journal of Broadcasting*, 15 (Spring 1971), 153–59.

28. Charles W. King, "Demographics, Spending and Leisure; A Critique," in Wilkie, *Advances in Consumer Research*, VI, 149–52.

29. Frederick W. Derrick and Alane K. Lehfeld, "The Family Life Cycle: An Alternative Approach," *Journal of Consumer Research*, 7 (September 1980), 214–17; and Patrick E. Murphy and William A. Staples, "A Modernized Family Life Cycle," *Journal of Consumer Research*, 6 (June 1979), 12–22.

30. John B. Lansing and Leslie Kish, "Family Life Cycle as an Independent Variable," *American Sociological Review*, 32 (October 1957), 514.

31. Richard B. Ellis, "Composite Population Descriptors: The Socio-Economic Life Cycle Grid," in Mary Jane Schlinger, ed., *Advances in Consumer Research* (Association for Consumer Research, 1974), II, 481–93.

32. A. Marvin Roscoe, Jr., and Jagdish N. Sheth, "Demographic Segmentation of Long Distance Behavior: Data Analysis and Inductive Model Building," in M. Venkatesan, ed., *Third Annual Conference of the Association for Consumer Research*, 1972, 258–78.

33. C. Milton Coughenour, "Functional Aspects of Food Consumption Activity and Family Life Cycle Stages," *Journal of Marriage and the Family*, 34 (November 1972), 656–64.

34. Ibid., 660.

35. Ibid., 662.

36. Wroe Alderson, *Dynamic Marketing Behavior* (Homewood, Ill.: Richard D. Irwin, 1965), 149.

37. Robert D. Hisrich and Michael P. Peters, "Selecting the Superior Segmentation Correlate," *Journal of Marketing*, 38 (July 1974), 60–63.

38. E. Laird Landon, Jr., and William B. Locander, "Family Life Cycle and Leisure Behavior Research," in Wilkie, *Advances in Consumer Research*, VI, 133–38; and Johan Arndt, "Family Life Cycle as a Determinant of Size and Composition of Household Expenditures," in Wilkie, *Advances in Consumer Research*, VI, 128–32.

39. William D. Wells and George Gubar, "Life Cycle Concept in Marketing Research," *Journal of Marketing Research*, 3 (November 1966), 355–63.

40. See, for example, Betty Yorburg, *The Changing Family* (New York: Columbia University Press, 1973).

THIRTEEN

Social Class and
Consumer Behavior

introduction

SOME form of class structure or social stratification has existed in all societies throughout the history of human existence. Therefore it is not surprising that even in America, the "land of equal opportunity," there is much evidence of social class groupings. As an indication of the presence of social classes in America, the people who are better educated or have more-prestigious occupations generally have greater status than people with little education or less-prestigious occupations. For example, the occupations of physician and lawyer are often more highly valued than those of truck driver and farmhand.[1] All four occupations, however, are necessary for our society's general well-being. Moreover, as will be discussed later, a wide range of differences in values, attitudes, and behavior has been shown to exist between members of different social classes.

The major questions we will explore in this chapter are: What is social class? What are its determinants? How is it measured? How do members of specific social classes behave? How do social-class-linked attitudes and behavior influence consumer behavior?

WHAT IS SOCIAL CLASS?

While social class can be thought of as a range of social positions—a continuum—on which each member of society can be placed, researchers have preferred to divide the continuum into a small number of specific social classes, or *strata*. Within this framework, the concept of social class is used to assign individuals or families to a social-class category. Consistent with this practice, *social class* is defined as *the division of members of a society into a hierarchy of distinct status classes, so that members of each class have relatively the same status and members of all other classes have either more or less status.*

To appreciate more fully the complexity of social class, we will briefly consider several underlying concepts pertinent to our definition.

All the people like us are We, and every one else is They.

RUDYARD KIPLING

"We and They" (1926)

Social Class and Social Status

Researchers often measure social class in terms of social status; that is, they define each social class by the amount of status the members of that class have in comparison with members of other social classes.

Status is frequently conceptualized as the relative rankings of members of each social class in terms of specific types of status factors. For example, relative *wealth* (amount of economic assets), *power* (the degree of personal choice or influence over others), and *prestige* (the degree of recognition received from others) are three popular status factors frequently employed in the estimation of social class.[2] As we will see later in our discussion of the measurement of social class, researchers often use selected aspects of wealth, power, and prestige to estimate social-class standing.

Social Class Is Hierarchical

Social-class categories are usually ranked in a hierarchy ranging from low status to high status. Thus members of a specific social class perceive members of other social classes as having either more or less status than they do. To many people, therefore, social-class categories suggest that others are either equal to them (about the same social class), superior to them (higher social class), or inferior to them (lower social class). The hierarchical nature of social class is encapsulated in the following quotation:[3]

> The members of a social class are basically people who see others in their own class level as people they can accept as equals, and with whom they can participate socially without feeling that they are out of their social niche. At the same time, people in a superior social class level are looked on as being of greater importance and as moving in circles that are generally unobtainable, and people below are people of inferior positions and with whom they are not interested in participating.

This hierarchical aspect of social class is important to marketers. Consumers may purchase certain products because they are favored by members of their own or a higher social class, and they may avoid other products because they perceive them to be "lower-class" products.

Social Class and Market Segmentation

The various social-class strata provide a natural basis for market segmentation for many products and services. In many instances, consumer researchers have been able to relate product usage to social-class membership. Thus marketers can effectively tailor their products, channels of distribution, and promotional messages to the needs and the interests of a specific social stratum.

Social Class and Behavioral Factors

The assignment of society's members into a small number of social classes has enabled researchers to note the existence of shared values, attitudes, and behavioral patterns among members *within* each social class, and differing values, attitudes, and behavior *between* different social classes. Consumer researchers have been able to relate social-class standing to consumer attitudes concerning specific products, and to examine social-class influences on the actual consumption of products.

Social Class as a Frame of Reference

Social-class membership serves as a frame of reference (i.e., a reference group) for the development of consumer attitudes and behavior. In the context of reference groups, we might expect members of a specific social class to turn most often to other members of the *same* social class for cues (or clues) as to appropriate behavior.

SOCIAL-CLASS CATEGORIES

There is little agreement among sociologists on how many distinct class divisions are necessary to describe adequately the social-class structure of the United States.[4] For example, most early studies divided the social-class organizations of specific communities into five-class or six-class social structures. However, other researchers have found nine-class, four-class, three-class, and even two-class schemes to be most suitable for their purposes. The choice of how many separate classes to use depends on the amount of detail the researcher believes is necessary to explain adequately the attitudes or behavior under study. Marketers are interested in the social-class structures of communities that offer potential markets for their products and in the specific social-class level of their potential customers. Table 13-1 illustrates the number and diversity of social-class schemes.

TABLE 13-1   Variations in the Number and Types of Social-Class Categories

two-category social-class schemes
—Blue-Collar, White-Collar
—Lower, Upper
—Lower, Middle

three-category social-class schemes
—Blue-Collar, Gray-Collar, White-Collar
—Lower, Middle, Upper

four-category social-class schemes
—Lower, Lower-Middle, Upper-Middle, Upper

five-category social-class schemes
—Lower, Working Class, Lower-Middle, Upper-Middle, Upper

six-category social-class schemes
—Lower-Lower, Upper-Lower, Lower-Middle, Upper-Middle, Lower-Upper, Upper-Upper

nine-category social-class schemes
—Lower-Lower, Middle-Lower, Upper-Lower Lower-Middle, Middle-Middle, Upper-Middle, Lower-Upper, Middle-Upper, Upper-Upper

Although most behavioral scientists tend to agree that social class is a valid and useful concept, there is no general agreement as to how to measure this complex social concept. To a great extent, researchers are uncertain as to what constitutes the underlying dimensions of social-class structure. To attempt to resolve this dilemma, researchers have employed a wide range of measurement techniques that they feel capture the spirit, if not the essence, of social class. Of course, no one can be certain that a particular approach does, in fact, fully measure the various complexities of social class. In many cases, however, social-class measures are believed to give a "fair" approximation.

Systematic approaches for measuring social class fall into the following three broad categories: subjective measures, reputational measures, and objective measures. These measures are described below and summarized in Table 13-2.

Subjective Measures

In the subjective approach to measuring social class, individuals are asked to estimate their own social-class positions. Typical of this approach is the following question:[5]

> If you were asked to use one of these four names for your social class, which would you say you belong in: the middle class, lower class, working class, or upper class?

The resulting classification of social-class membership is based on the participants' self-perceptions or self-images. Social class is treated as a "personal" phenomenon, one that reflects an individual's sense of belonging or identification with others.[6] This feeling of social-group membership is often referred to as *class consciousness*.

TABLE 13-2   Methods Used in the Measurement of Social Class

MEASUREMENT TECHNIQUE	METHOD EMPLOYED
Subjective	Self-perception
Reputational	Perception of others
Objective	Single- or composite-variable index based on:
	Occupation
	Education
	Income (source, amount)
	Quality of neighborhood
	Quality of dwelling
	Inventory of possessions

Subjective measures of social-class membership have been criticized because they tend to produce an overabundance of people who classify themselves as "middle class" (thereby understating the number of people—the "fringe" people—who would, perhaps, be more correctly classified as either "lower" or "upper" class), and because very few people elect to say "don't know" (thereby avoiding classification altogether).[7]

To date, subjective procedures have not been employed in consumer behavior studies. It is likely, however, that subjective perception of social-class membership, as a reflection of self-image, is related to product usage (see Chapter 6). Unfortunately, there is no available research that attempts to support this hypothesis.

Reputational Measures

The reputational approach for measuring social class requires participants to make judgments concerning the social-class membership of *others* within the community, rather than themselves.

Perhaps the best known of all reputational procedures is the "evaluated participation" approach, which uses the evaluations of selected community informants concerning the social-class membership of others in the community to determine the social-class structure of the community.[8] Note that while this method requires informants to evaluate other community members, the final task of assigning community members to social-class positions belongs to the trained researcher.

Sociologists have employed the reputational approach to measure social class in order to obtain a better understanding of the specific social-class structures of the communities under study. However, consumer researchers are concerned with the measurement of social class in order to obtain a better understanding of markets and marketing behavior, not of social structure. In keeping with this more-focused goal, the reputational approach has proved to be impractical.

Objective Measures

In contrast to the subjective and reputational measures of social class, which require people to evaluate their own class standing or that of other community members, *objective* measures (also called socioeconomic measures) require participants to answer several factual questions about themselves, their families, or their residence. In selecting objective measures of social class, most researchers draw on the following variables:

1. Occupation
2. Income (amount or source)
3. Education
4. Quality of neighborhood

5. Value of residence
6. Inventory or quality of possessions

Such socioeconomic measures of social class appeal to marketers because they seem to capture the basic characteristics that provide status within our society. These measures are also relatively simple to obtain. By adding a number of factual questions to a consumer survey, the researcher is able to develop a measure of social class for the respondents.

Socioeconomic measures of social class are of considerable value to marketers for segmenting their markets. The requirements for efficient market segmentation, remember, are identification, size, and accessibility (see Chapter 2). The marketing manager who has developed a socioeconomic profile of his or her target market can locate (i.e., identify and measure) this market by studying the socioeconomic data periodically issued by the U.S. Bureau of the Census. In order to reach a desired target market, the marketer simply has to match its socioeconomic profile to the audience profiles of selected advertising media. Socioeconomic audience profiles are regularly collected and routinely made available to potential advertisers by most of the mass media because of their ability to influence advertisers' media decisions. An example of such a profile can be seen in Table 13-3.

Objective measures of social class fall into two basic categories: single-variable indexes and composite-variable indexes.

TABLE 13-3   Profile, Smithsonian Subscriber Families, 1979

income		
Annual median income		$30,079
Annual average income		$40,817
Percent incomes over $25,000		64.0%
Percent incomes over $50,000		20.4%
Total college educated		87.5%
College grads	64.2%	
Attended college	23.3%	
occupation		
Total manager-administrator, professional, technical		82.5%
Management	37.0%	
Professional/technical	45.5%	
home ownership		
Median value of owned home		$71,916
Percent over $50,000 value		76.9%
Percent over $75,000 value		46.7%
Percent over $100,000 value		27.1%
investment holdings		
Own corporate stock		56.6%
Own real estate (other than homes)		32.2%
Own mutual funds		21.0%

Source: *Smithsonian* Magazine, Washington, D.C.

TABLE 13-4   Prestige Ratings of Occupational Titles in the United States, 1963

OCCUPATIONS	SCORES	OCCUPATIONS	SCORES	OCCUPATIONS	SCORES
U.S. Supreme Court Justice	94	Owner of a factory that employs about 100 people	80	Traveling salesman for a wholesale concern	66
Physician	93	Building contractor	80	Plumber	65
Nuclear physicist	92	Artist who paints pictures that are exhibited in galleries	78	Automobile repairman	64
Scientist	92			Playground director	63
Government scientist	91			Barber	63
State governor	91	Musician in a symphony orchestra	78	Machine operator in a factory	63
Cabinet member in federal government	90	Author of novels	78	Owner-operator of a lunch stand	63
College professor	90	Economist	78	Corporal in the regular army	62
U.S. representative in Congress	90	Official of international labor union	77	Garage mechanic	62
Chemist	89	Railroad engineer	76	Truck driver	59
Lawyer	89	Electrician	76	Fisherman who owns his own boat	58
Diplomat in the U.S. Foreign Service	89	County agricultural agent	76	Clerk in a store	56
Dentist	88	Owner-operator of a printing shop	75	Milk route man	56
Architect	88	Trained machinist	75	Streetcar motorman	56
County judge	88	Farm owner and operator	74	Lumberjack	55
Psychologist	87	Undertaker	74	Restaurant cook	55
Minister	87	Welfare worker for a city government	74	Singer in a nightclub	54
Member of the board of directors of a large corporation	87	Newspaper columnist	73	Filling station attendant	51
Mayor of a large city	87	Policeman	72	Dockworker	50
Priest	86	Reporter on a daily newspaper	71	Railroad section hand	50
Head of a department in a state government	86	Radio announcer	70	Night watchman	50
Civil engineer	86	Bookkeeper	70	Coal miner	50
Airline pilot	86	Tenant farmer—one who owns livestock and machinery and manages the farm	69	Restaurant waiter	49
Banker	85	Insurance agent	69	Taxi driver	49
Biologist	85	Carpenter	68	Farm hand	48
Sociologist	83	Manager of a small store in a city	67	Janitor	48
Instructor in public schools	82	A local official of a labor union	67	Bartender	48
Captain in the regular army	82	Mail carrier	66	Clothes presser in a laundry	45
Accountant for a large business	81	Railroad conductor	66	Soda fountain clerk	44
Public school teacher	81			Sharecropper—one who owns no livestock or equipment and does not manage farm	42
				Garbage collector	39
				Street sweeper	36
				Shoe shiner	34

Source: Robert W. Hodges, Paul M. Siegel, and Peter H. Rossi, "Occupational Prestige in the United States, 1925–1963," *American Journal of Sociology*, 70 (November 1964), 290–92, Copyright © 1964 by The University of Chicago. Reprinted by permission.

SINGLE-VARIABLE INDEXES

A single-variable index does not combine socioeconomic factors; instead, just one socioeconomic variable is used to evaluate social-class membership. Some of these variables are discussed below.

OCCUPATION.   Occupation (i.e., inferred occupational status) is the most widely accepted and best documented measure of social class. The importance of occupation as a social-class indicator is dramatized by the frequency with which people ask others whom they meet for the first time, "What do you do for a living?" Obviously, the response to such a question serves as a guide in evaluating and forming opinions of others.

Table 13-4 presents the results of a benchmark national study designed to estimate the relative prestige that people assign to some ninety basic occupational titles.[9] The findings of this study and similar studies are used by social-class researchers to assign status scores to occupations encountered in their research.[10]

Most observers will agree that the occupations at the top of the list in Table 13-4 tend to earn the greatest incomes and require the most formal education. As we move down the list of occupational rankings, we find that the amount of income and the amount of required formal education tend to decrease. This suggests that there is a rather close association between occupational status, income, and education.[11]

INCOME.   Individual or family income is another socioeconomic variable frequently used to approximate social-class standing. Researchers who favor income as a measure of social class use either *amount* of income or *source* of income.[12] Table 13-5 illustrates the types of categories used for each of these income variables.

While income is a popular estimate of social class standing, not all consumer researchers agree that income is an appropriate index of social class.[13] They argue that a blue-collar truck driver and a white-collar school teacher may both earn $18,000 a year, yet each will spend that income in a different way. Therefore, though both earn the same income, how they decide to spend that income reflects different values. To such researchers, it is the difference in values that is an important discriminant of social class between people, not the amount of income they earn. Table 13-6 vividly illustrates how two groups of consumers (labeled "passive" and "creative") with the same basic income can have quite different activities, interests, and opinions. Moreover, such differences are very likely to be reflected in consumer-related tastes and patterns.

OTHER VARIABLES.   Level of education, quality of neighborhood and dollar value of residence are rarely used as sole measures of social class; however, they are frequently used informally to support or verify social-class membership assigned on the basis of occupational status or income.

TABLE 13-5   Typical Categories Used for Assessing Amount or Source of Income

AMOUNT OF INCOME	SOURCE OF INCOME
Under $5,000 per year	Public welfare
$5,000-$9,999	Private financial assistance
$10,000-$14,999	Wages (hourly)
$15,000-$19,999	Salary (yearly)
$20,000-$24,999	Profits or fees
$25,000-$29,999	Earned wealth
$30,000 and over	Inherited wealth

TABLE 13-6 Comparison of Differences in Activities, Interests, and Opinions of Passive and Creative Consumers, Given the Same Income Level

	$10,000-15,000	
	passive	creative
Visited museum during past 6 months	18.5%	52.8%
Attended classical music concert, past 12 months	5.4	25.8
Member, or use, Book Rental or Book Club and/or Record Club	21.2	46.0
Read 5 or more non-fiction books in past 12 months	13.8	57.6
Ever taken Adult Education Courses	43.1	70.6
Are Negroes right about job opportunities being unequal	21.5	51.5
Chances of moving up in company in next 12 months (very good and excellent chance)	30.9	49.1
Had alcoholic beverage—other than beer or wine—outside home during past week	41.0	67.5

Source: Emanuel Demby, "Psychographics and from Whence It Came," in William D. Wells, ed., *Life Style and Psychographics* (Chicago: American Marketing Association, 1974), 16.

Finally, *possessions* have been used by sociologists as an index of social class. The best known and most elaborate social-class rating scheme for evaluating possessions is Chapin's Social Status Scale, which focuses on the presence of certain items of furniture and accessories in the living room (types of floor or floor covering, drapes, fireplace, library table, telephone, bookcases) and the condition of the room (cleanliness, organization, general atmosphere).[14] Conclusions are drawn about a family's social-class position on the basis of such observations. Since the scale was developed over forty-five years ago, a contemporary update is very much needed.

To conclude our examination of single-variable objective measures of social class, we will look at one example of how such variables are used in consumer behavior research. Table 13-7 presents the results of a study undertaken in a midwestern city of residents who used a local Coca-Cola bottler's can and bottle recycling center, and those who did not.[15] The findings revealed that users of the recycling center were most likely to have a family income in excess of $14,000 and a head-of-household who was a professional, with at least a college degree. In other words, the recycling center attracted a well-educated, professional, and higher-income family. When combined with other information

TABLE 13-7 Income, Occupation, and Education as They Relate to Use of Recycling Center

family income level	USES CENTER	DOES NOT USE CENTER
0–$9,000	25	51
10,000–13,999	20	19
14,000–19,999	31	16
20,000 and over	24	14
	100%	100%
	(N = 84)	(N = 74)
occupational level of family head		
Professional (Lawyer, M.D., professor, C.P.A., architect, etc.)	39	10
Manager, executive, self-employed manufacturer	11	11
Technical/engineer/artisan (Research asst., teacher, librarian, computer programmer, etc.)	22	27
Sales/clerical/owner of small retail store (white collar worker)	15	27
Craftsmen/service worker/farmer/ laborer (blue collar worker)	13	25
	100%	100%
	(n = 82)	(N = 67)
educational level of family head		
Four years of high school or less	13	41
Some college	14	25
Four years of college or more	73	34
	100%	100%
	(N = 84)	(N = 75)

Source: William H. Peters, "Who Cooperates in Voluntary Recycling Efforts?" in Thomas V. Greer, ed., *1973 Combined Proceedings* (Chicago: American Marketing Association, 1974), 507.

(e.g., attitudes), such insights could help the bottler make strategic decisions as to how to attract additional users to the facility.

COMPOSITE-VARIABLE INDEXES

Composite indexes strive to combine systematically a number of socioeconomic factors to form *one* overall measure of social-class standing. Such indexes are receiving increased attention from consumer researchers because they better reflect the complexity of social class than do single-variable indexes. We will now briefly review several of the more important composite indexes.

INDEX OF STATUS CHARACTERISTICS.   A classic composite measure of social class is Warner's Index of Status Characteristics (ISC).[16] The ISC is a weighted measure of the following socioeconomic variables: occupation, source of income (*not* amount of income), house type, and dwelling area (quality of neighborhood). Table 13-8 presents the specific seven-point rating scale used for each of the four variables and the weights by which they are adjusted.

SOCIOECONOMIC STATUS SCORES. Another composite social-class measure is the U.S. Bureau of the Census Socioeconomic Status Score (SES), which was developed for the 1960 census.[17] The SES combines three of the most basic socioeconomic variables: occupation, family income, and educational attainment. The appeal of the SES index is that it enables consumer researchers to compare their findings with census data. For this reason, it is not surprising that a major corporation like the American Telephone and Telegraph Company has used the SES as a model in its research on the residence telephone market.[18]

POTENTIAL RATING INDEX BY ZIP MARKET (PRIZM). A recently developed composite index combines geographic and socioeconomic factors (i.e., educa-

TABLE 13-8   Scores and Weights for Warner's Index of Status Characteristics

OCCUPATION (weight of 4)	SOURCE OF INCOME (weight of 3)	HOUSE TYPE (weight of 3)	DWELLING AREA (weight of 2)
1. Professionals and proprietors of large businesses	1. Inherited wealth	1. Excellent houses	1. Very high: Gold Coast, North Shore, etc.
2. Semi-professionals and officials of large businesses	2. Earned wealth	2. Very good houses	2. High: the better suburbs and apartment house areas, houses with spacious yards, etc.
3. Clerks and kindred workers	3. Profits and fees	3. Good houses	3. Above average: areas all residential, larger than average space around houses; apartment areas in good condition, etc.
4. Skilled workers	4. Salary	4. Average houses	4. Average: residential neighborhoods, no deterioration in the area
5. Proprietors of small businesses	5. Wages	5. Fair houses	5. Below average: area not quite holding its own, beginning to deteriorate, business entering, etc.
6. Semi-skilled workers	6. Private relief	6. Poor houses	6. Low: considerably deteriorated, rundown and semi-slum
7. Unskilled workers	7. Public relief and non-respectable income	7. Very poor houses	7. Very low: slum

Source: W. Lloyd Warner, Marchia Meeker, and Kenneth Eells, *Social Class in America: A Manual of Procedure for the Measurement of Social Status* (New York: Harper & Row, 1960), 123. Copyright © 1960 by Harper & Row, Publishers, Incorporated, Reprinted by permission.

TABLE 13-9   Ten Homogeneous Consumer Clusters and an Application of PRIZM

A. THE TEN HOMOGENEOUS ZIP-MARKET CLUSTERS

code	description
S1	Educated, affluent families in suburban owner-occupied homes
S2	Educated, affluent, semi-urban families and singles with university enclaves.
T1	Mobile, upper-middle, child-raising families in new suburbs and ex-urban towns
U1	Educated singles in hi-rise areas with university and artistic elements
S3	Middle-class, blue-collar families in industrial urban fringes
U2	Integrated middle-class families in dense urban areas
T2	Lower-middle to low-income families in mill and factory towns and blue-collar labor
R1	Minor cities and rural towns amidst farms and ranches across agricultural mid-America
U3	Low-income families in center-cities, row, and high-rise areas
R2	Unskilled, low-income families in rural towns and farms

B. COMPARISON OF CLUSTERS S1 AND R2

	S1		R2	
	% U.S.	index	% U.S.	index
Adults	8.07%	—	11.94%	—
Percent of Total Volume				
Table wine	15.59%	193	2.41%	20
Imported beer	11.19	139	1.54	13
Air trips	24.17	300	4.02	34
Traveler's checks	16.56	205	4.96	42
Single lens reflex camera	15.46	192	4.24	36
Hi-fi/stereo components	12.83	159	4.21	35
New cars—Japanese	15.22	189	3.59	30
New cars—European	17.09	212	3.08	26
New cars—domestic compacts	10.63	132	9.40	79
New cars—domestic station wagons	11.69	145	8.28	69
MAGAZINE IMPERATIVES				
% of total magazine imperatives	11.37%	141	8.42%	71
% penetration/coverage	45.58	—	22.82	—
TELEVISION IMPERATIVES				
% of total TV imperatives	5.61%	69	14.13%	118
% penetration/coverage	25.61	—	43.62	—

Source: Based on PRIZM/SMRB Product and Media Audience Profiles as they appear in Marvin M. Gropp, *Magazine Newsletter of Research* (New York: Magazine Publishers Association, December 1980), 2 and 3.

tion, affluence, family life cycle, mobility, ethnicity, housing, and urbanization) to form consumer segments, and it then locates concentrations of these consumer segments in terms of more than thirty-five thousand residential zip-code neighborhoods.[19] From this vast amount of information, ten PRIZM clusters were eventually derived (see Table 13-9A on page 359) and were related to a host of product and advertising media consumption information.

Table 13-9B lists a sample of the useful market segmentation insights that emerge from this geographic-socioeconomic composite variable. For instance, it indicates that while Cluster S1 (an upscale consumer segment) is only 8 percent of the U.S. population, it consumes over 15 percent of the table wine purchased in the United States (some 93 percent above average). In contrast, while Cluster R2 (a downscale consumer segment) is almost 12 percent of the population, it consumes less than 3 percent of the table wine (some 80 percent below average). Most important, the geographic locations of the various consumer clusters (and subclusters) are identified by a zip code. This enables marketers to pinpoint their marketing effort and to reach the desired social-class-related segments for their products.

OTHER COMPOSITE-VARIABLE INDEXES. Many other composite social-class measures are available to the consumer researcher. Table 13-10 identifies three of these indexes and the variables employed to establish their overall status scores.

AN APPLIED COMPARISON OF SINGLE
AND COMPOSITE INDEXES OF SOCIAL CLASS

The American Telephone and Telegraph Company has utilized a variety of single and composite indexes of social class in its efforts to more fully understand customer needs. The results it obtained from a study designed to

TABLE 13-10   Popular Composite Measures of Social Class

COMPOSITE INDEX	VARIABLES
Two-Factor Index of Social Position*	Occupation Education
Index of Urban Status (revised)†	Occupation (husband and wife) Education (husband and wife) Neighborhood of residence Quality of housing Church affiliation Community associations
Index of Cultural Classes‡	Occupation Education Home value (or amount of rent)

Sources: *Marie Haug, "Social-Class Measurement: A Methodological Critique," in Gerald W. Thielbar and Saul D. Feldman, eds., *Issues in Social Inequality* (Boston: Little, Brown, 1972), 433-38.

†Richard P. Coleman and Bernice L. Neugarten, *Social Status in the City* (San Francisco: Jossey-Bass, 1971).

‡James M. Carman, *The Application of Social Class in Market Segmentation* (Berkeley: Institute of Business and Economic Research, University of California Graduate School of business Administration, 1965).

provide information about long-distance calling behavior are presented graphically in Figure 13-1.[20] Three single-variable indexes—family income, education of the head-of-household, and occupation of the head-of-household—are compared with a composite Socioeconomic Status Scores Index modeled after the SES developed by the Bureau of the Census.

The single-variable studies found that families with incomes in excess of $10,000, those whose heads-of-household have more than a high-school education, and those whose heads-of-household have mid-to-high occupational status tend to spend *more* on long-distance calls than the average amount spent by all customers. Families classified by the SES (a composite-variable index) as lower class (composite scores between 10 and 44) and lower-middle class (scores between 45 and 69) tend to spend *less* on long-distance calls than the average amount spent by all customers, while families classified as upper-middle class (scores between 70 and 89) and upper class (scores between 90 and 99) tend to spend *more* on long-distance calls than the average amount spent by all

FIGURE 13-1   **Average Long-Distance Telephone Expenditures, by Socioeconomic Variables**   Source: A. Marvin Roscoe, Jr., and Jagdish N. Sheth, "Demographic Segmentation of Long Distance Behavior: Data Analysis and Inductive Model Building," in M. Venkatesan, ed., *Third Annual Conference of the Association for Consumer Research*, 1972, 262. Also, courtesy of the American Telephone and Telegraph Company.

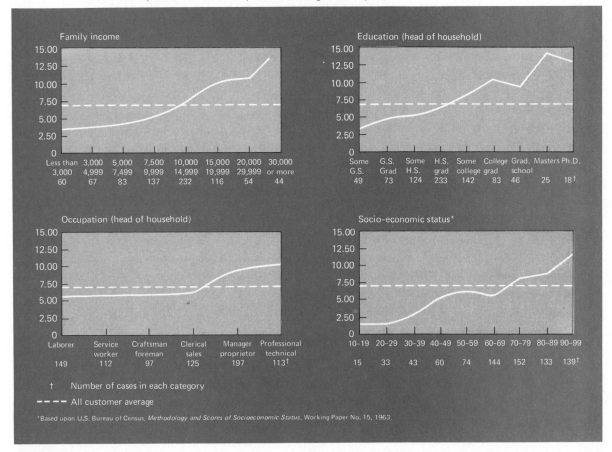

customers. These results demonstrate that the insights gained from several single-variable indexes and from a composite index tend to reinforce each other in terms of the information they provide concerning customer behavior.

Issues in the Measurement of Social Class

Before concluding our discussion of the measurement of social class, we will briefly consider two important issues: (1) the role of women in the measurement of social class, and (2) the relative efficiencies of social class and income to explain consumer behavior.

SOCIAL CLASS: THE MISSING IMPACT OF WOMEN

Researchers have traditionally tended to evaluate a family's social-class position exclusively in terms of the status of the *male* head-of-household. Although such an approach to measuring social class may have been adequate in previous decades, it is not appropriate today when so many women are actively pursuing higher education and are engaged in careers outside the home. Recent research has found that social-class position would have been categorized higher for an important segment of blue-collar families if the wife's educational and occupational levels had been used to calculate social class instead of the husband's.[21] For example, based on a composite index of education and occupation, one researcher reported: "Around a third of all dual-work families include a wife who has a higher social class level than her husband..."[22] A study concerned with the social-class structure of a large urban metropolitan area (Kansas City) found that the wife's educational level was more closely related to the family's income and social-class membership than the husband's educational level.[23]

These studies strongly suggest that the time is ripe to develop social-class measurement schemes that account for the educational and occupational levels of *both* spouses, or selectively employ the status score of the spouse with the *higher* educational and occupational attainment, or use as a status indicator the educational and occupational score of the spouse *most influential* in the consumption situation being examined. Some promising work on such broadened measures appears to be under way.[24]

COMPOSITE VERSUS SINGLE INDEXES

Considerable controversy exists regarding the relative merits of using a *single index* (e.g., income) versus a *composite index* of social class to explain consumer behavior. Two studies in particular have questioned the superiority of composite indexes as a determinant. The first study compared the efficiency with which income alone and a composite measure of social class accounted for the presence (or absence) of a relatively large number of common household products (toiletries, detergents, soft drinks, liquor, frozen and canned food).[25] With few exceptions, the evidence revealed that income was as good as or better than the composite measure of social class as a predictor of whether a family would have a specific product on hand. A follow-up study focused on the purchase of durable goods (furniture, appliances, family clothing) and selected consumer services (travel) during the previous year.[26] Again, for the overwhelming majority of products, income was found to be equal to or better than the composite measure as a determinant of whether a specific purchase was made during the preceding year.

Several studies have addressed themselves to identifying under what conditions composite indexes are better determinants of consumer behavior than income alone. One study compared the ability of *income* and *social class* (as determined by a composite index) to account for the use or nonuse and the frequency of use of fourteen entertainment activities (e.g., movies, skiing, golf, and specific types of dining out).[27] Income was found to be a superior predictor of use or nonuse, while the composite measure of social class was found to be a better predictor of frequency of use. For example, income rather than social class was positively related to whether a family did or did not "dine at expensive restaurants," while the composite measure of social class rather than income was positively related to the frequency of such dining out. This study suggests that the research designs of the earlier studies were deficient in examining only one variable ("having or not having" a product on hand) and that a composite measure of social class may have been a more effective predictor of the frequency of such purchases.

Another study examined the relationship between *income, social class,* and numerous *lifestyle* (psychographic) items (see Chapter 5).[28] The objective of this study was to determine whether lifestyle characteristics (which are generally assumed to reflect social class) are in fact more closely associated with a composite social-class index than with income alone. The findings support this hypothesis. Table 13-11 presents a sample of lifestyle items that were found to be strongly associated with social class.

TABLE 13-11   Selected Lifestyle Items That Were Found to Better Explain Social Class Than Income

LIFESTYLE ITEMS THAT ARE POSITIVELY ASSOCIATED WITH SOCIAL CLASS	LIFESTYLE ITEMS THAT ARE NEGATIVELY ASSOCIATED WITH SOCIAL CLASS
I enjoy going to concerts.	Somebody should stop all the protests that are going on.
I attend a bridge club regularly.	Long hair on boys should be banned.
I enjoy going through an art gallery.	I am a homebody.
I am usually an active member of more than one service organization.	If it was good enough for my mother, it is good enough for me.
I like ballet.	Any housewife who doesn't have a spring housecleaning is slovenly.
I think I'm a pretty nice looking person.	When I must choose between the two, I usually dress for comfort, not for fashion.

Source: Adapted from James H. Myers and Jonathan Gutman, "Life Styles: The Essence of Social Class," in William D. Wells, ed., *Life Style and Psychographics* (Chicago: American Marketing Association, 1974), 250-51.

While a debate about the relative merits of composite social-class measures and income as predictors of consumer behavior may seem to be academic, it has served to provoke a careful evaluation of the relationships between consumer behavior and social class. Out of such an assessment has come a better understanding of consumer behavior. Although more research is needed on this issue, it appears that which variable is the better predictor may be a function of how consumption behavior (as a dependent variable) is defined. Income may be a more suitable predictor of consumer behavior for acquisitive types of behavior—"having" or "not having." On the other hand, composite social-class indexes may be more predictive of expressive types of consumer behavior, such as which brands are purchased, the price that is paid, in what type of store the product is purchased, and how the product is used.[29] It is also likely that composite social-class indexes better reflect broad values such as the "inventory" or "bundle" of products that a family possesses, whereas income may better reflect the ownership of certain specific products.

A potentially interesting approach for circumventing the composite social-class versus income issue comes from the findings of several research studies, which suggest that the members of each social class be divided into subgroups on the basis of their relative incomes. The resulting *social class/relative income* variable embodies the notion that within any social class there is a wide range of incomes; some members are clearly better off than others. More specifically, consumers who have incomes *above* the average of all members of their social class can be considered "overprivileged," while those who have incomes *below* the average can be considered "underprivileged," regardless of which level of social class they represent.

Two studies concerned with automobile purchase behavior before the gasoline crisis of 1974 serve to illustrate how a *social class/relative income* variable can contribute to our understanding of consumer behavior. In the first study, it was found that *overprivileged* members of each of three social classes (upper-lower, lower-middle, and upper-middle) were the primary market for Pontiacs, Buicks, Oldsmobiles, Chryslers, and Cadillacs. The members of each social class with *average* incomes (i.e., neither overprivileged nor underprivileged) were found to be the major users of full-size Fords and Chevrolets, while those who were classified as "*underprivileged*" within each of the three social classes constituted the prime market for compact automobiles.[30]

In the second study, which was restricted to the examination of *size* of automobiles, overprivileged members of each specific social class tended to own full-size cars, while underprivileged members of each specific social class owned more compacts and intermediate-sized automobiles.[31] These results seem to indicate that a status hierarchy, based on income, may exist *within* each social class. Thus the blue-collar worker who is financially well off may make consumption decisions (at least for a conspicuous product like a car) that are more like those of affluent white-collar and professional workers than like those of blue-collar workers who earn less money. Other research that focuses on the price that consumers are willing to pay for coffee confirms the usefulness of the social class/relative income variable.[32]

A GENERAL PROFILE OF THE SOCIAL CLASSES

As indicated earlier, social science researchers have perceived social-class structure as consisting of from two to nine categories. A fairly discriminating division of social-class structure uses a six-class breakdown: upper-upper class, lower-upper class, upper-middle class, lower-middle class, upper-lower class, and lower-lower class. For purposes of discussion, it is easier to consider these classes as mutually exclusive categories; however, since we are classifying human beings—with their wide range of behavior and experience—it is important to remember that these classes are not really discrete but actually overlap when individuals possess characteristics of two adjacent strata.

In this section we have pieced together from various sources a consolidated portrait of the members of each of the six social classes listed above.[33] It should be kept in mind that each of the six profiles is only a generalized picture of the class. There may be people in any class who possess values, attitudes, and behavioral patterns that are a hybrid of two or more classes. Table 13-12 illustrates the distribution of the population within a six-category social-class scheme.

The Upper-Upper Class

Members of the upper-upper social class are typified by the small number of well-established families that make up the "inner circle" or "Social Register" of a community. The members of this highest-status class are the nucleus of the membership of the best country clubs and the sponsors of the major charitable events. They provide the leadership and funds for community civic and cultural activities, and they serve as trustees for local universities, colleges, and hospitals. In terms of occupation, members of this class are likely to head the major local financial institutions, to own or manage the major long-established businesses,

TABLE 13-12   Social-Class Distribution in Population

CLASS	PERCENT OF POPULATION
Upper-Upper } Lower-Upper }	.9
Upper-Middle	7.2
Lower-Middle	28.4
Upper-Lower	44.0
Lower-Lower	19.5
	100.0

Source: Adapted from *Motivation in Advertising*, by Pierre Martineau. Copyright 1957, McGraw-Hill Book Company. Used with permission of McGraw-Hill Book Company.

and to constitute the most prominent group of physicians, lawyers, and other key professionals within the community.

While such elite families have often accumulated money and property over the years, it is not the amount of their wealth, but the status and influence they have within the community, that sets them apart from others.

Since members of the upper-upper class are aware of the favorable position they occupy and over the years have become accustomed to their wealth, they are not likely to spend their money conspicuously. Indeed, though they have admirable lifestyles, they are unlikely to be ostentatious. Rather, they spend their money conservatively—e.g., they often wear tweeds and tailored clothing that whisper good taste and refinement rather than shout wealth. In this vein, Figure 13-2 presents an instructive group of "rules" on dressing well that reflect the merchandising philosophy of a distinguished clothing specialty store that caters to the tastes of upscale customers.

The Lower-Upper Class

The lower-upper class is primarily distinguishable from the upper-upper-class by its members' family standing, which is not elite. Lower-upper-class families are relatively new within the community or, if resident for a long time, have never quite been accepted by the upper crust of society. They have a lot of "new money;" in fact, their incomes are often greater than those of the upper-uppers. This supports the notion that income alone is not enough to determine a family's social-class position. Occupationally, lower-uppers are most likely to be successful business executives whose success is largely due to their own initiative. The members of the lower-upper class are also quite active in civic and philanthropic causes.

In contrast to the upper-upper class, members of the lower-upper class are likely to be conspicuous users of their new wealth. Their conspicuous consumption is an important symbol of their personal achievements. Lower-uppers are therefore most likely to be the major purchasers of large modern homes, to own luxury domestic and imported automobiles, to hold extravagant parties, to dress conspicuously, and to otherwise consume extravagantly. Both the upper-upper and lower-upper classes together constitute less than 1 percent of the population.

The Upper-Middle Class

The upper-middle class is comprised of families who possess neither family status nor unusual wealth. Their trademark, however, is that they are distinctly career-oriented. Occupationally, the upper-middle class consists of young successful professionals, owners of independent businesses, and corporate managers. Most members of this social class are college graduates, and many have professional or graduate degrees. Education and career advancement are therefore two very important ideals that members of this social class value, both for themselves and for their children. The upper-middle class are joiners; their

FIGURE 13-2   Advertisement Appealing to Upper-Class Customers

THE ELEMENTS OF STYLE

(Some advice on dressing well gleaned largely from Strunk and White)

IT'S easy to say what style is not. It is not, for example, fashion. (See Rule 1, below.) But when a friend asked us, the other day, to say what it is, the only answer we felt sure of was: our bread and butter. Perhaps because that answer was true, our inability to define the word rankled. So at last, prompted by some half-remembered sentences, we reached for our copy of The Elements of Style.*

This useful little book, as anyone who took Freshman English within the last twenty years probably knows, was written by William Strunk, Jr., and revised by E.B. White. Mr. White also added the final chapter, and it was there we found him describing style as "what is distinguished and distinguishing." That seemed a dandy definition to us. It certainly described what we look for in clothes. It also sent us hunting through the pages for other remarks which, perhaps with the change of a word or two, might shed as much light upon style in dress as they did upon style in writing. We found them. And you can find them below, together with some remarks of our own. Most of them are merely observations or reminders, but we phrased them as rules to preserve the book's flavor. Should the reader wish to know which rules are whose, we suggest he reach for his own copy of the little book.

RULE 1. Don't confuse style with fashion.

To recognize the difference, consider the Nehru jacket. When it came into fashion here, the men who wore it were all, presumably, fashionable. But it rarely conferred much style.

RULE 2. Don't confuse style with substance.

A coat that is cashmere on the hanger continues to be cashmere when it's worn. But style may appear or disappear with the wearer: when Nehru wore it, the Nehru jacket had style.

RULE 3. Don't imagine that time governs style.

Time only governs fashion. If you doubt this, look at some old portraits.

Unless you are familiar with the period, you won't know if the subject's clothes are in fashion. But you will know at once if they had style.

RULE 4. Choose some clothes that are not in fashion.

Clothes that are in fashion one year are often out the next. But clothes that are too distinctive merely to echo current dictates, provided they are not so different as to be eccentric, often anticipate fashion or remain independent of it. And, if well suited to the wearer, they will go on being distinguished and distinguishing year after year.

RULE 5. Avoid tame, colorless, hesitating, noncommittal clothes.

They may seem to offer safety by promising to say nothing about the wearer. But, by being anonymous, they say that he is timid, indecisive, and without a sense of style.

RULE 6. Avoid the pretentious, the exaggerated, the coy, and the cute.

Those first two words are tricky. Kings may wear ermine without offense. And there are men who can carry off a scarlet-lined opera cape or a ten-gallon hat. But if wearing such things makes you feel as though you are showing off or masquerading, don't. As to the coy and cute, we feel queasy when we see an adult male in love beads.

RULE 7. Be sparing of the tried and true.

Good serviceable clothes, like good serviceable words and phrases, become dull and ineffectual when used too often in the same way. A few familiar

classics may give a friendly ease to your wardrobe. But a wardrobe built entirely of classics is as tiresome as a vocabulary of clichés.

RULE 8. Remember that style is an increment in dress.

When we speak of a writer's style, we don't just mean his command of the relative pronoun. When we say a man dresses with style, we don't just mean we like the cut of his shirts.

RULE 9. Never sacrifice comfort to style.

The result is always self-defeating. Clothes that make you fidget can not be worn with style. If the coat pinches at the waist or the armhole, or rides up at the back of the neck, don't buy it. Or have it remedied. (We have a large staff of fitters to make sure the clothes we sell fit as they should.)

RULE 10. Dress in a way that comes naturally.

But don't be afraid to experiment: even Fred Astaire probably felt uneasy the first time he put on tails. Every well-dressed man, by the way he dresses, reveals something of his spirit, his habits, his capacities, his bias. So choose the clothes you are drawn to naturally. You will wear them better, and more often, than those you talk yourself into because they seem practical or look well on somebody else. But you may not find them in our store.

The clothes we carry reflect our spirit, our bias, our temperament. We collect them, just as we collect clothes for ourselves. If we find six sweaters of some wonderful kind, we'll buy them, even though six are all there are.

That sort of thing can make shopping in our store something of a treasure hunt. But it also means we can make no pretense of being able to dress every stylish man. To wear our clothes, Anthony Eden would have had to unbend a bit, Charles de Gaulle to lose some of his starch, and we doubt that we could ever have outfitted Adolph Menjou at all.

*The Elements of Style, Third Ed., by William Strunk, Jr. and E. B. White, MacMillan Publishing Co., Inc. 1979

Paul Stuart

Madison Avenue at 45th Street, New York, 10017

Courtesy of of Paul Stuart, Inc.

professional, community, and social activities parallel their strong need to achieve and their interest in education.

Although they are financially comfortable (with incomes frequently in the $35,000 to $80,000 range), they are not wealthy. However, they share a keen interest in the "better things in life" with members of the two upper classes. They attend the ballet, opera, and theater and are active in a wide range of other cultural activities.

Upper-middle-class families live in somewhat expensive, well-furnished modern homes, which serve as symbols of their achievement or as an indication that they are on the way up. They are therefore an important market for interior decorators and related home improvement services. Like the members of the lower-upper class, consumption is often conspicuous, though they do not possess enough money to satisfy all their consumption whims. They are highly interested in fashionable clothing and accessories and tend to buy expensive items like stereo equipment and cameras. Members of this class are very child-oriented in their consumption behavior. They tend to "purchase" art instruction, musical training, dance lessons, and other products or services designed to provide their children with the "tools" to get ahead. This social class represents about 7 percent of the population.

The Lower-Middle Class

The lower-middle class is relatively large (approximately 30 percent of the population) and is composed primarily of nonmanagerial white-collar workers (office workers, small-business owners) and high-paid blue-collar workers (plumbers, factory foremen). Its members can be categorized as "typical" Americans, located as they are at the bottom of the white-collar group and at the top of the blue-collar group. Their primary concern is achieving respectability and acceptance as good citizens, and these values are reflected in their attitudes toward their children. They want their children to be well behaved, and they are anxious that their sons be manly and their daughters ladylike. Lower-middle-class families are churchgoers and are often involved in church-sponsored activities and in fraternal organizations (Elks, Shriners, Masons, Odd Fellows).

Members of the lower-middle class frequently live in modest row houses in suburban neighborhoods. They tend to avoid extravagant home furnishings and prefer a comfortable, neat, clean, and "pretty" home. Lower-middle-class families are a major market for do-it-yourself products, which they employ to keep their homes in good repair. Their tastes in clothing parallel their tastes in home furnishings: They prefer a neat and clean appearance and tend to avoid clothing that is faddish or high-style.

The Upper-Lower Class

The upper-lower, or working, class is the largest social-class segment (approximately 45 percent of the population). It is solidly blue collar—and consists of skilled or semiskilled factory workers. While members of the lower-middle class seek respectability and advancement, members of the upper-lower class strive for security and to protect what they already have. Upper-lower-class members see work as a means to "buy" enjoyment rather than as an end unto itself, and they view union membership as the major way of attaining security. Although they are even more concerned than members of the lower-middle class that their children behave properly (like "little men" and "little ladies"), they are less likely to plan for their children's future in terms of a college education.

Upper-lower-class families, who earn relatively high union wages, tend to spend impulsively, for today, rather than to save and plan for the future. They are less interested in their home and personal looks and are more involved with purchasing items that make their leisure time enjoyable (TV sets, camping, sporting, hunting equipment). Working-class families are heavy TV watchers and were among the first to purchase television sets when they were introduced on the market.[34]

The working-class husband is likely to be active in local veterans', sporting, and hunting organizations. He has a strong "all-male" self-image; he is a sports enthusiast (baseball, boxing, and wrestling fan and a bowler), an outdoorsman (hunter and fisherman), and a heavy smoker and beer drinker. He also enjoys working around the house and relaxes by playing poker with the "boys." The working-class wife is primarily involved in her domestic role: with being a good mother and homemaker. She engages in limited social activity outside of the home, usually with a few friends who share her outlook on life. However, some recent evidence indicates that the horizon of the working-class woman may be expanding, and she may be acquiring greater interest in herself as a person and her place in the world outside her home.[35]

The Lower-Lower Class

The lower-lower class is at the bottom of the social spectrum and consists of poorly educated, unskilled laborers (dishwashers, gas station attendants, domestics). Members of this class quite frequently find themselves out of work and on some form of public assistance. Their dwellings are generally substandard and are often located in slum areas.

Many lower-lower-class women are "forced" to work (rather than desiring to work) because it is often easier for an unskilled woman to find employment than it is for an unskilled man. The life of the lower-lower-class family is frequently consumed with frustration, anger, and indifference. In this kind of environment, children are often poorly treated and punished for acts that parents of other classes are more likely to tolerate or even encourage. If members of this class are at all optimistic, they hope that somehow tomorrow will be better.

Members of the lower-lower class are largely disorganized in their approach to life and tend to live a day-to-day existence, spending what they have with no real thought for the future. For this reason, their ownership of TV sets, automobiles, and even expensive stereo sets reflects their attempts to escape the hopelessness and despair of their lives and to taste, at least superficially, a more desirable style of life.

Social-Class Mobility

Social-class membership in this country is not as hard and fixed as it is in some other countries and cultures. While individuals can move either up or down in social-class standing (when contrasted with the class position held by their parents), because of the availability of free education to all citizens and opportunities for self-development and self-advancement we primarily think in

369

terms of upward moves. Indeed the classic Horatio Alger tale of a penniless young man who managed to achieve great success in business and in life is depicted over and over again in popular novels, movies, and television shows. Because social mobility is possible in our society, the higher social classes often become reference groups for ambitious men and women of lower social status. The junior executive tries to dress like his boss; the middle manager aspires to belong to the president's club; the graduate of a free university wants to send his

FIGURE 13-3 Advertisement Suggesting Social-Class Mobility

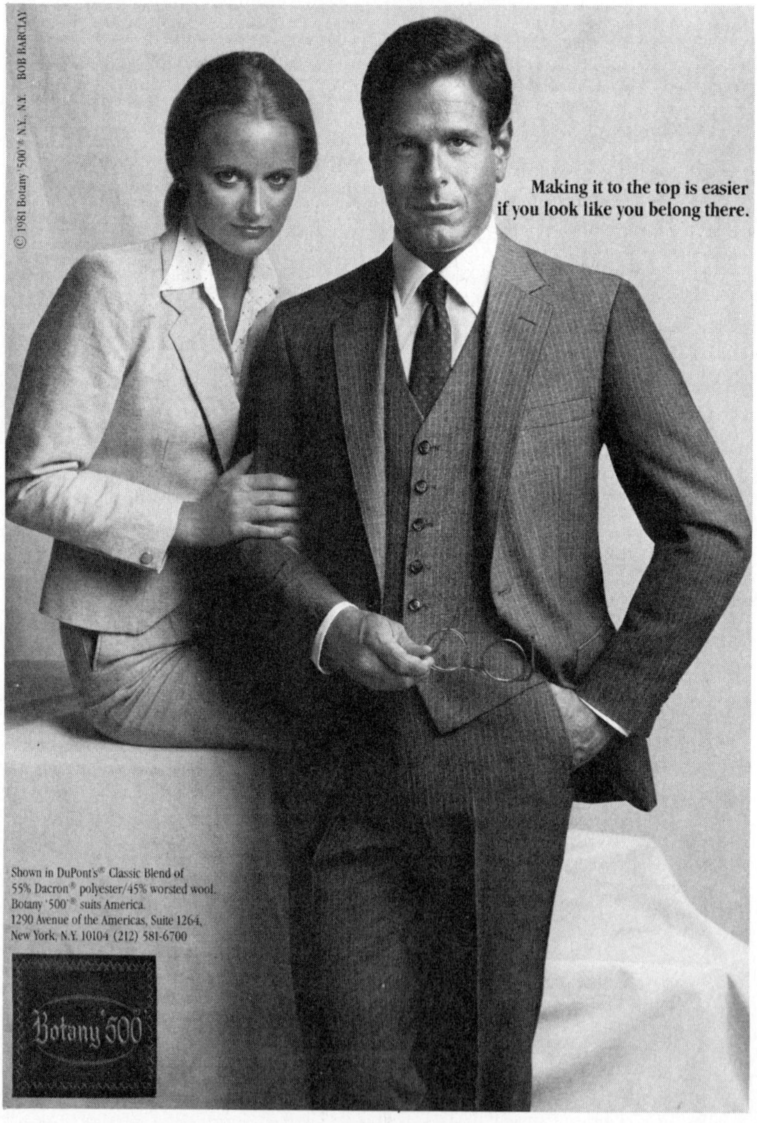
© 1981 Botany '500'® N.Y., N.Y. BOB BARCLAY
Making it to the top is easier
if you look like you belong there.
Shown in DuPont's® Classic Blend of
55% Dacron® polyester/45% worsted wool.
Botany '500'® suits America.
1290 Avenue of the Americas, Suite 1264,
New York, N.Y. 10104 (212) 581-6700
Botany '500'

Courtesy of Botany "500"

son to Princeton. The advertisement for Botany 500 in Figure 13-3 is consistent with this general view of life.

Some marketers, recognizing that individuals often aspire to membership in higher social classes, incorporate the symbols of higher-class membership (both as products and props) in their advertisements addressed to lower-social-class audiences. For example, they might advertise an Oldsmobile to lower-middle-class consumers, or golf clubs to lower-management ranks.

Although studies of human levels of aspiration (see Chapter 3) indicate that individuals may reasonably aspire to the class immediately above their own, it appears that aspirations that skip social classes tend to be unrealistic and fade away into fantasy. Therefore marketers must be careful not to incorporate symbols in their advertisements that are too far above the social-class status of their intended audience. Some years ago, a leading marketer of watches in the popular price range ran a campaign that featured such props as a man's top hat, beautiful crystal champagne glasses, and opera tickets in advertisements directed to a lower-middle-class market. This intended audience, however, could not identify with the situations depicted and did not respond; and higher-class audiences who noted this marketer's ads could not identify with an inexpensive watch. Thus the advertising campaign failed dismally.

Many advertisers make the same mistake. For example, advertisements for economy cars often show them parked in front of elaborate country homes. The viewer who identifies with the background is unlikely to identify with the car, and vice versa. Marketers should therefore pay closer attention to the relevance of their advertising symbols to the social class of their target audiences. Symbols that represent either the same social class or the class immediately above that of the target market are usually appropriate; symbols that skip to a higher social class or represent a lower social class are usually not effective.

CONSUMER BEHAVIOR APPLICATIONS OF SOCIAL CLASS

Social-class profiles provide a broad picture of the values, attitudes, and behavior that distinguish the members of various social classes. This information becomes much more useful to marketers, however, when it is related to consumption behavior. Therefore, in this section we change our focus and concentrate on specific consumer research that relates social class to the development of marketing strategy.

Clothing and Fashion

A Greek philosopher said, "Know, first, who you are; and then adorn yourself accordingly."[36] This bit of wisdom is relevant to clothing marketers today, since most people dress to fit their self-images, which include their perceptions of their own social-class membership. A study that examined the fashion interests of women found that all women respondents, regardless of social class, considered fashionable clothing to be important; however, upper- and middle-class women were found to be somewhat more involved in fashion than their lower-class counterparts. This was demonstrated by such factors as more active readership of fashion magazines, more frequent attendance at fashion shows, and more frequent discussions of fashion with others, particularly their friends and husbands.[37]

A study designed to compare working-class (lower-class) and middle-class women found that working-class women were more likely to consider "a dress for a special occasion" or "a trip to the beauty parlor" as a luxury than did middle-class women.[38] However, a comparison of these findings with an earlier study indicates that the percentage of working-class women who view such purchases as luxuries is declining, which suggests that fashion consciousness is becoming more important for lower-class women.[39]

Still further evidence that there are social-class differences regarding fashion is found in the usage of cosmetics. Research revealed that middle-class women are more likely to be heavy users of cosmetics than lower-class women.[40]

Differences in fashion interests between adjacent social classes are not strikingly evident because "...mass production and mass consumption have enabled most Americans to wear clothes, as well as to possess other artifacts, that are very much alike in *gross* appearance and quality."[41] More research is needed to examine the relationship between clothing purchase behavior and social-class membership.

Home Decoration

To the extent that a family's home is its castle, the decor of the home should provide clues to the family's social-class position. Of all the rooms in the home, the living room seems to best express how a family wants to be seen by those it entertains. Therefore, living-room furnishings are likely to be particularly sensitive to social-class influences. It will be recalled that Chapin's Social Status Scale uses the presence and condition of living-room furnishings to measure a family's social-class standing. The appropriateness of using living-room furnishings as a barometer of social-class standing is underscored by a leading consumer researcher who noted: "The living-room of a home is essentially the face you present the world of your friends and acquaintances, and the average housewife is consciously or unconsciously concerned with the impression it makes."[42]

Figure 13-4 presents a typology of social-class status based on the ownership of specific types of living-room furniture and accessories.[43] It classifies fifty-three living-room items or characteristics in terms of high or low social-class status and modern or traditional decor. This classification scheme results in four distinct groupings: (1) low-status traditional (upper-left quadrant), (2) high-status traditional (upper-right quadrant), (3) high-status modern (lower-right quadrant), and (4) low-status modern (lower-left quadrant). This type of classification scheme is useful to marketers of home-furnishing products concerned with developing products or promotional campaigns for specific target segments. For example, the location of television sets in the lower-left quadrant indicates that a television set in the living room is more likely to occur in lower-class households. Indeed, further analysis reveals that lower-class

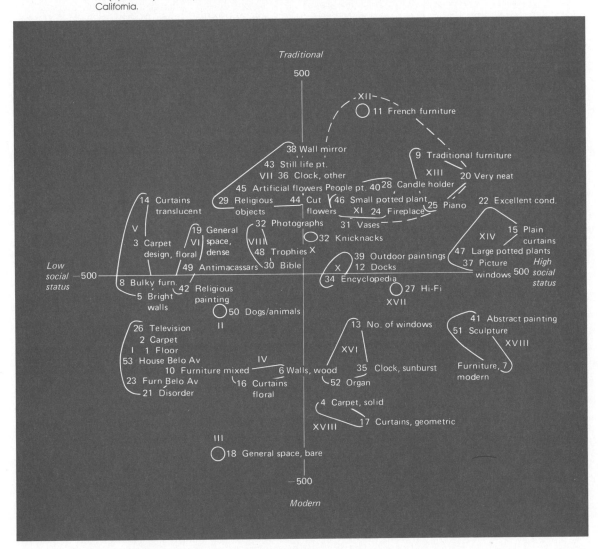

families are likely to place their television sets in the living room, while middle- and upper-class families usually place their television sets in the bedroom or family room.[44] The marketing implications of these findings suggest that advertisements for television sets targeted at the lower-class consumer should show the set in a living-room setting, while advertisements directed to middle- or upper-class consumers should show the set in either a bedroom or a family room.

A study undertaken by the American Telephone and Telegraph Company provides some additional insights into the relationship between style con-

TABLE 13-13   A Psychographic Profile of Style Consciousness in Home Furnishings by Socioeconomic Status

SELECTED STYLE CONSCIOUSNESS STATEMENTS	LOWER-CLASS AGREEMENT	LOWER-MIDDLE-CLASS AGREEMENT	UPPER-MIDDLE-CLASS AGREEMENT	UPPER-CLASS AGREEMENT
product-specific statements				
Phones should come in patterns and designs as well as colors.	60%	80%	63%	58%
A telephone should improve the decorative style of a room.	47	82	73	77%
Telephones should be modern in design.	58	85	83	89%
A home should have a variety of telephone styles.	8	46	39	51%
You can keep all those special phones, all I want is a phone that works.	83	67	68	56%
The style of a telephone is unimportant to me.	86	54	58	51%
general-lifestyle statements				
Our home is furnished for comfort not style.	96	87	79	79%
I have more modern appliances in my home than most people.	17	23	41	48%
I prefer colored appliances.	57	73	87	92%

Source: Adapted from A. Marvin Roscoe, Jr., Arthur LeClaire, Jr., and Leon G. Schiffman, "Theory and Management Applications of Demographics in Buyer Behavior," in Arch G. Woodside, Jagdish N. Sheth, and Peter D. Bennett, eds., *Foundations of Consumer and Industrial Buying Behavior* (New York: American Elsevier, 1977), 74-75.

sciousness in home furnishings and social class.[45] Table 13-13 above reveals that a significant difference in attitude exists among the four social classes studied concerning telephone design and basic style in home furnishings. An examination of the product-specific statements suggests that lower-middle-class consumers feel that telephones should improve the style of a room and be available in a variety of patterns and designs. In contrast, lower-class consumers simply express a desire for a telephone that works. Thus lower-middle-class consumers might be an important market for new, stylish telephones.. The results also indicate that upper-class consumers would be the best market for a variety of telephone styles, particularly those that are modern in design. The three general lifestyle statements tapped a broader aspect of home decorating interests; findings suggest that upper-middle-class consumers have a greater preference for style than comfort in home decorations and that they are also more likely than the other classes studied to buy colored appliances.

The Pursuit of Leisure

For many products and services, social-class membership is closely related to the choice of recreational and leisure-time activities. Research suggests that upper-class consumers are likely to attend the theater and concerts, to play bridge, and to attend college football games, while lower-class consumers tend to be avid television watchers and fishing enthusiasts and enjoy attending drive-in movies and baseball games.[46] Furthermore, the lower-class consumer spends more time on commercial types of activities (bowling, playing pool or billiards, visiting taverns) and craftsmanlike activities (model building, painting, woodworking projects).[47] A national survey of adult men, sponsored by the publishers of *Playboy* magazine, confirms many of these insights.[48] Table 13-14 reveals that for certain leisure-time interests and activities, the involvement levels of members of specific social classes are quite different.

For the marketer of on-draft and bottled beers, the lower-class consumer would appear to be a fruitful target market. This strategy implication is supported by the following description of the heavy in-tavern beer drinker, developed in a study undertaken for Schlitz Beer:[49]

Demographically we saw that the heavy user...derives his income from primarily blue-collar occupations. He is young and has at least a high school education. The major life style patterns that emerged indicated that the heavy beer drinker was probably more hedonistic and pleasure-seeking toward life than the non-drinker. He seemed to have less regard toward responsibilities of family and job. More than the non-drinker he tended to have a preference for a physical/male-oriented existence and an inclination to fantasize. Finally we found, not surprisingly, a great enjoyment of drinking, especially beer which he saw as a real man's drink.

TABLE 13-14   Adult Male Participation in Selected Leisure-Time Activities (Percentage Who Do This on a Regular Basis)

	LOWER CLASS	WORKING CLASS	LOWER-MIDDLE CLASS	UPPER-MIDDLE CLASS
Fishing, Hunting, Camping, Hiking, Backpacking	41	54	43	41
Swimming	23	30	32	33
Baseball/Softball	22	24	24	19
Tennis	9	12	18	26
Bicycling	15	13	16	18
Football	17	16	12	10
Jogging	7	11	11	17
Golf	5	8	15	23
Weight lifting	14	11	9	8
Motorboating	8	14	13	13
Motorcycling	14	16	11	7
Skiing	4	7	7	14
Racquetball, Handball, Paddleball	7	6	6	9
Distance running	3	6	6	4
Horseback riding	7	6	3	4
Social activities, such as dining, dancing, attending parties	40	54	54	66
Church or club activities	22	29	29	33
Volunteer work in the community	13	17	20	26
Political activities	6	6	9	15
Reading	38	49	55	73
Just do nothing	44	35	31	29

Source: *The Playboy Report on American Men* (Survey conducted by Louis Harris and Associates for Playboy Enterprises, New York, 1979), 53-54 and 57.

Figure 13-5 presents an example from the classic Schlitz "Gusto" advertising campaign designed to appeal to the heavy beer drinker.

Saving, Spending, and Credit

Saving, spending, and credit-card usage all seem to be related to social-class standing. For example, in response to a question that asked consumers what they would do if their income was doubled for the next ten years, upper-class respondents were more likely to specify some type of saving, particularly more risky investments. In contrast, lower-class respondents were more likely to spend their windfall income or save a portion of it in a nonrisk savings account.[50] These findings suggest that upper-class consumers are future-oriented and confident of their financial acumen, to the extent that they are more willing to invest in insurance, stocks, and real estate. In comparison, lower-class consumers are more concerned with immediate gratification; however, when they do save, they are primarily interested in safety and security.

A research project designed to compare the attitudes of working-class and middle-class women provides some further insights on social-class differences in this important area:[51]

> Working-Class women are relatively *anxious* about how they and other people handle money. They are uneasy about borrowing and thereby incurring financial obligations (which may not be paid back, at least not "on time," and thus lead to unpleasant recriminations—a "goof" indeed). They are fearful of the way men (husbands) handle money. And their feeling that young people should help their parents financially appears to indicate some willingness to become dependent in this area or perhaps a desire to continue being in control of the money earned by family members. The strong desire or need to "control the purse strings" suggests a primary anxiety about what (other) people will do when they have money in their hands. Impulsive Working-Class spending patterns make this anxiety understandable.
>
> Middle-Class women manifest appreciably greater self-assurance in this area: they are willing to borrow money (after all, they are likely to have the savings to "dig into" if there were ever difficulties in repaying a loan), and they are more easygoing about the prospect of money being in the hands of others—husbands and offspring. All of this suggests a more relaxed, carefree approach to money than typifies the Working-Class woman.

A study that focused on bank credit-card usage also illustrates how social-class influences consumer behavior.[52] Results indicated that members of the lower social classes tended to use their bank credit cards for installment purchases, while members of the upper social classes tended to be convenience users, paying their credit card bills in full each month. Furthermore, the lower-class purchasers sought out stores that would honor their cards and used the card to buy appliances and other major purchases. In contrast, the upper-class purchasers used their credit cards to buy gasoline or pay restaurant bills. In short, lower-class purchasers tend to use their credit cards to "buy now and pay later" for things that they might not otherwise be able to afford, whereas upper-class purchasers used their credit cards as a convenient substitute for cash.

FIGURE 13-5   Advertisement Targeted to the Heavy Beer Drinker

Courtesy of Jos. Schlitz Brewing Co.

Social Class and Communication

Social-class groupings differ in terms of how they transmit and receive communications, and in their media habits. Knowledge of these differences is invaluable to marketers who segment their markets on the basis of social class. It enables them to develop promotional strategies specifically designed to "penetrate" their prospects' perceptual screens.

COMMUNICATION PATTERNS

Evidence suggests that, in describing events, lower-class members portray their world in rather personal and concrete terms, while middle-class members are able to describe their experiences from a number of different perspectives.[53] The following responses to a question asking where the respondent usually purchased chewing gum illustrate how members of different social classes tend to see the world from different perspectives:[54]

> UPPER-MIDDLE-CLASS ANSWER: "At a cashier's counter or in a grocery store."
> LOWER-MIDDLE-CLASS ANSWER: "At the National or the corner drugstore."
> LOWER-CLASS ANSWER: "From Tony."

These variations in response indicate that middle-class consumers have a broader or more general view of the world, while lower-class consumers tend to see the world through their own immediate experience.

There also seem to be important social class differences in the *choice* of words used to describe things, people, and events. For example, one sociologist noted the following differences in word usage between lower- and upper-class members:[55]

LOWER-CLASS USAGE	UPPER-CLASS EQUIVALENT
evening	afternoon
dinner	lunch
supper	dinner

An awareness of such differences in language usage enables marketers to appeal more directly to their target markets in their advertising copy, their packaging, and their labeling.

Researchers have also perceived real differences in the general speech patterns of different social classes.[56] This finding suggests that advertisers, when considering announcers for their radio and television commercials, should carefully select those who project a social-class picture consistent with the target audience they are trying to reach.

Regional differences in terminology, choice of words and phrases, and patterns of usage tend to increase as we move down the social-class ladder.[57] Therefore, in targeting appeals to the lower classes, marketers should try to make certain that the language in their advertisement reflects any regional differences that might exist.

MEDIA EXPOSURE

There is evidence that selective exposure to various types of mass media differs by social class. Higher-class consumers tend to have greater exposure to magazines and newspapers than do their lower-class counterparts.[58] Lower-class consumers are likely to have greater exposure to publications that dramatize romance and the lifestyles of movie and television celebrities. For example, magazines such as *True Story* and *Photoplay* appeal heavily to blue-collar or working-class women, who enjoy reading about the problems, fame, and fortunes of others. In the selection of specific television programs and program types, higher-social-class members tend to prefer current events and drama, while lower-class individuals tend to prefer soap operas, quiz shows, and situation comedies.[59]

Retail Shopping

Consumer's shopping values, attitudes, and behavior are also influenced by their social class. For example, although most women tend to enjoy shopping, their reasons vary by social class. A study of the shopping behavior of Cleveland women found that the *acquisition* of new clothing and household products was the principal enjoyment received by lower-class shoppers. In contrast, upper-middle-class and upper-class shoppers tended to enjoy the *act* of shopping itself (store atmosphere and displays) and tended to shop more frequently than lower-class women.[60]

Furthermore, while department stores attract a large portion of shoppers from all social classes, there is a definite tendency for higher-class women to favor traditional department stores, and lower-class women to patronize mass merchandisers and "downtown" stores.[61] A detailed analysis of the type of department store preferred by women from different social classes is presented in Table 13-15. The evidence indicates that price appeal stores draw lower-class shoppers, broad appeal stores attract middle-class shoppers, and stores that feature a high-fashion image are preferred by upper-class shoppers.[62]

TABLE 13-15   Types of Department Store Favored, by Social Class

TYPES OF DEPARTMENT STORE	SOCIAL CLASS		
	lower class	middle class	upper class
Price Appeal Store	65%	33%	19%
Broad Appeal Store	28	42	12
High Fashion Store	7	25	69
Total	100%	100%	100%
Number of Respondents	(275)	(275)	(42)

Source: Adapted from Stuart U. Rich and Subhash C. Jain, "Social Class and Life Cycle as Predictors of Shopping Behavior," *Journal of Marketing Research*, 5 (February 1968), 48.

A study that investigated the retail preferences of different social classes found that upper-class consumers prefer department and specialty stores for items that they perceive to be socially risky but are willing to use discount stores for items that are not perceived to be socially risky.[63] On the other hand, lower-class consumers are willing to patronize discounters for products of both high and low social risk.

The study indicates that discounters have successfully developed acceptance across social-class boundaries for a wide range of products with low social risk. However, they have not attracted large numbers of upper-class consumers for products that can be classified as *socially risky* (such as clothing or conspicuous home furnishings). In terms of marketing, it would probably be a gross error for discounters to trade up their merchandise in an attempt to capture the upper-class consumer. Such a strategy would also run the risk of providing an atmosphere that might alienate the lower-class consumers who are their established customers.

Finally, there is evidence that in-home consumers—those who purchase from a catalog, by mail, or by telephone—are socioeconomically different from those consumers who rely solely on retail stores.[64] The results indicate that in-home consumers tend to have high family incomes, white-collar occupations, and more formal education than consumers who do not shop at home. These findings suggest that middle- and upper-class consumers are a fertile market for direct mail and telephone marketing.

Consumerism

Marketers, public policy makers, and private consumer advocates are becoming increasingly interested in the nature of consumer dissatisfaction. For this reason, consumer behavior studies are now beginning to receive attention from consumer policy researchers.

TABLE 13-16   Problem Categories of Hot Line Callers, by Social Class

	SOCIAL CLASS			
PROBLEM CATEGORY	low (n = 39)	middle (n = 66)	high (n = 45)	total (n = 150)
Prepurchase	13%	11%	20%	14%
Purchase transaction/ delivery	10	31%	31	27
Product performance	13	18	18	17
Guarantee/warranty/ contract	15	11	9	11
Service/repair	39	25	18	26
Deposits/credit/ collections	8	1	4	4
Other	2	3	0	1
	100%	100%	100%	100%

Source: Steven L. Diamond, Scott Ward, and Ronald Faber, "Consumer Problems and Consumerism: Analysis of Calls to a Consumer Hot Line," *Journal of Marketing*, 40 (January 1976), 60.

A study that examined the types of consumers who take advantage of a publicly sponsored consumer "hot line" found that lower-class callers reported considerably more service or repair problems; both middle- and upper-class callers complained about purchase and delivery problems; and upper-class callers were more likely to complain about deceptive or offensive advertisements.[65] Table 13-16 categorizes the callers by social class and type of problem.

These findings reveal significant social-class differences in the frequency and type of consumer complaints. They suggest that social-class analysis might be fruitful within the context of other consumer problem areas.

summary

Social stratification—the division of members of a society into a hierarchy of distinct social classes—exists in all societies and cultures. *Social class* is usually defined by the amount of status that members of a specific class possess in relation to members of other classes. Social-class membership often serves as a frame of reference (i.e., a reference group) for the development of consumer attitudes and behavior.

The measurement of social class is concerned with classifying individuals into social-class groupings. These groupings are of particular value to marketers, who use social classification as an effective means to identify and segment target markets.

There are three basic methods for measuring social class: subjective measurement, reputational measurement, and objective measurement. Subjective measures rely on an individual's self-perception, reputational measures rely on an individual's perceptions of others, and objective measures use specific socioeconomic measures, either alone (as a single-variable index) or in combination with others (as a composite-variable index). Composite-variable indexes combine a number of socioeconomic factors to form one overall measure of social-class standing.

Social-class structures range from two-class systems to nine-class systems. A frequently used classification system consists of six classes: upper-upper, lower-upper, upper-middle, lower-middle, upper-lower, and lower-lower. Profiles of each of these classes indicate that the socioeconomic differences between classes are reflected in differences in attitudes, in leisure-time activities, and in consumption habits. That is why segmentation by social class is of special interest to marketers.

Research has revealed social-class differences in clothing habits, home decoration, telephone usage, leisure-time activities, retail patronage, and saving, spending, and credit habits. Thus the astute marketer will differentiate product and promotional strategies for each social-class target segment.

Studies of consumer dissatisfaction reveal a relationship between social class and the types of problems consumers complain about. In summary, it would appear that social-class analysis holds enormous promise for marketers, public policy makers, and consumer advocates in terms of understanding, influencing, and improving the conditions for consumer behavior.

discussion questions

1. Give an example from your own experience of how social class may serve as a frame of reference for an individual's consumption behavior.
2. Marketing researchers have generally used the objective method to measure social class, rather than the subjective or reputational methods. Why has the objective method been preferred by researchers?
3. What is the principal drawback of evaluating a family's social-class position exclusively in terms of the male head-of-household?
4. Under what circumstances would you expect income to be a better predictor of consumer behavior than a composite measure of social class (based on income, education, and occupation)? On the other hand, when would you expect the composite social-class measure to be superior?
5. Identify either a men's or a women's clothing retailer in your local community that you feel appeals primarily to upper-middle-class shoppers. What is there about the store that makes you feel that it attracts this particular social class? How does this store differ from other stores that cater to lower-social-class shoppers?
6. If you were invited to a family's home for the first time, what factors might you consider in making an estimate of their social-class standing? Explain.
7. Assume that you are a marketing consultant for a small savings bank. What advice would you give the management of the bank about the use of social class as a variable for segmenting its market?
8. If you were asked by a local consumer protection agency to provide them with guidelines on how lower- and middle-class consumers differ in terms of consumer protection needs, what advice would you give them?

endnotes

1. Robert W. Hodges, Paul M. Siegel, and Peter H. Rossi, "Occupational Prestige in the United States, 1925–1963," *American Journal of Sociology* 70 (November 1964), 286–302.
2. David Popenoe, *Sociology*, 2nd ed. (Englewood Cliffs, N.J.: Prentice-Hall, 1974), 251–58.
3. Burleigh B. Gardner, "Social Status and Consumer Behavior," in Lincoln H. Clark, ed., *The Life Cycle and Consumer Behavior* (New York: New York University Press, 1955), 58.
4. Marcus Felson, "A Modern Sociological Approach to the Stratification of Material Life Styles," in Mary Jane Schlinger, ed., *Advances in Consumer Research* (Association for Consumer Research, 1975), II, 34.
5. Richard Centers, *The Psychology of Social Class* (New York: Russell and Russell, 1961), 233.
6. Ibid., 27.
7. Hadley Cantril, "Identification with Social and Economic Class," *Journal of Abnormal and Social Psychology*, 38 (January 1943), 75–79.
8. W. Lloyd Warner, Marchia Meeker, and Kenneth Eells, *Social Class in America: Manual of Procedure for the Measurement of Social Status* (New York: Harper & Brothers, 1960).

9. Hodges, Siegel, and Rossi, "Occupational Prestige."

10. Albert J. Reiss, Jr., Otis Dudley Duncan, Paul K. Hatt, and Cecil C. North, *Occupational and Social Status* (New York: Free Press, 1961).

11. Felson, "Modern Sociological Approach," 34.

12. Stephen J. Miller, "Source of Income as a Market Descriptor," *Journal of Marketing Research,* 15 (February 1978), 129–31.

13. Chester R. Wasson, "Is It Time to Quit Thinking of Income Classes?" *Journal of Marketing,* 33 (April 1969), 54–57.

14. F. Stuart Chapin, *Contemporary American Institutions* (New York: Harper, 1935), 373–97.

15. William H. Peters, "Who Cooperates in Voluntary Recycling Efforts?" in Thomas V. Greer, ed., *1973 Combined Proceedings* (Chicago: American Marketing Association, 1974), 505–8.

16. Warner, Meeker, and Eells, *Social Class in America.*

17. *Methodology and Scores of Socioeconomic Status,* Working Paper No. 15 (Washington, D.C.: U.S. Bureau of the Census, 1963).

18. Richard B. Ellis, "Composite Population Descriptors: The Socio-Economic/Life Cycle Grid," in Schlinger, *Advances in Consumer Research, II,* 481–93.

19. Marvin M. Gropp, *Magazine Newsletter of Research* (New York: Magazine Publishers Association, December 1980).

20. A. Marvin Roscoe, Jr., and Jagdish H. Sheth, "Demographic Segmentation of Long Distance Behavior: Data Analysis and Inductive Model Building," in M. Venkatesan, ed., *Third Annual Conference of the Association for Consumer Research,* 1972, 258–78.

21. Alvin B. Coleman, "Class Structure: A Comparison of Lower-Working and Upper-Middle Family Characteristics," *Clearing House,* 42 (April 1968), 470.

22. Marie R. Haug, "Social Class Measurement and Women's Occupational Roles," *Social Forces,* 52 (September 1973), 92.

23. Richard P. Coleman and Bernice L. Neugarten, *Social Status in the City* (San Francisco: Jossey Bass, 1971), ix.

24. See Arun K. Jain, "A Method for Investigating and Representing Implicit Social Class Theory," *Journal of Consumer Research,* 2 (June 1975), 53–59; Peter H. Rossi, William A. Sampson, Christine E. Bose, Guillermina Jasso, and Jeff Passel, "Measuring Household Social Standing," *Social Science Research,* 3 (1974), 169–90; and Terence A. Shimp and J. Thomas Yokum, "Extensions of the Basic Social Class Model Employed in Consumer Behavior," in Kent Monroe, ed., *Advances in Consumer Research* (Ann Arbor, Mich.: Association for Consumer Research, 1981), VIII, 702–07.

25. James H. Myers, Roger R. Stanton, and Arne F. Haug, "Correlates of Buying Behavior: Social Class vs. Income," *Journal of Marketing,* 35 (October 1971), 8–15.

26. James H. Myers and John F. Mount, "More on Social Class vs. Income as Correlates of Buying Behavior," *Journal of Marketing,* 37 (April 1973), 71–73.

27. Robert D. Hisrich and Michael P. Peters, "Selecting the Superior Segmentation Correlate," *Journal of Marketing,* 38 (July 1974), 60–63.

28. James H. Myers and Jonathan Gutman, "Life Style: The Essence of Social Class," in William D. Wells, ed., *Life Style and Psychographics* (Chicago: American Marketing Association, 1974), 235–56.

29. J. Michael Munson and V. Austin Spivey, "Product and Brand User Stereotypes among Social Classes," in Monroe, *Advances in Consumer Research,* VIII, 696–701.

30. Richard P. Coleman "The Significance of Social Stratification in Selling," in Martin L. Bell, ed., *Marketing: A Mature Discipline* (Chicago: American Marketing Association, 1961), 171–84.

31. William H. Peters, "Relative Occupational Class Income: A Significant Variable in the Marketing of Automobiles," *Journal of Marketing,* 34 (April 1970), 74–77.

32. R. Eugene Klippel and John F. Monoky, Jr., "A Potential Segmentation Variable for Marketers: Relative Occupation Class Income," *Journal of the Academy of Marketing Science*, 2 (Spring 1974), 351–56.

33. The social-class profiles in this section are drawn from a variety of sources, including Coleman and Neugarten, *Social Status;* and Harold M. Hodges, Jr.,"Peninsula People: Social Stratification in a Metropolitan Complex," in Clayton Lane, ed., *Permanence and Change* (Cambridge, Mass.: Schenkman, 1969), 5–36.

34. Saxon Graham, "Class and Conservatism in the Adoption of Innovations," *Human Relations*, 9 (February 1956), 91–100.

35. *A Study of Working-Class Women in a Changing World* (prepared for Macfadden-Bartell Corporation by Social Science Research, Inc., May 1973).

36. Epictetus, *Discourses* (2nd cent.), 31, trans. Thomas Higginson.

37. Stuart U. Rich and Subhash C. Jain, "Social Class and Life Cycle as Predictors of Shopping Behavior," *Journal of Marketing Research*, 5 (February 1968), 43–44.

38. *Study of Working-Class Women*, 154–55.

39. Ibid.

40. William D. Wells, "Seven Questions about Life Style and Psychographics," in Boris W. Bunker and Helmut Becker, eds., *1972 Combined Proceedings* (Chicago: American Marketing Association, 1973), 464.

41. Thomas E. Lasswell, *Class and Stratum* (Boston: Houghton Mifflin, 1965), 231.

42. Gardner, "Social Status," 60.

43. Edward O. Laumann and James S. House, "Living Room Styles and Social Attributes: The Patterning of Material Artifacts in a Modern Urban Community," *Sociology and Social Research*, 54 (April 1970), 324–27.

44. Ibid.

45. A. Marvin Roscoe, Jr., Arthur LeClaire, Jr., and Leon G. Schiffman, "Theory and Management Applications of Demographics in Buyer Behavior," in Arch G. Woodside, Jagdish N. Sheth, and Peter D. Bennett, eds., *Foundations of Consumer and Industrial Buying Behavior* (New York: American Elsevier, 1977), 67–76.

46. William R. Cotton, Jr., "Leisure and Social Stratification," in Gerald W. Thielbar and Saul D. Feldman, eds., *Issues in Social Inequality* (Boston: Little, Brown, 1972), 520–38.

47. Alfred C. Clarke, "Leisure and Occupational Prestige," *American Sociological Review*, 21 (June 1956), 305–6; and Robert B. Settle, Pamela L. Alreck, and Michael A. Belch, "Social Class Determinants of Leisure Activity," in William L. Wilkie, ed., *Advances in Consumer Research* (Ann Arbor, Mich.: Association for Consumer Research, 1979), VI, 139–45.

48. *The Playboy Report on American Men* (Survey Conducted for Playboy Enterprises, 1979).

49. Joseph T. Plummer, "Life Style and Case Studies," in Fred C. Allvine, ed., *1971 Combined Proceedings* (Chicago: American Marketing Association, 1972), 292.

50. Pierre Martineau, "Social Classes and Shopping Behavior," *Journal of Marketing*, 23 (October 1958), 128.

51. *Study of Working-Class Women*, 151.

52. H. Lee Mathews and John W. Slocum, Jr., "Social Class and Commercial Bank Credit Usage," *Journal of Marketing*, 33 (January 1969), 71–78.

53. Leonard Schatzman and Anselm Strauss, "Social Class and Modes of Communication," *American Journal of Sociology*, 60 (January 1955), 329–38.

54. Ibid., 337.

55. John Kenneth Morland, *Millways of Kent* (Chapel Hill: University of North Carolina Press, 1958), 192, 277.

56. Lasswell, *Class and Stratum*, 223–24.

57. Ibid., 221–22.

58. Leah Rozen, "Coveted Consumers Rate Magazines over TV: MPA," *Advertising Age*, August 20, 1979, 64.

59. Sidney J. Levy, "Social Class and Consumer Behavior," in Jospeh W. Newman, ed., *On Knowing the Consumer* (New York: John Wiley, 1966), 155.

60. Rich and Jain, "Social Class," 44.

61. Ibid., 45–46.

62. Ibid., 46.

63. V. Kanti Prasad, "Socioeconomic Product Risk and Patronage Preferences of Retail Shoppers," *Journal of Marketing*, 39 (July 1975), 42–47.

64. Peter L. Gillett, "A Profile of Urban In-Home Shoppers," *Journal of Marketing*, 34 (July 1970), 40–45.

65. Steven L. Diamond, Scott Ward, and Ronald Faber, "Consumer Problems and Consumerism: Analysis of Calls to a Consumer Hot Line," *Journal of Marketing*, 40 (January 1976), 58–62.

FOURTEEN

The Influence of Culture
on Consumer Behavior

introduction

THE study of culture is a challenging undertaking because its primary focus is on the broadest component of social behavior—an entire society. Thus, in contrast to the psychologist, who is principally concerned with the study of individual behavior, or the sociologist, who is concerned with the study of groups, the anthropologist is primarily interested in identifying the very fabric of society itself.

This chapter explores the basic concepts of culture, with particular emphasis on the role culture plays in influencing consumer behavior in the American society. We will first consider the specific dimensions of culture that make it such a powerful force in regulating human behavior. Then we will review several measurement approaches that researchers employ in their efforts to understand the impact of culture on consumption behavior. Finally, we will show how a variety of core American cultural values influence consumer behavior.

This chapter is concerned with the more general aspects of culture; the following chapter focuses on subcultures and on foreign cultures and will show how marketers can use such knowledge to shape and modify their marketing strategies.

WHAT IS CULTURE?

Given the broad and pervasive nature of culture, its study generally requires a global examination of the character of the total society, including such factors as its language, knowledge, laws, religion, food customs, music, art, technology, work patterns, products, and other artifacts which give the society its distinctive flavor. In a sense, culture is a society's "personality." For this reason, it is not easy to define its boundaries.

> *Culture is not an exotic notion studied by a select group of anthropologists in the South Seas. It is a mold in which we are all cast, and it controls our daily lives in many unsuspected ways.*
>
> EDWARD T. HALL
> The Silent Language (1959)

Since our specific objective is to understand the influence of culture on consumer behavior, we will define *culture* as the *sum total of learned beliefs, values, and customs which serve to regulate the consumer behavior of members of a particular society.*

The *belief* and *value* components of our definition refer to the accumulated feelings and priorities that individuals have about "things." More precisely, *beliefs* consist of the very large number of mental or verbal statements (i.e., "I believe that...") that reflect a person's particular knowledge and assessment of *something* (another person, a store, perhaps a product, a brand). *Values* are also beliefs. However, values differ from other beliefs in that they meet the following criteria: (1) they are relatively few in number; (2) they serve as a guide for "culturally appropriate" behavior; (3) they are enduring or difficult to change; and (4) they are widely accepted by the members of a society.[1]

Therefore, in a broad sense, both beliefs and values are "mental images" that affect a wide range of specific attitudes, which in turn influence the way a person is likely to respond in a specific situation. For example, the criteria that a person employs in evaluating alternative brands and his or her eventual conclusion concerning these brands are influenced by that person's beliefs and values.

Figure 14-1 presents a simple conceptualization of a consumer value system that consists of three interrelated belief components: (1) a *very* small number of global values that guide behavior across a wide range of situations; (2) a small number of domain-specific values that people acquire as part of their experience in specific situations (e.g., aspects of economic, social, and religious life); and (3) a large number of evaluative beliefs held about product categories

FIGURE 14-1   A Model of Consumers' Value-Belief Systems   Source: Donald E. Vinson, Jerome E. Scott, and Lawrence M. Lamont, "The Role of Personal Values in Marketing and Consumer Behavior," *Journal of Marketing,* 41 (April 1977), 46.

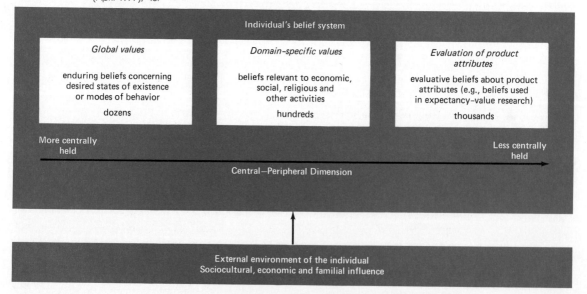

and brands that are important components of consumer attitudes. The figure also indicates that a consumer's belief system is produced and altered through exposure to the external environment.[2]

In comparison with beliefs and values, *customs* are overt modes of behavior that constitute culturally approved or acceptable ways of behaving in specific situations. Customs have been called "...behavior at its most commonplace."[3] For example, a consumer's routine behavior, such as shopping for food on Saturday or serving cream with coffee, involves customs. Thus, while beliefs and values are *guides* for behavior, customs are *usual* and *acceptable ways of behaving*.

Within the context of our definition, it is easy to see how an understanding of the beliefs, values, and customs of a society will enable marketers to accurately anticipate consumer acceptance of their products.

CHARACTERISTICS OF CULTURE

To more fully comprehend the scope and complexity of culture, we will now examine a number of its underlying characteristics.

The Invisible Hand of Culture

The impact of culture is so natural and so automatic that its influence on behavior is usually taken for granted. For example, when consumer researchers ask people why they do certain things, they frequently answer, "Because it's the right thing to do." This seemingly superficial response partially reflects the ingrained influence of culture on our behavior. Frequently, it is only when we are exposed to people with different cultural values or customs (e.g., when visiting a different region or a different country) that we become aware of how culture has molded our own behavior. The following statement dramatically illustrates the invisible nature of culture and the difficulties of objectively studying its impact on human behavior:

> It has been said that the last thing which a dweller in the deep sea would be likely to discover would be water. He would become conscious of its existence only if some accident brought him to the surface and introduced him to air. Man, throughout most of his history, has been only vaguely conscious of the existence of culture and has owed even this consciousness to contrasts between the customs of his own society and those of some other with which he happened to be brought into contact.[4]

Thus a true appreciation of the influence that culture has on our daily life requires some knowledge of at least one other society with different cultural characteristics. For example, to understand that brushing our teeth twice a day with flavored toothpaste is a cultural phenomenon requires some awareness that members of another society either do not brush their teeth at all or do so in a manner distinctly different from our own.

Culture Satisfies Needs

Culture exists to satisfy the needs of the people within a society. It offers order, direction, and guidance in all phases of human problem solving by providing "tried and true" methods of satisfying physiological, personal, and social needs. For example, culture provides standards and "rules" regarding when to eat and what is appropriate to eat for breakfast, lunch, dinner, and snacks, and what to serve to guests at a dinner party, a picnic, or a wedding.

Cultural beliefs, values, and customs continue to be followed so long as they yield satisfaction. However, when a specific standard no longer fully satisfies the members of a society, it is modified or replaced, so that the resulting standard is more in line with the current needs and desires of the society. Thus culture gradually but continually evolves to meet the needs of society.

Within a cultural context, a firm's products and services can be viewed as offering appropriate or acceptable solutions for individual or social needs. If a product is no longer acceptable because a value or custom related to its use does not adequately satisfy human needs, then the firm producing it must be ready to adjust or revise its product offerings. For example, as Americans have become more informal and relaxed in their style of living, there has been a strong movement away from formal dress customs. Astute clothing manufacturers responded by offering more casual clothing and thus were able to maintain or even improve their market position. Marketers who were not perceptive enough to note these changing lifestyles were likely to find themselves squeezed out of the market.

Culture Is Learned

Unlike our biological characteristics (e.g., sex, skin, hair color, and innate intelligence), we are not born "knowing" our culture. At an early age, however, we begin to acquire from our social environment a set of beliefs, values, and customs which constitute our culture. Culture is thus *learned* as part of social experience.

HOW IS CULTURE LEARNED?

In answering this question, anthropologists have identified three distinct types of cultural learning: (1) *formal learning,* in which adults and older siblings teach a young family member "how to behave"; (2) *informal learning,* in which a child learns primarily by imitating the behavior of selected others (family, friends, TV heroes); and (3) *technical learning,* in which teachers instruct the child in an educational environment as to *what* should be done, *how* it should be done, and *why* it should be done.[5]

A little girl who is told by her mother to stop climbing trees because "little girls don't do that" is *formally* learning a value that her mother feels is right. In contrast, if she "dresses up" by copying her mother or older sister, she is *informally* learning certain dress habits (see Figure 14-2). Finally, if she is given ballet lessons, she is experiencing *technical* learning.

Although a firm's advertising can influence all three types of cultural

FIGURE 14-2   Advertisement That Reinforces Informal Cultural Learning

Courtesy of Mainstream Bathing Suits

learning, it is likely that many product advertisements enhance *informal* cultural learning by providing the audience with a model of behavior to imitate. With a unique twist, Figure 14-3 provides another illustration of how informal learning can be utilized as part of a firm's marketing efforts. Employing a *reversal* of the popular expression "Like father, like son," Johnson and Johnson is attempting to communicate that if you judge a product good for your child, it may also be good for you—an adult. Increasing adult usage of the product offers one road to increasing sales and is an especially appropriate marketing strategy because of the decline in the annual birthrate in the United States.

The repetition of advertising messages also creates or reinforces cultural beliefs and values. For example, many advertisers continually stress the same

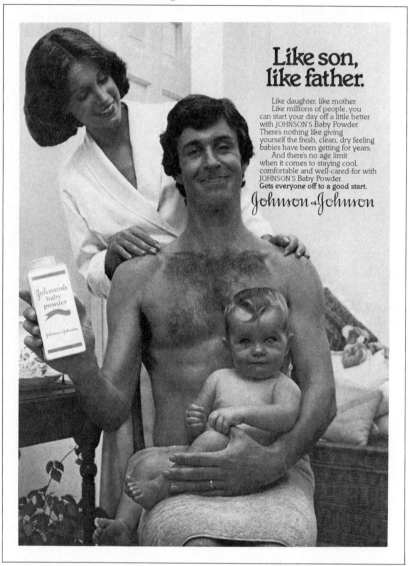

Courtesy of Johnson & Johnson Baby Products Co.

selected benefits as integral features of their products or brands. To illustrate,
ads for toothpaste often stress one or more of the following benefits: prevents
cavities, whitens teeth, makes the mouth feel better or taste fresher. After
decades of cumulative exposure to such potent advertising appeals, it is difficult
to say with any degree of certainty whether people *inherently* desire these benefits
from toothpaste or whether they have been *taught* by marketers to desire them.
In a sense, while specific product advertising may reinforce the benefits that
consumers want from the product (as determined by consumer behavior

research), such advertising also "teaches" future generations of consumers to expect the same benefits from the specific product category.

ENCULTURATION AND ACCULTURATION

In discussing the acquisition of culture, anthropologists often distinguish between the learning of one's own or "native" culture and the learning of some other culture. The learning of one's own culture is known as *enculturation*. In contrast, the learning of a new or foreign culture is known as *acculturation*. In the next chapter we will see that acculturation is an important concept for marketers who plan to sell their products to consumers with distinctly different cultures in foreign or multinational markets. In such cases, marketers must study the specific cultures of their potential target market in order to determine whether their products will be acceptable to its members, and how they can best communicate the characteristics of their products to persuade the target market to buy.

LANGUAGE AND SYMBOLS

To acquire a common culture, the members of a society must be able to communicate with each other through a common language. Without a common language, shared meaning could not exist and true communication would not take place (see Chapter 10).

To communicate effectively with their audiences, marketers must use appropriate symbols to convey desired product images or characteristics. These symbols can be *verbal* or *nonverbal*. Verbal symbols may include a television announcement or an advertisement in a magazine. Nonverbal communication includes the use of such symbols as figures, colors, shapes, and even textures to provide additional meaning to print or broadcast advertisements, to trademarks, and to packaging or product designs.

Basically, it is the symbolic nature of human language that sets it apart from all other animal communication. A *symbol* is anything that stands for something else.[6] Any word is a symbol. The word *table* calls forth a specific image related to an individual's own knowledge and experience. The word *fire* not only calls forth the notion of burning but also has the power to stir us emotionally, arousing feelings of warmth, danger, and fascination. Similarly, the word *Cadillac* has symbolic meaning—to some it suggests a fine luxury automobile, to others it implies wealth and status, to still others it may suggest a brand of dog food.

Because the human mind can process symbols, it is possible for a person to read an advertisement for a product such as a typewriter with a correction key (see Figure 14-4) and understand its purpose and how it works, even though he or she has never before used a typewriter with such a feature. The capacity to learn symbolically is primarily a human phenomenon; most other animals learn by direct experience. Clearly, the ability of humans to understand symbolically how a product or an idea may satisfy their needs makes it easier for marketers to sell the features and benefits of their products.

FIGURE 14-4   Advertisement Incorporating Symbolic Learning

It's called the correction key. And it's possibly the most important key on the keyboard. Because it fixes the mistakes all the other keys can make. And only one typewriter has it. The electric Sears Corrector.

It works like magic.

When a mistake pops up, just backspace, then press the correction key. As soon as you do, your mistake is gone. Then without backspacing, hit the key you want. Quick as that, you're on your way again. Your fingers never leave the keyboard.

There's more to the Corrector than a correction key.

As a matter of fact, there's a lot more. The Corrector has a 13½-in. carriage to handle charts and envelopes. An easy-to-change cassette ribbon. A tab key to set columns. A paper injector. A check protector. Your choice of pica or elite type. A full power keyboard that lets you type at full speed ahead. And Sears durability and reliability come as standard equipment.

Don't make a mistake.

Before you buy any typewriter, test the Corrector. You'll find it, along with all the others in our line, at most larger Sears retail stores. The Corrector is Sears Best. The one with a key difference.

Sears

Where America shops for Value

When you touch this key, mistakes disappear right before your eyes.

Courtesy of Sears, Roebuck and Co.

Inasmuch as a symbol may have several meanings, even contradictory ones, it is important that the advertiser ascertain exactly what the symbols are communicating to an intended audience. For example, the advertiser who uses a trademark depicting an old craftsman to symbolize careful workmanship may instead be communicating an image of old age, outmoded methods, and lack of style. The marketer who uses slang in an advertisement to attract a teenage audience must do so with great care. Slang that is misused or outdated will symbolically outdate the marketer's firm and product.

Price and channels of distribution are also significant symbols of the marketer and the marketer's product. For example, price often implies quality to potential buyers (see Chapter 6). For certain products, the type of store in which the product is sold is also an important symbol of quality. Thus all of the elements of the marketing mix—the product, its promotion, its price, and the stores at which it is available—are symbols that communicate ranges of quality to potential buyers.[7]

Culture Is Shared

To be considered a characteristic of a culture, a particular belief, value, or practice should not be the sole province of a few individuals; rather, it must be shared by a significant portion of the society. Accordingly, culture is frequently viewed as group customs that link together the members of a society.[8] And, of course, common language is the critical component of a culture which makes it possible for people to share values, experiences, and customs.

Various social institutions within a society transmit the elements of culture and make the sharing of culture a reality. Chief among such institutions is the family, which serves as the primary agent for enculturation—the passing along of basic cultural beliefs, values, and customs to society's newest members. A vital part of the enculturation role of the family is the consumer socialization of the young (see Chapter 12). This includes the teaching of such basic consumer-related values and skills as the meaning of money, the relationship between price and quality, the establishment of product tastes, preferences, and habits, and appropriate methods of response to various promotional messages.

In addition to the family, two other institutions traditionally share much of the responsibility for the transfer of selected aspects of culture—the school and the church. Educational institutions are specifically charged with imparting basic learning skills, history, patriotism, citizenship, and the technical training needed to prepare people for significant roles within society. Religious institutions provide and perpetuate religious consciousness, spiritual guidance, and moral training. Although it is in the family environment that the young receive much of their consumer training, the educational and religious systems reinforce such training through the teaching of economic and ethical concepts.

A fourth, frequently overlooked, social institution that plays a major role in the transfer of culture throughout society is the mass media. Given the extensive exposure of the American population to both print and broadcast media, and the easily ingested, entertaining format in which the contents of such media are usually presented, it is not surprising that the mass media are a powerful vehicle for imparting a wide range of cultural values.

Advertising is an important component of most mass media to which we are exposed daily. It not only underwrites or makes economically feasible the editorial or programming contents of the media but also transmits much about our culture. Without advertising, it would be almost impossible to disseminate information about products, ideas, and causes. A leading historian noted: "...advertising now compares with such long-standing institutions as the schools and the church in the magnitude of its social influence."[9]

Thus, while the scope of advertising is often considered to be limited to stimulating or altering the demand for specific products or services, in a cultural context advertising has the expanded mission of reinforcing established cultural values and aiding in the spread of new tastes, habits, and customs. In planning their advertising, marketers should therefore recognize that advertising is an important agent of social change in our society.

Culture Is Dynamic

In our discussion of the need-gratifying role of culture, we have noted that culture must change if it is to continue to function in the best interests of a society. We have also suggested that to effectively market an existing product, or develop promising new products, the marketer must carefully monitor the social-cultural environment.

This is not an easy task, since many factors are likely to produce cultural changes within a given society (new technology, population shifts, availability of scarce resources, wars, changing values, customs borrowed from other cultures). For example, a major cultural change in our society is the expanded role choices of American females. A number of factors have been cited in connection with this change, including increased educational opportunities, the availability of labor-saving devices which make homemaking less restrictive, the increased number of women in the labor force, the availability of new birth-control techniques, the efforts of female activist groups, and the enactment and enforcement of equal employment laws. Just which of these factors are basic forces in the shifting role of women in American society, and which are outgrowths that have their own impact on other areas of life, is difficult to say.

However, it is clear that the role choices of American women have definitely changed. More women are working outside the home, often in careers that once were considered exclusively male, and more women are active in social and athletic activities outside of the home. All this adds up to an increased blurring of traditional male-female sex roles. These changes mean that marketers must reconsider *who* are the purchasers and the users of their products (males only, females only, or both), *when* they do their shopping, *how* and *where* they can be reached by the media, and *what* new-product and service needs have been created.

Marketers who monitor cultural changes often find new opportunities to increase corporate profitability. For example, Yamaha was innovative when it first targeted its motorcycles to young women (see Figure 14-5). Not too long ago such a product and such an advertising approach would have been inappropriate, but today such a product is within the scope of female interests.

Marketers of life insurance, leisure wear, electric trains, and small cigars, among others, have attempted to take advantage of the dramatically shifting definition of what is "feminine." This sex-role shift has also had its impact on traditional male roles. For instance, today toy manufacturers are successfully marketing dolls to parents of little boys (Action Joe, Bionic Man).

Other aspects of the changing roles of women and their effect on consumer behavior patterns will be discussed in the next chapter as part of our examination of subculture.

Courtesy of Yamaha International Corp.

A wide range of measurement techniques have been employed to study culture. Some of these techniques have already been described in earlier chapters. For example, the projective tests used by psychologists to study motivation and personality (discussed in Chapters 3 and 4), and the attitude measurement techniques used by social psychologists and sociologists (Chapter 8), are relatively popular tools in the study of culture.

In addition, observational fieldwork, content analysis, and value measurement instruments are three data collection techniques that are frequently associated with the examination of culture. We will briefly discuss each of these techniques.

Observational Fieldwork

In studying a specific society, anthropologists frequently immerse themselves in the environment they wish to explore. As trained observers, they often select a small sample of people from a particular society and observe their behavior. Based upon their observations, they draw conclusions about the values, beliefs, and customs of the society under investigation.

To illustrate, if researchers were interested in how people shop for and select detergents, they might position trained observers in the detergent section of supermarkets and note the specific types of detergents selected (cold water versus hot water, liquid versus powdered) and the size and price of specific brands selected. The researchers might also be interested in the degree of indecision that accompanies the choice; that is, how frequently shoppers tend to hesitate (e.g., take packages off the shelf; read the labels, place them back again) before selecting the brand they purchase.

The distinct characteristics of field observation are: (1) it is performed within a natural environment, (2) it is sometimes performed without the subjects' awareness, and (3) it focuses only on observation of behavior. Thus, since the emphasis is on a natural environment and observable behavior, field observation concerned with consumer behavior is usually limited to in-store behavior, and only rarely to in-home preparation and consumption.

In some cases, instead of just observing behavior, researchers become *participant-observers*. Such researchers actually become an active member of the environment they are studying. For example, if a researcher were interested in examining how men select a new shirt, the researcher might take a sales position in a men's clothing store in order to observe directly and even interact with customers in the transaction process.

Both field observation and participant-observer research require highly skilled researchers who can separate out their own emotions from what they actually observe in their roles as researchers. Such techniques, however, can provide valuable insights which might not easily be obtained through survey research that simply asks consumers to answer questions about their behavior.

Content Analysis

Conclusions about a society, or some specific aspect of a society, can sometimes be drawn from an examination of the content of its messages. The *content analysis* approach, as its name implies, focuses on the content of verbal and pictorial communication (e.g., the copy and art components of an ad).[10]

Content analysis can be used as an objective means of determining whether social and cultural changes have occurred within a specific society. For instance, in the next chapter we discuss the results of several content analysis studies that were designed to determine how the roles of blacks and females, as depicted in magazine ads, have changed with the passage of time. Content analysis is equally useful to marketers and to public policy makers who are interested in comparing the advertising claims of competitors and other firms within a specific industry.

Value Measurement Survey Instruments

Anthropologists have traditionally observed the behavior of members of a specific society and *inferred* from such behavior the dominant or underlying values of the society. In recent years, however, there has been a gradual shift to measuring values *directly* by means of survey (or questionnaire) research. Researchers use data collection instruments called "value instruments" to ask people how they feel about such basic personal and social concepts as freedom, comfort, national security, and peace.

Research involving the relationship between people's values and their actions as consumers is still in its infancy. However, it is an area that is destined to receive increased attention, for it taps a broad dimension of human behavior that could not be effectively explored before the availability of standardized value instruments.

A promising instrument that has been employed in several consumer behavior studies is the Rokeach Value Survey.[11] This self-administered value inventory is divided into two parts, with each part measuring different, but complementary, types of personal values (see Table 14-1). The first part consists of eighteen "terminal" value items, which are designed to measure the relative importance of "end-states of existence" (i.e., personal goals). The second part consists of eighteen "instrumental" value items, which measure basic approaches an individual might follow to reach end-state values. Thus the first half of the measurement instrument deals with "ends," while the second half considers "means."

One of the first consumer studies to employ the Rokeach Value Survey examined the relationship between the thirty-six values and subjects' evaluations of automobile attributes (style, amount of service required, amount of pollution produced, economy of operation, and quality of warranty).[12] The findings revealed that specific values were associated with specific automobile attributes. For instance, the attribute *style* was found to be related to such terminal values as "a comfortable life," "an exciting life," and "pleasure." The attribute *amount of pollution produced* was found to be related to the terminal value "a world at peace" and the instrumental values "helpful" and "loving."

TABLE 14-1   The Rokeach Value Survey Instrument

TERMINAL VALUES	INSTRUMENTAL VALUES
A comfortable life (a prosperous life)	Ambitious (hard-working, aspiring)
An exciting life (a stimulating, active life)	Broadminded (open-minded)
A world at peace (free of war and conflict)	Capable (competent, effective)
Equality (brotherhood, equal opportunity for all)	Cheerful (lighthearted, joyful)
Freedom (independence, free choice)	Clean (neat, tidy)
Happiness (contentedness)	Courageous (standing up for your belief)
National security (protection from attack)	Forgiving (willing to pardon others)
Pleasure (an enjoyable life)	Helpful (working for the welfare of others)
Salvation (saved, eternal life)	Honest (sincere, truthful)
Social recognition (respect, admiration)	Imaginative (daring, creative)
True friendship (close companionship)	Independent (self-reliant, self-sufficient)
Wisdom (a mature understanding of life)	Intellectual (intelligent, reflective)
A world of beauty (beauty of nature and the arts)	Logical (consistent, rational)
Family security (taking care of loved ones)	Loving (affectionate, tender)
Mature love (sexual and spiritual intimacy)	Obedient (dutiful, respectful)
Self-respect (self-esteem)	Polite (courteous, well-mannered)
A sense of accomplishment (lasting contribution)	Responsible (dependable, reliable)
Inner harmony (freedom from inner conflict)	Self-controlled (restrained, self-disciplined)

Source: Milton Rokeach, *The Nature of Human Values* (New York: Free Press, 1973), 28.

In another study of automobile attributes, the values of college students and their parents were compared by means of the Rokeach Value Survey.[13] Not surprisingly, the results revealed that students and parents had different instrumental and terminal values concerning automobiles.

Specifically, the study found that students evaluated "an exciting life" and "pleasure" as particularly important values; whereas their parents gave higher ratings to values that reflected standards of social and individual responsibility—"national security," "a world of beauty," and "obedience." In terms of automobile attributes, students considered styling and speed to be important attributes and preferred compact cars; their parents rated such features as comfort, handling, service, and warranty as most important and preferred standard-sized cars.

Finally, another study that contrasts two groups of subjects in terms of their global values (as measured by the Rokeach Value Survey), various consumer beliefs and preferences, and social issues also found a logical pattern of results.[14] Specifically, Group I subjects drawn from students attending a university in a western state (which was characterized as "liberal") were compared with Group II subjects drawn from students attending a southern university (which was labeled "traditional"). As the consumer researchers had anticipated, and as the summary of results in Table 14-2 reveals, the distinctly different orientations of the two universities were reflected in the values, opinions, and preferences of their students: That is, Group I's responses seem to fit a more liberal or less traditional mold than those of Group II.

TABLE 14-2 Summary of Significant Differences between Groups Characterized as "Liberal" and "Traditional"

group I subjects (liberals)

GLOBAL VALUES	DOMAIN-SPECIFIC VALUES	AUTOMOBILE ATTRIBUTES	CONSUMER PRODUCTS	SOCIAL ISSUES
Exciting life	Durable products	Operate on unleaded gas	Compact cars	Air pollution
Equality	Non-polluting products	High speed capabilities	Outdoor recreation	Freedom of press
Self-respect	Health promoting products	Handling		Control of housing discrimination
Forgiving	Products easy to repair	Quality workmanship		
Intellectual	Quiet products	Advanced engineering		
Logical	Help eliminate environmental pollution	Low level pollution emission		

group II subjects (traditionals)

National security	Prompt service on complaints	Smooth riding	Standard-sized cars	Crime control
Salvation		Luxurious interior	Stylish attractive clothing	The drug problem
Polite		Prestige	Television	
Social recognition		Large size		
		Spacious interior		

Source: Donald E. Vison, Jerome E. Scott, and Lawrence M. Lamont, "The Role of Personal Values in Marketing and Consumer Behavior," *Journal of Marketing*, 41 (April 1977), 48.

The results of these and other studies suggest that the Rokeach Value Survey can be used by marketers to segment their markets by specific values and perceptions of specific product attributes.[15] Such information would be useful in developing new products for specific market segments.

SOCIAL-TREND TRACKING SERVICES

A related event in the application of value measurement to consumer behavior has been the appearance of a number of research services that feature the measurement of values, the tracking of social trends, and the identification of distinct consumer-value segments that reflect the various value-orientations of the American population. Two such research services merit our attention—the Yankelovich Monitor (conducted by Yankelovich, Skelly, and White) and the SRI Values and Lifestyles (VALS) Program (offered by SRI International). Both of these services have been successful in attracting the financial sponsorship of leading consumer goods marketers and their advertising agencies. Since these services are sold (subscribers generally pay in excess of $15,000 per year), and the results are therefore proprietary in nature, we can only highlight some of the

TABLE 14-3   A Sample of Social Trends Examined by the Yankelovich Monitor Service

Trend No. 1, Personalization

Monitor's measurement of the size of the group committed to Personalization comprises a series of scaled items including: (1) the emphasis placed on buying "products that reveal their style and personality"; (2) the need to add "one's own personal touch" to products; (3) the acceptance of nonconformity in appearance and life-style, even with some social and economic penalties; (4) the degree of desirability ascribed to being different from other people and showing it, rather than the value assigned to "fitting in."

Trend No. 10, New Romanticism

Monitor's measurement of the size of the group committed to New Romanticism is based on a series of scaled items including: (1) the recognition of a real need for "romance and mystery" in one's life; (2) the desire for "more excitement and sensation"; (3) the wish to "have lived in an age" when adventure and romantic concepts were in style.

Trend No. 14, Return to Nature

Monitor measures Return to Nature through a series of scaled items including: (1) the desire to live in a natural setting, i.e., in the country, as opposed to living in a city or its surrounding suburbs; (2) the perceived need to live in a way that is "closer to nature"; (3) the relative value to the individual of living in a "natural" way, as opposed to the benefits of widely available man-made modern conveniences.

Trend No. 33, Concern About Privacy

Monitor's measurement of Concern About Privacy is based on a series of scaled items including: (1) concern about maintaining one's right to privacy; (2) perceived violations of privacy by certain government agencies; (3) attitudes toward wiretapping under specified conditions; and (4) attitudes toward legislation designed to protect the consumer from perceived invasions of privacy by business.

Trend No. 44, Flirtation With Danger

Monitor's measurement of the size of the group committed to Flirtation With Danger consists of a series of scaled items covering: (1) the belief that the mastering of "dangerous" leisure activities can make one a better person; (2) interest in "dangerous" activities; (3) interest in taking potentially dangerous and/or illegal risks; (4) agreement that driving yourself to "the brink" is a path to better self-understanding.

Source: The Yankelovich Monitor, *Technical Description/Appendix* (New York: Yankelovich, Skelly and White, 1981), 50–58.

major features of these social-trend services from available and published sources.

The Yankelovich Monitor was first conducted in 1970 and has been updated annually since then. Its main purpose involves the tracking of over forty social trends (for examples see Table 14-3) and providing detailed information about the potential shifts in the size, direction, and implications of these trends to consumer marketing.[16]

By carefully interpreting the social trends and determining which demographic segments of the population are most affected by a particular group of trends, the Monitor service is capable of providing advanced insights as to the likely shift in demand for various product categories. For instance, researchers working with Monitor were able to forecast the shift away from "brown" whiskey (e.g., rye blends and Scotch) to "white" liquor (e.g., vodka and gin).[17] They based their prediction on the observation that young adults were seeking instant gratification (it takes time to develop a taste for Scotch), were concerned with health and fitness, were searching for novelty, and were generally less preoccupied with doing the "standard" or "correct" thing. All of this added up to the forecast that vodka and gin were going to become increasingly popular.

In contrast to Monitor, which does not stress any preconceived conceptual model of consumer segments, SRI's VALS features an explicit framework that is a composite of the models fostered by a number of leading behavioral theorists (e.g., Maslow, McClelland, Riesman, and Fromm).[18] The VALS model shown in Figure 14-6 consists of three major groups of consumers (which in turn are

FIGURE 14-6   **SRI's Values and Lifestyle Segments** Source: Thomas C. Thomas, "Values and Lifestyles—The New Psychographics?" (Paper presented at the Advertising Research Foundation Conference, New York, February 24, 1981), 6.

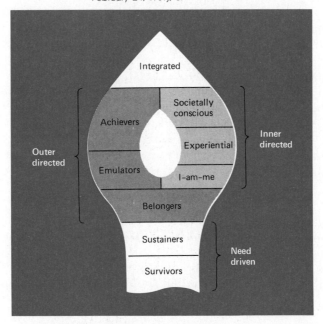

TABLE 14-4   A Profile of Selected Characteristics for the SRI VALS Consumer Segments

	MILLIONS OF ADULTS	MEDIAN AGE	MEDIAN HOUSE-HOLD INCOME	ETHNIC MINORITIES	ARE MORE EXPERIMENTAL THAN CONVENTIONAL	BELIEVE A WOMAN'S PLACE IS IN THE HOME
Survivors	6	66	Under $5,000	28%	15%	46%
Sustainers	11	32	$11,000	30	12	32
Belongers	57	51	$17,500	5	6	34
Emulators	16	28	$19,000	20	10	9
Achievers	37	42	$30,000	3	7	16
I-Am-Me	8	21	$10,000	8	29	7
Experiential	11	28	$22,000	5	33	5
Societally Conscious	14	37	$25,000	8	25	2

Source: Thomas C. Thomas, "Values and Lifestyles—The New Psychographics?" (Paper presented at the Advertising Research Foundation Conference, New York, February 24, 1981).

divided into nine specific segments). Table 14-4 summarizes a variety of published findings about the segments.

For many consumer goods marketers, tracking the shifts in the values and consumer behavior of one or more of the six segments that belong to the especially attractive inner- and other-directed groups is obviously important if they are to avoid misjudging their target market. As an example of how SRI's VALS Program has helped clients overcome problems in targeting their products and services, we can look at the experience that Merrill Lynch has had with its promotional campaign "Bullish on America."[19] The original "out-of-step" ads featured a herd of bulls. However, the symbolism of a "herd" was ultimately judged unsuitable for stimulating its target market—the *achievers*— who tend to view themselves as individualists. The solution was to drop the herd of bulls and to replace it with a single bull, and to change the promotional tag line to "A Breed Apart" (see Figure 14-7).

From these examples, it appears that standardized value and social-trend measurement instruments are a highly promising avenue for continued consumer behavior research, especially segmentation analysis. When combined with other behavioral variables examined in this book, values can be employed to predict shifts in consumption patterns. Such insights would be particularly useful in developing new-product concepts, repositioning existing products, and adjusting the firm's general marketing efforts.

AMERICAN CORE VALUES

What is the American culture? In this section we will try to identify a few core values that both affect and reflect the character of American society. This is a difficult undertaking for several reasons. First, the United States is a diverse

Where would a wise investor seek sound advice, attentive service, unbeatable information, and unmatched financial strength?

Merrill Lynch says, close to home.

Don't misunderstand. There's nothing wrong with searching far and wide for investment ideas. It's not easy to get rich these days.

But to search on your own is a full-time job-and-a-half. You have to read everything, digest it all, analyze the information, act on it...and do it fast, because opportunities become ancient history in precious little time.

Meanwhile, some of the best investment ideas are sitting practically on your doorstep, at a nearby office of Merrill Lynch.

We have the resources and the people to know, really *know*, investment opportunities as diverse as oil drilling partnerships and Treasury Bill futures, options and retirement plans.

Our research team is the best on Wall Street—in Wall Street's own opinion. And we make it easy to use that unrivaled resource: computer terminals at every Merrill Lynch office can instantly print out

A breed apart

up-to-the-minute opinions on more than 1200 stocks.

Best of all is the way we tailor our advice to your requirements. Before offering a single suggestion, your Merrill Lynch Account Executive will spend a long while listening. Finding out what you really need. Because the smartest investment plans—the plans most likely to succeed—start with a clear definition of where they want to go. Are you looking for security or the

opportunity to speculate? For current income or capital growth? What you tell us determines in large part what we tell you.

So we make a point of developing, for each customer, a sound long-term investment strategy, and we encourage you to stick with it and not be sidetracked by investment fads or temporary market aberrations. And we give you the security of knowing that we're going to stick with you and see you through to your goals. Merrill Lynch has more than $800 million in capital resources working for you, and we plan to be advising you long after all those fad investments have been written off.

So drop in at a nearby Merrill Lynch office and look over some of the brochures that explain our philosophy and way of doing things. Don't worry...we won't ask you to buy anything. In fact, we probably won't even let you, until we get to know you better.

Merrill Lynch

Courtesy of Merrill Lynch Pierce Fenner & Smith Inc.

country, consisting of a variety of subcultures (religious, ethnic, regional, racial, and economic groups), each of which interprets and responds to society's basic beliefs and values in its own specific way. Second, America is a dynamic society, one that has undergone almost constant change in response to its leadership role in the development of new technology. This element of rapid change makes it especially difficult to monitor changes in cultural values. Finally, the existence of contradictory values in American society is often somewhat confusing. For instance, Americans traditionally embrace freedom of choice and individualism, yet simultaneously they show great tendencies to conform (in dress, in furnishings, in fads, etc.) to the rest of society. In the context of consumer behavior, Americans like to have a wide choice of products and prefer those that uniquely express their personal lifestyles. Yet there is often a considerable amount of implicit pressure to conform to the values of family members, friends, or other socially important groups. It is difficult to reconcile such seemingly inconsistent values; however, their existence demonstrates that America is a complex society with numerous paradoxes and contradictions.[20]

In selecting the specific core values to be examined here, we were guided by three criteria:

1. The value must be pervasive. A significant portion of the American people must accept the value and employ it as a guide for their attitudes and actions.
2. The value must be enduring. The specific value must have influenced the actions of the American people over an extended period of time (as distinguished from a short-run "trend").
3. The value must be consumer related. The specific value must provide insights that help us understand the consumption actions of the American people.

Utilizing these criteria, we will now discuss a number of basic values that expert observers of the American scene consider the "building blocks" of that rather elusive concept we call the American Character.[21]

Achievement and Success

In our discussion of human needs and motives (Chapter 3), we pointed out that the need for achievement is often a propellant for individual behavior. In a broader cultural context, achievement is a central American value, with historical roots that can be traced to the traditional religious belief—the Protestant ethic—that hard work is wholesome, spiritually rewarding, and an appropriate end in itself. Indeed, substantial research evidence shows that the achievement orientation is closely associated with the technological development and general economic growth of the American society.[22]

Success is a closely related American cultural theme. However, achievement and success do differ. Specifically, achievement is its own direct reward (it is implicitly satisfying to the achiever), while success implies an extrinsic reward (such as financial or status improvements).

Both achievement and success influence consumption. They often serve as social and moral justification for the acquisition of goods and services. For example, "You owe it to yourself," "You worked for it," and "You deserve it" are popular achievement themes used by advertisers to coax consumers into purchasing their products. Figure 14-8 depicts an ad from an ongoing advertising campaign that stresses that its brand of Scotch is both a reward and a sign of success.

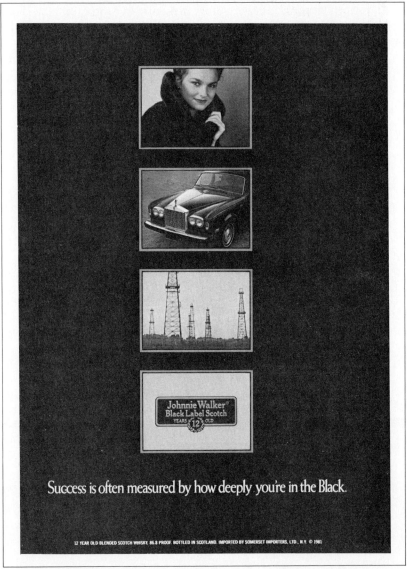

Courtesy of Somerset Importers, Ltd.

Activity

Americans attach an extraordinary amount of importance to being "active" or "involved." Keeping busy is widely accepted as a healthy and even necessary part of the American lifestyle. The hectic nature of American life is attested to by foreign visitors who frequently comment that they cannot understand why Americans are always "on the run" and seemingly are unable to relax.

In line with this popular perception of Americans, a national consumer behavior study asked consumers, "What would you do with an extra two hours in your day?"[23] Table 14-5 presents by rank and percentage the ten most frequently selected activities (including tied ranks) to which men and women would elect to devote the hypothetical additional time. While the findings indicate considerable male-female overlap in the ten activities selected, they also reveal that women include two activities in their top-ten list that are not included by men (i.e., spend time on "creative" activities and spend time shopping); whereas men uniquely included three activities in their top-ten list (i.e., home repairs, hunting and fishing, and work on their car).

Beyond these differences, it is interesting to look at the implications of how men and women differ in their two highest-ranked activities. Specifically, in promoting timesaving products to women, marketers might emphasize how their products would enable women to complete unfinished household tasks or give them more free time to read or study. In contrast, if marketers are interested in targeting their timesaving products to men, they might emphasize that these products would give them more free time to relax by themselves or more time to be with their families.

The premium placed on activity has had both a positive and a negative effect on the popularity of various products. For example, the main reason for the enormous growth of fast-food chains, such as McDonald's and Kentucky Fried Chicken, is that so many people want quick, prepared meals when they are out of the house and on the run. In contrast, one of the reasons for the decline in the consumption of eggs for breakfast is that Americans are usually too rushed

TABLE 14-5   The Top Ten Ranked Activities (In Response to How People Would Spend an Extra Two Hours)

ACTIVITY	FEMALES (N = 603)		MALES (N = 512)	
	percent	rank	percent	rank
Catch up on household chores, projects	61%	1	36%	4
Read, study	46	2	34	5
Rest, relax, loaf, sleep	45	3	54	1
Spend time with family, play with children	45	3	45	2
Spend time on *indoor* hobbies	44	4	25	10
Spend time on "creative" activities	41	5		
Listen to music, records, tapes	34	6	32	6
Socialize, visit friends	34	6	34	5
Spend time shopping	30	7		
Do gardening, landscaping	30	7	32	6
Watch television	29	8	40	3
Spend time on personal business and errands	28	9	27	8
Spend time on *outdoor* hobbies	25	10	31	7
Do repair work on the house			36	4
Go fishing or hunting			27	8
Work on car, motorcycle, other powered vehicles			26	9

Source: Douglass K. Hawes, "Time Budgets and Consumer Leisure-Time Behavior," in William D. Perreault, Jr., ed., *Advances in Consumer Research* (Atlanta: Association for Consumer Research, 1977), IV, 227.

in the morning to prepare and to eat a traditional breakfast. According to an egg industry executive, "There's nothing that could make most people sit down and eat a 25-minute breakfast ever again."[24]

Efficiency and Practicality

With a basic philosophy of down-to-earth pragmatism, Americans pride themselves on being efficient and practical. When it comes to efficiency, they admire anything that saves time and saves effort. In terms of practicality, they are generally receptive to any new product that can make tasks easier and can help solve problems. For example, Americans wholeheartedly accepted such a labor-saving institution as the sawmill, which was outlawed in England (where it was developed) for fear that it would create unemployment.[25]

Here in America, where mass production has been so ingeniously refined, it is now possible for a manufacturer of almost any product category to offer the public a wide range of interchangeable components. For example, a consumer can design his or her own "customized" wall treatment from standard components of compatible base, sides, color, front panels, and special-function shelves, at a cost not much greater than a completely standardized unit. The capacity of American manufacturers to create mass-produced components that offer the consumer a customized product has in some instances taken two basically contradictory concepts, "mass produced" and "customized," and blurred their differences.

Another illustration of Americans' attentiveness to efficiency and practicality is the extreme importance attached to *time*. Americans seem to be convinced that "time waits for no man," which is reflected in their habitual attention to being prompt. The frequency with which Americans look at their watches, and the importance attached to having an accurate timepiece, tend to support the American value of punctuality. The very rapid consumer acceptance of the food processor as a kitchen appliance is still another example of Americans' love affair with products that save time and effort in providing efficiency and practicality. As Figure 14-9 shows, marketers of such products stress the benefits of ease, accuracy, and timesaving.

Progress

Belief in progress is another watchword of American society. Indeed, America has been labeled a "cult of progress."[26] Its receptivity to progress appears to be closely linked to other core values already examined (achievement and success, efficiency and practicality) and to the central belief that people can always improve themselves, that tomorrow should be better than today.

In a consumption-oriented society such as the United States, progress often means the acceptance of change—new products or services designed to fulfill previously undersatisfied or unsatisfied needs. In the name of progress, Americans appear to be receptive to product claims that stress "new," "improved," "longer lasting," "speedier," "quicker," "smoother and closer," and

FIGURE 14-9   Advertisement Appealing to Efficiency and Practicality

IT'S THE BEST.
BUT IT KEEPS
GETTING BETTER.

There are few culinary experts or food editors who do not consider the Cuisinart® DLC-7E the finest food processor available for home use.

This machine features, as standard equipment, the revolutionary Large Feed Tube that lets you process food faster than ever, a bigger workbowl that lets you do more at one time and blades and discs of superior, exclusive design.

Now, this standard of the industry is even better.

Now it has an even more powerful and efficient motor designed to give you peak performance when you most need it — kneading dough or chopping a pound of meat. It delivers maximum power during heavy jobs.

This motor is a workhorse. The chopping blade is also improved. The hub is smaller

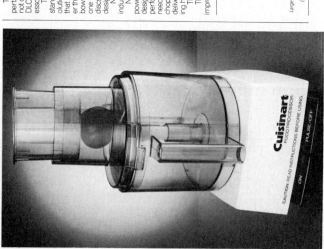

Standard Feed Tube Opening

Large Feed Tube Opening on DLC-7E and DLC-8E Models.
(Drawings Show Relative Size)

in diameter, significantly improving its dough kneading and chopping ability.

(Similar improvements have been incorporated into our DLC-8E model. It costs less, but has the same Large Feed Tube, same improved chopping blade, a larger than standard workbowl and, now, a more powerful, efficient motor.)

HOW A CUISINART FOOD PROCESSOR BECOMES A CUISINART FOOD PROCESSOR

Cuisinarts is a company with one major strength: engineering. And one principal love: cooking. Our criterion is that each Cuisinart product must make your life in the kitchen easier, more rewarding and six months after you have bought it, you must be thoroughly pleased that you did.

Behind our commitment

Six knobs around the edge of the disc project above the shredding teeth, preventing contact between teeth and cover.

to you is the Cuisinart Research and Development Group.

Seven years ago, when the founder of Cuisinarts, Inc. discovered the predecessor of what is now the Cuisinart food processor, it was not yet suitable for use in the American home. We modified it, but even our first models were primitive compared to our current machines.

Today's Cuisinart food processors are the result of the many patented innovations conceived by the Cuisinart Research and Development Group — a group that never stops looking for ways to make our products better.

Problem: Excessive pressure by inexperienced users caused shredding disc to shred the bottom of the cover.

Solution: (Patented.) We placed around the edge of the disc metal "dimples" which are higher than the shredding teeth. Result: unblemished covers and no plastic in your food.

Problem: Feed tube was too small to allow whole tomatoes, whole potatoes to be processed.

Solution: (Patented.) We invented the revolutionary Large Feed Tube that accepts food as big as many whole tomatoes, onions, oranges, even Idaho potatoes.

Problem: Collisions between food and ridge on slicing disc caused cracked and broken slices and too numerous crumbs.

The ridge behind the slicing blade is moved to the far end of a raised shelf, preventing slices from colliding with it.

Solution: (Patented.) We moved the ridge way back so that the slice falls free without ever touching the disc. Result: far more perfect slices.

As you can see, to the Cuisinart Research and Development Group, nothing is quite good enough. That's why even the best keeps getting better.

MORE INFORMATION.

For more about our food processors and the ease they bring to your cooking, write Cuisinarts, Inc., 411( ) West Putnam Avenue, Greenwich, CT 06830.

We'll also be pleased to send you information on our cookware, convection oven and our magazine, "The Pleasures of Cooking" (for those to whom cooking is a joy, a means of expression).

Cuisinart Food Processor

FIGURE 14-10   Advertisement Incorporating a Progress Appeal

Courtesy of General Electric Company

"increased strength." Figure 14-10 depicts an advertisement for a new light bulb that appeals to the core value of progress.

Material Comfort

For most Americans, material comfort signifies the attainment of "the good life"—a life that may include a self-defrosting refrigerator, a self-cleaning oven, an air conditioner, a hot tub, and an almost infinite variety of other convenience-oriented and pleasure-providing goods and services.

General acceptance of products that save time and labor is a rather new phenomenon for most Americans. In fact, for many Americans, the acceptance of convenience products has not been an emotionally easy task. People tend to have mixed feelings about the benefits of convenience products.[27] On the one hand, these products provide material comfort, which is symbolic of achievement and success. On the other hand, they produce anxiety and guilt, for they run counter to the notion of "hard work" as a symbol of self-worth.

A landmark consumer behavior study supports the contention that convenience products initially produce feelings of uncertainty and guilt. This study, reported in 1950 when instant coffee was still in its infancy, found that homemakers perceived women who used instant coffee as lazy housekeepers and poor wives. In contrast, users of regular grind coffee were perceived as thrifty and good wives.[28] This research suggests that convenience foods may sometimes be viewed with skepticism, and that people tend to judge others by the cultural acceptability of the products they own or use.

In response to our dynamic culture, Americans' values with regard to convenience products, particularly instant coffee, have shifted toward general acceptance during the past thirty years. Indeed, a replication of the original study described above indicated that the stigma attached to the use of instant coffee had disappeared.[29]

Although the use of convenience products by American households is now almost entirely culturally acceptable, many marketers are still reluctant to stress convenience in promoting their products. For example, in promoting Pampers (a disposable baby diaper), Procter and Gamble makes almost no reference to how easy or convenient the product is for mothers. Instead, it stresses how much softer, drier, and more comfortable the product is for baby. This copy approach avoids possible guilt feelings that she is selfishly using the product to satisfy her own needs rather than those of her baby.

AMERICA'S RESPONSE TO SHORTAGES

Until the early 1970s, many Americans felt that abundance and material comfort were inalienable "rights." However, the combined impact of actual and rumored shortages in such product categories as oil, natural gas, antifreeze, sugar, grain, and coffee has altered this blind optimism and made Americans realize that their personal comfort could be in danger.

Americans were shocked and frightened by the rationing, long lines, and curtailment of service station hours that occurred during the gasoline shortages of the mid-1970s. According to one consumer psychologist, gasoline shortage was perceived as "...a loss of freedom of mobility as well as a direct threat to Americans' life-style and even economic existence."[30] He identified the following five stages of "trauma" produced by the reality of scarcities:[31]

Stage 1: Consumers convince themselves that shortages cannot occur or are only temporary.

Stage 2: Consumers bargain or search for solutions.

Stage 3: Consumers become hostile—blaming government, business, ecologists, and other organizations or institutions.

Stage 4: Consumers realize that they are relatively helpless to deal with the shortages and become psychologically depressed.

Stage 5: Consumers begin to accept the reality of the shortages and reshape their attitudes and goals.

A resistance to full-sized "gas-eating" automobiles (which forced Detroit to offer a greater variety of compact and subcompact cars), taking vacations closer to home, making fewer shopping trips, and doing more in-home shopping by telephone or mail are ways in which consumers have attempted to deal constructively with the impact of higher gasoline prices and the realization that such shortages could occur again in the future.

When events such as the gasoline shortage occur—when companies find that raw materials and other supplies are no longer available in sufficient quantities to adequately satisfy existing demand—they must consider how they can responsibly deal with the problem of excess demand. The marketing task that exists when there is greater demand than supply has been characterized as *demarketing*.[32] The marketer's objective in demarketing is to discourage demand. When shortages are likely to be temporary, this task may be a short-run goal. When shortages are likely to be permanent, demarketing becomes a long-run goal. The scope of the demarketing effort may be the reduction of demand across all customers (general demarketing), or it may be targeted toward a specific segment of customers (selective demarketing).

In terms of consumer behavior, demarketing is not easily accomplished. It means that marketers must change existing consumption customs by encouraging people to alter their lifestyles. This is particularly difficult for a society such as ours, where consumers have acquired a strong appetite for material goods designed to make their lives more comfortable. To change these customs, marketers have to be extremely creative in designing marketing programs that motivate a historically affluent people to limit their consumption behavior. The highly creative advertisement for a subcompact, or "baby," limousine service in Figure 14-11 seems to effectively communicate the concept that "downsized" comfort and luxury may today be a reasonable alternative. One might speculate that the ad will not only be attractive to those affluent consumers who may find it intriguing to consider trading up from a taxi but, alternatively, may draw the attention of those consumers who feel uncomfortable about hiring a full-sized limousine.

Facing up to the reality that shortages and inflation are not likely to disappear and are symptomatic of a larger ecological problem, consumers will have to learn to conserve scarce natural resources for the benefit of their own physical and environmental well-being. Consumers must be persuaded to undertake more "responsible" consumption.[33] For example, Americans will have to learn to turn lights off in rooms that are vacant, refrain from doing less than full loads of laundry, and avoid many other forms of excessive or wasteful consumption.

An encouraging sign of progress is the work reported by several consumer researchers that identifies a small but growing segment of consumers known as *voluntary simplifiers*. These consumers make a conscious effort to elect lifestyles that attempt to maximize the amount of control that they will have over their own lives.[34]

Voluntary-simplifying consumers tend to be socioeconomically middle class. They subscribe to lifestyles that reflect five specific values: (1) material simplicity (nonconsumption-oriented patterns of use), (2) human scale (a desire for smaller-scale institutions and technologies), (3) self-determination (a desire to assume greater control over personal destiny), (4) ecological awareness

FIGURE 14-11   Advertisement Offering Alternative to Grand-Size Luxury

Courtesy of Manhattan Limousine

(recognition of the interdependency of people and resources), and (5) personal growth (a desire to explore and develop the "inner life").[35] Table 14-6 compares traditional lifestyles with simplifying lifestyles.

Recent research has suggested that there may be three distinct subsegments of voluntary simplifiers: (1) *conservers,* who were brought up in an environment that stressed the importance of being frugal and avoiding waste; (2) *crusaders,* who are primarily motivated to follow a simplifying lifestyle because they consider it to be socially responsible behavior; and (3) *conformists,* whose conserving is motivated by a variety of reasons, including guilt of being wealthy or a desire to be socially acceptable to other voluntary simplifiers.[36]

Responsible consumption is also likely to require public policies that stimulate selected forms of *deconsumption.* We can think of deconsumption as a policy consistent with voluntary simplicity, one that encourages consumers' selective curtailment or elimination of purchase activities. The appeals that are likely to be effective in gaining consumer cooperation in deconsuming include personal, environmental, political, or even nationalistic themes.

Individualism

Americans place a strong value on "being themselves." Self-reliance, self-interest, self-confidence, self-esteem, and self-fulfillment are all exceedingly popular expressions of individualism. The striving for such individualism seems

TABLE 14-6   A Comparison of Simplifying and Nonsimplifying Lifestyles

	SIMPLIFIERS	NONSIMPLIFIERS
value premises	Material sufficiency coupled with psychospiritual growth	Material growth
	People within nature, equilibrium	Man over nature
	Enlightened self-interest	Competitive self-interest
	Cooperative individualism	Rugged individualism
	Rational and intuitive	Rationalism
social characteristics	Smaller, less complex living and working environments	Large, complex living and working environments
	Reduction of material complexity	Growth of material complexity
	Appropriate technology	Space age technology
	Identity found through inner and interpersonal discovery	Identity defined by patterns of consumption
	Greater local self-determination coupled with emerging global institutions	Centralization of regulation & control at nation/state level
	More integrated work roles (e.g. team assembly, multiple roles)	Specialized work roles—through division of labor
	Balance of secular and spiritual	Secular
	Hand-crafted, durable, unique products	Mass-produced, quickly obsolete, standardized products
	"Spaceship Earth" ethic	Lifeboat ethic in foreign relations
	Cultural heterogeneity, eager acceptance of diversity	Cultural homogeneity, partial acceptance of diversity
	Laid-back, relaxed existence	High-pressure, rat-race existence
consumer behavior	Conservation society	Consumption society
	Quality of life	Hedonistic life
	Small is better	Big is beautiful
	Preference for quality	Preference for quantity
	Essential products	Luxury products
	More emphasis on durability	Less emphasis on durability
	Ecologically and environmentally more responsible	Ecologically and environmentally less responsible
	Preference for small, personal outlets (stores)	Preference for big outlets (stores)
	More receptivity to innovative outlets, e.g., flea markets, street vendors	Less receptivity to innovative outlets
	More do-it-yourself orientation	Less do-it-yourself orientation
	More co-op buying	Less co-op buying
	Print, radio orientation	Television orientation

Source: Avraham Shama, "How Marketers Can Cater to 'Voluntary Simplicity' Segment," *Marketing News*, March 21, 1980, 3.

FIGURE 14-12   Advertisement Stressing Individualism

Courtesy of Chesbrough-Ponds, Inc., owner of the registered trademarks PRINCE MATCHABELLI and CACHET

to be linked to the rejection of dependency.[37] That is, it is better to rely on one's self than on others.

In terms of consumer behavior, an appeal to individualism frequently takes the form of reinforcing one's own sense of identity with products or services that both reflect and emphasize that identity (including products like Perrier water and a host of fashion items that offer status designer labels).

Marketers with effective segmentation strategies often design their entire marketing mix—product, price, promotion, and retail channels—with the view of enhancing the feeling of individuality of selected audience segments. For example, advertisements for high-style clothing and cosmetics usually "promise" the reader that their products will emphasize the consumer's exclusive or distinctive character and will set him or her apart from others. An advertisement for cologne in Figure 14-12 states: "Cachet. As individual as you are." The body copy supports this individualistic theme with such statements as "Cachet is different on every woman who wears it."

Freedom

Freedom is another very strong American value, one that has historical roots in such democratic ideals as "freedom of speech," "freedom of the press," and "freedom of worship."

As an outgrowth of these democratic beliefs in freedom, Americans have a strong preference for *freedom of expression*—the desire to be one's self and to feel responsible solely to one's self. The advertisement for a men's cologne in Figure 14-13 appeals to the reader's desire for "adventurous freedom."

Americans also demonstrate a strong need for *freedom of choice*—the opportunity to choose from a wide range of alternatives. This preference is reflected in the large number of competitive brands and product variations that can be found on the shelves of the modern supermarket. For many products, consumers can select from a wide variety of sizes, colors, flavors, and even special ingredients (e.g., toothpaste with stannous fluoride or special whiteners, or toothpaste designed for sensitive gums).

Given all this choice, it may just be possible that American consumers are beginning to feel they have too much choice; making a selection from many competing brands can be difficult. One study found that consumers believed that "overchoice" existed for such product categories as facial tissue, margarine, breakfast cereal, cake mix, and laundry detergent.[38]

External Conformity

Although Americans deeply embrace freedom of choice and individualism, they nevertheless accept the reality of conformity. External conformity is a necessary process by which the individual adapts to society. It has been said that "no social organization, no culture, no form of institutionalized relationship whatever could exist without the process of interaction we call conformity."[39]

In the realm of consumer behavior, conformity (or uniformity) takes the form of standardized goods and services. Standardized products have been made possible by mass production. The availability of a wide choice of standardized products places the consumer in the unique position of being individualistic (by selecting specific products that his or her close friends do not have) or conforming (by purchasing a similar product). It is within this context that individualism and conformity exist side by side as choices for the American consumer.

Consumer dress behavior would seem to be a particularly potent and observable area of external conformity. A study that explored the relationship between male college students' dress patterns and their social-cultural attitudes

FIGURE 14-13   Advertisement Appealing to Freedom of Expression

found that students categorized as "radical" dressers (e.g., unkempt hair, unpressed or dirty clothing) were politically more liberal, had more permissive sexual attitudes, were more conscious of youth as a distinct social grouping, and were more likely to play down conventional male-female sex role differences than were members of the "traditionally" dressed student group.[40] This research suggests that dress behavior functions as a visible symbol of people's attitudes, which in turn may foster external conformity among those who wish to be associated with a specific point of view.

Humanitarianism

Americans are a generous people when it comes to those in need. They support with a passion many humane and charitable causes, and they sympathize with the "underdog" who must overcome adversity or get ahead by working hard.[41] This humanitarian spirit seems to extend to decisions concerning products and services. A classic illustration is the Avis promotional campaign that stressed that because Avis was only "number two" in the automobile rental business (behind Hertz), it had to "try harder" to satisfy its customers. (See Figure 14-14 for an early Avis advertisement.) This campaign and others like it often successfully enlist the empathy of a sufficient number of consumers to have a very favorable impact on sales.

Youthfulness

Americans tend to place an almost sacred value on youthfulness. This emphasis is a reflection of America's rapid technological development. In an atmosphere where "new" is so constantly stressed, being "old" is often equated with being "outdated." This is in contrast to traditional European, African, and Asian

FIGURE 14-14   **Advertisement Appealing for Support for the Underdog**

Avis is only No.2. But we don't want your sympathy.

Have we been crying too much? Have we overplayed the underdog?

We didn't think so till David Biener, 11 years old, sent us 35¢, saying, "It may help you buy another Plymouth."

That was an eye-opener.

So now we'd like to correct the false impression we've made.

We don't want you to reserve Avis cars for your clients because you feel sorry for us. Give us a chance to prove that a No. 2 can be just as good as a No. 1. Or even better. Because we have to try harder.

Maybe we ought to eliminate the negative and accentuate the positive.

Instead of saying "We're only No. 2 in rent a cars," we could say "We're the second largest in the world."

AVIS RENT A CAR
(address and phone number)

It hasn't come to this.

Courtesy of Avis Rent A Car System, Inc.

societies, where the elderly are revered for possessing the wisdom of experience, which comes with age.

"Youthfulness" should not be confused with "youth," which describes an age grouping. While there is obviously some relationship between age and youthfulness, we are really concerned with Americans' preoccupation with *looking* and *acting* young, regardless of their actual age. For Americans, youthfulness is a state of mind and a state of being, sometimes expressed as being "young at heart," "young in spirit," or "young in appearance."

A great deal of advertising is directed to people's sense of urgency about retaining their youth and to their fear of aging. Hand cream ads talk about "young hands," skin treatment ads state "I dreaded turning 30...," fragrance and cosmetic ads stress looking "sexy and young," and detergent ads ask the reader "Can you match their hands with their ages?" Such advertising themes reflect the American premium placed on youthfulness as they promise the consumer the benefits of youth.

TABLE 14-7   Summary of American Core Values

VALUE	GENERAL FEATURES	RELEVANCE TO CONSUMER BEHAVIOR
Achievement and success	Hard work is good; success flows from hard work	Acts as a justification for acquisition of goods ("You deserve it")
Activity	Keeping busy is healthy and natural	Stimulates interest in products that are time-savers and enhance leisure-time activities
Efficiency and practicality	Admiration of things that solve problems (e.g., save time and effort)	Stimulates purchase of products that function well and save time
Progress	People can improve themselves; tomorrow should be better	Stimulates desire for new products that fulfill unsatisfied needs; acceptance of products that claim to be "new" or "improved"
Material comfort	"The good life"	Fosters acceptance of convenience and luxury products that make life more enjoyable
Individualism	Being one's self (e.g., self-reliance, self-interest, and self-esteem)	Stimulates acceptance of customized or unique products that enable a person to "express his or her own personality"
Freedom	Freedom of choice	Fosters interest in wide product lines and differentiated products
External conformity	Uniformity of observable behavior; desire to be accepted	Stimulates interest in products that are used or owned by others in the same social group
Humanitarianism	Caring for others, particularly the underdog	Stimulates patronage of firms that compete with market leaders
Youthfulness	A state of mind that stresses being young at heart or appearing young	Stimulates acceptance of products that provide the illusion of maintaining or fostering youth

Core Values Not an American Phenomenon

The cultural values just examined are not all uniquely or originally American. Some of these values have been borrowed, particularly from European society, as people emigrated to the United States. Some values that originated in America are now part of the fabric of other societies. Furthermore, all Americans do not necessarily accept each of these values. We do suggest, however, that these values, when taken as a whole, do account for much of the American character. Table 14-7 lists the highlights of our discussion of American core values and their relevance to consumer behavior.

summary

The study of culture is the study of all apsects of a society—its language, knowledge, laws, customs, etc.—which give that society its distinctive character and personality. In the context of consumer behavior, *culture* is defined as the sum total of learned beliefs, values, and customs which serve to regulate the consumer behavior of members of a particular society. Beliefs and values are *guides* for consumer behavior; customs are usual and acceptable *ways of behaving*.

The impact of culture on society is so natural and so ingrained that its influence on our behavior is rarely noted. Yet culture offers order, direction, and guidance to members of society in all phases of their human problem solving. Culture is dynamic and gradually and continually evolves to meet the needs of society.

Culture is learned as part of social experience. As children, we acquire from our environment a set of beliefs, values, and customs which constitute our culture (i.e., we are "encultured"). These are acquired through formal learning, informal learning, and technical learning. Advertising enhances formal learning by reinforcing desired modes of behavior and expectations; it enhances informal learning by providing models for our behavior.

Culture is communicated to members of the society through a common language and through commonly shared symbols. Because the human mind has the ability to absorb and to process symbolic communication, marketers can successfully promote both tangible and intangible products and product concepts to consumers through mass media.

All the elements in the marketing mix serve to communicate symbolically with the audience. Products project images of their own; so does promotion (e.g., through the format of the advertisement and the media used); both price and retail outlets symbolically convey images concerning the quality of the product.

The elements of culture are transmitted by three pervasive social institutions; the family, the church, and the school. A fourth social institution that plays a major role in the transmission of culture is the mass media—both through editorial content and through advertising.

A wide range of measurement techniques have been employed to study culture. These include projective techniques, attitude measurement methods, field observation, participant observation, content analysis, and value measurement survey techniques.

A small number of core values of the American people appear to be relevant to the study of consumer behavior. These include achievement and success, activity, efficiency and practicality, progress, material comfort, individualism, freedom, conformity, humanitarianism, and youthfulness.

Since each of these values varies in importance to the members of our society, they provide an effective basis for segmenting consumer markets.

discussion questions

1. Distinguish between beliefs, values, and customs. Illustrate how the clothing a person wears, at different times or for different occasions, is influenced by custom.
2. Give an example from your own experience of each of the following types of cultural learning:
   a. Formal learning
   b. Informal learning
   c. Technical learning
3. Describe how the mass media participate in the transmission of cultural beliefs, values, and customs.
4. As the media planner for a largest advertising agency, you have been asked by top management to identify recent cultural changes that affect your selection of the media in which to place clients' advertising. List five cultural changes that you believe have bearing on the selection of television shows for different types of products.
5. How do achievement and success differ? Discuss the implication of these differences for marketing strategy.
6. Find advertisements that illustrate three of the core values summarized in Table 14-7. Describe your choices.
7. As a marketing consultant to one of the major oil companies, you have been asked to create a *demarketing* campaign. Outline your recommendations for a campaign to discourage wasteful use of oil products. Which American cultural values are affected?
8. Which basic American cultural values do you think would have an influence on the various types of automobiles that Americans buy? Explain.

endnotes

1. Milton Rokeach, *The Nature of Human Values* (New York: Free Press, 1973), 5; and Francesco M. Nicosia and Robert N. Myer, "Toward a Sociology of Consumption," *Journal of Consumer Research*, 3 (September 1976), 67.

2. Donald E. Vinson, Jerome E. Scott, and Lawrence M. Lamont, "The Role of Personal Values in Marketing and Consumer Behavior," *Journal of Marketing*, 41 (April 1977), 44–50.

3. Ruth Benedict, "The Science of Custom," *Century Magazine*, 117 (1929), 641.

4. Ralph Linton, *The Cultural Background of Personality* (New York: Appleton-Century-Crofts, 1945), 125.

5. Edward T. Hall, *The Silent Language* (Greenwich, Conn.: Fawcett, 1959), 69–72.

6. Raymond Firth, *Symbols: Public and Private* (Ithaca, N.Y.: Cornell University Press, 1973), 47.

7. M. Wayne DeLozier, *The Marketing Communications Process* (New York: McGraw-Hill, 1976), 163.

8. George Peter Murdock, *Culture and Society* (Pittsburgh: University of Pittsburgh Press, 1965), 81.

9. David M. Potter, *People of Plenty* (Chicago: University of Chicago Press, 1954), 167.

10. For a comprehensive discussion of content analysis, see Harold H. Kassarjian, "Content Analysis in Consumer Research," *Journal of Consumer Research*, 4 (June 1977), 8–18; Fred N. Kerlinger, *Foundations of Behavioral Research*, 2nd ed. (New York: Holt, Rinehart & Winston, 1973), 525–34; and Morris B. Holbrook, "More on Content Analysis in Consumer Behavior," *Journal of Consumer Research*, 4 (December 1977), 176–77.

11. Rokeach, *Nature of Human Values;* and Milton Rokeach, "Change and Stability in American Value Systems, 1968–1971," *Public Opinion Quarterly*, 38 (Summer 1974), 222–38.

12. Jerome E. Scott and Lawrence M. Lamont, "Relating Consumer Values to Consumer Behavior: A Model and Method for Investigation," in Thomas V. Greer, ed., *1973 Combined Proceedings* (Chicago: American Marketing Association, 1974), 283–88.

13. Donald E. Vinson and J. Michael Munson, "Personal Values: An Approach to Market Segmentation," in Kenneth L. Bernhardt, ed., *Marketing: 1776–1976 and Beyond* (Chicago: American Marketing Association, 1976), 313–17.

14. Vinson et al., "Role of Personal Values," 47–48.

15. J. Michael Munson and Shelby H. McIntyre, "Personal Values: A Cross Cultural Assessment of Self Values and Values Attributed to a Distant Cultural Stereotype," in H. Keith Hunt, ed., *Advances in Consumer Research* (Ann Arbor, Mich.: Association for Consumer Research, 1978), V, 160–66; J. Michael Munson and Shelby H. McIntyre, "Developing Practical Procedures for the Measurement of Personal Values in Cross-Cultural Marketing," *Journal of Marketing Research*, 16 (February 1979), 48–52; and Thomas J. Reynolds and James P. Jolly, "Measuring Personal Values: An Evaluation of Alternative Methods," *Journal of Marketing Research*, 17 (November 1980), 531–36.

16. The Yankelovich Monitor, *Technical Description/Appendix* (New York: Yankelovich, Skelly and White, 1981), 50–58.

17. Olivia Schieffelin Nordberg, "Lifestyle's Monitor," *American Demographics*, 3 (May 1981), 22; and B. G. Yovovich, "Finding the Answers," *Advertising Age*, July 20, 1981, 41–42 and 44.

18. Thomas C. Thomas, "Values and Lifestyles—The New Psychographics?" (Paper presented at the Advertising Research Foundation Conference, New York, February 24, 1981), 4.

19. Ibid., 31.

20. Lowell D. Holmes, *Anthropology* (New York: Ronald Press, 1965), 121.

21. Many of the ideas for the value concepts examined in this section were inspired by the comprehensive treatment in "Major Value Orientations in America," appearing in Robin M. Williams, Jr., American Society: A Sociological Interpretation (New York: Knopf, 1970), 438–504.

22. David C. McClelland, *The Achieving Society* (New York: Free Press, 1961), 150–51.

23. Douglass K. Hawes, "Time Budgets and Consumer Leisure-Time Behavior," in William D. Perreault, Jr., ed., *Advances in Consumer Research* (Atlanta: Association for Consumer Research, 1977), IV, 221–29.

24. Steve Lohr, "Hens Are Willing but People Aren't," *New York Times,* July 11, 1976, Sec. 3,1.

25. Henry Fairlie, *The Spoiled Child of the Western World* (New York: Doubleday, 1976), 79.

26. Williams, *American Society,* 468.

27. Edward M. Tauber, "How Market Research Discourages Major Innovation," *Business Horizons,* 17 (July 1974), 24.

28. Mason Haire, "Projective Techniques in Marketing Research," *Journal of Marketing,* 14 (April 1950), 649–56.

29. Frederick E. Webster, Jr., and Frederick Von Pechmann, "A Replication of the 'Shopping List' Study," *Journal of Marketing,* 34 (April 1970), 61–63. Also see Johan Arndt, "Haire's Shopping List Revisited," *Journal of Advertising Research,* 13 (October 1973), 57–61.

30. Joseph M. Kamen, "Learning of Scarcities May Depress Consumers," *Marketing News,* August 1, 1973, 3.

31. Ibid.

32. Philip Kotler and Sidney J. Levy, "Demarketing, Yes Demarketing," *Harvard Business Review,* November–December 1971, 74–80; Philip Kotler, "The Major Tasks of Marketing Management," *Journal of Marketing,* 37 (October 1974), 42–49; and David Cullwick, "Positioning Demarketing Strategy," *Journal of Marketing, 39 (April 1975), 51–57.*

33. George Fisk, "Criteria for a Theory of Responsible Consumption," *Journal of Marketing,* 37 (April 1973), 24–31.

34. Dorothy Leonard-Barton and Everett M. Rogers, "Voluntary Simplicity," in Jerry C. Olson, ed., *Advances in Consumer Research* (Ann Arbor, Mich.: Association for Consumer Research, 1980), VII, 28.

35. D. Elgin and A. Mitchell, "Voluntary Simplicity," *Co-Evolution Quarterly* (Summer 1977), 4–19. Also see Avraham Shama, "Marketing in a Slow-Growth Economy," (New York: Praeger, 1980), 110–25.

36. Leonard-Barton and Rogers, "Voluntary Simplicity," 32.

37. Holmes, *Anthropology,* 136.

38. Robert B. Settle and Linda L. Golden, "Consumer Perceptions: Overchoice in the Market Place," in Scott Ward and Peter Wright, eds., *Advances in Consumer Behavior* (Association for Consumer Research, 1974), I, 29–37.

39. Robert A. Nisbet, *The Social Bond* (New York: Knopf, 1970), 69.

40. L. Eugene Thomas, "Clothing and Counterculture: An Empirical Study," *Adolescence,* 8 (Spring 1973), 93–112.

41. Williams, *American Society,* 462.

FIFTEEN

Subcultural and Cross-Cultural Aspects of Consumer Behavior

introduction

CULTURE has a potent influence on all consumer behavior. Individuals are brought up to follow the beliefs, values, and customs of their society and to avoid behavior that is frowned upon or considered taboo. Marketers who incorporate an understanding of culture into their marketing strategies are likely to satisfy consumers more fully by providing them with added, though intangible, product benefits. However, culture, as a concept, has a very broad beamed focus in that it embraces total societies. To even better satisfy consumers, marketers have learned to segment society into smaller subgroups, or "subcultures," that are homogeneous in relation to certain customs and ways of behaving. These subcultures provide important marketing opportunities for astute marketing strategists.

Our discussion of subcultures, therefore, will have a *narrower* focus. Instead of examining the dominant beliefs, values, and customs that exist within an entire society, it will explore the marketing opportunities created by the existence of certain beliefs, values, and customs among specific subcultural groups *within* a society. Subcultural divisions based on nationality, religion, geographic locality, race, age, and sex often enable marketers to segment a market in terms of the specific beliefs, values, and customs shared by members of a specific subcultural group.

In the second section of this chapter we will *broaden* our scope of analysis and consider the marketing implications of cultural differences and similarities that exist between the people of two or more nations. Recognition of cross-cultural differences can provide expanded sales and profit opportunities for multinational marketers, who can tailor their marketing mix to the specific customs of each target nation.

SUBCULTURES

In the world of primitive tribal society, the same set of cultural values and customs prevails throughout the group; there are no subgroups with distinctive cultural traits. A society with such a highly unified culture is ruled by

Different men seek after happiness in different ways and by different means...

ARISTOTLE

Politics *(4th cent. B.C.)*

"commonness." All of its people worship the same god, all have a common racial background, and all eat the same kinds of food. Social organizations and institutions are extremely simple. In contrast, in a complex society like the United States, there is considerable diversity in religious beliefs, racial backgrounds, food customs, and other social practices and institutions. Indeed the members of a complex society belong to many different kinds of subcultural groups. It is such diversity that makes subculture a useful segmentation variable.

What Is Subculture?

A *subculture* can be thought of as *a distinct cultural group which exists as an identifiable segment within a larger, more complex society.*[1] The members of a specific subculture tend to possess beliefs, values, and customs that set them apart from other members of the same society. In addition, they adhere to most of the *dominant* cultural beliefs, values, and behavioral patterns of the overall society.

Thus the cultural profile of a society or nation can be viewed as a composite of two distinct elements: (1) the unique beliefs, values, and customs subscribed to by members of specific subcultures; and (2) the central core cultural themes that are shared by most of the population, regardless of specific subcultural memberships. Figure 15-1 presents a model of the relationship between two subcultural groups (easterners and westerners) and the larger culture. As the figure depicts, each subculture has its own unique traits, yet both groups share the dominant traits of the overall American culture.

Let us look at it another way. Each American is in large part a product of the "American way of life." However, each American is at the same time a member of various subcultures. For example, a fifteen-year-old girl may simultaneously be an Irish-Catholic, a teenager, and a southerner. We would expect that membership in each different subculture would provide its own set of specific beliefs, values, attitudes, and customs. Table 15-1 lists the typical subcultural categories and gives corresponding examples of specific subcultural

FIGURE 15-1   Relationship between Culture and Subculture

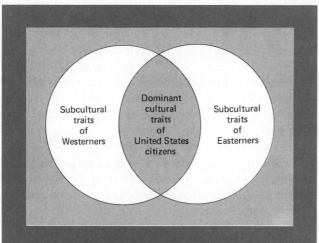

Subcultural
traits
of
Westerners

Dominant
cultural
traits
of
United States
citizens

Subcultural
traits
of
Easterners

TABLE 15-1   Subcultural Categories

SUBCULTURAL CATEGORY	ILLUSTRATIVE SUBCULTURE
Nationality (i.e., birthplace of ancestors)	Italian, Puerto Rican, Mexican
Religion	Mormon, Protestant, Jew
Region	Midwestern, Northern, Southern
Race	Black, White, Oriental
Age	Elderly, Teenage, Middle-age
Sex	Female, Male
Occupation	Carpenter, Lawyer, Schoolteacher
Social class	Lower, Middle, Upper

groups. This list is by no means exhaustive. For example, Boy Scouts, college students, "jet-setters," feminists, and intellectuals—in fact, any group that shares common beliefs and customs—may be classified as a subculture.

SUBCULTURES AS MARKET SEGMENTS

Subcultural analysis enables the marketing manager to focus on rather large and "natural" market segments. In carrying out such analyses, the marketer must determine whether the beliefs, values, and customs shared by members of a specific subgroup make them strong candidates for special marketing attention. According to one marketing expert, "Subcultures are the relevant units of analysis for market research. *They represent definable target groups for specific products and logical units for segmenting of larger markets.*"[2]

We will now examine the marketing implications of the following subcultural categories: (1) nationality, (2) religion, (3) geographic location, (4) race, (5) age, and (6) sex. (Occupational and social-class subgroups are discussed in detail in Chapter 13.)

Nationality Subcultures

With the exception of the American Indian, most U.S. citizens have their roots in European, African, South American, and Asian countries. In terms of numbers, most of these Americans can trace their family ancestry to Europe. During the period 1820 to 1978, over 60 percent of all the immigrants to the United States came from seven European countries: Germany, Great Britain, Ireland, Italy, Austria, Russia, and Sweden.[3]

While most Americans, especially those born in the United States, see themselves as "Americans," they frequently retain a sense of identification and pride in the language and customs of their ancestors.

When it comes to consumption behavior, this ancestral pride is manifested most strongly in the consumption of ethnic foods, in travel to the "homeland" country, and in the purchase of numerous cultural artifacts (ethnic clothing, art, music, foreign-language newspapers). It has been observed that interest in such goods and services has expanded rapidly as younger Americans attempt to better understand and more closely associate themselves with their ethnic roots.[4]

Unfortunately, with the exception of the Hispanic subculture, there is little information available about the consumption behavior of the many nationality subcultural groups found in the United States.

HISPANIC SUBCULTURES

Hispanic-Americans represent about 10 percent of the U.S. population and are the fastest-growing ethnic-minority group in the United States. With a 65 percent population increase during the 1970–80 decade, Hispanic-Americans now constitute a market force that includes more than 15 million people. Most important, they are not a single market, but rather a number of subcultural markets that correspond to their country of origin. In terms of country of origin, the three largest Hispanic subcultural groups consist of Mexican-Americans, Puerto Ricans, and Cubans. These subcultures are heavily concentrated geographically, with about 70 percent of their members residing in California, Texas, New York, and Florida.[5]

According to the available evidence, Hispanic-Americans are consumption-oriented and have a strong preference for major name-brand products.[6] Data from a classic comparison of the brand preferences of both Hispanic and Anglo consumers are listed in Table 15-2. These data, although not current, do suggest

TABLE 15-2   Estimated Brand Share Studies for Selected Products

PRODUCT	ANGLO	HISPANIC
Soaps (powdered or flakes)		
Tide	30.2	15.3
Cheer	15.0	42.3
Lipstick		
Revlon	26.5	21.0
Avon	23.9	50.7
Indigestion remedies		
Alka Seltzer	31.6	7.7
Pepto Bismol	31.3	65.4
Cold remedies		
Contac	54.1	45.5
Coricidin	20.3	9.1
Coldene	2.7	13.6
Dristan	10.8	0.0
Soft drinks		
Pepsi-Cola	25.0	52.4
Coca-Cola	25.0	33.0
Seven-Up	9.0	5.1
Cigarets		
Winston	31.1	7.0
Marlboro	7.3	21.6
Viceroy	2.2	12.5

Source: Reprinted with permission from the November 27, 1967, issue of *Marketing Insights.* Copyright 1967 by Crain Communications, Inc.

that Hispanic consumers' preferences among the leading brands in several major consumer-packaged-goods categories differ considerably from those of the general market. These results reflect not only the subcultural differences but the explicit efforts of such marketers as Anheuser-Busch, Pepsi-Cola, Chrysler, Gillette, Kraft, McDonald's, Colgate-Palmolive, Procter and Gamble, Scott Paper, and Bristol-Myers to penetrate the Hispanic markets via Spanish-language mass media.[7]

The Spanish language is the bridge that links the various Hispanic subcultures. However, though they share a common language, each of the major Hispanic subcultural groups has its own distinct beliefs, values, and customs (see Table 15-3). It has been suggested that ". . . what may be popular in New York [i.e., among Puerto Ricans] might fail in Miami [i.e., among Cubans]. . . ."[8] Thus a marketer may wish to segment the Hispanic market even further by appealing to the distinct cultural values of a specific nationality.

Religious Subcultures

Over 220 different organized religious groups reportedly flourish in the United States.[9] Of this number, the major Protestant denominations, Roman Catholicism, and Judaism are the principal organized religious faiths. The members of all these religious groups are at times likely to make purchase decisions that are influenced by their religious identity. However, as American life becomes increasingly secularized (i.e., as religion plays less of a central role in determining basic beliefs and values), adherence to traditional religious rules tends to diminish. Therefore it is likely that consumer behavior is most directly affected by religion in terms of products that are *symbolically* associated with the celebration of various religious holidays. For example, as the major gift-purchasing season of the year, Christmas is important to many marketers of consumer goods.

Although members of most major religions can be reached through religious publications, marketers are reluctant to do so because they feel uncomfortable about mixing religion and business.[10] However, it has been shown that advertising in religious media can be rewarding. Specifically, research concerned with measuring the impact of special-interest media aimed at Jewish households provides some striking insights about brand purchase behavior. The research that contrasts brand penetration in Jewish and non-Jewish households revealed that in the New York market, Maxwell House coffee is used in 61 percent of the Jewish homes (versus 33 percent of the non-Jewish homes); My-T-Fine puddings are used in 73 percent of the Jewish homes (versus 29 percent non-Jewish); and Star-Kist tuna is used in 35 percent of the Jewish home (versus 16 percent non-Jewish).[11]

Geographic or Regional Subcultures

The United States is a large country, one that enjoys a wide range of climatic and geographic conditions. Given the country's size and physical diversity, it is only natural that the American people have a sense of regional identification and use

TABLE 15-3   Hispanic-American Lifestyle Differences and Similarities

PERCENT WHO AGREE/STRONGLY AGREE WITH STATEMENTS	HISPANICS					UNITED STATES
	Total	Puerto Rico	Mexico	Cuba	Other	Total
Optimism in Improved Standard of Living It is becoming harder to be optimistic that our standard of living in the future is going to be better than it is now	61	67	58	60	66	77
Pleasure from Work I don't expect to get much pleasure from my work. Work is just what you do to earn a living	41	46	37	35	52	24
Materialism/Tangibles I prefer to spend money on tangible things that I can keep rather than on things that give me temporary enjoyment like a vacation and so on	61	75	55	51	74	48
Live for Today I try to have as much fun as I can now and let the future take care of itself	36	29	36	29	41	47
Feelings of Despair I often feel there is nothing in this world worth striving for	24	27	22	12	37	16
Interest in Change I need to satisfy my hunger for new experiences	62	55	61	65	68	62
Physical Attractiveness I need to keep up with the new styles	49	51	42	69	64	46
Physical Fitness We are all getting soft; it is more important today than ever to take special measures to maintain our health	86	92	85	79	86	90

Source: *Spanish USA: A Study of the Hispanic Market in the United States* (Study conducted by Yankelovich, Skelly and White for the Sin National Spanish Television Network, New York, June 1981), 10.

this identification as a way of describing others (e.g., He's a big Texan). Such labels often assist us in developing a mental picture—a stereotype—of the person in question.

Anyone who has traveled across the United States has probably noted many regional differences in consumption behavior. For example, coffee preferences differ in different sections of the country (e.g., black coffee in a *mug* typifies the West, while coffee with milk and sugar in a *cup* is especially popular in the East).[12] There are also geographic differences in the consumption of a staple food like bread. Specifically, in the South and Midwest, soft bread (white bread) is preferred, while on the East and West coasts firmer breads (rye, whole wheat, and French and Italian breads) are favored.[13]

Fashion tastes and preferences also seem to have a regional identity. Indeed, two major cities in the same state may even have quite different fashion orientations. For example, according to the chief executive officer of a leading Texas-based fashion specialty chain, Dallas has historically been more sophisticated and upbeat, whereas Houston has been more fundamental or practical in outlook. Therefore, he concludes, "In Dallas, you could sell the sizzle. In Houston, you had to sell the steak."[14]

Subcultural and Cross-Cultural Aspects of Consumer Behavior

There are few research studies available to document such differences in consumption patterns. Most academic consumer research focuses on single geographic areas (usually the locale of the researcher's university). However, the findings of a large-scale study of consumer lifestyles and buying preferences suggest that commercially sponsored studies can provide rich insights into the regional variations of consumer behavior. This study, which questioned two thousand male and two thousand female consumers, reported the following specific geographic differences.[15]

1. Southern men were more likely to use mouthwash or deodorants than eastern men.
2. Southern men were more likely to listen to western music than any other regional group, and least likely to read a Sunday newspaper. Also, a southern household was more likely to own a freezer than other regional households.
3. Western men tend to consume more cottage cheese, vitamins, and regular coffee than either easterners or southerners. A western family is also more likely to own a garbage-disposal unit.

To further illustrate how product usage varies in terms of geography, Table 15-4 shows the results of a study that sought to determine the percentage of households in each region that had made at least one wine purchase during the preceding twelve-month period. The results indicate a considerable amount of interregional variation in the degree of market penetration for wine. More precisely, only 20 percent of those residing in the East South Central States had purchased wine, whereas over 50 percent of those residing in the Pacific States had purchased wine. Overall, 38 percent of those participating in the study had purchased wine.

Such regional differences tend to dispel the myth sometimes held that American consumers are one big "mass" market and reinforce the need for market segmentation for a variety of goods and services.

TABLE 15-4   Regional Market Penetration of Wine Sales

REGION	PROPORTION OF HOUSEHOLDS PURCHASING WINE (%)
New England	47.3
Middle Atlantic	42.8
East North Central	39.5
West North Central	30.6
South Atlantic	35.2
East South Central	19.6
West South Central	30.8
Mountain	36.8
Pacific	52.6
All Regions	38.8

Source: Raymond J. Folwell, "Marketing to the Wine Consumer—An Overview," in Jerry C. Olson, ed., *Advances in Consumer Behavior* (Ann Arbor, Mich.: Association for Consumer Research, 1980), VII, 92.

Racial Subcultures

The major racial subcultures in the United States are white, black, Oriental, and American Indian. Although there are differences in lifestyles and consumer spending patterns among all of these groups, the vast majority of racial consumer research has focused on black-white consumer differences.

THE BLACK CONSUMER

Black consumers constitute the largest racial minority segment of the U.S. population (approximately 12 percent). This group of over 26 million consumers has too frequently been portrayed as a single, undifferentiated "black market," consisting of economically deprived consumers who have a uniform set of consumer needs. However, though a substantial portion of the black population is economically less well off than the white majority, there does exist an important and growing black middle class.[16] Therefore, just as the white majority has been divided into a variety of submarket segments, each with its own distinctive needs and tastes, so too can the black market be segmented. Unfortunately, there is not sufficient research data available concerning market segments within the total black market to examine them in detail. Instead, the following sections deal with more general consumer dimensions of the black subculture.

REACHING THE BLACK AUDIENCE. A question of central importance to marketers is, What is the best way to reach the black consumer? Traditionally, marketers have subscribed to one of two distinct marketing strategies. Some have followed the policy of running all their advertising in the general mass media in the belief that blacks have the same media habits as whites; others have followed the policy of running additional advertising in selected media directed exclusively to blacks.

Both of these strategies may be appropriate in specific situations and for specific product categories. For certain products of very broad appeal (e.g., aspirin, cold remedies, toothpaste), it is quite possible that the mass media (primarily television) may effectively reach all relevant consumers, black and white alike. However, for other products (e.g., food products), an advertiser may find that the general mass media do *not* communicate effectively with the relevant black market.

If marketers feel that a product is not realizing its potential among black consumers, they may supplement general advertising with black-targeted advertisements in magazines, newspapers, and other media directed specifically to blacks. If marketers are offering a product exclusively for the black market (e.g., a line of black cosmetics), they should probably spend the major part of their advertising budget in so-called black media, where it will most effectively reach the target audience.

Research that compared the media exposure habits of a national sample of black and white consumers found substantial differences in exposure to weekly and monthly magazines, and in TV viewing.[17] However, when the data were further analyzed in terms of income categories, some distinctly different conclusions emerged. Specifically, lower-income and higher-income black consumers displayed media exposure patterns similar to whites with comparable income levels. This finding initially suggests that black and white upper- and lower-income groups may be effectively reached through the same media. However, this does not take into account any differences in advertising appeals that may be appropriate between the two markets. The greatest number of black-white differences was found to exist among the middle-income classes. This suggests that marketers who wish to reach the middle-income black market should consider the use of black media such as *Jet* and *Ebony* magazines. Thus income seems to be a reasonable variable to use in segmenting the black market.

Several studies have compared the responses of black and white consumers to advertising and point-of-purchase promotions that feature all black models, all white models, or both black and white models ("integrated" promotions).[18] Not surprisingly, the majority of these studies indicate that black consumers tend to be more strongly in favor of ads that feature black models than white consumers. White consumers tend to respond either neutrally or positively to ads that feature black models. This research suggests that, while black consumers welcome ads that include black models, white consumers are unlikely to respond adversely to such ads.[19]

In part, this conclusion is supported by an experiment that measured the sales response of southern black and white consumers to supermarket displays that featured black only, white only, and black and white models.[20] Both black and white consumers were found to respond *equally* well to all three types of displays. It may be that black consumers do prefer to see more blacks in advertisements but are really indifferent to the model's race when it comes to the actual purchase situation.

A number of studies that employ content analysis (described in Chapter 14) have examined the frequency of use and the status roles of black models in general mass-media magazines. The findings indicate that during the twenty-year period from 1946 to 1965, blacks increasingly have been portrayed in higher-status occupations, and that the number of ads containing black models more than doubled in the five-year period 1965–69.[21]

Although these studies report some increases in the status portrayal and the frequency of use of black models in magazine ads, a more recent content analysis performed over a wide range of 1978 consumer magazines concluded that the percentage of black models being employed was still much lower than the relative percentage of blacks in the population.[22] However, the research did suggest that the status or role portrayal of blacks had advanced to the point where it was nearly equal in many ways to the portrayal of whites. Still further, related research reveals a trend toward increased employment of black models in TV commercials.[23] The study found that the inclusion of black models in TV ads is consistent with the percentage of blacks in the overall population.

DO BLACKS PAY MORE? This question is of prime interest to leaders of local black communities and government public policy makers concerned with the quality of life in such communities.

Most of the evidence on the question has focused on poor blacks living in central-city communities. A review of the topic suggests that supermarket chain stores charge the same prices in their stores located in black communities as they do in their stores located in predominantly white urban or suburban communities.[24] However, the research also indicates that small independent groceries located in black communities do charge more than the major supermarket chains, and therefore blacks who shop at these stores are likely to pay more.

Since almost all of these studies examined the "price asked" by retailers located inside and outside of black communities rather than the "price paid," it is difficult to determine whether black consumers actually do pay more. One study found that blacks tend to avoid the higher prices charged by small independent stores in their communities by shopping outside of their immediate community.[25] Another study, more rigorously designed, examined the actual prices paid by inner-city blacks, inner-city whites, and suburban whites for food and related items.[26] It found that inner-city blacks paid more than inner-city whites, and that both these groups paid more than suburban whites. However, the evidence failed to reveal whether the higher prices paid by blacks were due to discriminatory pricing practices. Instead, the researcher suggested that the additional amount paid by blacks (which averaged about 1 percent) was likely to have been a function of the fact that blacks more often bought the relatively higher-priced smaller sizes of the products studied.[27] These results indicate the need for effective consumer education for lower-income blacks.

PURCHASE MOTIVES AND BEHAVIOR. In terms of their basic drive as consumers, blacks have been characterized in terms of their motivation to strive (or not to strive) for middle-class values, as such values are reflected in the consumption of material goods.[28] According to this "striving" framework, the black consumer faces the dilemma of "...whether to strive against odds for middle-class values as reflected in material goods, or to give in and live more for the moment."[29] Strivers were identified as those black consumers who perceive that it is possible for them, in terms of present or expected incomes, to attain a middle-class lifestyle. Nonstrivers are described as those black consumers who feel financially blocked from such goals and who therefore do not seek the material goods associated with being "middle class."

A comparison of two groups of black students—one that strongly subscribed to basic American values and one that did not—provides some support for the "striver" notion.[30] The findings indicated that those black students who identified strongly with basic American values were more likely to be "strivers" (i.e., aspire to attain higher social-class status) than those who did not.

Segmentation of the black market on the basis of motivation suggests that the nonstrivers may constitute a distinct market segment. They have to be reached through copy appeals that differ from the traditional values stressed in most mass-media advertising. The striver-nonstriver framework also suggests that as more blacks acquire middle-class economic status, the striver segment of the black market will increase.

Other research studies that have explored the product preferences and brand purchase patterns of black consumers have found the following:

1. Black consumers usually favor popular brands, often the leading brand within a product category.[31] It has been proposed that this purchase pattern is due to two factors: (a) black consumers have a strong desire to impress others, and (b) buying the "best" is their strategy for coping with perceived risk.

2. Black consumers are loyal consumers; that is, they tend to establish definite brand preferences.[32] Brand loyalty may also be a strategy for avoiding perceived risk. Furthermore, it is a simple decision strategy which frees up time that would otherwise be spent searching for product information.

3. As an outcome of their loyalty to popular national brands, black consumers tend to be less willing than the general population to purchase private-label and generic products.[33] For marketers of established national brands, black consumers are therefore especially important target consumers. Drawing from a study of black consumers' supermarket shopping behavior, Table 15-5 presents the brand preferences for twelve major consumer product categories.

4. Research suggests that blacks are more likely than whites to be clothing innovators (i.e., to purchase new styles).[34] Other evidence indicates that within each income category, blacks are more likely than whites to own higher-priced automobiles.[35] It

TABLE 15-5   Black Consumers' Brand Preferences for Twelve Supermarket Product Categories

(UNIT VOLUME SHARE BASED ON PURCHASES IN SIMULATED SUPERMARKET)

Mouthwash		Flour		Mayonnaise	
Listerine	47.1%	Gold Medal	51.2%	Kraft	48.3%
Scope	23.4	Aunt Jemima	18.6	Hellmann's	31.4
Listermint	13.1	Pillsbury	18.6	Generic	13.3
Signal	10.1	Private label	10.1	Private label	7.0
Generic	6.3	Ceresota	1.5		
Hand & body lotion		**Coffee**		**Peanut butter**	
Vaseline Intensive		Maxwell House	41.6%	Skippy	43.0%
Care	43.1%	Folgers	36.3	Peter Pan	19.0
Jergens	18.4	Generic	9.6	Jif	16.1
J & J Baby Oil	12.8	Hills Bros.	8.9	Generic	11.6
Nivea	11.6	Private label	3.6	Private label	6.4
Private label	7.3			Smuckers	3.8
Wondra	6.8				
Frozen orange juice		**Paper towels**		**Cooking oil**	
Minute Maid	57.7%	ScotTowels	30.1%	Crisco	51.7%
Private label	18.5	Bounty	22.6	Wesson	21.4
Tropicana	18.4	Generic	20.2	Mazola	15.3
Snow Crop	5.4	Viva	20.1	Generic	8.1
		Private label	6.9	Private label	3.4
Detergents		**All-purpose cleansers (liquid)**		**Baked beans**	
Tide	54.7%	Pine Sol	38.4%	Campbell	60.0%
Cheer	20.4	Ajax	25.4	Generic	10.8
Fab	9.0	Lysol	16.3	B & M	10.6
Generic	8.0	Top Job	9.2	Heinz	10.3
Private label	4.3	Lestoil	6.4	Private label	8.3
All	3.5	Generic	4.3		

Source: Alphonzia Wellington, "Traditional Brand Loyalty," *Advertising Age* May 18, 1981, S-2, which is based on *Black Consumers' Response to Inflation: The Supermarket*, Copyright 1980 Wellington Group, Inc. Used with permission.

has been suggested that the purchase of socially conspicuous products serves to enhance the black consumer's self-image or self-worth.

Research that compared basic black/white values in terms of the Rokeach Value Survey (see Chapter 14) found that differences in values that exist between blacks and whites are primarily due to socioeconomic differences.[36] When the analysis controlled for income, only minor differences appeared between blacks and whites at the same socioeconomic levels.

Age Subcultures

All major age subgroupings of the population might broadly be thought of as separate subcultures. Within the context of the family life cycle, Chapter 12 examined the major age segments of the adult population. Each stage of the life cycle (bachelorhood, honeymooners, parenthood, postparenthood, and dissolution) could be considered a separate subculture, since important shifts occur in the demand for specific types of products and services.

In this section we will limit our examination of age subcultures to just two groups: the *young adult* and the *elderly*. These two age groups have been singled out because they are on opposite ends of the age spectrum of the adult population, and because their distinctive lifestyles qualify them for consideration as subcultural groups.

THE YOUNG ADULT MARKET

Many marketers perceive young adults to be a particularly desirable target audience because (1) they are on the threshold of adult life, (2) they are often anxious to spend the discretionary money at their disposal, and (3) they are still forming their purchase patterns and brand loyalties for many product categories.

WHO ARE THE YOUNG ADULTS? When we speak of young adults, we are referring to the segment of the population that is between eighteen and twenty-four years of age. According to U.S. Census Bureau figures, in 1980 there were approximately 30 million young adults, which constituted 13 percent of the total population.[37] It is expected that the size of this segment will increase slightly through the early 1980s and then begin to decline, so that by the year 2000 there should be approximately 25 million young adults, constituting about 9 percent of the population. This expected shrinkage in the size of the young adult market reflects the decline in birthrate that began in the early 1960s.[38]

It is helpful to think of the young adult market as consisting of three somewhat overlapping subgroups: (1) college students, (2) young singles, and (3) young marrieds. Following is a brief profile of each of these major subdivisions of the young adult market:

1. *College students.* Approximately 26 percent of the members of the young adult market are enrolled in college programs.[39] The majority of these students live at home or consider their parents' homes to be their permanent address. Many of

them have part-time jobs to meet their expenses and to provide them with spending money.

2. *Young singles.* Most of the members of the young adult segment are single (75 percent of the males and 59 percent of the females).[40] Moreover, available evidence indicates that members of this age segment tend to stay single longer than the same age group of a decade ago. Among the major reasons why they remain single longer are (1) the increased accessibility of college and graduate education, (2) the growing preference among young adults for extensive travel, (3) the desire among women to achieve an independent identity and career recognition, (4) changing attitudes toward the acceptability of premarital sexual behavior, and (5) the rising divorce rate, which tarnished the romantic image of marriage as an institution of never-ending love and fidelity.[41]

3. *Young marrieds.* This is a relatively small segment of the young adult market (about 4.5 million families are headed by a person under twenty-five).[42] At this early stage in the formation of their family units, the overwhelming majority of young marrieds live in rented dwellings and are just beginning to establish family-oriented consumption patterns.

CONSUMER CHARACTERISTICS OF THE YOUNG ADULT.   Most young adults are in a transitional stage between adolescence and "full" adulthood, where they will assume responsibility for a wide range of individual and family purchase behavior.

In terms of consumer behavior, young adulthood is a unique stage because most young adults still live at home, or temporarily at college, and rely on their parents for their primary support. Thus the money they have (either earned through part-time jobs or provided by their parents) is almost completely *discretionary.* This means that they are relatively free to spend their money on "luxury-type" items. For instance, young adults are heavy purchasers of books, records, stereo equipment, cameras, fashion clothing, hair driers, and a host of other personal-care and grooming products.[43]

The young adult market has been characterized as low in brand loyalties and high in new-product interests.[44] For marketers, these traits are extremely inviting, for they suggest that young people are a very receptive market.

A study that compared unmarried coeds from a large midwestern university with nearby housewives provides a unique opportunity to evaluate these two distinct market segments in terms of a number of important consumer behavior factors.[45] The coeds were found to have a higher level of perceived fashion opinion leadership than the housewives, were more likely to have received fashion advice from others, were more interested in fashion, and were more likely to be fashion innovators. The coeds had also read more news and fashion magazines, and fewer romance magazines, and watched less television.

Additional research to identify the unique consumption patterns of the young adult market segment would enable marketers to target their marketing efforts more directly to this group.

THE ELDERLY CONSUMER

Unlike the young adults, who are often glorified as a market segment, the elderly are frequently misunderstood and avoided.[46] The distorted image that some marketers have of the elderly has been aptly summed up as follows: "The tendency of marketers is either to treat the elderly, over-65, consumers as a more or less homogeneous group, or to pay virtually no attention to them at all."[47]

WHO IS THE ELDERLY CONSUMER?   In the United States, "old age" is officially assumed to begin with a person's sixty-fifth birthday (i.e., when the individual qualifies for full social security insurance and Medicare). However, research suggests that Americans who are seventy years old still tend to view themselves as "middle aged," and that it is only when they reach their seventy-fifth birthday that they begin to consider themselves to be "elderly."[48]

This and other research suggest that people's *perception* of their age may be more important in determining their behavior than their chronological age (i.e., the number of years lived or the time-distance from birth). In fact, people may at the same time have a number of different subjective or perceived ages (e.g., *feel-age,* how old a person feels; *look-age,* how old a person looks; *do-age,* how involved a person is in doing "things" favored by members of a certain age group; and *interest-age,* how similar a person's interests are to those of members of a certain age group).[49] Table 15-6 shows the percentage of elderly consumers who perceived themselves to be younger than their chronological age for four perceived age dimensions. The results support other research that indicates that elderly consumers are more likely to consider themselves *younger* than their chronological age. Still further, the mean percentages in the last column of the table show that as their chronological age increases, these elderly consumers are more likely to identify with a younger-perceived age grouping. For marketers, these findings suggest the importance of looking beyond chronological age to consumers' perceived ages when attempting to segment markets. Commenting on the need to go beyond chronological age, an advertising executive who specializes in the elderly market noted: "Some people are into looking young and others don't care—they just want to look good. Both attitudes are fine, but both require [different] creative responses..."[50]

The elderly are among the fastest-growing age segment in the American population. According to U.S. Census Bureau data, in 1980 there were approximately 25.5 million people sixty-five years of age and older, or about 11.3 percent of the population.[51] This age segment is expected to grow to approximately 31 million, or 12 percent of the population, by the year 2000. This expected growth in the elderly segment of the population can be explained

TABLE 15-6   Percentage of Elderly Expressing a Perceived Age That Is Younger Than Their Chronological Age

DECADE	FEEL-AGE	LOOK-AGE	DO-AGE	INTEREST-AGE	MEAN %
50's	54%	52%	69%	66%	60%
60's	67	63	77	71	70
70's	63	66	80	77	72
80's	74	68	79	84	76

Source: Benny Barak and Leon G. Schiffman, "Cognitive Age: A Nonchronological Age Variable," in Kent B. Monroe, ed., *Advances in Consumer Research* (Ann Arbor, Mich.: Association for Consumer Research, 1981), VIII, 604.

by the declining birthrate, improved medical diagnoses and treatment, and the resultant increase in general life expectancy.

A MISUNDERSTOOD MARKET.   Some marketers have an extremely narrow and inaccurate picture of the elderly consumer, which causes them to overlook the potential profit to be derived from catering to the needs of this special market segment. For example, marketers are often reluctant to research the elderly market in order to identify unsatisfied needs because they believe that, in general, the elderly cannot afford to buy new products or services. This stereotyped view of the elderly fails to recognize that today many older people do have sufficient funds available for products that could improve the quality of their lives. Indeed, available evidence suggests that the elderly are very willing to try new products, especially those designed to promote or maintain good health.[52] Furthermore, with more and more elderly consumers receiving the benefits of private pension funds in addition to social security and Medicare, this age segment is even more likely to be able to afford new products and services in the future.

It has been the retailer, rather than the manufacturer, who has been most attuned to the needs of the elderly and quickest to realize their value as customers. Retailers have recognized the elderly as a special market segment for the following reasons: (1) they are price sensitive, (2) they have comparatively more time and interest in shopping, and (3) they often view shopping as a social activity to be undertaken with friends or relatives.[53]

Large retail-food chains have been particularly sensitive to the needs of older consumers. For instance, Kroger, the large midwestern supermarket chain, has promoted a "Senior Citizens Club," which offers anyone who is over fifty-nine years of age and on a fixed income a special shopping program designed to cut food costs. Many of the major fast-food restaurant chains have also sponsored various promotional programs designed to attract the business of older consumers.[54]

Table 15-7 lists the results of an insightful study designed to pinpoint the major concerns and desires of older consumers when it comes to their dealing with retailers. The findings suggest that older consumers would especially like to see retail establishments offer a wider range of senior-citizen discount programs, to receive better treatment from retail personnel, and to see stores offer delivery services. Retailers wishing to attract and retain older consumers could use the points covered in the table as a kind of checklist against which to compare their own level of service.

THE NEEDS AND MOTIVATIONS OF ELDERLY CONSUMERS.   The elderly are by no means a homogeneous subcultural group. Available research suggests that, in terms of how they approach life, the elderly can be divided into three major subgroups: (1) *the reorganizers*—those who substitute new involvements for lost ones (e.g., shifting attention after retirement to family, church, social groups, and community activities); (2) *the focused*—those who become active in a selective or narrowed range of activities; and (3) *the disengaged*—those who become uninvolved or withdrawn.[55]

TABLE 15-7   What Do Older Consumers Want from Retailers?

CONCERNS AND DESIRES	AGE 55 TO 64	AGE 65 AND OLDER
Discounts	59.4%	53.0%
More courteous, dignified, patient treatment of older consumers	19.8	25.0
Assistance in locating products	18.9	18.1
Personal assistance	8.5	15.1
Improved store directories	7.5	3.0
Grouped products	2.8	2.2
Transportation services		
Transportation to and from stores	11.3	12.9
Delivery service	20.8	22.4
Price tags and labels		
Small or blurred price numerals	9.4	10.3
Small print on labels	2.8	4.3
Faster checkout provisions	10.4	6.5
Smaller packages for perishables	9.4	8.2
Rest facilities (chairs/benches)	6.6	7.8
Purchasing assistance		
Store personnel to provide detailed product information	2.8	5.2
Purchasing advice	9.4	5.6
Removal of products from displays	5.7	3.4
Parking and entrances		
Designated parking spaces	5.7	2.6
Entrance hazards	1.9	3.4
Package carryout	3.8	3.0

Source: Zarrel V. Lambert, "An Investigation of Older Consumers' Unmet Needs and Wants at the Retail Level," *Journal of Retailing*, 55 (Winter 1979), 43.

To develop special products and special promotional programs to meet the needs of these market segments, marketers must not only recognize their different approaches to life but also conduct research into their specific needs. Table 15-8 presents the findings of a study that asked a sample of elderly consumers to rank sources of satisfaction and dissatisfaction with life in old age. The results revealed that the elderly derive most satisfaction from meaningful social involvement and purposeful activity. On the other hand, they are most fearful of financial and physical dependency and of loneliness. These findings suggest that the elderly need products and services that help them feel that their lives are useful and socially enjoyable, and which reduce their fears of financial and physical dependency. Builders of retirement communities for the elderly have successfully recognized these needs by promoting the organized activities and the security measures their communities offer.

In aiming products at the elderly, marketers must be careful not to embarrass them and make them feel uneasy about their age. When Heinz found that many elderly people were buying baby food because of the small sizes and easy chewing consistency, it introduced a line of "senior foods." The new

Subcultural and Cross-Cultural Aspects of Consumer Behavior

**TABLE 15-8   A Ranking of Sources of Satisfaction and Dissatisfaction with
Life in Old Age**

SATISFACTIONS	RANK	DISSATISFACTIONS
Entertainment and diversions	1	Dependency—financial or physical
Socialization	2	Physical discomfort or sensory loss
Productive activity	3	Loneliness, bereavement
Physical comfort	4	Boredom, inactivity, confinement
Financial security	5	Mental discomfort or loss
Mobility and movement	6	Loss of prestige or respect
Good health and stamina	7	Fear of dying

Adapted from Margaret Clark and Barbara G. Anderson, *Culture and Aging: An Anthropological Study of Older Americans,* 1967. Courtesy Charles C. Thomas, Publishers, Springfield, Illinois.

product failed because elderly consumers were ashamed to admit that they required strained foods; instead, they preferred to buy baby food which they could always pretend they were buying for a grandchild.[56]

REACHING THE ELDERLY CONSUMER.   Relatively little is known about the specific media habits of the elderly consumer. However, it would seem that television should be a particularly good medium through which to reach the elderly. Television would appear to fulfill a number of distinct functions. It provides an escape from loneliness and boredom, a substitute for social interaction, and a means of maintaining a sense of participation in society. For these reasons, perhaps, the elderly tend to prefer TV programs that provide information, news, and current events (a way of keeping in touch with society).[57]

Sex as a Subculture

It may seem surprising to see sex (i.e., gender) included in a discussion of subcultures. Sex-related characteristics are not usually treated as subcultural differences. However, as one marketing expert has pointed out, this is a "notable omission."[58] Indeed, since sex roles are largely culturally determined, it is quite fitting to examine gender as a subcultural category. Moreover, given the extensive amount of attention that changing sex roles and sex discrimination have received in recent years, this is a timely issue.

SEX ROLES AND CONSUMER BEHAVIOR

All known societies assign certain traits and roles to males ("masculine" traits and roles) and others to females ("feminine" traits and roles). In the American society, for instance, aggressiveness, competitiveness, independence, and self-confidence are considered to be traditional masculine traits; while neatness, tactfulness, gentleness, and talkativeness are considered to be traditional feminine traits.[59] Similarly, in terms of role differences, women have historically been cast as homemakers with responsibility for child care, and men have been considered the providers or breadwinners.

While such traits and roles are no longer strongly associated with members of a specific sex, they are nevertheless still prevalent. Many advertisers still appeal to such sex-linked roles, and consumer tastes are frequently influenced by such sex-role factors.

CONSUMER PRODUCTS AND SEX ROLES.   Within every society, it is quite common to find products that are either exclusively or strongly associated with the members of one sex. In the United States, for example, shaving equipment, cigars, pants, ties, and work clothing were historically male products; whereas bracelets, hair spray, hair driers, and sweet-smelling colognes were generally considered to be feminine products. For most of these products, the sex link has either diminished or disappeared; while for others, the prohibition still lingers.

Granting that the line between "male only" and "female only" products has become blurred in recent years, research nevertheless indicates that males and females tend to impute a sex, or gender, to products.[60] Table 15-9 lists the results of a study that explored the gender that male and female respondents attribute to twenty-four products. For advertising executives, such insights suggest that they should consider not only the sex of their target market but also the *perceived* sex of the product category.

Other research has examined male acceptance of a traditionally feminine product (hair spray). It suggests that males with a strong masculine self-concept and those who are less anxiety-prone may be good prospects for products that initially had a feminine image.[61]

MASS MEDIA AND SEX ROLES.   A series of investigations have employed content analysis to examine the portrayal of women in mass-media advertising.[62] Generally, these studies indicate that women have not been depicted accurately

TABLE 15-9   Gender Ascribed to 24 Products

masculine-image products	feminine-image products	indeterminate products
Pocket knife	Umbrella	Key ring
Tool kit	Mouthwash	
Shaving cream	Fountain pen	
Cuff links	Sun glasses	
Poker chips	Sandals	
Brief case	Gloves	
Mechanical pencil	Bedroom slippers	
Blue jeans	Silk shirt	
Tennis shoes	Hair spray	
Nail clippers	Hand lotion	
	Baby oil	
	Nylon underwear	
	Scarf	

Source: Neil K. Allison, Linda L. Golden, Gary M. Mullet, and Donna Coogan, "Sex-Typed Product Images: The Effects of Sex, Sex Role Self-Image and Measurement Implications," in Jerry C. Olson, ed., *Advances in Consumer Research* (Ann Arbor, Mich.: Association for Consumer Research, 1980), VII, 606.

in terms of the range and scope of their current roles. For instance, general audience magazine advertisements have tended to stereotype women into four restrictive feminine roles:

1. *A woman's place is in the home.* Advertisements do not adequately represent the fact that about half of all American women work outside of the home.
2. *Women do not make important decisions or do important things.* Advertisements rarely depict women making non household decisions, nor do they show them engaged in meaningful activities outside of the home.
3. *Women are dependent and need men's protection.* Advertisements portray women as dependent rather than independent or interdependent beings.
4. *Men regard women primarily as sexual objects.* Advertisements show women being treated by men not as equal human beings, but rather as subordinate, "decorative" and/or sexual objects.[63]

Table 15-10 compares the roles portrayed by women in advertisements in 1958, 1970, 1972, and 1978. It reveals some modest improvement in the proportion of magazine ads that portrayed women in a working environment

TABLE 15-10   A Comparison of Working and Nonworking Roles of Women Portrayed in Advertisements

	1958 PERCENT*	1970 PERCENT†	1972 PERCENT‡	1978 PERCENT§
a. Working Roles				
Percent shown in a working environment	13.0	9.0	21.0	12.2
Occupational categories:				
High-level business	0.0	0.0	0.0	0.0
Professional	0.0	0.0	4.0	21.8
Entertainment, sports	11.1	58.0	23.0	30.4
Middle-level business	5.6	8.0	15.0	30.4
Secretarial, clerical	74.4	17.0	46.0	17.4
Blue collar	8.9	17.0	12.0	0.0
Total	100.0	100.0	100.0	100.0
b. Nonworking Roles				
Percent shown in a nonworking environment	87.0	91.0	79.0	87.8
Family	24.2	23.0	8.0	19.3
Recreational	28.3	46.0	36.0	19.3
Decorative	47.5	31.0	56.0	61.4
Total	100.0	100.0	100.0	100.0

Sources: Adapted from* Ahmed Belkaoui and Janice M. Belkaoui, "A Comparative Analysis of the Roles Portrayed by Women in Print Advertisements: 1958, 1970, 1972," *Journal of Marketing Research,* 13 (May 1976), 170–71.

†Alice E. Courtney and Sarah Wernick Lockeretz, "A Woman's Place: An Analysis of the Roles Portrayed by Women in Magazine Advertisements," *Journal of Marketing Research,* 8 (February 1971), 93–94.

‡Louis C. Wagner and Janis B. Banos, "A Woman's Place: A Follow-Up Analysis of the Roles Portrayed by Women in Magazine Advertisements," *Journal of Marketing Research,* 10 (May 1973), 214.

§Marc G. Weinberger, Susan M. Petroshius, and Stuart A. Westin, "Twenty Years of Women in Magazine Advertising: An Update," in Neil Beckwith et al., eds., *1979 Educators' Conference Proceedings* (Chicago: American Marketing Association, 1979), 345.

for the period between 1970 and 1972, and then a drop backward to below the 1972 and 1958 levels in 1978. However, there was a marked increase in the percentage of women portrayed in professional and middle-level business positions between 1972 and 1978, and a decline in the proportion of women depicted in secretarial, clerical, and blue-collar jobs. In the realm of nonworking roles, the increased portrayal of women was most evident in the depiction of women in a family-related role.

An experiment that required female subjects to create print ads for a variety of product categories provides some additional insights into the prevalence of traditional sex roles in advertising.[64] Each subject was supplied with a portfolio of pictures depicting women in five roles (neutral, family, career, sex-object, fashion-object) and was asked to match product pictures to female role pictures. The findings indicated no uniform selection of a single female role for all product categories. Instead, female subjects tended to select different role/product combinations, depending on the nature of the specific product. For instance, the *neutral* and *career* roles were preferred for personal and grooming products, while the *family* role was preferred for household and food products. However, there was no product category for which a *sex-object* role was considered the most appropriate role portrayal. For the advertiser, these results tend to confirm that there is no universal female role; rather, women should be portrayed in roles that are consistent with the environment in which the product is likely to be consumed.

Advertisers who have creatively appealed to the expanded role of contemporary women are likely to have their efforts rewarded. For example, Figure 15-2 presents an ad for Drambuie that challenges women to think for themselves when selecting a drink.

FEMINISM AND CONSUMER BEHAVIOR

What impact has the feminist movement had on the locus of family decision making? According to one study, a wife who has a "liberal" view of the female role (e.g., strongly favors sexual equality) is more likely to participate with her husband in family decision making.[65] In fact, for selected product categories, the equality-minded woman often played a *dominant* role in the decision-making process (e.g., she was more likely to influence the amount to be spent). In those households where the wife had either a "moderate" or a "conservative" view of the female role, husbands were more likely to dominate in a wide range of family purchase decisions.

The research also indicated that age and family income affect sex-role differences in family decision making. Specifically, younger "liberal" women from higher-income families were less likely to report husband-dominated decisions that those who were older and from lower-income families. In general terms, the results suggest that sex-role perceptions of married women reflect the amount of influence that either spouse has in family decision making.

As further evidence that many American women, especially younger and better-educated women, have broadened their horizons with regard to opportu-

FIGURE 15-2   Advertisement Appealing to an Expanded Female Role

Courtesy of W.A. Taylor & Co.

nities open to women during the past two decades, Figure 15-3 depicts the decline in the percentage of women who agree with the traditional belief that "A woman's place is in the home."

The relationship between various measures of feminist involvement and opinion leadership has also been examined.[66] Studies indicate that feminists may be an important force in the marketplace. For instance, one study found that women who were members of a feminist group (the National Organization of Women) were more likely to be opinion leaders than women who belong to nonfeminist women's organizations (Women's Democratic Club, Young Women's Christian Association, and League of Women Voters). Since opinion leaders influence the consumer attitudes and behavior of others, these findings suggest

FIGURE 15-3   Decline of the Traditional Feminine Outlook
Source: Fred D. Reynolds, Melvin R. Crask, and William D. Wells, "The Modern Feminine Life Style," *Journal of Marketing*, 41 (June 1977), 39.

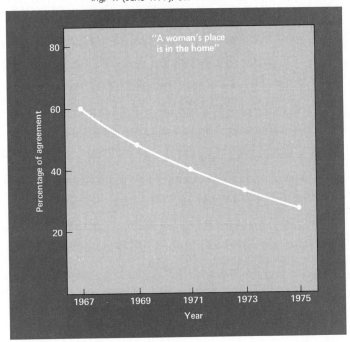

that marketers should explicitly consider feminist values and attitudes in developing promotional campaigns. Failure to do so may significantly impede the acceptance of new products and services for this growing market segment.

THE WORKING WOMAN

In recent years, marketers and consumer researchers have been increasingly interested in the working woman, especially the *married* working woman. They recognize that working wives are a large and growing market segment whose needs differ from those of women who do not work outside the home.

According to government sources, slightly more than half (51 percent) of all American women are now employed outside the home. Moreover, about 43 percent of all *married* women have jobs. Still more revealing, about 45 percent of all married women with *preschool children* are working. In fact, young married working women with young children are the fastest-growing segment in the female work force.[67]

These married working women have become an important market segment. However, marketers still know relatively little about how the dual demands of job and family influence consumer behavior.

WHY DO MARRIED WOMEN WORK?   Many social-cultural factors are responsible for why so many married women now work. Some of the chief factors are (1) the increased level of female educational attainment, (2) a need to supplement the husband's income, (3) the high divorce rate, (4) the growing conviction that women can simultaneously be mothers and have careers, (5) the growth in the number of service jobs that appeal to women, (6) the trend toward fewer children, and (7) the availability of products that make homemaking easier and less time consuming.[68]

CONSUMER BEHAVIOR AND WORKING WOMEN

A study based on a large sample of women living in a major southwestern metropolitan area compared the consumption behavior of working women and nonworking women.[69] The results indicated that working women were more likely than nonworking women to shop just once a week for their food needs and were more likely to do so either during evening hours or on Saturday. Working women were also found to spend less money at the supermarket; however, this may be explained by the greater likelihood that they eat out one or more times a week.

When it came to clothing shopping, working women were found to prefer self-service stores and evening shopping and to be store loyal; nonworking women were more likely to use newspapers to select clothing stores and other retailers and were more price conscious. Finally, working women were somewhat less likely than nonworking women to read a daily newspaper and tended to watch less television. Table 15-11 summarizes these and other differences found to exist between working women and nonworking women.

TABLE 15-11   Consumer Behavior Differences between Working Women and Nonworking Women

CONSUMER AREA	THE WORKING WOMAN IS MORE LIKELY TO	THE NONWORKING WOMAN IS MORE LIKELY TO
Food shopping	Shop once a week or less. Shop evenings or Saturdays. Spend $11–$25 per week.	Shop several times a week. Shop Monday or Thursday. Spend $26–$50 per week. Find newspaper food ads helpful.
Clothing shopping	Prefer self-service. Shop evenings. Shop same store.	Use newspaper to select store. Be price conscious. Be concerned with how flattering clothing is.
Services	Not use a maid. Not shop by mail-order catalog. Make more frequent use of vending machines. Eat out one or more times a week.	Use a maid once a week. Shop by mail-order catalog and by phone. Use cents-off coupons from newspapers.
Media exposure	Watch less than three hours of TV per day.	Read a newspaper daily.

Source: Adapted from Suzanne McCall, "Analytical Projections of Lifestyle Identification in Consumer Behavior," in Kenneth L. Bernhardt, ed., *Marketing: 1776–1976 and Beyond* (Chicago: American Marketing Association, 1976), 335.

Another study that compared working and nonworking women found that working women averaged fewer food-shopping trips in a given week than nonworking women.[70] In addition, working women were found to be more brand loyal. Because brand loyalty is a way of reducing shopping time, this finding is consistent with the finding that working women make fewer food-shopping trips each week.

For marketers, these studies suggest that working women make shopping a less time-consuming activity. They accomplish this "time economy" by shopping less often, and by being brand and store loyal. Not surprisingly, the working woman is also likely to do her shopping during evening hours or on the weekend.

To better account for the various factors that might contribute to why women work and to provide a richer market segmentation framework, it seems desirable to go beyond simply classifying women as either working or nonworking when studying their consumer behavior. To this end, it has been suggested that marketers would benefit from looking at four specific subgroups of working and nonworking women: (1) those homemakers who have *no* plans to work outside the home; (2) those homemakers who plan to work outside the home; (3) those working women who view their work as being "just a job"; and (4) those working women who consider their work to be a career. These different outlooks or orientations have been shown to be related to mass-media habits (e.g., career women are the heaviest radio listeners) and purchasing and shopping patterns (e.g., career women are the most deliberate and the most brand loyal in their shopping behavior).[71]

Subcultural Interaction

We have just examined six important subcultural categories. It should be remembered that all consumers are simultaneously members of more than one subcultural segment (for example, a consumer may be a young, Hispanic, Catholic, working wife living in the northeastern section of the country). For this reason, marketers should strive to understand how multiple subcultural memberships *interact* to influence their target consumers' relevant consumption behavior. Promotional strategy should not be limited to a single subcultural membership.

CROSS-CULTURAL CONSUMER ANALYSIS

In our examination of psychological, social, and cultural concepts, we have continuously pointed out how various segments of the American consuming public differ. If such diversity exists between segments of a *single* society, then even more diversity should exist among the members of two or more societies. International marketers must understand the differences inherent in different societies (i.e., cross-culturally) so that they can develop appropriate marketing strategies to effectively penetrate each foreign market of interest.

What Is Cross-Cultural Consumer Analysis?

In deciding whether to enter a foreign market, and how to approach that market, it is appropriate for the marketer to engage in cross-cultural consumer analysis. Within the scope of this discussion, we will define *cross-cultural consumer analysis* as the effort to determine *to what extent the consumers of two or more nations are similar or different*. Such analyses are designed to provide the marketer with sufficient understanding of the differences in psychological, social, cultural, and environmental characteristics to facilitate the design of effective marketing strategies for each of the specific countries involved.

SIMILARITIES AND DIFFERENCES AMONG PEOPLE

A major objective of cross-cultural consumer analysis is the determination of how consumers in two or more societies are similar, and how they are different. An understanding of the similarities and differences that exist between nations is critical to the multinational marketer, who must devise appropriate marketing strategies to reach the consumers in specific foreign markets. The greater the similarity between nations, the more feasible it is to employ similar marketing strategies in each nation. On the other hand, if the cultural beliefs, values, and customs of specific target countries are found to differ widely, then a highly *individualized* marketing strategy is indicated for each country.

Just how wise it would be for a firm to introduce its successful product in a number of foreign countries is likely to be heavily influenced by how similar the

FIGURE 15-4   **Cross-National Comparison of the Value Placed on Housecleaning** Source: Joseph T. Plummer, "Consumer Focus in Cross-National Research," *Journal of Advertising*, 6 (Spring 1977), 10.

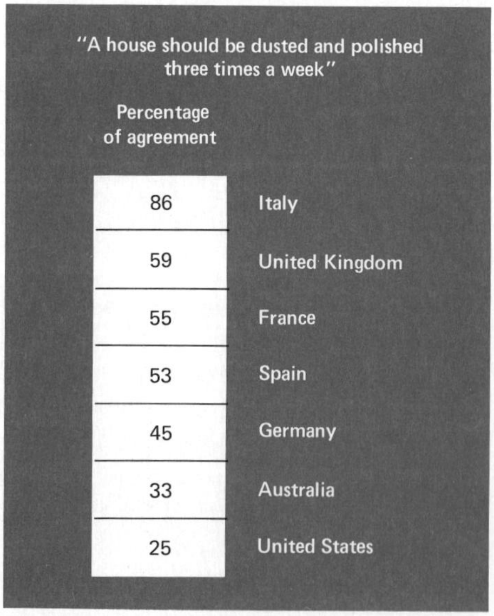

"A house should be dusted and polished three times a week"

Percentage of agreement

86	Italy
59	United Kingdom
55	France
53	Spain
45	Germany
33	Australia
25	United States

beliefs, values, and customs of the countries are that govern the use of the product. For example, the seven-country comparison in Figure 15-4 shows the percentage of consumers who agreed with the statement "A house should be dusted and polished three times a week." While much additional information is likely to be required, a multinational firm that was planning to market a new line of furniture polishes would be quite interested in such research for its potential usefulness in establishing the firm's marketing priorities.

Some marketers have argued that the world is becoming more and more similar and that standardized marketing strategies are therefore becoming increasingly feasible. Indeed, Philip Morris has successfully used the Marlboro cowboy all over the world (see Figure 15-5). Other companies, such as Coca-Cola and Volkswagen have frequently used the same marketing themes on a global basis.[72] However, other marketers have argued that differences between countries are sufficiently glaring to make "localized" marketing a more effective approach. For instance, Gervais-Danone experienced considerable difficulty in marketing various dairy products outside of its native France. Specifically, in Mexico the firm was on the edge of bankruptcy before it hit upon the correct advertising theme—one that recognized that Mexicans liked to use one particular cheese as a substitute for butter.[73]

A survey of multinational business executives found that individualized marketing efforts are becoming more common.[74] One marketing authority has

FIGURE 15-5   A Popular Advertising Theme Used Worldwide

aptly summed up the arguments as follows: "The only ultimate truth possible is that humans are both deeply the same and obviously different...."[75]

This book is based upon the very same thesis. Earlier chapters have attempted to point up the underlying similarities that exist between people, and the external influences that, at the same time, serve to differentiate them into distinct market segments. If we believe in tailoring marketing strategies to specific segments in the American market, it follows that we also believe in tailoring marketing strategies to the needs—psychological, social, cultural, and functional—of specific foreign segments.

ACCULTURATION IS A NEEDED MARKETING VIEWPOINT

Many American marketers make the strategic error of believing that "if Americans like it, then everyone will." Such a biased viewpoint increases the likelihood of marketing failures abroad. It reflects a complete lack of understanding of the unique psychological, social, cultural, and environmental characteristics of distinctly different cultures.

To overcome such a narrow and culturally myopic view, marketers must become *acculturated;* that is, they must learn everything that is relevant to the foreign cultures in which they plan to operate.

In a sense, acculturation is a dual process for marketers who are entering a foreign market with which they are not familiar. First, they must thoroughly orient themselves to the values, beliefs, and customs of the new society if they hope to be successful in marketing their products. Second, to gain acceptance of a culturally new product in a foreign society, they must persuade the members of that society to break with their own traditions. For example, a social marketing effort designed to encourage consumers in developing nations to employ artificial birth-control devices would require a dual acculturation process. First, the marketer must acquire an in-depth picture of the society's present attitudes and customs with regard to birth control; then the marketer has to devise promotional strategies that will persuade the target market to adopt the new practice in place of its traditional customs.

It stands to reason that the more similar the target society is to our own, the easier the process of acculturation. A study that focused on consumer acculturation found that foreign students who came from *developed* countries, with cultural heritages similar to the United States, were most likely to become acculturated; while those who came from *developing* nations were significantly less likely to adopt American consumption values and behavior.[76] Related research indicates that the interaction of personality factors and religious affiliation are useful in understanding consumer acculturation.[77]

DISTINCTIVE CHARACTERISTICS OF CROSS-CULTURAL ANALYSIS

The same research techniques used to study the American consumer are used to study consumers in foreign lands. In cross-cultural analysis, however, there is the additional burden that language and word usage often differ from nation to nation.[78]

To illustrate how important proper wording is in cross-cultural analysis, and the necessity of designing questionnaires that reflect a country's specific beliefs, values, and customs, consider the following:[79]

1. A six-nation study indicated that consumption of spaghetti and macaroni was substantially greater in France and West Germany than in Italy. Upon further consideration, however, the researchers realized that their question had asked about the purchase of "packaged and branded spaghetti" rather than about level of consumption. Since many Italians purchase their spaghetti loose, their responses in no way reflected their actual purchase or consumption of spaghetti. Thus the finding that Italians were lighter spaghetti consumers than the French and West Germans had no basis in fact.

2. A pretest of a seven-country study designed to discover whether married or engaged women had received an engagement ring identified the following problems with the wording of the original questionnaire: (a) the word "engaged" did not mean the same thing in all nations (e.g., for a young Italian or Spanish woman, it refers to a relationship with any man who has taken her out more than once); (b) the question "Do you own an engagement ring?" is not appropriate for all countries (e.g., in Germany it is a common practice for a young woman to receive a gold wedding band upon her engagement). These and other aspects of the questionnaire were modified to meet the specific cultural traits of each country studied.

To avoid such research design problems, marketers or consumer researchers must familiarize themselves with the culture and availability of research facilities in the countries that are being evaluated as potential markets. Table 15-12 lists eight basic factors that multinational marketers must consider in planning cross-cultural consumer research.

TABLE 15-12   Eight Basic Factors Influencing Cross-Cultural Analysis

FACTORS	EXAMPLES
Language differences	The words or concepts of a promotional theme may not translate adequately, and the meaning might be lost.
Differences in consumption patterns	Two countries may differ substantially in the level of consumption of a product.
Differences in potential market segments	The income or social class, age, and sex of consumers may differ dramatically in different countries.
Differences in the way that products or services are used	Two nations may use the same product or service in very different ways.
Differences in the criteria for evaluating products and services	The benefits that consumers seek from a product or service may differ from country to country.
Differences in economic and social conditions	The locus of family decision making may vary significantly from country to country.
Differences in marketing conditions	The types and quality of retail outlets may vary greatly between countries.
Differences in marketing research opportunities	High illiteracy rates or lack of telephones may inhibit data collection in certain countries.

Source: Adapted from Paul Howard Berent, "International Research is Different," in Edward M. Mazze, ed., *1975 Combined Proceedings* (Chicago: American Marketing Association, 1975), 295.

Marketing Mistakes: A Failure to Understand Differences

In most cases, the "gamble" in international marketing is not knowing if the product, the promotional appeal, the pricing policy, or the retail channels that are effective in America will also work in other countries and what specific changes should be made to ensure acceptance in each foreign market. To provide the reader with a vivid picture of the problems inherent to international marketing, we will briefly examine some international marketing blunders. These examples illustrate that a failure to tailor marketing strategy to the target market's distinctive cultural traits can lead to costly mistakes.

PRODUCT PROBLEMS

International marketers frequently neglect to modify their products to meet local customs and tastes. For example, one American marketer learned the hard way (through poor sales performance) that English homemakers were not interested in American-style cake mixes but preferred instead "...a tough, rather spongy item which was traditional for tea."[80] To avoid such problems, marketers must ascertain whether the physical characteristics of their products are acceptable to the new market. For instance, Nestlé learned that it was necessary to market more than sixty different formulations of Nescafé in order to meet local foreign coffee preferences.[81]

Products brought from Europe to the United States have also had problems. For example, the *Delacre* line of luxury biscuits proved too rich for American tastes, and its ingredients and promotional appeal have since been revised to make it more acceptable to Americans.[82]

Color is an extremely critical variable in international marketing because the same color frequently has different meanings in different cultures. To illustrate, a yellow cologne failed to sell in Africa because consumers believed that it was animal urine; however, it sold successfully when its color was changed to green.[83] Similarly, General Foods, which markets its Instant Maxwell House coffee worldwide in a red can, found that red was inappropriate in Japan, where it means "fire sale."[84]

PROMOTIONAL PROBLEMS

When communicating with consumers in different parts of the world, it is imperative that the promotional message be consistent with the language and customs of the specific society. Following are the kinds of problems that international marketers have faced in communicating with widely different customer groups.

The Seven-Up Company's highly successful "Uncola" theme, which was developed for the United States market, was considered inappropriate for many foreign markets because it did not translate well into other languages.[85] In its place, Seven-Up used a theme that featured a pair of white-gloved hands coming out of a green box. It was determined that this theme could easily be translated into the respective languages of some eighty countries.

In Japan, Seiko employed the headline "Like a Wind, I am the Color of a Bird" to introduce a new line of colored dial watches. To a Japanese consumer, this headline might mean "This watch is light and delicate. It perhaps floats on your hand like a seedpod on the wind. Or a bird. A hummingbird with its jewel-like colors, the colors of the watch itself."[86] Yet to most Americans, the headline would be meaningless.

Product names also cause considerable problems for international marketers. For instance, Pledge, the Johnson wax product, translated inappropriately in several European languages.[87] To avoid product name difficulties, marketers must often use different names in different countries. To this end, General Foods' Dream Whip in the United States is called Dream Topping in England and Copo Imperial in Venezuela.[88]

PRICING AND DISTRIBUTION PROBLEMS

International marketers must also adjust their pricing and distribution policies to meet local economic conditions and customs. For instance, in many developing nations where the average income is quite low, small-sized packages of products are often a necessity because consumers cannot afford the cash outlay required for the larger sizes popular in the United States and other affluent countries. Even in developed nations there are important differences. To illustrate, supermarkets are very popular in Switzerland, but in France, which is just across the border, consumers prefer smaller and more intimate stores for their grocery shopping.[89] Thus marketers must vary their distribution channels by nation.

The Need for Systematic Cross-Cultural Consumer Research

Until quite recently, the systematic study of marketing and of consumer behavior has been dominated by Americans, and therefore it was only natural that most marketing and consumer behavior research would focus on the United States. The following comment reflects the "state of the art" of cross-cultural consumer research: "With few exceptions, most of the current information on consumption patterns of people outside the United States is strictly observational and often emphasizes colorful idiosyncrasies rather than systematic behavioral modes."[90]

In response to the growing interest in multinational marketing, it is likely that academic consumer researchers, especially American and European scholars, will increasingly undertake systematic and conceptual research investigations designed to identify the psychological, social, and cultural characteristics of consumers in different societies.

summary

Subcultural analysis enables marketers to segment their market to meet the specific needs, motivations, perceptions, and attitudes that are shared by members of a specific subcultural group. A *subculture* is a distinct cultural group which exists as an identifiable segment within a larger, more complex society. Its members possess beliefs, values, and customs that set them apart from other members of the same society; at the same time, they hold to the dominant beliefs of the overall society. Major subcultural categories in this country include nationality, religion, geographic location, race, age, sex, and occupation. Each of these can be broken down into smaller segments which can best be reached through special copy appeals and selective media choices. In some cases (e.g., the elderly consumer), product characteristics can be tailored to the specialized needs of the market segment. Since all consumers are simultaneously members of several subcultural groups (e.g., a young, married, northern, Catholic working woman of Italian parentage), the marketer should try to determine how specific subcultural memberships interact to influence the consumer's overall purchase decisions.

With such diversity among the members of just one nation, it is easy to understand that numerous larger differences exist between members of different nations. If international marketers are to effectively penetrate selected foreign markets, they must understand the relevant similarities and differences that exist among the peoples of these countries. Such cross-cultural analyses will provide marketers with sufficient understanding of the psychological, social, cultural, and environmental characteristics of the countries in which they are interested to develop appropriate marketing strategies.

For some international marketers, *acculturation* may be a dual process: first, they must learn everything that is relevant to the society in which they plan to market; then they must persuade the members of that society to break with their own traditional ways of doing things to adopt the new product. The more similar the target society is to our own, the easier the process of acculturation. Conversely, the more different the target society, the more difficult the process of acculturation.

Some of the problems involved in cross-cultural analysis include differences in language, consumption patterns, needs, product usage, economic and social conditions, marketing conditions, and market research opportunities. There is an urgent need for more systematic and conceptual cross-cultural analyses concerning the consumption habits of foreign consumers. Such analyses will serve to identify increased marketing opportunities that will benefit both international marketers and the consumers they seek to serve.

discussion questions

1. Discuss the importance of subcultures in segmenting the market for food products.
2. What specific recommendations would you offer the management of a firm that produces household detergents on how they might more effectively reach (a) the Hispanic market and (b) the black market?
3. Describe two ways in which the changing lifestyles of young adults have influenced their behavior as consumers.
4. Illustrate how changes in traditional sex roles have provided opportunities to reposition products that have formerly been marketed exclusively to either males or females.
5. Describe two ways in which the changing roles of women have affected their decision making or purchasing behavior.
6. How can a multinational company use cross-cultural consumer analysis to design each factor in its marketing mix? Discuss.
7. If you wanted to name a new product so that it would be acceptable throughout the world, what cultural factors would you consider?
8. List four reasons why a product that is successful in one society might fail in another society.

endnotes

1. Robin M. Williams, Jr., *American Society: A Sociological Interpretation*, 3rd ed. (New York: Knopf, 1970), 415.
2. Gerald Zaltman, *Marketing: Contributions from the Behavioral Sciences* (New York: Harcourt, Brace & World, 1965), 8.
3. U.S. Immigration and Naturalization Service, *Annual Report* (Washington, D.C., 1979).
4. "Businesses that Ride a Rebirth of Ethnic Pride," *Business Week*, October 22, 1979, 149, 153, 156.
5. U.S. Department of Commerce, "More than Three-Fifths of U.S. Hispanic Population in California, Texas and New York, 1980 Census Shows," *Commerce News*, July 17, 1981.
6. "Spanish Speaking Are $20 Billion U.S. Market," *Advertising Age*, November 21, 1973, 56.
7. David Astor, "The Hispanic Market: An In-Depth Profile," *Marketing Communication*, July 1981, 15–19; and Kitty Dawson, "Advertising's Missed Opportunity: The Hispanic Market," *Marketing and Media Decisions*, January 1981, 68–69 and 132–136.
8. Chuck Wingis, "Spanish TV Net Grows, Looks to East," *Advertising Age*, August 18, 1975, 214.
9. *Yearbook of American and Canadian Churches* (Nashville, Tenn.: Abingdon, 1980), 231.
10. Arthur W. VanDyke, "Stop Killing Us with Kindness," *Journal of Marketing*, 40 (July 1976), 90–91.

11. Richard A. Jacobs, "Jewish Media Provide What Others Don't," *Advertising Age*, April 16, 1979, S-28.

12. Del I. Hawkins, Don Roupe, and Kenneth A. Coney, "The Influence of Geographic Subcultures in the United States," in Kent B. Monroe, ed., *Advances in Consumer Research* (Ann Arbor, Mich.: Association for Consumer Research, 1981), VIII, 713–17.

13. Subhash C. Jain, "Life Cycle Revisited: Applications in Consumer Research," in Mary Jane Schlinger, ed., *Advances in Consumer Research* (Association for Consumer Research, 1975), II, 42.

14. William K. Stevens, "Neiman-Marcus's Challenger," *New York Times*, August 6, 1981, D4.

15. Philip H. Dougherty, "Matching Products to Lifestyle," *New York Times*, April 21, 1976, 58. Also see William D. Wells and Fred D. Reynolds, "Psychological Geography," in Jagdish Sheth, ed., *Research in Marketing* (Greenwich, Conn: JAI Press, 1979), II, 345–57.

16. Herbert Allen, "Product Appeal: No Class Barrier," *Advertising Age*, May 18, 1981, S-4.

17. Parvat K. Choudhury, Francis J. Connelly, and Ronald Kahlow, "The Effect of Income on Black Media Behavior," in Kenneth L. Bernhardt, ed., *Marketing: 1776–1976 and Beyond* (Chicago: American Marketing Association, 1976), 422–25.

18. Mary Jane Schlinger and Joseph T. Plummer, "Advertising in Black and White," *Journal of Marketing Research*, 9 (May 1972), 149–53; John W. Gould, Norman B. Sigband, and Cyril E. Zoerner, Jr., "Black Consumer Reactions to 'Integrated' Advertising: An Exploratory Study," *Journal of Marketing*, 34 (July 1970), 20–26; Arnold M. Barban and Edward W. Cundiff, "Negro and White Response to Advertising Stimuli," *Journal of Marketing Research*, 1 (November 1964), 53–56; and Leah Rozen, "Black Presenter Makes a Difference," *Advertising Age*, October 13, 1980, 20.

19. Ronald F. Bush, Joseph F. Hair, Jr., and Paul J. Solomon, "Consumers' Level of Prejudice and Response to Black Models in Advertising," *Journal of Marketing Research*, 16 (August 1979), 341–45.

20. Paul J. Solomon, Ronald F. Bush, and Joseph F. Hair, Jr., "White and Black Consumer Sales Response to Black Models," *Journal of Marketing Research*, 13 (November 1976), 431–34.

21. Harold H. Kassarjian, "The Negro and American Advertising, 1946–1965," *Journal of Marketing Research*, 6 (February 1969), 29–39; and Harold H. Kassarjian, "Blacks in Advertising: A Further Comment," *Journal of Marketing Research*, 8 (August 1971), 392–93.

22. Ronald F. Bush, Alan J. Resnik, and Bruce L. Stern, "A Content Analysis of the Portrayal of Black Models in Magazine Advertising," in Richard P. Bagozzi et al., eds., *1980 Educators' Conference Proceedings* (Chicago: American Marketing Association, 1980), 484–87.

23. Ronald F. Bush, Paul J. Solomon, and Joseph F. Hari, Jr., "There Are More Blacks in TV Commercials," *Journal of Advertising Research*, 17 (February 1977), 21–25.

24. Donald E. Sexton, Jr., "Comparing the Cost of Food to Blacks and to Whites—A Survey," *Journal of Marketing*, 35 (July 1971), 40–46.

25. Charles S. Goodman, "Do the Poor Pay More?" *Journal of Marketing*, 32 (January 1968), 18–24.

26. Donald E. Sexton, Jr., "Do Blacks Pay More?" *Journal of Marketing Research*, 8 (November 1971), 420–26.

27. Ibid., 425–26.

28. Raymond A. Bauer, Scott M. Cunningham, and Lawrence H. Wortzel, "The Marketing Dilemma of Negroes," *Journal of Marketing*, 29 (July 1965), 1–6.

29. Ibid., 3.

30. Joseph F. Hair, Jr., Ronald F. Bush, and Paul S. Busch, "Acculturation and Black Buyer Behavior," in Edward M. Mazze, ed., *1975 Combined Proceedings* (Chicago: American Marketing Association, 1975), 253–56.

31. Kelvin A. Wall, "Positioning Your Brand in the Black Market," *Advertising Age*, June 18, 1973, 71; and Robert B. Settle, John H. Faricy, and Richard W. Mizerski, "Racial Differences in Consumer Locus of Control," in Fred C. Allvine, ed., *1971 Combined Proceedings* (Chicago: American Marketing Association, 1972), 629–33.

32. Bauer, Cunningham, and Wortzel. "Marketing Dilemma," 4; and Carl M. Larson, "Racial Brand Usage and Media Exposure Differentials," in Keith Cox and Ben M. Enis, eds., *New Measure of Responsibility for Marketing* (Chicago: American Marketing Association, 1968), 208–15.

33. Alphonzia Wellington, "Traditional Brand Loyal," *Advertising Age*, May 18, 1981, S-2.

34. Thomas S. Robertson, Douglas J. Dalrymple, and Michael Y. Yoshino, "Cultural Compatibility in New Product Adoption," in Philip R. McDonald, ed., *Marketing Involvement in Society and the Economy* (Chicago: American Marketing Association, 1969), 70–75.

35. Fred C. Akers, "Negro and White Automobile-Buying Behavior: New Evidence," *Journal of Marketing Research*, 5 (August 1968), 283–90.

36. Milton Rokeach and Seymour Parker, "Values as Social Indicators of Poverty and Race Relations in America," *Annals of the American Academy of Political and Social Science*, 388 (March 1970), 97–111.

37. U.S. Bureau of the Census, *1980 Census of Population: Supplementary Report*, PC80-S1-1 (Washington, D.C.: Government Printing Office, May 1981).

38. U.S. Bureau of the Census, *Current Population Reports*, Series P-25, No. 704, "Projections of the Population of the United States 1977 to 2050" (Washington, D.C.: Government Printing Office, July, 1977).

39. U.S. Bureau of the Census, *Current Population Reports*, Series P-20, No. 333, "School Enrollment—Social and Economic Characteristics of Students: October 1977" (Washington, D.C.: Government Printing Office, February 1977).

40. U.S. Bureau of the Census, *Current Population Reports*, Series P-20, No. 349, "Marital Status and Living Arrangements: March 1979" (Washington, D.C.: Government Printing Office, February 1980).

41. *The Life Cycle*, Trend Report No. 8 (New York: Institute of Life Insurance, February 1974), 11.

42. U.S. Bureau of the Census, *Current Population Reports*, Series P-20, No. 349, "Marital Status and Living Arrangements: March 1979" (Washington, D.C.: Government Printing Office, February 1980).

43. Melvin Helitzer and Carl Heyel, *The Youth Market* (New York: Media Books, 1970), 58.

44. Ibid., 18.

45. Stephen A. Baumgarten and John O. Summers, "A Comparison of the Predictors of Fashion Opinion Leadership across Two Populations," in Mazze, *1975 Combined Proceedings*, 429–32.

46. Lynn W. Philips and Brian Sternthal, "Age Differences in Information Processing: A Perspective on the Aged Consumer," *Journal of Marketing Research*, 14 (November 1977), 444–57.

47. Jeffrey G. Towle and Claude R. Martin, Jr., "The Elderly Consumer: One Segment or Many?" in Beverlee B. Anderson, ed., *Advances in Consumer Research* (Association for Consumer Research, 1976), III, 463.

48. Ethel Shanas, "What's New in Old Age?" *American Behavioral Scientist*, 14 (September–October 1970), 5.

49. Benny Barak and Leon G. Schiffman, "Cognitive Age: A Nonchronological Age Variable," in Monroe, *Advances in Consumer Research*, VIII, 602–606.

50. Theodore J. Gage, "Ads Targeted at Mature in Need of Creative Hoist," *Advertising Age,* August 25, 1980, S-5.

51. U.S. Bureau of the Census, *1980 Census of Population: Supplementary Report*, PC80-S1-1 (Washington, D.C.: Government Printing Office, May 1981).

52. Leon G. Schiffman, "Perceived Risk in New Product Trial by Elderly Consumers," *Journal of Marketing Research,* 9 (February 1972), 106–8.

53. Joseph Barry Mason and Brooks E. Smith, "An Exploratory Note on the Shopping Behavior of Low Income Senior Citizens," *Journal of Consumer Affairs*, Winter 1974, 204–9.

54. Philip H. Dougherty, "Age Is No Limit to Sambo's," *New York Times*, November 20, 1980, 35.

55. B. Neugarten, R.J. Havighurst, and S.S. Tobin, "Personality and Patterns of Aging," in B. Neugarten, ed., *Middle Age and Aging* (Chicago: University of Chicago Press, 1968), 173–77.

56. "The Power of the Aging in the Marketplace," *Business Week*, November 20, 1971, 52–58.

57. Lawrence Wenner, "Functional Analysis of TV Viewing for Older Adults," *Journal of Broadcasting,* 20 (Winter 1976), 77–88; and Rena Bartos, "Over 49: The Invisible Consumer Market," *Harvard Business Review,* January–February 1980, 140–48.

58. Frederick D. Sturdivant, "Subculture Theory: Poverty, Minorities and Marketing," in Scott Ward and Thomas S. Robertson, eds., *Consumer Behavior: Theoretical Sources* (Englewood Cliffs, N.J.: Prentice-Hall, 1973), 476.

59. Inge K. Broverman, Susan Raymond Vogel, Donald M. Broverman, Frank E. Clarkson, and Paul S. Rosenkrantz, "Sex Role Stereotypes: A Current Appraisal," *Journal of Social Issues,* 28 (1972), 63.

60. Neil K. Allison, Linda L. Golden, Gary Mullet, and Donna Coogan, "Sex-Typed Product Images: The Effects of Sex, Sex Role Self-Image and Measurement Implications," in Jerry C. Olson, ed., *Advances in Consumer Research* (Ann Arbor, Mich.: Association for Consumer Research, 1980), VII, 604–609.

61. George P. Morris and Edward W. Cundiff, "Acceptance by Males of Feminine Products," *Journal of Marketing Research,* 8 (August 1971), 372–74.

62. Alice E. Courtney and Sarah Wernick Lockeretz, "A Woman's Place: An Analysis of the Roles Portrayed by Women in Magazine Advertisements," *Journal of Marketing Research,* 8 (February 1971), 92–95; Louis C. Wagner and Janis B. Banos, "A Woman's Place: A Follow-up Analysis of the Roles Portrayed by Women in Magazine Advertisements," *Journal of Marketing Research,* 10 (May 1973), 213–14; and Ahmed Belkaoui and Janice M. Belkaoui, "A Comparative Analysis of the Roles Portrayed by Women in Print Advertisements: 1958, 1970, 1972," *Journal of Marketing Research,* 13 (May 1976), 168–72. Also see Marc G. Weinberger, Susan M. Petroshius, and Stuart A. Westin, "Twenty Years of Women in Magazine Advertising: An Update," in Neil Beckwith et al., eds., *1979 Educators' Conference Proceedings* (Chicago: American Marketing Association, 1979), 373–77.

63. Courtney and Lockeretz, "A Woman's Place," 94–95.

64. Lawrence H. Wortzel and John M. Frisbie, "Women's Role Portrayal Preferences in Advertisements: An Empirical Study," *Journal of Marketing,* 38 (October 1974), 41–46.

65. Robert T. Green and Isabella C. M. Cunningham, "Feminine Role Perception and Family Purchasing Decisions," *Journal of Marketing Research,* 12 (August 1975), 325–32.

66. Maureen Daly, *Feminism and Opinion Leadership* (Honors paper, Baruch College of the City University of New York, 1976).

67. U.S. Bureau of the Census, *Current Population Reports*, Series P-20, No. 363, "Population Profiles of the United States: 1980" (Washington, D.C.: Government Printing Office, June 1981).

68. Ibid.; and Suzanne McCall, "Analytical Projections of Lifestyle Identification in Consumer Behavior," in Bernhardt, *Marketing: 1776–1976 and Beyond*, 354–59.

69. McCall, "Analytical Projections."

70. Beverlee B. Anderson, "Working Women versus Non-Working women: A Comparison of Shopping Behavior," in Boris W. Becker and Helmut Becker, eds., *1972 Combined Proceedings* (Chicago: American Marketing Association, 1973), 355–59. Also see Susan P. Douglas, "Working Wife vs. Non-Working Wife Families: A Basis for Segmenting Grocery Markets?" in Anderson, *Advances in Consumer Research*, III, 191–98.

71. Rena Bartos, "What Every Marketer Should Know about Women," *Harvard Business Review*, May–June 1978, 73–85; and Elizabeth C. Hirschman, "Women's Self-Ascribed Occupational Status and Retail Patronage," in Monroe, *Advances in Consumer Research*, VIII, 648–54.

72. S. Watson Dunn, "Effect of National Identity on Multinational Promotional Strategy in Europe," *Journal of Marketing*, 40 (October 1976), 55.

73. "Yogurtizing a Market," *Advertising Age*, July 10, 1978, 94.

74. Ibid., 54.

75. Sidney J. Levy, "Myth and Meaning in Marketing," in Ronald C. Curhan, ed., *1974 Combined Proceedings* (Chicago: American Marketing Association, 1975), 555–56. Also see Saul Sands, "Can You Standardize International Marketing Strategy?" *Journal of the Academy of Marketing Science*, 7 (Spring 1979), 117–28.

76. Joseph Franklin Hair, Jr., and Rolph E. Anderson, "Culture, Acculturation and Consumer Behavior: An Empirical Study," in Becker and Becker, *1972 Combined Proceedings*, 426.

77. Leon G. Schiffman, William R. Dillon, and Festus E. Ngumah, "The Influence of Subcultural and Personality Factors on Consumer Acculturation," *Journal of International Business Studies*, 12 (Fall 1981), 137–43.

78. Robert T. Green and Philip D. White, "Methodological Considerations in Cross-National Consumer Research," *Journal of International Business Studies*, Fall/Winter 1976, 81–87; and W. Fred van Raail, "Cross-Cultural Research Methodology as a Case of Construct Validity," in H. Keith Hunt, ed., *Advances in Consumer Research* (Ann Arbor, Mich.: Association for Consumer Research, 1978), V, 693–701.

79. Paul Howard Berent, "International Research Is Different," in Mazze, *1975 Combined Proceedings*, 294.

80. Albert Stridberg, "U.S. Advertisers Win Some, Lose Some in Foreign Market," *Advertising Age*, May 6, 1974, 18.

81. J. Douglas McConnell, "The Economics of Behavioral Factors on the Multi-National Corporation," in Allvine, *1971 Combined Proceedings*, 263; and H. T. Parker, "International Markets Look Bright," *Advertising Age*, May 13, 1974, 53.

82. Stridberg, "U.S. Advertisers," 40.

83. Eliyahu Tal, "Advertising in Developing Countries," *Journal of Advertising*, 3 (Spring 1974), 21.

84. "GF International Moves to Centralized Policies," *Advertising Age*, February 25, 1974, 148.

85. Ramona Bechtos, "Man in the Green Box Sells 7UP in World Markets," *Advertising Age*, May 19, 1975, 25, 43, and 45.

86. Larry O'Neill, "How to Cope with 'Tokyo Trauma,'" *Advertising Age*, May 28, 1974, 32.

87. Stridberg, "U.S. Advertisers," 18.

88. "GF International Moves to Centralized Policies," 148.

89. Walter Weir, "What Americans Can Learn from Europe—Market Segmentation," *Advertising Age*, February 16, 1976, 41.

90. Robert T. Green and Eric Langeard, "A Cross-National Comparison of Consumer Habits and Innovator Characteristics," *Journal of Marketing*, 39 (July 1975), 34.

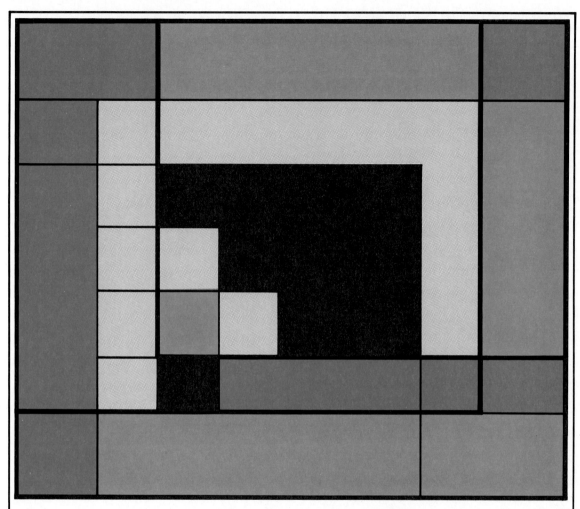

part four

THE CONSUMER'S DECISION-MAKING PROCESS

Part IV focuses on various facets of consumer decision making. The first two chapters are concerned with (1) the influence of informal social communication on consumer decision making, and (2) how consumers make decisions about new products and services. The next chapter takes a broader perspective and demonstrates, by means of a simple model, how the contributions of psychological, sociological, and cultural theory influence the consumer's consumption-related decisions. The final chapter in this section briefly reviews several comprehensive models of consumer decision making.

SIXTEEN

Personal Influence
and the Opinion
Leadership Process

introduction

ONSUMERS are often influenced by advice they receive from other people, especially in choosing products to buy and services to use. Just how powerful and important this type of consumer influence can be is pointed up by the following comment of an executive at a major film studio: "The only thing that makes a film successful or unsuccessful is word of mouth."[1]

This chapter describes the influence that friends, neighbors, acquaintances, fellow workers, and so forth, have on the individual's consumption behavior. It examines the nature and dynamics of this influence, called the *opinion leadership* process, and the personality and motivations of those who influence (i.e., *opinion leaders*) and those who are influenced (i.e., *opinion receivers*).

WHAT IS OPINION LEADERSHIP?

Opinion leadership is *the process by which one person (the opinion leader) informally influences the actions or attitudes of others, who may be opinion seekers or merely opinion recipients.* This influence is informal and verbal, but it may be supported by observing the actions of others. The informal flow of consumer-related influence between two people is sometimes referred to as product-related conversation, or word-of-mouth communication.

As Chapter 10 points out, this kind of influence takes place as informal, interpersonal communication. The key characteristic of such communication is that it takes place between two or more people, none of whom represents a commercial selling source. Interpersonal communication implies personal, or face-to-face, communication, although it may also take place by telephone.

One of the parties in an informal communications encounter is usually dominant in terms of offering advice or information about a specific product or product category, such as which of several brands is best, or how a particular

---

The art of conversation is the art of hearing as well as of being heard

WILLIAM HAZLITT

*"On The Conversation of Authors," The Plain Speaker
(1826)*

product may be used. That person, the opinion leader, may become an opinion receiver when another product or product category is discussed.

Individuals who actively seek information and advice about products are sometimes called opinion seekers. For purposes of simplicity, the term *opinion receiver* will be used in the following discussion to identify both those who actively seek product information from others and those who receive unsolicited information.

Simple examples of opinion leadership at work include the following:

1. When his hot water heater fails, a man calls his neighbor for the name of "a good plumber."
2. While two friends watch Sunday's football game, one suggests to the other that a new type of TV antenna might bring the set into sharper focus.

Most studies of opinion leadership are concerned with the identification and measurement of the behavioral impact that opinion leaders have on the consumption habits of others.

DYNAMICS OF THE OPINION LEADERSHIP PROCESS

The opinion leadership process is very dynamic. This section discusses those specific dimensions of opinion leadership that make it a powerful consumer force.

Credibility

Opinion leaders are a highly credible source of product-related information because they are usually perceived as being neutral (and thus objective) concerning the information or advice they dispense. Their intentions are perceived as being in the best interests of the opinion recipients, since they receive no compensation for the advice and apparently have no "ax to grind." Because opinion leaders often base their product advice on firsthand experience, the advice reduces the perceived risk or anxiety inherent in new-product trial for opinion receivers. Since opinion leaders are often unaware that they are influencing others, their product-related advice can be considered "soft sell."

Positive and Negative Product Information

Information provided by marketers tends to invariably be favorable to the product; thus the very fact that opinion leaders provide both favorable and unfavorable information adds to their credibility. An example of unfavorable, or negative, product information is, "...the problem with front-loading washers is that you can't add clothes to a wash already started."

Information and Advice

Opinion leaders are the source of both information and advice. They may simply talk about their experiences with a product, relate what they know about a product, or, more aggressively, advise others to buy or to avoid a product. Some examples of the kinds of product-related information that opinion leaders are likely to transmit during a conversation include the following:

1. Which of several brands is best: "The Norelco electric shaver gives a very close shave."
2. How a person might best use a specific product: "If you drain the gas out of your lawnmower in the fall, it starts up much more readily in the spring."
3. Which is the best place to buy a product: "Syms has a good selection of designer clothing at discount prices."
4. Who provides the best product-related service: "F&G Opticians will make up a new pair of glasses while you wait."

Opinion Leadership Is a Two-Way Street

A person who is an opinion receiver in one product category may become an opinion leader in another. Consider the following example. An individual contemplating the purchase of a new car may seek information and advice from other people to reduce her indecision about which car to select. Once the car has been bought, however, she may experience postpurchase dissonance and have a compelling need to talk favorably about the purchase to other people to confirm the fact that she made a wise choice.

An opinion leader may also be influenced by an opinion receiver as a result of their product-related conversation. For example, a person may tell a friend about a favorite seafood restaurant and, in response to questions from the opinion receiver, come to realize that the restaurant is really too large, too noisy, and somewhat overpriced.

Opinion Leadership Is Category-Specific

Opinion leadership tends to be category-specific; that is, opinion leaders often "specialize" in certain product categories about which they offer information and advice. When other product categories are discussed, they may reverse their roles and become opinion receivers. Thus a person who is considered an expert gardener may be an opinion leader in terms of this subject to others; yet, when it comes to financial investments, the same person may seek advice from others—perhaps even from someone who has received the gardening advice.

The Motivations Behind Opinion Leadership

To understand opinion leadership, it is necessary to appreciate the motivations of those who participate in informal product-related conversations. To this end, we will review the underlying motivations of those who receive and those who provide product-related information and advice.

THE NEEDS OF OPINION RECEIVERS

Opinion leaders fulfill a number of needs for opinion receivers. First, they are providers of new-product or new-usage information. Second, they reduce the perceived risk of the opinion seekers by endorsing—usually on the basis of firsthand knowledge—a specific product or brand. Third, they serve to reduce the search time entailed in the identification of a needed product or service. Moreover, opinion receivers can be certain of receiving the approval of a person whose opinion they obviously respect when they follow that person's advice or product endorsement.

For all of these reasons, consumers often look to friends, neighbors, and other acquaintances for product information. One story reported:

> the source of information most frequently consulted by durable goods buyers were friends and relatives...More than 50 percent of all buyers turned for advice to acquaintances and in most instances also looked at durable goods owned by them. Even more striking is the finding that a third of durable goods buyers bought a brand or model that they had seen at someone else's house...[2]

Not only are opinion receivers attempting to satisfy a variety of needs by engaging in product-related conversations, but there is evidence that the type of person from whom opinion receivers prefer to acquire their information varies, depending on cultural background.[3] Specifically, some researchers found that white Americans and British subjects tended to select close friends of similar age as sources of advice; whereas Chinese subjects preferred an opinion leader who had acquired authority and respect as a group standard bearer or as a male head-of-family. In contrast, black Americans were drawn to individuals who had achieved a degree of notoriety or who were typecast by the press as charismatic. Finally, Indian subjects were prone to select individuals who were recognized as possessing a strong philosophical outlook. These findings suggest that subcultural and cross-cultural factors (see Chapter 15) are likely to influence the traits judged desirable in an opinion leader.

THE NEEDS OF OPINION LEADERS

What motivates a person to talk about a product or service? Motivation theory suggests that people may provide information or advice to others in order to satisfy some basic need of their own (see Chapter 3). This notion is supported by a study of 255 consumers, which reported that "nobody will speak about products or services unless the talking itself, or the expected action of the listener, promises satisfaction of some kind—popularly speaking, unless he gets something out of it."[4]

However, opinion leaders may be unaware of their own underlying motives. As suggested earlier, opinion leaders may simply be trying to reduce their own postpurchase dissonance. If a man buys a new lawnmower and then is uncertain as to the widsom of his choice, he may try to reassure himself by "talking up" the lawnmower's virtues to others. In this way, he relieves his own psychological discomfort; furthermore, if he can influence a friend or neighbor to also buy that brand, he confirms his own good judgment in selecting the product first. Thus the opinion leader's motivation may really be one of self-confirmation—what has been referred to as self-involvement.[5] Furthermore, the information or advice opinion leader's dispense may serve to gain attention, help them to achieve status, assert their superiority, demonstrate their awareness and expertise, enable them to feel innovative, and give them the feeling of having inside information and of "converting" less-adventurous souls.[6]

In addition to *self*-involvement, the opinion leader may also be motivated by *product*-involvement, *other*-involvement, and *message*-involvement.[7] Opinion leaders who are motivated by *product*-involvement may find themselves so enthused or so disappointed with a product that they simply must tell others about it. Those who are motivated by involvement with *others* have a need to share product-related experiences with those others. In this type of situation, opinion leaders use their product-related conversation as an expression of friendship, neighborliness, and love.

The pervasiveness of advertising in our society encourages *message*-involvement, in that individuals who are bombarded with advertising messages and slogans tend to discuss them and the products they are designed to sell. Such word-of-mouth conversation is typified by the line "If you've got it, flaunt it" promoted by one of the airlines and widely repeated by consumers.

Table 16-1 compares the motivations of opinion receivers with those of opinion leaders.

TABLE 16-1   A Comparison of the Motivations of Opinion Receivers and Opinion Leaders

OPINION LEADERS	OPINION RECEIVERS
1. *Self-Involvement Motivations:* a. To reduce postpurchase uncertainty or dissonance b. To gain attention or status c. To assert superiority and expertise d. To feel like an adventurer e. To experience the power of "converting" others	1. *Self-Involvement Motivations* a. To reduce the risk or uncertainty of making a purchase commitment b. To reduce search time; e.g., to avoid the necessity of shopping around
2. *Product-Involvement Motivations:* To express satisfaction or dissatisfaction with a product or service	2. *Product-Involvement Motivations:* a. To learn how to use or consume a product b. To learn what products are new in the marketplace
3. *Other-Involvement Motivations:* To express neighborliness and friendship by discussing products or services that may be useful to others	3. *Other-Involvement Motivations:* To buy products that have the approval of others, therefore ensuring acceptance
4. *Message-Involvement Motivations:* To express one's reaction to a stimulating advertisement by telling others about it	

Consumer researchers are interested in identifying and measuring the impact of the opinion leadership process on consumption behavior. In measuring opinion leadership, the researcher has a choice of four basic measurement techniques: (1) the self-designating method, (2) the sociometric method, (3) the key-informant method, and (4) the objective method. We will briefly review each of these measurement methods in terms of its strengths, its weaknesses, and its applications to consumer research.

Self-Designating Method

In the self-designating method, respondents to a consumer survey are asked to evaluate the extent to which they have provided others with information about a product category or specific brand or have otherwise influenced the purchase decisions of others.

Figure 16-1 shows three types of self-designating question formats that can be used to determine a respondent's opinion leadership activity. The first consists of a single question, while the other two consist of a series of questions. The use of multiple questions enables the researcher to determine a respondent's opinion leadership more reliably on the basis of a series of supporting statements.

In most cases where researchers use the self-designating method, they divide consumer respondents into two categories: those who influence others (opinion leaders), and those who do not influence others (non-opinion leaders). While this two-category classification scheme is simple and easy to use, it does not realistically reflect the extent to which an individual might function as an opinion leader. Some people classified as nonleaders may truly have no influence on others, while other nonleaders may actually influence the consumption decisions of other people to some degree. Therefore it would be more realistic to employ a classification scheme consisting of three or more categories, one that explicitly considers a *range* of opinion-leading activity—e.g., those who *never* or *infrequently* influence others, those who *more frequently* influence others, and those who are *highly influential* opinion leaders.

The self-designating technique is used more frequently than other methods for measuring opinion leadership because consumer researchers find it easy to include in market research studies. However, because this method relies on consumers' self-evaluation of their opinion leadership activity, it may be open to bias should respondents perceive "opinion leadership" (even though the term is not used) to be a desirable characteristic and thus overestimate their own roles as opinion leaders.[8]

Sociometric Method

The sociometric method measures the person-to-person informal communication of consumers concerning products or product categories. In this method, respondents are asked to identify (1) the specific individuals (if any) to whom

FIGURE 16-1 **Self-Designating Method of Measuring Opinion Leadership** Sources: *Alvin J. Silk, "Overlap among Self-designated Opinion Leaders: A Study of Selected Dental Products and Services," *Journal of Marketing Research*, 3 (August 1968), 255–59. †John O. Summers, "The Identity of Women's Clothing Fashion Opinion Leaders," *Journal of Marketing Research*, 7 (May 1970), 178–85. ‡Fred D. Reynolds and William R. Darden, "Mutually Adaptive Effects of Interpersonal Communication," *Journal of Marketing Research*, 8 (November 1971), 449–54.

Single-Question Approach

a. Have you recently been asked your advice or opinion about ___*___ ?[a]

    Yes _____ No _____

    Respondents answering "yes" are classified as opinion leaders.

In one survey using this single question approach, opinion leadership for the following dental products and services were determined: electric toothbrushes, toothpastes, mouthwashes, and dentists.

Multiple-Question Approaches

a. In general do you like to talk about ___*___ with your friends?[b]

    Yes _____ 1   No _____ 2

b. Would you say you give very little information, an average amount of information, or a great deal of information about ___*___ to your friends?

    You give very little information   1
    You give an average amount of information   2
    You give a great deal of information   3

c. During the past six months, have you told anyone about ___*___ ?

    Yes _____ 1   No _____ 2

d. Compared with your circle of friends, are you less likely, about as likely, or more likely to be asked for advice about ___*___ ?

    Less likely to be asked   1
    About as likely to be asked   2
    More likely to be asked   3

e. If you and your friends were to discuss ___*___ , what part would you be most likely to play? Would you mainly listen to your friends' ideas or would you try to convince them of your ideas?

    You mainly listen to your friends' ideas   1
    You try to convince them of your ideas   2

f. Which of these happens more often? Do you tell your friends about ___*___ , or do they tell you about ___*___ ?

    You tell them about ___*___   1
    They tell you about ___*___   2

g. Do you have the feeling that you are generally regarded by your friends and neighbors as a good source of advice about ___*___ ?

    Yes _____ 1   No _____ 2

Please read the following sentences and place the number that most closely responds to the correct answer in the space following. The range of answers is 1 through 5, as follows:

    1—strongly agree
    2—agree
    3—neither agree nor disagree
    4—disagree
    5—strongly disagree

a. My friends and neighbors often ask my advice about clothing fashions. _____[c]

b. I sometimes influence the types of clothes my friends buy. _____

c. My friends come to me more often than I go to them about clothes. _____

d. I feel that I am generally regarded by my friends as a good source of advice about clothing fashions: _____

e. I can think of at least two people whom I have told about some clothing fashion in the last six months. _____

*Insert relevant product or product category.

they provided advice or information about the product or brand being studied, and (2) the specific individuals (if any) who provided *them* with advice or information about the product or brand being studied. In the first instance, if respondents identify one or more individuals whom they have provided with some form of product information, they are tentatively classified as opinion leaders. The researcher then seeks to validate this determination by interviewing the individuals named by the primary respondents and asking them to recall whether or not they did, in fact, receive such product information.

In the second instance, respondents are asked to identify individuals who provided them with information about a product under investigation. Individuals so designated by the primary respondent are tentatively classified as opinion leaders. Again, the researcher attempts to validate this determination by asking the individuals so named whether or not they did, in fact, provide the relevant product information.

Thus, if Consumer A reports that information or advice concerning a specific product was received from Consumer B, then Consumer B must confirm that such information or advice was given to Consumer A. In this way the sociometric method validly identifies the opinion leaders and opinion receivers in product-related conversations.

SOCIOMETRIC RESEARCH DESIGNS

In using the sociometric method, researchers have two options in terms of research design: They can study a self-contained community, or they can elect to study a more widespread respondent sample. If they study a specific community that has definite physical boundaries (such as all the residents in a particular housing project), they will find it relatively simple to verify product-related conversations. If they choose a more widespread respondent sample, they must be prepared to trace the web of word-of-mouth contacts by seeking out all individuals named by the primary respondent group, regardless of where they are located. The few consumer studies that have used the sociometric method have elected to study "intact" or self-contained communities because such research is so much less costly and easier to manage.

CONSUMER BEHAVIOR APPLICATIONS

An early application of the sociometric approach to the study of consumer behavior examined opinion leadership among wives of graduate students living in university-sponsored housing.[9] The intact community provided the opportunity to measure the flow of word-of-mouth conversation concerning a new brand of coffee and the subsequent impact of such conversation on the trial of the new product. The researcher found that wives who received favorable comment or information concerning the product were more likely to try it than those who received either no information or negative information. This pioneering study concluded that positive informal communication promotes the acceptance of new products among members of a given community.

Figure 16-2 illustrates the type of questioning employed in the sociometric research approach. It presents a series of questions used in a study of opinion leadership among elderly consumers residing in a retirement community.[10]

The objective of the study was to determine the impact of product-related informal communication on community members' subsequent decisions to purchase or not to purchase a new salt substitute. The results of this study indicated that individuals who provided others with information or advice

FIGURE 16-2   Sociometric Questioning Approach to Assess Informal Communication about a New Product

A. *Providing Information to Others*

1. Did you tell anyone, living here at Kissena I, about the "Brand X" salt substitute?

   yes _____   no _____

2. If "yes"
   Which person did you first tell about the salt substitute?

   First Name   Family Name   Apt. or Floor

   _____   _____   _____

3. Which other people, living here at Kissena I, did you tell about the "Brand X" salt substitute?

   (Space for three other names and locations)

4. Did you suggest that they try or not try the "Brand X" salt substitute?

   Try _____   Not Try _____   Other _____

B. *Receiving Information from Others*

1. What was the first thing you remember hearing about the "Brand X" salt substitute?

2. Do you remember who made this first comment about "Brand X" salt substitute?

   yes _____   no _____

3. If "yes," what was her name?

   First Name   Family Name   Apt. or Floor

   _____   _____   _____

4. Does she live here at Kissena I?

   yes _____   no _____

5. Did this person recommend that you *try* or *not try* the "Brand X" salt substitute?

   Try _____   Not Try _____   Other _____

6. If the respondent bought "Brand X" salt substitute, then ask:

   "Did this conversation occur before or after you bought the "Brand X" salt substitute?

   Before _____   After _____   Do not remember _____

7. Can you name any other persons, living at Kissena I, who have mentioned the "Brand X" salt substitute to you?

   (Space for three other names and locations)

concerning the new product (the opinion leaders) and those who received positive information or advice from others concerning the new product (the opinion receivers) were both more likely to have purchased it than those who did not engage in an exchange of informal information about the product.[11]

Key-Informant Method

A third way to measure opinion leadership is through the use of a key informant—a person who is keenly aware or knowledgeable about the nature of social communication among members of a specific consumer group. This person, the key informant, is asked to identify those individuals in the group who are most likely to be opinion leaders.

The key informant does not have to be a member of the group under study (for example, a professor may serve as the key informant for a college class). This research method is relatively inexpensive, since it requires that only one individual—or at most several individuals—be intensively interviewed, while the self-designating and sociometric methods require that an entire consumer sample or community be interviewed. However, the key-informant method is generally not used by marketers because of the difficulties inherent in identifying an individual who can *objectively* identify opinion leaders in a relevant consumer group.

The key-informant method would seem to be of greatest potential use in the study of industrial or institutional opinion leadership. For example, a firm's salespeople might serve as key informants in the identification of specific customers who are most likely to influence the purchase decisions of other firms in their industry. Similarly, the purchasing agent of a specific firm might serve as a key informant by providing an outside salesperson with the names of those persons in his or her organization who are most likely to influence the purchase decision.

In the study of consumers, possible key informants include influential community members such as the mayor, the president of a local club, the head of the PTA, or a prominent local retailer.

Objective Method

The objective method of determining opinion leadership is much like a controlled experiment. It involves the deliberate placement of new products or new-product information with selected individuals and then tracing the resultant web of interpersonal communication that occurs concerning the relevant product.

An intriguing study designed to measure the influence of opinion leaders in household matters provides a unique example of the objective method.[12] Fifteen friendship groups of women living in a self-contained community were individually interviewed via the sociometric method to assess their level of opinion leadership with regard to household management matters. The women who scored *highest* as opinion leaders in each of nine groups were chosen to serve as opinion-leader confederates (i.e., to cooperate with the researcher). In each of the other six groups, the women who scored *lowest* in opinion leadership were also chosen to serve as opinion-leader confederates. This research design enabled the researcher to compare the influence exerted by those identified as opinion leaders with the influence exerted by those identified as nonleaders when all were placed in a "controlled" situation to serve as opinion leaders.

All fifteen participants selected by the researcher to function as opinion leaders were provided with new freeze-dried food items and were asked to serve them to their families. They were also asked to give samples of the new food products to all other members of their friendship groups and to suggest that they, in turn, serve the items to their families.[13]

The results indicated that those individuals who received the new food items from "natural" opinion leaders tended to echo the leaders' opinions concerning the new product. Conversely, those individuals who received samples of the new food items from artificially created opinion leaders shifted away from the opinion leaders' sentiments. These findings suggest that true opinion leaders are capable of altering group members' opinions in the direction of their own opinions, whereas nonleaders (those who score low in opinion leadership studies) may adversely influence those whom they attempt to influence.

Table 16-2 presents an overview of each of these four methods of measuring opinion leadership.

A PROFILE OF THE OPINION LEADER

Just who are opinion leaders? Can they be recognized by any distinctive characteristics? Can they be reached through any specific media? Marketers have long sought answers to these questions, for if they are able to identify the relevant opinion leaders for their products, they can direct their promotional efforts to these leaders, confident that they in turn will influence the consumption behavior of others. For this reason, a number of consumer researchers have attempted to develop a realistic profile of the opinion leader. This has not been easy to do. It was pointed out earlier that opinion leadership tends to be category-specific; that is, an individual who is an opinion leader in one product category may be an opinion receiver in another product category. Thus the generalized profile of opinion leaders can only be considered in the context of specific product categories.

Knowledge and Interest

It has been suggested that shared interest is the foundation upon which most informal communication is based.[14] However, some studies indicate that opinion leaders probably possess a keener level of interest in the product category than

TABLE 16-2   Methods of Measuring Opinion Leadership—Advantages and Limitations

OPINION LEADERSHIP MEASUREMENT METHOD	DESCRIPTION OF METHOD	SAMPLE QUESTIONS ASKED	ADVANTAGES	LIMITATIONS
1. Self-designating method	Each respondent is asked a series of questions to determine the degree to which he perceives himself to be an opinion leader.	Do you influence other people in their selection of products?	Measures the individual's own perceptions of his opinion leadership.	Dependent upon the objectivity with which respondents can identify and report their personal influence.
2. Sociometric method	Members of a social system are asked to whom they go for advice and information about a product category.	Whom do you ask? Who asks you for information about that product category?	Sociometric questions have the greatest degree of validity and are easy to administer.	Very costly analysis is often very complex. Requires a large number of respondents. Not suitable for sample designs where only a portion of the social system is interviewed.
3. Key-informant method	Carefully selected key informants in a social system are asked to designate opinion leaders.	Who are the most influential people in the group?	Relatively inexpensive and less time consuming than the sociometric method.	Informants who are not thoroughly familiar with the system would provide invalid information.
4. Objective method	Artificially places individuals in the position to act as opinion leaders and measures results of their efforts.	Have you tried the product?	Measures individual's ability to influence others under controlled circumstances.	Requires the establishment of an experimental design and the tracking of the resulting impact on the participants.

Reprinted with permission of Macmillan Publishing Co., Inc. from *Communication of Innovations*, by Everett M. Rogers and F. Floyd Shoemaker. Copyright © 1971 by The Free Press, a Division of The Macmillan Company.

do opinion receivers.[15] Because of their interest, opinion leaders are likely to be better informed; and because of their knowledge, others may turn to them for their relative expertise. This tends to be true regardless of whether the basic motivation of the opinion leaders is self-involvement, product-involvement, or other-involvement.

A study designed to relate opinion leadership to perceived knowledge and degree of interest in the subject was conducted among four hundred members of a consumer buying panel in Los Angeles. The researchers found a moderate-to-strong relationship between opinion leadership and interest in household furnishings, and a strong relationship between opinion leadership and knowledge about cosmetics and personal care.[16] In another study, researchers reported that interest in fashion was a relatively stable predictor of opinion leadership in the area of male clothing fashions.[17]

Other research suggests that chief among the characteristics that distinguish opinion leaders from nonleaders is their unique *involvement* with the subject of interest.[18] Compared with nonleaders in a particular product category, opinion leaders read more about related consumer issues, are more knowledgeable about related new-product developments, participate more often in related consumer activities, and derive greater satisfaction from these product-related activities.

Consumer Innovators

Consistent with their greater interest in a product category, consumer opinion leaders are more likely to try new products.[19] Thus opinion leaders tend to speak with some authority when providing advice to others who have not as yet tried the new product.

A study of consumer innovators (identified as the first 10 percent to adopt one or more of such consumer durable goods as color television or stereo equipment) found that about half of the individuals identified as innovators claimed to have shown the purchased product to others, and that more than 60 percent of those to whom they showed the product later purchased it.[20] In another study, it was reported that innovators in the use of a new automotive diagnostic service (those who used it during its first two months of operation) claimed to have been asked their opinion more often about a variety of topics than did a comparable random sample.[21] Ninety percent of the innovators also reported telling at least one other person about the experience within a few days after using the automotive service; of this number, almost half reported telling two or more people. Another study found that 33 percent of the innovators in the adoption of Touch-Tone telephones claimed that they could name at least one other person who bought the innovation because of their influence.[22]

Research conducted on behalf of the film industry confirms the close bond between innovators and their influence on others' consumption actions.[23] Specifically, frequent moviegoers who attend a movie within its first two weeks of release have been found to influence the attendance of their friends. Similarly, a study of subscribers to a community cable television service found that those individuals who were the first to sign up were more likely to be TV opinion leaders.[24] These studies indicate that consumer innovators are likely to be opinion leaders in their area of innovation.

Very few studies have explored the relationship between personality and opinion leadership. Of those that have, most have focused on the subject of women's clothing fashions.

An obvious characteristic of the consumer opinion leader is a willingness to talk about a product-related topic. For example, women's fashion opinion leaders have been found to talk more about fashion, and to more often interpret fashion trends for friends, than do nonleaders.[25]

This characteristic of willingness to talk is supported by evidence that indicates that fashion opinion leaders possess greater *assertiveness* and *emotional stability,* which enable them to speak out more readily on topics in which they feel competent. Furthermore, their self-perception as being *more likeable* and *less depressive* may encourage their active participation in social conversations.[26]

One researcher reported that fashion opinion leaders tended to be more *progressive, outgoing* (less shy), and *susceptible to change* than nonleaders.[27] Another study found a significant relationship between *general self-confidence* and fashion opinion leadership.[28]

However, other researchers have reported finding no significant relationships between opinion leadership and such personality variables as *sociability, social presence, self-acceptance, socialization, communality,* and *flexibility.*[29] Obviously, further research is needed to resolve these inconsistencies.

Several personality characteristics of opinion leaders would appear to bridge specific product-related contexts. Among these are *self-confidence* and *gregariousness* (i.e., sociability). It may be that, to advise others, individuals must first have confidence in themselves and their ideas. Several studies have reported that opinion leaders scored higher in terms of local friendships than did nonleaders.[30] This is not surprising when one considers that opinion leaders must be involved in social interaction in order to function.

Attitudes and Intention

Too little attention has been given to the role that attitudes play in the probability that consumers will (or will not) serve as opinion leaders. One field study found that consumers who liked a "new" brand of coffee they were asked to sample were more inclined to talk about it than those who did not like it (i.e., who held unfavorable attitudes).[31] The study also revealed that consumers who proclaimed a willingness or intention to buy the product when it became available were more likely to have talked to others about the brand than those with a negative intention. Finally, heavy coffee users were found to be more likely to initiate word-of-mouth conversation about the new brand than light or infrequent users.

If this link between attitude–intention behavior and opinion leadership were to be confirmed through additional research, it would provide further support for the common-sense notion that creating and maintaining a strong favorable attitude for a product, especially a new brand, should be a critical marketing goal.

Media Habits

A number of interdisciplinary studies concerned with opinion leadership and the diffusion of information have concluded that opinion leaders make greater use of mass media—they tend to use "more impersonal and technically accurate" and more "cosmopolitan" (i.e., widespread) sources of information than non-leaders.[32] Few studies within the marketing or consumer behavior literature have been able to confirm these findings. Rather, opinion leaders have been found to have much greater readership of special publications devoted to the specific product category in which the opinion leader "leads." For example, a study of automotive opinion leadership concluded that "opinion leaders will read media directly related to their consumer topics more often than nonleaders."[33] Therefore, placing ads in special-interest publications like *Car and Driver, Motor Trend,* and *Road and Track* not only serves to inform car buffs about new models and accessories that may be of personal interest but also places them in a better position to make recommendations to the relatives, friends, and neighbors who turn to them for advice. In their role as opinion leaders, car buffs frequently influence the nonleaders' acceptability of new automotive items.[34]

Other research has found a significant relationship between women's fashion leadership and high exposure to fashion magazines.[35] Thus the opinion leader would appear to have greater exposure to media relevant to his or her area of interest than would nonleaders, though not necessarily greater exposure to mass media in general. Additional research is needed to determine the opinion leaders' usage of both mass and class (i.e., special-interest) media.

Social Characteristics

As with other characteristics of the opinion leader, social characteristics appear to depend upon the topic of interest. In most marketing studies, the opinion leader has been found to belong to the same socioeconomic group (social class) as the opinion receiver. This is not surprising; it would seem reasonable to expect an individual to turn to someone within the same social group for information or advice concerning a specific product category.[36] Similarly, opinion leaders would be most likely to give information or advice to those people with whom they regularly engage in informal communication, the people within their own social stratum.

TABLE 16-3   Sociological Characteristics of Women's Clothing Fashion Opinion Leaders

Greater Physical Mobility	Greater Organizational Affiliation
More Social Communication	Greater Participation in Formal Social Activities
More Organizational Memberships	Greater Participation in Informal Social Activities
More Organizational Participation	Greater Participation in Sporting Activities
More Organizational Offices Held	More Total Social Activity Participation

Source: Adapted from John O. Summers, "The Identity of Women's Clothing Fashion Opinion Leaders," *Journal of Marketing Research,* 7 (May 1970), 180.

A study of women's fashions found that opinion leaders tended to have greater physical mobility and thus a greater opportunity for exposure to new and different fashion ideas.[37] This study also found opinion leaders to be higher in social communications, organizational affiliations, and participation in social activities.[38] Table 16-3 summarizes findings concerning the sociological characteristics of opinion leaders for women's fashions.

Demographic Characteristics

A number of studies indicate that informal communication generally flows between people of similar age. This characteristic is again category-specific. For example, one research study concerned with moviegoing found that opinion leaders and opinion receivers could be classified into three broad age categories.[39] It also found that 66 percent of all informal communication concerning movies occurred among people of the same age category. A study of women's clothing fashions showed that opinion leaders tended to be younger and have more education, higher incomes, and higher occupational status.[40] Another study found that individuals tend to seek advice from older people regarding the selection of a physician.[41] Further analysis of these data revealed that parents tend to seek advice regarding physician selection from other parents with children of approximately the same age and number.

These studies suggest that for specific areas of interest, people may seek information and advice from people whom they perceive to be highly qualified informants. In the context of physician selection, older people may be perceived as having more information and experience. In the context of women's fashions, younger people, those with higher incomes, and/or those with higher occupational status may be perceived as being more qualified informants.

In summary, it is difficult to construct a generalized profile of the opinion leader outside of the context of a specific category of interest. However, on the basis of the limited evidence available, as shown in Table 16-4, opinion leaders, across categories, tend to be higher in the following attributes: innovativeness, greater willingness to talk, self-confidence, and gregariousness. Within the context of specific subject areas, opinion leaders tend to have greater interest in and knowledge of the product category and more exposure to relevant special-interest media. They also tend to belong to the same socioeconomic and age groups as the opinion receivers.

TABLE 16-4   Profile of Opinion Leaders

GENERALIZED ATTRIBUTES ACROSS PRODUCT CATEGORIES	CATEGORY-SPECIFIC ATTRIBUTES
Innovativeness	Interest
Willingness to talk	Knowledge
Self-confidence	Special-interest media
Gregariousness	exposure
	Same age
	Same social status
	Social exposure outside group

Opinion leadership is not a rare phenomenon. Often more than one-third of the people studied in a consumer research project are classified as opinion leaders.[42] One researcher reported that almost half (47.5 percent) of his respondents identified themselves as opinion leaders in one or more of the product categories he investigated.[43] In another study, only 31 percent of the 976 respondents did not qualify as opinion leaders in at least one of six product areas examined.[44]

The frequency of consumer opinion leadership tends to suggest that people are sufficiently interested in at least one product or product category to talk about it and give advice concerning it to others.

This leads to some interesting questions: Is opinion leadership generalized? Do opinion leaders in one product category tend to be opinion leaders in other product categories? Consumer researchers have concerned themselves with these questions in their search for a generalized profile of the opinion leader.

Overlap of Opinion Leadership

A number of studies have investigated the overlap of opinion leadership across several product categories. A study of five dental product and service categories did not yield statistically significant evidence of opinion leadership overlap, although it did generate some evidence for this trend.[45]

Another study concluded that opinion leadership tends to overlap across certain combinations of interest areas. The researchers noted that opinion leadership overlap was highest among product categories that involved similar interests (large and small appliances, women's clothing fashions and cosmetics, personal grooming aids, household cleansers and detergents, and packaged food products).[46]

Self-designated female opinion leaders who were members of a national consumer panel were questioned about sixteen categories of consumer spending.[47] The findings of this study supported the hypothesis that opinion leadership overlaps product areas in which the opinion leaders' interests overlap (for example, in buying and preparing food, or in new clothing styles and furnishing a home).

The above evidence indicates that opinion leaders in one product area are often opinion leaders in related areas in which they are also interested.

THE OPINION LEADERSHIP ENVIRONMENT

Product-related discussions between two people do not take place in "thin air" or in a vacuum. Two people are not likely to meet and spontaneously break into a discussion in which product-related information is sought or offered. Rather, product discussions generally occur within relevant situational contexts—e.g., when a specific product or a similar product is being used or served, or as an outgrowth of a more general discussion which in some way touches upon the product category.[48] Thus, if two co-workers are discussing the forthcoming office Christmas party and one asks, "What are you going to wear?" their discussion might eventually lead to one asking the other for advice on the appropriateness of a new style or fashion. In this situation, the opinion leader will provide information to the opinion receiver as an outgrowth of a conversation concerning the office party that they both plan to attend.

A study of 134 randomly selected homemakers concerning their awareness of a new coffee product (Maxim Freeze-Dried Coffee) revealed that discussions concerning the new product were most likely to come up in food-related contexts.[49] Table 16-5 presents data indicating that 79 percent of the respondents who *provided* information about Maxim to others did so in a food-related context, while 75 percent of the respondents who reported *receiving* such information did so in a food-related context.

Opinion Leaders Are Friends or Neighbors

It is not surprising that opinion leaders and opinion receivers are often friends, neighbors, or work associates, since existing friendships provide numerous opportunities for conversation concerning product-related topics. It is also true that physical proximity is likely to increase the occurrences of product-related conversations.[50] A community center, for example, increases the opportunities

TABLE 16-5   Situational Contexts of Interpersonal Influence with a New Coffee Product

	INFORMATION GIVEN	INFORMATION RECEIVED	TOTAL
food related context			
Drinking coffee	25%	38%	30%
Drinking Maxim	9	—	6
Conversation concerning food	35	29	33
Shopping for food	5	8	6
Eating	5	—	3
Subtotals:	79%	75%	78%
non-food context			
Spontaneously given	7%	17%	11%
Spontaneously received	—	4	1
Viewing/hearing Maxim ad	5	4	4
Unclear	9	—	6
Subtotals:	21%	25%	22%
Totals:	100%	100%	100%

Source: Russell W. Belk, "Occurrence of Word-of-Mouth Buyer Behavior as a Function of Situation and Advertising Stimuli," *Combined Proceedings* (Chicago: American Marketing Association, 1971), 420.

for neighbors to meet and engage in informal communication concerning product-related topics.

The importance of physical proximity in the opinion leadership process was supported in the study concerning interpersonal influence in physician selection.[51] Analysis revealed that 11 percent of the participants in two-person discussions (i.e., dyads) were members of the same club, 15 percent belonged to the same church, 15 percent were employed by the same company, 27 percent lived within one block of each other, and 67 percent had visited the other person's home.

Additional support for the importance of physical proximity in informal product-related conversations comes from a study of word-of-mouth influence among elderly residents in a high-rise retirement community. The study found that 81 percent of the exchange of information and advice occurred between persons who lived on the same floor; the remaining 19 percent occurred between residents living one floor apart.[52]

The private home appears to be the most frequent setting for product discussions. A study of four different types of consumer products (see Table 16-6) revealed that such discussions are more likely to take place in the afternoon and are most likely to occur between two people rather than in a larger group.[53]

The foregoing studies demonstrate that product-related conversations generally occur between friends, neighbors, or work associates who have some physical proximity in a situational context relevant to the product under discussion.

TABLE 16-6   Social Settings for Interpersonal Communications

	PRODUCT CATEGORY				
	durable press clothing	new type of nylon hose	new snack food	electric toothbrush	total
physical location					
Private home	65%	50%	74%	77%	69%
Other	35	50	26	23	31
	100%	100%	100%	100%	100%
time of day					
Morning	30%	28%	20%	26%	27%
Afternoon	44	44	35	38	40
Evening	26	28	45	36	33
	100%	100%	100%	100%	100%
number of participants					
Two	72%	77%	54%	63%	66%
More than two	28	23	46	37	34
	100%	100%	100%	100%	100%
Number of respondents	(843)	(247)	(477)	(560)	(2,127)

Source: Adapted from John O. Summers, "New Product Interpersonal Communication," *Combined Proceedings* (Chicago: American Marketing Association, 1971), 432.

How does information provided by the mass media reach and influence the total population? Several theories suggest that the opinion leader is a vital link in the transmission of information and influence.

Two-Step Flow of Communication Theory

A study of voting behavior some thirty-five years ago concluded that ideas often flow from radio and print to opinion leaders and from them to the less-active sections of the population.[54] This so-called *two-step flow of communication* theory portrayed opinion leaders as direct receivers of information from impersonal mass-media sources, who in turn transmitted (and interpreted) this information to the masses. This theory views the opinion leader as a *middleman* between the impersonal mass media and the majority of society.

The major contribution of the two-step flow of communication theory was that it demonstrated that social interaction between people serves as the principal means by which information is transmitted, attitudes are developed, and behavior is stimulated. The theory rejected the notion that mass media alone influenced the sale of products, political candidates, and ideas to a mass audience.

Figure 16-3 presents a model of the two-step flow of communication theory. Information is depicted as flowing in a single direction (i.e., one way) from the mass media to the opinion leaders (Step 1), and then from the opinion leaders (who interpret, legitimize, and transmit the information) to friends, neighbors, and acquaintances, who constitute the "masses" (Step 2).

The two-step flow of communication theory is insightful in that it illustrates how people acquire information about issues of interest. However, it no longer seems to be an accurate portrayal of the flow of information and influence. The need for modification of this theory is in large part based upon advances in communication technology and more recent research evidence, which suggests that:[55]

1. Mass media may inform both opinion leaders and opinion receivers; however, the opinion receiver is more likely to be influenced by the opinion leader than by the media.

FIGURE 16-3   Two-Step Flow of Communication Theory

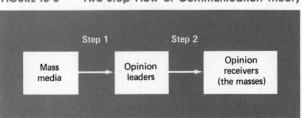

Step 1   Step 2

Mass media → Opinion leaders → Opinion receivers (the masses)

2. Not all interpersonal communication is initiated by opinion leaders and directed to opinion receivers. Very often those who are receivers may initiate the interpersonal communication by requesting information or advice from the opinion leaders.

3. Those who receive information and advice *from* others (i.e., opinion receivers) are more likely to offer advice *to* others (including opinion leaders) than those who do not receive advice from others.

4. Opinion leaders are more likely than those who are nonleaders to both receive and seek advice from others.

Multistep Flow of Communication Theory

It is apparent that the two-step flow of communication theory does not fully account for the complexity of interpersonal communications. A more recent model depicts the transmission of information from the media as a *multistep flow of communication.* The revised model takes into account the fact that information and influence are often two-way processes in which opinion leaders both influence and are influenced by opinion receivers.

Figure 16-4 presents a model of the multistep flow of communication theory. Steps 1a and 1b depict the flow of information from the mass media simultaneously to opinion leaders, opinion receivers, and information receivers (who neither influence nor are influenced by others.) Step 2 shows the transmission of information and influence from opinion leaders to opinion receivers. Step 3 reflects the transfer of information and influence from opinion receivers to opinion leaders.

MARKETING IMPLICATIONS OF THE MULTISTEP THEORY

Research evidence provides support for the multistep theory of communication.[56] It suggests that interpersonal communication cannot be neatly dichotomized into dominant, all-powerful opinion leaders and passive opinion receivers. For the marketing practitioner, the multistep flow of communication theory suggests that it is important to identify and reach opinion leaders because of the critical roles they play in transmitting information and influence about products to opinion receivers. However, the theory also suggests that it is equally important to identify and reach individuals who are the receivers or seekers of product advice, for these individuals are likely to function eventually as opinion

FIGURE 16-4   Multistep Flow of Communication Theory

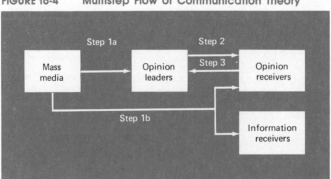

leaders themselves. As one astute observer remarked: "...it appears that rather than distinguishing among opinion leaders and followers, one should distinguish among consumers engaging in more or [in] less personal communication about the product."[57]

A BROADER APPROACH TO INTERPERSONAL COMMUNICATION

A few consumer studies have combined measures of opinion leadership and opinion seeking to form a richer picture of the interpersonal communication process than is possible by examining opinion leadership alone. These studies have used the following four-way categorization of interpersonal communication:[58]

1. The *socially integrated*: those who score high on both opinion leadership and opinion seeking
2. The *socially independent*: those who score high on opinion leadership and low on opinion seeking
3. The *socially dependent*: those who score low on opinion leadership and high on opinion seeking
4. The *socially isolated*: those who score low on both opinion leadership and opinion seeking

This typology is basically consistent with the multistep flow of communication theory. The four interpersonal communication groups are formed by cross-classifying consumers in terms of their responses to questions designed to establish the extent to which they are opinion leaders and/or opinion seekers (see Table 16-7). The advantage of this four-way classification over the traditional two-way classification (i.e., opinion leaders vs. nonleaders) is that it distinguishes those consumers who transmit and/or seek information and advice from those who neither transmit nor seek advice and information.

TABLE 16-7   Four-Way Categorization of Interpersonal Communication

		OPINION SEEKING SCORES	
		high	low
OPINION LEADERSHIP SCORES	high	Socially Integrated	Socially Independent
	low	Socially Dependent	Socially Isolated

Source: Leon G. Schiffman and Steven P. Schnaars, "The Consumption of Historical Romance Novels: Consumer Aesthetics in Popular Literature," in Elizabeth C. Hirschman and Morris Holbrook, eds., *Symbolic Consumer Behavior* (Ann Arbor, Mich.: Association for Consumer Research, 1980), 49.

TABLE 16-8   Representative Results of the Four-Way Categorization of Interpersonal Communication

	STAINLESS STEEL BLADES*	HOUSEHOLD CLEANSERS AND DETERGENTS†	COSMETICS AND PERSONAL GROOMING AIDS†	DIET FOOD PRODUCTS‡	WOMEN'S CLOTHING FASHIONS§	HISTORICAL ROMANCE NOVELS‖	AUDIO EQUIPMENT#
Socially integrated	14%	21%	22%	28%	32%	38%	51%
Socially independent	4	6	4	16	18	24	14
Socially dependent	35	35	40	21	18	8	25
Socially isolated	47	38	34	35	32	30	10
Total	100%	100%	100%	100%	100%	100%	100%

Sources: Adapted from the following:

*Jagdish N. Sheth. "Word-of-Mouth in Low Risk Innovations," *Journal of Advertising Research*, 11 (June 1971), 17.

†John O. Summers and Charles W. King, "Interpersonal Communication and New Product Attitudes," *Proceedings* (Chicago: Fall Conference, American Marketing Association, 1969), 295.

‡Leon G. Schiffman, "Social Interaction Patterns of the Elderly Consumer," *Proceedings* (Chicago: Fall Conference, American Marketing Association, 1972), 446.

§Fred D. Reynolds and William R. Darden, "Mutually Adaptive Effects of Interpersonal Communication," *Journal of Marketing Research*, 8 (November 1971), 451.

‖Leon G. Schiffman and Steven P. Schnaars, "The Consumption of Historical Romance Novels: Consumer Aesthetics in Popular Literature," in Elizabeth C. Hirschman and Morris Holbrook, eds., *Symbolic Consumer Behavior* (Ann Arbor, Mich.: Association for Consumer Research, 1980), 50.

#Leon G. Schiffman et al., "Interpersonal Communication: An Opinion Leadership/Opinion Seeking Composite Approach," *1975 Combined Proceedings* (Chicago: American Marketing Association, 1975), 230.

To illustrate how the four-way classification scheme can be employed to compare interpersonal communication patterns for different products, Table 16-8 lists the results of seven consumer behavior studies in terms of the interpersonal communication scheme. It reveals that most consumers are involved in some form of product-related conversation, and that the percentage of respondents in each of the four groups tends to vary by product category.

Most important, the four-way classification scheme enables us to see patterns that would otherwise be masked if we simply contrasted opinion leaders with nonleaders. For example, Table 16-8 indicates that with the exception of audio-equipment buyers (the only really big-ticket item in the study), consumers of historical romance novels are the most socially integrated; that is, more of them engage in interpersonal communication than do consumers of the other product categories studied. Furthermore, very few of the historical romance readers are socially isolated. Both of these findings provide support for the frequent contention that despite the absence of substantial advertising budgets, historical romances attain widespread consumer acceptance due to word-of-mouth communication.

Cross-tabulating the four interpersonal communication groups with other consumer-relevant factors (e.g., demographics, personality traits, attitudes, and psychographics) offers additional insights into the dynamics of interpersonal communication. To illustrate this, Table 16-9 presents a cross-tabulation of the

TABLE 16-9   Relationships between Interpersonal Communication Typology and Significant Consumer Behavior Variables

	SOCIALLY INTEGRATED	SOCIALLY INDEPENDENT	SOCIALLY DEPENDENT	SOCIALLY ISOLATED
I went to a club meeting	38%	21%	67%	37%
I went out to dinner at a restaurant	96	88	83	76
I like to think I am a bit of a swinger	56	35	50	17
TV is my primary form form of entertainment	29	49	25	52
I like romantic movies	94	64	83	83
I often seek out the advice of my friends regarding brands and products	57	29	42	29
My friends and neighbors often come to me for advice about products and brands	68	56	50	34
Age (% under 30)	55	32	25	21
Education (% with schooling beyond H.S.)	57	50	92	67

Source: Leon G. Schiffman and Steven P. Schnaars, "The Consumption of Historical Romance Novels: Consumer Aesthetics in Popular Literature," in Elizabeth C. Hirschman and Morris Holbrook, eds., *Symbolic Consumer Behavior* (Ann Arbor, Mich.: Association for Consumer Research, 1980), 50.

four interpersonal communication groups and a variety of popular consumer behavior variables. The outcome is a profile of each of the four types of communicators. For example, the results reveal that the socially integrated exhibit the following characteristics:[59]

They are younger and less educated.
They eat out more frequently.
They tend to view themselves as "swingers."
TV is less likely to be their primary form of entertainment.
They like romantic movies.
They tend to seek out the advice of others regarding various products and brands.
They are likely to have others come to them for advice concerning various products and brands.

This single example indicates that the four-way interpersonal communication typology is capable of providing additional and richer insights into the dynamics of word-of-mouth communication.

OPINION LEADERSHIP AND THE FIRM'S PROMOTIONAL STRATEGY

Marketers have long been aware of the powerful influence that opinion leadership exerts on consumer behavior. They try to encourage word-of-mouth communication and other favorable informal conversations concerning their products because they recognize that consumers place more credibility in informal communication sources than in paid advertising. The seeking of product information and advice also tends to be the most widely used consumer strategy for reducing perceived risk.

One marketing strategist suggested that new-product designers exploit the effectiveness of word-of-mouth communication by deliberately designing products to have word-of-mouth potential. He said that new products "should give customers something to talk about, and to talk with—a powerful advantage idea that can be expressed in words."[60] Examples of new products that have had such word-of-mouth potential include Rubik's Cube, the Polaroid camera, Diet-Rite Cola, the Sylvania flashcube, the Water Pik, Contac, Crest toothpaste, and the "pill." These revolutionary products "sold themselves," as consumers sold them to each other by word of mouth.

In some instances where informal word of mouth did not spontaneously emerge from the uniqueness of the product or its marketing strategy, marketers have deliberately attempted to stimulate or to simulate opinion leadership.

Advertisements That Stimulate Opinion Leadership

Advertisements designed to get consumers to "tell your friends how much you like our product" are one way in which marketers have used advertising to increase product-related discussions. The objective of a promotional strategy of

490

stimulation is to run advertisements that are sufficiently interesting and informative to provoke consumers into discussing the virtues of the product with others. For example, Ben Kahn, the well-known furrier, has sponsored a series of advertisements designed to increase the consumer's expertise in the selection of fine furs. Figure 16-5 illustrates how such an advertisement can provide the

FIGURE 16-5   Advertisement Designed to Stimulate Informal Communication

Courtesy of Ben Kahn Furs Corp.

consumer with sufficient knowledge and self-confidence to enable her to give advice on the selection of a mink coat.

Advertisements That Stimulate Opinion Leadership

A firm's advertisements can also be designed to simulate product discussion by portraying people in the act of informal communication. Such a promotional tactic has the characteristic of suggesting that it is appropriate to discuss a particular subject or product. For example, a simulated informal communication encounter between two women has been employed in the television advertising campaign for a feminine hygiene product to persuade women to discuss their use or contemplated use of this personal-care product. Such simulations also reduce the need for consumers to actually seek product advice from others.

An even more penetrating application of advertising designed to simulate informal communication is shown in Figure 16-6. This Hunt-Wesson Foods advertisement depicts a group of consumers in a "chain of communication" dispelling the false rumor that Hunt's products are owned by a rich Texan of the same name.

Word of Mouth May Be Uncontrollable

Although most marketing managers believe that word-of-mouth communication is extremely effective, one problem they sometimes overlook is the fact that such informal communication is not easy to control. Negative comments—rumors that are untrue—can sometimes sweep through a population to the detriment of the product in question.

Following are some of the more common rumor themes that have beset firms, and in certain cases have unfavorably influenced sales: (1) the product was produced under unsanitary conditions; (2) the product contained an unwholesome or culturally unacceptable ingredient; (3) the product functioned as an undesirable depressant or stimulant; (4) the product included some cancer-causing element or agent; and (5) the firm was owned or influenced by an unfriendly or misguided foreign country, governmental agency, or far-out religious cult.

Combatting unfounded rumors is a difficult task. For example, for years Du Pont was plagued by the rumor that Teflon (a resin used to coat cookware) gave off lethal fumes when heated. The rumor claimed that an unidentified machinist took one puff from a cigarette contaminated by a little Teflon and died within five minutes. At one point, Du Pont's public relations department was answering twenty letters a day from worried stockholders and customers, but still the rumor persisted. Finally, Du Pont had one of its most distinguished scientists present a carefully documented paper at a technical meeting which detailed the exhaustive tests that Du Pont had conducted over the years to establish Teflon's safety. A booklet based on his speech was then distributed by the "tens of thousands" to the consuming public. After many years, the rumor finally died out. It is interesting to speculate about the number of lost sales that resulted from that unfortunate rumor.

FIGURE 16-6   Advertisement Depicting Word-of-Mouth Communication

Courtesy of Hunt-Wesson Foods, Inc.

More recently, some of the companies that have had to deal with damaging rumors include General Foods, Life Savers, McDonald's, Procter and Gamble, Squibb, and Warner-Lambert.[61] Most of these firms have found that rumors cannot generally be ignored. Instead, they must be responded to quickly before they spread out of control. Sometimes ads have been employed to refute rumors and to demonstrate how unfounded they are.

The Creation of Opinion Leaders

Marketing strategists agree that promotional efforts would be most effective if they could segment their markets into opinion leaders and opinion receivers relevant to their product category. Then they could direct their promotional messages directly to the people most likely to "carry the word" to the masses. However, because of the difficulties inherent in identifying appropriate opinion leaders, some researchers have suggested that it might be more fruitful to "create" product-specific opinion leaders.

In one study, a group of socially influential high-school students (class presidents, sports captains, etc.) were asked to become members of a panel that would rate new rock-and-roll phonograph records. As part of their responsibility, panel participants were encouraged to discuss their record choices with friends. Preliminary examination suggested that these influentials would not qualify as opinion leaders for records because of their relatively meager ownership of the product category.[62] However, by encouraging their interest, some of the records that the group evaluated made the top-ten charts in the cities where they lived, but these same records did not make the top-ten charts in any other city. This study suggests that product-specific opinion leaders can be created by taking socially involved or influential people and deliberately increasing their enthusiasm for a product category.

summary

Opinion leadership is the process by which one person (the opinion leader) informally influences the actions or attitudes of others, who may be opinion seekers or merely opinion recipients. Opinion receivers perceive the opinion leader as a highly credible source of product information who, because of his or her presumed objectivity, can help reduce their search time and their perceived risk. Opinion leaders, in turn, are motivated to give information or advice to others in part because it enhances their own status and self-image, and because such advice tends to reduce their own postpurchase dissonance. Other motives include product-involvement, other-involvement, and message-involvement.

Market researchers identify opinion leaders by the self-designated method, the key-informant method, the sociometric method, and the objective method. Studies of opinion leadership indicate that the phenomenon tends to be product-specific; that is, individuals "specialize" in a product or product category in which they are highly interested and involved. An opinion leader for one product category may be an opinion receiver for another.

Generally, opinion leaders are gregarious, self-confident, innovative people who like to talk. They acquire information about their areas of interest through avid readership of special-interest magazines and by new-product trial. Their interests often overlap adjacent product areas; thus their opinion leadership may extend into related areas.

The opinion leadership process usually takes place among friends, neighbors, and work associates who have frequent physical proximity and thus ample opportunity to hold informal product-related conversations. Such conversations usually occur naturally in the context of the product-category usage.

The two-step flow of communication theory, developed some thirty-five years ago, highlighted the role of interpersonal influence in the transmission of information from the mass media to the population at large. This theory provides the foundation for a revised *multistep flow of communication* model, which takes into account the fact that information and influence are often two-way processes, and that opinion leaders both influence and are influenced by opinion receivers.

Marketers recognize the strategic importance of segmenting their audiences into opinion leaders and opinion receivers for their product categories. In this way, they can direct their promotional efforts to the more influential segments of their markets, with some confidence that these individuals will in turn transmit this information to those who seek product advice. Marketers have found that they can also "create" opinion leaders for their products by taking socially involved or influential people and deliberately increasing their enthusiasm for a product category.

discussion questions

1. Why is the opinion leader a more credible source of product information than a product advertisement?
2. As a marketing research consultant, you have been asked by a manufacturer of a new brand of instant coffee to identify the opinion leaders for this product category. Which one of the following measurement techniques would you recommend: self-designating method, sociometric method, key-informant method, or objective method? Explain your selection.
3. Why would a consumer who has just made an important purchase attempt to influence the purchase behavior of others?
4. Is an opinion leader for stereo equipment likely to be an opinion leader for fashion clothing? Discuss.
5. A manufacturer of automobile parts is interested in adding a new product to its existing line of automobile products. Using Table 16-4 as a guide, identify and

discuss those category-specific attributes of an opinion leader that you feel would be particularly useful in planning a marketing strategy.

6. The two-step flow of communication theory has been modified to portray more accurately the flow of information. Briefly describe this modification and explain its relevance to the marketing decision maker.

7. Assume that you have been asked by a major sporting goods retailer to prepare a promotional campaign that would *simulate* word-of-mouth conversation. What type of promotional story line might you recommend? Explain why you think it would be effective.

8. Find an advertisement that attempts to *stimulate* word-of-mouth conversation. Explain why you believe the marketer used this appeal in the advertisement.

endnotes

1. Aljean Harmetz, "For Films, Word of Mouth Means Success," *New York Times*, November 27, 1978, C13.

2. George Katona and Eva Mueller, "A Study of Purchase Decisions, in Lincoln H. Clark, ed., *Consumer Behavior* (New York: New York Unviersity Press, 1955), 45.

3. Stephen C. Cosmas and Jagdish N. Sheth, "Identification of Opinion Leaders across Cultures: An Exploratory Assessment" (Urbana-Champaign: University of Illinois, May 1978), Working Paper No. 123.

4. Ernest Dichter, "How Word-of-Mouth Advertising Works," *Harvard Business Review*, 44 (November-December 1966), 148.

5. Ibid., 149–51.

6. Ibid.

7. Ibid., 149–52.

8. For an assessment of the various opinion leadership measurement procedures, see Jacob Jacoby, "Opinion Leadership and Innovativeness: Overlap and Validity," in M. Venkatesan, ed., *Proceedings 3rd Annual Conference* (Association for Consumer Research, 1972), 642–49; George Brooker and Michael J. Houston, "An Evaluation of Measures of Opinion Leadership," in Kenneth L. Berbhardt, ed., *1976 Educators' Proceedings* (Chicago: American Marketing Association, 1976) 564–67; and Danny N. Bellenger and Elizabeth C. Hirschman, "Identifying Opinion Leaders by Self-Report," in B.A. Greenberg and D.B. Bellenger, eds., *1977 Educators' Proceedings* (Chicago: American Marketing Association, 1977), 341–44.

9. Johan Arndt, "Role of Product-Related Conversations in the Diffusion of a New Product," *Journal of Marketing Research* 4 (August 1967), 292–94.

10. Leon G. Schiffman, "Sources of Information for the Elderly," *Journal of Advertising Research*, 11 (October 1971), 33–37.

11. Ibid., 35.

12. John G. Myers, "Patterns of Interpersonal Influence in the Adoption of New Products," in Raymond M. Haas, ed., *Proceedings* (Chicago: American Marketing Association, 1966), 750–57.

13. Ibid., 756–57.

14. Elihu Katz and Paul F. Lazarsfeld, *Personal Influence* (New York: Free Press, 1955), 32.

15. For example, see David B. Montgomery and Alvin J. Silk, "Patterns of Overlap in Opinion Leadership and Interest for Categories of Purchase Activity," in Phillip R.

McDonald, ed., *Proceedings* (Chicago: American Marketing Association, 1969), 377–86; and James H. Myers and Thomas S. Robertson, "Dimensions of Opinion Leadership," *Journal of Marketing Research,* 9 (February 1972), 41–46.

16. Myers and Robertson, "Dimensions of Opinion Leadership," 42–43.

17. William R. Darden and Fred D. Reynolds, "Predicting Opinion Leadership for Men's Apparel Fashions," *Journal of Marketing Research,* 9 (August 1972), 324–28.

18. Lawrence G. Corey, "People Who Claim to Be Opinion Leaders: Identifying Their Characteristics by Self-Report," *Journal of Marketing,* 35 (October 1971), 48–53.

19. For example, see John O. Summers, "The Identity of Women's Clothing Fashion Opinion Leaders," *Journal of Marketing Research,* 7 (May 1970), 178–85; Steven A. Baumgarten, "The Innovative Communicator in the Diffusion Process," *Journal of Marketing Research,* 12 (February 1975), 12–18; and Jacoby, "Opinion Leadership and Innovativeness," 647.

20. William Lazer and William E. Bell, "The Communication Process and Innovation," *Journal of Advertising Research,* 6 (September 1966), 7.

21. James F. Engel, Robert J. Kegerreis, and Roger D. Blackwell, "Word-of-Mouth Communication by the Innovator," *Journal of Marketing,* 33 (July 1969), 15–19.

22. Thomas S. Robertson, "Determinants of Innovative Behavior," in Reed Moyers, ed., *Proceedings* (Chicago: American Marketing Association, 1967), 331.

23. Harmetz, "For Films, Word of Mouth Means Success," C13.

24. John H. Holmes, "Communication Patterns and the Diffusion of a Consumer Innovation: Preliminary Findings," *Proceedings of the Second Annual Meeting* (Baltimore: Association for Consumer Research, 1971), 459–63.

25. Summers, "Identity of Women's Clothing," 183.

26. Ibid., 181.

27. Ibid.

28. Fred D. Reynolds and William R. Darden, "Mutually Adaptive Effects of Interpersonal Communication," *Journal of Marketing Research,* 8 (November 1971), 449–54

29. Thomas S. Robertson and James H. Myers, "Personality Correlates of Opinion Leadership and Innovative Buying Behavior," *Journal of Marketing Research,* 6 (May 1969), 164–68.

30. For example, see Summers, "Identity of Women's Clothing," 181; and Leon G. Schiffman and Vincent Gaccione, "Opinion Leaders in Institutional Markets," *Journal of Marketing,* 38 (April 1974), 51.

31. John H. Holmes and John D. Lett, Jr., "Product Sampling and Word of Mouth," *Journal of Advertising Research,* 17 (October 1977), 35–40.

32. For example, see Bruce Ryan and Neal C. Gross, "The Diffusion of Hybrid Seed Corn in Two Iowa Communities," *Rural Sociology,* 8 (March 1943), 15–24; and Verling C. Troldahl and Robert Van Dam, "Face-to-Face Communication about Major Topics in the News," *Public Opinion Quarterly,* 29 (Winter 1965), 626–32.

33. Corey, "People Who Claim to Be Opinion Leaders," 51.

34. Stuart Elliot, "How to Reach the Automobile Buff," *Advertising Age,* June 22, 1981, S-16.

35. Reynolds and Darden, "Mutually Adaptive Effects," 450; and Summers, "Identity of Women's Clothing," 185.

36. For example, see Sidney P. Feldman, "Some Dyadic Relationships Associated with Consumer Choice," in Haas, *Proceedings,* 758–75; and Sidney P. Feldman and Merlin C. Spencer, "The Effect of Personal Influence in the Selection of Consumer Services," in Peter D. Bennett, ed., *Proceedings* (Chicago: American Marketing Association, 1965), 440–52.

37. Summers, "Identity of Women's Clothing," 180.

38. Ibid.

39. Katz and Lazarsfeld, *Personal Influence,* 305–6.

40. Summers, "Identity of Women's Clothing," 179.

41. Feldman and Spencer, "Effect of Personal Influence," 71.

42. For example, see Corey, "People Who Claim to Be Opinion Leaders"; Charles W. King and John O. Summers, "Overlap of Opinion Leadership across Consumer Product Categories," *Journal of Marketing Research,* 7 (February 1970), 43–50; and Alvin J. Silk, "Overlap across Self-designated Opinion Leaders: A Study of Selected Dental Products and Services," *Journal of Marketing Research,* 3 (August 1966), 253–59.

43. Silk, "Overlap across Self-designated Opinion Leaders," 257.

44. King and Summers, "Overlap of Opinion Leadership," 46.

45. Silk, "Overlap across Self-designated Opinion Leaders," 258.

46. King and Summers, "Overlap of Opinion Leadership," 48–50.

47. David B. Montgomery and Alvin J. Silk, "Clusters of Consumer Interests and Opinion Leaders' Spheres of Influence," *Journal of Marketing Research,* 8 (August 1971), 317–21.

48. Russell W. Belk, "Occurrence of Word-of-Mouth Buyer Behavior as a Function of Situation and Advertising Stimuli," in Fred C. Allvine, ed., *Proceedings* (Chicago: American Marketing Association, 1971), 419–22.

49. Ibid.

50. For example, see William H. White, "The Web of Word of Mouth," *Fortune,* November 1954, 140–43.

51. Feldman, "Some Dyadic Relationships," 768–71.

52. Leon G. Schiffman, "Social Interaction Patterns of the Elderly Consumer," in Boris W. Becker and Helmut Becker, eds., *Combined Proceedings* (Chicago: American Marketing Association, 1972), 451.

53. John O. Summers, "New Product Interpersonal Communication," in Fred C. Allvine, ed., *Combined Proceedings* (Chicago: American Marketing Association, 1971), 428–33.

54. Paul F. Lazarsfeld, Bernard Berelson, and Hazel Gaudet, *The People's Choice,* 2nd ed. (New York: Columbia University Press, 1948), 151.

55. For example, see Thomas S. Robertson, "Purchase Sequence Response: Innovators vs Non-Innovators," *Journal of Advertising Research,* 8 (February 1968), 47–52; Summers, "New Product Interpersonal Communication," 429–30; Reynolds and Darden, "Mutually Adaptive Effects," 451; Jagdish N. Sheth, "Word-of-Mouth in Low Risk Innovations," *Journal of Advertising Research,* 11 (June 1971), 15–18; and Schiffman and Gaccione, "Opinion Leaders," 51–52.

56. Robertson, "Purchase Sequence Response," 47–52; Summers, "New Product Interpersonal Communication," 429–30; Reynolds and Darden, "Mutually Adaptive Effects," 451; Sheth, "Word-of-Mouth in Low Risk Innovations, 15–18; and Schiffman and Gaccione, "Opinion Leaders," 51–52.

57. Flemming Hansen, "Backwards Segmentation Using Hierarchical Clustering and Q Factor Analysis," in Venkatesan, *Proceedings 3rd Annual Conference,* 226.

58. Reynolds and Darden, "Mutually Adaptive Effects," 450; Schiffman, "Social Interaction Patterns," 447; Leon G. Schiffman, Joseph F. Dash, and William R. Dillon, "Interpersonal Communication: An Opinion Leadership/Opinion Seeking Composite Approach," in Edward M. Mazze, ed., *Combined Proceedings* (Chicago: American Marketing Association, 1975), 228–32; and Leon G. Schiffman and Steven P. Schnaars, "The Consumption of Historical Romance Novels: Consumer Aesthetics in Popular Literature," in Elizabeth C. Hirschman and Morris Holbrook, eds., *Symbolic Consumer Behavior* (Ann Arbor, Mich.: Association for Consumer Research, 1980), 46–51.

59. Schiffman and Schnaars, "Consumption of Historical Romance Novels," 50.

60. James J. Sheeran, "'Me-Too' Marketing Mania," *New York Times*, March 11, 1973, 17.

61. Robert Levy, "Tilting at the Rumor Mill," *Dun's Review*, July 1981, 52–54.

62. Joseph R. Mancuso, "Why Not Create Opinion Leaders for New Product Introduction?" *Journal of Marketing*, 33 (July 1969), 20–25.

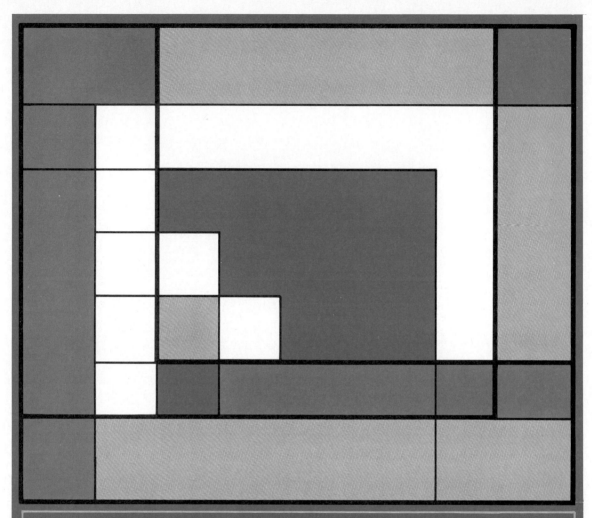

SEVENTEEN

Diffusion of Innovations

introduction

THIS chapter examines a major aspect of consumer behavior—the acceptance of *new* products and services. The introduction of new products is vital to both the consumer and the marketer. For the consumer, new products represent an increased opportunity for better satisfaction of personal, social, and environmental needs. For the marketer, new products provide an important mechanism for keeping the firm competitive and profitable.

Our framework for exploring consumers' acceptance of new products is drawn from the area of research known as the *diffusion of innovations*. Actually, the study of the diffusion of innovations is interdisciplinary in scope and has its earliest roots in anthropology and rural sociology. Other disciplines, such as communications, education, medical sociology, and marketing, have more recently investigated selected aspects of diffusion. Table 17-1 lists the kind of topics and units of analyses examined by these various behavioral disciplines.

The central interests of consumer researchers who have specialized in the diffusion of innovations have been to better understand (1) how the acceptance of a new product spreads within a market, and (2) the individual consumer decision-making process that led up to the acceptance or rejection of a new product.

Within the scope of our discussion of the diffusion of innovations, we will concentrate on two closely related processes: (1) the diffusion process and (2) the adoption process. In the broadest sense, the diffusion process is a *macro* process which is concerned with the spread of a new product (an innovation) from its source to the consuming public. In contrast, the adoption process is a *micro* process which focuses on the stages through which an individual consumer passes in making a decision to accept or reject a new product. In addition to these two interrelated processes, we will present a profile of *consumer innovators*— those consumers who are the first to purchase a new product. The ability to identify and reach this important group of consumers plays a major role in the success or failure of a marketer's new-product marketing efforts.

> *We have learned so well how to absorb novelty that receptivity itself has turned into a kind of tradition—"the tradition of the new."*
>
> RICHARD HOFSTADTER
>
> Anti-Intellectualism in American Life (1963)

TABLE 17-1   Type of Diffusion of Innovation Studies Undertaken, by Discipline

DISCIPLINE	TYPICAL INNOVATIONS STUDIED	MAIN UNIT OF ANALYSIS
Anthropology	Technological ideas (e.g., steel ax)	Tribal or peasant villages
Early sociology	City manager government, postage stamps, "ham" radios	Communities or individuals
Rural sociology	Agricultural ideas (e.g., weed sprays, hybrid seed, fertilizers) and health ideas (e.g., vaccinations, latrines)	Individual farmers in rural communities
Education	Kindergartens, driver training, modern math, programmed instruction	School systems or teachers
Medical sociology	Medical drugs, vaccinations, family-planning methods	Individuals
Communications	News events, agricultural innovations	Individuals
Marketing	New products (e.g., a coffee brand, the touch telephone, clothing fashions)	Individual consumers

Reprinted with permission of Macmillan Publishing Co., Inc. from *Communication of Innovations*, by Everett M. Rogers and R. Floyd Shoemaker. Copyright © 1971 by The Free Press, a Division of The Macmillan Company.

THE DIFFUSION PROCESS

The diffusion process is concerned with the general dimension of how innovations spread—how they are assimilated—within a market. More precisely, the *diffusion process* is the *process by which the acceptance of an innovation* (a new product, new service, new idea, new practice) *is spread by communication* (mass media, salespeople, informal conversations) *to members of a social system* (a target market) *over a period of time.* This definition includes the four basic elements of the diffusion process: (1) the innovation, (2) the channels of communication, (3) the social system, and (4) time. Each of these elements will be considered in turn.

The Innovation

Defining a "product innovation" or a "new product" is not an easy task. The various approaches that have been used to define a *new product* can be classified as firm-oriented, product-oriented, market-oriented, and consumer-oriented.

A *firm-oriented* approach treats newness of a product from the perspective of the company producing or marketing the product; that is, if it is "new" to the company, it is considered to be *new.* This definition of newness ignores whether or not the product is actually new to the marketplace (i.e., to both competitors and consumers). Consistent with this view, exact duplicates or modifications of a competitor's product would qualify as new. While this definition of "newness" has considerable merit if the objective is to examine the impact that a "new" product has on the firm, it is not especially useful if the goal is to understand consumer acceptance of a new product.

In contrast, a *product-oriented* approach focuses on the features inherent in the product itself, and the effects these features are likely to have on consumers' established usage patterns. One product-oriented framework considers the extent to which a new product is likely to be disruptive to the consumer's already established behavioral patterns. It defines three types of product innovations: continuous, dynamically continuous, and discontinuous.

1. A *continuous* innovation has the least disrupting influence on established patterns. It involves the introduction of a *modified* product, rather than a totally new product. Examples: fluoride toothpaste, new automobile models, concentrated liquid detergents.
2. A *dynamically continuous* innovation is somewhat more disruptive than a continuous innovation, but it still does not alter established behavioral patterns. It may involve the creation of a new product or the modification of an existing product. Examples: the electric toothbrush, the correcting typewriter, the electric hand-held game, the erasable-ink pen.
3. A *discontinuous* innovation requires the establishment of new behavioral patterns. Examples: television, pocket calculators, home computers.[1]

In another product-oriented approach, the extent of "newness" of a product is defined in terms of how much impact its physical features or attributes are likely to have on user satisfaction.[2] Thus the more satisfaction a consumer derives from a new product, the higher it ranks on the scale of "newness." This concept leads to the classification of products as *artifically new, marginally new,* or *genuinely new.* A genuinely new product would have features that satisfy the user in a manner that differs significantly from that of an older product. New products that have been judged to possess enough "newness" to qualify as genuinely new products include nonrefrigerated prepared salad spreads, frozen breakfasts, canned puddings, and instant omelet mixes. The advertisement in Figure 17-1 is designed to pinpoint the benefits of a new telephone service.

A *market-oriented* approach judges the newness of a product in terms of how much potential exposure consumers have to the new product. Two market-oriented definitions of product innovation have been used quite extensively in consumer studies:

1. A product is considered new if it has not been purchased by more than a relatively small (fixed) percentage of the potential market.
2. A product is considered new if it has only been available on the market for a relatively short (specified) period of time.

Both of these market-oriented definitions are basically subjective because they leave to the researcher the task of establishing the degree of sales penetration within which it is appropriate to call the product an innovation (such as the first 5 percent to use the new product) or how long a product can be on the market and still be considered "new" (such as the first three months the product is available). These approaches have been useful to consumer researchers in their attempts to

FIGURE 17-1   Advertisement Stressing the Benefits of a New Service

Courtesy of American Telephone and Telegraph Co.

study the diffusion of innovations. Table 17-2 gives some examples of how products have been defined as innovations in terms of these two market-oriented schemes.

Some researchers have suggested that a *consumer-oriented* approach is the most appropriate way to define an innovation.[3] Within the context of this approach, a new product is any product that a potential consumer judges to be new. In other words, newness is based on the consumer's *perception* of the product, rather than on physical features or market realities. Although the consumer-oriented approach has been endorsed by some advertising practition-

TABLE 17-2   Examples of Market-Oriented Definitions of Innovation

SCHEME	INNOVATION	DEFINITION
Percent of target market to purchase	Various durable goods (e.g., color TV)*	The first 10% to purchase
	Touch-Tone telephones†	The first 10% to purchase
Extent of time on the market	Automobile diagnostic center‡	The first three months after the opening of the center
	Ladies' fashion hats§	The five-and-one-half-month period from August through mid-January

Sources: *William E. Bell, "Consumer Innovators: A Unique Market for Newness," in Stephen A. Greyser, ed., *Toward Scientific Marketing* (Chicago: American Marketing Association, 1963), 85–87.

†Thomas S. Robertson, "Determinants of Innovative Behavior," in Reed Moyer, ed., *Changing Marketing Systems* (Chicago: American Marketing Association, 1967), 328–32.

‡James F. Engel, Roger D. Blackwell, and Robert J. Kegerreis, "Consumer Use of Information in the Adoption of an Innovation," *Journal of Advertising Research*, 9 (December 1969), 3–8.

§Charles W. King, "Fashion Adoption: A Rebuttal to the 'Trickle Down' Theory," in Greyser, *Toward Scientific Marketing*, 108–25.

ers and marketing strategists, it has received little systematic attention from consumer researchers.

PRODUCT CHARACTERISTICS THAT INFLUENCE DIFFUSION

All new products are not equally susceptible to consumer acceptance. For example, some products seem to catch on almost overnight (e.g., personal audio equipment like the Sony Walkman), whereas other innovations take a very long time to gain acceptance (e.g., organ donor programs). Some new products never seem to achieve widespread consumer acceptance (e.g., light whiskeys, Polavision, or quadratic sound systems).

It would reduce the uncertainties of product marketing if marketers could anticipate how consumers will react to their products. For example, if a marketer knew that a product contained features that were likely to retard its acceptance, the marketer would either develop a marketing strategy that would compensate for these features or decide not to market the product at all. While there are no precise formulas by which marketers can evaluate a new product's acceptance, diffusion researchers have identified five product characteristics that seem to influence consumers' acceptance of new products: (1) relative advantage, (2) compatibility, (3) complexity, (4) trialability, and (5) observability.[4]

Relative advantage is the degree to which potential customers *perceive* a new product as superior to existing substitutes. For example, the seal of approval awarded to Crest toothpaste in the mid-1960s by the American Dental Association was a strong relative advantage. Mothers of young children concerned with tooth decay were impressed by this first-time endorsement, as evidenced by a dramatic increase in sales within a relatively short time. However, since product perception is highly selective, it is likely that young, single adults who are primarily interested in toothpastes that whiten their teeth and freshen their breath, did not perceive the ADA approval as a relative advantage. The advertisement in Figure 17-2 dramatically illustrates the relative size advantage of a camera.

In addition to unique product features, a promotional program that includes cents-off coupons, two-for-one sales, and a variety of special services also has the potential of being perceived by consumers as a relative advantage and may lead to increased acceptance.

Compatibility is the degree to which potential consumers feel that a new product is consistent with their present needs, values, and practices. For example, male university students who shaved daily took a shorter period of time to decide to try a new type of blade than did less-frequent shavers.[5] These results suggest that when a new product is compatible with existing needs and experience, it is likely to enjoy increased acceptance. A new cream designed to

FIGURE 17-2   Advertisement Depicting a Product's Relative Advantage

Courtesy of the Pentax Corporation

remove facial hair might be simpler to use than a razor, but it is less likely to receive mass acceptance because (1) it would require a major adjustment in behavior, and (2) it would not be consistent with the values most males possess with regard to the ritual of shaving.

Complexity is the degree to which a new product is difficult to comprehend or use. Clearly, the easier it is to understand and use a new product, the greater the likelihood that it will be accepted. For example, the acceptance of such convenience products as TV dinners, premixed alcoholic drinks, and instant mashed potatoes is generally due to their appeal to consumers' desires for ease of preparation and use. Card games like poker and gin rummy are played by a greater segment of the population than bridge and canasta because they are less complex.

Trialability is the degree to which a new product is capable of being tried on a limited basis by consumers. The greater the opportunity to try a new product, the easier it will be for consumers to evaluate it. The inherent quality of the product ("no soapy mess") and its low cost (especially when a trial coupon is offered) make it relatively easy to try a new liquid hand soap product (see Figure 17-3). On the other hand, durable items such as major appliances are difficult, if

FIGURE 17-3   **Classification of Households by Type of Change in Trial Purchase**   Source: Robert W. Shoemaker and F. Robert Shoaf, "Behavioral Changes in the Trial of New Products," *Journal of Consumer Research,* 2 (September 1975), 107.

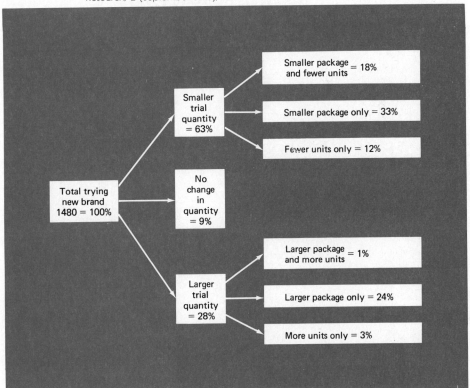

not impossible, to try without making a major commitment. This may explain why publications like *Consumer Reports* are so widely used for their ratings of infrequently purchased durable goods.

As a general rule, it would seem that frequently purchased household products tend to have qualities that make trial relatively easy.[6] Figure 17-4 indicates that 63 percent of the consumers studied made a trial purchase of a new brand in a smaller quantity than they usually purchased (33 percent bought a smaller package and 18 percent purchased both a smaller size and fewer units). For the marketer of household products, these findings suggest that it may be

FIGURE 17-4   New-Product Advertisement That Stresses Trial

Courtesy of Softsoap Division of Minnetonka, Inc.

wise to offer a new product in smaller-than-typical sizes initially in order to stimulate trial.

Because it recognized the importance of trialability, Gillette undertook a massive promotional campaign to introduce the Trac II razor blade. It mailed a free razor handle and single Trac II blade to a large segment of the adult male population. By supplying the free, reusable razor handle, Gillette was able to establish an almost instantaneous replacement market for its new Trac II blades. Similarly, Beecham launched its Aqua-fresh toothpaste in the United States by mailing a free sample to some 45 million homes. This mammoth program to gain large-scale trial, when coupled with a massive introductory advertising campaign, rocketed the brand to second place in sales. Test drives for automobiles, money-back guarantees, and free samples also enhance the acceptance of products by making consumer trial easy.

Observability (or communicability) is the ease with which a product's benefits or attributes can be observed, imagined, or described to potential consumers. Products that have a high degree of social visibility, such as fashion items, are more easily diffused than products that are used in private, such as a new brand of toothpaste. Similarly, a tangible product is more easily promoted than an intangible product (i.e., a service).

To date, only a few studies have examined the influence of these five innovation characteristics on consumers' trial of new products. The first consumer study to examine these five characteristics found that relative advantage, compatibility, trialability, and observability were positively associated with consumers' intentions to buy a variety of new product concepts.[7] This study did not examine actual purchase behavior. However, its findings were supported by subsequent studies that used actual purchase data.[8]

It must be recognized that each of these product attributes is dependent on consumer perception. A product that is *perceived* as having a strong relative advantage, as fulfilling present needs and values, as easy to try on a limited basis, and as simple to understand and to see (and/or examine), is more likely to be purchased than a product that is not so perceived.

The Channels of Communication

How quickly a product innovation spreads through a market depends to a great extent on communication between the marketer and the consumer, and communication between consumers. For this reason, researchers interested in diffusion have paid particular attention to the transmission of product-related information through various channels of communication, and to the impact of the messages and the channels on the adoption or rejection of new products. Of central concern has been the influence of both impersonal sources (e.g., advertising and editorial matter) and interpersonal sources (e.g., salespeople and informal opinion leaders). In fact, most of our discussion of personal influence and the opinion leadership process (see Chapter 16) is based on evidence that is part of the general tradition of diffusion research.

One major stream of communication research has focused on the relative importance of certain *types* of information sources on early-versus-later adoption of new products. Specifically, the following generalizations gleaned from the general diffusion literature are important to marketers:[9]

1. Early adopters have more change-agent contact (e.g., with salespeople) than later adopters.
2. Early adopters have greater exposure to mass-media communication channels than later adopters.
3. Early adopters seek information about innovations more frequently than later adopters.
4. Early adopters have greater knowledge of innovations than later adopters.
5. Early adopters have a higher degree of opinion leadership than later adopters.

We will discuss these generalizations in greater detail in our examination of the consumer innovator.

The Social System

The diffusion of a new product usually takes place in a social setting—frequently referred to as a *social system*. Within the framework of consumer behavior, the terms *market segment* or *target market* are equivalent to the term *social system* used in diffusion research. Regardless of what it is called, however, a social system is a physical, social, or cultural environment to which people belong and within which they function. For example, for a new hybrid seed corn, the social system might consist of all farmers in a number of local communities; for a new drug, the social system might consist of all physicians within several specified cities; for a new special-diet product, the social system might include all residents of a geriatric community.[10] As these examples indicate, the social system serves as the boundary within which the diffusion of a new product is examined.

The orientation of a social system, with its own special values or norms, is likely to influence the acceptance or rejection of new products. If the social system is "modern" in orientation, the acceptance of innovations is likely to be high. In contrast, if a social system is "traditional in orientation," innovations that are perceived as radical or as infringements on established custom are likely to be avoided. According to one authority, the following characteristics typify a "modern" social system:[11]

1. A positive attitude toward change.
2. An advanced technology and skilled labor force.
3. A general respect for education and science.
4. An emphasis on rational and ordered social relationships rather than on emotional ones.
5. An outreach perspective, in which members of the system frequently interact with outsiders, thus facilitating the entrance of new ideas into the social system.
6. The system's members can readily see themselves in quite different roles.

These orientations (modern or traditional) may be national in scope and influence members of an entire society, or they may exist at the local level and influence only those who live in a specific community. The critical issue is that a social system's orientation is the "climate" in which marketers have to operate in attempting to gain acceptance for their new products. For example, the United States has in recent years experienced a rapid increase in the introduction of food products that stress natural ingredients (i.e., which contain no artificial ingredients or preservatives, such as natural ice cream, health breads, and natural cereals). For these new products to be successful, the prevailing values of a sufficient number of consumers must agree with the concept of natural ingredients.

Time

Time is the backbone of the diffusion process. It pervades the study of diffusion in three distinct but interrelated ways: (1) in *purchase time,* (2) in the identification of *adopter categories,* and (3) in the *rate of adoption.*

PURCHASE TIME

Purchase time is concerned with the amount of time that elapses between the consumer's initial awareness of a new product and the point at which the consumer purchases it or rejects it. The purchase of an expensive camera will serve to illustrate how a consumer's decision might progress over time.[12] Figure 17-5 shows an average purchase time frame and pinpoints the influence of various communications sources on the first-time purchaser of an expensive camera. An examination of the overall time frame reveals that it takes about twelve months from contact with an opinion leader (a friend or relative who is perceived to be knowledgeable about photography and who introduces the idea of the purchase of an expensive camera) to the actual purchase.

The figure illustrates how long and complex a process consumer decision making can be, and how different information sources become important at

FIGURE 17-5   **Time Frame for First-Time Purchasers of Expensive Cameras**

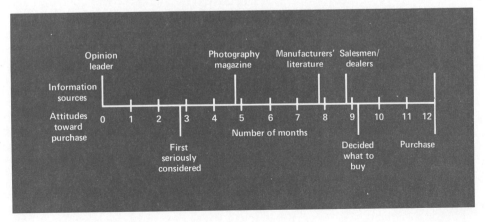

TABLE 17-3   Adopter Categories

ADOPTER CATEGORY	DESCRIPTION	RELATIVE PERCENTAGE WITHIN THE POPULATION WHICH EVENTUALLY ADOPTS
Innovators	"Venturesome"—willing to accept risks	2.5
Early adopters	"Respectable"—regarded by many others in the social system as a role model	13.5
Early majority	"Deliberate"—willing to consider innovation only after peers have adopted	34.0
Late majority	"Skeptical"—overwhelming pressure from peers needed before adoption occurs	34.0
Laggards	"Traditional"—oriented to the past	16.0
		100.0

Reprinted with permission of Macmillan Publishing Co., Inc. from *Diffusion of Innovations*, by Everett M. Rogers. Copyright © The Free Press, 1962.

successive stages in the process. Purchase time is an important concept because the average time a consumer takes to adopt a new product is a predictor of the overall length of time that will be required for the new product to be diffused throughout the market. For example, when the individual purchase time is short, a marketer has reason to expect that the overall rate of diffusion will be faster than when the individual purchase time is long, as in the purchase of a new camera. Thus, individual purchase time is an indicator of the total amount of time necessary for a product to achieve widespread adoption.

ADOPTER CATEGORIES

The concept of adopter categories involves the determination of a classification scheme that indicates where a consumer stands in relation to other consumers in terms of when he or she adopted a new product. Five adopter categories are frequently cited in the diffusion literature: (1) innovators, (2) early adopters, (3) early majority, (4) late majority, and (5) laggards.[13] Table 17-3 describes each of these adopter categories and estimates their relative proportions within the total population that eventually adopts the new product.

As Figure 17-6 indicates, the adopter categories take on the characteristics of a normal distribution (i.e., a bell-shaped curve). It is based on the sociologists' assumption that 100 percent of the members of the social system under study (the target market) will eventually accept the product innovation.[14] This assumption is *not* in keeping with marketers' experiences, since very few, if any, products fit the needs of all potential consumers. For example, theoretically all American women could be expected to color their hair. In reality, however, a relatively small proportion of adult females use hair coloring, and it would be unrealistic for the hair-coloring industry to expect that all women eventually will. For this reason, it is important to think of an additional category, that of *nonadopters*. A "nonconsumer" category is in accord with marketplace reality, in that not *all* potential consumers do adopt a product innovation.

FIGURE 17-6 **The Sequence and Proportion of Adopter Categories Among the Population that Eventually Adopts** Reprinted with permission of Macmillan Publishing Co., Inc. from *Diffusion of Innovations,* by Everett M. Rogers. Copyright © The Free Press, 1962.

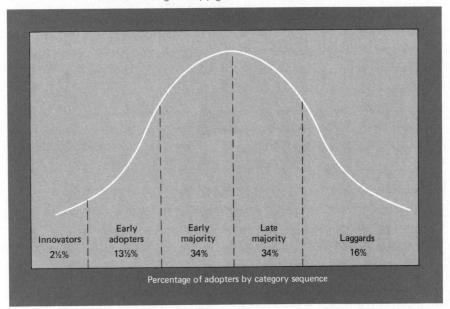

For these reasons, consumer behavior studies usually avoid using the classic five-category adopter scheme. However, there is not as yet any generally accepted alternative procedure for defining adopter categories.[15] Instead, as Table 17-4 on page 514 indicates, consumer researchers have employed a variety of adopter schemes, most of which consist of two or three categories that compare *innovators* or *early triers* with *later triers* or *nontriers.* As we will see, this focus on the innovator or early trier has produced some important generalizations which have practical significance for marketers planning the introduction of new products.

RATE OF ADOPTION

The rate of adoption is concerned with how long it takes for a new product to be adopted by members of a special social system; that is, how quickly a new product is accepted by those who will adopt it. Recent research has shown that the speed of adoption for new products has generally been increasing (i.e., getting shorter).[16]

The diffusion of television sets provides an illustration of this concept. Figure 17-7 compares the growth in the total number of United States households with the growth in television-owning households for the thirty-two-year period 1950–81. Note the very rapid rate of adoption of television sets between 1950 and 1958, and the emergence of multiset homes as an important market segment since 1958. The ownership of color television sets is shown as having a very low rate of adoption within the ten-year period 1955–64, probably due to their high sales price, the lack of color programming, and consumers'

TABLE 17-4   Types of Adopter Categories Used in Marketing Diffusion Studies

INNOVATION	ADOPTER CATEGORIES	RESEARCHERS' DEFINITIONS OF CATEGORIES
New brand of regular coffee*	Pioneers	The first 12% (or first two days)
	Early adopters	The next 18% (third to ninth day)
	Late adopters	The next 12% (tenth to sixteenth day)
New movie†	Innovators	Those who attended opening night
	Early adopters	Those who attended the fourth night
	Late adopters	Those who attended the sixth night
Automobile diagnostic center‡	Innovators	Those who used the center during its first three months of operation
	Nonadopters	A random sample drawn from the same city
A new health food (a salt substitute)§	Innovators	Those who used the product during a two-week trial period
	Noninnovators	Those who did not use the product during the trial period

Sources: *Johan Arndt, "Role of Product-Related Conversations in the Diffusion of a New Product," *Journal of Marketing Research*, 4 (August 1967), 291–95.

†Johan Arndt, "A Cold Blooded Analysis of Movie-Going as a Diffusion Process," *Markedsokonomic*, March 1969, 90.

‡James F. Engel, Roger D. Blackwell, and Robert J. Kegerreis, "Consumer Use of Information in the Adoption of an Innovation," *Journal of Advertising Research*, 9 (December 1969), 3–8.

§Leon G. Schiffman, "Perceived Risk in New Product Trial by Elderly Consumers," *Journal of Marketing Research*, 9 (February 1972), 106–8.

perceived functional risk (see Chapter 6). Since 1965, however, there has been a dramatic acceleration in the acceptance of color television sets.

In the marketing of new products, the objective is usually to gain very wide acceptance of the product as quickly as possible. The reasons why marketers desire a rapid rate of product adoption include the following:

1. To penetrate the market and establish market leadership (obtain the largest share of the market) before competition takes hold. A penetration policy is usually accompanied by a relatively low introductory price designed to discourage competition from entering the market.

2. To demonstrate to the channels of distribution (wholesalers and retailers) that the product is worthy of their full and continued support.

Under certain circumstances, marketers might prefer to avoid a rapid rate of adoption for a new product. For example, marketers who wish to employ a pricing strategy that will enable them to recoup their development costs quickly might follow a *skimming* policy—they first make the product available at a very high price to consumers who are willing to pay "top dollar" and then gradually lower the price in a series of steps designed to attract additional market segments at each price reduction.

FIGURE 17-7 **32 Years of Television Growth** Source: Reprinted with permission from the April 19, 1976 issue of *Advertising Age.* Copyright 1976 by Crain Communications Inc. Also, courtesy of Television Bureau of Advertising and McCann Erickson, Inc.

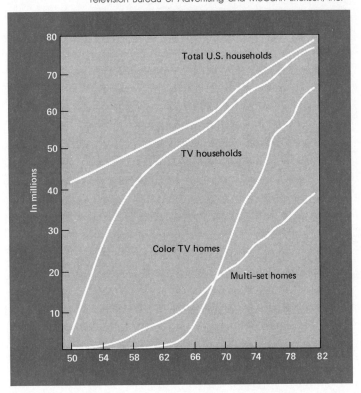

THE ADOPTION PROCESS

The second major process within the overall scope of the diffusion of innovations is the *adoption process*. The focus of this process is the stages through which an individual consumer passes in arriving at a decision *to try* or *not to try, to continue using* or *to discontinue using* a new product.

Stages in the Adoption Process

It is often assumed that the consumer moves through five stages in arriving at a decision to purchase or reject a new product: (1) awareness, (2) interest, (3) evaluation, (4) trial, and (5) adoption (or rejection).[17]

AWARENESS. During this first stage, consumers are exposed to the product innovation. This exposure is somewhat neutral, since they are not yet sufficiently interested in the product to search for additional product information.

INTEREST.   When consumers develop an interest in the product or product category, they search for information about how the innovation can benefit them.

EVALUATION.   Based upon their stock of information, the consumers draw conclusions about the innovation or determine whether further information is necessary. The evaluation stage thus represents a kind of "mental trial" of the product innovation. If the evaluation is satisfactory, the consumer will actually try the product innovation; if the mental trial is unsatisfactory, the product will be rejected.

TRIAL.   At this stage, consumers actually use the product innovation on a limited basis. Their experience with the product provides them with the critical information they need to adopt or reject.

ADOPTION.   Based upon their trials and/or favorable evaluation, the consumers decide to use the product on a full rather than limited basis or they decide to reject it.

The adoption process provides a framework for determining which types of information sources consumers find most important at specific decision stages. For example, a study of early users of the first automobile diagnostic

FIGURE 17-8   The Relative Importance of Different Types of Information Sources, by Adoption Process Stages

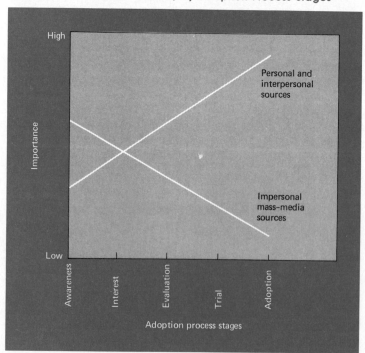

center in a midwestern city found that *mass-media sources* (magazines and radio publicity) were most important for disseminating general knowledge about such services and awareness of the specific service offered in the city. However, early users' final pretrial information was drawn primarily from informal discussions with *personal sources.*[18]

A study concerned with the acceptance of stainless steel blades among university students found that the mass media were the principal sources of initial product awareness, while informal sources (friends and relatives) were influential in the final decision to try the new type of blade.[19] A study designed to examine the influence of various information sources on the *rejection* of a new clothing style found that mass media served as the main source of awareness for women concerning the style, while informal sources were most influential at the evaluation stage.[20]

These and other studies support the notion that impersonal mass-media sources tend to be most valuable for creating initial product awareness; however, as the purchase decision progresses, the relative importance of these sources declines while the relative importance of interpersonal sources (friends, salespeople, and others) increases. Figure 17-8 depicts this relationship.

Criticisms of the Adoption Process

Although the adoption process model has been instructive for consumer researchers, it has been criticized because of the following limitations:

1. It does not adequately acknowledge that a need or problem recognition stage may precede the awareness stage.
2. It does not adequately provide for the rejection of a product after its trial (i.e., a consumer may never advance from the trial stage to the adoption stage but may reject the product after trial or never use the product on a continuous basis).
3. It does not adequately recognize that evaluation occurs throughout the decision-making process and not solely at the "evaluation" stage.
4. It does not adequately account for the possibility that the five stages may not always occur in the specific order suggested (e.g., trial may occur before evaluation); nor does it consider that some of the stages may, in fact, be skipped (e.g., in the case of consumer durables, such as a refrigerator, there may be no opportunity for trial).
5. Finally, it does not explicitly include *postpurchase evaluation.* This evaluation may lead to a strengthened commitment, or it may lead to a decision to discontinue use of the product.[21]

The Innovation Decision Process

To overcome these limitations, the traditional adoption process model has been updated into a more general decision-making model—the *innovation decision process.* The four stages of the revised adoption process model are:

1. *Knowledge.* Consumers are exposed to the innovation's existence and gain some understanding of how it functions.
2. *Persuasion.* Consumers form a favorable or unfavorable attitude toward the innovation.

3. *Decision.* Consumers engage in activities that lead to a choice to adopt or reject the innovation.
4. *Confirmation.* Consumers seek reinforcement for their innovation decision but may reverse this decision if exposed to conflicting messages about the product.[22]

Figure 17-9 depicts in diagrammatic form the operation of the innovation decision process. Very briefly, the model suggests that a number of individual consumer (i.e., receiver) and environmental (i.e., social system) variables influence the reception of information about the product innovation during the *knowledge* stage. At the *persuasion* stage, the consumer is further influenced by communications sources and by perceptions of the characteristics of the innovation (its relative advantage, compatibility, complexity, trialability, and observability). Additional information received during the *decision* stage enables the consumer to assess the innovation and decide whether to adopt or reject it. The final stage, *confirmation,* is also influenced by communication sources; it is at this stage that consumers evaluate their purchase experiences, look for support for their behavior, and decide to continue or discontinue using the product.

The innovation decision process model appears to be more comprehensive than the earlier adoption process model and eliminates many of its basic limitations. It is also much more attuned to the realities faced by the marketer who is launching a new product.

FIGURE 17-9   **The Innovation Decision Process** Reprinted with permission of Macmillan Publishing Co., Inc. from *Communication of Innovations,* by Everett M. Rogers and Floyd Shoemaker. Copyright © 1971 by The Free Press, a Division of The Macmillan Company.

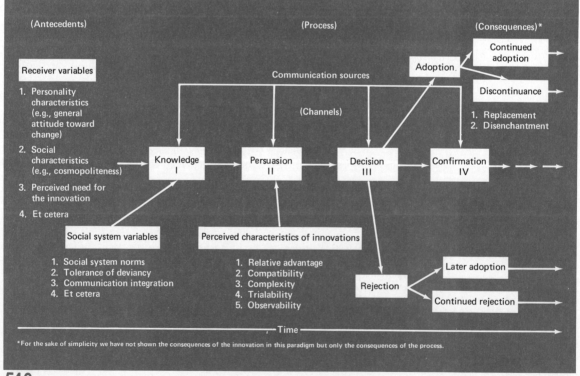

A PROFILE OF THE CONSUMER INNOVATOR

Who is the consumer innovator? What characteristics set the innovator apart from later adopters and from those who never purchase? How can the marketer reach and influence the innovator? These are key questions to the marketing practitioner about to introduce a new product or service.

Defining the Consumer Innovator

Consumer innovators can be defined as the relatively small group of consumers who are the earliest purchasers of a new product. The problem with the definition, however, centers on the concept "earliest," which is, after all, a relative term. Sociologists have treated this issue by sometimes defining *innovators* as the first 2.5 percent of the social system to adopt an innovation. In a good number of marketing diffusion studies, however, consumer researchers have *derived* the definition of the consumer innovator from the status of the new product under investigation. For example, if the researcher assesses the new product as an innovation for the first three months of its availability, then he or she defines the consumers who purchase it during this period as consumer innovators.

Other researchers have defined innovators in terms of their *innovativeness,* that is, their purchase of some minimum number of new products from a selected group of new products. In a study of the adoption of new fashion items, innovators were defined as those consumers who purchased more than one fashion product from a group of ten new fashion products; noninnovators were defined as those consumers who purchased only one or none of the new fashion products.[23] In other instances, researchers have defined innovators as those falling within an arbitrary proportion of the total market (e.g., the first 10 percent of the population in a specified geographic area to buy the new product).

Interest in the Product Category

Not surprisingly, researchers have found that consumer innovators are much more interested than either later adopters or nonadopters in the product category that they are among the first to purchase. For example, the earliest purchasers of the rotary-engined Mazda automobile were found to have substantially greater interest in automobiles (they enjoyed looking at auto magazines and were interested in the performance and functioning of automobiles) than those who purchased different small cars during the same period, or those who purchased the Mazda during a later period.[24]

Furthermore, consumer innovators are more likely than noninnovators to seek out information concerning their specific interests from a variety of informal and mass-media sources.[25] Contrary to what might be expected, consumer innovators do not seem to be impulsive purchasers; rather they seem to give greater deliberation to the purchase of new products than noninnovators.[26]

The Innovator Is an Opinion Leader

In discussing the characteristics of the opinion leader (see Chapter 16), we indicated a strong tendency for consumer opinion leaders to be innovators. Within our present context, it is worthwhile to note that an impressive number of studies on the diffusion of innovations have found that consumer innovators are likely to provide other potential consumers with information and advice about new products, and that those who receive such advice frequently follow it. Thus, in the role of opinion leader, the consumer innovator often influences the acceptance or rejection of new products.[27] If the innovator is enthusiastic about a new product and encourages others to try it, the product is likely to receive broader and quicker acceptance. On the other hand, if consumer innovators are dissatisfied with a new product and discourage others from trying it, its acceptance will be severely handicapped and it may die a quick death. With products that do not generate much excitement (either positive or negative), consumer innovators may not be sufficiently motivated to provide advice; in such cases, the marketer not only has to rely almost entirely on mass media and personal selling to influence future purchasers but the absence of *informal* influence is likely to result in a somewhat slower rate of acceptance (or rejection) for the new product. Since motivated consumer innovators can evidently speed up acceptance or rejection of a new product, they can thereby influence its eventual success or failure.

Personality Traits

In Chapter 4 we examined the personality traits that distinguish the consumer innovator from the noninnovator. In this section we will briefly highlight what researchers have learned about the personality of the consumer innovator.

First, consumer innovators have been found to be *less dogmatic* than noninnovators.[28] They tend to approach new or unfamiliar products with considerable openness and little anxiety. In contrast, noninnovators seem to find new products threatening, to the point where they prefer to delay purchase until the product's success has been clearly established.

Consistent with their open-mindedness, consumer innovators have also been found to be *inner-directed;* that is, they rely on their own values or standards in making a decision about a new product.[29] In comparison, noninnovators are *other-directed,* tending to rely on others for guidance on how to respond, rather than trusting their own personal values or standards. There is some research evidence that the initial purchasers of a new model automobile were inner-directed, and that later purchasers of the same model tended to be other-directed.[30] This suggests that as acceptance of a product progresses from early to later adopters, there is a gradual shift in the personality type of adopters from inner- to other-directedness.

Finally, in terms of *category width,* which purports to measure an individual's risk-handling orientation (see Chapter 4), the consumer innovator has been found to be a broad categorizer, while the noninnovator tends to be a narrow categorizer.[31] Broad categorizers tend to try many new products, even though, by doing so, they subject themselves to the risk of trying unsatisfactory products. On the other hand, narrow categorizers are so afraid of making poor product choices that they limit their trial of new products, even though this means they may forgo the benefits of desirable new products. However, for trivial or "artificially" new products (such as a new-flavored dessert), the narrow categorizer may adopt more quickly than the broad categorizer.[32] This suggests that the true consumer innovator does not respond to superficially different products but tends to single out substantially different products.

To sum up, consumer innovators seem to be more receptive to the unfamiliar; they are more willing to rely on their own values or standards than on the judgments of others. They are also willing to run the risk of a poor product choice in order to increase their exposure to new products. For the marketer, the personality traits that distinguish innovators from noninnovators suggest the need for separate promotional campaigns for innovators and for later adopters. Consumer innovators are more likely to react favorably to informative or fact-oriented advertising that appeals to their increased interest in the product category, and to readily evaluate the merits of a new product on the basis of their own personal standards. To reach noninnovators, it would seem appropriate to feature reference group settings and to use a recognized and trusted expert or celebrity to appeal to their other-directed responsiveness to those with authority.

Venturesomeness

Venturesomeness is a broad-based measure of a consumer's willingness to accept the risk of purchasing new products. Measures of venturesomeness have been used to evaluate a person's general values or attitudes toward trying new products. Typical questions include:

> Do you prefer to (1) try a new food product when it first comes out or (2) wait and learn how good it is before trying it?
> How do you feel about buying new things that come out for the home?
> When I am shopping and see a brand of heavy-duty detergent I know of but have never used, I am (very anxious or willing to try it), (hesitant about trying it), or (very unwilling to try it).[33]

Research that has examined venturesomeness has generally found that consumers who indicate a willingness to try new products tend to be consumer innovators (as measured by their actual purchase of new products). On the other hand, consumers who express a reluctance to try new products are in fact less likely to purchase new products. Therefore venturesomeness seems to be an effective barometer of actual innovative behavior.

Perceived Risk

Perceived risk, discussed in detail in Chapter 6, is another measure of a consumer's tendency to try new brands or products. Specifically, perceived risk can be thought of as the degree of uncertainty or fear as to the consequences of a purchase that a consumer feels when considering the purchase of a new product. For example, consumers experience uncertainty when they are concerned that a new product will not work properly or will not be as good as other alternatives.

Research on perceived risk and the trial of new products overwhelmingly indicates that the consumer innovator is a low-risk perceiver.[34] Consumers who perceive little or no risk associated with the purchase of a new product are much more likely to purchase it than consumers who perceive a great deal of risk. In other words, high-risk perception limits innovativeness.

Consistent with their greater venturesomeness and lowered risk perception, consumer innovators are also likely to believe that they learn about innovations earlier than others. They also tend to be more intrigued with the prospect of "newness" than are noninnovators.[35]

Purchase and Consumption Characteristics

Consumer innovators have purchase and usage traits that set them apart from noninnovators. Studies have shown that consumer innovators are *less* brand loyal, that is, *more* apt to switch brands. For example, with regard to a new brand of regular coffee, consumer innovators were found to be less loyal to established brands of coffee than noninnovators.[36] Similarly, in a study of the diffusion of new grocery products, innovators were found to be less loyal to established brands than later adopters.[37] It is not surprising that innovators tend to be less brand loyal, for brand loyalty would seriously impede their willingness to try new products.

Consumer innovators are also more likely to be *deal-prone* (i.e., to take advantage of special promotional offers such as free samples and cents-off coupons). Not surprisingly, consumers who are deal-prone have generally been found to be less brand loyal.[38] Consumer innovators are also likely to be heavy users of the product category in which they innovate.[39] For example, two different studies of the diffusion of new brands of coffee found that consumer innovators either purchase larger quantities of coffee or consume more cups of coffee daily than noninnovators.[40] The study of the diffusion of stainless steel blades (described earlier) found that respondents who were heavy shavers (i.e., daily shavers) and more experienced at shaving were more likely to be innovators (i.e., to take less time to make a decision to try the new product) than either occasional or less-experienced shavers.[41]

These studies indicate a positive relationship between innovative behavior and heavy usage. They suggest that consumer innovators not only are an important market segment from the standpoint of being the first to use a new product but also represent a substantial market in terms of the quantity of the product used. However, their propensity to switch brands and to respond positively to promotional "deals" also suggests that they will continue to use a specific brand only so long as they do not perceive that a new and potentially better alternative is available.

Are There Generalized Consumer Innovators?

Do consumer innovators in one product category tend to be consumer innovators in other product categories? The answer to this strategically important question is a guarded "no." The few studies that have specifically attempted to measure the overlap of innovativeness across product categories

522

have noted some degree of overlap, particularly between product categories that seem to be related to the same basic interest area. The overlap, however, does not seem to be sufficiently strong to warrant a marketing strategy that would treat innovators of diverse product categories as members of the same basic market segment.[42]

There seems to be much stronger evidence that consumers who are innovators in regard to one new food product or one new appliance are more likely to be innovators for other new products within the same product category.[43] In other words, although no single or generalized consumer-innovativeness trait seems to operate *across* broadly different product categories, evidence suggests that consumers who innovate *within* a specific product category will innovate again within the same product category. For the marketer, these findings indicate that it may be good marketing strategy to target a new product to those consumers who were the first to try other products within the same basic product category.

Media Habits

In launching a new product, it is desirable that the marketer be able to identify specific mass media that will reach the consumer innovator. To accomplish this task, the marketer has to determine whether consumer innovators selectively expose themselves to any specific types of media that could be used to reach them more effectively.

Research studies that have compared the media habits of innovators and noninnovators suggest that innovators have somewhat greater total exposure to magazines. For example, in a study of the earliest users of a new automobile diagnostic center, innovators were found to be more likely than noninnovators to subscribe to more than five magazines.[44] In a study that compared early and later adopters of women's fashion hats, it was also found that early adopters had greater total magazine exposure than later adopters.[45]

Certain evidence indicates that consumer innovators are likely to have greater exposure to *special-interest* magazines devoted to the product category in which they innovate. For example, a study of female fashion innovators found that innovators had greater exposure to magazines such as *Glamour* and *Vogue* than noninnovators.[46] Similarly, two studies of male fashion innovators found that innovators had greater exposure to male special-interest publications such as *Playboy* and *Penthouse*.[47] Studies outside the realm of fashion have also found that innovators are more likely to read special-interest magazines. For example, women who were early adopters of household cleansers and detergents had greater exposure to magazines devoted to the home (e.g., *Better Homes and Gardens* and *Good Housekeeping*).[48] Though innovators tend to have greater total magazine exposure than noninnovators, it would be more efficient for the marketer to attempt to reach them through appropriate *special-interest* magazines relevant to their specific product category rather than through general-interest magazines. Special-interest magazines frequently point to the fact that they reach innovative consumers in their own ads aimed at prospective advertisers (see Figure 17-10).

A number of studies reveal that consumer innovators are likely to have *less* exposure to television than noninnovators.[49] However, a study of male fashion

Courtesy of The Redbook Publishing Co.

innovators revealed that the innovators were somewhat more interested in watching TV sports programs than noninnovators. A study that examined the media exposure patterns of innovators in six product categories found that the large-appliance innovator watched less television than the noninnovator; however, no difference was found in television viewing for any of the other five product categories examined.[50] These studies suggest that the mass appeal of television does not make it a particularly effective medium for reaching consumer innovators in all product categories.

Studies concerning the relationship between innovative behavior and exposure to other mass media, such as radio and newspapers, have been too few in number and too varied in results to provide any useful conclusions. Definitive research in this area would provide marketers with more comprehensive guidelines as to where to reach the consumer innovator.

Social Characteristics

Available evidence indicates that consumer innovators are more socially accepted and socially involved than noninnovators. For example, a number of studies reveal that consumer innovators are more socially integrated within the community than noninnovators. Specifically, push-button telephone innovators were found to be better accepted by others and to have more social involvement with other members of the community than noninnovators.[51] A diffusion study that examined the acceptance of a new brand of regular coffee found that residents who were well integrated into the community (i.e., those who received more sociometric citations as a "relatively close friend") were quicker to adopt the new product than residents who were less integrated (see Figure 17-11).[52]

FIGURE 17-11   **Relationship between Time of First Purchase and Number of Citations Received as "Relatively Close Friend"**   Source: Adapted from Johan Arndt, "Role of Product-Related Conversations in the Diffusion of a New Product," *Journal of Marketing Research*, 4 (August 1967), 293.

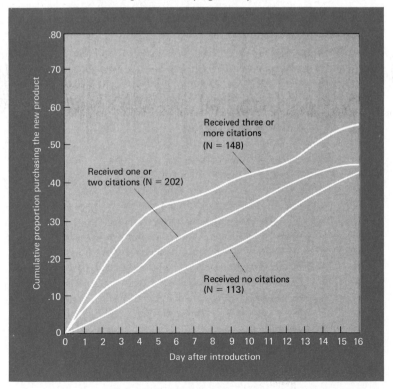

TABLE 17-5 Comparative Profiles of the Consumer Innovator and the Noninnovator or Later Adopter

CHARACTERISTIC	INNOVATOR	NONINNOVATOR (OR LATER ADOPTER)
Product interest	More	Less
Opinion Leadership	More	Less
Personality:		
Dogmatism	Open-minded	Closed-minded
Social character	Inner-directed	Other-directed
Category width	Broad categorizer	Narrow categorizer
Venturesomeness	More	Less
Perceived Risk	Less	More
Purchase and Consumption Traits:		
Brand loyalty	Less	More
Deal proneness	More	Less
Usage	More	Less
Media Habits:		
Total magazine exposure	More	Less
Special-interest magazines	More	Less
Television	Less	More
Social Characteristics:		
Social integration	More	Less
Social striving (e.g., social, physical, and occupational mobility)	More	Less
Group memberships	More	Less
Demographic Characteristics:		
Age	Younger	Older
Income	More	Less
Education	More	Less
Occupational status	More	Less

Evidence also indicates that consumer innovators are *social strivers*—that is, they are more socially mobile (aspire to move up the social-class ladder), they are more physically mobile (have relocated more often), and they are more occupationally mobile (have changed jobs more often) than noninnovators.[53]

Innovators are likely to belong to more social groups and organizations than noninnovators. For example, in two separate studies, female fashion innovators were found to belong to more formal organizations than later adopters or noninnovators.[54] Innovators in the acceptance of a community antenna television system (CATV) were found to hold more memberships and to be more involved in social and civic clubs, professional associations, and organized church groups than later adopters.[55]

The greater social acceptance and involvement of consumer innovators may in part explain why they function as effective opinion leaders.[56]

Demographic Characteristics

It is reasonable to assume that the age of the consumer innovator is related to the specific product category in which he or she innovates; however, many studies have found consumer innovators to be younger than either later adopters or noninnovators.[57] The inconsistency between our expectations and recent evidence is no doubt a function of the fact that many of the products selected for examination (fashion, convenience grocery products, new automobiles) are particularly attractive to younger consumers.

Available evidence indicates that the consumer innovator has more formal education, has a higher personal or family income, and is more likely to have a higher occupational status (i.e., to be a member of a profession or have a managerial position) than later adopters or noninnovators.[58] In other words, innovators tend to be more up-scale than other consumer segments.

The profile in Table 17-5 summarizes the major differences between the consumer innovator and the later adopter or noninnovator.

summary

The diffusion process and the adoption process are two closely related concepts concerned with the acceptance of new products by consumers. The diffusion process is a *macro* process, which focuses on the spread of an innovation (a new product, a new service, a new idea) from its source to the consuming public. The adoption process is a *micro* process, which examines the stages through which an individual consumer passes in making a decision to accept or reject a new product.

The term *innovation* can be defined in a firm-oriented sense (if it is new to the marketing firm), in a product-oriented sense (as a continuous innovation, a dynamically continuous innovation, or a discontinuous innovation), in a market-oriented sense (by how long the product has been on the market or by the percentage of the potential target market that has purchased it), and in a consumer-oriented sense. Market-oriented definitions of innovation are most useful to the study of the diffusion and adoption of new products.

Five product characteristics influence the consumer's acceptance of a new product: (1) its *relative advantage* over existing products; (2) its *compatibility* with the consumer's present needs, values, and practices; (3) its *complexity;* (4) its *trialability* (how easy it is to try on a limited basis); and (5) its *observability* or *communicability* (the ease with which it can be viewed by or described to potential consumers).

Diffusion researchers are concerned with two aspects of communication: the channels through which word of a new product is spread to the consuming public, and the types of messages that influence the adoption or rejection of new products. Diffusion is always examined within the context of a specific social system, such as a target market, a community, a region, or even a nation.

Time is an integral consideration in the diffusion process. Researchers are concerned with the amount of time required for an individual consumer to adopt or reject a specific new product (*purchase time*), with the percentage of the target market who have adopted the new product by a given time period (the *rate of adoption*), and with the identification of sequential adopter categories. The five adopter categories are *innovators*, *early adopters*, *early majority*, *late majority*, and *laggards*.

Marketing strategists try to control the rate of adoption in accordance with their new-product pricing policies. Marketers who wish to penetrate the market in order to achieve market leadership try to achieve wide adoption in as short a period as possible with low prices; those who choose a skimming pricing policy deliberately plan a longer adoption process.

The traditional adoption process model describes five stages through which an individual consumer passes in arriving at the decision to adopt or reject a new product: awareness, interest, evaluation, trial, and adoption. The newer *innovation decision process* model is a more general decision-making model which focuses on four stages of adoption: knowledge, persuasion, decision, and confirmation. Both models offer a framework for determining the importance of various information sources on consumers at the various decision stages.

Marketers are vitally concerned with identifying the consumer innovator so that they may initially direct their new-product promotional campaigns to the people who are most likely to try new products, to adopt them, and to influence others in the target market. Consumer research has identified a number of consumer-related characteristics and personality traits that distinguish consumer innovators from later adopters. These serve as useful variables for the segmentation of markets for new-product introductions.

discussion questions

1. What are the essential differences between "product," "market," and "consumer" oriented definitions of a *new* product? Which definition do you feel is most suitable for the marketer? Why?

2. Describe how the manufacturer of a new type of cosmetic remover might use knowledge of the following five product characteristics to speed up the acceptance of the new product:
   a. Relative advantage
   b. Compatibility
   c. Complexity
   d. Trialability
   e. Observability

3. An appliance manufacturer is considering the introduction of a new microwave oven that cooks food three times as fast as competitive ovens while selling at about the same price. Identify those product characteristics that will influence the new oven's rate of acceptance.

4. Describe three dimensions of *time* that make it a particularly important factor in the diffusion of a product.

5. How might a firm alter its promotional appeal to effectively reach members of each of the following adopter categories:
   a. Innovators
   b. Early adopters
   c. Early majority
   d. Late majority
   e. Laggards

6. Compare and contrast the *adoption* and *diffusion* processes. How are these two processes interrelated?

7. How would a profile of the *consumer innovator* assist a marketer planning a mass-media advertising campaign for a new line of male cosmetics? Be specific in your recommendations.

8. Select three characteristics of the consumer innovator summarized in Table 17-5. For each of these consumer characteristics, indicate how a marketer might effectively use the profile information to positively influence the adoption process.

endnotes

1. Thomas S. Robertson, "The Process of Innovation and the Diffusion of Innovation," *Journal of Marketing,* 31 (January 1967), 14–19.

2. James H. Donnelly, Jr., and Michael J. Etzel, "Degrees of Product Newness and Early Trial," *Journal of Marketing Research,* 10 (August 1973), 295–300.

3. Everett M. Rogers and F. Floyd Shoemaker, *Communication of Innovations,* 2nd ed. (New York: Free Press, 1971); and Gerald Zaltman and Ronald Stiff, "Theories of Diffusion," in Scott Ward and Thomas S. Robertson, eds., *Consumer Behavior: Theoretical Sources* (Englewood Cliffs, N.J.: Prentice-Hall, 1973), 416–68.

4. Rogers and Shoemaker, *Communication of Innovations,* 138–55.

5. Jagdish N. Sheth, "Perceived Risk and Diffusion of Innovation," in Johan Arndt, ed., *Insights into Consumer Behavior* (Boston: Allyn & Bacon, 1968), 173–88.

6. Robert W. Shoemaker and F. Robert Shoaf, "Behavioral Changes in the Trial of New Products," *Journal of Consumer Research,* 21 (September 1975), 104–9.

7. Lyman E. Ostlund, "The Role of Product Perceptions in Innovative Behavior," in Philip R. McDonald, ed., *Marketing Involvement in Society and the Economy* (Chicago: American Marketing Association, 1969), 259–66.

8. Lyman E. Ostlund, "Perceived Innovation Attributes as Predictors of Innovativeness," *Journal of Consumer Research,* 1 (September 1974), 23–29; and Duncan E. LaBay and Thomas C. Kinnear, "Exploring the Consumer Decision Process in the Adoption of Solar Energy Systems," in *Consumer Behavior and Energy Use* (Banff, Alberta, Canada: Banff Centre, 1980), U1–U21.

9. Rogers and Shoemaker, *Communication of Innovations,* 371–75.

10. Bruce Ryan and Neal C. Groas, "The Diffusion of Hybrid Seed Corn in Two Iowa Communities," *Rural Sociology,* 8 (March 1943), 15–24; James Coleman, Elihu Katz, and Herbert Menzel, "The Diffusion of an Innovation among Physicians," *Sociometry,* 20 (December 1957), 253–70; and Leon G. Schiffman, "Perceived Risk in New Product Trial by Elderly Consumers," *Journal of Marketing Research,* 9 (February 1972), 106–8.

11. Rogers and Shoemaker, *Communication of Innovations,* 32–33. Also see Elizabeth C. Hirschman, "Consumer Modernity, Cognitive Complexity, Creativity and Innovativeness," in Richard P. Bagozzi et al., eds., *Marketing in the 80's: Changes and Challenges* (Chicago: American Marketing Association, 1980), 135–39.

12. Based upon *The Decision-Making Process in Purchasing Expensive Photographic Equipment* (a study conducted for *Popular Photography* by MPI Marketing Research, Inc., 1974).

13. Everett M. Rogers, *Diffusion of Innovations* (New York: Free Press, 1962), 185.

14. Ibid., 152–59.

15. Robert A. Peterson, "A Note on Optional Adopter Category Determination," *Journal of Marketing Research,* 10, No. 3 (August 1973), 325–29.

16. Richard W. Olshavsky, "Time and the Rate of Adoption of Innovations," *Journal of Consumer Research*, 6 (March 1980), 425–28.

17. Rogers, *Diffusion of Innovations* 81–86.

18. James F. Engel, Roger D. Blackwell, and Robert J. Kegerreis, "Consumer Use of Information in the Adoption of an Innovation," *Journal of Advertising Research*, 9 (December 1969), 3–8.

19. Sheth, "Perceived Risk and Diffusion," 185; and Jagdish N. Sheth, "Word-of-Mouth in Low Risk Innovations," *Journal of Advertising Research*, 11 (June 1971), 15–18.

20. Fred D. Reynolds and William R. Darden, "Why the Midi Failed," *Journal of Advertising Research*, 12 (August 1972), 39–44.

21. Rogers and Shoemaker, *Communication of Innovations*, 104–5.

22. Ibid., 103.

23. John Jay Painter and Max L. Pinegar, "Post-High Teens and Fashion Innovation," *Journal of Marketing Research*, 8 (August 1971), 368–69.

24. Lawrence P. Feldman and Gary M. Armstrong, "Identifying Buyers of a Major Automotive Innovation," *Journal of Marketing*, 39 (January 1975), 47–53.

25. James F. Engel, Robert J. Kegerreis, and Roger D. Blackwell, "Word-of-Mouth Communication by Innovator," *Journal of Marketing*, 3 (July 1969), 15–19; and Thomas S. Robertson, "Purchase Sequence Responses: Innovators vs. Non-Innovators," *Journal of Advertising Research*, 8 (March 1968), 47–52.

26. Engel, Blackwell, and Kegerreis, "Consumer Use of Information," 5.

27. For example, see Johan Arndt, "Role of Product-Related Conversations in the Diffusion of a New Product," *Journal of Marketing Research*, 4 (August 1967), 291–95; and Thomas S. Robertson, "Determinants of Innovative Behavior," in Reed Moyer, ed., *Changing Marketing Systems* (Chicago: American Marketing Association 1968), 328–32.

28. Jacob Jacoby, "Personality and Innovativeness Proneness," *Journal of Marketing Research*, 8 (May 1971), 244–47; Kenneth A. Coney, "Dogmatism and Innovation: A Replication," *Journal of Marketing Research*, 9 (November 1972), 453–55; and J.M. McClurg and I.R. Andrews, "A Consumer Profile Analysis of the Self-Service Gasoline Customer, *Journal of Applied Psychology*, 59 (February 1974), 119–21.

29. James H. Donnelly, Jr., "Social Character and Acceptance of New Products," *Journal of Marketing Research*, 7 (February 1970), 111–13; and Painter and Pinegar, "Post-High Teens." 369.

30. James H. Donnelly, Jr. and John M. Ivancevich, "A Methodology for Identifying Innovator Characteristics of New Brand Purchasers," *Journal of Marketing Research*, 11 (August 1974), 331–34.

31. Donald T. Popielarz, "An Exploration of Perceived Risk and Willingness to Try New Products," *Journal of Marketing Research*, 4 (November 1967), 368–72; Donnelly and Etzel, "Degrees of Product Newness," 299; and James H. Donnelly Jr., Michael J. Etzel, and Scott Roeth, "The Relationship Between Consumers' Category and Trial of New Products," *Journal of Applied Psychology*, 57 (May 1973), 335–38.

32. Donnelly and Etzel, "Degrees of Product Newness," 299.

33. Schiffman, "Perceived Risk," 107; Thomas S. Robertson, "Consumer Innovators: The Key to New Product Success," *California Management Review*, 10 (Winter 1967), 28; and Edgar A. Pessemier, Philip C. Burger, and Douglas J. Tigert, "Can New Product Buyers Be Identified?" *Journal of Marketing Research*, 4 (November 1967), 352.

34. For example, see Arndt, "Role of Product-Related Conversations," 294; and Schiffman, "Perceived Risk," 107–8.

35. Engel, Blackwell, and Kegerreis, "Consumer Use of Information," 5; and McClurg and Andrews, "Consumer Profile Analysis," 120.

36. Johan Arndt, "Profiling Consumer Innovators," in Johan Arndt, ed., *Insights into Consumer Behavior* (Boston: Allyn & Bacon, 1968), 79.

37. Kenneth Uhl, Roman Andrus, and Lance Poulsen, "How are Laggards Different? An Empirical Inquiry," *Journal of Marketing Research,* 7 (February 1970), 52.

38. Arndt, "Profiling Consumer Innovations," 79; David B. Montgomerey, "Consumer Characteristics Associated with Dealing: An Empirical Example," *Journal of Marketing Research,* 8 (February 1971), 118–20; and Leon G. Schiffman and Clifford J. Neiverth, "Measuring the Impact of Promotional Offers: An Analytic Approach," in Thomas V. Greer, ed., 1973 *Combined Proceedings* (Chicago: American Marketing Association, 1974), 256–60.

39. James W. Taylor, "A Striking Characteristic of Innovators," *Journal of Marketing Research,* 14 (February 1977), 104–7.

40. Ronald E. Frank and William F. Massy, "Innovation and Brand Choice: The Folger's Invasion," in Stephen A. Greyser, ed., *Toward Scientific Marketing* (Chicago: American Marketing Association, 1964), 106; and Arndt, "Profiling Consumer Innovators," 79.

41. Sheth, "Perceived Risk and Diffusion," 188.

42. John O. Summers, "Generalized Change Agents and Innovativeness,"*Journal of Marketing Research,* 8 (August 1971), 313–16; and Thomas S. Robertson and James H. Myers, "Personality Correlates of Opinion Leadership and Innovative Buying Behavior," *Journal of Marketing Research,* 6 (May 1969), 164–68.

43. Schiffman, "Perceived Risk," 107; and Robertson, "Consumer Innovators," 28.

44. Engel, Blackwell, and Kegerreis, "Consumer Use of Information," 4.

45. Charles W. King, "Communicating with the Innovator in the Fashion Adoption Process," in Peter D. Bennett, ed., *Marketing and Economic Development* (Chicago: American Marketing Association, 1965), 429.

46. John O. Summers, "Media Exposure Patterns of Consumer Innovators," *Journal of Marketing,* 36 (January 1972), 43–49.

47. John J. Painter and Kent L. Granzin, "Profiling the Male Fashion Innovator—Another Step," in Beverlee B. Anderson, *Advances in Consumer Research* (Association for Consumer Research, 1976), III, 43; and William R. Darden and Fred D. Reynolds, "Backward Profiling of Male Innovators," *Journal of Marketing Research,* 9 (February 1974), 79–85.

48. Summers, "Media Exposure Patterns," 47–48.

49. King, "Communicating with the Innovator," 428; Painter and Granzin, "Profiling the Male Fashion Innovator," 43; and Painter and Pinegar, "Post-High Teens," 369.

50. Summers, "Media Exposure Patterns," 45–47.

51. Robertson, "Purchase Sequence Responses," 49.

52. Arndt, "Role of Product-Related Conversations," 293.

53. Robertson, "Consumer Innovators," 29; Painter and Granzin, "Profiling the Male Fashion Innovator," 42; and Louis E. Boone, "The Search for the Consumer Innovator," *Journal of Business,* 43 (April 1970), 138.

54. King, "Communicating with the Innovator," 430; and Painter and Pinegar, "Post-High Teens," 369.

55. Boone, "Search for the Consumer Innovator," 138.

56. Mary C. Harrison and Alvin C. Burns, "The Role of Social System Membership in the Adoption of a New Department Store," in Subhash C. Jain, ed., *Research Frontiers in Marketing: Dialogues and Directions* (Chicago: American Marketing Association, 1978), 139–42.

57. For example, see Feldman and Armstrong, "Identifying Buyers," 50; McClurg and Andrews, "Consumer Profile Analysis," 120; and William E. Bell, "Consumer Innovators: A Unique Market for Newness," in Stephen A. Greyser, ed., *Toward Scientific Marketing* (Chicago: American Marketing Association, 1963), 90–93.

58. For example, see Robert J. Kegerreis and James F. Engel, "The Innovative Consumer: Characteristics of the Earliest Adopters of a New Automotive Service," in McDonald, *Marketing Involvement in Society and the Economy,* 357–61; Feldman and Armstrong, "Identifying Buyers," 50; Bell, "Consumer Innovators," 90–93; and Boone, "Search for the Consumer Innovator," 138.

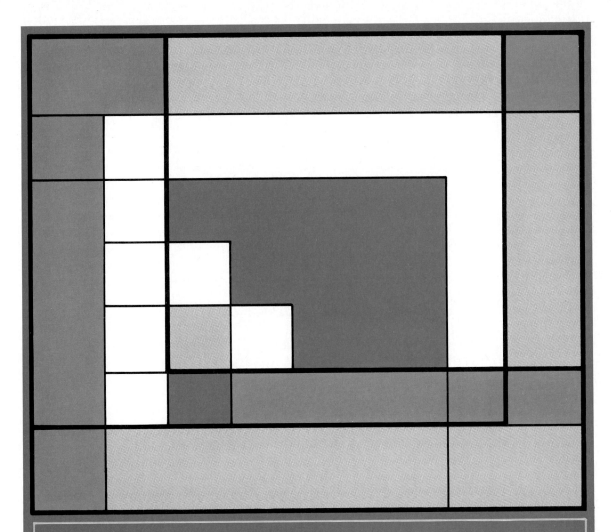

EIGHTEEN

Consumer
Decision Making

HIS chapter ties together the relevant psychological, social, and cultural concepts developed throughout the book into a framework for understanding how consumers make decisions. Unlike Chapter 17, which examined the dynamics of *new* product adoption, this chapter takes a broader perspective and examines consumer decision making within the context of *all* types of purchase choices, ranging from the purchase of new products to the selection of old and established products.

WHAT IS A DECISION?

Each of us makes numerous decisions every day concerning every aspect of our everyday lives. However, we generally make these decisions without stopping to think about *how* we make them, about what is involved in the decision making itself. In the most general terms, a *decision* is *the selection of an action from two or more alternative choices.*[1] In other words, in order for a person to make a decision, there must be a choice of alternatives available. To illustrate, if a person has a choice between making a purchase and *not* making a purchase, or a choice between Brand X and Brand Y, we can say that this person is in a position to make a decision. On the other hand, if the consumer has no alternatives from which to choose, but rather is literally *forced* to make a particular purchase (e.g., purchase Brand X), then this single "no-choice" action does not consitute a decision. A "no-choice" decision is often popularly referred to as a "Hobson's choice."

In actuality, a no-choice purchase or consumption situation is very rare in American society. It will be recalled from our discussion of core cultural values (Chapter 14) that Americans often think of *freedom* as being expressed in terms of the existence of a wide range of consumer choices. Thus, if there is almost always a choice, then there is almost always an opportunity for consumers to make decisions.

> *Nothing is more difficult, and therefore more precious, than to be able to decide.*
>
> *NAPOLEON I*
>
> Maxims (1804-15)

TABLE 18-1   Types of Purchase Decisions

DECISION CATEGORY	ALTERNATIVES	
Basic purchase decision	To purchase a product (or service)	Not to purchase a product (or service)
Brand purchase decisions	To purchase a specific brand	To purchase another brand
	To purchase one's usual brand	To purchase another established brand (possibly with special features)
	To purchase a new brand	To purchase one's usual brand or some other established brand
	To purchase a standard quantity	To purchase more or less than a standard quantity
	To purchase an on-sale brand	To purchase a non-sale brand
	To buy a national brand	To buy a store brand
Channel purchase decisions	To purchase from a specific type of store (e.g., a department store)	To purchase from some other type of store (e.g., a discount store)
	To purchase from one's usual store	To purchase from some other store
	To purchase in-home (by phone or catalog)	To purchase in-store
	To purchase from a local store	To purchase from a store requiring some travel (out-shopping)

Table 18-1 summarizes various types of purchase-related decisions. While this list is not exhaustive, it does serve to demonstrate that the scope of consumer decision making is much broader than the mere selection of one brand from a number of brands.

THREE VIEWS OF CONSUMER DECISION MAKING

Before presenting a simple model of how consumers make decisions, we will pause to consider several models of man that depict consumer decision making in distinctly different ways. The term *model of man* refers to a general perspective held by a significant number of people concerning how (and why) individuals behave as they do. Specifically, we will examine the following consumer-related models of man: (1) economic man, (2) passive man, and (3) cognitive man.

Economic Man

In the field of theoretical economics, which portrays a world of perfect competition, the consumer is often characterized as an "economic man"—that is, one who makes *rational decisions*. This model has been attacked by consumer researchers for a number of reasons. To behave rationally in the economic sense, a consumer would have to be aware of all available product alternatives, would have to be capable of correctly ranking each alternative in terms of its benefits and its disadvantages, and would have to be able to identify the one best alternative. However, consumers do *not* generally have enough information, or sufficiently accurate information, or even an adequate degree of involvement or motivation to make perfect decisions.

According to a leading social scientist, the *economic man* model is unrealistic for the following reasons: (1) man is limited by his existing skills, habits, and reflexes, (2) man is limited by his existing values and goals, and (3) man is limited by the extent of his knowledge.[2] Thus consumers operate in an imperfect world, one in which they do not maximize their decisions in terms of such economic considerations as price-quantity relationships, marginal utility, or indifference curves. Indeed the consumer is often simply unwilling to engage in extensive decision-making activities and will instead settle for a "satisfactory" decision, one that is "good enough."[3] For this reason, the economic model of man is often rejected as too idealistic and too simplistic.

Passive Man

Quite opposite to the economic man model is the *passive man* model, which depicts the consumer as basically submissive to the self-serving interests and promotional efforts of marketers. The following statement captures the flavor of the passive model of man:

> The image of man implied in advertising and in modern sales methods is one of a passive person, open and vulnerable to external and internal stimuli leading to spending. The unconscious becomes a vehicle for directing economic behavior. The prototype is the dissatisfied, restless housewife who, after husband and children have left for the day, visits the department store, lets herself be titillated by the exhibited goods, and spontaneously, without clear-cut wants and purpose succumbs to the lure of salesmanship and buys something she does not "really" need and will later regret having bought.[4]

As this quotation implies, consumers are sometimes perceived as impulsive and irrational purchasers, ready to yield to the arms and aims of marketers. At least to some degree, the passive model of the consumer was subscribed to by the hard-driving supersalesman of old, who was trained to regard the consumer as an object to be manipulated. The following excerpt from a 1917 salesmanship text dramatically illustrates the long-held belief in the dominance of the salesman over the unresisting, somewhat passive consumer:

> In the development of the selling process, there are four distinct stages. First, the salesman must secure the prospect's undivided attention. Secondly, this attention must be sustained and developed into interest. Thirdly, this interest must be ripened into desire. And fourthly, all lingering doubts must be removed from the prospect's mind, and there must be implanted there a firm resolution to buy; in other words, the sale must be closed.[5]

This view of prospective consumers implies that if they do not buy, it is only because the salesmen (or marketers) have failed to manipulate them properly.

The principal limitation of the *passive model of man* is that it fails to recognize that the consumer plays an equal, if not dominant, role in many buying situations by seeking out information about product alternatives and selecting the product that appears to offer the greatest satisfaction. All that we know about motivation (Chapter 3), selective perception (Chapter 6), learning (Chapter 7), attitudes (Chapter 8 and 9), communication (Chapter 10), and opinion leadership (Chapter 16) serves to support the proposition that consumers are *not* objects of manipulation. Therefore this simple and single-minded view should also be rejected as an unrealistic model of consumer behavior.

Cognitive Man

The third model portrays the consumer as *cognitive man* or *problem solver*. Within this framework, consumers are frequently pictured as either receptive to or actively seeking out products or services to fulfill their needs and enrich their lives. This model of man focuses on the *processes* by which consumers seek and evaluate information about selected brands and retail outlets.

Because *choice* is an inherent factor in consumer behavior, risk is frequently a component of the cognitive or problem-solving model. Chapter 6 discusses several types of consumer-perceived risk (functional risk, economic risk, social risk, psychological risk) and the strategies consumers adopt for handling risk (e.g., collecting information about alternatives, patronizing specific retailers, brand loyalty). Such strategies depict the consumer as a problem solver, attempting to effectively dispel the risk perceived in making choices.[6]

In contrast to the economic man model, the cognitive model more realistically portrays the consumer as *unlikely* to even attempt to obtain all available information about all available choice alternatives. Instead, the consumer's information-seeking efforts are likely to cease when what is perceived to be a sufficient amount of information is obtained concerning some of the alternatives—enough information to enable an "adequate" decision to be made. Consumer information-processing research reveals that consumers frequently develop short-cut decision rules (called heuristics) to ease the decision-making process.[7] Some consumer researchers have even suggested that consumers can suffer from too much information—information overload.[8]

In a sense, the cognitive or problem-solving model depicts a consumer who is somewhere between the extremes of the economic man and passive man models—a consumer who does not possess complete knowledge and therefore cannot make *perfect* decisions, but one who nevertheless actively seeks information and attempts to make *satisfactory* decisions.

The cognitive model seems to capture the essence of a well-educated and involved consumer who seeks information upon which to base consumption decisions. Our discussions of specific aspects of consumer decision making throughout the book have generally depicted a consumer who is consistent with the cognitive or problem-solving model.

A SIMPLE MODEL OF CONSUMER DECISION MAKING

In this section we will present a simple model of consumer decision making that reflects the picture of the cognitive or problem-solving consumer. Our primary purpose in depicting this model is to tie together many of the ideas discussed throughout this book on consumer decision making. The model is not designed to provide an exhaustive picture of the complexities of a consumer decision; rather, it is designed to synthesize and coordinate relevant concepts into a significant whole. The model (see Figure 18-1) has three major components: *input, process,* and *output.*

FIGURE 18-1   A Simple Model of Consumer Decision Making

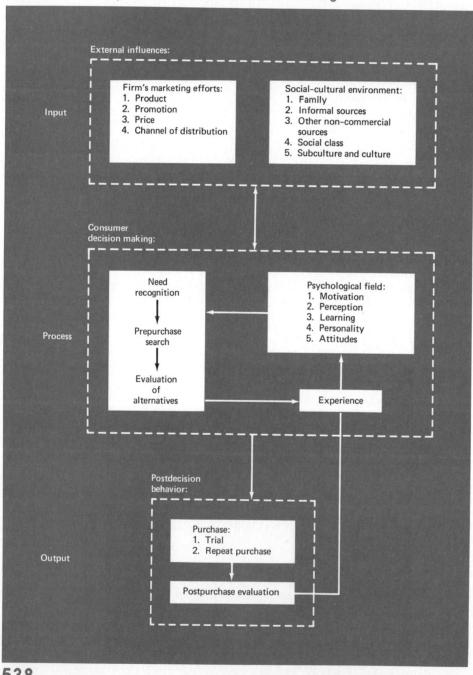

Input

The input component of our consumer decision-making model consists of external influences that serve as sources of information about a particular product and influence a consumer's product-related values, attitudes, and behavior. Chief among these input factors are the marketing-mix activities of organizations that are trying to communicate the benefits of their products to potential consumers, and nonmarketing social-cultural influences which, when internalized, affect the consumer's purchase decisions.

MARKETING INPUTS

The firm's marketing activities constitute a direct attempt to reach, inform, and persuade consumers to buy and use its products. These inputs to the consumer's decision-making process take the form of specific marketing-mix strategies which consist of (1) the product itself (including its package, warranties, and guarantees), (2) mass-media advertising, personal selling, and other promotional efforts, (3) pricing policy, and (4) the selection of distribution channels to move the product from the manufacturer to the consumer.

It is important to remember that ultimately the impact of a firm's marketing efforts is in large measure governed by consumers' perception of these efforts. This should serve to remind marketers that they must be alert to consumers' perceptions and must not merely rely on the intended impact of their marketing messages.

SOCIAL-CULTURAL INPUTS

The second type of input, the social-cultural environment, also exerts a major influence on the consumer. Social-cultural inputs (examined in Part III) consist of a wide range of noncommercial influences. For example, the comments of a friend, usage by a family member, an editorial in the paper, or an article in *Consumer Reports* are all specific and direct noncommercial sources of information. The influences of one's social class, culture, or subculture, though less tangible, are nevertheless important input factors that are internalized and affect how consumers judge products, and which products they eventually buy. Indeed the unwritten codes of conduct communicated by culture indicate which purchases are considered "right" or "wrong." For example, until the mid-1950s, most men would not be seen wearing a red sweater; today, males wear clothing of every imaginable hue. Until the mid-1960s, few women would wear slacks to the office; a decade later, pantsuits were common attire.

Unlike the firm's marketing efforts, social-cultural inputs do not necessarily *support* the purchase of a specific product. Instead, they may influence consumers to *avoid* the product by underscoring its negative features. For example, when fashion designers tried to introduce a longer hemline style some years ago, they were unable to do so because of widespread informal negative discussions among women.[9]

The cumulative impact of each firm's marketing efforts, the influence of family, friends, and neighbors, and society's existing code of behavior are all inputs that are likely to affect what consumers purchase and how they use what they buy. Since these influences may be directed *to* the individual or actively sought *by* the individual, a two-headed arrow is used to link the input and process segments of the model (Figure 18-1).

Process

The process component of our model is concerned with how consumers make decisions. To understand this process, we must consider the influence of many of the psychological concepts that were examined in Part II. The *psychological field* represents the internal influences that affect the consumer's decision-making process (what consumers need or want, their awareness of various product choices, their information-gathering activities, and their evaluation of alternatives). As pictured in the process component, the act of making a consumer decision consists of three stages: (1) need recognition, (2) prepurchase search, and (3) evaluation of alternatives.

Before we examine these three stages in detail, let us consider the idea that there are *levels of consumer decision making*, in that not all consumer decision situations receive (or require) the same degree of consumer effort.

LEVELS OF CONSUMER DECISION MAKING

If all purchase decisions required extensive effort, consumer decision making would be an exhausting process that left little time for anything else. On the other hand, if all purchases were routine, they would tend to be monotonous and would provide little pleasure or novelty. On a continuum of effort ranging from very high to very low, we can distinguish three specific levels of consumer decision making: (1) extensive problem solving, (2) limited problem solving, and (3) routinized response behavior.[10]

EXTENSIVE PROBLEM SOLVING. When consumers have no established criteria for evaluating a product category or specific brands within the category, or have not narrowed down the number of brands they will consider to some small manageable subset (the evoked set), their decision-making efforts can be classified as *extensive problem solving*. At this level, the consumer needs a great deal of information in order to establish a set of criteria on which to judge specific brands, and a correspondingly large amount of information concerning each of the brands to be considered.

LIMITED PROBLEM SOLVING. At this level of problem solving, consumers have already established the basic criteria for evaluating the product category and the various brands within the category. However, they have no fully established preferences concerning a select group of brands. Their search for additional information is more like "fine tuning;" they have to gather additional brand information in order to discriminate among the various brands.

ROUTINIZED RESPONSE BEHAVIOR. At this level, consumers have had some experience with the product category and a well-established set of criteria with which to evaluate the brands in their evoked sets. In some situations, they may search for a small amount of additional information; in others, they simply review what they already know.

Just how extensive a consumer's problem-solving task is depends on how well established are his or her criteria for selection, how much information he or she has about each brand being considered, and how narrow is the set of brands (the evoked set) from which the choice will be made. Clearly, extensive problem solving implies that the consumer must seek a greater amount of information in order to make a choice, while routinized response behavior implies a minimum or no need for additional information.

Let us now turn to the three stages of the process component of the model.

NEED RECOGNITION

The recognition of a need is likely to occur when a consumer is faced with a problem that he or she desires to solve, such as which style of refrigerator to order for the planned renovation of a kitchen or what to do when a refrigerator breaks down and has to be replaced.

For instance, within the context of the refrigerator that breaks down, the recognition of a need is the realization by the consumer that there is a difference between "what is" (e.g., a nonfunctioning refrigerator) and "what should be" (a refrigerator that keeps foods cold). Thus a consumer who is confronted with the reality that her present refrigerator is not working must quickly make plans to either repair or replace it. If her refrigerator is relatively new or the estimated repair cost is low, she will probably have it repaired. If it is old or estimated repair costs are excessive, its malfunction will serve to trigger a search for information about various brands, types, styles, and sizes of regrigerators; an estimate of how much she can afford to spend on a new refrigerator; and a mental listing of retail outlets from which she might make the purchase.

PREPURCHASE SEARCH

The prepurchase search state begins when a consumer perceives a need that might very well be satisfied by the purchase and consumption of a product. A sign that a consumer is in this stage is the sense of a need for information upon which to base a choice. This need could simply require the consumer to bring from his or her memory (long-term storage) the recollection of past experiences that might provide adequate information for the present choice. On the other hand, if the consumer has had no prior experience, it could require extensive search of the outside environment for useful information upon which to base a choice.

The consumer usually searches his or her memory (the "psychological field" depicted in the model) before seeking out external sources of information regarding a given consumption-related need. In this sense, past experience is an *internal* source of information. The greater the relevant past experience an individual possesses, the less the external information the consumer is likely to need in order to reach a decision. However, for many consumer decisions, it is likely that a combination of both past experience (internal sources) and marketing and noncommercial information (external sources) is used before a decision is reached.

How much information a consumer will gather also depends on various situational factors. For example, the consumer with a malfunctioning refrigerator may need to replace it immediately; thus her search will be limited. She may rely primarily on past experience if she was satisfied with the performance of her old refrigerator. In this case, she would probably attempt to identify the retailers in her area that carry "her" brand. She might turn to the *Yellow Pages* for a listing of authorized appliance dealers who sell the brand she wants. If the refrigerator happens to be a store brand, such as Sears's Cold Spot, her search will be even simpler: She has only to visit the store to examine the current models and make her choice. If she has the time to consider a variety of brands, she might also turn to the *Yellow Pages,* this time to make a list of local appliance stores in which to look. She might even visit the library to acquire information about makes and models of refrigerators rated by *Consumer Reports.*

The amount of relevant prior experience and other situational factors are important determinants of the extent of external search that a consumer undertakes before making a purchase decision. Table 18-2 lists the product,

TABLE 18-2   Factors That Are Likely to Increase Prepurchase Search

product factors
Long interpurchase time (a long-lasting or infrequently used product)
Frequent changes in product styling
Frequent price changes
"Volume" purchasing (large number of units)
High price

situational factors
Experience:
  First time purchase
  No past experience because the product is new
  Past experience within the product category has been unsatisfactory
Social Acceptability:
  The purchase is for a gift
  The product is socially visible
Value-related Considerations:
  Purchase is discretionary rather than necessary
  All alternatives have both desirable and undesirable consequences
  Family members disagree on product requirements or evaluation of alternatives
  Product usage deviates from important reference group
  The purchase involves ecological considerations

personal factors
Demographic Characteristics of Consumer:
  Well educated
  High income
  White-collar occupation
  Under 35 years of age
Personality:
  Low dogmatic (open-minded)
  Low risk perceiver (broad categorizer)
  Other Personal Factors:
  High product involvement
  Enjoyment of shopping and search

Adapted from Donald H. Granbois, "The Role of Communication in the Family Decision Making Process," in Stephen A. Greyser, ed., *Toward Scientific Marketing* (Chicago: American Marketing Association, 1964), 50–56.

situational, and personal factors that are likely to *increase* the amount of information search a consumer will undertake as part of the decision-making process.

EVALUATION OF ALTERNATIVES

When evaluating potential alternatives, consumers tend to employ two types of information: (1) a "list" of brands from which they plan to make their selection, and (2) the criteria that they will use to evaluate each brand. In our discussion of product perception (Chapter 6), we noted that those brands from which a person will make a choice are called the *evoked set*. The evoked set is generally only a part—a subset—of all the brands of which the consumer is aware; these brands are, in turn, frequently only a segment of all the brands available on the market.[11] Making a selection from a *sample* of all possible brands is a human characteristic that helps simplify the decision-making process.

The criteria consumers employ in evaluating the brands that constitute their evoked sets are usually expressed in terms of product attributes that they feel are important to them. Examples of product attributes that consumers might employ as criteria in evaluating nine product categories are listed in Table 18-3.

The evoked set of our consumer in need of a new refrigerator might consist of the following three brands of refrigerators: General Electric, Frigidaire, and Sears's Cold Spot. She might consider the following criteria or attributes in evaluating the three alternatives: color, brand name (trustworthiness), size (interior and exterior), special features (e.g., an automatic ice

TABLE 18-3 Product Attributes Used as Purchase Criteria for Six Product Categories

BRASSIERES	LIPSTICK	MOUTHWASH
Comfort	Color	Color
Fit	Container	Effectiveness
Life	Creaminess	Kills germs
Price	Prestige factor	Price
Style	Taste/flavor	Taste/flavor
ORANGE JUICE (FROZEN)	**TOILET TISSUE**	**TOOTHPASTE**
Nutritional value	Color	Decay prevention
Packaging	Package size	Freshens mouth
Price	Price	Price
Taste/flavor	Strength	Taste/flavor
Texture	Texture	Whitens teeth
TIRES	**AUTOMOBILES**	**SHOES**
Safety	Durability	Fit
Service policy	Safety	Care
Durability	Appearance	Durability
Ride	Ride	Style
Traction	Repairs	Comfort

Source: Derived from Frank M. Bass and William L. Wilkie, "A Comparative Analysis of Attitudinal Predictions of Brand Preference," *Journal of Marketing Research*, 10 (August 1973), 263; and Andrew A. Mitchell, J. Edward Russo, and Meryl Gardner, "Strategy-Induced Low Involvement Perception of Advertising" (Working paper, Carnegie-Mellon University, August 1979).

maker), and style, Table 18-4 lists these brands and attributes and indicates the consumer's hypothetical evaluation for each brand in terms of each of the attributes. For instance, when it comes to the availability of suitable colors, General Electric is rated "best," followed by Frigidaire and then Sears's Cold Spot. The consumer may then weigh each attribute in terms of which is more important to her. Thus, if color *and* size are most important, she may choose the Frigidaire over the General Electric model.

CONSUMER DECISION RULES, OR HEURISTICS.   Consumer decision rules (also commonly referred to as heuristics, decision strategies, consumer information-processing strategies, etc.) are procedures employed by consumers to facilitate brand (or other) choices. Such rules serve to reduce the burden of making complex decisions by providing guidelines or routines that make the process less taxing.

Consumer decision rules have been broadly classified into two main categories: *compensatory* and *noncompensatory decision rules*.[12] In following a compensatory-type decision rule, a consumer evaluates each brand option in terms of each attribute considered to be relevant and computes a weighted or summated score for each brand.

The computed "score" reflects each brand's relative merit as a potential purchase choice. There is an assumption that the consumer will generally select the brand that scores highest among the alternatives evaluated.

A unique feature of a compensatory decision rule is that it allows a positive evaluation of a brand on one attribute to balance out a negative evaluation on some other attribute. For example, a positive assessment of a particular brand of headache remedy in terms of speed of relief may offset an unacceptable assessment of its total amount of relief.

In comparison, noncompensatory decision rules do not allow consumers to balance a positive evaluation of a brand on one attribute against a negative evaluation of the same brand on some other attribute. For instance, in the case of the headache remedy, a negative (unacceptable) rating on the total amount of relief would *not* be offset by the positive evaluation on speed of relief. Instead, the brand of headache remedy would be disqualified from any further consideration.

TABLE 18-4   A Consumer's Hypothetical Refrigerator Brand-Attribute Ratings

BRANDS	color	brand name	size	special features	style
		CRITERIA OR ATTRIBUTES			
General Electric	10*	9	5	7	8
Frigidaire	8	6	7	4	3
Sears's Cold Spot	6	8	5	6	8

*The consumer's evaluations are on a 10-point scale, where a higher number indicates a higher rating.

Numerous noncompensatory rules are described in the consumer behavior literature. We will briefly consider three noncompensatory rules: conjunctive, disjunctive, and lexicographic.[13]

1. CONJUNCTIVE RULE.　In employing this decision rule, a consumer establishes a separate minimally acceptable level as a cutoff point for each attribute. If any particular brand falls below the cutoff point on any one attribute, it is eliminated from further consideration.

Since the conjunctive rule can produce more than one acceptable alternative, it becomes necessary in such cases to apply an additional decision rule in order to arrive at a final selection. For instance, one simple solution is for the consumer to accept the first satisfactory brand as the final choice. The conjunctive rule seems to be particularly useful for quickly reducing the number of alternatives to be considered and then applying some other, perhaps more refined, decision rule as a way to arrive at a final choice from among the surviving alternatives.

2. DISJUNCTIVE RULE.　The disjunctive rule has been referred to as the "mirror image" of the conjunctive rule.[14] In employing this decision rule, a consumer also establishes a separate minimally acceptable level as the cutoff point for each attribute (which may be higher than the one normally established for a conjunctive rule).[15] In this case, if a brand alternative meets or surpasses the cutoff established for any one attribute, it is accepted. Here again, a number of brands might surpass the cutoff point, producing a situation where another decision rule is required. If this occurs, the consumer may accept the first satisfactory brand as the final choice or employ some other, perhaps more suitable, decision rule.

3. LEXICOGRAPHIC RULE.　In employing this decision rule, a consumer first ranks the attributes in terms of their perceived relevance or importance. The consumer then compares the various brand alternatives in terms of the single attribute that is considered most important. If one brand scores sufficiently high on this top-ranked attribute (regardless of the score on any of the other attributes), it is selected and the process comes to a halt.

On the other hand, if there are two or more surviving brand alternatives with effectively the same ratings, the process is repeated with the second-highest-ranked attribute (and so on) until a point is reached where one of the brands is selected because it exceeds the others on a particular attribute.

In employing the lexicographic rule, the highest-ranked attribute (the one employed first) may reveal something about the individual's basic consumer or shopping orientation. For instance, a "buy the best" rule might indicate that a consumer is *quality oriented;* a "buy the most prestigious brand" rule might indicate that a consumer is *status oriented;* a "buy the least expensive" rule might reveal that the consumer is *economy-minded.*

We have considered only the most basic of an almost infinite number of possible consumer decision rules. Most of the decision rules described here can be combined to form new variations—e.g., conjunctive-compensatory, conjunctive-disjunctive, or disjunctive-conjunctive. In addition, we would expect that for many purchase decisions, the consumer would maintain in long-term memory an overall evaluation of the brands in his or her evoked set. This would make assessment by individual attributes unnecessary. Instead, the consumer would simply select the brand with the highest perceived overall rating. This type of synthesized decision rule has been labeled the *affect referral* rule and may represent the simplest of all rules.[16]

Table 18-5 captures the essence of each of the decision rules described in this section by revealing the kind of "mental statement" that a consumer might make in considering the choice of a refrigerator.

In discussing consumer decision rules, we have assumed that a choice is made among the brands being evaluated. Of course, a consumer may also conclude that *none* of the alternatives offer sufficient benefits to warrant their purchase. If this were to occur with a necessity like a regrigerator, the consumer would probably either lower her expectations and settle for the best of the available alternatives or seek additional information about other brands, hoping to find one that more closely meets her criteria. If the purchase is more discretionary in terms of time (such as an oil painting for the living room), the consumer would probably postpone the purchase. In such a case, information gained from the experience up to that point would be transferred to long-term storage (in the psychological field) and would be retrieved and reintroduced as input when, and if, the consumer regained interest in making such an acquisition.

DECISION RULES AND MARKETING STRATEGY. Since marketers generally strive to convince consumers to purchase their brand rather than the other

TABLE 18-5   Hypothetical Usage of Popular Decision Rules in Making a Purchase Decision

DECISION RULES	MENTAL STATEMENT
Compensatory rule	"I chose the refrigerator that came out best when you balanced the good ratings with the bad ratings."
Conjunctive rule	"I chose the refrigerator that didn't have any bad features."
Disjunctive rule	"I chose the refrigerator that excelled in at least one attribute."
Lexicographic rule	"I looked at the feature that was the most important to me and chose the refrigerator that was best on that attribute. If two or more of the refrigerators were about equal on that attribute, I then looked at the second most important attribute to break the tie."

Source: Adapted from Michael Reilly and Rebecca H. Holman, "Does Task Complexity or Cue Intercorrelation Affect Choice of an Information Processing Strategy? An Empirical Investigation," in William D. Perreault, Jr., ed., *Advances in Consumer Research* (Atlanta: Association for Consumer Research, 1977), V, 187.

brands available, an understanding of which decision rules consumers are likely to choose is useful in formulating the marketing effort.[17] For example, a marketer familiar with the decision rule that consumers are likely to employ could prepare a promotional message in a format that would faciliate the processing of information, or the promotional message might even suggest how the consumers should make a decision. The advertisement in Figure 18-2 provides a guide for readers on "how to buy a typewriter." The "clip and save" format is designed to encourage readers to take the ad with them when they actually go shopping for a typewriter and evaluate alternative brands. This advertisement not only provides information about typewriters but also suggests the criteria the decision maker should use in arriving at a choice. Finally, it makes a strong selling point: "More people prefer Smith-Corona electric portables than all other brands combined. After these tests, we think you'll know why."

FIGURE 18-2   Advertisement Suggesting Criteria for Decision Making

Courtesy of Smith-Corona Group of SCM Corporation

Output

The output portion of the model is concerned with two closely associated kinds of postdecision activity: (1) purchase behavior and (2) postpurchase evaluation. The objective of both of these activities is to increase the consumer's satisfaction with his or her purchase.

PURCHASE BEHAVIOR

Consumers make two types of purchases: trial purchases and repeat purchases. If a consumer purchases a product (or brand) for the first time, and buys a smaller quantity than is usual for him or her, such a purchase would be considered a trial. Thus, trial is the exploratory phase of purchase behavior in which consumers attempt to evaluate a product through direct use. Research evidence indicates that when consumers purchase a new brand about which they may be uncertain, they tend to purchase a smaller quantity than they would if it were a familiar brand.[18] Trial, of course, is not always feasible. For example, with most durable goods (dishwashers, air conditioners, refrigerators), a consumer usually moves directly from evaluation to a long-term commitment through purchase, without the opportunity for an actual trial.

If the consumer evaluates the trial of a new product in a product category that has been purchased on a regular basis (food products, cigarettes, beauty and health aids) as satisfactory or better than other brands the consumer is likely to repeat the purchase. Repeat purchase behavior is closely related to the concept of *brand loyalty,* which most firms try to encourage because it ensures them of stability in the marketplace. Therefore, unlike trial, in which the consumer uses the product on a small scale, a repeat purchase signifies that the product basically meets with the consumer's approval and that the consumer is willing to use it in larger quantities.

POSTPURCHASE EVALUATION

As consumers use a product, particularly during a trial purchase, they evaluate its performance in light of their own expectations. For this reason, it is difficult to separate the trial of a product from the postpurchase evaluation of the product. The two go hand in hand.

An important component of postpurchase evaluation is the reduction of uncertainty or doubt that the consumer might have about the selection. Consumers, as part of their postpurchase analysis, try to reassure themselves that their choice was a wise one; that is, they attempt to reduce *postpurchase cognitive dissonance* (see Chapter 9) by adopting any one of the following strategies: (1) they may rationalize the decision as being wise, (2) they may seek out advertisements that support their choice and avoid those of competitive brands, (3) they may attempt to persuade their friends or neighbors to buy the same brand (and thereby confirm their own beliefs), or (4) they may turn to other satisfied owners for reassurance.

The degree of postpurchase analysis that consumers undertake is likely to depend on the importance of the product decision and the experience acquired in using the product. If the product lives up to their expectations, that is, if they are basically satisfied, then they will probably buy it again.[19] However, if the product's performance is disappointing and does not meet expectations, then they will search for more suitable alternatives. Thus the consumer's postpurchase evaluation "feeds back" as *experience* to the consumer's psychological field and serves to influence future related decisions.

summary

The consumer's decision to purchase or reject a product is the moment of final truth for the marketer. It signifies whether the marketing strategy has been wise, insightful, and effective, or whether it was poorly planned and missed the mark. Thus marketers are particularly interested in the consumer decision-making process. In order for a consumer to make a decision, there must be more than one alternative available to him or her. (The decision *not* to buy is also an alternative.)

Theories of consumer decision making vary, depending on the researcher's own assumptions about the nature of humankind. The various "models of man" (economic man, passive man, and cognitive man) depict consumers and their decision-making processes in distinctly different ways.

A simple consumer decision-making model ties together the psychological, social, and cultural concepts examined in Parts II and III into an easily understood framework. This decision model has three distinct sets of variables: input variables, process variables, and output variables.

Input variables that affect the consumer's decision-making process include commercial marketing efforts as well as noncommercial influences from the consumer's social-cultural environment. The decision *process* variables are influenced by the consumers' own psychological fields, which affect their recognition of a need, their prepurchase search for information, and their evaluation of alternatives. The *output* phase of the model includes the actual purchase (either trial purchase or repeat purchase) and postpurchase evaluation. Both prepurchase and postpurchase evaluation feed back in the form of *experience* into the consumer's psychological field and serve to modify future decision processing.

discussion questions

1. Briefly describe how a consumer is assumed to make a decision in terms of the economic, passive, and cognitive models of man.
2. Give an example (not mentioned in the text) of a product that you believe is influenced, either positively or negatively, by the social-cultural environment. Explain.

3. Identify three different products that you believe require reasonably intensive prepurchase search by a consumer. Then, using Table 18-3 as a guide, identify the characteristics of these products that make intensive prepurchase search likely.

4. Discuss the role of a consumer's evoked set in evaluating brand alternatives.

5. Describe a recent purchase you have made in terms of the model of consumer behavior presented in Figure 18-1.

6. Describe the general characteristics of extensive, limited, and routinized decision making.

7. Using a product that you are familiar with, distinguish between compensatory and noncompensatory decision rules.

8. Select a newspaper or magazine advertisement that attempts to provide the consumer with a decision stragegy to be followed in making a purchase decision. Explain the decision strategy.

endnotes

1. This definition is similar to the one suggested in Irwin D. J. Bross, *Design for Decision* (New York: Free Press, 1953), 1.

2. Herbert A. Simon, *Administrative Behavior*, 2nd ed. (New York, Free Press, 1965), 40.

3. James G. March and Herbert A. Simon, *Organizations* (New York: John Wiley, 1958), 140–41.

4. Walter A. Weisskopf, "The Image of Man in Economics," *Social Research*, 40 (Autumn 1973), 560.

5. John G. Jones, *Salesmanship and Sales Management* (New York: Alexander Hamilton Institute, 1917), 29.

6. For interesting ideas on consumer decision strategies, see Lawrence X. Tarpey, Sr., and J. Paul Peter, "A Comparative Analysis of Three Consumer Decision Strategies," *Journal of Consumer Research*, 2 (July 1975), 29–37.

7. James R. Bettman, *An Information Processing Theory of Consumer Choice* (Reading Mass.: Addison-Wesley, 1979).

8. Jacob Jacoby, Donald E. Speller, and Carol A. Kohn, "Brand Choice Behavior as a Function of Information Load, *Journal of Marketing Research*, 11 (February 1974), 63–69; "Brand Choice Behavior as a Function of Information Load: Replication and Extension, *Journal of Consumer Research*, 1 (June 1974), 33–42.

9. Fred D. Reynolds and William R. Darden, "Why the Midi Failed," *Journal of Advertising Research*, 12 (August 1972), 39–44.

10. John A. Howard and Jagdish N. Sheth, *The Theory of Buyer Behavior* (New York: John Wiley, 1969), 46–47.

11. Howard and Sheth, *Theory of Buyer Behavior*, 26.

12. Peter Wright, "Consumer Choice Strategies: Simplifying vs. Optimizing," *Journal of Marketing Research*, 12 (February 1975), 60–67; and Bettman, *Information Processing Theory*, 176–85.

13. Ibid.

14. Wright, "Consumer Choice Strategies," 61.

15. Bettman, *Information Processing Theory*, 181.

16. Wright, "Consumer Choice Strategies," 66; Bettman, *Information Processing Theory*, 179.

17. Peter L. Wright, "Use of Consumer Judgment Models in Promotional Planning," *Journal of Marketing*, 37 (October 1973), 32.

18. Robert W. Shoemaker and F. Robert Shoaf, "Behavioral Changes in the Trial of New Products," *Journal of Consumer Research*, 2 (September 1975), 104–9.

19. For example, see Ralph L. Day, "Extending the Concept of Consumer Satisfaction," in W.D. Perreault, ed., *Advances in Consumer Research* (Atlanta: Association for Consumer Research, 1977), IV, 149–54; Richard L. Oliver, "A Cognitive Model of the Antecedents and Consequences of Satisfaction Decisions," *Journal of Marketing Research*, 17 (November 1980), 460–69; John E. Swan and Lind Combs, "Product Performance and Consumer Satisfaction: A New Concept," *Journal of Marketing*, 40 (April 1976), 26–33; and Robert A. Westbrook, "A Rating Scale for Measuring Product/Service Satisfaction," *Journal of Marketing*, 44 (Fall 1980), 68–72.

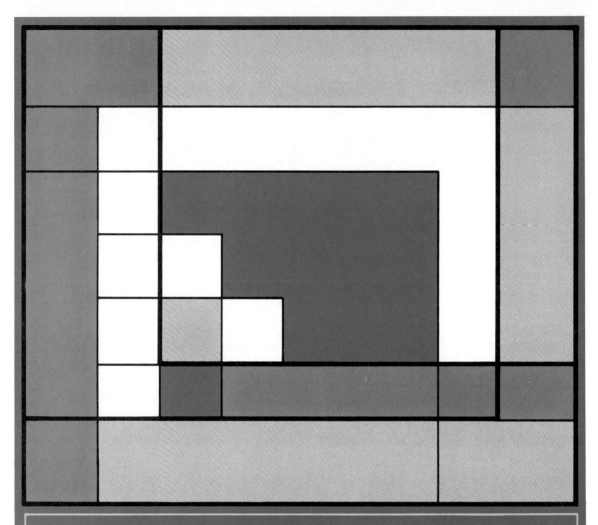

NINETEEN

Comprehensive Models
of Consumer
Decision Making

introduction

Ｉ NTEREST in comprehensive models of consumer behavior is a
rather recent phenomenon. Within a relatively short time (since the mid-fifties),
a variety of models have been proposed by consumer researchers.[1] It is the
purpose of this chapter to set out and to briefly examine a number of
comprehensive models of consumer buyer behavior. These models reflect an
effort to order and integrate the huge number of bits and pieces of knowledge
that are now known about consumer behavior. They also serve as an indication
that the consumer behavior discipline has attained some degree of academic
maturity.

We will examine five specific models that have contributed to an understanding of the dynamics of consumer behavior. The first three models focus on
consumer decision making, especially on how individual consumers arrive at
brand choices. The fourth model deals with family decision making. Particular
attention is given to factors that influence the extent and nature of family
members' contributions to a purchase decision. The final model takes a
consumer information-processing perspective. It focuses on the cognitive
aspects of information search and processing and indicates how consumers
employ information to arrive at various types of buying decisions.

Some of the more complex consumer behavior models were originally
designed primarily to tie together the contents of a specific consumer behavior
book. Others were conceived to capture the dynamics of consumer decision
making and to provide a framework for consumer researchers interested in
testing various dimensions of the models. Taken together, they provide insights
for the design of future research to increase our understanding of consumer
behavior.

The models discussed in this chapter illustrate the "state of the art" of
integrative models of consumer behavior. We have attempted to keep our
discussion of the components, variables, and interrelationships of the various
parts of each model as simple as possible, even at the risk of understating the
uniqueness or richness of a specific model. The reader who desires a complete
description of any of these models is encouraged to consult the original sources.

The whole of science is nothing more than a refinement of everyday thinking.

EINSTEIN

Out of My Later Years, 1950

The Nicosia model focuses on the relationship between the firm and its potential consumers.[2] In the broadest terms, the firm communicates with consumers through its marketing messages (its advertising), and consumers communicate with the firm by their purchase responses. Thus the Nicosia model is *interactive* or *circular* in design: The firm tries to influence the consumers, and the consumers—by their actions (or inaction)—influence the firm.

In its full-blown form, the Nicosia model is an elaborate computer flowchart of the consumer decision-making process. For our purposes, it is sufficient to examine a *summary* flowchart which highlights the full model. As depicted in Figure 19-1, the Nicosia model is divided into four major fields: (1) the span between the source of a message and the consumer's attitude, (2) search and evaluation, (3) the act of purchase, and (4) feedback. A brief discussion of each of these four fields and related subfields follows.

Field 1: The Consumer's Attitude Based on the Firm's Messages

The first field of the Nicosia model is divided into two subfields. Subfield One includes aspects of the firm's marketing environment and communications effort that affect consumer attitudes, such as product attributes, competitive environment, characteristics of relevant mass media, the choice of a message appeal or theme, and characteristics of the target market.

Subfield Two specifies various dimensions of the consumer's predispositions (e.g., personality and experience) that mediate the individual's reception of the firm's messages. The output of the first field is an *attitude* toward the product based on the consumer's interpretation of the message.

Field 2: Search and Evaluation

The second field of the Nicosia model deals with the search for relevant information and the evaluation of the firm's brand in comparison with other alternatives. The output of this stage is motivation to purchase the firm's brand. (Of course, evaluation could also lead to rejection of the firm's brand; however, the model illustrates a positive response.)

Field 3: The Act of Purchase

In the third field, the consumer's motivation toward the firm's brand results in actual purchase of the brand from a specific retailer.

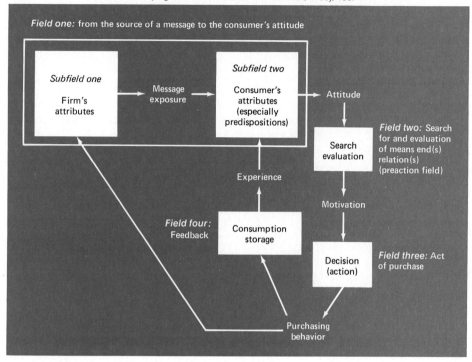

FIGURE 19-1   **Summary Flowchart of the Nicosia Model of Consumer Decision Processes**   Source: Francesco M. Nicosia, *Consumer Decision Processes* (Englewood Cliffs, N.J.: Prentice-Hall, 1966), 156.

Field 4: Feedback

The final field consists of two important types of feedback from the purchase experience; one to the firm in the form of sales data, and the other to the consumer in the form of experience (satisfaction or dissatisfaction). The consumer's experience with the product affects the individual's attitudes and predispositions concerning future messages from the firm.

HOWARD-SHETH MODEL

The Howard-Sheth model is a major revision of an earlier systematic effort to develop a comprehensive theory of consumer decision making.[3] This model explicitly distinguishes between three levels of learning or stages of decision making: (1) extensive problem solving, (2) limited problem solving, and (3) routinized response behavior. Table 19-1 summarizes the main characteristics of each of these three stages of decision making.

TABLE 19-1   Characteristics of the Three Stages of Decision Making

STAGE	AMOUNT OF INFORMATION	SPEED OF DECISION
Extensive Problem Solving	Large	Slow
Limited Problem Solving	Medium	Medium
Routinized Response Behavior	Small	Fast

Source: John A. Howard, *Consumer Behavior: Application of Theory* (New York: McGraw-Hill, 1977), 10.

A simplified version of the basic Howard-Sheth model is shown in Figure 19-2. The model consists of four major sets of variables: (1) inputs, (2) perceptual and learning constructs, (3) outputs, and (4) exogenous (i.e., external) variables (not depicted in Figure 19-2). A brief description of each of these sets of variables follows.

Inputs

The input variables consist of three distinct types of stimuli or information sources in the consumer's environment. Physical brand characteristics (*significative* stimuli) and verbal or visual product characteristics (*symbolic* stimuli) are stimuli supplied by the marketer in the form of product or brand information. The third type of stimulus is provided by the consumer's social environment (family, reference groups, and social class). All three types of stimuli provide inputs concerning the product class or specific brands to the prospective consumer.

Perceptual and Learning Constructs

The central component of the Howard-Sheth model consists of psychological variables that are assumed to operate when the consumer is contemplating a decision. While these constructs are the "heart" of the model, Howard and Sheth treat them as abstractions that are not operationally defined or directly measured. Some of the variables are perceptual and are concerned with how the consumer receives and processes information acquired from the input stimuli and other parts of the model. For example, "stimulus ambiguity" occurs if a consumer is unclear about the meaning of information received from the environment, and "perceptual bias" occurs if the consumer distorts the information received so that it fits the individual's established needs or experiences.[4]

There are also learning constructs, which include the consumer's goals, information about brands in the evoked set, criteria for evaluating alternatives, preferences, and buying intentions. The proposed interaction (linkages) between the various perceptual and learning variables and the variables in the other segments of the model give the Howard-Sheth model its distinctive character.

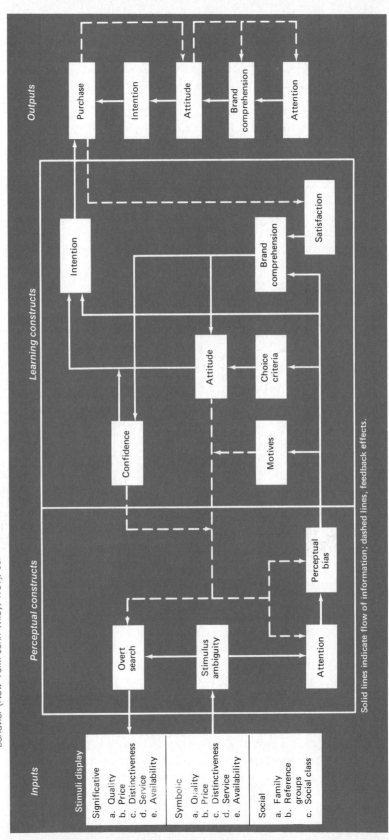

FIGURE 19-2   Simplified Version of the Howard-Sheth Model of Buyer Behavior   Source: John A. Howard and Jagdish N. Sheth, *The Theory of Buyer Behavior* (New York: John Wiley, 1969), 30.

Inputs

Stimuli display

Significative
a. Quality
b. Price
c. Distinctiveness
d. Service
e. Availability

Symbolic
a. Quality
b. Price
c. Distinctiveness
d. Service
e. Availability

Social
a. Family
b. Reference groups
c. Social class

Perceptual constructs

Overt search

Stimulus ambiguity

Attention

Perceptual bias

Confidence

Motives

Attitude

Choice criteria

Brand comprehension

Satisfaction

Intention

Learning constructs

Outputs

Purchase

Intention

Attitude

Brand comprehension

Attention

Solid lines indicate flow of information; dashed lines, feedback effects.

Outputs

The model indicates a series of outputs that correspond in name to some of the perceptual and learning construct variables (attention, brand comprehension, attitudes, intention) in addition to the actual purchase.

Exogenous Variables

Exogenous variables are not directly part of the decision-making process and are not shown in the model presented here. However, because external variables influence the consumer, they should concern the marketer's segmentation efforts. The important exogenous variables include the importance of the purchase, consumer personality traits, time pressure, and financial status.

In an effort to understand the underlying relationships among the variables, Howard and Sheth have tested the model with actual data on consumer decision making.[5] The first test focused on the instant breakfast market.[6] It found that consumers are quite systematic in their use of information and in their establishment of attitudes about brands.

Another test of the model examined consumers' decisions to purchase a Vega automobile.[7] From their analysis of the data, the researchers concluded that informal influence (particularly information acquired from friends) was more critical than information gained from advertisements.[8] However, while advertising was found to be a relatively ineffective information source, exposure to a Vega advertising message did have some impact on comprehension of the Vega's features and on the intention to purchase. Additional research on a wider range of products and services is needed to obtain a better picture of the strengths and limitations of commercial and noncommercial information sources on various aspects of the consumer decision-making process.

ENGEL-KOLLAT-BLACKWELL MODEL

The Engel-Kollat-Blackwell model of consumer behavior was originally designed to serve as a framework for organizing the fast-growing body of knowledge concerning consumer behavior.[9] Like the Howard-Sheth model, it has gone through a number of revisions aimed at improving its descriptive ability and clarifying basic relationships between components and subcomponents.[10] Figure 19-3 presents a recent version of this comprehensive model, which consists of six vertically organized sections: (1) decision process stages, (2) information input, (3) information processing, (4) product-brand evaluations, (5) general motivating influences, and (6) internalized environmental influences. A brief description of each of these sections follows.

FIGURE 19-3 **The Engel-Kollat-Blackwell Model of Consumer Behavior** Source: James F. Engel, Roger D. Blackwell, and David T. Kollat, *Consumer Behavior*, 3rd ed. (Hinsdale, Ill.: Dryden Press, 1978), 556.

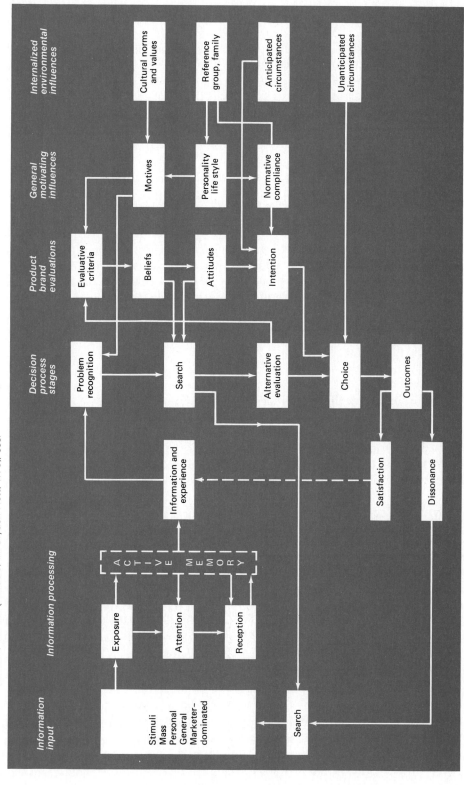

Decision Process Stages

The central focus of the model is on five basic decision process stages: (1) problem recognition, (2) search, (3) alternative evaluation, (4) choice, and (5) outcomes. How many of these stages actually figure in a specific purchase decision depends on how extensive is the problem-solving task. For example, in "extended decision process behavior," the consumer is assumed to pass through all five stages; in "habitual decision process behavior," the consumer is assumed to advance directly from internal search to actual purchase.

Information Input

Feeding into the information-processing section of the model are various forms of information from marketing and nonmarketing sources. After passing through the consumer's active memory, which serves as a filter, the information is depicted as having its initial influence at the problem recognition stage of the decision-making process. The model reveals that search for external information is also activated if either additional information is required in order to arrive at a choice or the consumer experiences dissonance because, the chosen alternative is assessed to be less satisfactory than was originally expected.

Information Processing

The information-processing section of the model consists of the consumer's *selective* exposure, attention, and reception (i.e., comprehension and retention) of incoming marketing and nonmarketing information. As indicated in the model, before a message can be utilized, the consumer must be exposed to it, must attend to it, and must receive it. Thus, as shown in Figure 19-3, these three perceptual dimensions provide information that the active memory filters or selectively processes before it is allowed to pass through to permanent or long-term memory as information and experience.

Product-Brand Evaluations

The product-brand evaluations section of the model is linked most closely with the alternative evaluation stage of the decision process. It is comprised of four dimensions: (1) evaluative criteria, (2) beliefs, (3) attitudes, and (4) intention. This section of the model accounts for the assessment of various alternatives before arriving at a final purchase decision.

General Motivating Influences

This section of the model is comprised of two basic elements: (1) motives that trigger the specific evaluative criteria that the consumer employs in assessing alternatives, and (2) personality and lifestyle traits that help produce the consumer's general behavioral patterns. In addition, there is normative compliance (the presence of felt social pressure), which reflects the impact of the consumer's personality and lifestyle on intention to buy.

Internalized Environmental Influences

The last section of the model consists of environmental influences as they have been accepted or responded to by the consumer. The general environmental factors noted are (1) cultural norms and values that impact on motives, (2) reference groups and family factors that influence personality and lifestyle, (3) anticipated circumstances that affect intention to buy, and (4) unanticipated circumstances that may block or alter consumer decision making.

SHETH FAMILY DECISION-MAKING MODEL

The three comprehensive models presented thus far all focus on *individual* consumer decision making. An alternative perspective considers the family and its members as the appropriate consumer decision-making unit as reflected in the Sheth family decision-making model in Figure 19-4.[11] The left side of the model depicts separate psychological systems, which represent the distinct predispositions of the father, mother, and other family members. These separate predispositons lead into "family buying decisions," which may be either individually or jointly determined.

The right side of the model lists seven factors that influence whether a specific purchase decision will be autonomous or joint: (1) social class, (2) lifestyle, (3) role orientation, (4) family life-cycle stage, (5) perceived risk, (6) product importance, a l (7) time pressure. The model suggests that joint decision making tends to prevail in families that are middle class, newly married, and closely knit, with few prescribed family roles. In terms of product-specific factors, it suggests that joint decision making is more prevalent when there is a great deal of perceived risk or uncertainty, when the purchase decision is considered to be important, and when there is ample time to make a decison.

BETTMAN'S INFORMATION-PROCESSING MODEL OF CONSUMER CHOICE

A more recent comprehensive model of consumer behavior is Bettman's information-processing model of consumer choice.[12] This model approaches consumer choice from a distinctly cognitive and information-processing point of view.

Consistent with this perspective, the consumer is portrayed as possessing a limited capacity for processing information. Thus, when faced with a choice, the consumer rarely (if ever) undertakes very complex analyses of available alternatives. Instead, as suggested by the model, the consumer typically employs

Comprehensive
Models of
Consumer Decision
Making

FIGURE 19-4 **Sheth Family Decision-Making Model** Source: Figure 2.1 "A Theory of Family Buying Decisions," (pp. 22–23) from *Models of Buyer Behavior* by Jagdish N. Sheth (Harper & Row, 1974).

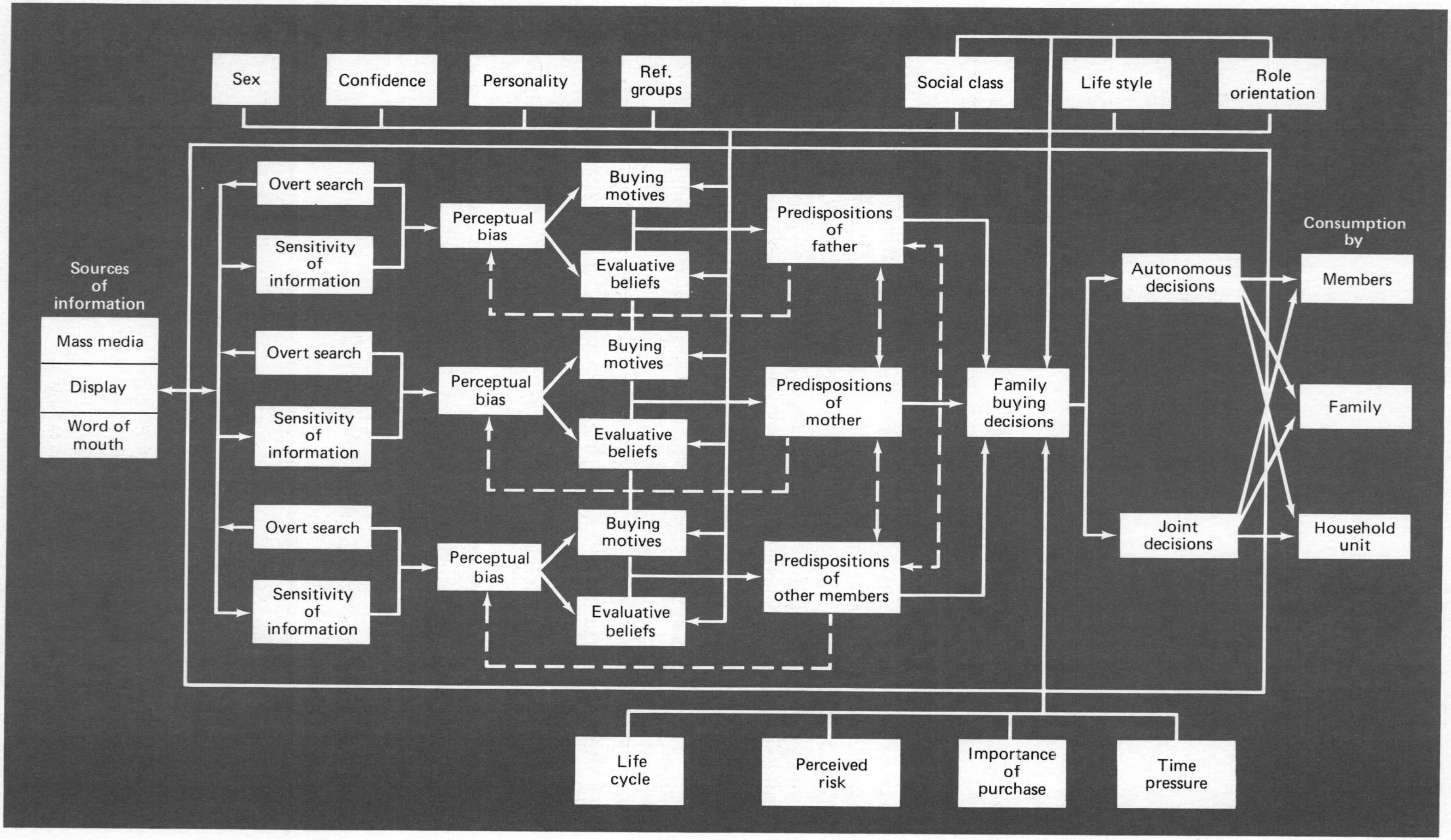

simple decision strategies or heuristics. These simplifying decision rules assist the consumer in arriving at a choice by providing a means of sidestepping the overly burdensome task of assessing all the information available about all the alternatives.

In its complete form, the Bettman model consists of a number of interrelated flowcharts that depict the various dimensions of the consumer choice process. The overview of the Bettman model in Figure 19-5 contains all of its basic components: (1) processing capacity, (2) motivation, (3) attention and perceptual encoding, (4) information acquisition and evaluation, (5) memory, (6) decision processes, and (7) consumption and learning processes.[13] In addition,

FIGURE 19-5 **The Bettman Information-Processing Model of Consumer Choice** Source: James R. Bettman, *An Information Processing Theory of Consumer Choice* (Reading, Mass.: Addison-Wesley, 1979), 17.

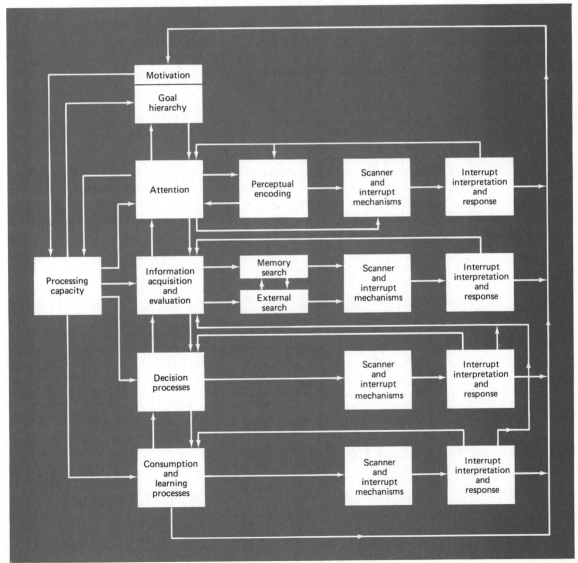

the model includes, at appropriate points, mechanisms that continually scan the environment and receive and respond to interruptions.

Processing Capacity

The processing capacity component of the Bettman model is founded on the notion that individuals have only a limited capacity for processing information. Thus, in making choices, consumers are likely to find complex computations and extensive information processing to be particularly difficult or burdensome tasks. To deal with these demands, consumers are likely to select choice strategies or rules of thumb that make alternative selection an easier and less-taxing process.

As depicted in Figure 19-5, the process capacity component influences the other major components of the model. This suggests important implications for the kinds and scope of choice strategies that consumers are likely to employ in evaluating alternatives and choosing among them. More precisely, it impacts on the *allocation* of the limited processing capacity and sets the stage for the selection of simple choice rules as an effective way of adjusting to these constraints.

Motivation

Since consumer choice in the Bettman model is conceived as being purposeful (i.e., designed to achieve one or more goals), motivation is a central component. Motivation influences both the direction and the intensity of consumer choice and stimulates the consumer to seek information required to evaluate alternatives and to make a choice (e.g., a purchase).

Motivation provides momentum by means of two basic mechanisms: (1) the hierarchy-of-goals and (2) an interrupting and scanner mechanism. The hierarchy-of-goals mechanism is a dynamic force in the form of a series of intermediate subgoals that lead to a desired end state—a choice. The hierarchy-of-goals mechanism is consistent with the notion of limited capacity: It suggests that as a consumer gains experience in a particular choice area, he or she will no longer have to employ an elaborate hierarchy of goals to arrive at a decision. Instead, acquired experiences eventually provide the consumer with the basis for employing less-demanding decision rules. Thus the goal hierarchy mechanism channels the consumer's efforts in making a choice. Because the companion scanner and interrupt mechanisms are linked to all the components of the Bettman model, they will be discussed after we have considered the other components.

Attention and Perceptual Encoding

The attention and perceptual encoding components are closely tied and are heavily influenced by the consumer's goal hierarchy. As conceived in the Bettman model, there are two types of attention: *voluntary attention*, which is a conscious allocation of processing capacity to current goals and *involuntary attention*, which is more of an automatic response to disruptive events (e.g., conflicting views or newly acquired complicating information). Each of these quite different types of attention influences how individuals progress in reaching goals and making choices.

The perceptual encoding element of the model is an extension of the attention component. It accounts for the process by which the consumer organizes and interprets those stimuli that have been attended to, and it may provide insights as to the need for additional information.

Information Acquisition and Evaluation

Within the context of the Bettman model, the consumer undertakes external search to the extent that information now available in memory is judged to be inadequate. After acquiring information, it is evaluated and its suitability or usefulness is assessed. The consumer continues to acquire additional information until all relevant information has been secured, or until the consumer perceives any additional effort to be "too costly" in terms of time or effort.

Memory

Memory is the component of the Bettman model through which all information flows. More precisely, memory is where a consumer first begins the search (internal search) for information on which to base a choice. If the internal information is insufficient, then the consumer undertakes external search.

As part of the dynamics of memory, information is stored either in short-term storage (which is limited in capacity and is where information is processed) or in long-term storage.

Decision Processes

The Bettman model stresses that different types of choices are normally made in conjunction with the fulfillment of specific components of the model (e.g., choice of goals and choice of information to be acquired). Thus the choices made during the decision processes component are a particular form of choice rather than *the* choice. Specifically, the decision processes component deals with the application of heuristics or rules of thumb in the evaluation of and selection among alternatives (e.g., selecting a specific brand).

This portion of the model emphasizes that the specific heuristics a consumer employs are influenced by both individual factors (e.g., personality differences) and situational factors (e.g., urgency of the decision). Therefore it is unreasonable to assume that a particular decision rule will consistently be employed by the same consumer in different situations, or by different consumers in the same situation.

CONSUMPTION AND LEARNING PROCESSES

The consumption and learning component of the Bettman model is concerned with the future utilization of the experiences acquired after the purchase choice has been made and the selected alternative has been consumed. Such consumption experiences not only serve the consumer as a form of information to be applied to future choice situations but also provide the basis for developing or refining his or her heuristic. Thus, as an outgrowth of this component, a consumer's postpurchase and postconsumption evaluations are stored for repeat or related future use.

SCANNER AND INTERRUPT MECHANISMS

As we have already mentioned, throughout the Bettman model there are scanning and interrupting mechanisms that receive all kinds of messages from the consumer's environment. The scanner is continuously open to relevant information from the environment, whereas the interrupt mechanism is a device designed to deal with messages that tend to interfere with the progress of making a particular choice.

Cast in this light, the scanner is receptive to information, whereas the interrupt mechanism deals with messages that are more or less "forced" on the consumer. However, both mechanisms are capable of delaying the achievement of goals associated with a particular choice process and of diverting attention to a completely different area of choice (e.g., a more-pressing problem).

Of all the consumer behavior models presented here, only the Howard-Sheth model has been subjected to more than a minimum of systematic testing. To the best of our knowledge at the time of this writing, the Engel-Kollat-Blackwell model has received only modest small-scale testing, while the Nicosia model, the Sheth family model, and the Bettman information-processing model have not been tested at all. Given the still rather primitive "state of the art," it may be some time before comprehensive decision-making models are adequately tested and applied.[14]

Nevertheless, comprehensive models of consumer behavior are likely to receive periodic attention because they serve to tie together what is known about consumers and their choice processes, and because they provide a framework or starting point for more modest consumer research projects.

summary

Consumer behavior models describe the decision-making or choice processes of consumers. Comprehensive models of consumer behavior include the Nicosa model, the Howard-Sheth model, the Engel-Kollat-Blackwell model, the Sheth family decision-making model, and the Bettman information-processing model.

As the study of consumer behavior progresses and becomes a mature, scientific discipline, it is likely that consumer researchers will continue to find the development and testing of these and other comprehensive models of consumer behavior a useful synthesizing device. Knowledge of how individuals and family units make consumption decisions is important to students of human behavior, to students of marketing behavior, and to the public policy planners who shape the environment in which we all must function.

discussion questions

1. Describe a recent purchase that you have made in terms of the Nicosia model of consumer decision processes presented in Figure 19-1.
2. Describe a recent purchase that you have made in terms of the Howard-Sheth model of buyer behavior presented in Figure 19-2.
3. Describe a recent purchase that you have made in terms of the Engle-Kollat-Blackwell model of consumer behavior presented in Figure 19-3.
4. Describe a recent purchase that you have made in terms of the Sheth family decision-making model presented in Figure 19-4.
5. Describe a recent purchase that you have made in terms of Bettman's information-processing model of consumer choice presented in Figure 19-5.
6. Briefly describe the major implications of the Bettman model's assumption that consumers have only a limited capacity for processing information.
7. Taken as a group, describe three strengths and three weaknesses of comprehensive models of consumer decision making.
8. How would you expect marketing executives to react to the comprehensive models of consumer decision making described in this chapter?

endnotes

1. Several other noteworthy comprehensive models are not reviewed here: Alan R. Andreason, "Attitudes and Customer Behavior: A Decision Model," in Lee Preston, ed., *New Research in Marketing* (Berkeley: Institute of Business and Economic Research, University of California, 1965), 1–16; Flemming Hansen, *Consumer Choice Behavior* (New York: Free Press, 1972); and Frederick E. Webster, Jr., and Yoram Wind, "A General Model for Understanding Organizational Buying Behavior," *Journal of Marketing*, 36 (April 1972), 12–19.
2. Francesco M. Nicosia, *Consumer Decision Processes* (Englewood Cliffs, N.J.: Prentice-Hall, 1966), esp. 156–88.
3. John A. Howard and Jagdish N. Sheth, *The Theory of Buyer Behavior* (New York: John Wiley, 1969), esp. 24–49.
4. Ibid., 36–37.
5. For example, see John U. Farley, John A. Howard, and L. Winston Ring, *Consumer Behavior: Theory and Applications* (Boston: Allyn & Bacon, 1974); Donald R. Lehmann et al., "Some Empirical Contributions to Buyer Behavior Theory," *Journal of Consumer Reseach*, 1 (December 1974), 43–55; John A. Howard, *Consumer Behavior: Application of Theory* (New York: McGraw-Hill, 1977); John U. Farley and Donald R. Lehmann, "An Overview of Empirical Applications of Buyer Behavior System Models," in William D. Perreault, Jr., ed., *Advances in Consumer Research* (Atlanta: Association for Consumer Research, 1977), IV, 337–41; and Michel Larsche and John A. Howard, "Nonlinear Relations in a Complex Model of Buyer Behavior," *Journal of Consumer Research*, 6 (March 1980), 377–88.
6. Stanley E. Cohen, "Ads a 'Weak Signal' in Most Buying Decisions: Howard," *Advertising Age*, June 12, 1972, 3 and 78.
7. Ibid., 78.
8. Ibid.
9. James F. Engel, David T. Kollat, and Roger D. Blackwell, *Consumer Behavior*, New York: Holt, Rinehart & Winston, 1968), 40.

10. James F. Engel, David T. Kollat, and Roger D. Blackwell, *Consumer Behavior*, 3rd ed. (Holt, Rinehart & Winston, 1978), 556.

11. Jagdish N. Sheth, "A Theory of Family Buying Decisions," in Jagdish N. Sheth, ed., *Models of Buying Behavior* (New York: Harper & Row, 1974), 17–33.

12. James R. Bettman, *An Information Processing Theory of Consumer Choice* (Reading, Mass.: Addison-Wesley,1979).

13. For a detailed flowchart, see ibid., 38–39.

14. For a discussion of the problems of testing consumer behavior models, see Gerald Zaltman, Christian R. A. Pinson, and Reinhard Angelman, *Metatheory and Consumer Behavior* (New York: Holt, Rinehart & Winston, 1973); and Shelby D. Hunt, *Marketing Theory* (Columbus, Ohio: Grid, 1976).

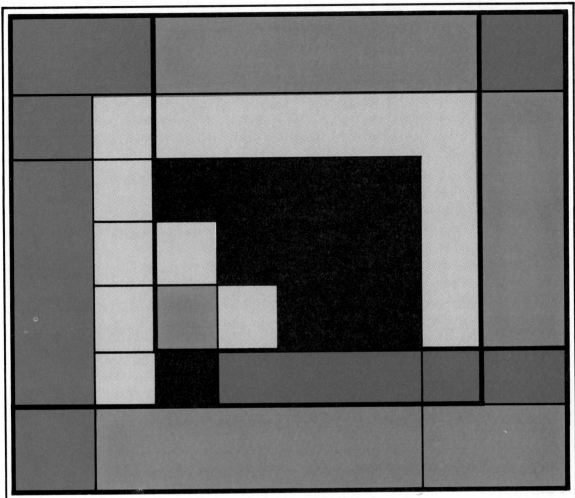

part five

BROADENING THE CONCEPT OF CONSUMER BEHAVIOR

Part V describes the application of consumer behavior research findings to public policy issues. The extension of consumer behavior research techniques to the non-profit sector has enabled the government and such organizations as hospitals, museums, and political parties to better serve the needs of clients, voters, and the general public.

TWENTY

Consumer Behavior Applications for Public Policy and Nonprofit Organizations

introduction

I N addition to the impetus given to the study of consumer behavior by developments in marketing philosophy and practice, the field has also grown in response to public policy needs and the extension of marketing concepts to nonbusiness areas. Specifically, the rise of the consumer movement, the increased demand for more consumer information and education, and the adoption of marketing techniques by nonprofit organizations have all contributed to expanding the scope of consumer behavior research.

CONSUMER PROTECTION

The consumer movement that emerged in the late 1960s endeavored to correct the imbalance that had developed in the marketplace between buyers and sellers. Consumer advocates complained of shoddy and hazardous products. Furthermore, they claimed that products were being sold by misrepresentation—through deceptive advertising and packaging, high-pressure salesmanship, and inadequate warranties—on credit terms that disguised their true costs. In response to these complaints, Congress passed some major pieces of legislation designed to protect consumers, and state and local governments enacted dozens more.

Although the need for consumer legislation was widely supported, the effectiveness of such legislation in safeguarding consumer rights has been somewhat uneven. Consider the truth-in-lending law. This law was passed to ensure that consumers are made aware of the true rates of interest they are charged for buying on credit. The law was intended to aid low-income consumers in particular, who most often rely on credit purchases. However, research has shown that only 34 percent of those who made a purchase on credit after passage of the law could report the true interest charges they agreed to pay; moreover, low-income shoppers were among those who were least aware of finance charges.[1]

Public sentiment is to public officers what water is to the wheel of the mill.

HENRY WARD BEECHER

Proverbs from Plymouth Pulpit, *1887*

Many policymakers now concede that legislation like truth-in-lending, while well-intentioned, was passed with little consideration of actual consumer behavior. They agree that research into consumers' attitudes and habits concerning their purchase behavior should have been a necessary precondition to the enactment of any consumer legislation and should be a requisite basis for remedying the faults in current laws.[2]

Two government agencies that have used consumer behavior studies to aid in policymaking decisions are the Federal Trade Commission (FTC) and the Food and Drug Administration (FDA). Both agencies have concerned themselves in recent years with the regulation of advertising—an area in which consumer abuse has frequently been charged. Officials from both agencies have asked for consumer behavior research that clarifies the meaning of "deceptive advertising," proposes remedies for such advertising, and measures the effectiveness of proposed remedies.[3] This is a prime example of the potential application of consumer behavior research to the development of consumer protection policies.

Deceptive Advertising and Consumer Research

Both the FTC and the FDA have the power to halt any advertising they consider to be deceptive; yet over the years, no single definition of what constitutes deception in advertising has evolved. Each case brought before either regulatory agency has been decided on an *ad hoc* basis—that is, on its own merits—so that advertisers have not been able to discern any broad guidelines as to what would be considered improper or deceptive advertising. To remedy this situation, consumer behavior studies have been conducted to clarify the meaning of deception. One recent study distinguished three categories of deception: (1) unconscionable lies, in which completely false claims are made and intended; (2) claim/fact discrepancies, in which some relevant qualifications of a claim are omitted, resulting in misrepresentation; and (3) claim/belief discrepancies, in which no deceptive claim is explicitly made, but a deceptive belief is created.[4]

Of the three categories, the one that is probably the most insidious is the last form of deception. Industry watchdog agencies frequently guard against outright lies and insufficiently documented claims, but the clever manipulation of words to foster a misleading belief is more difficult to police. For example, a candy bar that is portrayed in its advertising as "wholesome" implies that it meets basic FDA requirements for vitamins and other nutrients, whether or not it does, in fact, do so.

How can the FTC or the FDA determine whether a false belief has been created among consumers? Consumer behavior research offers some promising answers, but requires some creativity in design. In one study, subjects were exposed to product claims that might lead to the formation of false beliefs; then they were exposed to corrected claims for the same products. After some experimentation, the researchers developed a technique that reportedly enabled them to spot the existence of false beliefs, trace those beliefs to specific ads (not just to generalized misimpressions that consumers might have held prior to seeing the ads in question), and measure the specific level of false belief created by the ads. Adoption of this technique would enable advertisers to pretest their

Consumer Behavior
Applications for
Public Policy and
Nonprofit
Organizations

573

advertising prior to widespread media release, and to revise any ads that research indicated would be misleading. The same technique would permit the FTC and the FDA to predetermine the strength of a misleading advertising case before deciding whether or not to prosecute.[5]

Corrective Advertising and Consumer Research

In situations where the FTC has determined that an advertisement is deceptive, it has ordered the advertiser to cancel the ad and to run a series of so-called corrective ads in an effort to eliminate any residual effects of the misleading claims on consumers. For example, the Warner-Lambert Company was ordered to run corrective advertising from September 4, 1978, through February 1, 1980, for its product Listerine, which for years had been deceptively promoted as a cold remedy. (See Figure 20-1.) The corrective ads state that Listerine does not help to prevent colds or sore throats or lessen their severity.

The main purpose of corrective advertising is to dispel mistaken impressions created by misleading advertising and to help consumers make more informed product decisions. (An implicit purpose is to impose sanctions designed to discourage marketers from either deliberately or thoughtlessly sponsoring such ads.) However, consumer behavior research into the effectiveness of corrective advertising in achieving its primary purpose has come up with some mixed results. For example, research has found that although deceptive claims are less widely believed after corrective advertising has been implemented, loyal brand users tend to ignore such ads and remain loyal, instead of changing their beliefs or their buying patterns.[6] In a recent follow-up study of the Listerine corrective advertising, the FTC reported that although the ads had had some impact, many people have continued to use the product as a remedy for sore throats and colds.

Research has also revealed that some consumers tended to overgeneralize the corrective message, so that they disbelieved all subsequent advertising claims, both for the brand and for the product category.[7] Thus it appears that corrective advertising has the potential for being both ineffective and overly effective. Consumer behavior research designed to determine consumer responses to suggested corrective ads *before* the fact may be one way to effectively assist consumers without needlessly harming a broad category of products.

Consumer Information

Laws and regulatory agencies are needed to protect basic consumer rights. But beyond protection, consumers need information and education to enable them to make better buying decisions. Increasingly, government policymakers and consumer advocates are recognizing that they cannot protect consumers against every possible marketing abuse, and that the consumers' best defense is better knowledge of the product. Today more than thirty federal agencies, as well as state and local agencies, are designing consumer education programs and

Consumer Behavior
Applications for
Public Policy and
Nonprofit
Organizations

FIGURE 20-1   A Corrective Advertisement for Listerine

LISTERINE®

"BRIDE"

ANNCR: Where will you be . . . when your mouthwash stops working?

FATHER: Here come the guests. (SFX: CLOUD)

BRIDE: Dad . . . bad breath.
FATHER: But I used . . .
BRIDE: Should have used Listerine.

ANNCR: Listerine works hours longer than the number two mouthwash.

While Listerine will not help prevent colds or sore throats or lessen their severity - -

Listerine's strong formula keeps your breath clean for hours.

It kills the germs that can cause bad breath.

(MUSIC UP & UNDER)
FATHER: What a day!
BRIDE: What a Dad!

ANNCR: Listerine Antiseptic. You can bet your breath on it.

Courtesy of Warner-Lambert Company

disseminating consumer information. Table 20-1 lists some of the programs that various government units have instituted to make more information available to consumers. Consumer behavior research has proved useful to the implementation and evaluation of many of these programs. Three areas in which a great deal of research has been done are unit pricing, nutritional labeling, and energy conservation labeling.

TABLE 20-1   Recent or Prospective Information Disclosure Requirements

TYPE OF DISCLOSURE	IMPLEMENTED RECENTLY	LIKELY TO BE IMPLEMENTED IN THE FUTURE
1. Comparative prices	—Truth in lending —Unit pricing —Automobile list prices —Truth in life insurance —Costs of operation of appliances and automobiles —Prescription prices	—Truth in consumer leasing
2. Comparative performance and efficiency	—Nutrition labeling of food products —Lumen and life data for light bulbs —Stereo amplifier power output —Octane labeling —Automobile performance (vehicle stopping distance, acceleration and passing ability, and tire reserve load) —Automobile gas mileage —Appliance energy consumption and comparative efficiency —Appliance performance —Tire mileage, stopping ability, and high-speed resistance to heat —Sun screen efficacy of suntan preparations	—Carpet and upholstery wear characteristics —Quality grade labels for food products —Standards of drug efficacy —Detergent efficacy —Vocational school drop-out rate
3. Ingredients (including additives)	—Cosmetics —Food —Liquor —Phosphate content of detergents —Labeling of fat content in food	—Presence of pesticides —Pigment content of paint —Labeling to explain purpose of food ingredients and additives
4. Life/perishability	—Open dating of foods —Expiration dates for drug potency	—Appliance durability and life —Automobile damage susceptibility and repair costs
5. Warnings/clarifications	—Cigarette health hazards —Lack of efficacy of vitamins —Flammability (children's sleepwear)	—Flammability of cellular plastic insulation

TABLE 20-1   Continued

TYPE OF DISCLOSURE	IMPLEMENTED RECENTLY	LIKELY TO BE IMPLEMENTED IN THE FUTURE
6. Form and usage of product/ terms of contract and warranties	—Size standards (i.e., TV screens and refrigerators) —Truth in warranties and service contracts —Tire construction and load rating —Care labeling for clothing —Net and drained weights of canned and frozen food	—Standards specifying amount of product to use (i.e., detergents) —Terms of land sales contracts —Truth in imports (country of origin) —Truth in savings (interest payments) —Disclosure of manufacturer, packer, and distributor of food products

Source: Updated and adapted from George S. Day, "Assessing the Effects of Information Disclosure," *Journal of Marketing*, 40 (April 1976), 43.

UNIT PRICING

Supermarket shoppers often confront the difficult task of determining which is the best buy among the various brands and package sizes available. Is a 30-ounce house brand of detergent at 89 cents a wiser purchase than a 48-ounce national brand at $1.29? To aid consumers, several states have instituted unit pricing, which requires the storekeeper to list the price per unit (e.g., per ounce) for each brand and size carried.

Consumer behavior researchers have conducted several studies over the past ten years to determine the degree to which consumers use unit pricing and how useful it is to them. Early surveys reported that the system was not extensively used, particularly by the shoppers it was supposed to help most—the poor and the elderly.[8] However, a more recent study of a program that had been in operation for six years showed extensive use by all types of shoppers.[9]

Besides documenting its use, studies have been devoted to discovering the best way to display unit price information. It has been suggested that posted price lists near displays are more effective than individual shelf tags for every brand and size.[10] Subsequent research has revealed that both methods produce savings for consumers, since they encourage switching to cheaper store brands. The listing format produces more savings, however, apparently because it makes comparisons easier.[11]

NUTRITIONAL LABELING

The concept of nutritional labeling covers a broad spectrum of programs and proposals for apprising consumers of the nutritional value of the foods they buy. In 1975, the FDA ordered marketers to list on their labels the vitamin, protein, carbohydrate, and fat content of all processed foods for which nutritional claims are made. In 1980 it proposed extending the labeling disclosure requirement to additional products and to additional information. The FTC has also proposed a rule requiring disclosure of nutritional information in food advertising.[12]

In evaluating the effects of current labeling requirements, consumer behavior researchers have found that consumers rarely consult such labels. Only about 25 percent of all consumers are aware of nutritional labels, and even fewer understand how to interpret them.[13] Recent research lends little support to the notion that a different format for labeling would be more effective in conveying such information.[14] Many consumers lack the background to understand the labels, and without more education, they may not benefit from nutritional advertising. Significantly, the FDA's proposed rule for additional labeling also contains the suggestion that a consumer education program be initiated.

ENERGY CONSERVATION LABELING

Since the beginning of the energy crisis in the early 1970s, the federal government has been concerned about energy conservation. To make citizens more energy conscious, the FTC initiated a program requiring the manufacturers of seven major appliances to clearly label the energy efficiency of their products. (See Figure 20-2.) The labels show the average yearly operating cost as well as a range of high-to-low operating costs. In addition, consumers can obtain a table showing various usage and utility rates so that they can estimate their individual costs for using the appliances.

FIGURE 20-2   Energy Efficiency Label

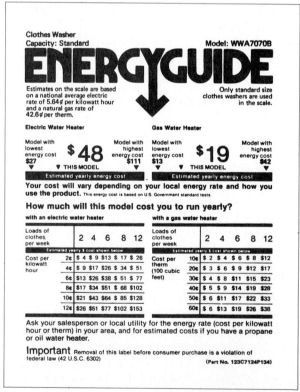

Courtesy of General Electric Company

Consumer Behavior
Applications for
Public Policy and
Nonprofit
Organizations

578

As with the nutritional labeling program, consumer behavior studies have been conducted to test the efficacy of energy labels. Research has shown that such information is effective in shifting consumers away from energy inefficient appliances and increasing their preference for models with lower operating costs.[15]

A support program using advertising to encourage energy conservation has not proved to be as successful as the labeling program. Research on the effectiveness of different conservation messages has shown that people lack involvement and interest in the issue of energy conservation, and that advertisements are only marginally successful in increasing their interest.[16] However, the decontrol of energy prices, and the subsequent increase in consumer costs, have made consumers more aware of the need to conserve. This awareness can be buttressed by more formal consumer education programs.

Consumer Education

In order for consumer information programs to have the greatest impact on their intended audiences, more extensive consumer education is needed. Without such education, further protective legislation may prove to be a wasted effort.

How best to carry out such consumer education has been the subject of a number of research studies. Of the suggestions that have been made, three are particularly noteworthy.[17] The first involves instituting a labeling program for all goods to certify quality. A cooperative effort by government officials, businesspeople, consumer spokespersons, and academic researchers would be needed to establish the standards to be summarized on the labels. Such uniform labeling would give consumers a basis for making product comparisons while shopping.

Another suggestion that has been proposed to advance consumer education involves the development of computerized data banks containing product information (e.g., local prices, availability, and product test results) and general educational information (e.g., the meaning of nutritional information). Consumers could tap into such information banks by means of home computers or cable television, two recent technological developments which are receiving increasingly wide distribution and acceptance.

Another very appealing suggestion for increasing consumer information is to make consumer education mandatory in the public-school system. At present, only a few states have such programs, and the content varies widely. Consumer behavior researchers could make a substantive contribution to the field of consumer education by designing appropriate curricula for such programs.[18]

NONPROFIT MARKETING

In addition to aiding public policymakers in formulating consumer protection policies and disseminating information, consumer behavior research has helped nonprofit organizations to better serve their publics. The notion that nonprofit organizations, like commercial organizations, have clients with varying needs that require differentiated marketing efforts, is relatively new. Nevertheless, in the decade or so since the idea was introduced, all sorts of organizations—from political parties and government bodies to colleges, welfare agencies, hospitals, and museums—have adopted a consumer behavior approach.

The "product" that these organizations are trying to sell is usually a service or an idea that they want the public to use or adopt. Moreover, the "price" the public pays is often nonmonetary (such as a vote or a museum visit), and the

FIGURE 20-3   Nonprofit Marketing: Example of Museum Advertising

Copyright© 1981 The Greek Ministry of Culture and Sciences. Reprinted with permission.

Consumer Behavior
Applications for
Public Policy and
Nonprofit
Organizations

580

methods used to sell the service or idea are often nontraditional (e.g., special events or public service films).[19] In not-for-profit marketing, just as in commercial marketing, studies of consumer (client) behavior are useful in both devising marketing programs and measuring their effectiveness. Examples of consumer behavior research in the nonprofit sector can be found in the marketing of social causes, health services, and political ideas (see Figure 20-3).

Social Marketing

Social marketing uses marketing concepts and techniques to win adoption of socially beneficial ideas.[20] Its purpose may be merely to change attitudes in a given target market or, more ambitiously, to alter behavior.

Advertising campaigns that attempt to alert teenagers to the dangers of drugs are an example of social marketing. Consumer behavior studies have been conducted to determine the kinds of messages that are most effective in conveying the dangers of drug taking, and advertising research has been conducted to assess the effects of specific ads on changing attitudes about drugs. For example, one study of high-school students tested the effects of three variations of a commercial: (1) the threat of serious versus minimal harm (e.g., death versus parental disapproval); (2) the drawing of an explicit conclusion versus no summary statement at the end; and (3) the presentation of the message in a monologue versus a dialogue format. The study concluded somewhat surprisingly that the threat of serious harm was no more effective than that of lesser harm, and that a dialogue format had no more effect than a monologue format. It did find, however, that explicit conclusions must be drawn in order for the ads to have any influence. Another unexpected finding was that although the initial effect of the ads was to engender negative attitudes toward drugs, repeated exposure to the commercials usually weakened rather than strengthened such attitudes.[21] Thus some drug-abuse information programs may unintentionally defeat their own purpose by "overkill"—a finding that only careful research was able to uncover.

The example of social marketing in Figure 20-4 is designed to encourage companies to hire disadvantaged people who "turned their lives around."

The National Highway Traffic Safety Administration has had a long-running advertising campaign designed to convince the public to wear seat belts. Behavioral studies have been conducted to determine both actual usage and more effective promotional techniques to encourage usage. The research showed that less than 25 percent of the drivers whose cars were equipped with seat belts actually used them. One study also indicated that drivers were most likely to wear seat belts if a close friend had been injured in a crash. This fact suggested a possible theme for an advertising campaign to encourage seat belt usage—the threat of serious injury. Various advertisements employing this theme were test-marketed on a small scale, and observational studies of those exposed to the commercials were then conducted. The research revealed that the commercials had little effect on changing the behavior of nonusers.[22] It is likely that people think that a car crash "can't happen to me" until they actually do see it happen to a close friend. Even though this social marketing effort was

Consumer Behavior
Applications for
Public Policy and
Nonprofit
Organizations

581

FIGURE 20-4   An Example of Social
Marketing

HOW'D YOU LIKE TO HIRE SOMEONE WHO TURNED HIS LIFE AROUND?

It makes a lot of sense. Because that person is motivated to succeed. And isn't that the kind of man or woman you want working for your business?

Since it began, Opportunities Industrialization Centers—OIC—have helped more than 600,000 people turn their lives around. To change from drifting along to pursuing productive careers.

OIC is a non-profit organization that offers free help to anyone who needs it. Besides basic education and marketable skills, OIC teaches people to believe in themselves and their unique abilities.

Thousands of the country's top corporations work directly with OIC. And all of them help us find jobs for the best employees anywhere—OIC graduates.

How about your business? You'll be helping yourself when you help one of them. Contact Elton Jolly, National Executive Director, OICs of America, Inc., 100 W. Coulter Street, Philadelphia, PA 19144, (215) 849-3010.

OPPORTUNITIES
INDUSTRIALIZATION
CENTERS OF
AMERICA, INC.

HELP SOMEBODY BE SOMEBODY.

Courtesy of Opportunities Industrialization Centers of America, Inc.

unsuccessful, consumer behavior research in exposing the ads' ineffectiveness before large-scale campaigns were conducted probably saved taxpayers a great deal of money.

Public Health Marketing

The provision of health care services is an important segment of the nonprofit sector, with expenditures for health care accounting for close to 10 percent of the gross national product. Hospitals, nursing homes, clinics, and federal, state, and local health agencies have recently discovered the value of consumer research in identifying the needs of patients. Information from such research helps them plan for better use of facilities and more widespread use of existing programs.

Research into the behavior of dental patients in the Houston area provides one example of the usefulness of marketing techniques in the field of health care. The study revealed that social class plays a role in determining whether dental checkups are regularly sought. Middle-class patients were far more likely than working-class patients to seek routine dental care. In neither group, however, did the majority of patients have checkups at six-month intervals, as recommended by the American Dental Association.

The researchers who conducted this study theorized that dental facilities were underutilized because of fear, and because the service was dispensed so impersonally. To dispel such fear and create more personal contacts, they selected patients from both the working class and the middle class and had them fill out reminder cards in their own handwriting, to be mailed to them in six months. After the mailing, personal phone calls were made to suggest an appointment date, thus taking the initiative away from the patient. The experiment resulted in an increase in the number of people in both social classes who made a dental appointment in response to the reminder card and telephone followup. By reducing the effort required to secure such services, demand for dental checkups was increased. The same technique could be applied, the researchers suggested, to other types of routine preventive health services, such as childhood immunization and annual physical examinations.[23]

Political Marketing

Candidates for political office and those interested in promoting political causes also recognize the value of consumer research. Candidates are interested in knowing the psychological and sociological profiles of those likely to vote for them, and the issues most important to those voters in a given campaign. Political activists concerned with winning the approval of a particular idea (e.g., tax reform or "pro-choice") also find it useful to research voters carefully in order to tailor their messages to appropriate segments.

Consumer research techniques proved quite useful, for example, in an effort by organized labor in Missouri to defeat a proposal outlawing union shops. Labor leaders were afraid that a massive voter turnout, which might be generated by a TV advertising campaign on the issue, would bring out enough unfriendly votes to pass the anti-union-shop amendment. Thus their task was to find union sympathizers among the general public and promote the importance of voting to that segment alone.

Research into past voter patterns revealed likely classes of voters who could be identified by income, education, and other sociological traits. To find out where such voters lived, researchers divided the state into block groups and assembled demographic data (available from census records) on the residents of each block group. This information was then matched with the data already collected on pro-union sympathizers. The block groups with the best match were selected for a get-out-the-vote campaign via direct mail. The election resulted in a clear victory for organized labor.[24]

Political marketing is by far the most controversial area in which behavioral research is conducted. The potential for manipulation of the voter by politicians or special interest groups is undeniable. On the other hand, to the extent that candidates and activists can better attune themselves to voter preferences, improved government should result. Like other areas of consumer behavior research, voter behavior studies offer the promise of a deeper understanding of voter needs and the development of improved voter communication programs.

summary

The field of consumer behavior has grown substantially in the past decade in response to public policy needs and the adoption of marketing techniques by nonprofit organizations. Consumer research has uncovered new ways to protect and inform consumers and has revealed weaknesses in previous public policy programs directed at consumers. Government regulatory agencies such as the Federal Trade Commission and the Food and Drug Administration now use consumer behavior studies to aid them in policy making. New applications for consumer behavior research are found in such public policy areas as unit pricing, nutritional labeling, and energy conservation labeling.

The extension of consumer behavior studies to the nonprofit sector has enabled such organizations as colleges, hospitals, museums, and political parties to better serve the needs of clients, voters, and the general public. Consumer behavior findings are used to assist such organizations in developing better techniques for "selling" the public on socially beneficial issues and programs, and identifying ways to improve the delivery of health-care services. Consumer behavior research enables political parties and candidates to tailor their platforms to the needs of their constituents.

discussion questions

1. Regulations and laws designed to protect the consumer have been developed since the late 1960s. Explain the need for these laws. Have they been effective? Why or why not?

2. Consumers need to be informed about products and services so that they can make better product decisions. Explain this statement in relation to (1) unit pricing, (2) nutritional labeling, and (3) energy conservation.

3. Discuss three ways to improve consumer education. Which do you think would be the most effective? Why?

4. List and discuss at least three social marketing campaigns that have been run in the last year. Do you think they were effective?

Consumer Behavior
Applications for
Public Policy and
Nonprofit
Organizations

584

5. Is political advertising beneficial to society or does it gloss over the essential issues? Explain your answer.

6. Is nonprofit marketing a useful tool in terms of social and health issues? Support your answer with examples.

7. Develop a campaign strategy to promote a drug rehabilitation center in your neighborhood, taking into consideration the fact that you might have local opposition.

8. Give three examples of what you think may be deceptive advertising. Do you think corrective advertising campaigns would be useful in counteracting their impact on consumers?

endnotes

1. George S. Day, "Assessing the Effects of Information Disclosure Requirements," *Journal of Marketing,* 40 (April 1976), 46; and Homer Kripke, "Gesture and Reality in Consumer Credit Reform," in David A. Aaker and George S. Day, eds., *Consumerism: Search for the Consumer Interest,* 2nd ed. (New York: Free Press, 1974), 218–24.

2. Alan R. Andreasen and Gregory D. Upah, "Regulation and the Disadvantaged: The Case of the Creditors' Remedy Rules," *Journal of Marketing,* 43 (Spring 1979), 75–83.

3. See Robert F. Dyer and Terence A. Shimp, "Enhancing the Role of Marketing Research in Public Policy Decision Making," *Journal of Marketing,* 41, (January 1977), 63–67.

4. David M. Gardner, "Deception in Advertising: A Conceptual Approach," *Journal of Marketing,* 39 (January 1975), 42.

5. J. Edward Russo, Barbara L. Metcalf, and Debra Stephens, "Toward an Empirical Technology for Identifying Misleading Advertising," in Richard J. Harris, ed., *Information Processing Research in Advertising* (Hillsdale, N.J.: Lawrence Erlbaum Associates, 1982).

6. James R. Taylor and Thomas C. Kinnear, "Corrective Advertising: An Empirical Tracking of Residual Effects," in Richard P. Bagozzi et al., eds., *Marketing in the 80's: Changes and Challenges* (Chicago: American Marketing Association, 1980), 416–18.

7. Michael B. Mazis and Janice E. Adkinson, "An Experimental Evaluation of a Proposed Corrective Advertising Remedy," *Journal of Marketing Research,* 13 (May 1976), 178–83.

8. See James M. Carman, "A Summary of Empirical Research on Unit Pricing in Supermarkets," *Journal of Retailing,* 48 (Winter 1972–73), 63–71; Hans R. Isakson and Alex R. Maurizi, "The Consumer Economics of Unit Pricing," *Journal of Marketing Research,* 10 (August 1973), 277–85; and John S. Coulson, "New Consumerists' Breed Will Fade Away," *Marketing News,* mid-June 1971, 5.

9. Bruce F. McElroy and David Asker, "Unit Pricing Six Years After Introduction," *Journal of Retailing,* 55 (Fall 1979), 44–57.

10. J. Edward Russo, Gene Krieser, and Sally Miyashita, "An Effective Display of Unit Price Information," *Journal of Marketing,* 39 (April 1975), 11–19.

11. J. Edward Russo, "The Value of Unit Price Information," *Journal of Marketing Research,* 14 (May 1977), 193–201.

12. Reed Moyer and Michael D. Hutt, *MacroMarketing,* 2nd ed. (New York: John Wiley, 1978), 83; Lynn E. Densford, "FDA Bureau Head Advocates Major Changes in

Consumer Behavior
Applications for
Public Policy and
Nonprofit
Organizations

585

Package Labeling," *Progressive Grocer,* 59 (February 1980), 31–32; and Tyzoon T. Tykbjee, "Affirmative Disclosure of Nutrition Information and Consumers' Food Preferences," *Journal of Consumer Affairs,* 13 (Winter 1979), 206–23.

13. R.J. Lenahan et al., "Consumer Reaction to Nutritional Labels on Food Products," *Journal of Consumer Affairs,* 7 (Summer 1973), 1–14; and George S. Day, "Assessing the Effects of Information Disclosure Requirements," *Journal of Marketing,* 40 (April 1976), 42–52.

14. Stephen A. Goodwin and Michael Etgar, "Alternate Organizational Formats for Nutritional Information: Processing and Policy Normative Perspectives," in *Marketing in the 80's,* 412–15.

15. Dennis L. McNeill and William L. Wilkie, "Public Policy and Consumer Information: Impact of the New Energy Labels," *Journal of Consumer Research,* 6 (June 1979), 1–10.

16. Gordon H.G. McDougall, "Alternate Energy Conservation Appeals: Relative Effects," in *Marketing in the 80's,* 432–35.

17. These suggestions can be found in Hans B. Thorelli and Jack L. Engledow, "Information Seekers and Information Systems: A Policy Perspective," *Journal of Marketing,* 44 (Spring 1980), 19–21.

18. Some guidelines for establishing such a curriculum can be found in George P. Moschis, "Formal Consumer Education: An Empirical Assessment," in William L. Wilkie, ed., *Advances in Consumer Research* (Ann Arbor, Mich.: Association for Consumer Research, 1979), VI, 456–59.

19. These and other differences between business and nonbusiness marketing are explored in Michael L. Rothschild, "Marketing Communications in Nonbusiness Situations, or Why It's So Hard to Sell Brotherhood Like Soap," *Journal of Marketing,* 43 (Spring 1979), 11–20.

20. See Karen F.A. Fox and Philip Kotler, "The Marketing of Social Causes: The First 10 Years," *Journal of Marketing,* 44 (Fall 1980), 24–33.

21. Paul C. Feingold and Mark L. Knapp, "Anti-Drug Abuse Commercials," *Journal of Communication,* 27 (Winter 1977), 20–28.

22. Leon S. Robertson et al., "A Controlled Study of the Effect of Television Messages on Safety Belt Use," *American Journal of Public Health,* 64 (November 1974), 1074–80; and Leon S. Robertson, "Consumer Response to Seat Belt Use Campaigns and Inducements: Implications for Public Health Strategies," in Beverlee B. Andersen, ed., *Advances in Consumer Research* (Cincinnati: Association for Consumer Research, 1976), III, 287–89.

23. Betsy D. Gelb and Mary C. Gelly, "The Effects of Promotional Techniques on Purchase of Preventive Dental Care," *Journal of Consumer Research,* 6 (December 1979), 305–8.

24. Warren Weaver, Jr., "A Pinpoint System Is Developed for Finding Voters for an Issue," *New York Times,* February 3, 1979, 16.

Consumer Behavior
Applications for
Public Policy and
Nonprofit
Organizations

586

GLOSSARY

Absolute Threshold. The lowest level at which an individual can experience a sensation.

Acculturation. The learning of a new or "foreign" culture.

Achieved Role A role expected of an individual as the result of some factor concerned with his or her personal attainment, such as level of education, income, occupational status, or marital status.

Achievement Need. The need for personal accomplishment as an end in itself.

Acquired Needs. Needs that are learned in response to one's culture or environment (such as the need for esteem, prestige, affection, or power). Also known as *psychogenic* or *secondary needs.*

Activation Research. A theory of human learning that holds that much consumer behavior is biologically determined; i.e., that is "nature" rather than "nurture."

Actual Self Concept. The image that an individual has of himself or herself as a certain kind of person, with certain characteristic traits, habits, possessions, relationships, and behavior.

Adaptation. In the field of perception, the term refers specifically to "getting used to" certain sensations, becoming accommodated to a certain level of stimulation.

Adopter Categories. A sequence of categories which describes how early (or late) a consumer adopts a new product in relation to other adopters. The five typical adopter categories are: innovators, early adopters, early majority, late majority, and laggards.

Adoption Process. The stages through which an individual consumer passes in arriving at a decision to try (or not to try), to continue using (or to discontinue using) a new product. The five stages of the traditional adoption process are: awareness, interest, evaluation, trial, and adoption.

Affective Component. The part of the tricomponent attitude model that reflects a consumer's emotions or feelings (favorable or unfavorable) with respect to an attitude-object.

Affect Referral Rule. A simplified decision rule whereby consumers make a product choice on the basis of their previously established overall ratings of the brands considered, rather than on specific attributes.

Affiliation Need. The need for friendship, for acceptance, and for belonging.

Aggressive Individual. One of three personality types identified by Karen Horney. The aggressive person is one who moves against others (e.g., who competes with others).

Aided Recall Measures. A technique used to measure advertising awareness, in which a respondent is asked if he or she remembers seeing an advertisement for a specific product category.

AIOs. Psychographic variables that focus on activities, interests, and opinions.

Ascribed Role. A role expected of an individual as the result of factors over which he or she has no control, such as age, sex, family, race, or religion.

Aspirational Group. A group to which a nonmember would like to belong.

Assimilation-Contrast Theory. A theory of attitude change which suggests that consumers are likely to accept only moderate attitude changes. If the change suggested is too extreme, the contrast with presently held attitudes will cause total rejection of the entire message. Because an extreme belief-changing message is likely to be perceived as more extreme than it actually is, it is likely to be rejected.

Attitude. A learned predisposition to respond in a consistently favorable or unfavorable manner with respect to a given object.

Attitude-Toward-Behavior Model. A model that proposes that a consumer's attitude toward a specific behavior is a function of how strongly he or she believes that the action will lead to a specific outcome (either favorable or unfavorable).

Attitude-Toward-Object Model. A model that proposes that a consumer's attitude toward a product or brand is a function of the presence of certain attributes and the consumer's evaluation of those attributes.

Attribution Theory. A theory concerned with how people assign causality to events and form or alter their attitudes as an outcome of assessing their own or other people's behavior.

Autonomic Decisions. Family purchase decisions in which either the husband or the wife makes the final decision.

Avoidance Group. A group with which a nonmember does not identify and does not wish to be identified.

Awareness. The first stage of the traditional adoption process.

Bachelorhood. The first stage of the family life cycle, in which young single adults set up their own housekeeping arrangements apart from their parents.

Balance Theory. An attitude-change theory that assumes that individuals attempt to avoid inconsistency and, instead, seek consistency or harmony, by placing conflicting attitudes in balance.

Behavioral Learning Theories. Theories based on the premise that learning takes place as the result of observable responses to external stimuli. Also known as *stimulus-response theory*. See Conditioned Learning and Instrumental Conditioning.

Beliefs. Mental or verbal statements that reflect a person's particular knowledge and assessment about some idea or thing.

Benefits Segmentation. A form of psychological segmentation based on the kinds of benefits consumers seek in a product.

Bettmen's Information Processing Model. One of several comprehensive models of consumer behavior.

Brand Loyalty. Consistent purchase or preference of one brand or service in a specific product category.

Category Width. The range or number of choices a person tends to consider when making product decisions. Broad categorizers are more likely to risk a poor product choice in order to maximize their chances of making good choices; narrow categorizers prefer to limit their purchase decisions to known and safe choices.

Classical Conditioning. See Conditioned Learning.

Closure. A principle of Gestalt psychology that stresses the individual's need for completion. This need is reflected in the individual's subconscious reorganization and perception of incomplete stimuli as complete or whole pictures.

Cognitive Component. The part of the tricomponent attitude model that represents the knowledge, perception, and beliefs that a consumer has acquired with respect to an attitude-object.

Cognitive Dissonance. A theory of attitude change that suggests that consumers act to relieve the discomfort or dissonance that occurs when they receive conflicting information concerning a belief or an attitude.

Cognitive Learning Theory. A theory that holds that the kind of learning most characteristic of human beings is problem solving, based on mental processing, which enables individuals to gain some control over their environment.

Cognitive Man Model. A model of man that portrays consumers as active seekers of information that will enable them to make satisfactory purchase decisions.

Communication. The transmission of a message from a sender to a receiver by means of a signal of some sort sent through a channel of some sort.

Comparative Reference Group. A group whose norms serve as a benchmark for highly specific or narrowly defined types of behavior. See also Normative Reference Group.

Comparison Advertising. Advertising that explicitly names or identifies one or more competitors of the advertised brand for the purpose of claiming superiority, either on an overall basis or in selected product attributes. Also called *comparative advertising*.

Compatibility. The degree to which potential consumers feel that a new product is consistent with their present needs, values, and practices.

Compensatory Decision Rule. A type of decision rule whereby consumers evaluate each brand option in terms of each relevant attribute and then select the brand with the highest weighted score.

Complexity. The degree to which a new product is difficult to comprehend and/or use.

Compliant Individual. One of three personality types identified by Karen Horney. The compliant person is one who moves toward others (e.g., one who desires to be loved, wanted, and appreciated by others).

Composite-Variable Index. An index that combines a number of socioeconomic variables (such as education, income, occupation) to form one overall measure of social class standing. See also Single-Variable Index.

Conative Component. The part of the tricomponent attitude model that reflects a consumer's likelihood or tendency to behave in a particular way with regard to an attitude-object. Also referred to as *"intention to buy."*

Concentrated Marketing. Marketing a product or service to a single segment with a unique marketing mix (price, product, promotion, method of distribution).

Concept. A mental image of an intangible trait, characteristic or idea.

Conditioned Learning. According to Pavlovian theory, conditioned learning results when a stimulus that is paired with another stimulus that elicits a known response serves to produce the same response by itself.

Conformity. The extent to which an individual adopts attitudes and/or behavior that are consistent with the norms of a group to which he or she belongs or would like to belong.

Conjunctive Rule. A noncompensatory decision rule in which consumers establish a minimally acceptable cutoff point for each attribute evaluated. Brands that fall below the cutoff point on any one attribute are eliminated from further consideration.

Construct. A term that represents or symbolizes an abstract trait or characteristic, such as motivation or aggression.

Consumer Behavior. The behavior that consumers display in searching for, purchasing, using, evaluating, and disposing of products, services and ideas.

Consumer Decision Rules. Procedures adopted by consumers to reduce the complexity of making product and brand decisions.

Consumer Education. Programs designed to improve consumer knowledge to help them make better buying decisions.

Consumer Heuristics. See Consumer Decision Rules.

Consumer Involvement. The extent to which consumers are concerned with a particular purchase decision and consider it to be important to them.

Consumer Learning. The process by which individuals acquire the purchase and consumption knowledge and experience they apply to future related behavior.

Consumer Protection Legislation. Consumer-oriented laws that attempt to correct any power imbalance that exists between buyers and sellers.

Consumer Socialization. The process by which an individual first learns the skills and attitudes relevant to functioning as a consumer.

Consumers. A term used to describe two different kinds of consuming entities: *personal consumers* (who buy goods and services for their own use or for household use), and *organizational consumers* (who buy products, equipment, and services in order to run their own organizations).

Contactual Group. A formal or informal group with which a person has regular face-to-face contact and with whose values, attitudes, and standards he or she tends to agree.

Content Analysis. A method for systematically and quantitatively analyzing the content of verbal and/or pictorial communication. The method is frequently used to determine prevailing social values of a society.

Continuous Innovation. A "new" product entry that is an improved or modified version of an existing product rather than a totally new product. A continuous innovation has the least disruptive influence on established consumption patterns.

Corrective Advertising. Advertising designed to eliminate any residual effects of misleading advertising claims made by marketers.

Cross-Cultural Consumer Analysis. Research designed to determine to what extent the consumers of two or more nations are similar in relation to specific consumption behavior.

Cues. Stimuli that give direction to consumer motives; i.e., that suggest a specific way to satisfy a salient motive.

Cultural Anthropology. The study of human beings that traces the development of core beliefs, values, and customs that are passed down to individuals from their parents and grandparents.

Culture. The sum total of learned beliefs, values, and customs that serve to regulate the consumer behavior of members of a particular society.

Customs. Overt modes of behavior that constitute culturally approved or acceptable ways of behaving in specific situations.

Deceptive Advertising. Advertising that presents or implies false or misleading information to the consumer.

Decision. A choice made from two or more alternatives.

Decision Time. Within the context of the diffusion process, the amount of time required for an individual consumer to accept or reject a specific new product.

Deconsumption. A policy that encourages consumers to curtail or eliminate usage of a particular brand or product category.

Defensive Attribution. A principle that suggests consumers are likely to accept credit for success (internal attribution), and to blame others or outside events for failure (external attribution).

Demarketing. The marketing task of discouraging consumers or consumer segments from purchasing selected goods.

Demographic Segmentation. The division of a total potential market into smaller subgroups on the basis of such objective characteristics as age, sex, marital status, income, occupation, or education.

Demography. The vital and measurable statistics of a population.

Dependent Variable. A variable whose value will change as a result of a change in another (i.e., independent) variable. For example, consumer purchases are a dependent variable subject to level and quality of advertising (independent variables).

Depth Interview. A research technique designed to uncover consumers' underlying attitudes and/or motivations through lengthy and relatively unstructured interview.

Detached Individual. One of three personality types identified by Karen Horney. The detached person is one who moves away from others (e.g., who desires independence, self-sufficiency, and freedom from obligations).

Differential Threshold. The minimal difference that can be detected between two stimuli. Also known as the *j.n.d.* (*just noticeable difference*). See also Weber's Law.

Differentiated Marketing. Marketing a product or service to several segments, using a specifically tailored product, promotional appeal, price, and/or method of distribution for each.

Diffusion Process. The process by which the acceptance of an innovation is spread by communication to members of a social system over a period of time.

Disclaimant Group. A group in which a person holds membership or has face-to-face contact, but of whose values, attitudes and behavior he or she disapproves.

Discontinuous Innovation. A dramatically new product entry that requires the establishment of new consumption patterns.

Disjunctive Rule. A noncompensatory decision rule in which consumers establish a minimally acceptable cutoff point for each relevant product attribute so that any brand meeting or surpassing the cutoff point for any one attribute is considered an acceptable choice.

Dissolution. The final stage of the family life cycle with only one surviving spouse.

Distributed Learning. Learning spaced over a period of time to increase consumer retention. See Massed Learning.

Dogmatism. A personality trait that reflects the degree of rigidity a person displays toward the unfamiliar and toward information that is contrary to his or her own established beliefs.

Drive. An internal force that impels a person to engage in an action designed to satisfy a specific need.

Dynamically Continuous Innovation. A new product entry that is sufficiently innovative to have some disruptive effects on established consumption patterns.

Economic Man Model. A model of man that depicts the consumer as a perfectly rational being who objectively evaluates and ranks each product alternative and selects the alternative that gives the best value.

Ego. In Freudian theory, the part of the personality that serves as the individual's conscious control. It functions as an internal monitor that balances the impulsive demands of the *id* and the social-cultural constraints of the *superego*.

Ego-Defensive Function. A component of the functional approach to attitude-change that suggests that consumers want to protect their self-concepts from inner feelings of doubt.

Emotional Motives. Motives or goals based on subjective criteria, such as love, pride, fear, affection, or self-esteem.

Encoding. The process by which individuals select and assign a word or visual image to represent a perceived object.

Enculturation. The learning of the culture of one's own society.

Engel-Kollat-Blackwell Model. One of several comprehensive models of consumer behavior.

Evaluation. The third stage of the traditional adoption process, in which the consumer either draws conclusions about a product innovation or determines if further information is needed.

Evaluation of Alternatives. A stage in the consumer decision-making process in which the consumer appraises the benefits to be derived from each of the product alternatives being considered.

Evoked Set. The specific brands a consumer considers in making a purchase choice in a particular product category.

Expected Self-Concept. How individuals expect to see themselves at some specified future time.

Exploratory Qualitative Phase. The phase of an in-depth segmentation study in which usage patterns, buying habits, benefits sought, and attitudes consumers have about a product class are examined.

Exploratory Quantitative Phase. The phase of an in-depth segmentation study in which brand similarities, consumer attitudes, perceptions of brand images, and preferences are measured.

Extended Family. A household consisting of a husband, wife, offspring, and at least one other blood relative.

Extensive Problem Solving. A search by the consumer to establish the necessary product criteria to evaluate knowledgeably the most suitable product to fulfill a need.

Extinction. The point at which a learned response ceases to occur because of lack of reinforcement.

Extrinsic Cues. Cues external to the product, such as price, store image, or brand image, that serve to influence the consumer's perception of a product's quality.

Family. Two or more persons related by blood, marriage, or adoption who reside together.

Family Branding. The practice of marketing a whole line of company products under the same brand name.

Family Gatekeeper. A family member who controls the flow of information to the family about products or services, thereby regulating the related consumption decisions of other family members.

Family Influencer. A family member who provides product-related information and advice to other members of the family, thereby influencing related consumption decisions.

Family Life Cycle (FLC) .A progression of stages through which most families pass, including such traditional stages as bachelorhood, honeymooners, parenthood, post-parenthood, and dissolution.

Fatigue. See Habituation, Wear-Out.

Focus Group. A qualitative research method in which about eight to ten persons are interviewed simultaneously and which is designed to benefit from group interaction.

Foot-in-the-Door Technique. A theory of attitude change that suggests individuals form attitudes that are consistent with their own prior behavior.

Formal Group. A group that has a clearly defined structure, specific roles and authority levels, and specific goals (e.g., a political party.)

Formal Interpersonal Communication. Direct communication between a person representing a profit or nonprofit organization and one or more others (e.g., a discussion between a salesman and a prospect).

Freudian Theory. A theory of personality and motivation developed by the psychoanalyst Sigmund Freud. See Psychoanalytic Theory.

Functional Approach. An attitude-change theory that classifies attitudes in terms of four functions: the utilitarian function, the ego-defensive function, the value-expressive function, and the knowledge function.

Generic Goals. The general classes or categories of goals that individuals select to fulfill their needs. See Product-Specific Goals.

Geographic Segmentation. The division of a total potential market into smaller subgroups on the basis of geographic variables. (e.g. region, state, or city).

Gestalt. A German term meaning "pattern" or "configuration" which has come to represent a school of psychology upon which various principles of perceptual organization are based. See also Perceptual Organization.

Goals. The sought-after results of motivated behavior. One fulfills a need through achievement of a goal.

Group. Two or more people who interact either on a regular or irregular basis in their pursuit of individual or common goals.

Group Cohesiveness. The extent to which group members tend to "stick together" and follow group norms.

Group Norms. The implicit rules of conduct or standards of behavior which members of a group are expected to observe.

Habit. A consistent pattern of behavior performed without considered thought. Consistent repetition is the hallmark of habit.

Habituation. The mechanism by which an individual systematically ignores those stimuli (e.g., products or advertising messages) that are predictable or readily recognizable because of excessive repetition. See also Wear-Out.

Hierarchy of Needs. See Maslow's Need Hierarchy.

High Involvement. The level of involvement where consumers judge a purchase decision to be important enough to engage in extensive search activity for information prior to making a decision.

Honeymooners. A stage of the family life cycle consisting of young married couples with no children.

Howard-Sheth Model. One of several comprehensive models of consumer behavior.

Hypothesis. A tentative statement of a relationship between two or more variables.

Hypothetical Construct. See Construct.

Id. In Freudian theory, the part of the personality that consists of primitive and impulsive drives that the individual strives to satisfy.

Ideal Self Concept. How individuals would like to perceive themselves (as opposed to Actual Self Concept—the way they actually do perceive themselves).

Impersonal Communication. Communication directed to a large and diffuse audience, with no direct communication between source and receiver. Also known as *mass communication.*

Independent Variable. A variable that can be manipulated to effect a change in the value of a second (i.e., dependent) variable. For example, price is an independent variable that often affects sales (the dependent variable).

Index of Status Characteristics (ISC). A measure of social class that weights occupation, source of income (not amount), house type, and dwelling area into one single index of social class standing. Also called *Warner's ISC.*

Inept Set. Brands that a consumer excludes from purchase consideration.

Inert Set. Brands that a consumer is indifferent towards because they are not perceived as having any particular advantage.

Informal Group. A group of people who see each other frequently on an informal basis, such as weekly poker-players or social acquaintances.

Informal Interpersonal Communication. Direct communication between two or more persons who are friends, neighbors, relatives, or coworkers.

Information Overload. A dysfunctional situation in which the consumer is presented with too much product- or brand-related information.

Information Processing. A cognitive theory of human learning patterned after computer information processing which focuses on how information is stored in human memory and how it is retrieved.

Innate Needs. Physiological needs for food, water, air, clothing, shelter, and sex. Also known as *biogenic* or *primary* needs.

Innovation-Decision Process. An update of the traditional *adoption process* model consisting of the following four stages: knowledge, persuasion, decision, and confirmation.

Innovativeness. A measure of a consumer's willingness to try new products.

Innovator. An individual who is among the earliest purchasers of a new product.

Institutional Advertising. Advertising designed to promote a favorable company image rather than to promote specific products.

Instrumental Conditioning. A form of learning based on a trial-and-error process, with habits formed as the result of positive experiences resulting from certain responses or behaviors. See also Conditioned Learning.

Interest. The stage of the traditional adoption process in which the consumer actively seeks out information concerning a new product innovation.

Interpersonal Communication. Communication that occurs directly between two or more people by mail, by telephone or in person.

Intrinsic Cues. Physical characteristics of the product (such as size, color, flavor, and aroma) that serve to influence the consumer's perceptions of product quality.

Involvement. See Consumer Involvement.

Joint Decisions. Family purchase decisions in which the husband and wife are equally influential. Also known as *syncratic decisions.*

Just Noticeable Difference (j.n.d.) The minimal difference that can be detected between two stimuli. See also Differential Threshold and Weber's Law.

Key Informant Method. A method of measuring various aspects of consumer behavior (such as opinion leadership or social class) whereby a knowledgeable person is asked to classify individuals with whom he or she is familiar into specific categories.

Knowledge Function. A component of the functional approach to attitude-change theory that suggests consumers have a strong need to know and understand the people and things with which they come into contact.

Lampert Pollimeter. A simple scaling device used in attitude research that operates much like a common sliderule.

Learning. The process by which individuals acquire the knowledge and experience they apply to future purchase and consumption behavior.

Level-of-Processing Theory. An information-processing theory that holds that the more involving information is, the deeper the level of processing to which it is subjected, and the better it is understood and retained.

Lexicographic Rule. A noncompensatory decision rule in which consumers first rank product attributes in terms of their importance, then compare brands in terms of the attribute considered most important. If one brand scores sufficiently high, it is selected; if not, the process is continued with the second ranked attribute, and so on.

Life-style. See Psychographic Characteristics.

Limited Problem Solving. A limited search by a consumer for a product that will satisfy his or her basic criteria from among a selected group of brands.

Long-term Store. In Information-processing theory, the stage of real memory where information is organized, reorganized and retained for relatively extended periods of time.

Low Involvement. The level of involvement where consumers judge a purchase decision to be unimportant or trivial, and therefore engage in little information search prior to making a decision.

Manufacturer's Image. The way in which consumers view (i.e., perceive) the "personality" of the firm that produces a specific product.

Marketing. Activities designed to enhance the flow of goods, services, and ideas from producers to consumers in order to satisfy consumer needs and wants.

Marketing Concept. A consumer-oriented philosophy that suggests that satisfaction of consumer needs and wants should provide the focus for product development and marketing strategy in order for the firm to meet its own organizational goals.

Marketing Mix. The unique configuration of the four basic marketing variables (product, promotion, price, and channels of distribution) over which a marketing organization has control.

Market Segmentation. The process of dividing a potential market into distinct subsets of consumers and selecting one or more segments as a target market to be reached with a distinct marketing mix.

Maslow's Need Hierarchy. A theory of motivation that postulates that individuals strive to satisfy their needs according to a basic hierarchical structure, starting with physiological needs, then moving on to safety needs, social needs, egoistic needs, and finally self-actualization needs.

Mass Communication. See Impersonal Communication.

Massed Learning. Compressing the learning schedule into a short time span to accelerate consumer learning. See Distributed Learning.

Mass Marketing. The practice of offering a single product and marketing mix to the whole target market.

Medium. A channel through which a message is transmitted (e.g., a television commercial, a newspaper advertisement, or a personal letter).

Membership Group. A group to which a person either belongs or qualifies for membership.

Message. The thought, idea, attitude, image, or other information that a sender wishes to convey to an intended audience.

Model. A simplified representation of reality designed to show the relationships between the various elements of a system or process under investigation.

Motivation. The driving force within individuals that impels them to action.

Motivational Research. Qualitative research designed to uncover consumers' subconscious or hidden motivations. The basic premise of motivational research is that consumers are not always aware of the basic reasons underlying their actions.

Multiattribute Attitude Models. A group of attitude models that examine the composition of consumer attitudes in terms of selected product attributes or beliefs.

Need Recognition. The realization by the consumer that there is a difference between "what is" and "what should be."

Negative Reinforcement. An unpleasant or negative outcome that serves to discourage a specific behavior.

Neo-Freudian Personality Theory. A school of psychology that stresses the fundamental role of social relationships in the formation and development of personality.

Nicosia Model. One of several comprehensive models of consumer behavior.

Noncompensatory Decision Rule. A type of consumer decision rule whereby a positive evaluation of a brand attribute does not compensate for (i.e., is not balanced against) a negative evaluation of the same brand on some other attribute.

Nonprofit Marketing. The use of marketing concepts and techniques by nonprofit organizations such as museums or government agencies to impart information, ideas, or attitudes to various segments of the public.

Normative Reference Group. A group that influences the general values or behavior of an individual. See Comparative Reference Group.

Nuclear Family. A household consisting of a husband and wife and at least one offspring.

Objective Measurement of Social Class. A method of measuring social class whereby individuals are asked specific socioeconomic questions concerning themselves or their families. On the basis of their answers, people are placed within specific social class groupings.

Observability. The ease with which a product's benefits or attributes can be observed, visualized, or described to potential customers.

Observational Research. A research procedure in which the actual behavior of consumers in the marketplace is measured.

Opinion Leader. A person who informally influences the attitudes or behavior of others.

Opinion Leadership. The process by which one person (the opinion leader) informally influences the actions or attitudes of others, who may be opinion seekers or merely opinion recipients.

Opinion Leadership Overlap. The degree to which people who are opinion leaders in one product category are also opinion leaders in one or more other categories.

Opinion Receivers. Individuals who either actively seek product information from others or receive unsolicited information.

Optimizing Decision Strategy. A strategy whereby a consumer evaluates each brand in terms of significant product criteria. See also Simplifying Decision Strategy.

Optimum Stimulation Level (OSL). The level or amount of novelty or complexity that individuals seek in their personal experiences. High OSL consumers tend to accept risky and novel products more readily than low OSL consumers.

Organizational Consumer. A purchasing agent (or group) employed by a business, government agency, or other institution, profit or nonprofit, that buys the goods, services, or equipment necessary for the organization to function.

Parenthood. A stage of the family life cycle consisting of married couples with at least one child living at home.

Participant Observer. A researcher who becomes an active member of the environment he or she is studying.

Passive Man Model. A theory of man that depicts the consumer as a submissive recipient of the promotional efforts of marketers.

Perceived Quality. The quality attributed to a product by the consumer on the basis of various informational cues associated with the product. See Intrinsic Cues and Extrinsic Cues.

Perceived Risk. The degree of uncertainty perceived by the consumer as to the consequences or outcome of a specific purchase decision.

Perception. The process by which an individual selects, organizes, and interprets stimuli into a meaningful and coherent picture of the world.

Perceptual Blocking. The subconscious screening out or blocking of stimuli that are threatening or inconsistent with one's needs, values, beliefs, or attitudes.

Perceptual Defense. The process of subconsciously distorting stimuli to render them less threatening or inconsistent with one's needs, values, beliefs, or attitudes.

Perceptual Mapping. A research technique that enables marketers to plot graphically consumers' perceptions concerning product attributes of specific brands.

Perceptual Organization. The subconscious ordering and perception of stimuli into groups or configurations according to certain principles of Gestalt psychology.

Personal Consumer. The individual who buys goods and services for his or her own use, for household use, for the use of a family member, or for a friend. (Sometimes referred to as the *ultimate consumer* or *end user.*)

Personality. The inner psychological characteristics that both determine and reflect how a person responds to his or her environment.

Personality Scale. A series of questions or statements designed to measure a single personality trait.

Personality Test. A pencil-and-paper test designed to measure an individual's personality in terms of one or more traits or inner characteristics.

Political Marketing. The use of marketing concepts and techniques by candidates for political office and by those interested in promoting political causes.

Positioning. Establishing a specific image of the attributes of a brand in relation to competing brands. See also Product Positioning.

Positive Reinforcement. A favorable outcome to a specific behavior that strengthens the likelihood that the behavior will be repeated.

Postparenthood. A stage of the family life cycle consisting of older married couples whose children live permanently apart from them.

Postpurchase Dissonance. Cognitive dissonance that occurs after a consumer has made a purchase commitment. Consumers resolve this dissonance through a variety of strategies designed to confirm the wisdom of their choice.

Postpurchase Evaluation. An assessment of a product, based on actual trial.

Potential Rating Index by Zip Market (PRIZM). A composite index of geographic and socioeconomic factors expressed in residential zip code neighborhoods from which consumer segments are formed.

Power Need. The need to exercise control over one's environment, including other persons.

Prepotent Need. An overriding need, from among several needs, that serves to initiate goal-directed behavior.

Prepurchase Search. A stage in the consumer decision making process in which the consumer perceives a need and actively seeks out information concerning products that will help satisfy that need.

Price-Quality Relationship. The perception of price as an indicator of product quality (e.g., the higher the price, the higher the perceived quality of the product).

Primacy Effect. A theory that proposes that the first (i.e., the earliest) message presented in a sequential series of messages tends to produce the greatest impact on the receiver. See also Recency Effect.

Primary Data. Information that is collected through surveys, interviews, or questionnaires for a specific research project.

Primary Group. A group of people who interact (e.g., meet and talk) on a regular basis, such as members of a family, neighbors, or co-workers.

Primary Needs. See Innate Needs.

Product Image. The "personality" that consumers attribute to a product or brand.

Product Line Extension. A marketing strategy of adding related products to an already established brand (based on the Stimulus Generalization Theory).

Product Positioning. A marketing strategy designed to project a specific image for a product.

Product-Specific Goals. The specifically branded or labeled products that consumers select to fulfill their needs. See Generic Goals.

Projective Techniques. Research procedures designed to identify consumers' subconscious feelings and motivations. These tests often require consumers to interpret ambiguous stimuli such as incomplete sentences, cartoons, or inkblots.

Psychoanalytic Theory. A theory of motivation and personality which postulates that unconscious needs and drives, particularly sexual and other biological drives, are the basis of all human motivation and personality.

Psychographic Characteristics. Intrinsic psychological, social-cultural and behavioral characteristics that reflect how an individual is likely to act in relation to consumption decisions. (Also referred to as *lifestyle or activities, interests, and opinion (AIO) characteristics*).

Psychographic Instrument. A series of written statements designed to capture relevant aspects of a consumer's personality, buying motives, interests, attitudes, beliefs, and values.

Psychological Segmentation. The division of a total potential market into smaller subgroups on the basis of intrinsic characteristics of the individual, such as personality, buying motives, lifestyle, attitudes, or interests.

Psychology. The study of the intrinsic qualities of individuals, such as their motivations, perception, personality, and learning patterns.

Quantitative Probability Phase. The phase of an in-depth segmentation study that identifies the prime segments to be pursued in such terms as members' behavior, attitudes, demographic characteristics or media habits.

Rate of Adoption. The percentage of potential adopters within a specific social system who have adopted a new product within a given time frame.

Rate of Usage. The frequency of use and repurchase of a particular product.

Rational Motives. Motives or goals based on economic or objective criteria, such as price, size, weight, or miles per gallon.

Recency Effect. A theory that proposes that the last (i.e., most recent) message presented in a sequential series of messages tends to be remembered longer. (See Primacy Effect.)

Recognition Measure. A research technique in which the consumer is shown a specific advertisement and is asked whether he or she remembers having seen it.

Reference Group. A person or group that serves as a point of comparison (or reference) for an individual in the formation of either general or specific values, attitudes, or behavior.

Rehearsal. The silent, mental repetition of material. Also, the relating of new data to old data to make the former more meaningful.

Reinforcement. A positive or negative outcome that influences the likelihood that a specific behavior will be repeated in the future in response to a particular cue or stimulus.

Relative Advantage. The degree to which potential customers perceive a new product to be superior to existing alternatives.

Reliability. The degree to which a measurement instrument is consistent in what it measures.

Repeat Purchase. The act of repurchasing the same product or brand purchased earlier.

Reputational Measurement of Social Class. A method of measuring social class whereby knowledgeable community members are asked to judge the social-class position of other members of their community. See Key Informant Method.

Response. The reaction of an individual to a specific stimulus or cue.

Retrieval. The stage of information processing in which individuals recover information from long-term storage.

Rokeach Value Survey. A self-administered inventory consisting of eighteen "terminal" values (i.e., personal goals) and eighteen "instrumental" values (i.e., ways of reaching personal goals.)

Role. A pattern of behavior expected of an individual in a specific social position, such as the role of mother, daughter, teacher, or lawyer. One person may have a number of different roles, each of which is relevant in the context of a specific social situation.

Routinized Response Behavior. A habitual purchase response from among a small group of product alternatives based on predetermined criteria.

Secondary Data. Data that has been collected for reasons other than the specific research project at hand.

Secondary Group. A group of people who interact infrequently or irregularly, such as two women who meet occasionally in the supermarket.

Secondary Needs. See Acquired Needs.

Selective Attention. A heightened awareness of stimuli relevant to one's needs or interests.

Selective Exposure. Conscious or subconscious exposure of the consumer to certain media or messages, and the subconscious or active avoidance of others.

Self-Designated Method. A method of measuring some aspect of consumer behavior (such as opinion leadership) in which a person is asked to evaluate or describe his or her own attitudes or actions.

Self-Image. The image a person has of himself or herself as a certain kind of person with certain characteristic traits, habits, possessions, relationships, and behavior.

Self-Perception Theory. A theory that suggests that consumers develop attitudes by reflecting on their own behavior.

Self-Report Attitude Scales. The measurement of consumer attitudes by self-scoring procedures, such as Likert scales, semantic differential scales, or rank-order scales.

Self-Reports. Pen-and-pencil "tests" completed by individuals concerning their own actions, attitudes, or motivations in regard to a subject or product under study.

Sensation. The immediate and direct response of the sensory organs to simple stimuli (e.g., color, brightness, loudness, smoothness).

Sensory Receptors. The human organs (eyes, ears, nose, mouth, skin) that receive sensory inputs.

Sensory Store. According to information-processing theory, the place in which all sensory inputs are housed very briefly before passing into the short-term store.

Sheth Family Decision-Making Model. One of several comprehensive models of consumer behavior.

Short-Term Store. In information-processing theory, the stage of real memory in which information received from the sensory store for processing is retained briefly before passing into the long-term store or forgotten.

Simplifying Decision Strategy. A strategy whereby the consumer evaluates alternative brands in terms of one relevant criterion. Also see optimizing decision strategy.

Single-Component Attitude Model. An attitude model consisting of just one overall affective, or feeling, component.

Single-Variable Index. The use of a single socioeconomic variable (such as income) to estimate an individual's relative social class. Also see Composite-Variable Index.

Sleeper Effect. The tendency for persuasive communication to lose the impact of source credibility over time (i.e., the influence of a message from a high credibility source tends to decrease over time, and the influence of a message from a low credibility source tends to increase over time).

Social Character. In the context of consumer behavior, a personality trait that ranges on a continuum from inner-directedness (reliance on one's own "inner" values or standards) to other-directedness (reliance on others for direction).

Social Class. The division of members of a society into a hierarchy of distinct status classes, so that members of each class have relatively the same status and members of all other classes have either higher or lower status.

Social-Cultural Segmentation. The division of a total potential market into smaller subgroups on the basis of sociological or cultural variables, such as social class, stage-in-the-family life cycle, religion, race, nationality, values, beliefs, or customs.

Social Marketing. The use of marketing concepts and techniques to win adoption of socially beneficial ideas.

Social Psychology. The study of how individuals operate in a group.

Socioeconomic Status Scores (SES). A social class measure used by the United States Bureau of the Census which combines occupational status, family income, and educational attainment into one measure of social class standing.

Sociology. The study of groups.

Sociometric Method. A method of measuring opinion leadership whereby the actual pattern of person-to-person informal communication is traced.

Source. The initiator of a message.

SRI Values and Lifestyle Program (VALS). A research service that tracks marketing-relevant shifts in the beliefs, values and lifestyles of a sample of the American population that has been divided into a small number of consumer segments.

Status. The relative prestige accorded to an individual within a specific group or social system.

Stimulus. Any unit of input to any of the senses. Examples of consumer stimuli include products, packages, brand names, advertisements, and commercials. Also known as *sensory input.*

Stimulus Discrimination. The ability to select a specific stimulus from among similar stimuli because of perceived differences.

Stimulus Generalization. The inability to perceive differences between slightly dissimilar stimuli.

Storage. The stage in information processing in which individuals organize and reorganize information in long-term memory received from the short-term store.

Store Image. Consumers' perception of the "personality" of a store and the products it carries.

Subculture. A distinct cultural group that exists as an identifiable segment within a larger, more complex society.

Subjective Measurement of Social Class. A method of measuring social class whereby people are asked to estimate their own social class position.

Sublimation. The manifestation of repressed needs in a socially acceptable form of behavior; a type of defense mechanism.

Subliminal Embeds. Symbols implanted in print advertisements that are designed to appeal to consumers below the level of their conscious awareness.

Subliminal Perception. Perception of very weak or rapid stimuli received beneath the level of conscious awareness.

Superego. In Freudian theory, the part of the personality that reflects society's moral and ethical codes of conduct. See also Id and Ego.

Supraliminal Perception. Perception of stimuli at or above the level of conscious awareness.

Symbolic Group. A group with which an individual identifies by adopting its values, attitudes, or behavior despite the unlikelihood of future membership.

Theory. A hypothesis or group of hypotheses that offers an explanation of behavior.

Theory of Reasoned Action. A comprehensive theory of the interrelationship among attitudes, intentions, and behavior.

Three-Hit Theory. A theory which proposes that the optimum number of exposures to an advertisement to induce learning is three: (1) to gain consumers' awareness; (2) to show the relevance of the product; and (3) to show its benefits.

Trait. Any distinguishing, relatively enduring way in which one individual differs from another.

Trait Theory. A theory of personality that focuses on the measurement of specific psychological characteristics.

Trial. The fourth stage of the traditional adoption process in which the consumer tries the product innovation on a limited basis.

Trialability. The degree to which a new product is capable of being tried by consumers on a limited basis (e.g., through free samples or small size packages).

Trial Purchase. A type of purchase behavior in which the consumer purchases a product (usually in a small size) in order to evaluate it.

Tricomponent Attitude Model. An attitude model consisting of three parts: a cognitive (knowledge) component, an affective (feeling) component, and a conative (doing) component.

Two-Step Flow of Communication Theory. A communication model that portrays opinion leaders as direct receivers of information from mass media sources who in turn interpret and transmit this information to the general public.

Unaided Recall Measures. An advertising measurement technique in which respondents are asked to recall advertisements they have seen, with no cues as to the identity or product class of the advertisement to be recalled. Often used to measure the influence of timing on learning schedules.

User Behavior Segmentation. The division of a total potential market into smaller subgroups in terms of rate of usage or brand preference.

Utilitarian Function. A component of the functional approach to attitude-change theory that suggests consumers hold certain attitudes partly because of the brand's utility.

Validity. The degree to which a measurement instrument accurately reflects what it is designed to measure.

Value-Expressive Function. A component of the functional approach to attitude-change theory that suggests that attitude express consumers' general values, lifestyle and outlook.

Value Instruments. Data collection instruments used to ask people how they feel about basic personal and social concepts such as freedom, comfort, national security, or peace.

Values. Relatively enduring beliefs, that serve as guides for what is considered to be "appropriate" behavior, and that are widely accepted by the members of a society.

Variable. A thing or idea that may vary (i.e., assume a succession of values).

Venturesomeness. A personality trait that measures a consumer's willingness to accept the risk of purchasing innovative products.

Voluntary Simplifiers. A small but growing segment of consumers that select lifestyles designed to maximize the amount of control they have over their own lives.

Warner's Index of Status Characteristics. See Index of Status Characteristics (ISC).

Wear-Out. The point at which repeated exposure to a stimulus, such as an advertising message, no longer has a positive or reinforcing influence on attitudes or behavior.

Weber's Law. A theory concerning the perceived differentiation of similar stimuli of varying intensities (i.e., the stronger the initial stimulus, the greater the additional intensity needed for the second stimulus to be perceived as different).

Yankelovich Monitor. A research service that tracks over forty social trends, and provides information as to shifts in size and direction, and resulting marketing implications.

AUTHOR INDEX

SUBJECT INDEX